CARDINAL BEAUFORT

Engraving of Cardinal Beaufort's Seal of Arms.

CARDINAL BEAUFORT

A Study of Lancastrian Ascendancy and Decline

G. L. HARRISS

Clarendon Press · Oxford
1988

Oxford University Press, Walton Street, Oxford OX2 6DP
Oxford New York Toronto
Delhi Bombay Calcutta Madras Karachi
Petaling Jaya Singapore Hong Kong Tokyo
Nairobi Dar es Salaam Cape Town
Melbourne Auckland
and associated companies in
Berlin Ibadan

Oxford is a trade mark of Oxford University Press

Published in the United States
by Oxford University Press, New York

British Library Cataloguing in Publication Data
Harriss, G. L. (Gerald Leslie)
Cardinal Beaufort: a study of Lancastrian ascendancy and decline.
1. England. Beaufort, Henry, 1374–1447
I. Title
942.04'092'4
ISBN 0-19-820135-4

Library of Congress Cataloging in Publication Data
Harriss, G. L.
Cardinal Beaufort: a study of Lancastrian ascendancy and decline.
Bibliography: p. Includes index.
1. Beaufort, Henry, 1374–1447. 2. Statesmen—Great Britain—Biography. 3. Cardinals—Great Britain—Biography. 4. Lancaster, House of. 5. Great Britain—Politics and government—1399–1485. I. Title.
DA247.B39H37 1988 942.04'3'0924 [B] 88–5206
ISBN 0–19–820135–4

Set by Pentacor Limited, High Wycombe, Bucks
Printed in Great Britain
at the University Printing House, Oxford
by David Stanford
Printer to the University

PREFACE

BIOGRAPHY is unfashionable and suspect.[1] For the medieval period it may seem a folly and a fraud. Sixty years ago K. B. McFarlane judged it so: 'The historian cannot honestly write biographical history; his province is rather the growth of social organisations, of civilisation, of ideas.' As he explained, 'the formal records alone survive; behind them lies a tangle of human motives, in many cases a petty affair, in others historically of the first importance—and these are not revealed'. It was the abandoned dissertation on Cardinal Beaufort, centred on an examination of his loans to Henry VI, which produced this verdict, although it later yielded two important articles, both of them highly illuminating studies of the cardinal's personality.[2]

My own work on Beaufort began in the early 1960s with a study of the character of his loans. It was resumed some ten years ago with the purpose of assessing his political contribution to the fortunes of the house of Lancaster. Linked to the royal house by birth, his abilities and ambition won him a central role in the formulation and execution of royal policy, while the accidents of Henry V's early death and his own longevity conferred on him the unique status of elder statesman and mentor of three kings. In this sense Beaufort's life epitomized the story of Lancastrian ascendancy and decline, and his death was felt to cut the last link with the foregoing age. To approach the history of this period through his career is necessarily to distort its pattern in some degree; but in some crucial respects it presents the past with greater veracity by emphasizing the contingent and unforeseeable, and the effects of human passions and failings on events. Above all it illuminates at crucial points the options and choices which faced Beaufort and others. As will become apparent, the framework of ideological, political, military, and financial determinants is by no means ignored. Is political biography of this kind possible for the medieval period? I can only say that in Beaufort's case his words and actions afford just sufficient evidence for an interpretation of his character and policies, though any probing of his personal psychology must remain very tentative. This matters the less in that his thoughts and work centred predominantly on his political and financial concerns. Second to these was his concern for his family, and I have endeavoured to set the careers of his

[1] 'It is despised by the hard and practised by the soft in one discipline after another': Eric Homberger in *The Times Higher Educational Supplement*, 9 Oct. 1987, p. 11.

[2] An account of McFarlane's work on Beaufort is given in J. P. Cooper's introduction to K. B. McFarlane, *The Nobility of Later Medieval England* (Oxford, 1973), pp. viii–x.

brothers and nephews in parallel with his own. Over all, Beaufort's life was not without an epic quality. His vision of a Lancastrian ascendancy had something of grandeur, if more of the grandiose; his steadfast commitment to it, through successive stages of a disintegration which he strove vainly to halt, and severe personal reverses, evinced both dignity and courage. Only his death saved him from witnessing the nemesis of the Lancastrian empire and crown, and of the Beaufort family.

My abiding debt as a late medieval historian is to Bruce McFarlane, to whose memory this study of Beaufort is offered, though I cannot recall that I ever discussed the cardinal with him. With Karl Leyser's kind permission I have used McFarlane's dissertation on Beaufort and his unpublished lecture on the political crisis of 1432. I have also received much assistance from a number of scholars on particular points. I trust that I have acknowledged all of these in the footnotes, but any failure to do so arises from inadvertence, not ingratitude. I wish to acknowledge in particular the generosity of Mr Gervase Belfield in putting his notes at my disposal, and of all those who have made my visits to Winchester and Bishop's Waltham so pleasurable and rewarding. I am grateful to those who have allowed me to consult and cite their theses and for stimulating conversations about the Beauforts with Dr Michael Jones. I have taken the decision not to use his thesis on the career of Edmund Beaufort in France since his important researches into French archives deserve publication in their own right. Finally, I must record my indebtedness to my colleagues at Magdalen who have enabled me to have two periods of study leave in which to draft and then complete this book.

CONTENTS

LIST OF ILLUSTRATIONS

ABBREVIATIONS

BIHR	*Bulletin of the Institute of Historical Research*
BJRL	*Bulletin of the John Rylands Library*
BRUO	*Biographical Register of the University of Oxford*
BL	British Library
BN	Bibliothèque Nationale
Cal. L. Bk.	*Calendar of Letter Books of the City of London*
CAD	*Catalogue of Ancient Deeds*
CCM	Canterbury Cathedral Muniments
CCR	*Calendar of Close Rolls*
CCh. R	*Calendar of Charter Rolls*
CFR	*Calendar of Fine Rolls*
Chron. Angl.	*Incerti Scriptures Chronicon Angliae*
CIM	*Calendar of Miscellaneous Inquisitions*
Concilia	*Concilia Magnae Britanniae*
CP	*Complete Peerage*
CPL	*Calendar of Papal Letters*
CPR	*Calendar of Patent Rolls*
CSL	*Calendar of Signet Letters*
DKR	*Reports of the Deputy Keeper of the Public Records*
EHR	*English Historical Review*
Fasti	*Fasti Ecclesiae Anglicanae*
HMC	*Historical Manuscripts Commission*
HRO	Hampshire Record Office
IPM	Inquisitions Post Mortem
Kal. and Inv.	*Kalendars and Inventories of the Treasury of Receipt*
LAO	Lincoln Archives Office
LQR	*Law Quarterly Review*
NRO	Norfolk Record Office
PPC	*Proceedings and Ordinances of the Privy Council*
PRO	Public Record Office
Rot. Parl.	*Rotuli Parliamentorum*
RDP	*Lords Report on the Dignity of a Peer*
Reg. CS	*Register of the Common Seal of St Swithun's Priory*
Royal Wills	*A Collection of Royal Wills*
SCH	*Studies in Church History*
SR	*Statutes of the Realm*
TRHS	*Transactions of the Royal Historical Society*
WAM	Westminster Abbey Muniments

I

The Emergence of the Beauforts

ALTHOUGH Henry Beaufort knew the day of his birth and liked to celebrate it, we remain uncertain even of the year.[1] John of Gaunt's liaison with Catherine Swynford, daughter of Sir Payn Roelt, the Hainaulter who had come to England in the service of Queen Philippa, had begun sometime after she became governess to his children on the death of the Duchess Blanche in 1369. Catherine had married the Lincolnshire knight Sir Hugh Swynford in 1368 at the age of eighteen, and before she was widowed by his death in battle in 1372 she had borne him two children. The first of her offspring by Gaunt, named after his father, was probably born in the same year, following the duke's own marriage to Constance of Castile. The births, of Henry in about 1375, and of Thomas and Joan in 1377 and 1379, suggest that it was only after Gaunt's great march to Bordeaux in 1373–4 that the relationship with Catherine was resumed, and it was in these years that rumours of it reached the chroniclers.[2] Between the births of the first and second of the duke's bastards, Constance had borne him a son and a daughter, but the son died in infancy and Constance had no further children, leaving Gaunt to father subsequent issue from his sturdier Low Countries mistress. By Constance's death, in 1394, Gaunt's family comprised the children of Blanche, namely his son Henry of Bolingbroke aged 28, and his two daughters, Philippa and Elizabeth, married respectively to João I of Portugal and John Holand, earl of Huntingdon; the daughter of Constance married to Enrique III of Castile; and the four Beauforts.

From the first the Beauforts were accorded a place in the family group alongside the true blood. When Henry of Bolingbroke was admitted to the fraternity of Lincoln Cathedral in February 1386, it was in the company of John Beaufort and Thomas Swynford, and some diet lists of Gaunt's household from the early 1390s show the Beaufort brothers in residence for various periods.[3] On reaching manhood, John demonstrated his military aptitude alongside Bolingbroke in the jousts at St Ingelvert in the spring of 1390, though when Bolingbroke found himself denied passage through France, John did not join him on the *Reyse* in Prussia but proceeded on the

[1] T. F. Kirby, 'The Oratory of the Holy Trinity at Barton in the Isle of Wight', *Archaeologia*, 52 (1890), 311.

[2] S. Armitage-Smith, *John of Gaunt*, 390–1, 462–3.

[3] *Chaucer Life Records*, ed. M. C. Crow and C. C. Olson, 91; East Sussex Record Office, Glynde MS. 3469, m. 6, 7, 11, 12 (I owe this reference to Dr S. K. Walker).

duke of Bourbon's Barbary crusade in the company of the chamber knights, Clifford, Nevill, Clanvowe and Courtenay. He was in Lincolnshire to meet Bolingbroke on his return in the spring of 1391, but did not form part of his company for the prolonged expedition to the Holy Land in 1392–3. Instead, he seems to have joined the Lithuanian crusade in 1394 and could have fought at the battle of Lettow.[4] It was a mark both of John's military ability and of the political accord between Gaunt and the king that Richard made him a king's knight in June 1392 with an annuity of 100 marks to add to that of £100 from his father.[5] The foundations of Henry's clerical career were also laid by royal and ducal patronage. He had rooms in Peterhouse, Cambridge in 1388–9, and in Queen's college, Oxford in 1390–1 and 1392–3, his move being probably determined by his collation to the prebends of Sutton-cum-Buckingham and Thame in the winter of 1389–90. This had been by royal grant and, together with the prebend of Ricall and the wardenship of the free chapel at Tickhill in the gift of his father, provided maintenance for his studies.[6]

The royal favour shown to the young Beauforts reflected the close alliance between Richard II and John of Gaunt following the latter's return from Castile in November 1389. In the main this marked Gaunt's recognition that the young king could no longer be subject to restraint and that it was safer and more profitable to support than to oppose the development of royal power. He hoped to exercise a restraining influence over Richard himself and the former Appellants, and saw the Lancastrian family and affinity as forming a link between the court and the nobility. But Gaunt's own family interests were equally to be served by Richard's dependence upon him. In February 1390 he was granted the *Jura Regalia* of the palatinate of Lancaster in tail male, and in March he was made duke of Aquitaine for life.

In the next five years the possibility of creating an appanage in Aquitaine, perhaps for the Beauforts or his grandchildren, lured Gaunt into supporting Richard's search for a final peace with France. By June 1393 he and Gloucester returned from negotiations in Leulinghem with the outline of a territorial settlement which set generous boundaries to the duchy of Aquitaine. But the definition of its status in a peace treaty was bound to revive the latent fear of the Gascons that the duchy might in time become separated from the English crown. They had been alerted to this when the grant of 1390 breached the principle that the duchy should only be held by the king's eldest son and from the crown of England, and their

[4] *Expeditions to Prussia and the Holy Land made by Henry, Earl of Derby*, ed. L. Toulmin Smith (Camden Ser., 1894), pp. xiii, xxxviii, 100; J. L. Kirby, *Henry IV of England*, p. 91.

[5] *CPR 1396–9*, 63; PRO, DL 28/3/2 fo. 10.

[6] *BRUO* i. 140; J. Le Neve, *Fasti Ecclesiae Anglicanae, 1300–1541*, Lincoln, 113, 116.

alarm was increased by a French proposal in 1392 that it should become the appanage of Gaunt and his heirs, to be held from the French crown. This French move to separate Aquitaine from England was rebuffed by the English council and the negotiations of 1393 proceeded on the basis that Richard should do homage for the ownership of the duchy and Gaunt for the usufruct. But rumours and suspicions of Gaunt's intentions were widespread in England and Gascony, prompting the formal defiance of his authority in the duchy in April 1394. It led him to make a prolonged visit commencing in November 1394, on which he was accompanied by John Beaufort.[7] Constance's death in March of that year had given further point to such plans, for it opened the way to marriage with his long acknowledged and honoured mistress; that would entail making appropriate provision for her children without damage to the estate of the true heirs. But by the summer of 1395 plans for a ducal appanage, whatever their substance, were fast becoming unrealistic. Gaunt had bowed to the Gascons' objections and ultimately relinquished his title in 1398. Even so, Richard then appointed John Beaufort as his lieutenant in the duchy for seven years.[8]

After 1393 the acquiescence of the former Appellants in Richard's exercise of royal authority ceased, and the political harmony which Gaunt had sought to create began to dissolve. Arundel's growing alienation from Richard was paralleled by his own quarrel with Gaunt in 1394, and by 1396 Gloucester had come out in open opposition to the terms of the long truce with France. These years saw both the rapid enlargement of a royal affinity in Cheshire and the consolidation of a group of young nobility as Richard's favoured and pledged supporters. The emergence of a 'court' party comprising York, Rutland, Kent, Huntingdon, the young Salisbury, and some of the lesser baronage and chamber knights, had serious implications for Gaunts own influence over Richard and for the political 'amnesty' of the last five years, of which he had been the architect and in which the future of his own line, in the person of Bolingbroke, was directly at stake. His reception at court was less than cordial, but his response was to strengthen further his ties with Richard and his courtiers rather than distance himself from them. He attended the court constantly in these years witnessing every charter before July 1398.[9] Since his eldest son was not part of this new court circle, Gaunt seems to have intended that John Beaufort should represent Lancastrian influence there, renewing his association with the chamber knights which had been interrupted by accompanying his father to Aquitaine.

Gaunt's marriage to Catherine Swynford in Lincoln Cathedral in

[7] J. J. N. Palmer, *England, France, and Christendom, 1377–1399*, ch. 8–10. For John Beaufort's presence, see PRO, C 61/104 m. 7.

[8] C 61/105 m. 9, 11. [9] Armitage-Smith, *John of Gaunt*, 390; PRO, C 53/166, 167.

February 1396, undoubtedly with the king's prior approval, transformed the position and prospects of the Beauforts. It brought their legitimation, by papal bull in September, and by royal patent approved in the parliament of February 1397. John had attended Richard at the meeting with Charles VI at Calais in November 1396, and on 10 February 1397 was created earl of Somerset, thereby paving the way for his marriage with Margaret Holand, daughter of Thomas, earl of Kent, later in the year.[10] Gaunt's gratitude for these favours was for the moment matched by Richard's own need for his support in the impending confrontation with Gloucester and Arundel, already foreshadowed by their refusal to attend council. Gaunt, with Henry of Derby at his side, was to throw the weight of his authority as steward behind the proceedings against Gloucester and Arundel in the parliament of September 1397, while the new earl of Somerset joined with the other courtier earls as latter-day Appellants. Richard's celebration of his revenge was marked by the distribution of new dignities among the group, John's elevation to the rank of marquis of Dorset fittingly placing him after the dukes of the royal blood and above the newly ennobled earls. At the same time he and his new wife were granted in fee-tail eleven manors in Staffordshire, Northamptonshire, Wiltshire, and Norfolk, formerly of the earl of Warwick.[11] With the promotion of his eldest son as duke of Hereford and his new son-in-law as earl of Westmorland, Gaunt probably felt that the security of his family had been safeguarded against Richard's deep-seated sense of outrage over the events of ten years before. But in the tense weeks that followed the dissolution of parliament, rumours of a conspiracy against the house of Lancaster abounded, and faced with Mowbray's allegations of Richard's enmity, Gaunt once more sought safety in strengthening his ties with the court and contriving the isolation and ruin of his son's former associate.[12] York, Aumale, and Surrey became Hereford's pledges in the period preceding the appointed duel, while Norfolk remained in prison, conspicuously unable to find any who would act for him. In the will which Gaunt drew up shortly afterwards, he included York and Aumale among his supervisors and Worcester and Wiltshire as executors.[13] Both Gaunt and Somerset were members of the parliamentary committee set up to advise the king on the Hereford-Norfolk quarrel, and in the following months each received marks of Richard's favour and confidence. Already in November 1397 John had been made constable of Wallingford castle for life; to this was added on

[10] *CPL 1362–1404*, 545; *Rot. Parl.* iii. 343; *CPR 1396–9*, 86. Somerset was given precedence after the Earl Marshal but before the earl of Warwick.

[11] *CPR 1396–9*, 211; *CCR 1396–9*, 344; *CIM 1392–9*, nos. 283, 301.

[12] A. Tuck, *Richard II and the English Nobility*, 208; *Chronicles of London*, ed. C. L. Kingsford, 53–4.

[13] *Testamenta Eboracensia*, ed. J. Raine, i (Surtees Soc., 1836), 223–39; J. B. Post, 'The obsequies of John of Gaunt', *Guidhall Studies in London History*, 5 (1981), 2.

31 January 1398 the constableship of Dover and wardenship of the Cinque Ports. On 9 May 1398 he was appointed admiral of the north and west and on 2 September, two weeks before the fateful duel at Coventry, king's lieutenant in Aquitaine for seven years.[14] Gaunt himself, on 8 August was made hereditary constable of the new principality of Chester along with Aumale as chamberlain and Salisbury as steward.[15]

If these grants seemed to confirm Richard's goodwill towards the house of Lancaster, the blow of Hereford's banishment fell all the harder on his ageing father. It spelled the failure of his assiduous cultivation of the king's favour, a policy which had protected his interests as long as Richard needed his support, but served decreasingly to do so as there emerged a curial nobility of the king's own creation. By the autumn of 1398 the once all-embracing Lancastrian interest had become dangerously isolated. When Gaunt died in the following February, it was the courtiers Exeter, Aumale, Surrey, and Wiltshire who became the custodians of the Lancastrian lands. Yet even in disinheriting Hereford, Richard displayed his ambivalence towards the house of Lancaster. For the new custodians were chosen from Gaunt's executors or relatives, and their tenure was limited 'until Hereford or his heir should have sued the lands out of the king's hands, or have had another grant thereof from the king'. Should Hereford's heir find favour with Richard he might expect restoration.[16] The king looked for an acquiescent and dependent nobility who would receive their lands at his hands and enjoy them by his continued favour. Lancastrian power was too autonomous; Hereford already had the look of a potential heir to the crown, and an alternative king. The Beauforts posed no such threat, and Richard confirmed both Catherine's jointure and Gaunt's grants to the marquis of Dorset.[17] They owed their advancement to Richard himself and their future could only be in service to the crown. John certainly had no choice but to remain at court and, as one of the committee of 1398, to witness and assent both to Richard's revocation of the original permission for Hereford to take livery of his inheritance by attorney, and to the sentence of perpetual banishment. This opened up an ominous rift within the Lancastrian family, even though the fact that John was not given custody of any of the estates avoided any suggestion of an ultimate transfer of the inheritance to the distaff line.

There is virtually no indication how relations stood between Gaunt's heir and the Beauforts before his death, but in providing for his third family Gaunt had taken particular care to avoid any permanent disinheritance of

[14] *CPR 1396–9*, 289, 334, 410, 432; C 61/105 m. 9.

[15] R. R. Davies, 'Richard II and the principality of Chester, 1397–9' in *The Reign of Richard II*, ed. C. M. Barron and F. R. H. du Boulay, 266.

[16] *CFR 1391–99*, 293–7, 303.

[17] *CPR 1396–99*, 516, 532, 555.

his eldest son.[18] On 11 February 1397 he received royal licence to make a jointure to Catherine of the estate which he had received in 1372 in recompense for the surrender of Richmond. This comprised Knaresborough, Tickhill, and High Peak with manors in Sussex (notably Pevensey), and elsewhere. Henry of Derby was one of the duke's feoffees for this settlement, and since the grant followed that of 1372 providing remainder to the heirs of Gaunt's body, and not those of him and Catherine jointly, the lands would be reintegrated with the full Lancastrian inheritance upon her death. At the same time the Beauforts' legitimation placed them in the line of succession should the senior line fail or be disinherited, while the grant included a contingent remainder to the king.[19]

Even before his marriage Gaunt had taken steps to endow the Beauforts. In December 1391 he granted John some Northamptonshire manors extended at £88 p.a. and in 1394 he purchased the reversion of a group of Somerset manors from William, earl of Salisbury, for 5,000 marks.[20] It was this estate which determined John's new title, and on Salisbury's death in June 1397 two parts of these lands were transferred to him and his wife Margaret Holand, the remaining third being retained as dower by the Countess Elizabeth until 1415. In his will Gaunt distinguished the duchy lands forming Catherine's jointure from those which he had purchased for the endowment of her and her sons. A codicil provided that the grants made to her in fee were to pass to Thomas Beaufort with reversion to John and Joan and the right heirs, while John was to have the lands already granted him, with any residue of acquired lands going to Thomas.[21] Thomas, for the moment, was landless and his expectations from Catherine were small, though he was receiving an annuity of 300 marks at the time of Gaunt's death and was bequeathed 1,000 marks in the will. John's landed income was no more than that of a prosperous knight, supplemented by an annuity from Gaunt of £100 and the bequest of £1,000.[22] John's uncertain prospects and frequent absence before 1396 had perhaps caused him to defer marriage, but Joan and Thomas had already found marriages within the ranks of the more important knights of the Lancastrian affinity. Joan, already betrothed in 1386, was married in 1392 to Sir Robert Ferrers of Oversley, but his death and that of Margaret, wife

[18] Gifts by Henry of Derby to John Beaufort are recorded in DL 28/1/6 fo. 10.

[19] *CPR 1396–9*, 76, 516; *CCR 1396–9*, 365–6; *Sussex Feet of Fines*, ed. L. F. Salzman (Sussex Rec. Soc., 1916), 207; R. Somerville, *History of the Duchy of Lancaster*, 135 n. 3.

[20] In Northants: Oveston, Maxey, Eydon, and half of Brampton Parva (*CPR 1391–6*, 15; PRO, C 137/80); in Somerset: Curry Rivel, Martock, Langport, and the hundreds of Abdyke and Bulston (*CPR 1391–6*, 529; DL 28/32/21).

[21] Armitage-Smith, *John of Gaunt*, 420–36.

[22] DL 28/3/2/. A receiver-general's account for 1396–7 in Leeds central library (GC DL/3 fo. 6) records an annuity to Thomas of 100 marks. In 1402 Thomas had confirmation of an annuity of 300 marks in Norfolk granted by Gaunt in 1399 (*CPR 1401–5*, 98) and this was being paid in 1407 (Norwich Public Library MS NRS 11061).

of Sir Ralph Nevill, in 1396 enabled her to take Nevill as her second husband in November of that year.[23] Her advancement to the rank of countess in 1397 was a mark of Richard's favour to Gaunt rather than to the Nevills. By then Thomas Beaufort was married to Margaret, granddaughter and heiress of another Lancastrian retainer, Sir Robert Nevill of Hornby. She was still under age, living in the house of the duchess with her own governess and clothing allowance.[24]

Gaunt's direct endowment of the Beauforts had thus been limited; he had rather sought provision for them through royal favour, taking advantage of Richard's open-handedness and need for his uncle's support. John's accumulation of offices, dignities, and grants of land has already been discussed. By July 1397 Thomas was being retained for life by the king with an annuity of 100 marks, and in the following year he benefited from Norfolk's banishment, receiving custody of the castle and lordship of Castle Acre in Norfolk.[25] There is no evidence that he accompanied Richard to Ireland in 1399. Henry's career likewise blossomed from the time of his father's marriage. At the end of 1396 he secured the deanery of Wells by papal provision with permission to let it and the prebendary of Wedmore to farm while he continued his studies at Oxford. If this promotion was influenced by his brother's new territorial associations, it was to his family's traditional connection with the chapter at Lincoln that he owed his elevation to the episcopate. On 27 February 1398 Boniface IX provided him to the see, having on the same day translated the aged John Buckingham to Coventry and Lichfield, itself vacated by the translation of Richard Scrope to York. It is difficult to know who instigated these changes. Scrope was at this moment on a mission to the Curia and it is uncertain whether the pope was acting in response to his or the king's wishes. Nor is Richard likely to have requested the removal of the harmless if failing Buckingham, an action which the shocked Walsingham subsequently ascribed to the machinations of Gaunt.[26] Undoubtedly the duke had marked out the see for his own. He and his wife were munificent donors to the cathedral, in whose fraternity both their families were enrolled.[27] He was anxious to capitalize on royal and papal favour, to establish the second as he had the elder Beaufort while he lived. Buckingham was managing to survive far too long, resisting suggestions

[23] *Chaucer Life Records*, 91; *CP* xii. 547: Somerville, *Duchy of Lancaster*, 53 n. 5.

[24] Leeds central library MS GC DL/3 fo. 14v; *CP* ix, 491; Armitage-Smith, *John of Gaunt*, 436.

[25] *CPR 1396–9*, 171, 414.

[26] *BRUO* i. 140; R. G. Davies, 'Richard II and the Church in the years of the 'tyranny'', *Journal of Medieval History*, 1 (1974), 345–53. Walsingham says explicitly 'ob Ducis reverentiam et amorem', *Historia Anglicana*, ed. H. T. Riley ii (Rolls Ser., 1864), 228.

[27] C. Wordsworth, 'Inventories of plate, vestments etc., belonging to the cathedral church of the Blessed Mary of Lincoln', *Archaeologia*, 53 (1893), 19, 24; Davies, 'Richard II', 353; *Chaucer Life Records*, 91.

that he should resign. Indeed he even refused translation, continuing to perform his duties in the diocese as late as 11 June. Not until he had been offered retirement at Christ Church Canterbury did he make way for Henry Beaufort to take over on 3 July, and on 12 July render fealty and receive the temporalities at the Lancastrian castle of Tutbury.[28] Beaufort thus entered the episcopate as a political appointee, witness to an alliance of self-interest between Lancaster and the crown which was soon to be shattered. How Richard viewed the appointment is not known, but the removal of Archbishop Arundel had made it plain that in future the spiritual and political authority of the bishops was to be exercised in obedience to the royal will.

At the age of 23 Henry Beaufort was not wholly unqualified for the office of bishop. He had taken deacon's orders on 7 April 1397 and having completed the arts course at Oxford had commenced the study of theology, supported by his deanery and prebends in the dioceses of Lincoln, York, and Salisbury. The importance of his scholastic training should not be underrated. It was to show itself in the formal construction and rhetorical style of his public addresses in parliament, convocation, and diplomatic meetings, which always received commendation, and was conjoined with a natural and persuasive eloquence. His patronage, given to a circle of distinguished scholars who served as his officials, his acquisition of books, and his benefactions to colleges and the university, were all fruits of a strong association with Oxford formed in these years. If distinction of birth recommended his election as chancellor of the university in April 1397, this also reflected his evident ability and devotion to its interests[29]. All these offices except the wardenship of Tickhill were surrendered on his consecration as bishop in July 1398.

His association with Oxford of course continued *ex officio* and doubtless accounted for his inclusion on the university committee appointed in January 1399 to advise the crown on its response to the French proposal for a mutual withdrawal of obedience from the rival popes. Rejecting withdrawal, the committee put forward schemes for a general council which would enforce cession. It was Beaufort's first introduction to the conciliar problem.[30]

In the following month Gaunt's death imposed duties of a different kind. As Beaufort accompanied the funeral cortège from Northampton on its way to the interment at St Paul's, early in March 1399, we have the first glimpse of the young bishop in a conflict over jurisdiction with the abbey of

[28] Davies, loc. cit.

[29] *CPL* v. 26; C. E. Mallett, *History of the University of Oxford*, i. 248, 277; *Snappes Formulary*, ed H. E. Salter (OHS, 1924), 4, 11, 37, 332; J. R. McGrath *A History of the Queen's College*, i. 117.

[30] M. Harvey, 'Solutions to the Schism; a study of some English attitudes, 1378 to 1409' (*Kirchengeschichtliche Quellen u. Studien*, 12 (1983)), 102–4.

St Albans. The abbey, though admitting the cortège, feared to compromise its exemption from episcopal jurisdiction by permitting Beaufort to celebrate, and armed with a royal monition to the bishop, required him to give a formal indemnity to the abbey. Bishop Beaufort refused, and the abbot consequently declined to admit or provide lodging for the bishop or his mother. In this tense and unseemly situation, Bishop Braybrook advised Beaufort to give the required indemnity. The obsequies were then duly celebrated in the abbey church and hospitality offered to the bishop, who on the following day fulfilled his father's bequest of certain vestments to the convent. But Bishop Henry did not forget the incident, and on his first visitation early in the next reign the abbot found it advisable to placate him by permitting him to exercise his episcopal functions and by making him a gift of a ring which he coveted, containing a portion of the holy cross.[31] His installation at Lincoln probably took place in the first part of May 1399 when he also appointed Master John Burbache his vicar-general in spirituals in preparation for his own departure to Ireland in Richard's train.[32] Up to this date there is no indication that he frequented the court, and the only occasion on which he witnessed charters was when the court was nearby at Windsor in April. His inclusion among the group of court bishops who accompanied the king may have been as hostage for his brother or perhaps as tutor to his nephew, Bolingbroke's heir.[33]

Had Gaunt anticipated the verdict of exile which Richard II was to impose on his eldest son, the appointment of John as lieutenant in Aquitaine two weeks earlier might have struck him as ominous. Richard's removal of both supports was to quicken his demise, and Gaunt was in fact dead even before the date scheduled for John's departure, 1 April 1399. His death may have occasioned John's delay; he had been recruiting his ships and retinue throughout the winter, and Richard now sanctioned a short postponement until 30 April.[34] The council then ordered him to remain in attendance for a further forty days, for the safeguard of the realm. On 23 June, with Lancaster's invasion imminent, he drew £2,400 from the exchequer for the wages of the force he was taking to Aquitane. Thus, when the news of Henry's landing reached the council, Somerset was at the head of the only body of troops retained by the crown in southern

[31] *Gesta Abbatum Monasterii Sancti Albani*, ed. H. T. Riley, iii (Rolls Ser., 1869), 274–7, 438–40, 455, 472–4. Gaunt's interment at St Paul's was on 16 Mar.; J. B. Post, 'Obsequies', 3.

[32] Lincoln Archives Office, Reg. Beaufort, fo. 1v–68v. Letters of Burbache while Beaufort was '*agentis in remotis*', dated 5 July 1399, are in *The Register of Philip Repingdon*, ed. M. Archer, ii (Cant. & York Soc., 1963), 235. For Burbache, see *BRUO* i. 305–6.

[33] C 53/167, 23 April–1 May. He named his attorneys on 20 May, *CPR 1396–9*, 553, 569. In the latter part of 1398 he had mainly been at the episcopal manors of Sleaford and Stowe: Reg. Beaufort; PRO C 85/110.

[34] *CPR 1396–9*, 432, 588; *Winchester College Muniments*, ed. S. Himsworth, no. 10680, records payments to his troops at Plymouth in December 1398; yet protections for his retinue were still being issued on 6 July 1399: C 61/105, 106.

England. Whether his loyalty was suspect is difficult to know. On 12 July he received £200 from the exchequer for the wages of 100 lances and 200 archers for twenty days' service, and joined the duke of York who was assembling an army at St Albans.[35]

The two commanders decided to move westwards to Wallingford, where the queen resided and of which John was constable, gathering further reinforcements from the shires. Richard's councillors moved with the army, pressing on to Bristol to await the king's arrival from Ireland as the south-westerly direction of Henry of Lancaster's advance became known. While they fortified the city, York and Somerset encamped outside and prepared to face Lancaster's swollen army. They were certainly outnumbered and probably demoralized by the speed of his movements and the welcome he had received. York in effect decided to surrender for a free pardon, and went to Berkeley to meet his cousin. When it was Somerset's turn 'pour venir a mercy pour avoir paix a son frere', Northumberland and Hotspur sought to have him executed. Only Henry's intervention, claiming that his brother had always been his friend and had secretly sent letters to him abroad, saved his life.[36] The story may well be true; at least it accurately represents the ambivalent role that Somerset had been required to play over the past year when his quasi-attachment to the court and acquiescence in the seizure of Lancaster's inheritance could have fatally prejudiced him in the eyes of his half-brother. An ability to maintain an appearance of loyalty to divergent masters had enabled John Beaufort to survive the revolution of 1399. He had displayed cool mastery in his deception of the Ricardian courtiers and in the timing of his final shift to loyalty. The first crisis in the fortunes of the Beauforts had been surmounted, and their further advancement would depend on how far they vindicated the trust which their royal half-brother placed in them.

In the 1399 parliament John was among the former Appellants who stood charged with subscribing to the appeal, the death of Gloucester, the judgements on Arundel and Warwick, the exile of Bolingbroke, and the repeal of the patent in 1399. Although he seems to have avoided the recriminations, the throwing down of gages, and story-telling that then took place, he was separately examined like the rest and made answer like them that he had acted under compulsion. He claimed that he was ordered to join in the appeal when seated at dinner with Richard II in Nottingham castle and was in ignorance of it until then; that he did not partake of the sentence of exile, and agreed to the revocation of the patent out of fear.

[35] PRO SC 8/214/10688; E 403/562; *CPR 1399–1401*, 410.

[36] *Chronicque de la traison et mort de Richard Deux, Roy Dengleterre*, ed. B. Williams, 38–9. Bagot likewise claimed to have been in secret correspondence with Henry: *Chronicles of London*, 53.

With the rest, he suffered loss of his dignity and the surrender of his grants.[37]

The reconstitution of the Lancastrian family was unwelcome to the Percies, whose dominance in the next three years inhibited the advancement of the Beauforts in royal service. The Percies had lent support to Henry of Lancaster because Richard II had threatened their control of the north. Their price was the surrender into their hands of all the major military commands on the border and in North Wales. In addition Northumberland became constable and his son justiciar of Chester and North Wales, while his brother Thomas, earl of Worcester, not merely retained the grants and dignities he had received from the deposed king, but was now appointed admiral. By contrast John Beaufort had to relinquish his marquisate and restore to the earl of Warwick most of the lands he had received in 1397; he ceased to be constable of Dover and no more was heard of his appointment as lieutenant in Aquitaine. The earl of Westmorland received Mowbray's office of marshal and was granted the honour of Richmond, but was effectively excluded by the Percies from the area of his natural influence. But while the military commands rested in the hands of the Percies, Henry filled the principal administrative and court offices with trusted members of the Lancastrian affinity. The chancellor, treasurer, three principal household officers, and the king's chamberlain had all been his or Gaunt's servants; only the keeper of the privy seal, Richard Clifford, survived from the service of Richard II. John Beaufort joined this group by his appointment as chamberlain in November 1399, an office that kept him at Henry's side and, in effect, at the centre of government.[38]

For the first four years of the reign Henry governed through his entourage. He was only occasionally at London where the continual council remained, composed initially of the three great officers of state, the earl of Worcester, Sir John Cheyne, and John Doreward.[39] Its responsibilities were largely administrative and executive, the king communicating his orders or observations either by trusted messengers or by signet letters and bills endorsed by the chamberlain.[40] But the council could also meet away from London, in the king's presence, as it did on 10 April 1401 at Leeds castle, and on such occasions Somerset formed part of it. More

[37] *Chronicles of London*, 52–9; *Annales Ricardi Secundi et Henrici Quarti* in *Johannis de Trokelowe* etc., ed. H. T. Riley (Rolls Ser., 1865), 303–18; *Rot. Parl.* iii 450–2.

[38] Kirby, *Henry IV*, 71–3, 258–60; A. R. Rogers, 'The political crisis of 1401', *Nottingham Medieval Studies*, 12 (1968), 85–96; *CPR 1399–1401*, 79, 192; PRO, E 28/7 18 Nov. 1399.

[39] A. L. Brown, 'The Commons and the Council in the reign of Henry IV', *EHR* 79 (1964), 1–30, and in more detail in 'The Privy Seal in the early fifteenth century', D.Phil. thesis (Oxford, 1957).

[40] A. L. Brown, 'The authorization of letters under the Great Seal', *BIHR* 37 (1964), 125–56, and thesis pp. 22–28; *CSL* 30–1; *CCR 1399–1402*, 225–8, 245. There are numerous endorsement by Somerset in the files E 28/7, 9, 10, 11.

informally his advice and that of others with the king must often have influenced Henry's decisions, notably in the crucial distribution of patronage. Who was at Henry's side is very difficult to know. The list of those most frequently witnessing royal charters in the first years shows a fairly well defined group, composed of the archbishop of Canterbury, the bishops of London, Winchester, Lincoln, and Exeter, the duke of York, the earls of Northumberland, Somerset, and Westmorland, and Lords Grey of Ruthin, Roos, and Willoughby.[41] In these Henry IV put greatest reliance, and the consistent appearance of the Beauforts among them is significant. Yet charters were mostly issued on restricted occasions and afford no guide to those who were habitually in the king's presence. Thus Henry Beaufort witnessed only on occasions when he was in London for meetings of parliament and great councils. In the intervening periods he apparently resided at one or other of his episcopal manors, from where his letters are dated.[42] His itinerary and that of the royal household in no way coincide, although the absence of episcopal instruments for the summer of 1400 may indicate that he accompanied the royal army on the Scottish campaign. When the bishop visited London he stayed at the episcopal residence in the Old Temple; otherwise his favourite manor house seems to have been that of Lydington in Rutland. He spent most of the academic year, from the commencement of the Michaelmas term 1401 to May 1402, at Oxford, where he was on occasion honourably regaled at Queen's, his old college, and on 25 March conducted an ordination in the college chapel.[43]

Particularly after the revolt of January 1400 the number of those whom Henry could trust among a depleted nobility was severely limited. As chamberlain John must have shared the imminent danger to Henry and his family at the Epiphany revels at Windsor, and joined in the resistance organized at London and the pursuit of the conspirators as they fled westwards. His share in the confiscations that followed was the lands of Ralph, Lord Lumley, later valued at 540 marks, together with goods to the value of 200 marks and the two Devon manors of Sandford and Aller Peverel belonging to Sir William Asthorp, later valued at £80 p.a.[44] After five years of enjoyment of the Lumley lands he surrendered them to John, Lord Lumley, for £1,000, but the Devonshire manors became permanent

[41] C 53/168–74; A. L. Brown, 'The reign of Henry IV' in *Fifteenth Century England*, ed. S. B. Chrimes, C. D. Ross, R. A. Griffiths, 1–28.

[42] Beaufort was in London in Oct.–Nov. 1399 (parliament), Feb. and May–July 1400 (council), Jan.–Mar. 1401 (parliament), Aug. 1401, Feb. 1402 (councils), and Apr.–May 1402 (the king's marriage). His movements outside London are recorded in LAO, Reg. Beaufort, fos. 1^{v}–68^{v} (memoranda) and incidentally in *York Memorandum Book*, ed. J. W. Percy (Surtees Soc., 1973), 166; *Peterborough Local Administrations*, ed. W. T. Mellows (Northants Rec. Soc., 1939), 222, 229. (I owe these references to Mr G. Belfield.)

[43] McGrath, *Queen's College*, 131 n. 3; LAO, Reg. Beaufort, fo. 105.

[44] *CPR 1399–1401*, 173, 281; *CPR 1401–5*, 3, 17; *CCR 1399–1402*, 269; *CIM 1399–1422*, 44 no. 57.

parts of the Beaufort estates. The fatal involvement of the Holand earls of Huntingdon in the rising of 1400 also yielded some spoils to the Beauforts. Huntingdon's widow, Elisabeth of Lancaster now married the king's knight, Sir John Cornewaile, and was able to retain control of her former husband's estates and the custody of her children, making Dartington a centre of Lancastrian influence in the west country.[45] The lands of the earldom of Kent, now burdened with two dowagers, were distributed during the minority of Edmund as rewards. Henry Beaufort was granted the custody of the Lincolnshire lands and recovered a loan of £100 in plate, while Thomas was granted forfeited Holand manors in Kent, Sussex, and Hampshire, as well as receiving the custody of the lands of Baldwin Frevill valued at 400 marks p.a.[46] Having received these significant accretions to their resources, the eldest and youngest Beauforts were required to equip themselves for Henry IV's Scottish expedition in the summer, John leading a force of 39 lances and 160 archers, Thomas one of 5 lances and 24 archers.[47] Even so, John found himself compelled to borrow from Richard Whittington to meet the outlay.[48] Henry, as we have seen, may well have accompanied them. Along with the other bishops at the council in February at which the expedition was discussed, he had agreed to make a personal contribution at the rate of a clerical tenth by way of loan; his failure to do so may suggest that he went in person instead.[49]

The expedition had a political as well as military context. It had been mounted following the Scots' invasion of November 1399 to assert royal claims over Scotland and support the Percies' territorial ambitions across the border. At the same time it was a demonstration, within Percy country, of the size and strength of the royal affinity. For this large army was raised not by indenture but by summoning all who had a personal bond with the king as magnates, retainers, and annuitants. The large contingent of the earl of Westmorland recalled his importance for border defence, even though he held no permanent command there; similarly the numerous retinues of the household knights and esquires dispelled any impression that their service was merely in court or administration. It was the first occasion when all those who had received fees and annuities in the massive distribution of patronage in the early months of the reign were mobilized for royal service, and their presence on the expedition was made a condition of continued payment.[50] In this sense the Scottish expedition had—or was intended to have—a similar significance to Richard II's Irish

[45] *CPR 1399–1401*, 483, 550; E 28/8 9 May 1400.

[46] *CPR 1399–1401*, 176, 194, 206, 247; *CCR 1399–1402*, 435; *CIM 1399–1422*, 208, no. 379.

[47] PRO, E 101/43/3 m. 2; *CCR 1399–1402*, 39–40, *CFR 1399–1405*, 85.

[48] PRO, E 404/20/129.

[49] *PPC* i. 105.

[50] A. L. Brown, 'The English campaign in Scotland, 1400' in *British Government and Administration*, ed. H. Hearder and H. R. Loyn, 40–54.

expedition of 1394–5. In this demonstration of the loyalty and strength of the royal affinity the chamberlain had a central role, advising upon, and sometimes witnessing, the grants of annuities, and it was he and Waterton who were entrusted with the great seal of gold used for the *rotulus viagii*. Moreover, on its return in September part of the army accompanied the king on a circuit of North Wales, in a show of strength following Glyndwr's attack on a prominent member of the court, Lord Grey of Ruthin. Somerset was undoubtedly with the king because on 8 November he received a grant of Glyndwr's forfeited lands, and on the same day the custody of lands to the value of 800 marks during the minority of Fulk Fitzwarin.[51] This did not foreshadow service in Wales; he returned to London for a meeting of the council in December, preparatory to parliament, and to supervise the arrangements for the Emperor Manuel's visit to the court at Eltham over Christmas.[52]

The following two years brought a steadily developing crisis in the relations of Henry IV and the Percies. As they sought to tighten their grip on the administrative and household offices, and over the military commands in Wales and the northern border, the king increasingly drew support from the families linked to the house of Lancaster by blood or traditional loyalty. Among these the Beauforts became steadily more prominent. Henry was rendered additionally vulnerable by parliamentary criticism of his excessive expenditure on the household, deepening financial embarassment, and military ineffectiveness. In this the Percies made common cause with the Commons. In the parliament of January 1401 the crown's request for taxation produced the demand for a named and sworn council. This was conceded, although the identity of its members can only be deduced from subsequent attendances. It is doubtful whether it included either of the Beauforts, who were present in the next two years only at meetings of the great council. But Northumberland and Worcester, some lesser bishops, and five of the household knights and esquires did attend more frequently.[53] More material was the change of the major household officers. Worcester recovered the office of steward which he had held under Richard II, while the treasurer and controller of the household and the king's chamberlain, all long standing Lancastrian servants, were also replaced by former servants of Richard. Among the great officers of state John Scarle surrendered the chancellorship to Richard's former chancellor Bishop Edmund Stafford, while Henry IV's confidant John Norbury was replaced by Allerthorpe as treasurer. These changes clearly represented something more than the re-introduction of

[51] *CPR 1399–1401*, 380, 386, 500; *CCR 1399–1402*, 242.

[52] E 28/8 18 Dec. 1400.

[53] Somerset was present at council on 5 Nov. 1401 at Hertford and 31 Mar. 1402 at Westminster: PRO C 81/1398, C 81/1540/17. See in general Brown, 'The Commons and the Council', loc. cit. and Rogers, 'The political crisis of 1401' loc. cit.

experienced officials, or a magnate reaction against men of insufficient status. Criticism of Henry's excessive reliance on his Lancastrian familiars had united the interests of the Commons and the Percies, both of whom felt the immediate effects of royal insolvency, as cash revenue dropped, assignments soared, and fictitious loans began to climb. The administrative and fiscal autonomy of the household was checked and placed under the surveillance of a Percy as steward, while the Commons looked to the enlarged and sworn council under Northumberland as a guarantor of good governance. Somerset survived these changes, and his loyal services and those of Rutland were formally recognized as having purged the charges brought against them at the first parliament of the reign.[54]

The threat of war in Wales, Scotland, and France placed Henry IV's finances under further strain and helped to worsen his relations with the Percies. In Wales, the Tudor brothers' capture of Conwy in April 1401 opened a two-year period which saw English authority repudiated over large areas. The capture of Lord Grey of Ruthin in April 1402, and of Sir Edmund Mortimer in June, revealed the vulnerability of the marcher lordships, while the failure of two royal expeditions in the autumns of 1401 and 1402 showed the futility of these expensive demonstrations of military strength. Until 1403, although Prince Henry exercised an intermittent and nominal command at Chester, the control of operations remained largely in the hands of the Percies. Hotspur became king's lieutenant in North Wales on 31 March 1402, and in South Wales the earl of Worcester was made lieutenant and the prince's governor. His ambitious plan for a concerted attack on the Welsh heartland from north and south never took effect, and the spread of the revolt necessitated a new policy.

Emphasis was now placed on containing the rebellion by a sustained military presence, and in particular on preventing its spread to the marches. The organization of these under the young earls of Arundel and Stafford as the king's lieutenants in July 1402, and the appointment of Lord Grey of Codnor and the new Lord Charleton of Powys to defend South Wales in August, marked the first phase of a policy which was taken to its logical conclusion when Prince Henry indented as the king's lieutenant for the whole of Wales for one year from 1 April 1403 with a force of four barons, twenty knights, 500 men-at-arms, and 2,500 archers.[55] Although the earl of Worcester's retinue was by far the largest in this force, the nucleus was the prince's household, and this vesting of the prince, not yet 16, with overall command signalled a clear displacement of the Percies in this area. For the prince's apprenticeship in Wales was to do more than

[54] A. Steel, *The Receipt of the Exchequer*, 83–4; J. M. W. Bean, 'Henry IV and the Percies', *History*, 44 (1959), 212–27: *Rot. Parl.* iii. 460.

[55] W. R. M. Griffiths, 'The military career and affinity of Henry prince of Wales, 1399–1413', M.Litt. thesis (Oxford, 1980), 14; *Foedera, Conventiones, et Litterae*, ed. T. Rymer, viii. 291; *CPR 1401–5*, 216; E 404/18/300.

introduce him to the arts of war; it was to forge close ties with a group of young nobility who were to become his political associates. Those named as lieutenants and captains in the marches were the most eminent, and into this circle came Thomas Beaufort, who, in August 1402, received his first military command as captain of Ludlow.[56] Bishop Henry was forging a less orthodox connection, for at about this time he fathered his only known bastard, Joan, by Alice, the recently widowed Lady Charleton of Powys and daughter of the late earl of Arundel.[57] The prince's appointment also signified the hardening of the royal attitude against the readiness of the Percies to accommodate the grievances of the Welsh and come to terms with Glyndwr. Mortimer's recognition of Glyndwr in December 1402, and Henry's refusal to ransom him, helped to signal the divergence of the Percies from the household and marcher lords, who organized the ransoming of Lord Grey and who backed the king's refusal to deal with the Welsh except as rebels.[58]

As in Wales, so too in the north, the inability of the Percies to contain the military situation led to increased royal intervention. Throughout the winter of 1401–2 Henry had striven for an extension of the Scottish truce, and during this period had transferred the keeping of Roxburgh castle from the hands of Hotspur first to Lord Grey of Codnor and then to the earl of Westmorland. The Percies' victory at Homildon Hill in the summer opened up the question of how this was to be exploited. Hotspur's refusal to surrender his prisoner, the earl of Douglas, clearly signalled their ambition to secure the Douglas lands and establish themselves astride the border. On 2 March Henry was compelled to sanction this by the formal grant of the Douglas lands, and soon after Hotspur advanced to Cocklaw. In fact the Percies found that they had overreached themselves, for they could not on their own face the fully mobilized Scottish royal army. Yet they had no wish to appeal for royal intervention, which would undermine their autonomy and control in the borders. Hoping to raise an army under their own command at royal expense they demanded the payment of their dues from the crown, but Henry's response was to move north in early July with a force designed to assist the Percies in meeting the Scottish challenge. It does not seem that he was anticipating their revolt, but this had become their only alternative to military defeat by the Scots or subordination to royal authority.[59]

[56] *CPR 1401–5*, 140. In May 1402 he had been present at the appointment of an embassy to negotiate Prince Henry's marriage *Foedera*, viii 257.

[57] K. B. McFarlane, 'At the deathbed of Cardinal Beaufort', in *England in the Fifteenth Century*, 135 n. 113.

[58] *CPR 1401–5*, 155–6, 171, 213; *Rot. Parl.* iii. 487. However in Feb. 1403 Henry authorized the council to prepare peace negotiations with Glyndwr to placate the Percies: *CSL* 108.

[59] P. McNiven, 'The Scottish policy of the Percies and the strategy of the rebellion of 1403', *BJRL* 62 (1980), 498–530.

The growing importance of the younger nobles and members of the king's family was also visible in the military and diplomatic measures taken in the face of growing French hostility. For nearly two years the presence of Queen Isabella guaranteed the continuance of the truce with France, but already in January 1401 the hostility of the duke of Orléans was manifested in the grant of the duchy of Guyenne to the Dauphin Louis, and by the summer the English position there had become critical with the defection of the count of Foix. The Gascons' loyalty to the new dynasty was indeed uncertain. The residual hostility to Gaunt, uncertainty about Henry IV's intentions, and latent fears of the separation of the duchy from the English crown, combined to produce a highly unstable situation. Henry met this by appointing the earl of Rutland lieutenant for three years, as one 'who after his sons was closest in blood and friendship'.[60] Earlier, in April 1401, Somerset had been appointed captain of Calais, at a time when French attacks on English shipping were increasing, leading to a general breakdown of the maritime truces.[61] These two appointments, the reverse of what might have been expected, revealed Henry's discernment and priorities. Not merely would Gascon fears have been revived by Somerset's reappointment; Henry depended too greatly on him as one of the small group of nobility bound by family ties and political fortune to the Lancastrian house, and needed to retain his services in an English context. By November 1401, Somerset was at Calais, accompanied by the bishop of Rochester, to negotiate with French commissioners for the preservation of the truce.[62]

But if this removed for the present the Beauforts' expectations of establishing themselves in France, it facilitated their association with the Percies in the king's personal diplomacy. Somerset, as chamberlain, and Worcester, as steward, were entrusted with the return of Isabella in August 1401, and Somerset was present, with the three Percies, at Henry's proxy wedding to Joan of Navarre in April 1402, when Henry Bowet officiated. In June 1402 Somerset accompanied Henry's daughter Blanche to Heidelberg for her marriage with Rupert, duke of Bavaria and king of the Romans, while in May Henry and Thomas Beaufort had witnessed the appointment of proctors for the marriages of Princess Philippa and the Prince of Wales.[63] On 6 November 1402 Somerset and Worcester, accompanied this time by the bishop of Lincoln, sailed to Brittany to conduct Joan to England. Landing at Falmouth on 3 February 1403, they

[60] M. Vale, *English Gascony, 1399–1453*, 38–43.

[61] E 101/68/182, E 101/69/309; *CCR 1399–1402*, 536; C. J. Ford, 'Piracy or policy: the crisis in the Channel, 1400–1403', *TRHS* 29 (1979), 63–78.

[62] *Diplomatic and Scottish Documents*, nos. 342, 355, 362. The truce was ratified in Aug. 1402 and Aug. 1403.

[63] *PPC* i. 136; *CCR 1399–1402*, 364; Kirby, *Henry IV*, 138–40. A document in *Cotton Ms. Galba B.I*, ed. E. Scott and L. Gilliodts-van-Severen, 90 implies that Henry Beaufort was on the mission to Germany, but his register shows him in England in July 1402.

proceeded to Winchester where, on 7 February, Henry Beaufort officiated at the marriage of his royal half-brother in the cathedral.[64]

Three weeks later Beaufort succeeded Edmund Stafford as chancellor. It seems unlikely that Stafford was dismissed, since he was closely enough connected with the court group to be one of Somerset's feoffees for all his lands in April 1402 together with Henry Beaufort, Bishop Bowet, Thomas Langley, and Henry Merston.[65] Bowet had recently become treasurer in succession to Allerthorpe, and Langley had succeeded Clifford as keeper of the privy seal in November 1401. Unlike the courtier Beauforts, these men were career administrators. Henry Beaufort's attendance at the council had been infrequent, only five recorded occasions between April and October 1402. If Beaufort's appointment was in the tradition of Arundel and Courtenay, there is every reason to believe that his abilities were recognized as matching his birth.

He had a somewhat more prominent role in the parliament which sat during October and November 1402. This witnessed Northumberland's delivery of his prisoners, and the Commons coupled their thanks with commendation of Prince Henry and the king for their service in Wales. But the Commons' main concern, as that of the king, was the grant of taxation, and it was probably for the discussion of this and their lengthy common petition that they sought a committee of lords with whom to intercommune. The Speaker, Sir Henry Retford, was a Lincolnshire knight well known to the Beauforts, and the four earls, bishops, and barons named for this purpose included both the earl of Somerset and the bishop of Lincoln. The renewal of the wool subsidy and tunnage and poundage, and the grant of a whole tenth and fifteenth, indicated their success in reaching agreement on the Commons' proposals for financial reforms. These included the reservation of feudal incidents to the exchequer, restraints of grants of annuities, and resumption of alien priories. Their concern over the decline of the customs was expressed in a number of petitions for the tightening up of collection, the enforcement of bullion regulations, and the maintenance of the monopoly of the Calais staple[66]. All these were matters on which Henry Beaufort was to be in recurrent negotiations with the parliaments of the next forty years. He was also one of the royal emissaries who persuaded convocation to make a generous grant of one and a half clerical subsidies in October.[67]

While the mood in the country was changing to one of disillusion with

[64] E 404/19/309; E 101/320/38. Beaufort's retinue numbered 46 esquires and 74 archers, headed by John, Lord Berkeley. A. W. Goodman, 'The marriage of Henry IV and Joan of Navarre' (pamphlet, 1934).

[65] *CPR 1401–5*, 95.

[66] *Rot. Parl.* iii. 486–7, 491, 495, 500, 508–10.

[67] *Concilia Magnae Britanniae et Hiberniae*, ed. D. Wilkins iii. 270–2; A. R. Rogers, 'Clerical taxation under Henry IV', *BIHR* 46 (1973), 128.

the new regime, that of the Commons remained constructive, even though some of its members must have been aware of the critical condition of royal finances at the end of the king's September campaign. The summer had brought a further worsening of the prolonged financial crisis, with cash receipts reaching their lowest level of the reign and considerable default on assignments, particularly to the Percies. The largest borrowing operation of the reign was launched, raising £16,824 in this term. That exhausted the king's credit and when, in September, the treasurer sought to borrow again for the costs of the royal expedition in Wales, he reported a general refusal to lend on the security of the king's jewels unless lenders were given express permission to sell them if the exchequer defaulted on repayment.[68] These difficulties no doubt accounted for Bowet's resignation half-way through the parliament and his replacement, possibly through Northumberland's influence, by Guy Mone, a former servant of Richard II. Almost certainly he was not Henry IV's choice, for in September 1403 after the Percy revolt he was replaced by the king's courtier friend William, Lord Roos.

Henry Beaufort's departure from Oxford in the summer of 1402 meant the end of his hitherto mainly pastoral and academic activities as he moved towards the centre of politics and administration. By the time he became chancellor he must have been fully aware of the difficulties, financial and political, facing Henry IV. Although the grants of parliament and convocation eased the position at the exchequer, it was Henry's inability and unwillingness to meet the demands of the Percies that provoked the first crisis of the reign. Henry IV had sought to accommodate their ambitions within his government, placing in their hands the defence of the north and the safety of his eldest son, and engaging them fully in his personal diplomacy and councils. Even while others came increasingly to share the king's confidence and be entrusted with responsibilities, from none of these spheres were the Percies excluded to the very moment of their revolt. Henry acted as if he fully trusted them. Nevertheless they could see their dominance of office and royal policy daily weakening, and read the signs of an emerging Lancastrian family group composed of Henry's sons, the Beauforts, and the Nevills, linked to the young earls of Warwick, Arundel, and Stafford.[69] Although Northumberland was prominent in the proceedings of the 1402 parliament, as Worcester had been in those of 1401, the court interest had secured the ransoming of Lord Grey, and in the Commons someone promoted a petition for the restoration of Somerset to the rank of marquis. Somerset tactfully declined on the ground that it was an alien title, but such a proposal, affording recognition of his

[68] Steel, *Receipt*, 86–7; Bean, 'Henry IV and the Percies', 223; C 81/1540/40.

[69] *Incerti Scriptores Chronicon Angliae*, ed. J. A. Giles, (hereafter *Chron. Angl.*) 31 notes the hostility of the Percies to the *milites curiales*.

blood relationship with the king and giving him precedence over the other earls, is unlikely to have endeared him to the Percies.

It is tempting to see this as the first of a series of occasions over the next twenty years when the Commons apparently spontaneously commended one or other of the Beauforts for their services to the king and the realm, and to note that this was the first parliament in which Thomas Chaucer, later their mouthpiece in the Commons, sat. Chaucer's relations were closest with Bishop Henry, whose sensitivity to the affinity of the Beauforts to the royal house was to surface on occasions throughout his career. Was the petition an incautious expression of his ambition, which Somerset was forced to disclaim? Somerset had no doubts of the king's special favour, for on 26 November 1401 Henry IV had acted as godfather to his eldest son Henry, and granted the infant an annuity of 1,000 marks at the exchequer in lieu of lands—an overdue recompense for John's own lack of endowment on his elevation to the peerage by Richard II.[70]

The rise of the Beauforts had been neither swift nor inevitable. It had taken place over a full six years from 1397 to 1403 and had been punctuated by periods of uncertainty and danger. At all points it had depended on the favour of the dukes of Lancaster and the crown, and was determined by the changing relationship between these. Gaunt had procured their legitimation as a point of personal honour, but it enabled him to use the Beauforts as a link with the group of Richard's courtier nobles from which Bolingbroke was, perhaps by his own choice, excluded, and to forge and strengthen alliances with the Holands and Nevills. Richard did not extend to them the enmity he nursed towards Bolingbroke, and as the price of Gaunt's support he advanced their careers and accorded them a measure of trust. But by 1399 the price of royal protection had come to be the acceptance of Richard's disinheritance of Gaunt's heir. In this acute division of loyalties John could plead that he had very little choice. There is no indication that he, or Richard, envisaged the supplanting of the true heirs by the Beauforts, nor that Bolingbroke harboured suspicions of this. Gaunt had been careful not to disinherit his eldest son in providing for his new family, and although there is little evidence of close connections between Henry and John prior to 1399, the Beauforts had been reared in the Lancastrian family group and had ties of loyalty and gratitude to it. John acted circumspectly if with some ambivalence in 1399, but Henry IV had every inducement to accept his professions of fidelity, surrounded as he was by a nobility riddled and depleted by treachery and dominated by the military power of the Percies. Throughout the first four years of the reign, while Henry IV strove to maintain his independence of the Percies, Somerset as chamberlain was at the head of the group of officials and

[70] *CPR 1401–5*, 276.

nobility who formed the royal entourage, and, because Henry IV rarely attended the council at Westminster, he became the principal source of advice and the channel for patronage. His endorsement is found frequently on petitions of all kinds in these years. Apart from his diplomatic missions, he was probably rarely absent from the king's side.

His rewards were varied, and not always productive. The grants from the forfeited Beauchamp and Lumley lands had to be surrendered, while the Glyndwr estates can have produced little in his lifetime. His own landed income was probably little in excess of 1,000 marks p.a., and he had difficulty in collecting his annuity of £1,000. He was awarded the custody and marriage of some important heirs in his latter years, but the yield of these is impossible to assess.[71] All this, together with the profit of his office, was probably sufficient to maintain his estate; but as the grant of 1,000 marks p.a. to his son shows, it did not constitute sufficient endowment on which a family with a high precedence in the peerage could be founded. He was one of the service nobility, not a territorial magnate who could draw on traditional loyalties or forge bastard feudal ties. It is doubtful if he had recruited many retainers. The fact that, despite his military aptitudes, he had rendered service almost wholly at court reflected Henry IV's wishes and the dominance of the Percies, but it also distinguished him from the new generation of marcher lords who gathered round Prince Henry. His younger brother Thomas had been given a foothold in this company, but his prospects were still those of a knightly scion of a noble house. Bishop Henry's career showed no signal advance under the new dynasty until 1402, perhaps because his personal connections had been closer to the prince than to his father; he was not a courtier, and could not boast administrative experience, as could Lancastrian churchmen such as Bowet, Bubwith, and the aspiring Langley, and he had had little opportunity to demonstrate his talents in council. Nevertheless his ability, as much as his ambitions, must have been evident in 1403 when Henry IV made him chancellor, perhaps at Somerset's suggestion. Despite the jealousy of the Percies, the Beauforts had moved gradually towards the centre of power as relatives of the king.

It is unlikely that Somerset took part in the battle of Shrewsbury, for he had gone to Calais in March and had probably remained there throughout May and June for the negotiations over the renewal of the truce.[72] As

[71] His main grants had come in 1400 from the forfeited Glyndwr, Lumley, and Asthorp lands, valued at 300 marks p.a., 540 marks p.a., and £80 p.a. respectively, and the custody of the Harrington lands at 800 marks. (*CPR 1399–1401*, 381, 500; *CPR 1401–5*, 17, 19). Lumley recovered his lands in 1405 on payment of £1,000: (ibid., 503). For the list of his lands see Appendix II. The above valuation is mainly based on the account of 1419–20 rather than the IPM and omits the Glyndwr lands. In 1408 and 1410 he had the custody of the lands of Ivo Fitzwarin and Walter Fitzwalter: *CPR 1405–8*, 468; *PPC* i. 329.

[72] *CPR 1401–5*, 276; *CIM 1399–1422*, 133 no. 257.

captain of Ludlow Thomas Beaufort must surely have been present. Henry Beaufort was in London where, on 18 July, as chancellor he opened the king's letter written from Burton on Trent the previous day, summoning all lords, knights, and esquires to his side against the Percies, and passed it to the council with a note probably in his own hand for the issue of letters.[73] After the battle the Percies' offices were distributed among the Lancastrian supporters, including the young nobility who over the past year had grouped around the prince. The control of the north was vested in Westmorland as warden of the West March, and John of Lancaster, under his tutelage, as warden of Berwick and the East March. In Wales the new duke of York was made lieutenant in the south, and Arundel in the north, while the earl of Arundel, with Lords Berkeley, Burnell, Charleton, and Audley, were appointed governors of the march, and Warwick, who had recently received livery of his inheritance, was made captain of Brecon. It was with this group that Thomas, still constable of Ludlow, was to play an increasingly important role in the following years. Although the Beauforts did not themselves directly benefit from the spoils of the Percies, Henry IV's victory as certainly opened a new phase in their careers as had Gaunt's marriage or Richard's fall.

[73] *PPC* i. 208–9. The subscription and signature may well be in Beaufort's hand: BL Cotton MS. Cleopatra F.III, fo. 145.

2

The Challenge to the Dynasty, 1403–1407

HENRY IV survived the revolt of the Percies only to enter the most dangerous and wearing period of his reign. Much of Wales threw off English authority; the French attacked the south coast and Wales, invaded Gascony; and made preparations for a major assault on Calais; a series of plots among the nobility culminated in the second Percy rebellion of 1405. The war in the channel and the consequent disruption to trade with Flanders harmed the merchant community and undermined royal finances as wool exports fell during the years 1403–5. The crown's military and financial difficulties in turn provoked criticism in parliament where the Commons sought to limit household expenditure and royal patronage and to reserve taxation for the defence of the sea. In all these fields—war, rebellion, commercial relations, and parliament—the Beauforts rendered important services to Henry IV, helping to ensure his survival and winning his gratitude and favour. But the stress of these years undermined Somerset's health as it did that of the king.

Following the return of Isabella, French hostility to Henry IV's rule had become increasingly overt. In August 1402 and March 1403 Louis d'Orléans issued a personal challenge to Henry as a usurper, and in the following years French raids on the south coast and Wales posed a continual danger. Even more menacing was the threat to Calais and English trade with Flanders. The undeclared war in the Channel, initiated by the French fleet sent to Scotland in 1402, continued with mounting losses in 1403 and precipitated a crisis in relations with the Four Members of Flanders. The English government endeavoured to maintain a sharp distinction between French and Flemish merchants as legitimate objects of English piracy, and one of Henry Beaufort's first preoccupations as chancellor was to reach a new agreement with the Flemish in March 1403, giving guarantees of protection and recompense for losses. This was strictly enforced by the council in the following months. Even so, in July the Flemish were forced to take reprisals against the activity of English pirates such as Hawley and Mixto by impounding English merchandise in Sluys valued at £10,000. For the moment this put an end to the promise of a commercial truce with the duke of Burgundy, to which Charles VI had given formal approval only the previous month. The mutual economic dependence of Flanders and England, and the desirability of preserving the immunity of commercial ties from the impending Anglo-French war, was well recognized on both sides; however by the end of 1403 Philip was becoming unable to detach himself from the warlike preparations of the count of Saint-Pol for an attack on Calais.[1]

From late November 1403 the council was giving the highest priority to the defence of Calais, and was considering estimates for two sizeable fleets, of 1,000 men-at-arms and 2,000 archers, under Sir Thomas Beaufort and Lord Berkeley, to keep the northern and western approaches. Thomas Beaufort at once began to organize convoys of merchantmen between the Tyne and Thames and, following the grant of a tax for the safeguard of the sea in the spring parliament of 1404, he indented to serve for six months with a force of 900 men. This mustered early in June and patrolled the straits for thirteen weeks.[2] This action seems to have deterred the French fleets gathered at Harfleur and Sluys, and to have frustrated the proposed blockade of Calais by the fleet of the count of Saint-Pol assembled at Gravelines. To the same parliament John petitioned for the payment of his arrears as captain of Calais, amounting at the end of 1403 to £11,423, and warned of possible treachery among the garrison when the truce expired on 3 March. He was promised reinforcements and payment from the first money available, and soon after he crossed to Calais, taking personal command and remaining there probably throughout the summer.[3] But the problem remained critical; the parliamentary grant proved ineffective and in August Somerset's lieutenant, Richard Aston, again appealed for money. The council assigned him 5,000 marks on the clerical tenth and proposed to allocate to Calais half the wool subsidy for the following five years, but even so the garrison's wages were two full years in arrears. With the French fleet poised for invasion throughout the autumn of 1404, Somerset sent Aston to report the urgency of the situation to the Coventry parliament, while at Calais the English commissioners, armed with personal instructions from the chancellor, strove to keep lines open with the Four Members, settling grievances as they arose and making representations against the warlike preparations of Orléans and the count of Saint-Pol.[4]

Both the Beauforts returned to England in the winter of 1404–5, John being afflicted with illness, while Thomas prepared for further service in Wales. To meet the continuing threat to Calais, the council proposed for

[1] C. J. Ford, 'Piracy or Policy', 73–7; S. D. Pistono, 'Flanders and the Hundred Years' War: the quest for the *trêve marchande*', *BIHR* 49 (1976), 185–97; id., 'The Accession of Henry IV: the effects on Anglo-Flemish relations, 1399–1402', *Tijdschrift voor Geschiedenis*, 89 (1976), 465–74; Michael Nordberg, *Les Ducs et la royauté*, 131–51; *Royal Letters of Henry IV*, ed. F. C. Hingeston (Rolls Ser., 1860), i. 214–25; *CPR 1401–5*, 273.

[2] PRO, E 28/12, 28 Nov.; E 101/69/311 (indenture); E 101/44/20 (account); E 34/13 6 May gives a slightly larger force; *CPR 1401–5*, 393, 396–7, 401, 432.

[3] *CSL* no. 167; *Rot. Parl.* iii. 534. Somerset had returned to England by Oct. 1404: E 28/15.

[4] *Letters of Henry IV*, i. 281, 284–98; *PPC* i. 233; *Foedera*, viii. 374; *CPR 1401–5*, 404, 413; *CCR 1402–5*, 391; *Cotton Galba B.I.*, 112.

the new year a large seaborne force of 2,000 men at arms and 3,000 archers, this time under the supreme command of Somerset, with Thomas Beaufort and Lord Berkeley as lieutenants.[5] But Somerset's recuperation was slow, and on 20 February Thomas of Lancaster was commissioned admiral in his place.[6] It was his force which conducted a damaging raid on Sluys and Cadsand, ravaging Picardy and Normandy in May 1405. John himself returned to Calais with reinforcements in April and on 12 May he successfully repulsed Saint-Pol's assault on the fortress of Marck, taking numerous prisoners.[7] Together these victories relieved the immediate threat to Calais and justified the priority which the council had given to its defence. Although temporarily halting the negotiations with the Flemish, they ultimately opened the way to a commercial truce with the new duke of Burgundy. John the Fearless, like his father, might be tempted by the prospect of capturing Calais, and might even on occasion compel or persuade the Four Members to support such an enterprise. Yet once that possibility was ruled out both commercial and political interests dictated a permanent settlement with England. The commissioners appointed to negotiate with Burgundy in March 1405 included Somerset's half-brother Sir Thomas Swynford, the keeper of Calais, and they had achieved a preliminary settlement by October. In the following year Somerset's lieutenants, Aston and Swynford, were joined by a rising protégé of Henry Beaufort, John Catrik, and finally negotiated a one-year truce in November, which John the Fearless confirmed in March 1407. This formed the basis for a series of extensions to the end of the reign and into the next.[8]

It seems clear that the three Beauforts had acted in close association in this phase of Anglo-Flemish relations. As chancellor from February 1403 to March 1405, Henry had encouraged the council to protect and recompense Flemish merchants in the summer of 1403 and must have directed the subsequent negotiations with the duke and the towns. He had shaped the council's response to the French threat to Calais, the presentation of its policy in parliament, and the raising of money to implement it. John's captaincy of Calais placed him inescapably at the centre of the military crisis, but he was also continuously involved in negotiations for the prolongation of the truce and its enforcement. Thomas was afforded his first independent command at sea, prefiguring his later appointment as admiral of England. In all this the Beauforts' Hainault

[5] *PPC* i. 244–6, 260. Thomas actually indented on 21 Jan. 1405 to serve at sea for a quarter-year from 1 Feb., but this was superseded by the appointment of Thomas of Lancaster: E 101/69/312. Somerset was in council on 9 Dec. 1404: *CIM 1399–1422*, 155 no. 287.

[6] *PPC* i. 263; *Foedera*, viii. 388.

[7] *CSL* no. 295; E 28/20 1 Apr.; *Foedera*, viii. 397; Brown, thesis, 24; *CCR 1402–5*, 448.

[8] R. Vaughan, *John the Fearless*, 22–4; *Letters of Henry IV*, i. 306–8; *Foedera*, viii. 391, 443.

parentage may have been a significant element, giving them a natural interest in the area and an affinity to its people whom most Englishmen tended to despise and mistrust. For although the principal diplomatic exchanges were with the French and Burgundian courts, it had been an important feature of English policy to keep open the contacts with the burgesses of the Four Members of Flanders, discussing and sharing fears in plain and non-diplomatic language. Out of the dangers and tensions of these years was born the enduring commercial alliance with John the Fearless with all its political implications for future Anglo-French relations. For Henry Beaufort it marked the start of his connections with the merchant community and of his concern with the maintenance of commercial ties with Flanders.

His chancellorship likewise coincided with a crisis in Anglo-Hanseatic relations and prepared the way for a permanent agreement. Hanseatic resentment at the penetration of English cloth, particularly in Danzig, had led the Prussians to abrogate the treaty of 1388 even before Henry IV's accession, and the further problem of piracy in the years 1402–3 brought a Prussian embassy to London in September 1403 for discussions with Bishop Beaufort and Lord Roos. As relations deteriorated, with further acts of piracy in 1404, it was decided at the Coventry parliament to dispatch Sir William Sturmy and John Kington to Prussia in an attempt to settle all outstanding difficulties. By the time they arrived the Lübeck Diet had formally severed all trade with England; but the mutual recognition that this served the interests of neither side led, by October 1405, to an initial agreement which, by 1409, had been transformed into a formal treaty. This guaranteed reciprocal rights to merchants and established the English right to trade freely in Prussia. Here again, the settlement reached was to endure for the next quarter century.[9]

In Wales, however, it proved as difficult as ever to make headway. The revolt of the Percies and the hostilities with France provided Glyndwr with the opportunity to extend his control into south-west Wales during the latter part of 1403. Shortage of money prevented Henry IV from following up his victory at Shrewsbury, and after a brief expedition to Carmarthen in 1403 he left a large garrison there under the command of Somerset, as lieutenant in South Wales. This was a temporary appointment, for in October Somerset and Thomas Beaufort wrote to the king urging the appointment of the duke of York, who took command in November, releasing the Beauforts for the defence of the sea and Calais.[10] In 1404 Glyndwr, now formally allied with the French, captured Aberystwyth and

[9] M. M. Postan, 'The Economic and Political Relations of England and the Hanse from 1400 to 1475', in E. Power and M. Postan (edd.), *Studies in English Trade in the Fifteenth Century*, 108–10; *Letters of Henry IV*, i. li–lv, 354–62; *CCR 1402–5*, 288.

[10] Griffiths, thesis, 29; *CPR 1401–5*, 295, 298–9; *CCR 1402–5*, 111, 473; *PPC* i. 217.

Harlech, extended his control into Glamorgan, and forced the prince of Wales and his commanders back to the marches. Throughout the year lack of money confined them to short sallies to relieve and supply beleaguered garrisons. One such was at the end of November to relieve Coity castle, when Thomas Beaufort rejoined the prince for a five-day expedition and then remained to defend the area. Early in 1405 preparations began for a renewed English offensive in the summer and when, on 6 March, the prince was commissioned king's lieutenant in North Wales for a year, Sir Thomas Beaufort was given the custody of Carmarthen, Cardigan, and Newcastle Emlyn with the command of 190 men-at-arms and 950 archers. Some of these were drawn from the garrisons under his command at Hereford and Monmouth.[11] As second in command to the king's lieutenant in South Wales, Lord Bergevenny, Thomas was entrusted with a dangerously isolated but vital area of English lordship. As a result he played no part in the English victories at Grosmont in March and Usk in May, though he and Lord Grey of Codnor joined the force which the prince led to Yorkshire for the suppression of the Scrope–Mowbray rising. Beaufort's garrisons, thus denuded, were unable to resist the French landing at Milford Haven in August and the offensive which brought Glyndwr almost to the gates of Worcester. Despite the king's incursion to relieve Coity once again in September, the year closed with the prospect of a long struggle throughout 1406 to regain control of South Wales.

In April 1406 the prince was again appointed lieutenant in Wales and the march and throughout the summer English lordship was steadily re-established in Gower, Glamorgan, and Carmarthen. Thomas Beaufort had certainly rejoined his old associates, Lord Grey of Codnor and Lord Charleton of Powys, in these campaigns, though the details of his service are unknown. In September he was appointed keeper of Wigmore castle, and he and Grey controllers of the prince's receipts. Anglesey was recaptured after a sustained effort in November and though Glyndwr still held Harlech and Aberystwyth, Welsh resistance was virtually confined to the Snowdonia redoubt. This probably marked the end of Sir Thomas Beaufort's service in Wales; in August 1407 he and Lord Grey were with the king at Nottingham and he is not named among those present at the siege of Aberystwyth.[12] Nevertheless he had, for a crucial period, worked closely with that group of marcher lords around Prince Henry—Arundel, Warwick, Audley, Talbot, Grey, and Charleton—who, like him, were embarking on military careers which would reach fulfilment in the conquest and defence of Normandy under Henry V. His presence among them as his elder brother's representative (for he held no lands there

[11] Griffiths, thesis, 32–7; *PPC* i. 252; *CPR 1405–8*, 6, 8; *CSL* nos. 247, 332.

[12] By Sept. 1406 he was with Prince Henry and Lord Grey in South Wales: *CPR 1405–8*, 215, 219, 363; Griffiths, thesis, 45.

himself), introduced him to a brotherhood in arms out of which were soon to grow political loyalties.

The third element in this co-ordinated attempt to destabilize and overthrow the Lancastrian regime was treachery and rebellion among the nobility. Although this could exploit the discontent and disillusion with Lancastrian government which the strains of war, the restraints on trade, and the collapse of royal finance fostered, its driving force was essentially dynastic. Psychologically and politically the revolt of the Percies had reinforced Henry IV's dependence on his own family and those traditionally loyal to Lancaster, and his acts of clemency and reconciliation could do little to stop a growing cleavage between them and the former Ricardians. Between the battle of Shrewsbury in July 1403 and the execution of Archbishop Scrope in May 1405, Henry lived with the continual evidence of conspiracies and rebellions. When this materialized in Northumberland's revolt, the involvement of Archbishop Scrope, Mowbray, and Bardolf took the king by surprise. Mowbray, despite his recent service in Wales, had grievances against the Lancastrian circle, for Westmorland held his hereditary office of marshal of England, and Warwick's recent vindication of his claim to precedence perhaps made Mowbray fear for his tenure of Gower. The archbishop represented another strand of opposition to the court. His manifesto, echoing complaints in the parliament of 1404 against the costs of the household, the greed of the courtiers, the burden of taxes, and non-payment for purveyances, like his programme for conciliating the Welsh and restoring harmony between the lords, reveals him as the mouthpiece of Northumberland. His further claim, to be defending the liberties of the church, followed a period of eighteen months in which, under hostile pressure from the court, convocation had been forced to grant taxation on an unprecedented scale.[13]

At the Worcester council in September 1403, where both John and Thomas Beaufort were present, the bishops had been induced to make loans for the campaign in Wales, Henry Beaufort advancing 100 marks.[14] To provide for the repayment of these Arundel hastily summoned convocation in October, where the clergy voted an additional half-tenth. In April 1404 the southern convocation was harangued by royal commissioners, and under threat of the land tax granted in the January parliament being applied to church lands and incomes, it granted a tenth and a subsidy on exempt benefices. Convocation again met on 24 November following the Coventry parliament which had made the most generous grant of the

[13] For the Mowbray–Beauchamp dispute, see R. E. Archer, 'The Mowbrays: Earls of Nottingham and Dukes of Norfolk, to 1432', D.Phil. thesis (Oxford, 1984), chs. 2, 3. For Scrope, see P. McNiven, 'The betrayal of Archbisop Scrope', *BJRL* 54 (1971–2), 173–213: *Anglia Sacra*, ed. H. Wharton, ii (1691), 362–8.

[14] E 404/19/248.

reign. Whether Walsingham's story, that certain knights in the parliament proposed the appropriation of the church's temporalities for a year, is accurate or not, the bishops certainly faced renewed demands for loans. In making a grant of three additional half tenths the clergy stipulated that they should be relieved from further taxation for the period of the grant, and not be harassed by councils, parliaments and other bodies. The northern convocation made similar grants in June and December. Practically the whole of these taxes went to the wardrobe, the chamber, or the defence of Calais. Indeed with the lay taxes placed under the control of war treasurers, the king, his household, and his captains looked directly to church revenues to supply their needs. Complaints that the king's entourage was placing unbearable exactions on the realm were widespread.[15]

Archbishop Scrope's manifesto attacking the courtiers and calling for a reform of royal government, and his treasonous association with the Percy–Glyndwr rebellion, provoked the courtiers to an act of political revenge. When, on 3 June 1405, Henry IV rode into the courtyard of Pontefract castle where Scrope was being held following his surrender to the earl of Westmorland, he was accompanied by Lord Grey of Codnor and Sir Thomas Beaufort, who had brought forces from the Welsh march. The archbishop descended bearing his crozier, symbol of his spiritual role and the protection afforded by his cloth. Angered by this, Thomas Beaufort seized it, and after a brief struggle wrenched it from the archbishop's grasp and carried it to the king. Next day he, Lord Grey, and Sir John Stanley, the steward of the household, were appointed to a commission of oyer and terminer to try all the persons involved in the rebellion, while Thomas Beaufort and the earl of Arundel were invested with the authority of marshal and constable of England to hold a treason trial under the law of arms. Early on 8 June Archbishop Arundel arrived in York, having ridden post haste from London on hearing of Henry's intention. He pleaded with the king, insisting on the principle of clerical immunity respected by Richard in his own case. One chronicler tells us that he was answered by a certain knight of the royal household who warned Henry that if Archbishop Scrope were allowed to live 'all of us will desert you'.[16] Might this have been Sir Thomas Beaufort? At least the story pinpoints the crisis of confidence between the king and his retainers. Now that the critics of the household had revealed themselves as traitors, it was scarcely surprising that Henry should bow to the demands of those who

[15] Rogers, 'Clerical taxation', 128–32; A. K. McHardy, 'Clerical taxation in fifteenth-century England', in B. Dobson (ed.), *The Church, Politics and Patronage in the Fifteenth Century*, 174–83; *Annales R. II et H. IV*, 391–4; Walsingham, *Hist. Angl.* ii. 265–7; *Chron. Angl.* 44; *CPR 1401–5*, 309.

[16] *Annales R. II et H. IV*, 409; *Eulogium Historiarum Sive Temporis Chronicon*, ed. F. S. Haydon, iii (Rolls Ser., 1863), 407; *PPC* i. 260–2; *CPR 1405–8*, 65.

had protected and served him throughout the years of danger. While Archbishop Arundel briefly rested from fatigue the execution went ahead. Its consequences were not expunged for another ten years.

By this date Henry Beaufort had resigned the chancellorship which he had held for exactly two years from the end of February 1403. His most important political work had been the handling of the two parliaments of 1404. Both were dictated by the king's desperate need for money as the customs steeply declined while military and domestic expenses soared. Despite the imminence of the French threat and the urgent need to check the deteriorating position in Wales, the Commons were ready to dispute Henry's demand for taxation. They insisted on regarding him as a well-endowed king, and the defence of the marches as the responsibility of the resident lords. In part these were debating points, but they also reflected their conviction that the subsidies had been misspent and insufficient done to defend the realm. Convinced that the cost of the household was excessive, the Commons further asked that it should be 'put in good and moderate governance' and supported from crown revenues rather than taxation, and that annuities on these revenues be resumed. This was a politically explosive issue, for Henry IV had relied for his survival on an inflated royal retinue.[17] The Commons' discontents with the household were probably also fostered by the Percy faction which still retained some influence. A newsletter sent from the parliament to Durham depicts the Speaker as laying the blame for disaffection in the realm on certain counsellors who led and advised the king out of sheer malice.[18] Finally as we have seen the king's entourage was also feared and hated by churchmen.

As chancellor, Henry Beaufort's task was to secure grants of taxation and to defend the crown's record without exacerbating these divisions, and in particular to prevent an alignment of the factious with the merely critical. His opening sermon on 14 January took as its theme the familiar simile of the realm as a body, of which the clergy formed the right side, the temporal lords the left, and the 'communialte du Roialme' the other members; all were locked in mutual dependence. The king, he said, desired the advice, counsel, and assent of all the estates, for good government depended on wise counsel. He then recited the problems which had dominated the past year—external threats, relations with Ireland and Scotland, and the Percies' rebellion—and charged Lords and Commons to provide for the future.[19] This was the cue for the Speaker, Sir

[17] *Rot. Parl.* iii. 527b; *Eulogium*, iii. 399; A. R. Rogers, 'Henry IV, the Commons and taxation', *Medieval Studies*, 31 (1969), 56–7.

[18] C. M. Fraser, 'Some Durham documents relating to the Hilary Parliament of 1404', *BIHR* 34 (1961), 198.

[19] *Rot. Parl.* iii. 522; Fraser, op. cit. 197.

Arnold Savage, to table the Commons' complaints of misgovernment, to which the chancellor and the treasurer were sent to reply. Speaking 'molt discretement', Beaufort outlined the costs for defence and the household during the coming year, on the basis of the estimates given to the council in December. Evidently this did not satisfy the Commons, for they asked that some of them should appear before the Lords for a further statement on the position in Wales and for answers to their own points. They developed their attack on annuities and the cost of the household, and sought to bargain for a resumption of royal grants or a reduction of the rate of the customs in return for taxation.[20]

The turning point of the parliament may have come with Savage's proposal, at the end of January, for another affirmation of loyalty from the Lords and the admission of Northumberland to make his answer and receive pardon for his 'trespass against the crown'. Despite Archbishop Arundel's angry interjection and the king's momentary threat of an adjournment—countered by Savage's warning that the Commons might refuse to reassemble—both these were agreed to. A week later some token dismissals from the household were made, the chancellor announced the pardon of Northumberland, and he and Westmorland were formally reconciled.[21] Detailed negotiations now began on the terms of a grant, and by 1 March Archbishop Arundel could present to the Commons an allocation of crown revenues for the household which met their ideal that the king should live of his own. He also promised a commission to reform the household, and the commitment of the Commons' grant of a 5 per cent tax on incomes to four war treasurers, to ensure that it was spent primarily on the safeguard of the sea.[22] At the same time a council named in parliament, as a guarantee of good government, included both John and Henry Beaufort. The crown had thus conceded, at least formally, the Commons' whole programme of financial reform in return for a novel subsidy of uncertain yield. It had been the longest and most assertive parliament that Henry IV had yet encountered, and Beaufort seems to have needed Arundel's backing in handling the Commons. Yet it must have helped that the Beauforts were known by the Commons to favour the safeguarding of the sea and the provision for Calais, and the chancellor's personal commitment to this was expressed in his contribution of 2,000 marks to the loans now raised on the security of the parliamentary grant. This sum was delivered to the treasurers of war on 18 May, and repayment was assigned to him on the second part of the income tax and the clerical tenth in Lincolnshire due in October. Initiating a pattern which was to be

[20] *Rot. Parl.* iii. 523–4; *Eulogium*, iii. 399–400.

[21] Fraser, op. cit. 198–9; *Rot. Parl.* iii. 525.

[22] Rogers, 'Commons and taxation', 62, 64–6; *Annales R. II et H. IV*, 380–1; *Rot. Parl.* iii. 528.

developed in later years, Henry Beaufort's loan was applied to the cost of the fleet under his brother Thomas's command.[23]

During the following months the Commons' measures for the rigid allocation of revenue for the household and for war, and the failure of their experimental tax, combined to bring the exchequer to a state of paralysis and compelled the king to summon another parliament in October 1404. This was held at Coventry, in the Lancastrian heartland, where the king had been advised to spend the summer, keeping a watchful eye on the north and the Welsh marches and awaiting a possible French invasion. Beaufort's address repeated the theme of the king's desire for good counsel, but although he again spoke 'molt discretement', the tone was sterner. He told parliament bluntly that its predecessor had done nothing to provide for the suppression of the Welsh rebellion, and he revealed the failure of the tax. Meanwhile the French and Bretons were threatening to land on English shores, and Guyenne was under attack. For all these speedy provision had to be made, and next day he urged the Commons to set aside all other business and make an immediate grant. This they did, granting a full subsidy, with a second in 1405, and renewing the wool subsidy. Yet they remained critical. Treasurers of war were again appointed although one, Lord Furnival, was Westmorland's brother, while the other, Sir John Pelham, was a chamber knight and an old retainer of Gaunt. They also made the collection of the second subsidy depend on the first having been effectively employed.[24] However, in making extreme demands for a resumption of all lands and revenues granted since 1367, and the appropriation of church lands for a year, the Commons played into the king's hands. The first was deflected by the council's cosmetic proposal for a year's moratorium on the annuities of all who had failed to perform their required service; the second provoked Archbishop Arundel to denounce *ad hominem* the knights who had secured grants of alien priories.

It must have fallen to Bishop Beaufort as chancellor to defend the property and privileges of the church, and convince the Commons of the reality of the crown's needs and the effectiveness of its military actions. Here the successful defence of Calais and the sea by his two brothers, and his own loan, were his best credentials. Half-way through the parliament, on 23 October, the Commons, in asking the king to elevate his sons in rank and reward the duke of York, also commended to the king the 'estates' of John and Thomas Beaufort. For John, at least, this resulted in a successful petition for the annuity of 1,000 marks, awarded to his son Henry, to be

[23] E 101/43/38 file ii; E 101/44/20; *CPR 1401–5*, 392; *CCR 1402–5*, 401, 415; *CFR 1399–1405*, 251–64.

[24] *Rot. Parl.* iii. 545–6; T. E. F. Wright, 'Royal Finance in the latter part of the reign of Henry IV of England, 1406–13', D.Phil. thesis (Oxford, 1984), 19; *CFR 1399–1405*, 294.

increased to £1,000 and granted to himself in tail male.[25] By the close of the Coventry parliament the crown had recovered the political initiative, and secured an assured revenue for the coming year on the basis of which it could plan a military offensive in Wales and in the straits. Although Henry Beaufort's own contribution is difficult to identify, there are perhaps just sufficient hints that his own mixture of tact and firmness, and his family's identification with the naval and commercial interests so prominent in the Commons' minds, had enabled him to establish a rapport with them and win their confidence.[26]

Henry Beaufort's regular attendance at council had begun with his appointment as chancellor, but it was only briefly interrupted by his resignation. Between October 1404 and August 1405 he is recorded as attending forty-three times as chancellor and fourteen times after he had surrendered office. In the two years following his resignation Henry was present at almost half the recorded meetings, more than any other councillor not holding office. John, too, despite his military preoccupations, attended between one-third and one-quarter of all recorded meetings during the period when his brother was chancellor—far more than any other member of the nobility—and in the following two years his record of attendance was surpassed only by the duke of York.[27] Both brothers were members of the council named in the parliaments of May and December 1406, and were paid for their attendance from December 1405. The Beauforts were in this repect filling the place occupied by the Percies before 1403, for the fact that until 1406 the council was predominantly composed of members of the household, officials, and career churchmen gave its small aristocratic element a special significance. One or other of the Beauforts was usually in attendance on the king, for although the chancellor did not accompany Henry IV on the summer and autumn campaigns of 1403, following the spring parliament of 1404 in London he accompanied the court in the midlands, attended the Coventry parliament, and returned to the London area during the early months of 1405.[28]

In the midst of these migrations the bishop had found time to issue an award, from Huntingdon on 30 July 1404, in the long-running dispute between the dean and chapter of Lincoln, and he paid a last visit to Lincoln itself at the end of the year.[29] For on 19 November 1404 he was translated

[25] *Rot. Parl.* iii. 547–50; Walsingham, *Hist. Angl.* ii. 264–6; *Annales R. II et H. IV*, 393.

[26] The Speaker, Sir William Sturmy, had worked closely with both Somerset in 1402 and with Bishop Beaufort in 1404 in negotiations with the Emperor and the Flemings: see J. S. Roskell, *Parliament and Politics in late Medieval England*, iii. 96–7.

[27] Brown, 'Commons and Council', 30; thesis, 21.

[28] *CPR 1410–5*, 412, 403 ff.; *CCR 1402–5*, 370, 377. Somerset's presence in council is recorded in E 28/14 (May 1404), E 28/15 (Oct. 1404), *CIM 1399–1422*, 155 (Dec. 1404).

[29] *The Statutes of Lincoln Cathedral*, ed. A. Bradshaw and C. Wordsworth, i. 96, 261, ii. 249–55. PRO C 85/110 m. 47–58 shows him at Lincoln in Nov. to Jan.

to Winchester, receiving the temporalities on 14 March 1405. With a career in central government firmly in prospect, he was the natural successor to a see held by Edington and Wykeham. For although it was the occasion for his resignation of the chancellorship, it brought no respite from royal service. Henry Beaufort was with the king at Windsor in April 1405 and at Worcester in May, rejoining the council at Pontefract in August to deal with the aftermath of the rising.[30] By October he had returned to Southwark, resuming his place at council meetings in November, and though he spent the first two months of 1406 in Hampshire, followed by an embassy to Calais in the spring, thereafter the exigencies of parliament and council kept him at his palace in Southwark from which he was so often to rule his diocese in the next forty years. It was here that on 24 January 1407 he gave a sumptuous banquet following the marriage of his brother-in-law Edmund, earl of Kent, to Lucia Visconti.[31]

The parliament of 1406 was the longest of the reign, and was marked by the Commons' most determined effort to force financial reform on the king as the price of their grant of taxation. Although this involved a more fundamental and specific limitation of royal authority than in any previous parliament of the reign, the Commons achieved this not through the support of a baronial faction hostile to the court and dynasty, but through a council composed of those whom the king could trust and whom the Commons could depend on to ensure effective expenditure on defence. The Beauforts met both these requirements.

The immediate need was for money to meet the imminent military threats. The new chancellor, Bishop Langley, in whose consecration Beaufort had recently assisted, and whom he may have chosen as his successor, outlined the dangers in Wales, Gascony, Ireland, and the north, and reiterated the need for good counsel to make provision for them. More than any of these, it was the appearance of a French fleet at the mouth of the Thames which demonstrated the royal ineffectuality in defence. The Commons under their Speaker, Sir John Tiptoft, were in no mood to trust further royal promises, and had regained confidence in their programme of financial and political reform. Tiptoft was ready to commend those who fought: the prince and commanders in Wales, the earl of Somerset at Calais; but he complained that, despite the large grants made at Coventry, neither the Welsh rebellion nor the French threat had been mastered. Inasmuch as it was the Commons who paid for the war, they now insisted that the taxes should be wholly applied to defence, that crown revenues should make a larger contribution, that financial officials should be kept

[30] PRO, PSO 1/2/51, PSO 1/3/51, 99, 103; Brown, 'Authorization of Letters', 144 n. 1; HRO, Reg. Beaufort, fos. 1–3 records licences issued from Farnham in these months, presumably by his official. In Apr. 1405 Beaufort paid £600 from the temporalities to the crown: E 28/20 10 Apr.

[31] *Concilia*, iii. 281–4; *Register of Repingdon*, i. 75: *CP* vii. 161 note *e*.

under closer scrutiny, and that the council should make itself responsible for the new taxes to be granted. As before, this programme was accompanied by demands for a reduction in the cost and size of the household, and an attack in particular on the 'raskaille' who composed it. Yet this was less an attack on a court faction than a demand that the burden of the court on subjects should be lessened, and that it should not be supported from taxes granted for war.[32]

It was to the council above all that the Commons looked to implement these reforms. On 22 May, half-way through the second session, a council was named comprising most of the frequent attenders in the previous year. Its principal responsibility was defined as being the conservation of the rights of the crown, the increase and collection of royal revenues, and the maintenance of the king's estate. In effect its task was to supervise royal government, notably in the matter of royal grants, which were to pass only by its authority. This restriction on royal patronage was to be accompanied by the review of all grants of farms and wardships and the suspension of pardons of debts, and the Commons further demanded that all grants from crown revenues should be repealed and applied to household expenses. To many, if not all, of these the councillors were sympathetic, though Archbishop Arundel protested that they would not serve unless the Commons provided sufficient resources. In the event they did so despite the meagre provision for the household, which the Commons made conditional on the council's furtherance of reforms.[33] The council at once set to work in the spirit of the Commons' demands. On 28 June a commission was set up, on which Henry Beaufort was named, to investigate the value of lands at farm and the concealment of revenue by the crown's local officials, and on 8 July the collectors of the customs were summoned before it. Even so its main preoccupation was the shortage of revenue following the Commons' refusal of a grant. Canterbury convocation, under pressure from parliament and from delegates sent by the king, proved more amenable, and on 10 May had granted a tenth and a poll tax payable in November. On the security of this and the wool subsidy loans were raised under a general commission for the defence of the English church and realm.[34] By 28 July a total of £12,085 had been raised from a restricted circle of lenders, mainly the city of London, native and foreign merchants, and the treasurer. Bishop Beaufort contributed £600, a measure of the wealth of his new see and his membership of the council, rather than of any direct family interest.[35]

In fact, apart from interim payments to Prince John, the household, and

[32] *Rot. Parl.* iii. 567–92, 597.

[33] Brown, 'Commons and Council', 12 ff.; Wright, thesis, 59–80.

[34] *CPR 1405–8*, 53–5, 199; *CFR 1405–13*, 35; *Concilia*, iii. 284; Rogers, 'Clerical taxation', 133–4; Wright, thesis, 48 ff.

[35] Steel, *Receipt*, 94; *CPR 1405–8*, 214; *Foedera*, viii. 448; PRO E 401/638. Repayment was made on the first half of the clerical tenth in his diocese.

Ireland, the main expenditure during the summer was on the dispatch of Princess Philippa to Norway for her marriage to King Eric. Although the Commons had effectively denied the crown a subsidy for the space of a whole year, they reassembled on 17 October in an ungenerous and suspicious mood, while the king seemed to have set his face against further concessions. Some kind of crisis led up to Tiptoft's demand on 18 November that the council should be charged to tell the king openly about the misgovernment of the realm, but on 27 November Henry formally reasserted his confidence in the councillors named in May by reappointing them. However on 8 December the treasurer of the household was dismissed, economies were agreed, and the household knights and esquires were removed from the council, which the prince of Wales had begun to attend. The king now accepted thirty-one reform ordinances over which the obscure struggle of the previous weeks had presumably been fought. These constituted a detailed attempt to repair royal finances. They proposed the close control of revenue officials, a suspension of all grants from crown revenues until the next parliament and their application to the expenses of the household, a reduction of household expenses, the expulsion of its alien members, and the exercise of close control over its officials. The key appointment here was that of Tiptoft himself to be treasurer of the household, the first layman to hold that office. The principal resistance had probably come from the king; the council itself had lent qualified support to the Commons' programme, only contesting the demand for a repeal of the grants which it had sanctioned since the beginning of parliament. Here too it eventually gave way, though a special exception was made for the grant to the earl of Somerset of the wardship and marriage of the heir of Lord Fitzwalter, in deduction of his exchequer annuity. The council also agreed, under protest and at the king's command, to take an oath to observe the articles. For the Commons the acid test was whether the council would spend effectively the subsidy which they were now offering. Tiptoft's last-minute demand that the councillors should swear to refund the grant if it were misspent was unacceptable to the king and the council, and under threats by Henry IV the Commons had to give way.[36]

The changes of December 1406 brought to an end a period marked by a high degree of continuity in the membership of the council and a close identity of the council and the court. The new magnate council, meeting regularly in London while the king remained at some suitable residence with a reduced household, enjoyed a greater measure of autonomy and had an acknowledged responsibility to parliament. A new pattern of government began to emerge. Council records survive for only the first

[36] *Rot. Parl.* iii. 580–603; Walsingham *Hist. Angl.* ii. 273; *PPC* i. 295–6; Brown, 'Commons and Council'; Rogers, 'Commons and taxation', 66–7; Wright, thesis, 82–3 considers Walsingham's story improbable.

months of 1407, but they show that all those named in December attended, except for Lords Burnell and Roos and Sir John Tiptoft, who probably remained with the king at Hertford and accompanied him on his summer pilgrimage to the Lancastrian shrine of St John of Bridlington. Archbishop Arundel emerged as the leader of the new council, replacing Langley as chancellor on 30 January, while the sudden death of Lord Furnival in March led to the eventual appointment of Bishop Bubwith as treasurer. The influence of the Beauforts was diminished by both these changes, and by Arundel's growing personal influence over the sick and remorseful king.

Yet for so long as Calais stood in jeopardy the council would have to heed the demands of the earl of Somerset. The need to safeguard shipping to Calais, and the town itself, had been the background to all the sessions of the 1406 parliament. In March the Commons had authorized the formation of two armed fleets, captained by merchants, and financed from the wool subsidy and tunnage and poundage for a half-year. By October however, the council had become disillusioned with them and on 20 November the admirals were formally dismissed and Somerset was appointed in their place.[37] The choice was dictated by the renewed threat to Calais which had arisen earlier in the year when John the Fearless agreed to co-operate with the duke of Orléans in a twin attack on Bordeaux and Calais. In the May session Tiptoft drew attention to the shortage of victuals at Calais, and the arrears of the garrison's wages, asking that Somerset and other captains should be instructed to take up their commands. In fact it was the Commons' own refusal of taxation, and their application of tunnage and poundage and one quarter of the wool subsidy to the merchants' fleet, which left Calais largely deprived of money in the summer of 1406.[38] Some reinforcements were sent, and preparations were made for a royal expedition to relieve it in October. In the event the unresolved parliamentary crisis kept both the king and Somerset at Westminster, while John the Fearless's proposed attack failed to materialize. Despite his failure to go to Calais, Somerset's appointment as captain of Calais was renewed and extended for a further six years.[39]

In December the council released a total of £8,586 for the payment of the garrison, and early in 1407 rumours of a fresh Burgundian threat led to orders for the mobilization of the royal affinity. Then, as the military crisis passed, the council began to give priority to a new campaign in Wales.[40] By early in February the council was ready to endorse an allocation of £11,375

[37] *Rot. Parl.* iii. 569–70, 602–3, 610; *Foedera*, viii. 439, 455; *CCR 1405–9*, 156; Wright, thesis, 90–2.

[38] J. L. Kirby, 'Calais sous les Anglais, 1399–1413', *Revue du Nord*, 37 (1955), 19–30; *Rot. Parl.* iii. 573, 576; *PPC* i. 260. For the council's provision for Calais in 1405, see E 28/19 19 Mar., E 28/20 24 Apr.

[39] Vaughan, *John the Fearless*, 23–4; *Foedera*, viii. 456; E 101/69/318, E 404/22/211, 261, 285.

[40] *Letters of Henry IV*, ii. 145–7; *Foedera*, vii. 466; E 404/22/285; Wright, thesis, 116–22.

for a six month campaign in Wales while providing £7,481 for the needs of Calais. The garrison had already lobbied the council for satisfaction of its arrears, and must have deemed the provision insufficient, for on 9 March they seized wool as security for payment. For the moment the death of Lord Furnival and the closure of the exchequer over Easter inhibited action, but immediately after Easter a great council set about raising loans. Altogether over £15,000 was borrowed from the Staplers, merchants, and royal officers on the security of the customs and under the bonds of the lords of the council, including both the Beauforts. A sum of £19,620 was then paid over to the treasurer of Calais in two instalments in May and June.[41] A new treasurer was appointed, Richard Merlawe, whose connections with the Beauforts went back to 1405 when he acted as treasurer to Thomas Beaufort's fleet, and by August Somerset had been able to reassume his command of the garrison and negotiate compensation with the Hanse for the wool they had lost.[42] Henry Beaufort did not himself contribute to the loan despite the threat to his brother's captaincy; perhaps an indication that his days at the centre of government were already numbered. The mutiny thus caused the council to reverse its priorities, but it also coincided with the end of the threat to Calais, which had been the preoccupation of John Beaufort and of the Commons. For by March 1407 John the Fearless had agreed to a formal Anglo-Burgundian truce, and became further committed to this after the murder of the duke of Orléans later in the year.

The council, led by Arundel, and strengthened by the presence of the prince, was now free to give the highest priority to the needs of Wales. On 12 May the prince indented for six months' service, and on 1 June received a first instalment of £6,825 in wages for the recapture of Aberystwyth.[43] Although he was cheated of its recovery in September, the campaign left no doubt that the reduction of it and Harlech was only a matter of time. By 1407 the threat to Gascony had also been lifted by the failure of Orléans to capture Bordeaux in the last months of 1406, and following his assassination in December 1407 a truce was secured which in April 1408 was extended to the whole of France. The danger of Scottish incursions had likewise diminished with the young king a prisoner in English hands, and in February 1408 the defeat of the earl of Northumberland and Lord Bardolph at Bramham Moor marked the end of the challenge from the Percies.

The alleviation of these tensions was already producing a shift in political

[41] J. L. Kirby, 'The council of 1407 and the problem of Calais', *History Today*, 5 (1955), 44–52; id., *Henry IV* 211–13; Wright, thesis, 126, 138–9; *CPR 1405–8*, 321, 336, 341; E 404/22/285/464, 502; *CAD* iv. 16, v. 429.

[42] *CPR 1408–13*, 189; *HMC, 5th Report*, Appendix, 443.

[43] Griffiths, thesis, 44; *HMC, 4th Report*, Appendix, 194; *PPC* ii. 108; E 404/22/285, 503; E 403/591.

influence within the council, which became apparent when parliament met at Gloucester in October 1407. Although it was Archbishop Arundel who, as chancellor, spoke for the king, stressing his care for his subjects and their corresponding obligation to provide for the common defence, the Commons chose as their Speaker Thomas Chaucer, the Beauforts' cousin-german, constable of the bishop's castle at Taunton, and receiver of his lands in Somerset.[44] There was an immediate clash over the council's accountability for the subsidy granted at the last parliament. Although the council agreed to render account of its own free will, the chancellor protested that it deserved the thanks of the Commons for its diligent labours and readiness to pledge its own credit, and gave notice that it now wished to be discharged from the oath taken at the last parliament. Chaucer entered the usual demands for the protection of shipping and the suppression of the Welsh rebellion by the marcher lords, and asked for a committee of the council to intercommune with the Commons on these matters, naming both the Beauforts. Neither on these matters, nor over the Commons' protest against the council designating the size of their grant, was there intensive dispute, and the council secured the subsidy and a half which it had proposed, spread over three years, in return for a promise to ask for no further taxation until 1410. Although certainly less than the council had hoped for, this offered the prospect of planning expenditure and restoring financial solvency in a situation where military demands had become less urgent. It was to this that Prince Henry was to address himself in the following years. The council could claim to have stabilized its relationship with the Commons and freed itself of accountability to them. It was no longer bound, in regard to either its composition or its powers, by the acts of the 1406 parliament. Under the powerful leadership of the prince and the archbishop it was free to act and evolve as a more independent entity than at any previous point in the reign.[45]

From early in 1406 the king's illness had prompted demands for a definition of the rights of succession of his still unmarried and mostly untitled sons. In the second session of parliament in May Speaker Tiptoft had raised the question of whether this should be vested in Prince Henry and his brothers in tail male or in their heirs general. The decision to restrict it to male heirs and embody this in a statute was an important innovation. Then on the final day of the parliament, 22 December, again on Tiptoft's petition, the succession was restored to the heirs of their bodies. What motives and what interests occasioned these changes remains unclear.[46] Most directly affected was Prince Henry, negotiations for whose

[44] Roskell, *Parliament and Politics*, iii. 157–60.

[45] *Rot. Parl.* iii. 608–12; Wright, thesis, 150–5.

[46] *Rot. Parl.* iii. 574, 582; P. McNiven, 'Legitimacy and consent: Henry IV and the Lancastrian title, 1399–1406', *Medieval Studies*, 44 (1982), 470–88.

marriage to the former Queen Isabella, linked to a truce or peace, had been conducted by Henry Beaufort in Calais during April and May. According to Monstrelet, the English had advanced a suggestion that Henry IV might resign the throne in the event of such a union. The story must be treated with caution; although not without plausibility as part of a manœuvre to stave off French attack, it would have been an incautious and unauthorized offer.[47] Beaufort had few ties with the prince, who was himself not yet 20 and wholly inexperienced in government. Yet if Henry IV and his sons should die without heirs, the crown could well be disputed between the young earl of March, the suspect duke of York, and John earl of Somerset, who had ranked next after York in the witnesses to the act of succession. Whether it was such considerations, or whether concern for the succession of his own heirs to his dignities, on 10 February 1407 John petitioned for an exemplification of Richard II's patent of legitimation. This was now reissued but with an interlineation specifically excluding the Beauforts from the royal succession. Although immediately of little practical moment, it was a pointed reminder of the gulf between them and the heirs of the whole blood and, if indeed the result of Arundel's intervention as chancellor, another pointer to the growth of rivalries within the council.[48]

Yet their strenuous service to the crown had brought material rewards. In January 1404 Somerset had received a gift of 500 marks to enable him to clear his debts from the 1400 Scottish expedition, and in May 1405 he was granted the office of keeper of Clarendon park. In October 1406 the council awarded him the wardship and marriage of the heir of Lord Fitzwalter in deduction of his £1,000 annuity, and in May 1407 on surrendering his office of admiral to his brother-in-law, the young earl of Kent, he received a life grant of Corfe castle, previously held by the Holands.[49] In 1407 Somerset seems to have decided that his days of active service were over, for he was appointed to the bench in a series of counties where he held lands. The ill health which forced him to relinquish his command turned his thoughts to his heir's inheritance, and in June 1407 he made a jointure in his Devon and Somerset lands for his wife Margaret, with remainder to his sons.[50] Thomas, meanwhile, had secured a substantial endowment as reward for his service against the rebels in 1405 in the shape of the honour of Wyrmegey in Norfolk, formerly of Lord

[47] Enguerran de Monstrelet, *Chronique* ed. L. Douët-d'Arcq, i (Paris, 1857), 126 places the negotiations in Paris and names the ambassadors wrongly. Besides Beaufort they were Lord Camoys, John Catrik, and John Norbury: *Foedera*, viii. 432–5. Warrants: E 404/21/304, 311, E 404/22/239; his account in PRO E 364/40 rot. B shows him absent from London 26 Mar. to 22 May.

[48] *CPR 1405–9*, 284; *Excerpta Historica*, ed. S. Bentley, 152 ff.

[49] *CCR 1402–5*, 400, 459, 491; *CPR 1405–8*, 244, 275, 291, 323, 335; *CPR 1408–13*, 189; E 404/20/129.

[50] *CPR 1405–8*, 342.

Bardolph. This was granted to him for life in October 1405 but regranted in tail male in May 1408.[51] Henry Beaufort's reward had been promotion to the see of Winchester, the monks' choice of their prior, Thomas Neville, being overridden by papal mandate of 19 November 1404.[52] The Beauforts' advance in these years had been steady rather than spectacular, and the landed endowment of John and Thomas remained inevitably disparate to their quasi-royal status and military office. But royal favour and trust had lifted them to an eminence scarcely predictable a decade earlier.

Henry Beaufort's establishment at Winchester quickly led to an increase in his influence in the church. The early years of the reign had seen few episcopal vacancies; but from 1404 there occurred a series of deaths and translations which provoked fierce competition between rival candidates and their patrons, accentuated by disputes between the crown and the papacy. Beaufort's own election, and that of Repingdon to succeed him at Lincoln, were almost the only ones not delayed by these conflicts. Between August 1404 and October 1407 there were vacancies in the sees of Durham, Lincoln, London, Norwich, Rochester, Salisbury, Wells, Winchester, Worcester, and York and of these London, Salisbury, and York saw more than one appointment. The principal candidates were a group of able royal clerks, highly trained as diplomats and administrators, but including men of piety and learning. Langley, Repingdon, and Hallum were recruits to the episcopate; Beaufort, Bowet, Bubwith, Clifford, and Young received promotion. The final dispositions reflected the pressures of the king and the archbishop (though exercised at times in different directions), and the independent views and wishes of the pope. But there are also signs that Beaufort had his own candidates and was beginning to carry some weight. His agents handled negotiations at Rome at important stages: in August 1405 his chancellor, John Catrik, was sent to Rome to procure papal approval for Langley's election to York, and when this was quashed in May 1406 and Langley was provided to Durham, Henry IV sent Sir John Cheyne and Henry Chichele to the Curia to secure the see for Bowet against Hallum, whom Innocent VII had provided. Chichele, again, was a protégé of Beaufort. Beaufort also tried to prevent the acceptance by Tottington of Gregory XII's bull of provision to Norwich against the wishes of Henry IV, procuring his temporary imprisonment under the statute of Provisors. Finally, it was perhaps one of his candidates, Thomas Peverel of Llandaff, who secured the see of Worcester when Richard Clifford was translated to London.[53] Clifford himself, at any rate by his death, was

[51] Ibid. 105, 443.
[52] *Reg. CS* 23, 28.
[53] R. G. Davies, 'After the execution of Archbishop Scrope: Henry IV, the Papacy, and the English Episcopate, 1405–8', *BJRL* 56 (1977), 40–74.

sufficiently close to Beaufort to appoint him supervisor of his will. These early signs of Beaufort's endeavours to build a body of supporters among the episcopate may have contributed to the growing coolness between him and Archbishop Arundel.

During four critical years, from 1403 to 1407, Henry IV had depended more upon the Beauforts than on any others to sustain his throne. The immaturity and inexperience of his sons and of the representatives of the older magnate families identified with the house of Lancaster—Fitz Alans, Beauchamps, and Staffords—thrust the Beauforts into prominence, while the dynastic challenge to the house of Lancaster gave added significance to their own membership of the royal family. Their particular responsibility had been the defence of Calais and the safeguard of the sea routes with Flanders, and to this the council had given military and financial priority. But John, and more frequently Thomas, had also served in Wales, while their brother-in-law, the earl of Westmorland, had held the north. Only York, among the higher nobility, was available for comparable military commands, and he soon forfeited Henry IV's trust. Politically the crisis of these years centred on the extensive royal affinity, on which Henry relied in the face of treachery and rebellion. Thomas Beaufort was prominent among those household knights whose personal loyalty to the king was tested and fortified by shared dangers, but who became the targets of criticism by both the Commons and churchmen. The Commons, faced with mounting war expenditure, made the reduction of household expenses and the resumption of annuities their principal demands; the church, fearing that the crown's financial needs would be also fuelled by anticlericalism, lent its voice to demands for more economical government. The rifts thus opened might well have been exploited by the crown's enemies. The Beauforts, Henry in particular, were peculiarly well placed to reconcile these interests, allay distrust, and work for harmony. While he was chancellor Bishop Beaufort probably stood higher in royal confidence than did Archbishop Arundel, and both he and John were among the half-dozen magnates and bishops who regularly attended the council, composed predominantly of household knights and clerks. At the same time both enjoyed the confidence of the Commons, being repeatedly named in parliament as councillors, and twice being chosen as members of an intercommuning committee. As chancellor Henry presided over two of the most critical parliaments of the reign, securing from the October parliament of 1404 the most generous grants of taxation in the reign, without bowing to demands for disendowment of the church.

The fact that the crown survived not merely military challenges but severe parliamentary criticism, near bankruptcy, and the king's own incapacitating illness, was largely due to the solidarity of the small group of its committed supporters. Those who did service in Wales, the north, on the sea, and in Calais were, for the most part, those who were also members of the council and the royal entourage. They were a tightly knit group, not split by treachery or faction, to whom the king could entrust his dignity and estate even to the point of committing to them some of his prerogative powers when compelled by ill health and parliamentary criticism in 1406. In this group the Beauforts were both prominent and ubiquitous, moving between court, camp, parliament, and council as the occasion demanded, and available to serve on embassies for the marriages of the king and members of his family. In this sense they took over something of the role which the Percies had played in the early years of the reign, though unlike the Percies they inherited no traditional territorial base or long-rooted loyalties. Indeed their dependence on royal favour and vulnerability to the shifts of fashion made their relationship to the royal house particularly sensitive. Their role was to be pillars beneath the throne earning their dignities by strenuous service. But it was the crown which supported them, not they the crown, and the propitious circumstances which had enabled them to stake a claim to royal gratitude were now passing. The king's sons were growing to manhood and the circle of active, able, young nobility was rapidly enlarging: to the parliament of 1407 seven earls were summoned. The opportunities for military service had declined, and John was now too sick to put to sea. The council, headed by the prince and with Arundel as chancellor, was no longer an extension of the king's entourage; its greater autonomy could prove a recipe for greater factionalism. In the light of such developments the prominence and favour enjoyed by the Beauforts had, by the winter of 1407, begun to look less assured.

3

The Prince's Faction, 1408–1413

No two years are more obscure in the history both of Henry IV's reign and of the fortunes of the Beauforts than those between the close of the Gloucester parliament in December 1407 and the ministerial changes which preceded the parliament of January 1410. Although the council named in the parliament of 1406 was not reappointed at Gloucester, nor its powers renewed, its programme of financial reform and conciliar control provided the framework for policy in the following years. By providing taxation in regular instalments until Easter 1409, and prohibiting any further grants until 1410, parliament and convocation had set the council the task of planning a fixed budget over a defined period. This was assisted by the decline of the military emergency, which made financial planning more feasible and permitted a reconsideration of priorities in expenditure. Yet the programme overall was at the mercy of changes in the composition and authority of the council, and these were particularly influenced by the king's uncertain health culminating in a severe illness in the latter part of 1408. As the personal influence of Archbishop Arundel over the king was confronted by the rising ambitions of Prince Henry, factions hardened and were eventually manifested in the dismissal of the principal officers of state and the institution of a new council in the winter of 1409–10. In that council the Beauforts achieved a renewed prominence and the bishop declared himself a firm adherent of the prince. It is less easy to say whether he contrived the removal of Arundel and how far the conflict was between rival policies as well as parties.

The financial strategy of the council was laid down in a meeting of the great council from the end of January to mid-February 1408, at which both John and Henry Beaufort were present. Throughout 1407 the needs of Calais and the Welsh war had been given priority and payments to the household had been deliberately restricted; in consequence complaint of the failure to pay for purveyances was heard at both parliament and council.[1] Conforming to the Commons' financial ideals, the council assigned the revenue from casualties and farms for the support of the household for two years. Conscious that these would be insufficient for its requirements, the council further authorized assignments to the wardrobe and chamber on both halves of the lay and clerical subsidies due before Michaelmas to the sum of £16,680, with a further £4,000 from the wool

[1] *Rot. Parl.* iii. 609; E 404/23/229, 251.

subsidy.[2] These measures reflected Henry IV's own renewed influence and were certainly contrary to the Commons' traditional views that direct taxation was granted solely for defence. Yet they also commanded support in the council, which for the next three years maintained a policy of supporting the household from taxation, eventually accepted tacitly by parliament. In November 1408, a sum of £10,000 from the third part of the lay subsidy due in February 1409 formed part of the household's total annual allocation of 23,000 marks, to be replaced in the next annual allocation in November 1409, when no direct taxation was available, by a proportionate sum from the wool subsidy. Following the parliament of 1410 the council authorized the use of direct taxation for an even greater proportion of household expenses.[3]

At the same time the Calais lobby remained articulate and influential. No specific provision had been made at the Gloucester parliament for its finance, but at the end of January 1408 Somerset warned the council of the plight of the garrison and the possibilities of its desertion or a further seizure of the Staplers' wool. He secured an immediate grant of £1,500 and on 17 February the council agreed to re-establish the allocation of half the wool subsidy for the wages of Calais, to run until 1 November 1409.[4] Somerset received backing from the Staplers, who put in their own petition, answered by the council at a meeting on 2 March at which the prince and Henry Beaufort, though not Somerset, were present. The Staplers now secured repayment of their loans of 1407 from the customs, and asked for safeguards against further seizures of wool by the garrison, the maintenance of their monopoly of wool exports, the prolongation of the truce with Burgundy, and the safeguard of the sea promised at the Gloucester parliament.[5] Indeed the council was already in process of indenting with the earl of Kent for a sizeable force to keep the sea from April to October at a cost of £9,990.[6] Kent formally replaced Somerset as admiral in May, but his death in the attack on Briac in mid-September returned the office to the Beauforts, with the appointment of Sir Thomas as admiral a week later. At the same time the council made provision for the defence of the other frontiers of the realm. The Northumberland–Bardolph invasion led it to warrant £7,000 to John of Lancaster, and £2,500 to the earl of Westmorland two days before the battle of Bramham Moor.[7]

The main military effort in 1408 was designed to be in Wales, for which

[2] *CPR 1405–8*, 408; E 404/23/ 268, 273–4, 284. This pattern of spending is analysed by Wright, thesis, 157–76.

[3] *CPR 1408–13*, 35, 50; E 404/24/234.

[4] E 28/23 30 Jan.; E 404/23/294–5.

[5] *PPC* i. 305; *CPR 1405–8*, 414. The truce was extended for three years in June, Somerset being one of the conservators: *Foedera*, viii. 530, 541.

[6] E 404/23/305.

[7] E 404/23/272, 275–6.

the prince indented on 8 March for six months' service from 1 April receiving £12,051. 13*s*. 4*d*.[8] Aberystwyth was recaptured by early September and Harlech alone remained in Welsh hands, but the prince did not stay in Wales beyond the end of the year. Finally the council made generous and elaborate arrangements for financing Prince Thomas in Ireland, who now indented to serve from 1 May for three years at an annual retainer of 7,000 marks plus the payment of his arrears in three equal instalments.[9]

The great council of February 1408 thus attempted to allocate revenue between the principal charges up to the following Michaelmas; it did so under competing pressures from the king, the king's sons Henry, John, and Thomas, the earl of Somerset, and the Staplers. The indentures made for payment of the sums appointed to each regulated in detail the sources from which revenue was to be drawn and the order of preference of their competing claims. Having thus made a determined attempt to lay down authoritative guidelines for the exchequer, the council dispersed, and for the rest of the summer the direction of policy fell to the officers of state, notably Archbishop Arundel, under whose care the sick king rested at Mortlake during June and July.[10] The choice of Sir John Tiptoft to replace Bishop Bubwith as treasurer on 14 July reflected the growth of Arundel's influence, although the circumstances of the change are obscure. Bubwith was a friend of Beaufort, but Tiptoft was undoubtedly more efficient and was both *persona grata* with the king and closely identified with the policy of financial restraint initiated in 1406.

After the council Somerset returned to Calais arriving, according to one source, at the moment when the garrison, on an ill-advised sally into Picardy, found themselves surrounded and outnumbered by the enemy. John is said to have mustered the soldiers' wives in Calais and led them, as a relief force, to the rescue of their husbands.[11] Bishop Henry at once retired to his diocese, where he remained throughout the summer. Late in March, from his manor at Bishop's Waltham, he announced his intention of making a visitation of St Swithun's, and next month he conducted his first ordinations since his accession to the see. The visitation was scheduled for 15 September but, three days before that date, Beaufort wrote from Highclere that the business of church and state necessitated his immediate return to London.[12] He had briefly attended the convocation which met at St Paul's in late July, at which it had been agreed to put pressure upon

[8] E 404/23/310.

[9] *PPC* i. 313–18; E 404/23/309.

[10] *CSL* no. 717; P. McNiven, 'The problem of Henry IV's health', *EHR* 100 (1985), 761–72. Bishop Beaufort entertained the king at Southwark in 1408: S. Toy, 'Winchester House, Southwark', *Surrey Arch. Coll.* 49 (1946), 75.

[11] *Chron. Angl.* 54–5. Somerset was at Calais by early July: *CIM 1399–1422*, 204, no. 378.

[12] *Reg. CS*, 36, 39; HRO, Reg. Beaufort, fo. 321.

Gregory XII to attend the proposed council at Pisa for healing the schism. The payment of papal dues was to be suspended, and Beaufort with Lord Scrope and others was delegated to convey this to Gregory. The embassy never went, and Beaufort's register shows him back at Highclere by late August.[13] It may have been the impending visit of Cardinal Uguccione to secure support for the council at Pisa that brought Beaufort back again to London, although it was not until the end of October that the cardinal addressed a meeting of the great council and clergy and ultimately secured royal backing for the *via concilii* and the dispatch of an English delegation.[14] This, led by Hallum, with Chichele and Langley among the other bishops, included a number of ardent reformers and represented a clearly defined party within the church which enjoyed Arundel's support. Beaufort's omission from it is not surprising, for he had few connections with these, and had shown scant interest in reform. In June 1409 the council of Pisa elected Alexander V in place of the two 'deposed' occupants of the Holy See, and the English delegation returned in July, provided with extensive privileges as part of their reward. Then on 27 August Gregory XII, in a last bid to save his own influence in England, named the bishop of Winchester as legate a latere in England with special powers to work on behalf of the unity of the church against the newly elected Alexander.[15] There is no evidence, and little likelihood, that Beaufort had courted this, or that he ever claimed or used the powers. But Gregory's perception that Beaufort had distanced himself from the reforming group in the English church and had ambitions for an authority higher than that of Canterbury may well have been accurate.

Beaufort's own diplomatic milieu in 1409 was in the negotiations for a permanent peace with France, for which the current dominance of the duke of Burgundy at the French court held out some prospect. The truce negotiated during the course of 1407–8 had been largely the work of Langley, Sir Thomas Erpingham, John Catrik, and Hugh Mortimer, and Langley was at first commissioned to lead the peace delegation early in 1409. When he was transferred to Pisa his place was taken by Henry Beaufort.[16] Catrik conducted three embassies to France and Picardy in the course of 1409, Beaufort accompanying him on those of May and September which secured an extension of the truce from May 1410.[17]

While Henry Beaufort had spent the summer of 1409 either in France or

[13] *Concilia*, iii. 308–10; Reg. Beaufort, fo. 37, 40–1; Harvey, 'Solutions to the Schism', 138–42.

[14] *St Albans Chronicle*, ed. V. H. Galbraith, 31, 148–52; *Foedera*, viii. 547; R. L. Storey, *Thomas Langley and the Bishopric of Durham*, 26–8; Harvey, 'Solutions to the Schism', 143–74.

[15] *CPL* vi. 99; C. Eubel, *Hierarchia Catholica Medii Aevi*, i. 526 n. 6.

[16] Storey, *Langley*, 26. The truce was concluded in Sept. 1408: C 47/30/9; PRO, *Diplomatic and Scottish Documents*, 180; *Foedera*, viii. 586; E 404/24/465.

[17] *Foedera*, viii. 599–601; *CSL* no. 740; E 404/24/36; E 364/45 rot. 4.

in Hampshire, there is scattered evidence that Sir Thomas was firmly established at court. From February 1408 the king had ordered him to attend about his person, assigning him a residence at Stratford Langhorne near London, and a year later he, Langley, Tiptoft and Sir John Stanley witnessed the king's grant of Queenborough to Archbishop Arundel at Greenwich.[18] He was gradually moving into the place occupied by his ailing brother who, in July 1408, appointed him captain of Calais castle, and in September procured for him the vacant post of admiral.[19] Somerset himself remained firmly in Henry IV's favour, receiving a life annuity of £40 in August 1408 and in September the reversion to him and his heirs of the lands of Ivo Fitzwarin to be held in tail male from the crown. But he does not appear among the small group, numbering Arundel, York, Langley, Tiptoft, and members of the household, who attended Henry IV in his critical illness and witnessed his will on 21 January.[20] Prince Henry had hurried to his father's bedside, and Thomas returned precipitately from Ireland in March; then as the king recovered, the political scene enlarged and the influence exercised for the last year by this group, and pre-eminently by Arundel, began to be challenged. Significantly, in May, and again early in November 1409, special writs were sent to the marcher lords who were the natural followers of Prince Henry—Arundel, Warwick, Charleton of Powys, Grey of Codnor and Grey of Ruthin—ordering them to remain at their posts.[21] By August, although the prince had joined the council, it still consisted of the great officers and members of the household, while Thomas with his company from Ireland had attached himself to the royal household and was insisting on the payment of his arrears of wages.[22] These incipient political rivalries may have been suspended during the jousts between the Garter knights and some Hainaulters at Smithfield in August 1409 organized by the earl of Somerset, who, like the king, had recovered his health and now acquitted himself honourably; but by the autumn the renewed activity of the council was leading to a clash of wills.[23] Was it also a clash of policies?

The broad financial strategy adopted in the great council of February 1408 was adhered to for the next year, but by Easter 1409 the last instalments of the lay and clerical subsidies granted in 1407 had been paid and the council faced conditions of financial stringency in the latter part of the year. In the Easter term its cash receipts were the lowest for four years, and by Michaelmas it was evident that current revenue was inadequate to

[18] *CPR 1405–8*, 393; *CCR 1405–9*, 498.

[19] *Catalogue des rolles gascons, normans, et francais*, ed. T. Carte, ii. 196.

[20] *CPR 1405–8*, 465, 468; *A Collection of Royal Wills*, ed. J. Nichols, 203.

[21] *Foedera*, viii. 588, 611.

[22] *PPC* i. 320.

[23] *Chron. Angl.* 56–7; *Gregory's Chronicle*, ed. J. Gairdner, 105; *Chronicle of London*, ed. N. H. Nicolas, 91.

support the level of charges, and that parliament would have to be asked for another injection of direct taxation. On 26 October the king summoned parliament to meet at Bristol on 27 January. In this climate of general financial stringency priorities became politically charged. A new allocation for the household, the greater part of which was to be drawn from the wool subsidies, reduced its income to the equivalent of 20,000 marks p.a. This in turn meant that the allocation of the wool subsidy to Calais had to be cut from one-half to one quarter from 2 November.[24] After Easter only minimal sums had been paid to the commanders on the northern border and for operations in Wales, but by contrast Prince Thomas on 27 May had secured an assignment of £7,666. 13*s*. 4*d*. in payment of his arrears.[25]

Competition for financial preference fuelled the dissensions which were appearing between the court and the council, as Henry IV began to reassert his authority over expenditure, and within the council between Archbishop Arundel and the Prince of Wales. The prince had completed his task in Wales and his eyes were now fixed on his inheritance in England. His father's illness and the return to court of his favoured younger brother determined him to assert his own political leadership of the council. In August the prince, with the backing of the council, tried to put pressure on Thomas to surrender the lieutenantship of Ireland and relieve the royal household of the support of his retinue, but this failed.[26] By November the council had become fatally divided: though it began to borrow on a large scale for a Welsh expedition, the prince complained that the money had not reached him, while an 'appointment' which it made for the expenditure of the wool subsidies was never implemented by Arundel and Tiptoft.[27] Tiptoft's resignation on 11 December and Arundel's ten days later, when the king arrived in London, marked the resolution of a struggle between prince and archbishop over political control and financial priorities. This did not involve the royal power. and there is no evidence for any conflict between Henry IV and his eldest son. The prince and his associates were in no sense an anti-court faction. Both John and Thomas Beaufort, who were on the council in August, enjoyed the confidence of the king, while Henry Beaufort had few previous contacts with the prince. Throughout the first part of December 1409 the bishop seems to have resided at his manor at Esher, possibly moving to Southwark only in the New Year.[28] Rather, what the Beauforts could offer Prince Henry was what he and his marcher associates lacked: administrative, conciliar, and diplomatic experience, contacts with the court, and the confidence of the Commons in parliament.

[24] *CPR 1408–13*, 151; *CCR 1409–13*, 31; E 404/25/203; Wright, thesis, 183–92.

[25] Wright, thesis, 370 table 40a; E 401/649; Steel, *Receipt*, 98–9.

[26] *PPC* i. 319–20; *Foedera*, viii. 591, 608.

[27] Steel, *Receipt*, 99; *Cal. L. Bk. I*, 82–3; *CCR 1409–13*, 25, 51. The situation is analysed thoroughly in Wright, thesis, 192–7.

[28] HRO, Reg. Beaufort, fos. 50^v–1.

The conciliar revolution was only half complete when parliament met, and the first test of the prince's authority would be whether he could command the generosity of the Commons. In broad terms he proposed to offer them guarantees of the 'good governance' which they had repeatedly demanded if they, in return, would guarantee a regular income from taxation: this being essentially a restatement of the bargain struck in 1406 and 1407. Now he was seeking a more assured and adequate financial basis. According to one chronicler, parliament and convocation were to be asked for an outright grant of an annual subsidy for the rest of the reign.[29] The Commons' normal response to such a proposal would be to insist that direct taxation should be restricted to exceptional necessities, to reaffirm that the hereditary revenues of the crown should be used to support royal government and not dispersed in gifts, and to look for assurances of good government from a named council. But on this occasion a strident and well organized anticlerical lobby seized on the demand for a permanent endowment of the crown to advocate seizure of the church's temporalities which would yield an annual revenue to the king of £20,000. This was accompanied by a barrage of anticlerical petitions.[30]

It is possible that the existence of this anticlerical feeling influenced the choice of Arundel's successor as chancellor. There was an unprecedented delay in filling both the major offices of state. By 6 January Henry, Lord Scrope of Masham, had been appointed treasurer, but when parliament met on 27 January no chancellor had been named. The natural choice was Henry Beaufort; it was he who opened the parliament and set forth the king's needs, and once again his cousin, Thomas Chaucer, was elected Speaker on the following day. But on 31 January his brother Thomas was appointed, possibly against his own wishes, for he was a man of the sword rather than of the robe and had focused his ambitions on his office as admiral. Several factors made him, at this juncture, a more suitable candidate than his brother. The king might have stood out against the appointment of Arundel's junior and rival, whereas Thomas, as a knight of the king's household and a former companion of the prince, was acceptable to both. Moreover, to the anticlerical lobby in parliament, Henry Beaufort may have epitomized the worldly and wealthy prelacy they wished abolished, whereas Thomas had the reputation of a critic of ecclesiastical wealth and immunity. Yet this must have made him an uneasy colleague for Lord Scrope, whose pious devotion to his martyred uncle cannot have endeared him to one of the latter's judges.

Henry Beaufort opened parliament with a 'most discreet and wise' speech on the respective obligations of rulers and subjects, dwelling on the obedience and love owed to a ruler, the proper expression of which was the

[29] *St Albans Chron.* 56.

[30] Ibid. 52–6; *Chronicles of London*, 65–8; *Rot. Parl.* iii. 625, 632, 644.

assistance to be rendered in time of need.[31] He cited as the most pressing problems the threats to the truces with Scotland, France, and Burgundy. The renewed danger to Calais, with which the Beauforts were closely identified, may also have commended the appointment of Thomas as chancellor, for within a week he had been ordered to take reinforcements to Calais and at the same time to negotiate with the French admiral over infractions of the truce.[32] Despite a pointed warning from the king against dishonest and contentious proposals, the Commons seem to have spent all of the first session pursuing their scheme for disendowment, and were only released on the eve of Palm Sunday on the express undertaking to be more diligent in providing for the defence of the realm and marches on their return.[33] If the chaotic first session reflected the prince's still uncertain authority, in the second Thomas Chaucer's leadership proved more effective, although the Commons remained critical and tenacious in their demands. These centred on the safeguard of the truces and the sea, the provision of sufficient revenue for the household, and the establishment of a new council.

Even before parliament met the council had ordered a stop-gap payment for Calais and when, following the death of Somerset at the end of the first session, the captaincy was transferred to the prince of Wales, his influence secured the raising of the Calais part of the wool subsidy from one to three quarters.[34] The Commons could be assured that the new administration would give the highest priority to the defence of Calais, the safeguard of the sea, and the establishment of durable truces. Their own remedy for the persistent insolvency of the household—the application of revenue from escheats and other casualties for the discharge of household debts, with penalties against persons receiving grants of such—was grudgingly accepted by the king who saw it as a limitation on his patronage. On the other hand the Commons tacitly accepted the policy of 1408, of allocating a large part of taxation for household expenses; for they now reserved 20,000 marks from direct and indirect taxation for the king's use, this being in effect for household expenses. This was an important concession in practice.[35]

All these demands, which were contained in eighteen articles presented by the Commons on 23 April, were preceded by a request for a new council to be named and sworn in parliament. On 2 May it was reported that, besides the three officers of state, this would comprise the prince, the

[31] *Rot. Parl.* iii. 622.

[32] E 28/23 7 Feb.; *Foedera*, viii. 620, 622; Carte, *Catalogue*, 199. The threat to Calais reached its climax in Apr. 1410 when the armament gathered at Saint-Omer was destroyed by fire: *St Albans Chron.* 57; *Chronique du réligieux de St Denys*, ed. L. Bellaguet, iv. 312.

[33] *Rot. Parl.* iii. 623.

[34] Ibid. 625, 627; *Foedera*, viii. 629; E 404/25/184; C 76/94 m. 31.

[35] Ibid. 625, 627, 635; Wright, thesis, 210–11.

bishops of Winchester, Durham, and Bath, the earls of Arundel and Westmorland, and Lord Burnell. A week later Westmorland and Langley, both more attached to the king than to the prince, were replaced by Chichele and Warwick, leaving the council the preserve of the prince's friends.[36] Having reached agreement on the demands of the Commons, the prince now looked for that generous and assured supply of taxation needed to sustain the provision of good governance, without which he declined to serve. The grant of three half-subsidies was only half what he had sought, though it marked the Commons' recognition that an annual contribution from direct taxation was becoming essential. Thus the prince's first administration had been launched even if, from the different standpoints of both king and Commons, it was on probation. For so great was the mutual distrust and suspicion between these two that their half-confidence in the prince alone provided a basis for effective government. In obtaining this only the Beauforts had the necessary links with the court on the one hand and the Commons on the other. Thomas and Henry Beaufort, and their cousin Thomas Chaucer, were the real architects of the prince's emergence into politics. The bishop was probably also instrumental in securing a corresponding grant from the Canterbury convocation early in March. He may well have been among the *legati domini regis* who asked for one at the opening session; he was certainly present during the subsequent examination of the Lollard John Badby, in whose trial and execution the prince took a personal interest.[37] Though disappointed of the chancellorship, Henry Beaufort was well placed to establish himself as the prince's chief adviser and reap abundant reward in the following reign.[38]

The new council found itself in a difficult position. Despite the general accord with parliament, the fact remained that no lay or clerical taxes were payable until the autumn of 1410, which would be eighteen months since the last had been collected, and arrears had accumulated on all the major standing charges. One of the first acts of the new treasurer, in February, had been to cancel existing assignments on the customs, change the collectors, and order them to bring their receipts to the exchequer; but wool exports were sluggish and the exchequer's cash receipts remained low throughout the summer term.[39] Moreover, the treasurer's action had produced an additional crop of invalid tallies. The council could do little to improve the immediate situation, but it sought to restore confidence by meeting current obligations with assignments on the lay and clerical taxes and wool subsidies due in the autumn, while borrowing to meet its

[36] *Rot. Parl.* iii. or *Foedera*, viii. 632, 634.

[37] *Concilia*, iii. 324–9; Rogers, 'Clerical taxation', 136.

[38] HRO, Eccles. II 159412, the pipe roll for 1409–10 records a visit of Prince Henry to Bishop's Waltham probably late in August 1410 when Beaufort was in residence (Reg. Beaufort, fo. 62^v^.)

[39] *CCR 1409–13*, 25–6, 31; *CFR 1405–13*, 162–4, 170–2; Steel, *Receipt*, 99.

immediate needs. For the moment nothing could be done to satisfy arrears. Throughout June and July it met in almost daily session, receiving statements of arrears, and estimates of future charges, and allocating prospective revenue between different claimants.

The household was given an annual allocation from direct taxation and three quarters of the wool subsidy was assigned to Calais, both under the authority of parliament. The current wages of John of Lancaster and the earl of Westmorland in the north, where the truce stood in danger, were paid from the taxes due after Michaelmas.[40] Nothing could be done to meet the £9,000 owed for the wages of Calais, or John's arrears. As for the claims of Thomas, amounting to £13,407, the council did no more than authorize reassignment of his dishonoured tallies, for £5,016. It declined to meet either his arrears or his current salary unless he returned to Ireland. Neither Ireland nor Thomas stood high in the council's scale of preference.[41]

Far greater importance was attached to operations in Wales and upon the sea. On 19 June Prince Henry was reappointed as king's lieutenant and, although he did not go in person, a small force was sent there in the summer at a cost of £4,480.[42] Even more pressing was the need for a fleet to safeguard the sea, not against the French—with whom the truce had been extended to November, enforced by Prince Henry and Sir Thomas Beaufort as conservators—but against the earl of Mar in the north and John Prendergast, operating off East Anglia. In June the council was still uncertain about the size of the fleet and the period of its operations, but by July it had authorized payment for nineteen and a half weeks at a cost of £6,241. 18*s*. 6*d*. Probably not all of this was paid and the period of service had to be cut short. Thomas Beaufort indented as admiral on 29 July for a succession of short periods up to eighteen weeks in all, with a small flotilla of twenty ships and just over a thousand men. He received £2,004 as wages on 17 July and a week later a further £2,066 was warranted.[43] Whether he himself went to sea is uncertain; probably he remained at Lynn, fulfilling his dual roles as chancellor and admiral, for commissions were issued to Robert Umfraville as his lieutenant in the north and to John Blount in the west.[44] The cost of the fleet had to be met from loans, for which a general commission was issued in all shires on 14 June. Bishop Beaufort was named as sole commissioner in Hampshire, Berkshire, Wiltshire, and Oxfordshire, which were assessed at £1,000; but this was a formality since he had already loaned this sum from his own resources on 9 June as part of

[40] *PPC* i. 331–3, 336–7, 342, 352, ii. 17; E 404/25/367–8, 379, 382; Wright, thesis, 223–4.

[41] *PPC* i. 339–47, 352, ii. 15; E 404/25/375, E 404/26/10; Wright, thesis, 225–6.

[42] *PPC* i. 339; E 404/25/371, 381. Loans raised for this: *PPC* i. 342, ii. 114.

[43] *PPC* i. 327–8, 346; E 101/69/2/33 (indentures); E 403/605; E 404/25/389. Though warranted, the sum was not in fact paid: Wright, thesis, 230-1.

[44] *CPR 1409–13*, 228. By December Umfraville was owed £1,700: E 404/26/211.

a total of £4,340 received at the exchequer. He had tallies on the lay subsidy collectors in Hampshire and Wiltshire, reinforced by orders to the collectors to give him preference over all other payments.[45]

The need to make urgent provision for these military demands had complicated, but not obscured, the council's long-term apportionment of its predictable revenue from taxation. When, at the end of July, it came to review the allocations made from the subsidies over the preceding weeks, an overall deficit was revealed. Various measures for reducing the cost of the marches and Calais over the next two years seem to have been considered, and a cutback made on the allocation for Gascony. But the council also initiated some of the economies and restraints which the Commons had advocated. It ordered a review of annuities, on the basis of merit, and an investigation into concealment of revenue by local collectors. In November it began to distrain for knighthood, imposing fines as a contribution to household expenses.[46] In all, therefore, the summer of 1410 had seen a vigorous and sustained attempt by the council to get a grip on royal finance and fulfil its pledges to the Commons to defend Wales, Calais, and the sea, make the household solvent, and tighten up on fiscal administration. Councillors had attended regularly and worked hard; the record of Bishop Beaufort's presence in the council is confirmed by his register, which shows him resident at Southwark until well into August.[47]

Beaufort returned to Southwark in October and remained there throughout the winter of 1410–11, presumably attending meetings of the council, although few of these are recorded. The king stayed in his Lancastrian estates, at Kenilworth and Leicester. On 19 March 1411, the end of the exchequer Michaelmas term, a great council met in the king's presence at Lambeth to review the allocation of revenue for the current year. On this occasion financial planning proceeded not from estimates of likely costs but from what revenue was due during the year Michaelmas 1410–11.[48] The council divided this into the wool subsidy and revenue from all other sources. Three-quarters of the wool subsidy were still reserved for Calais and this enabled its current needs to be met and a contribution to be made to the payment of arrears.[49] The relatively favourable treatment of Calais, however, meant that all the remaining charges for defence had to be met from the other quarter of the wool subsidy, and this left a deficit of

[45] *CPR 1409–13*, 205, 240; *PPC* i. 335, 343, 347–9, ii. 14; E 404/25/388; E 401/652. Discussed by Wright, thesis, 215–21.

[46] *PPC* i. 341–2, 344–7, 349–52; *CPR 1408–13*, 228; *CCR 1409–13*, 52; *Foedera*, viii. 656, 685; *Issues of the exchequer*, ed. F. Devon, 315, 317. Wright, thesis, 232–55 gives a detailed analysis of expenditure in these months.

[47] HRO, Reg. Beaufort, fos. 62 r–v, 69.

[48] *PPC* ii. 6–17. For an extended discussion of this, see Wright, thesis, 257–74.

[49] The treasurer's accounts show that Calais received £35,000 in the period Dec. 1409 to Mar. 1412: Kirby, 'Calais sous les Anglais', 27, 30. Warrants: E 404/26/220, 241, 246. Peacetime wages were estimated at £27,250 for 1410–12 and arrears at £9,000: *PPC* i. 352.

£12,115. The council endeavoured to reduce this by cutting the allocation for Guyenne from £6,618 to £2,666, but approved the payment of the other charges as far as the money would stretch. From all the remaining revenues falling due by Michaelmas 1411—including a half-tenth from the clergy and tunnage and poundage—the council aimed to meet the expenses of the household and the costs of administration. The deficit on this account was predicted to be £3,924. Broadly speaking, therefore, the council continued to give priority to Calais and the household and thereafter to the northern marches. But even after slashing the allocation for Guyenne it found itself budgeting for a total deficit of around £12,000. Rather than anticipate the lay subsidy due at Martinmas 1411, the council pruned still further the costs of the northern marches and Ireland,[50] and imposed a restraint of annuities from the crown revenues, to be applied from 1 May, only to be relaxed when a surplus had been achieved.[51]

The great council of March 1411 thus shows that the prince's administration was maintaining the momentum and principles of the financial policy of 1410, which was itself a continuation of that of 1408. The allocation of revenue for the coming year or half-year on the basis of prepared estimates, the general priority given to Calais and the household, the readiness to support the latter from taxation, the attempts to increase the efficiency of revenue collection, and to reduce the amount paid out in annuities—all these were continuing features of financial policy under the prince's direction. Moreover, in 1411, despite the predicted deficit and the inability to reduce the accumulated debt, the council firmly resisted the temptation to borrow or to anticipate revenue from the next financial year. The Michaelmas term 1410–11 had seen genuine and fictitious loans almost vanish from the receipt roll, and doubtless the following roll if it had survived would confirm this trend.[52] The council was planning for a balanced budget, even if it had not achieved this by the time it was dismissed.

The council also sought to implement its promises to parliament to seek permanent truces with Burgundy and Scotland. In November 1410 it appointed negotiators for a three-year truce with Burgundy and issued safe conducts to Burgundian envoys, and on 27 May 1411 the truce was duly prolonged for three years. These negotiations also sought a better enforcement of the mercantile truce with Flanders, for which Prince Henry and Thomas Beaufort were again appointed conservators in June.[53] The

[50] The warrants for these commanders are in E 404/26/210, 243–4, 247, 363; new indentures made with John and Thomas are E 101/69/336, 337.

[51] *CCR 1409–13*, 148.

[52] Steel, *Receipt*, 100.

[53] *PPC* ii. 3; *Foedera*, viii. 660–1, 687–9; *Cotton Galba B.I.*, 302–4 (no. 133); 312 (no. 136). Thomas Beaufort was also conservator of the truce with Brittany: PRO *List of Diplomatic Docts*. 181.

principal threat came again from the piracy of John Prendergast, whose seizure the council had ordered in March. This had not happened and on 11 May the prince and the chancellor, fearing that the truce negotiations would be jeopardized, made themselves responsible for his arrest. On 15 May Thomas Beaufort received wages of £1,000 and, having left London on 7 May, returned on 12 June with Prendergast and William Longe as prisoners, though he deferred resuming his duties as chancellor until a week later.[54] His prompt and effective action had guaranteed the renewal of the vital Burgundian truce, for five years from 15 June. This formed part of a general policy of pacification. In the winter of 1410–11 negotiations were being pursued with Castile, with Sigismund, king of Hungary, and with the Master of the Teutonic Knights. With France the truces continued to be of short span and in a localized area, but in July 1411 Chichele, Lord Beaumont, Sir John Cheyne, and Catrik were commissioned to explore the possibility of a general peace.[55] Similarly in the north John of Lancaster and the earl of Westmorland were given power in April 1411 to renew the truce for a further two years. Both sides were anxious for a greater degree of stability, and after a year of negotiations a truce was concluded in May 1412 to last until Easter 1418.[58] In the first half of 1411, therefore, the policy of the prince and the council was to strengthen the peace, master the problem of piracy, and reduce the costs of defence.

This policy was put in jeopardy by the outbreak of civil war in France which had been threatening since the Orléanist defiance of Duke John in September 1410. By the time the Orléanists issued the manifesto of Jargeau in July 1411, both sides had sought and obtained allies. John, having concluded the truce with England, was exploring a more binding treaty, linked with marriage. The English council were discussing his proposal in August, and on 1 September instructions were issued in the name of the king and the prince to the earl of Arundel, Hugh Mortimer, and Catrik to explore Burgundy's terms for an alliance. The English purpose was not, at this stage, to exploit the divisions in France for its own advantage, but rather to maintain Burgundy's influence in France against the hostile intervention which had characterized Orléanist policy since the beginning of the reign. In a word, the English attitude remained defensive, and no far-reaching claims, or demands of allegiance, were advanced. Even the prospect of recovering lands in Guyenne was militarily remote.[57] Henry IV's personal support for an expedition to sustain Burgundy was manifested in mid-August by the order to all holding annuities from the king to muster in London on 23 September, and preparations for his

[54] *CPR 1408–13*, 316, 318; *CCR 1409–13*, 224; J. H. Wylie, *History of England under Henry IV*, iv. 24.

[55] *Foedera*, viii. 655–9, 665–74, 696; *PPC* ii. 24–6.

[56] E. W. M. Balfour-Melville, *James I, King of Scots*, 45–9.

[57] *PPC* ii. 19–24; Vaughan, *John the Fearless*, 87–92.

crossing were continuing as late as 3 September. But over the next two weeks he changed his mind, certainly about his own participation, and probably against any intervention.[58] Possibly John the Fearless had made it plain that he wanted auxiliaries rather than a royal expedition with all its diplomatic complications, and Henry IV had taken offence. For it was seemingly on the king's withdrawal that the Burgundian ambassadors appealed to Prince Henry who, against his father's will, mounted a private expedition under the leadership of his principal retainer, the earl of Arundel.[59]

The prince's defiance of his father provided the occasion for the latter to reclaim power. On 21 September, at almost exactly the moment when the earl of Arundel's expedition sailed, Henry IV summoned parliament to meet on 3 November. Its assembly had been agreed by the council in August, to meet the costs of the royal voyage, but it now served to accomplish and authorize a change of ministry.[60] The prince's response to this may have been, as some chroniclers suggest, to secure the support of a number of lords for the king's abdication. The story that this was on the advice of Henry Beaufort may well be true, for when parliament met it was once again Thomas Chaucer who was elected Speaker, and in accepting his formal protestation, the king gave pointed warning that he would have no 'novelties' in this parliament.[61] The success of Arundel's *force de frappe* at Saint-Cloud on 8 November may have temporarily strengthened the prince's hand, though it goes unmentioned in the parliament roll. Throughout the month there was an obscure struggle in which the Commons urged the need for good governance and commended the council, while the prince, in a veiled reproach to the Commons for their parsimony, declared that he could have done more had they been more liberal. But ultimately the Commons could not sustain a council which had lost the king's confidence, and on 30 November it was formally thanked and dismissed.

In the first half of December the king consolidated his position and was able, on the final day of parliament, to annul the 'article of restraint' made in the last parliament, almost certainly the restriction of feudal revenues to the payment of household debts, as being contrary to his liberties and prerogatives. The king had finally mastered a restive Commons who, acknowledging that he bore a heavy heart towards the present and previous parliaments, sought an assurance that he held them loyal and

[58] *CCR 1409–13*, 166, 240–1; Wylie, *Henry IV*, iv. 37–9.

[59] *Gregory's Chron.* 106; *Great Chronicle of London*, ed. A. H. Thomas and I. D. Thornley, 90; P. McNiven, 'Prince Henry and the English political crisis of 1412', *History*, 65 (1980), 4–5.

[60] Wright, thesis, 286.

[61] *Chron. Angl.* 63; *Eulogium*, iii. 421; *An English Chronicle 1377–1461*, ed. J. S. Davies, 37; *Rot. Parl.* iii. 647. Gloucester was to revive the allegation against Beaufort in 1426.

faithful subjects. At the same time they purchased a general pardon with the grant of a novel income tax, which they placed at the king's free disposal.[62] Finally came the replacement of the great officers. Lord Scrope was relieved of the treasurership and ordered to prepare a statement of his receipts and expenditure by 8 January, and Sir Thomas Beaufort surrendered the chancellorship on 21 December.[63] As chancellor he had opened parliament with a speech which, if it showed traces of his brother's academic training, also emphasized the obedience and honour due to the king, and throughout the parliament he remained the spokesman for the king's wishes. He may even have co-operated in Henry's reassertion of power, for he had stayed close to the court during the summer, and had never forfeited Henry's confidence. He was certainly unlikely to have backed any plan to force the king's abdication. Probably he surrendered the chancellorship with some relief, more particularly because on 3 March 1412 he was made admiral for life, and four months later created earl of Dorset.

Under the prince's leadership the council had demonstrated a well-defined character and programme. In defence its priorities had been the defence of Calais and the sea and a closer alliance with Burgundy, while domestically it had sought to ensure the solvency of the royal household within the general context of tight budgetary planning of current revenue and expenditure. In large measure its objectives were those of the Commons, while its methods had been inherited from the experience of the council under Archbishop Arundel. If the prince himself had brought greater dynamism and thoroughness to its work, the necessary continuity and experience within the council was supplied by Henry Beaufort. In none of these matters did the prince himself, or those whom he had introduced, have previous experience. Indeed in this predominantly youthful council only Bishop Bubwith was senior to Beaufort in years and none surpassed him in experience of high office. There is good reason to credit Beaufort with decisive influence over the prince at this critical stage of the latter's political education. For the lessons which Henry now learned were of paramount importance for his later conduct of government as king. Throughout his reign he set the highest store on maintaining the confidence of the Commons, the credit of the exchequer, and the channels and markets for English wool and cloth. Beaufort had devoted himself to promoting 'good governance' as a bond between crown and subjects and had established himself as a prominent member of the rapidly growing circle of the prince's friends who became the natural heirs to political power when the old king finally died.

[62] *Rot. Parl.* iii. 647–8, 658. As Wright (thesis, 287) points out, the Commons were far from generous in their renewal of the wool subsidy.

[63] E 28/23, 19 Dec.

Immediately after the dissolution of parliament Bishop Henry retired to Farnham, and although he made brief appearances at Southwark in February, May, and October of 1412, the remainder of that year was spent in Hampshire, at the episcopal residences at Farnham, Highclere and Wolvesey. His total withdrawal from the political scene gave him the opportunity to conduct ordinations at Winchester, in February and April, and regulate the affairs of the college, where he more than once dined. Otherwise his register gives no evidence of exceptional pastoral activity.[64] By contrast, Thomas Beaufort remained in touch with the court and was soon involved in preparations for the expedition to aid the Armagnac lords. It is probable that Prince Henry too remained in London to welcome the Burgundian envoys, with whom discussions over his projected marriage were still in train during the early spring.[65] But it was the influence of Clarence and Archbishop Arundel, once again chancellor, which ensured the acceptance of the rival offers from the Armagnac lords by the beginning of May. The treaty of Bourges was signed on 18 May and was endorsed by the king's four sons two days later.[66] It offered such a striking fulfilment of the royal claims in Aquitaine, and the healing of the traditional enmity between Orléans and Lancaster, that it is easy to believe that the old king, under Archbishop Arundel's influence, saw it as a last crowning mercy and vindication of his troubled reign. Prince Henry's attitude may well have been ambivalent. Some free-lance troops had gone to Burgundy in the spring, but the danger of Burgundian reprisals against Calais and English shipping was real, and steps were taken to send money to Calais, to warn the Four Members to observe the truce, and to extend the truce with Scotland.[67] Moreover Thomas of Lancaster had already staked out his claim to take part, and on 11 May Sir Thomas Beaufort, as admiral, was instructed to prepare ships for his passage. By the middle of the month, if not earlier, the king himself had resolved to lead the expedition, ordering his affinity to muster in London by mid-June and, probably by the date of signing the treaty, had agreed that Prince Henry should accompany him with a force of his own.[68]

[64] HRO, Reg. Beaufort, fos. 89–97; for previous ordinations by Beaufort in Sept. 1409 and May 1410, see *Register of Robert Rede* ii. 361; T. F. Kirby, *Annals of Winchester College*, 122–3, 172–3, 177. In Mar. 1412 he suspended his proposed visitation of Chertsey abbey, recognizing the convent's exemption: *Chertsey Abbey Cartularies*, part i (Surrey Rec. Soc., 1915), 38 no. 53.

[65] *Foedera*, viii. 715, 721.

[66] Ibid. 738, 743. On 22 and 31 May letters from Prince Henry speak of his earlier promise to assist Burgundy with numbers of troops, but of regretfully bowing to the king's decision: J. Pocquet du Haut Jussé, 'Une renaissance littéraire au cour d'Henri V', *Revue historique*, 224 (1960), 329–38.

[67] *CCR 1409–13*, 328; *St Albans Chron*. 65; *PPC* ii. 28–30; *Foedera*, viii. 728, 737.

[68] E 404/27/394; *CCR 1409–13*, 339. When the Armagnac lords wrote to the English commanders from Blois on 16 Sept. 1412 their letters were addressed to Henry IV and Prince Henry: BL Harley MS 431 fo. 105 r–v.

The treaty of Bourges had fixed the size of the English force as 1,000 men-at-arms and 3,000 archers, costing about £6,000 per month. By the latter part of May the difficulty of finding the first quarter's wages for this force had become clear. In particular the exchequer could see no way in which Prince Henry's own company could be paid for.[69] Perhaps a reduction in the size of the prince's contingent was suggested, for, according to his later manifesto, it was this which induced him to leave London for his Welsh and Cheshire lands in early June to find ways and means of increasing his force. It was during his absence that Henry IV was persuaded to withdraw from the expedition himself and appoint Thomas of Lancaster as its commander, on 8 June.[70] It spelt the exclusion of Prince Henry and was a direct affront to his dignity and repute, which he might well attribute to his enemies at court and construe as indicative of a wish to change the succession. His march to London with his supporters was indeed a political demonstration and not an insurrection; it was not aimed at reversing the king's decision, and he did not secure Archbishop Arundel's dismissal, although he was promised that his detractors would be tried and judged at the next parliament.

During Prince Henry's visit to London, from 30 June to 11 July, Sir Thomas Beaufort was created earl of Dorset and Thomas of Lancaster duke of Clarence. Prince Henry was a witness to neither.[71] Whether he resented Dorset's participation in the expedition is an open question. Dorset and York had indented two days after Thomas of Lancaster, and between them were to take half the total force.[72] Thomas's earldom gave recognition to his status as a joint commander and was reward for his support. In the event the exchequer met the cost by negotiating a loan of 10,000 marks from the city of London at the beginning of June followed by others from bishops, abbots, and chancery officials, probably at the instigation of Archbishop Arundel. In all £11,900 was raised.[73]

The fact that in Prince Henry's absence the council both raised money and sealed indentures which effectively excluded his participation points to a conspiracy against him in which Arundel as chancellor, Pelham (a retainer of the duke of York) as treasurer, Clarence, York, and Thomas Beaufort must at least have connived. The expedition had finally sailed on 9 August and the prince must have felt himself tricked and vulnerable. On 23 September he again came to London 'with an huge pepyll' to answer

[69] The figure of £6,000 is from Kirby, *Henry IV*. 244. *PPC* ii. 33–4 provides the only direct evidence that Prince Henry, as he claimed, intended to go on the expedition. Cf. McNiven, 'Prince Henry and the crisis of 1412', 9.

[70] *St Albans Chron*. 65–6; *Foedera*, viii. 745.

[71] Kirby, *Henry IV*, 243–4.

[72] *Foedera*, viii. 749–50; E 404/27/414, 415, 419.

[73] *Foedera*, viii. 747–9, 761–2, 766–7; *PPC* ii. 31–2; *CPR 1408–13*, 403, 419, 421: Wright, thesis, 303.

charges in council that he had retained large sums due to the Calais garrison. He cleared himself, but during October the council conducted an examination of present and former treasurers and victuallers of Calais, including Reginald Curteys, the victualler until 1407, who was now a retainer of Bishop Beaufort. Perhaps it was this that brought the bishop to Southwark in these weeks; perhaps also to rebuild his relations with the prince, whose succession to the throne he impatiently anticipated. Nevertheless neither the prince nor Bishop Beaufort are recorded as attending the council, and the king's generosity in his last months was directed towards the knights and esquires who surrounded his bed.[74]

Neither Thomas nor Henry Beaufort seem to have benefited directly from their membership of the council during 1410 and 1411. It is true that, as chancellor, Thomas was given an additional 800 marks p.a. beyond the fees of office, but this was done on the recommendation of the council and was a reflection of his own limited resources.[75] He received no further grants of land or wardships, although he was able to enter some of the lands of Baldwin Frevell granted earlier. His principal advancement came indeed after his surrender of the chancellorship. On 3 March 1412 his post of admiral of the north and west held since 1408 was converted into a life grant of the admiralty of England, Ireland, and Aquitaine. His creation as earl of Dorset on 5 July brought the customary £20 annuity from the exchequer but no promise of further endowment.[76]

His brother John's search for patronage remained assiduous and successful to the last. Following the grant of the reversion of the lands of Ivo Fitzwarin valued at 300 marks p.a. on 4 September 1408, he and Thomas Brounflete procured a grant to themselves of the keeping of all the lands of the recently deceased Edmund, earl of Kent, including those descending to the earl of March through his mother Eleanor Holand, during his minority. Brounflete was treasurer of the household, and the grant was made while Henry was convalescing at Hugh Waterton's house in London. Within weeks it was cancelled and the estates were apportioned between Kent's widow and the other Holand heiresses.[77] In August of 1409 John secured the marriage of Humphrey, son of Walter Fitzwalter, the custody of whose lands he had been granted in 1406, in deduction of his exchequer annuity of £1,000, and in October he succeeded in converting half of this sum to an annuity on the petty custom in London. It is probable that all these grants were the fruit of his direct contact and friendship with the king, but the advent of the prince's administration confirmed his

[74] *Chronicles of London*, 95; *PPC* ii. 34–40; Kirby, *Henry IV*, 246. For Curteys, see *CPR 1408–13*, 454; HRO, Reg. Beaufort fo. 129. For rewards to Pelham, Norbury, and Brounflete, see *CPR 1408–13*, 363, 369, 404–5, 410, 459.

[75] *CPR 1408–13*, 219, 282; *PPC* i. 338.

[76] *CPR 1408–13*, 97, 228; *CCR 1409–13*, 128.

[77] *CPR 1405–8*, 468; *CFR 1405–13*, 116, 135–6.

position. On 8 January 1410 his life grant of Corfe was converted into one in tail male, and in a meeting of the council at the prince's house, Coldharbour, on 8 February 1410, with the chancellor and treasurer present, he was permitted to draw 2,000 marks from the Fitzwalter lands in payment of the arrears of his exchequer annuity.[78] This was within six weeks of his own death, which occurred, probably following a heart attack, in the early hours of Palm Sunday in the hospital of St Katherine by the Tower.

John had successfully established the Beauforts among the curial nobility, yet his character emerges less clearly than those of his brothers, or of his sons who bore the same title. His salient qualities were military prowess and loyalty to Henry IV. From his youthful participation in the jousts of St Ingelvert and the Barbary crusade in 1390, to his reputed leadership of the English knights who triumphantly met the challenge of a company of Hainaulters in single combat before the court at Windsor in the year before his death, Somerset was foremost among the English nobility in cultivating the chivalric tradition.[79] In this he emulated Henry of Bolingbroke, and their common devotion to crusade and tournament, fortified by membership of the Garter, established a personal bond which was tested and proved in the trauma of 1399–1400. With Henry's accession to the throne John's qualities as a soldier had to be displayed in more mundane exercises. He had joined the Scottish expedition in the first year of the reign and was briefly lieutenant in Wales in 1403, but his main theatre was to be the defence of Calais and the northern sea. That was a heavy responsibility which, in the years from 1403 to 1407, took him repeatedly to Calais, not infrequently involving armed skirmishes in the march and Picardy. Both the king and the Commons felt assured of the safety of Calais in his hands. Henry's favour and confidence was already displayed in 1399 by Somerset's appointment as chamberlain, a post which made him not merely the vehicle for royal patronage, but the most habitual and influential counsellor at the king's side. He was entrusted with embassies, particularly for the royal marriages, but also those to safeguard links with Burgundy and Flanders. For all this his rewards in lands and money were considerable; they were well earned, but it is also true that circumstances had favoured his rise. For in the early years of the reign he and Westmorland were the only fully adult members of the nobility whom Henry IV could trust. The fortunes of the Beauforts necessarily stood or fell with those of Lancaster, and John, perceiving this, sought to demonstrate his loyalty through unwearying service and personal fidelity, which he maintained into the years when the king had become a shadow of his former self. Nor is there any hint in him of the jealousy or resentment

[78] *CPR 1408–13*, 89, 142, 144, 147; *PPC* i. 329; C 139/160.
[79] *Chron. Angl.*, 55–6.

of the true blood which is discernible in his brother Henry. Having shared with his monarch the responsibility for the defence of the new royal dynasty, and having marked out the path of loyalty and service on which the fortunes of his own family would have to be built, it was fitting that he should be buried in the choir of Canterbury cathedral near where his royal master was shortly to lie.

At the time of his death Earl John held lands worth some £1,000 p.a., half of them in his own right. These comprised the Northamptonshire and Leicestershire manors granted by John of Gaunt in 1391; the Somerset properties which Gaunt had purchased from the earl of Salisbury in 1395; and the lands in Devon of the forfeiture of William Asthorp which he had received from Henry IV in 1400. Beyond these were properties of lesser value: the lordship of Corfe, the manor of Orwell in Cambridgeshire, and the Glyndwrdwy lands of uncertain yield. As one of the five coheirs of Edmund, earl of Kent (d. 1408), his countess Margaret brought lands which complemented these geographically: a group of manors in Somerset, the manors of Buckby and Torpell in Northants, and a valuable estate at Deeping in Lincolnshire.[80] She inherited further Holand lands at the death of Elizabeth, relict of John, earl of Kent, in 1411.[81] Most of this quite sizeable estate remained in her hands on John's death, including her own lands, her dower, and a jointure in the Devon lands for which John had enfeoffed Bishop Henry and others in 1407.[82] Indeed on 21 April 1410, by the king's special grace, Margaret was granted the keeping of all John's lands except Corfe castle, during the minority of her son Henry.[83] As a young widow in enjoyment of a substantial estate, the countess would have no difficulty in finding a second husband. The question was to what extent this would impair the expectations of her son. In May the boy was brought to the king's presence and on 20 June his mother was awarded his keeping until the age of 15, with an annual allowance of 200 marks, though his marriage was reserved to the king.[84] Then, on 16 August, exactly five months after John's death, the pope issued a mandate to Archbishop Arundel and Bishop Beaufort to grant a dispensation for the marriage of Margaret to Thomas of Lancaster, if this was the king's will.[85] Significantly this was said to be at the petition of both Thomas and Prince Henry, suggesting that the transfer of all the estates into Margaret's hands in the preceding weeks had been with this marriage in prospect.

80 *CFR 1405–13*, 135; *CCR 1409–13*, 248. Buckby was held for life of the duchy of Lancaster, and yielded £83 p.a. His IPM is C 137/80. The figure represents the actual yield in 1420–1; WAM, 12163. See Appendix II.

81 *CP* vii. 150; *CFR 1405–13*, 212; *CCR 1409–13*, 248.

82 *CPR 1405–8*, 342; *CCR 1409–13*, 133, 128-9.

83 *CPR 1408–13*, 186; *CFR 1405–13*, 185–6.

84 Devon, *Issues*, 314; *CPR 1408–13*, 210.

85 *CPL* vi. 212–13.

Such a marriage placed in jeopardy much of the Beaufort inheritance. Thomas of Lancaster was young and vigorous and had already fathered a bastard son. Margaret, still under thirty, had borne six children since 1401.[86] Any children of the new marriage would be of the full blood-royal and in succession to the throne; almost certainly they would be preferred at the expense of her first family. Even if there were no children, Thomas would enjoy his wife's own lands, dower, and jointure during her life and would not easily relinquish them if he were left a widower. That would leave the young Henry as heir to only a small fraction of his father's estate, possibly for the greater part of his life. For the royal family Margaret's remarriage was an opportunity to provide for Thomas at no expense to the crown or the royal patrimony; for the Beauforts it was a disaster, threatening them with deprivation of Margaret's inheritance and with dispersal of their laboriously acquired gains. Did the papal mandate come as a bombshell? Bishop Henry may have had forewarning and procured his inclusion, for he now seems to have used his powers to obstruct or refuse the issue of the dispensation. On 10 November 1411 a fresh papal mandate, again at the petition of Prince Henry, was directed to the papal nuncio Antonio di Pireto, who was being sent to England to recruit Thomas of Lancaster into a crusade against the rival pope, Gregory XII. Pireto arrived in England in March 1412 and Margaret and Thomas were subsequently married in May, on the eve of Clarence's departure to Aquitaine.[87] They now received a new grant, vesting them jointly with the custody of the heir's lands and his marriage, without any render to the crown, and providing for the reversion of the dower lands to Thomas. This immediately followed his elevation as duke of Clarence and appointment as king's lieutenant in Aquitaine. Clarence was assuming the mantle of Somerset, enjoying for the present not only the custody of the young Henry's lands and body but also his annuity of 1,000 marks.[88]

Bishop Henry had been powerless to protect his nephew's interests in the estates; but in his last hours, John had, by a nuncupative will, constituted Henry his sole executor of all his goods, with his wife Margaret as supervisor.[89] Apart from requiring him to reward his servants and discharge his debts, he gave no other instructions and left no earlier will. According to one chronicle, which has Beaufort connections, John's personal wealth amounted to £20,000 and to this Clarence laid claim to half. Bishop Beaufort resisted this, with the backing of the prince of Wales,

[86] She was said to be 30 and more in 1416 (*CP* vii. 156 n. *e*). Her first child was born in 1401.

[87] *CPL* vi. 249; *Eulogium*, iii. 419–20.

[88] *CFR 1405–13*, 213–4; *CPR 1408–13*, 422. This replaced a grant of 16 July 1411 to Margaret alone. She was now exonerated from the annuities on the estates: *CPR 1408–13*, 359, 382, 391–3, 414–6. WAM 12163 shows Clarence's receipt of Beaufort annuities.

[89] *Royal Wills*, 208–14.

and the dispute was eventually settled by mediation or arbitration of other lords. It must have occurred in the first half of 1412, following Clarence's marriage and before Beaufort secured a pardon as executor on 13 July.[90] By the terms of the settlement Bishop Henry retained at least part of the money, and undertook to pay 200 marks annually for the maintenance of Somerset's children in Clarence's household.[91] The prince's belated support of Beaufort interests against his brother may have been influenced by his own dismissal from the council, for hitherto he had consistently furthered the endowment of Thomas at the Beauforts' expense. For Bishop Henry it must have been a telling demonstration of his family's vulnerability and of the reality of the gulf that divided them from the royal house. He himself was now head of his family, the defender of its interests, while his brother Thomas, by his closer ties to the court, elevation to the peerage, and qualities as a military commander, was well placed to succeed to John's role. Beaufort influence in camp and council chamber was set to re-emerge in the new reign, and if the attempts to build up a hereditary landed estate had been endangered, advancement in royal service was to open up new opportunities.

These years had seen a steady, if modest, growth in Bishop Beaufort's influence within the church. At a national level this had been held in check by Arundel's dominance, and the absence of any vacancies in the episcopate from 1407 to 1413 meant that patronage had to be exercised at a lower and local scale. Since Winchester was a monastic chapter, the bishop's direct patronage was small. Both the prior, Thomas Neville, and the archdeacon, Nicholas Daniel, had been appointed by Wykeham, but the death in 1410 of John Campeden, the able and devoted warden of the Hospital of St Cross and archdeacon of Surrey, allowed Beaufort to appoint John Forest to the former and John Catrik to the latter office.[92] Catrik was a Yorkshireman whose connection with Beaufort probably went back to Oxford.[93] His first promotion had been to a canonry in the Lincolnshire diocese in 1401, and in Winchester Beaufort had rewarded him with the mastership of St Mary Magdalen hospital at Esher and the rectory of Farnham. From 1405, when he became Beaufort's chancellor, until 1411 he was repeatedly employed on embassies with Beaufort, and to the duke of Burgundy and the Flemish towns. Forest too had been a prebendary in Lincoln and moved south with Beaufort, though his main benefice was at Middleton Stoney in Oxfordshire.

In the absence of secular patronage in his own diocese, Beaufort sought it in neighbouring ones, particularly those where he could influence the

[90] *Chron. Angl.* 62; *CPR 1408–13*, 420.
[91] WAM 12163 fo. 9.
[92] *Reg. CS* 47.
[93] The following biographical details of Catrik, Forest, Polton, Stokes, Stafford, Hody, Keton, and Medford are taken from BRUO *sub nominibus*.

bishop or dean and chapter. It was exercised most strongly at Wells, where he had been dean and Bubwith was now bishop; less strongly in Salisbury. Beaufort became the natural patron of Thomas Polton, archdeacon of Taunton since 1395, who also held canonries in Wells and Salisbury and numerous benefices, but whose main service was at the papal Curia. John Stokes, on the other hand, was just at the outset of his diplomatic career, and the Wells canonry and the rectory of Cobham, Surrey, to which he was instituted by Beaufort in 1410 were his first preferments. John Stafford, the natural son of Sir Humphrey Stafford of Southwick, was another who was commencing his career within the region with a canonry at Wells, though there is no clear evidence of Beaufort patronage; but John Hody, a bondman of Lord Audley who sent him to Oxford, had become a canon of Wells by 1407 and vicar of Queen Camel, Somerset's manor in 1408, and held a number of other livings in Dorset and Somerset. Robert Keton, Wykeham's last chancellor, had held the rectory of Cobham, Surrey from 1404 to 1410 and a canonry at Wells, and was to be Beaufort's vicar-general in 1426. Beaufort exercised far less influence in the Salisbury diocese under Hallum. Walter Medford was his principal link here. Under his brother, as bishop, he had become chancellor of the diocese and archdeacon of Berkshire, and in 1413 he succeeded Catrik as Beaufort's chancellor. As far as one can judge, Beaufort's patronage was principally extended to those whose careers lay in administration or diplomacy; unlike Hallum, he does not seem to have had in his circle any interested in conciliar reform or scholarship.

The Beauforts' lay following was likewise localized and of not more than middling status.[94] The scattered nature of Earl John's estates made it unlikely that he could ever influence significantly the political loyalties of a region, and his preoccupations at court and at Calais gave him neither the opportunity nor inducement to do so. Many of his annuitants were those who had served him at Calais or as admiral: at Calais his lieutenants were Sir John Ashton, Richard Ashton and Thomas Pickworth, while Thomas Thorley, Reginald Curteys, William Flete, Robert Frampton and John Gerard were among his officials. Sir William Bowes, an important northern figure, drew £20 p.a. from John's manor of Orwell (Cambs.), and Richard Boyton, sheriff of Somerset and Dorset in 1405 and 1409, 20 marks from Martock (Som.). William Tybenham, his lieutenant at Corfe, John Burton, Thomas Waryn, and Hugh Lutterell were other west country retainers.[95] Many of these—Lutterell, Tybenham, Boyton, Frampton, Curteys, Flete, and Burton—were also servants or associates of Bishop

[94] A list of Beaufort's officers and servants is available in A. J. Elder, 'A study of the Beauforts and their estates, 1399–1450', Bryn Mawr doctoral thesis (1964), Appendix III.

[95] Names of many annuitants are in C 137/80; others in *CCR 1405–8*, 94, 119, 415–16; *CPR 1408–13*, 221, 359, 382, 391–3, 415–16.

Henry. The main episcopal officials were Richard Wyot, steward, Thomas Chaucer, constable of Taunton, and John Clipsham, constable of Farnham, John Swetely and Nicholas Maunce, receivers of the Taunton bailiwick, William Tybenham, bailiff of Hampshire, and William Fauconer, bailiff of Overton. John Arnold and later John Foxholes were treasurers of Wolvesey, William Norton treasurer of the household, and John Prewes clerk of the household.[96] Among local gentry receiving annuities from the episcopal manors were John Wilcotes and John Golafre in Oxford, John St Loo and Robert Fitzjames in Somerset, John Uvedale and Percival Sonday in Hampshire, and somewhat surprisingly the Yorkshire knight Sir Robert Plumpton, who drew £20 p.a. from Witney.[97] Some of these like Chaucer, Wyot, Golafre, Fitzjames, Uvedale, and Fauconer, were of sufficient standing to represent their shires in parliament, and Wyot and Boyton were sheriffs. Chaucer was clearly the central figure linking the two areas where Beaufort influence was strongest, in Oxford and Somerset, and the focus for the bishop's supporters in the Commons.

96 These are mainly from the pipe rolls for 1406 and 1416: HRO, Eccles. II, 159410, 159419; also *Reg. CS* 31, 35–7, 401.

97 *Reg. CS* 31, 34, 42, 50; *CFR 1413–22*, 42; *Plumpton Correspondence*, ed. T. Stapleton (Camden Ser., 1839), p. xlii.

4

In the Service of Henry V, 1413–1417

HENRY V began his reign acutely conscious of the insecurity of his position. The long-standing enmity of the families who had opposed his father and the more recent rivalries among the royal family itself were a breeding ground for treachery, while the revival of Armagnac power brought a renewed threat of hostility from France. Henry's response was to place the key defensive posts in the hands of those already closely associated with him as prince. Warwick was appointed captain of Calais despite the claims of Clarence who was already captain of Guines, while Arundel—Henry's other principal retainer as prince of Wales—was made constable of Dover and warden of the Cinque Ports. Through his lieutenants Arundel also kept a firm grip on the Welsh marches, while two other of the prince's retainers, Sir Thomas Stanley and John, Lord Talbot were in succession lieutenants of Ireland, a post which Clarence had surrendered. The new earl of Dorset took his place in the group when his life tenure of the office of admiral of England was confirmed in June 1413, and in April 1414 his custody of Calais castle was renewed for three years. In the north John of Lancaster, created duke of Bedford, remained warden in the east march, with the earl of Westmorland in the west march. But Bedford, complaining that he was owed £13,000 from the past eleven years, was anxious to surrender his command.[1] He was temporarily succeeded by the duke of York in September 1414, although Henry V ultimately had in view the restoration of the Percy heir. The prime responsibility for the defence of the north thus fell to Westmorland, whose role in monitoring the loyalty of the young Henry Percy was foreshadowed by the latter's marriage to Joan Beaufort's second daughter Eleanor, in October 1414. During the Agincourt expedition Westmorland guarded the north while Bedford acted as regent.

Dorset in fact spent the first year of the reign in Aquitaine, another area of traditional Beaufort interest. On the news of Henry IV's death, Clarence had returned at once to England, bringing the count of Angoulême as security for the payment of 150,000 *écus* under the agreement signed with the Armagnac lords at Buzançais in November 1412. York, who had been lieutenant of Aquitaine in 1401, may have expected to take over his command, for on 18 June 1413 he received letters of protection for staying in Aquitaine a further year. But it was Dorset

[1] *CPR 1413–16*, 29; C 76/96 m. 1; indenture for Calais castle, 16 July 1414: E 101/69/3/355. For Clarence's interest in Calais, see *Rot. Parl.* iv. 13 (40). For Bedford's debt: *PPC.* ii. 136–8.

who, on 26 June, was empowered to receive the oaths of homage to Henry V and who was appointed lieutenant for six months on 22 July. York then returned with his retinue.[2] The choice of Dorset coincided with the reversal of the alliances of 1412. At first he had co-operated with Armagnac and Albret against the pro-Burgundian count of Foix, and in the early summer took the castle of Soubise and defeated a Burgundian force sent from Paris. But as Paris slipped from Burgundian control the Armagnac lords repudiated the agreement with Henry IV, and on 21 July the duke of Berri was appointed lieutenant in Guyenne. Dorset found himself facing a major assault on Soubise, where he had placed Sir John Blount as his lieutenant. It and Taillebourg fell at the end of the year, but on 29 January 1414 Dorset secured a truce for one year and prepared to return, though he was not back in England until mid-July.[3]

He had conducted the defence of the duchy without Burgundian help and hampered by lack of money. Clarence had secured an *impôt* from the reluctant estates of Bordeaux to be levied in 1413–14, but efforts to collect this had been fruitless despite the insistence of Henry V.[4] When William Clifford, the new constable of Bordeaux, sailed from England in August 1413, he brought with him £5,600 for the wages of Dorset's retinue. This was probably drawn from the £10,626 raised in loans on 14 and 17 July, including 2,000 marks from Bishop Beaufort.[5] Henry V was still determined that the duchy should also contribute to its own defence, and in February 1414 Dorset convened the estates and secured the grant of a *fouage* of two francs to pay his salary and the wages of his retinue for three months after the expiry of his original indenture. This was expected to yield 25,000 *écus*, but it too proved uncollectable, and Dorset and his troops returned to England bitter about their lack of pay. He at once sought the king's assistance, himself writing to the *Jurade* on 25 July 1414, and following this with letters from Henry V on 17 August and 15 October. Meanwhile he was pressing the exchequer for the balance of his wages for his six months' service, amounting to £5,397, and this was finally warranted in February 1415, while he was on embassy to the French court. Exactly a year later, when the mayor of Bordeaux arrived to offer belated congratulations to Henry V on his accession, Dorset came to London from the beleaguered Harfleur and with royal support extracted 10,000 crowns from the mayor in final satisfaction of his claims.[6]

[2] *CPR 1413–16*, 94; *PPC* ii. 129; *Foedera*, ix. 27–8, 42.

[3] Vale, *English Gascony*, 67–9; J. H. Wylie, *The Reign of Henry V*, i. 134–6, 139, 142; *Chronicle of London*, ed. Nicholas, 95–6.

[4] Wylie, *Henry V*, i. 116–7; *PPC* ii. 129; *Foedera*, ix. 32–4.

[5] Wylie, *Henry V*, i. 123 n. 7, 147–8; E 401/658; Steel, *Receipt*, 149; *Concilia*, ii. 338, 351; *CFR 1413–22*, 31.

[6] *PPC* ii. 129; Vale, *English Cascony*, 69; Wylie, *Henry V*, i. 126–8, 142. Dorset claimed 29,000 *écus* in all, having advanced 4,000 of his own money; he was paid Mar. 1415–16: *CPR 1413–16*, 281.

Just as Henry V entrusted the principal commands to those who had served him as prince of Wales, so he filled the offices of state with Bishop Beaufort as chancellor and the earl of Arundel as treasurer. No formal council was named and only Arundel and Beaufort are recorded as drawing salaries. Of the lay lords, the earl of Warwick and Lords Fitzhugh and Scrope were members from the start, to be joined after 1415 by Dorset, Salisbury, and York. The court office of chamberlain of England was given to the king's youngest brother Humphrey but Westmorland reluctantly surrendered the office of marshal to the traditional claims of John Mowbray on the latter's marriage to Joan Beaufort's eldest daughter Catherine in 1412.[7] The fecundity of Joan Beaufort was thus utilized to link the dissident houses of Percy and Mowbray to the quasi-royal stock, and a further link forged by the marriage of Joan's eldest son to Salisbury's daughter and heir in 1420. The Nevills and Beauforts took their place in the Lancastrian *familia* immediately beyond the brothers of the royal blood, with the role of reconciling and uniting the nobility under the new king. For although those he fully trusted were few, Henry was ready to extend royal favour impartially and to restore lost dignities as the reward of loyal service. Frequent meetings of parliament and great councils kept the nobility as a whole in touch with the king's unfolding plans.

Henry V attached equal importance to his relations with his non-noble subjects and evidently saw, and consciously used, parliament as a means of securing their active support. That support could certainly not be assumed, for the suspicion and ill will which his father had shown in 1411 still rankled with the Commons in the first parliament of 1413. Yet in recalling the vain promises of good governance made by his father, they were at the same time signalling their expectations from the young king and his new chancellor, Bishop Beaufort, who had consciously promoted a programme of solvency and security in the years 1410–12. Beaufort's opening speech to the Commons—delivered 'molt sagement et discretement'— desired their good counsel for the sustenance of the king's estate, for good governance and the maintenance of the laws, and for the cherishing of friendly foreigners but resistance to the enemies of the realm. As the parliament progressed, evidence of the new king's determination to review fiscal administration, restrain annuities in favour of household expenses, provide redress against sheriffs and officials, and bring justice to all aggrieved—all matters close to the Commons' hearts—brought a change of their mood. In return for a general pardon they granted the wool subsidies for four years, tunnage and poundage for one, and a whole lay subsidy.[8] It was a very adequate accession grant, more generous than the half-subsidy a year granted in 1410, which Henry had regarded as insufficient.

[7] *PPC* ii. 125–70; C 53/180–5; E 28/30; *CPR 1413–16*, 17. Cf. Brown, thesis, ii. 208; J. I. Catto, 'The King's Servants', in G. L. Harriss (ed.), *Henry V, The Practice of Kingship*, 88–9.
[8] *Rot. Parl.* iv. 4, 7, 10, 12–13.

When the second parliament met at Leicester in May 1414 Beaufort could extol the king's role in meeting and defeating the threat from Lollardy, and call on parliament to provide for its eradication. The principal theme of the Leicester parliament was law-keeping, the chancellor choosing as his text 'he has set his heart to keep the laws'. A new statute of riots was introduced which empowered the chancellor to remedy any failure by sheriffs and justices of the peace to deal with riots and maintenance by issuing a commission of enquiry and ordering the appearance of those named under subpoena. This legislation, and another act vesting the appointment of justices of the peace in the chancellor and council, was the prelude to a vigorous campaign of law enforcement in the disturbed west midlands on which Henry V embarked immediately after the close of the parliament. Parallel action was also taken at Leicester to curb piracy, with a new statute of truces forbidding private redress under the penalty of treason, and requiring all breaches of the peace to be reported to the conservators of the truces. The chancellor's appellate jurisdiction over Staple towns and responsibility for the protection of alien merchants, brought disputes involving the statute to his arbitration, and in 1416 he was given authority to issue letters of mark when all attempts to secure reparations had failed.[9] In all this Beaufort was moving in a familiar field, and one which he had at heart, ensuring the safety of English commerce to Calais and Flanders, and the maintenance of good relations with the Four Members. At the commencement of the parliament Beaufort had made it plain that in view of their previous grant the Commons would not be asked for a further lay subsidy, though he hinted that their gratitude for the king's present forbearance might be displayed on a later occasion. Nevertheless, the Commons now granted tunnage and poundage to run with the wool subsidy for the next three years.[10]

In the Leicester parliament Beaufort had worked closely with the Speaker, Sir Walter Hungerford, well known to him as a Wiltshire man and chief steward of the southern parts of the duchy of Lancaster. But in the following parliament, in November, it was once again his own cousin Thomas Chaucer, who was elected to that office. To this crucially important parliament Beaufort presented the king's decision to prosecute his rights in France as the logical culmination of his efforts to restore order in the realm and ensure the rights of his subjects. Taking as his text 'while we have time let us work for good', he declared that there was a time for peace, a time for war, and a time for work. Affirming the righteousness of the king's cause, he called on subjects to provide wise counsel, strong military support, and a copious subsidy, reminding them that the greater the king's patrimony became the less he would need to ask his subjects for

[9] Ibid. iv. 15, 22, 24–5, 50, 104; E. Powell, 'The restoration of law and order', in Harriss (ed.), *Henry V*, 53–74.

[10] *Rot. Parl.* iv. 16.

aid. But the Commons listened to this eloquent and forceful statement with some reservations, and joined the lords in urging the king first to seek his rights by negotiation. The chancellor had probably hoped to secure a double subsidy payable within the following year with which to launch the royal expedition; instead the Commons granted subsidies payable at Purification 1415 and 1416. That would at least allow loans to be raised on their security. The price of this grant was another general pardon, this time embracing offences against the statute of liveries.[11]

In the last parliament which he addressed as chancellor, in November 1416, Beaufort recalled the pattern of these early parliaments of the reign. In the first, he claimed, the king had established peace and good government in the realm; in the second he had made good and necessary laws; in the third he had secured assent for the recovery of his just rights in France.[12] Henry V and Beaufort (and their contributions are not easily separable) had fostered the impression that they were implementing a programme of government expressly modelled on the ideals of princely rule. This gave the Commons confidence in their leadership, while their readiness to take advice and heed grievances won the Commons' co-operation. In each of the chancellor's speeches the Commons' role—to complain, to counsel, to assent, and to provide—was firmly defined, and the unusually brisk and purposeful tempo of these parliaments (lasting respectively less than four weeks, exactly four weeks, and less than three weeks), like their harmonious character, must primarily be attributed to Beaufort's management and sensitivity to the Commons' opinions.

Of these we can be certain that Beaufort was kept well informed by a small group of his followers in the lower house. In addition to Chaucer himself, his fellow MP for Oxfordshire, John Wilcotes, had sat in all these parliaments, and John Golafre had represented Berkshire in the first two, while Richard Wyot had twice represented Buckinghamshire and once Middlesex. The fact that Lewis John sat once for Hampshire and another time for Taunton suggests that his later known connection with Beaufort was already formed, and the same may be true of William Flete, the MP for Hertfordshire, while John Arnold and John Uvedale who represented Hampshire in 1413 were both episcopal officials. With other leading knights like Walter Hungerford, John Tiptoft, Humphrey Stafford, William Sturmy, John Cheyne, John Arundell, and William Fillol, Beaufort was already well acquainted.[13]

Many of these men were also among the sheriffs and justices of the peace in whose selection the chancellor had a decisive voice. Wyot was sheriff of

[11] *Rot. Parl.* iv. 34–5, 40; *PPC* ii. 140–2, 150; Roskell, *Parliament and Politics*, ii. 95–136, iii. 151–92.

[12] *Rot. Parl.* iv. 94.

[13] *Members of Parliament*, 278–88.

Bedfordshire and Buckinghamshire in 1410 and 1416, Chaucer of Hampshire in 1413, where he was followed by John Uvedale in 1414; Wilcotes was sheriff of Oxfordshire in 1415 and Lewis John of Essex in 1416, while another servant, Richard Boyton, occupied the office in Somerset in 1416. Yet they also served either before or after Beaufort's chancellorship, and as members of the shire élite, were in no way intruded by him. Nor is it possible to discern the chancellor's peculiar influence in appointments to the bench; indeed in most shires the commissions appointed at the beginning of the reign continued with little or no change until 1417. What these names do indicate is Beaufort's close contact with leading members of the gentry in whose hands rested the government and representation of a swathe of southern shires. The only development which might be attributed to the chancellor's own initiative was the issue of commissions of array to the clergy. Reviving a practice last adopted in 1410, commissioners were sent to all dioceses to array the able-bodied clergy, the bishops being instructed to conduct the musters and certify into chancery the numbers arrayed by 16 July 1415. From eleven dioceses 11,769 clergy were thus arrayed.[14]

It is less easy to draw a distinctive picture of Beaufort's work within the chancery itself, for much of it was routine in character and what was not routine was often of an informal nature that has left no trace in the records. A handful of Henry V's signet letters to the chancellor in 1414 survive, but give no hint of the personal relationship between the two men, unlike those from Henry IV to Archbishop Arundel.[15] This may be a valid reflection of their shared dedication to the tasks of government above all else. The king's personal intervention in law enforcement, and preference for making the existing agencies more effective, meant that there was no dramatic expansion of the chancellor's jurisdiction to supplement the processes of common law, such as took place in the second part of the reign when Henry V was overseas.[16] Yet the chancellor's power to compel the attendance of misdoers and deal with them speedily, was actively employed by Beaufort, provoking a petition in the first parliament of 1416 that parties were being summoned before the chancellor by writs of subpoena on matters terminable at common law. This embodied a genuine grievance, that defendants found themselves put under sureties in vexatious suits; but allegations that the growth of chancery business deprived the crown of profits, monopolized the time of justices, and

[14] B. McNab, 'Obligations of the Church in English society: military arrays of the Clergy, 1369–1418', in W. C. Jordan, B. McNab, and T. F. Ruiz (edd.), *Order and Innovation in the Middle Ages*, 293–314.

[15] *CSL*, nos. 778, 783, 785.

[16] *Select Cases in Chancery, 1364 to 1471* (Selden Soc., 10, 1896), ed. W. P. Baildon, introduction; A. D. Hargreaves, 'Equity and the Latin side of Chancery', *LQR* 68 (1952), 486–90. For royal action, see *CSL* nos. 783, 772–3, *Rot. Parl.* iv. 27–8; *CCR 1413–19*, 43.

involved examination on oath according to the practice of canon and civil law, clearly betrayed the vested interests of the common-law courts.[17] The growing demand for the chancellor's justice probably had two origins. First, the statute of riots would have brought an increase in the issue of subpoenas and the imposition of sureties by the chancellor.[18] Secondly, enfeoffments to use were increasingly practised among the ranks of middling landowners, and the interests of the *cestui que* use were not adequately safeguarded at common law.[19]

For several reasons it is impossible to measure meaningfully the scope of these developments during Beaufort's periods of office. The surviving file of petitions addressed to the bishop of Winchester as chancellor contains 357 items.[20] They are mostly undated, and cover the eight years of his tenure between 1403 and 1426, while a few may date from Waynflete's time (1456–60). The annual average under Beaufort is less than half that under John Stafford (1432–43).[21] Even allowing for the hazards of survival and the existence of unknown quantities of oral petitions, it is clear that the chancellor's jurisdiction was still in its infancy. None the less, it was a precocious child, as a broad analysis of the matters referred to him and the language employed can demonstrate. Of the 300-odd petitions which can with fair certainty be ascribed to Beaufort's chancellorship, and are not too fragmentary to use, 101 allege assault, intimidation, perversion of justice, and wrongful imprisonment, or ask for sureties against such. Almost the same number (105) are connected with real estate, both in matters terminable at common law and in those involving trusts. Here feoffments, settlements, leases, mortgages, the execution of wills, detention of muniments, enforcement of arbitration, and problems of wardships, marriages, and dower were matters brought into chancery. A third broad group, numbering 69, concerned mercantile transactions, the enforcement of bonds, debts, and detinue, allegations of forgeries, ransoms and wages of war, and redress for aliens, notably over seizures of goods and debts. Here the chancellor had a statutory jurisdiction, recently reinforced by the

[17] *Rot. Parl.* iv. 86. For earlier petitions, see ibid. iii. 267, 323, 446, iv. 95.

[18] N. Pronay, 'The Chancellor, the Chancery, and the Council at the end of the fifteenth century', in H. Hearder and H. R. Loyn (edd.), *British Government and Administration*, 97; J. C. Bellamy, *Criminal Law and Society in Late Medieval and Tudor England*, 61–3; E. Powell, 'The King's Bench in Shropshire and Staffordshire in 1414' in W. Ives and A. H. Manchester (edd.), *Law, Litigants and the Legal Profession*, 94–103.

[19] *Select Cases in Chancery*, pp. xxxviii–ix; J. L. Barton, 'The medieval use', *LQR* 81 (1965), 569–70; M. E. Avery, 'The history of the equitable jurisdicition of the chancery before 1460', *BIHR* 42 (1969), 139–41; Peggy Jefferies, 'The medieval use as family law and custom', *Southern History*, 1 (1979), 50–6.

[20] PRO C 1/6. Other petitions addressed to Beaufort are in files 1 and 2. Some have been printed in *Select Cases in Chancery* (nos. 111–16) and others in *Calendar of the Proceedings in Chancery* (Rec. Comm., 1827), vol. i., pp. xiii–xiv, xix–xx. See too J. H. Fisher, and M. Richardson, *An Anthology of Chancery English*, 165, 171–3.

[21] Avery, op. cit. 130–1; Pronay, op. cit. 89–90.

statute of truces. Finally there were a variety of ecclesiastical causes (20) and a small number (9) of cases involving royal officers. These categories overlapped, some cases involving more than one matter. But the fact that the main areas of chancery's later jurisdiction are all fully represented cautions against attributing its rise to the emergence of any one type of business.[22]

Similarly, the variety of petitioners reveals how widespread and popular resort to the chancellor had become. Petitions came from the king himself as guardian of his wards' lands, members of the nobility such as Lords Latimer and Scrope and Lady Despenser, numbers of knightly families, corporations both lay, like the mayor and aldermen of London and the barons of the Cinque Ports, and ecclesiastical, like the abbey of St Mary's, York. Humbler petitioners included small merchants and artisans in towns, the men of a hundred, individual soldiers, clerks, widows, servants, and prisoners, all seeking redress or grace. Some of those petitioning had direct connections with Beaufort himself. His secretary Richard Petworth alleged that Robert Vyell had ousted him from a chantry to which he had been appointed by William Fillol; other petitions came from his tenants or the servants of his officials. One petition alleged the invasion of the lands of his nephew John, earl of Somerset, and the detention of documents from the executors of the duke of Clarence; another claimed that lands of his ward, Lord Beaumont, had been attacked, while a third petitioner, asking for the protection of an enfeoffment to her use, claimed Beaufort as one of her feoffees. Stephen Barbour, imprisoned in the gaol of the abbot of St Albans, piteously sought pardon for speaking words against Beaufort himself.[23]

How these cases were handled, what procedures were employed, who heard and sifted the evidence, and under what law judgement was rendered are all matters on which there is virtually no evidence. Many petitions ask for defendants to be subpoenaed and a few for the examination of other 'loial et credibles persones'. Although some petitions sue for grace under the traditional formula 'pur Dieu et en oeuvre de charite', many others complain that no remedy can be obtained at common law and (particularly in those suing for enforcement of bonds) ask for remedy 'as law, reason and conscience demand', a phrase which had first appeared in 1391. It was increasingly recognized that in matters of conscience and natural justice the chancellor could act outside the common-law courts. In 1419 Henry V ordered the chancellor to do 'right and equite' to the parties in a dispute, and an undated petition to Beaufort

[22] For similar analyses, see Avery, op. cit. 132–44; Pronay, op. cit. 92–6; J. A. Guy, 'The development of equitable jurisdictions, 1450–1550' in *Law, Litigants and the Legal Profession*, 81–3.

[23] C 1/6 nos. 268, 177, 127, 194, 324, 178.

described the chancery itself as 'this high court of conscience'.[24] But what proportion of cases might be construed as 'equitable' at this period would be hazardous to guess, and to what extent procedures and judgement before the chancellor were influenced by civil law is equally obscure, for scarcely any record of process or sentence survives earlier than 1440. When Beaufort as chancellor sat in Westminster hall he did so with the justices, and when he delegated judgement to the master of the rolls it was not to one who was a civil lawyer. Beaufort himself lacked such training, and largely dispensed a justice ancillary to the common-law courts, to which he certainly referred some of the suits that came before him.[25] Yet the variety and importance of these suits clearly reflect confidence in his authority and judgement, and this is not surprising. Beaufort was an adept and respected arbitrator; he was frequently chosen as an executor or trustee; he was one of the greatest landlords in England, and also in close touch with important mercantile interests; while, finally, he had the strenuous backing of a king winning a reputation for speedy justice and the suppression of self-help. At this stage it is to the personal qualities of the chancellor, rather than to the emergence of a new type of law, that the growth of the judicial work of chancery should be ascribed, and it was the personal standing of Beaufort and Langley that laid the foundations in the years 1413–26 of the court of chancery's subsequent continuous development.[26]

In two other spheres, both characteristic, we get glimpses of Beaufort at work, namely as diplomat and loan-raiser. Although the concurrent negotiations with the French court and the duke of Burgundy during 1413–14 were conducted by others, the chancellor was certainly privy to the discussions with the French and Burgundian envoys at Leicester, and his direct interest in the attempt to pin Burgundy to an English alliance at the appointment of Ypres in July 1414 is indicated by the presence of Thomas Chaucer on this embassy.[27] Dorset's return to England in July 1414 was marked by his formal inclusion into the council, and he may have joined

[24] *Rot. Parl.* iii. 297; *Calendar of proceedings in Chancery*, loc. cit. For the chancery as a 'court of conscience', see C 1/6 no. 42, and cf. *Select Cases in Chancery*, no. 123 (C 1/68 no. 3).

[25] For recent views on the development of 'equitable' jurisdiction, see J. B. Post, 'Equitable resorts before 1450', in *Law, Litigants and the Legal Profession*, 68–79; Guy, op. cit. 83. For the chancellor's role in arbitration, see E. Powell, 'Arbitration and the law in England in the late Middle Ages', *TRHS* 33 (1983), 64–6. Beaufort delegated the examination of witnesses to John Frank, master of the rolls, in 1426: C 1/6 no. 135; M. E. Avery, 'An evaluation of the effectiveness of the Court of Chancery under the Lancastrian Kings', *LQR* 86 (1970), 84–97 for this and other procedures. Cases referred by Beaufort to the King's Bench are noted on some plea rolls e.g. KB 27/658 (Mich. 4 Henry VI) Rex. rot. 9.

[26] For the personal role of the chancellor, see Avery, op. cit. *LQR* 86 (1970), 85–9, 92–3; Fisher and Richardson, *Chancery English*, 157; for Langley: Storey, *Langley*, 41–2. Dr E. Powell has pointed out to me that in the series of chancery subpoena files the change to initiation and return of writs in chancery alone (as distinct from king and council and council in chancery) occurred during Henry V's reign: *Chancery Files*, List and Index Soc. 130 (1976), 91.

[27] *Foedera*, ix. 102, 137, 150.

Langley and Courtenay on the second embassy to Paris early in 1415, which moderated English demands to comprise the lands of the treaty of Brétigny and half Provence, with the counties of Beaufort and Nogent. A further indication of the Beaufort interest in the area was an optimistic report reaching Bordeaux that this embassy had agreed on terms for Henry V's marriage with Catherine, and that Dorset and the Constable d'Albret were to come to Guyenne to arrange a settlement there. Yet there is little doubt that the English ambassadors understood their mission as being to justify Henry's cause to opinion at home by demonstrating the French intransigence.[28] Although the council, which received the report of the embassy on 12 April, drew up instructions for continuing negotiations with France, three days later a great council of twenty-eight lay lords and fifteen spiritual heard the chancellor 'wisely and compendiously' recite the course of negotiations with France, their fruitless result, and the king's firm decision to recover his inheritance and the lost rights of the crown by an expedition. Through their spokesman, the earl of Dorset, the lords registered their support for this and agreed to receive security for their second quarter's wages. Next day Bishop Beaufort outlined the arrangements for the government and the safeguard of the realm in the king's absence. Rates of wages for service in France and Guyenne were laid down, and Salisbury was offered command in the latter.[29]

As preparations for the expedition gathered momentum Beaufort moved to Winchester to prepare Wolvesey palace as the king's headquarters. It was here that the final negotiations with the French envoys, led by the archbishop of Bourges, took place in early July, at which Beaufort acted as the king's spokesman. They culminated in Beaufort's declaration of the insufficiency of the French offers, and the formal reassertion of the totality of the English claims and Henry V's determination to enforce them, which provoked the archbishop to a display of scorn and anger.[30] Beaufort's great presence, eloquence, and mastery of his argument was undoubtedly demonstrated to advantage on such public occasions. But in the same month we also glimpse his aptitude for diplomatic evasion and polite obstruction as he dealt with envoys from the Grand Master of the Teutonic Order who were seeking payment of long-standing compensation, promised by the king in 1410. They had no chance of securing this with the king's resources already insufficient for his immediate needs, yet it was important to avoid hostilities or reprisals of any kind at this point. The envoys first caught the chancellor as he was taking horse for Winchester and were directed by him to the keeper of the privy seal, who referred

[28] *CPR 1413–16*, 231; *Foedera*, ix. 186; Wylie, *Henry V*, i. 437–44.

[29] *PPC* ii. 155–8. In fact Sir John Tiptoft was ultimately appointed lieutenant in Guyenne: ibid. 167.

[30] Wylie, *Henry V*, i. 487–91; *Chron. St Denys*, v. 513.

them to the clerk of the council. The council itself remitted them to the chancellor, who when they reached him at Winchester, offered apologies for their inconvenience and sent them back to the council in London. But without instructions from the king the council would do nothing and they once more returned to Winchester where, after the departure of the French embassy, Beaufort secured them an interview with the king, who gave them a vaguely worded promise of a favourable reply. Only later, in London, did Beaufort temper their discouragement with a promise of actual payment provided that they were willing to accept it in long instalments. By then Beaufort was probably also performing the functions of the treasurer following the death of Arundel on 13 October.[31]

The first part of the lay and clerical subsidies granted in November 1414 had been used to pay those who indented for service in April, but for the payment of their second quarter's wages on 4 July the council agreed to deliver jewels to the nobility and to raise loans on a massive scale.[33] Already on 14 March, Beaufort, Bedford, Gloucester, and York had come to a meeting with the London aldermen at the Guildhall to persuade them to advance the sum of 10,000 marks, and two months later Beaufort, Arundel, and Dorset reminded the representatives of the Italian banks in London of their need for royal protection, and demanded substantial loans under threat of imprisonment.[33] A large-scale exercise to raise loans in the country was now launched, probably under the chancellor's direction. Early in May royal servants went down to the shires with signet letters addressed to individuals and corporations asking each for specific sums for the payment of the troops' wages. Although lenders were offered jewels as surety of repayment, promised by 1 January 1417, no source was specified and many either refused to lend or to deliver the sums they had promised. Not surprisingly, some important towns, bishops, and officials also insisted on assignments on the customs. Beaufort thus extracted a promised loan of £100 from the corporation of Salisbury by a mixture of the threat of royal displeasure and the promise of assignment on the customs.[34] When Beaufort himself lent £2,000 on 8 June he received jewels as security, which he was at liberty to retain if repayment had not been made within a year. In this he was treated the same as the other leading curial bishops and members of the lay nobility. But though he had no repayment from the exchequer, he seems to have recovered some and possibly all of his loan from the revenues of the duchy of Lancaster in which he and others had

[31] Wylie, *Henry V*, i. 494–8; *Hanserecesse, 1256–1430*, ed. K. Koppmann, vi. 147–50. *Cal. L. Bk. I*, 159.

[32] *PPC* ii. 151, 167; *Foedera*, ix. 257; *CPR 1413–16*, 329.

[33] *PPC* ii. 165–6; *Foedera*, ix. 271, 284, 312; *Cal. L. Bk. I*, 135; H. T. Riley, *Memorials of London Life*, 603–4.

[34] *Foedera*, ix. 241, 268, 284–6; *CPR 1413–16*, 342, 354, 367; *Cal. L. Bk. I*, 158; *Kal. and Inv.*, ii. 241; *HMC, Var.*, iv. 193; H. Nicolas, *History of the Battle of Agincourt*, Appendix III.

been enfeoffed by the king before his departure.[35] The total raised in loans during the summer—£18,300 excluding those from the chamber—was impressive testimony to the energies of the chancellor and his associates and the pressures they exerted; it was in fact the highest total since Richard II's Irish expedition of 1394–5.[36]

Henry V's appreciation of Beaufort's financial acumen and integrity was shown within two weeks of his accession when, as one of an inner group of the king's advisers, he was made responsible for discharging Henry's debts as prince—including a sum of £826. 13*s*. 4*d*. borrowed from Beaufort himself.[37] In December 1413 he and the duke of York were made administrators for Henry's annual subvention of 1,000 marks towards the completion of the nave of Westminster abbey, and in June 1414 he and Chichele were appointed supervisors of the fund of 25,000 marks for the discharge of Henry IV's will. It was no surprise that on the eve of his departure for France Henry V named him and Dorset among the feoffees of the major part of the duchy of Lancaster lands and the moiety of the Bohun inheritance for the performance of his will, and that two days later he was named principal executor.[38] Dorset, Fitzhugh, and the under-treasurer John Rothenal were also enfeoffed with lands from the alien priories for the building of the king's new Brigettine foundation at Syon. The Sheen Charterhouse, in whose foundation Bishop Beaufort had been involved,was already in being, and Dorset's own sympathies with the Carthusians found expression in his re-foundation of the Carthusian house at Hinckley in Leicestershire, charged to pray for his soul and that of Henry V.[39]

Such evidence of royal confidence elicited the same from others of the nobility. When in December 1414 the duke of York prepared to mortgage Oakham to Sir William Bourchier to meet the cost of building Fotheringhay, Bourchier, who had accompanied Dorset on the French embassies, chose the two Beauforts, the duke of Gloucester, and Sir Thomas Erpingham as his feoffees. The preparations for the royal expedition led a number of the nobility to place lands in feoffment either to raise money or to perform their wills, and Beaufort and Langley were used in turn by the Earl Marshal, the duke of Gloucester, and the duke of York.[40]

Royal favour also brought some material benefits to the Beauforts, although under Henry V these were characteristically modest. In September

[35] E 401/667; E 28/31 2 June; *PPC* ii. 167; DL 42/17/book ii, fo. 29; *CPR 1413–16*, 350, 356–7; *CPR 1422–9*, 472.

[36] Steel, *Receipt*, 151–2.

[37] *CPR 1413–16*, 17, 329; Devon, *Issues*, 329.

[38] *CPR 1413–16*, 146, 197, 356–7; *Foedera*, ix. 289–93.

[39] *CPR 1413–16*, 355, 358, 395; J. Cloake, 'The Charterhouse of Sheen', *Surrey. Arch. Coll.* 71 (1977), 149.

[40] *CPR 1413–16*, 270, 319, 338, 350; Devon, *Issues*, 336, 340.

1414 Dorset received the custody of the lands of William, Lord Roos, with the marriage of the heir during the minority, without render to the king; they were worth some £650 p.a. and he was to enjoy them until 1418.[41] Lord Roos had been Beaufort's colleague as treasurer in 1403 and Dorset's associate on the commission to try Archbishop Scrope; it is likely that his heir John, aged 18, was in Dorset's retinue on the Agincourt expedition. Bishop Beaufort likewise secured the profitable custody of the lands of Henry de Beaumont on 1413 and successfully retained the lands of Walter Fitzwalter as executor of John, earl of Somerset until the death of the heir Humphrey in 1415.[42]

Just as Henry V's accession brought the Beauforts to the very centre of royal government and favour, so Archbishop Arundel's death permitted the bishop's influence to expand within the church. Beaufort's close association with Chichele, Courtenay, and Langley in royal service reflected, at this stage, genuine bonds of friendship between them. Langley had chosen Beaufort to assist at his consecration as bishop of Durham, and it was from Beaufort that Chichele received the pallium in 1414 in the presence of Gloucester, Huntingdon, March, and Warwick.[43] Whether Beaufort desired the primacy for himself is not easy to decide. Winchester was the richer, but status and authority may have seemed more tempting at this point and he probably remained jealous of Chichele's dignity until his own promotion to one higher. Whatever Beaufort's own feelings, Henry V was not minded to advance his worldly kinsman, preferring as a pastoral leader the pious and scholarly Chichele. Courtenay, too, was Henry V's choice when the see of Norwich fell vacant a month after his accession. A man of similar temperament and career to Chichele, though of aristocratic lineage, he had enjoyed Beaufort's patronage from the start of his career, and shared a common affiliation to Queen's college dating from the period in 1402–3 when Beaufort resided in Oxford.[44] Chichele's promotion provided the opportunity for Beaufort to secure the see of St David's for his chancellor Catrik, and then, less than a year later, advance him to Lichfield on the death of Burghill. When Courtenay died in September 1415 from dysentery contracted at Harfleur, it was again a candidate with strong Beaufort connections, John Wakering, Thomas Beaufort's deputy as chancellor and newly made keeper of the privy seal, who succeeded. Both Catrik and Wakering were proved and able servants of the

[41] *CPR 1413–16*, 235–6; *CCR 1413–19*, 168, 230; *CP* xi. 102. SC 6/1121/13 is an account of the Roos lands for 1421–2 when they were again in the king's hands.

[42] *CFR 1413–22*, 42; *CPR 1413–16*, 170–1. The heir, John Beaumont, was aged 4 in 1413 and Beaufort retained custody of the lands until 1427: *CP* ii. 61; *CPR 1422–9*, 524. Walter, Lord Fitzwalter had livery in 1421: *CP* V. 483. For Beaufort's dispute with John Doreward over the Fitzwalter lands, see Roskell, *Parliament and Politics*, i. 61.

[43] Storey, *Langley*, 28; E. F. Jacob, *Archbishop Henry Chichele*, 20.

[44] *BRUO* ii. 500–2; Beaufort had the custody of the temporalities of Norwich during the vacancy.

Lancastrian crown, and their appointments reflected the firm control Henry V exercised over episcopal appointments during the triple schism in the papacy and the hiatus of conciliar rule. The election of the elderly Carmelite Stephen Patrington to Chichester in 1415 was likewise the king's reward for a lifetime's service to the house of Lancaster. Although Henry was master in his own church and had his own view of the role of the episcopate, these appointments are evidence of the influence which Beaufort had come to exercise in this sphere. He was certainly pressing the claims of his protégés at a lower level. It must have been through Beaufort's influence that his secretary Richard Petworth obtained canonries in Lincoln and Chichester in March 1415.[45] In July 1415 Beaufort issued a commission for the arrest of Prior Neville of Winchester and his detention in the Tower. He had opposed Beaufort's election, but it is also possible that he was implicated in the Southampton plot, for he was never released, and his resignation followed at once. The new prior, elected on Beaufort's mandate, was Thomas Shirebourne, whose brother John was already the bishop's 'servitour'.[46]

Thomas, earl of Dorset had indented to serve in the Agincourt expedition with a retinue of the same size as that of the duke of York. Unlike those of some other commanders his preparations are hidden from us, though it is certain that he recruited his former lieutenants in Aquitaine, Sir John Blount, John Fastolf, and John Massey, and his indentures survive with a number of other captains who were to make careers for themselves in France, including Sir Robert Brewes, John Banastre, John Harplay, and William Oldhall.[47] We can only speculate what were his costs, and how these were met. Unlike York and Mowbray he made no enfeoffment of his lands, which were indeed too few either to mortgage or to protect from escheat. Throughout May 1415 he continued in the council: as admiral he ordered the empressment of ships, and under his command the fleet sailed from Southampton water on 12 August. At Harfleur Dorset took up his station near Graville. By mid-September the besieging army, already reduced by dysentery, decided to mount an assault, which brought an offer to negotiate from the garrison. Dorset, Lord Fitzhugh, and Sir Thomas Erpingham were empowered to receive the surrender, and, on Henry V's instructions, the keys of the town were handed to Dorset, who on 22 September was appointed its captain.[48] While the king embarked on his hazardous march to Calais, Dorset was left with 300 men-at-arms and 900

[45] *BRUO* iii. 1471; Nottingham University, Middleton MS Mi C 5a.

[46] *Reg. CS*, 33–56; *CPR 1413–16*, 409. See too the case of Richard Bruton, canon of Wells: *Gesta Henrici Quinti*, ed. F. Taylor and J. S. Roskell, 190.

[47] His own indenture does not survive, though for the size of his retinue see E 404/31/278 and Nicolas, *Agincourt*, 373. His account is in E 364/56 m. 7, and indentures with his retinue in E 101/69/488–505.

[48] Wylie, *Henry V*, ii. 48, 57; *Gesta HV*, 50; *Chronicles of London*, 119.

archers to hold the town. Agincourt was fought on 25 October and by 23 November Henry had arrived back in London. There could be no immediate threat to Harfleur, and on 18 November and again on 19 December Dorset made far-reaching sallies into Normandy, bringing in supplies and ransoming large numbers of peasantry who were caught up in these sweeps. But the garrison would need significant reinforcement from England if it were to face a French assault in the spring. On 25 November the council recommended the urgent despatch of fodder and authorized the garrison's wages to a sum of £3,640 from the second part of the lay subsidy due on 13 December. It asked the king what instructions should be sent to Dorset, but Henry decided to recall him for consultation.[49] Dorset was in London during January and February, signing fresh indentures with Lord Grey of Wilton, Sir John Blount, John Fastolf, Janico D'Artas, and John and Thomas Carew. Reginald Curteys became victualler of Harfleur, Thomas Barneby the treasurer, and Simon Flete his controller. All of these had previously served with Dorset or Henry, prince of Wales. He returned with 900 men at arms and 1,500 archers and on 20 February was paid the wages for the garrison, amounting to £4,892.[50] The visiting mayor of Bordeaux, who was now induced to pay part of the taxes granted in 1413, testified to the king's 'great faith' in Dorset, now appointed lieutenant in Normandy. On his passage through Winchester the priory of St Swithun granted him confraternity 'on account of his special devotion to and affection for them'.[51]

Dorset soon showed that he could be rash as well as courageous. On 9 March, accompanied by his principal captains, Fastolf, Blount, Carew, and D'Artas, and possibly half the garrison, he conducted a foraging raid into Normandy, only to find himself trapped and brought to battle by the count of Armagnac. Dorset lost heavily at the fiercely fought engagement at Valmont on 11 March, and though on the retreat to Harfleur (with himself among the wounded) he managed to inflict losses on the French, the whole operation only hastened the close siege of the town.[52] Repeated requests were sent to England for supplies, culminating in representations to the council by Barneby and Curteys on 14 April that the town would be compelled to surrender in June if no aid were forthcoming. A small task force was sent under the earl of Huntingdon to revictual the town while a large army of 7,000 men was being raised for three months' service with the king. Its muster was fixed for 22 June at Southampton, and on 6 June the exchequer delivered over £20,000 in assignments on the lay subsidy due at

[49] R. A. Newhall, *The English Conquest of Normandy, 1416–24*, 8; *Chronicles of London*, 123; *PPC* ii. 184.

[50] C 76/98 m. 1–8; Devon, *Issues*, 345; Wylie, *Henry V*, ii. 332.

[51] Wylie, *Henry V*, ii. 57 n. 1; *Reg. CS* 58.

[52] *The Chronicle of John Strecche*, ed. F. Taylor *BJRL* 16 (1932), 159–61; *Gesta HV*, 115–21; Wylie, *Henry V*, ii. 335–6.

Whitsun.[53] These preparations were suspended while negotiations were pursued at Beauvais, and only when these failed and the French assault on Harfleur was imminent did the fleet sail under Bedford. The battle of the Seine was fought on 15 August. By that time the garrison at Harfleur had endured a five month siege, and despite the supplies brought in in May, they had been reduced to eating their horses and some had died of starvation. Dorset's tenacity and discipline must have been tested, and Henry's confidence in him justified; yet there must have been moments when his own confidence in the arrival of the relief force was sorely tried.

On 30 August the garrison received its wages and shortly afterwards Dorset sailed for Calais, where he joined the meeting between Henry, Sigismund, and John the Fearless, though it is unlikely that he was made party to the secret understanding reached between them. He returned to England on 16 October, where his brother opened parliament three days later. At the end of that parliament Dorset was advanced to the dukedom of Exeter, invested with the Order of the Garter, and granted £1,000 p.a. in tail male. The patent declared that the title was reward for good service to the king on both sides of the sea, while the grant of money was made at the request of the Commons and with the assent of the Lords. But according to the St Albans Chronicle, when the Lords were asked their pleasure, they declared it to be too slight a gift for one who had merited so much. Certainly the title was the more significant, since it raised Dorset into the circle of dukes of the royal blood, according to the Beauforts the position occupied by the Holands under Richard II.[54] The young earl of Huntingdon, who had so recently succoured Dorset, was thereby now debarred from recovering the title which his family had lost in 1399. Only Dorset's childlessness eventually restored it to the Holands, and though this may have been anticipated in 1416, it could not be guaranteed. But Huntingdon received his own reward by his full restoration to his father's dignity and entailed estates on reaching his maturity in the following March. The rewards of loyalty and service were thus nicely related to individual expectations.

Bishop Beaufort must have rejoiced in his brother's safety and honour. Immediately after the king's departure to France writs had been issued for parliament to assemble on 21 October 1415. On 29 September it was prorogued to 4 November. The decision was probably taken by Henry V on the fall of Harfleur on 22 September, and may well reflect his intention to be in England for its opening, on the assumption that his passage to Calais would not be challenged. As it was, Beaufort was able to announce the news of Agincourt at St Paul's Cathedral on 29 October, a week before the opening of parliament, at which he adduced the two victories as the

[53] *PPC* ii. 198–202; *Foedera*, ix. 355–6; E 401/672, E 403/624.

[54] *CPR 1416–22*, 50, 53; *CP* v. 202; *St Albans Chron.* 102–3. *CCR 1413–19*, 329.

verdict of the Almighty on the justice of Henry's cause. Taking as his text 'as he has done to us, so let us do to him', Beaufort called on the Commons for further assistance, and they at once advanced to December the collection of the second part of the lay subsidy, on the security of which Beaufort now loaned 1,000 marks for the costs of the king's reception.[55] Further, taking their cue from the chancellor, and reciting in almost identical words the king's great exploits, financial sacrifices, and need for money, they granted the wool subsidy and tunnage and poundage for his life, and raised the aliens' subsidy from 50*s.* to 60*s.* This had double significance. It was a symbolic affirmation of the Commons' view of Henry V as a just ruler and hence of the legitimacy of his title to the English throne. The only precedent for such a grant was that made to Richard II in 1398 under duress and was remembered as evidence of his tyranny. Henry's rule was the reverse of that, and Beaufort underlined this by prefacing his celebration of the king's victories by a long discourse to 'touchant la bone governance', which emphasized his measures for justice and the maintenance of the peace: 'sine justicia non regitur respublica'. Secondly it underwrote royal finance and credit with a permanent and substantial revenue and marked a step towards Henry's unavowed but probable objective of an annual direct subsidy free of parliamentary consent. For the coming year the Commons again provided a whole lay subsidy payable at Martinmas 1416. Although the Speaker, Richard Redmayne, was closely attached to the duke of Bedford, it can scarcely be doubted that it was the chancellor who had contrived these unexampled grants, in a parliamentary session lasting just eight days, the shortest since those of 1366 and 1369.

In a letter written to Henry V during that week, which can be ascribed with a high degree of probability to Beaufort, the king was assured that he need have no worries about the expected grants of subsidies from both parliament and convocation.[56] With measured rhetoric the writer rejoices in the happy auspices of the new reign, declaring that the glory and honour of this famous realm of England, long lulled to sleep and forgotten, had awoken to a new spring after the winter, bringing a savour of sweetness to its well-wishers, but terror to its enemies. Henry's victories surpass those of Maccabees; his reign excels those of Saul, David, Solomon, and Alexander. Yet such victories, though to the glory of the English nation and the eternal memory of the king's name, must be ascribed not to his hand, but to that of God, whose minister he is. God had chastised the English with mortality at

[55] *Rot. Parl.* iv. 62–3; Wylie, *Hery V*, ii. 232; *Cal. L. Bk. I*, 144; E 401/669 5 Nov. for the delivery of the loan.

[56] BL Add. MS 46846 fo. 61, printed in *Letters of Queen Margaret of Anjou*, ed. C. Monro (Camden Soc., 1863), 1–6. For the probable identification of the author as Beaufort see G. L. Harriss, 'Henry Beaufort, Cardinal of England', in D. Williams (ed.), *England in the Fifteenth Century*, 112.

Harfleur precisely to demonstrate his authorship of their victory at Agincourt: the king must therefore eschew pride, cruelty, and revenge, and show humility, thankfulness, and clemency. He should be encouraged to prosecute his rights further and finish what he had begun, seeking a just and permanent peace. Such themes were soon commonplace in the circle of the royal chaplains, and became embodied in the *Gesta*, but this is their first coherent statement in the aftermath of Agincourt. The chancellor's influence over parliament was probably extended to convocation, for when this met on 18 November its very first act was, as the writer predicted, to grant two tenths, payable at Martinmas 1416 and 1417. Convocation further provided for the keeping of St George's feast as a greater double, and held a requiem mass for the English slain at Harfleur and Agincourt.[57]

The council's immediate concern had been to arrange a triumphal reception for Henry on his arrival in London on 23 November. As the lengthy description of the pageant given in the *Gesta* makes plain, this was a visual exposition of the themes in the letter sent to Henry early in November. Although the construction of the set pieces was the work of the corporation and the guilds, the symbolism—apart from the giants representing the city's jurisdiction which welcomed the king—expounded the theme of England as the chosen instrument of God's will. Representations of St George, the Realm of England, the English kings, martyrs, and confessors, marked the route, and at all stages texts and canticles gave thanks to God, and God alone, for the victory. Henry's own meditative and quiet demeanour showed that he had taken to heart the homily on humility, and ascribed his triumph to God.[58] Thus in the three and a half weeks since the news was received was the myth of Agincourt born, a myth of the invincibility not of the king but of his cause, the justice of which had been manifested by God through the inequalities of the battle. It was to be propagated throughout Europe, reiterated in parliament, affirmed by the king himself, and echoed in the songs and chronicles of his subjects, who were to cling to it with an obstinate desperation as Henry's empire slowly crumbled in the years after his death. If, as it seems, it was Bishop Beaufort who first expounded and orchestrated this apologia, it was perhaps the most far-reaching of his achievements as Henry V's chancellor, and one with whose consequences he was to live for the rest of his life.

The same themes were once more elaborated in Beaufort's opening sermon to the next parliament which assembled on 16 March. His speech, as summarized in the *Gesta*, insisted on the need to continue with the war until it was brought to a successful conclusion, and the French recognized the triple verdict which God had pronounced in the battles of Sluys,

[57] *Register of Henry Chichele*, ed. E. F. Jacob iii. 3–7.
[58] *Gesta HV*, 101–13.

Poitiers, and Agincourt. God had rendered the French incapable of hurting the English by depriving them of Calais and Harfleur, their natural bravery, and their military resources. They should beware of flouting God's judgement further, and speedily acknowledge the justice of the English claims lest total ruin befall them.[59] After three weeks parliament was prorogued until 4 May to await Sigismund's visit, but must have been dissolved by 22 May when Henry took Sigismund to Windsor for the emperor's admission to the Order of the Garter. The celebration which initiated the double feast of St George and included a notable banquet with 'sotelties' fashioned in his honour, were designed to impress the royal viewpoint on the emperor, as was the *Gesta* itself which was commissioned in association with his visit, and composed within the circle of the royal chancery and chapel. Beaufort himself, as prelate to the Order of the Garter, had a central role in the liturgical ceremonies, and was seated next but one to the emperor at the banquet.[60]

He must also have been closely involved in the diplomatic negotiations with Sigismund which preceded the treaty of Canterbury, and it was in the company of the king and the emperor that he embarked for Calais on 4 September, handing over the seal to Simon Gaunstede, keeper of the chancery rolls. At Calais Henry V was trying to extend the diplomatic isolation of France begun in the treaty of Canterbury, and persuade Burgundy into an alliance and recognition of his title. He probably used the double argument that God had delivered judgement on the French and that his further conquests of French territory would vindicate his claims. None was better placed than Beaufort to urge these arguments on the duke of Burgundy and to draft a promise of alliance along these lines.[61] John was probably too wily to accede, but a fair understanding of their respective intentions and mutual interests was established.

Beaufort's first task on return from Calais was to address parliament, the last he would face as Henry's chancellor. The *Gesta* emphasizes his comprehensive review of the summer's negotiations as a prelude to his declaration that the only course left was again the divine arbitrament of battle. But evidently this formed part of a much more complex and wide-ranging justification of the king's government. In a breath-taking simile he likened Henry's labours to those of the Holy Spirit, who created the world in six days and rested on the seventh. In the course of five parliaments the king had accomplished what he was bound to do by his coronation oath; he had established justice and good governance at home, and pursued his just rights by negotiation and the sword. Yet since his adversary refused to accept God's verdict, war was the only route to a just peace. As in 1414 the

[59] *Gesta HV,* 123–7.
[60] Ibid. xxvii, 132–3; *Foedera*, ix, 336; *Gregory's Chron.* 113.
[61] *Foedera*, ix. 394, 425, 427.

chancellor now sought a double subsidy with which to launch the royal expedition. This time the Commons were more, though still not wholly amenable. A double subsidy was granted, three-quarters of which was payable in February 1417, with the remainder at Martinmas. The Commons prohibited the advancement of the last instalment, though loans could be raised on its security; these would be principally from churchmen, since the nobility were expected to accompany the king. For this, the most burdensome of their grants to Henry V, the Commons exacted some significant concessions: the imposition of hosting laws on aliens, the emasculation of the statute of truces, another comprehensive pardon, and harsher enforcement of the penalties against those accepting higher wages under the statute of Cambridge.[62] Roger Flore, the Speaker at this parliament, was already well known to Beaufort as a co-feoffee of the duke of York, but whether in the last three parliaments the chancellor had built up a following among the knights is impossible to say, since virtually none of the returns survive. Whether or not he employed the arts of 'management' in this sense, it seems a fair inference from the series of his highly characteristic sermons, the measured and sensitive concessions to the Commons' interests, the generally harmonious and consistently brief sessions, and the increasingly liberal grants, that he had won the trust and respect of the Commons, and had turned parliament into an effective agent of royal policy. Convocation had already been in session for ten days when, on the day parliament opened, Beaufort appeared, accompanied by the Earl Marshal, the prior of St John of Jerusalem, and Henry Ware. It may have been his first appearance there, for he was not accustomed to concelebrate with the archbishop at the opening mass. He came to demand a subsidy on behalf of the king, and spoke urbanely, offering the clergy gracious words, then remained behind for the discussion when the nobles withdrew. A week later convocation met the king's wishes, giving a lead to the Commons by its grant of a double subsidy payable at February and April 1417.[63]

These grants put at the king's disposal in the early part of 1417 some £75,000, and by the end of March almost £82,000 had been received in cash at the exchequer. Just over this sum was sent down to Salisbury and Southampton where the musters were being held.[64] Wages were not the only costs of the expedition. The council also had to find money to strengthen Harfleur, to requisition ships for transport, and to equip a fleet for a half-year to guard the sea.[65] Some captains were still owed wages for the second quarter of the Agincourt campaign and held jewels as security;

[62] *Gesta HV*, 179; *Rot. Parl.* iv. 94–104.

[63] *Reg. Chichele*, iii. 21–7.

[64] Steel, *Receipt*, 154–5; E 403/630 15 July 1417 has payments for tellers sent to Southampton 26 May–15 July.

[65] *PPC* ii. 208, 218; Wylie and Waugh, *Henry V*, iii. 44–5.

the exchequer was ordered to come to terms with them quickly.[66] Delays in assembling the transport fleet at Southampton and in forming some retinues led to the muster being deferred until the last week of May and then the first week of June. Finally it awaited Huntingdon's victory over the Genoese carracks at the Chef de Caux on 29 June for the channel to be clear, though even then it was not until 30 July that the king set sail.[67]

From early in the year it had been evident that, with all the careful husbandry of the exchequer's resources, loans would have to be raised on a large scale. Letters were sent out to large numbers of churchmen and lay landowners, who were not accompanying the king, to 'warn and require' them to lend specified sums.[68] Although over two hundred contributed, more than half the total of £19,539 comprised a loan of £10,000 made by the city of London, for which repayment was arranged from the customs in the port, under security of the Pusan collar and half the sword of Spain.[69] As delays and costs began to multiply from the middle of May, and the exchequer's cash revenue fell to a trickle, a second appeal for loans became necessary. Letters warning that the expedition would be jeopardized if the money were not found for the second quarter's wages were sent out to a wide circle of potential lenders, and royal agents were dispatched to the shires to induce men to lend. Many proffered excuses of poverty, but in the end a further £31,595 was raised from almost 300 lenders.[70] Most of the smaller sums were repaid from the forthcoming half-subsidy at Martinmas, but the larger loans had to be charged on the customs and subsidies. These were already charged with the wages of the Calais garrison and lenders were likely to wait two years before they recovered their money from this source.[71] It is in this context of the king's acute need for money to launch the expedition, and the exhaustion of all other sources of credit, that we must place Beaufort's massive loan of £14,000, which far surpassed any of his previous contributions and those of other lenders.

The loan was probably negotiated at a meeting of the council between 8 and 12 June, when it was delivered into the king's chamber and entered on the receipt roll, although the patent embodying the terms of repayment was not issued until 18 July. By this Beaufort was granted all the customs and subsidies from the port of Southampton (though only after existing assignments and annuities had been paid), with the authority to nominate

[66] *PPC* ii. 222–9; *Foedera*, ix. 416. The figure of £30,413 for the arrears of the Agincourt campaign given in Wylie and Waugh, *Henry V*, iii. 38 n. 12, 47 relates in fact to the prests for the next voyage: E 403/627 11 Mar.

[67] *PPC* ii. 213, 231–2; *CCR 1413–19*, 433–4; Wylie and Waugh, *Henry V*, iii. 47–50.

[68] C. L. Kingsford, 'An historical collection of the fifteenth century', *EHR* 29 (1914), 512; R. A. Newhall, 'The war finances of Henry V and the duke of Bedford', *EHR* 36 (1921), 174.

[69] Steel, *Receipt*, 154–5; *Cal. L. Bk. I* 176; *CPR 1416–22*, 47, 67.

[70] *CSL* no. 805 (cf. *Foedera*, ix. 241); E 28 /32 10 July; *Foedera*, ix. 461–4, 499–500; Steel, *Receipt*, 156–7.

[71] *Cal. L. Bk. I* 202, 214; *CPR 1416–22*, 234, 279.

one of the collectors and the assurance that no other grants would be made from this source. As pledge for his eventual repayment he was to hold the king's gold crown.[72] These terms were similar to those accorded to the city of London, but they gave no prospect of speedy repayment. Over the years since Michaelmas 1414 the Southampton customs had averaged £2,184 p.a. and between Michaelmas 1417 and the end of the reign they were to yield a total of £11,040 to the exchequer. Beaufort was therefore not likely to recover his money for at least seven years. What induced him to make a loan of this size? Any suggestion that he was primarily interested in financial gain may safely be ruled out. All the evidence points away from the theory that these loans to the crown incorporated a significant element of concealed interest; in any case the predictably long delay in repayment would have made this less attractive than other opportunities for investment. That his appointment of one collector enabled him to smuggle wool, or otherwise defraud the crown, likewise remains a hypothesis and is against probability.[73]

Instead, the loan must be seen in its political context. The king's expedition marked the fruition of a policy which, over the past four years, Beaufort had formulated and, to an unknown but perhaps appreciable degree, directed. As chancellor he had been unremittingly engaged in the king's business; he had expounded the king's rights and insisted on the king's duty to realize them; he had gloried in Henry's victories and interpreted them as God's judgement on the French. He had successfully urged these views on parliament and convocation and had secured the financial resources to launch three major expeditions across the Channel. His hand can equally be traced in the tortuous foreign policy designed to confuse and isolate the French, while consolidating the alliances with Burgundy and the Empire which he had always favoured. Moreover there can be little doubt that Beaufort saw Henry V as the saviour of the house of Lancaster and the realm of England. He had been impatient for his succession, believing that it would bring a renewal of good governance and a revival of national pride, and the past four years had confirmed his judgement. Now, as the king's just endeavour approached its final phase, all subjects were being asked and required to give their utmost aid. For Beaufort now to match his advocacy and industry in the king's cause with his own wealth would set the seal on his family's identification with the fortunes of the house of Lancaster, and would win the king's boundless gratitude. Any explanation of Beaufort's loan and its consequences must therefore see it as the logical culmination of his work as Henry V's chancellor. Yet this alone can scarcely explain its size and its sequel, for a

[72] *PPC* ii. 232; *CPR 1416–22*, 112, 372; E 401/677 12 June. PRO, E 356/17 m. 28^{v}–29^{v}, E 356/18, m. 26;

[73] G. L. Harriss, 'Cardinal Beaufort, patriot or usurer?', *TRHS* 20, (1970), 129–48.

loan of one-third or one-quarter of this sum would have far surpassed those of other lenders and have been a sufficient measure of his official obligation. If Beaufort was placing a very large proportion of his wealth at the king's service with uncertain guarantees of repayment, was this under some degree of duress? It is clear that Henry V was in desperate need for money and was putting pressure on all who had wealth to lend, and that he had pushed his chancellor to the very limit. Yet there is no indication that Beaufort had in any degree occasioned the king's displeasure or, having fallen into disgrace, was now purchasing the king's pardon.[74] He had been continually in council until early March, had officiated at Windsor at the feast of St George, and throughout June and July he followed the king between the centres where the host was being gathered in Hampshire and Wiltshire.[75] To explain the size of Beaufort's loan we must shift the perspective away from his chancellorship to its sequel. For six weeks later, and a week after receiving his patent for repayment, Beaufort surrendered the great seal and prepared to go on pilgrimage. The signs are that he anticipated a prolonged absence from England, as his career entered a new phase and a wholly different area of activity.[76]

[74] Beaufort did secure a pardon on surrendering the great seal, but this was a routine act of prudence: *Foedera*, ix. 741.

[75] *PPC* ii. 212–20; *CPR 1416–22*, *passim*; he was at Downton on 11 July: HRO, Eccles. II, 159419.

[76] Work was suspended on building the new chapel at Bishop's Waltham and not resumed until early in Henry VI's reign: ex. inf. Dr J. N. Hare.

5

Disgrace and Restoration, 1417–1422

HENRY BEAUFORT left England in August 1417 to resolve a crisis in Henry V's conciliar diplomacy.[1] The plan of 1416, to isolate the French, win over Sigismund, and pave the way for wider recognition of the justice of English claims, had become the victim of its own success. Sigismund had returned to Constance in January flaunting Henry V's livery, assured of the full backing of the English delegation led by Hallum, and confident that he could mould the council to his will. He thereby alienated the cardinals and the Italian, French, and Spanish delegations. By April, the council was rent by the animosity between the French and English, and as Henry V's invasion loomed, Sigismund's authority was called in question. As the process for Benedict XIII's deposition gathered momentum, so the question of the election of a new pope became the focus for these divisions. Sigismund's attempts to stifle this met with little success, and while Hallum strenuously supported his demand that all consideration of an election should await the achievement of reform, others among the English delegation were known to favour the Castilian proposal for an electoral college formed from the cardinals and the nations.[2] Unlike Hallum, who was deeply committed to Sigismund's plans, Bubwith and Catrik (now advanced to Lichfield) were royal clerks first and reformers second, and both had close links with Beaufort as had those added to the English delegation in July 1416, namely Clifford, bishop of London, Wakering, now bishop of Norwich, and Thomas Polton, dean of York.[3] Although the reports which they sent back to the chancellor in the first half of 1417 have not survived, it is reasonable to assume that Beaufort was well informed about the increasing divisions between the nations and among the English delegation at the time when his great loan was made in early July. Certainly by 18 July when his patent for repayment was issued and he received licence to resign the chancellorship and go on pilgrimage, the

[1] On the feast of St Agapitus (18 Aug.) he and thirty-two of his companions as pilgrims were admitted to the confraternity of Canterbury: BL Arundel MS 68 fo. 62^{v}. One of Beaufort's last acts as chancellor was to exted the truce with Burgundy until 1419, and he wrote from Bruges on 4 Sept. to seek redress for Flemish merchants who were victims of English piracy, and about the treasurer of Calais: *PPC* ii. 234–5.

[2] J. H. Moody and K. M. Woody (edd.), *The Council of Constance*, trans. L. R. Loomis, 311–53; *Foedera*, ix, 434; C. J. Hefele, *Histoire des conciles*, ed. and trans. H. Leclerq, vii. 427–38; C. M. D. Crowder, 'Some aspects of the English Nation at the Council of Constance', D.Phil. thesis (Oxford, 1953).

[3] *Foedera*, ix. 370; *BRUO* iii. 1494, 1744; Crowder, thesis, 118–20, 308–11.

need for a shift in English policy and consequently the need to override Hallum was becoming evident; for on that day a letter by Henry V referred to resistance among the delegation to his earlier instructions and enjoined conformity to the decisions of the majority.[4] Should the Anglo-German alliance come to be seen as an obstructive faction, it would forfeit any influence over the choice of the new pope. An initiative was needed to break the threatened deadlock between Sigismund and the cardinals, and the English were well placed to do this by swinging their support behind the movement for an election, with a good chance of thereby influencing the choice of the new pope and winning his gratitude.

This was to be Beaufort's mission, and it is important to stress that it was no individual enterprise but must have been the considered response of the king and the chancellor to the events at Constance between April and July 1417. The suggestion for it may well have emanated from Beaufort himself, but the scheme had features which would have commended it to Henry V. For Beaufort's 'pilgrimage' echoed Henry's own proclaimed intention to go to Jerusalem as his father had done, and lent credibility to his protestation that only the obstinacy of the French, in withholding recognition of his just claims, prevented him from leading a crusade for its recovery. The special honour which Henry accorded to St George, the deliverer of Christendom, and his own claim to be heir to St Louis, bespoke the pretensions of the house of Lancaster, now manifested in its spiritual representative. Beaufort's royal blood, his eloquence in expounding the king's cause, and his familiarity with Sigismund all fitted him uniquely for this mission. At the same time it concurred happily with his own interests.

The departure of the king and the greater part of the nobility to France was an obvious point at which to lay down the burdens he had shouldered for the past four years. The work of the council at home would be lighter but of reduced importance. Beaufort had no personal ties with Bedford, and though his brother Exeter was likewise remaining in England, he would be mainly guarding the north. To have stayed in England as chancellor, or to have resigned as chancellor and devoted himself to his diocese, would have been to place himself in a backwater, even if both courses gave better prospects for the repayment of his loan. Instead he saw his role as being to win recognition for English claims upon a wider stage and from a supreme authority, be it pope or council. He was to lead the English diplomatic offensive, parallel to Henry's military one.

Beaufort's immediate task was to detach the English delegation from the German position without alienating Sigismund, from whom Henry still looked for military support against Charles VI. In fact Hallum's death on

[4] *Foedera,* ix. 466; C.M.D., Crowder, 'Correspondence between England and the Council of Constance, 1414–18', *SCH* I (1964) 154–206.

4 September, when Beaufort was still in Bruges, facilitated the English desertion of Sigismund, which was accomplished by Catrik with remarkable promptitude on the following day.[5] Others of Sigismund's Italian allies now abandoned him, but even as the impetus towards an election gathered momentum, so the need to reconcile Sigismund and the triumphant cardinals and procure a unanimous choice became imperative. Here the role of the English as mediators was invaluable. It was Bubwith, Catrik, Polton, and Fleming who effected a settlement with the cardinals on 19 September, and it was the same group who suggested at the beginning of October that the council make an approach to Beaufort, by then at Ulm, in the hope of reconciling the general wish to proceed to election with Sigismund's adherence to the principle that this should be preceded by reform. Sigismund with three cardinals rode out to welcome Beaufort. Doubtless the ground had been well explored, but it was thanks to Beaufort's *facunda persuasio* that Sigismund accepted the face-saving formula which was now proposed: that the council should decree that reform of the Curia should follow the election; that agreed reforms should be promulgated forthwith; and that a commission should determine the method of election.[6]

The way was now open for negotiations on how the electoral college would be formed and for lobbying in support of the candidates. Beaufort himself could hardly fail to be one; he was said to be Sigismunds's favoured choice and the English were suspected of making secret deals on his behalf. It soon became evident that neither an English nor a French candidate could command unanimity and that, since the Germans and Spanish were likewise mutually antipathetic, an Italian was inescapable. None the less, on the first scrutiny on 10 November national loyalties were indulged, and Beaufort, among a number of others, received some votes. The second scrutiny on the following day reduced this to four, the most favoured being Odo Colonna for whom the English delegation had voted en bloc. Colonna received fewer of the cardinals' votes than any other, but had strong support from the English and German nations and some Italians, though only one vote from the French. His apparent neutrality between the contending wings of the council made him acceptable to both, while his reputed pliability and gratitude to the English encouraged expectations that he would be favourable towards the royal cause.[7] Beaufort had every reason to congratulate himself on the success of his mission, for he had procured the election of a suitable pope while retaining Sigismund's

[5] *Council of Constance*, 396; Crowder, thesis, 374–84.

[6] *Council of Contance*, 403, 406; *St Albans Chron.* 10; Hefele, *Conciles*, vii. 456–8. The English delegation claimed that Beaufort had considerable influence with Sigismund.

[7] *Council of Constance*, 407, 417, 426–8; Crowder, thesis, 398–404; *St Albans Chron.* 108; *Acta Concilii Constanciensis*, ed. H. Finke, iii. 148, 152; cf. T. Gascoigne, *Loci E Libro Veritatum*, ed. J. E. Thorold Rogers, 155.

goodwill, and had freed him to join Henry V's war—though in fact Sigismund now went home to deal with the Hussite revolt.

Yet this was only the first phase of the grand design, the ultimate objective of which was to win recognition of Henry's title to the French throne from the pope as from the emperor. It was a policy of high risks. Hitherto English propaganda had laid much emphasis on the notion that God was the arbiter of kings' quarrels in battle, since they had no temporal superiors on earth. If a restored papacy was to be invited to pronounce on the justice of these rival claims, it became essential to build upon the gratitude of the new pope and extend English influence in the Curia. As Henry V himself recognized, this could best be done through the medium of a resident cardinal who could exercise some influence over papal policy. Once again the choice was obvious, and neither Beaufort nor Henry could have found it surprising that on 18 December 1417 Martin V named Henry Beaufort for the cardinalate. What was unlooked for was that the bull conferred on him the title of legate a latere, and that this was followed by a further bull permitting him to hold the see of Winchester in *commendam* and by a grant of exemption from the jurisdiction of the see of Canterbury.[8]

Humphrey, duke of Gloucester later attributed Beaufort's acquisition of these dignities and powers to his ambition, and so probably did Henry V, who must have felt that his uncle had won approval for the mission to Constance in order to practice a deception on him. That Beaufort coveted the rank of cardinal there can be no doubt, for it would restore his precedence over his younger brother, recently made a duke, and over the bourgeois born Chichele whom he had formerly patronized but who was now his ecclesiastical superior. Yet it seems unlikely that Beaufort had planned or expected promotion of the kind he received. In so far as he and the king had considered his future role in the bustle of preparations for the Normandy campaign it had probably been in terms of a number of options ranging from the papal throne itself to a cardinalate which would give leadership and weight to the already influential English delegation at the council and the Curia. Henry V's remark that he needed to have 'promoters of his own nacion' at the Curia suggests that he envisaged Beaufort's role as that of a representative of English interests in Rome. This had been the role of previous English cardinals, and even now non-curial cardinals holding commendatory sees were virtually unknown.[9] Yet Beaufort had no wish to exchange the wealth of Winchester for a share in the uncertain and exiguous revenues of the sacred college, and he

[8] McFarlane, *England in XV Century*, 80–1. According to Wharton, *Anglia Sacra*, i. 800, who used the now damaged copy in Cotton MS Tib. B. VI, fo. 61, Martin V did not name a see, and promised to publish the bull at the earliest opportunity.

[9] Harriss, 'Henry Beaufort, Cardinal of England', 111, 118.

presumably anticipated with some confidence that his blood affinity, unremitting service to the king, and potential influence with the pope, would ensure that his case would be regarded as exceptional. Nor would it necessarily have served the king's interests for the see of Winchester to be filled by papal provision with another less able and willing to place its wealth at the service of the king's enterprise. Moreover, if Beaufort was destined to remain outside England, his retention of Winchester as a cardinal would pose no threat to Chichele's authority or the king's control of the English church.

It is therefore difficult to believe that it was either the cardinalate or the retention of his see that made Beaufort's promotion unacceptable to Henry V. It was rather his appointment as legate, with its implication of the papal intention to tax and discipline the English church, that alarmed the king and archbishop and led Henry to forbid acceptance of the bulls. Henry had exercised a close, paternalistic control over the church, promoting men who combined spiritual integrity with belief in royal leadership. Neither he nor Beaufort had foreseen that Martin's twin objectives would be the restoration of papal finances and the recovery of the powers lost to national churches since the commencement of the schism. Martin intended the new cardinal to be the instrument for recovering 'the pristine liberty of the church in England', but in this he seriously misjudged his man, believing Beaufort to be a more zealous churchman than in fact he was. There is nothing in Beaufort's previous or subsequent career to suggest that he had any personal interest either in the reform of the church or the restoration of its rights, and certainly he had little stomach for a fight to overturn the statute of provisors. If Beaufort found himself unexpectedly designated to implement a policy for which he had little taste, and which he must have known to be obnoxious to English sentiments and interests, he perhaps still reckoned that his own standing with the king might secure royal acquiescence in the form, if not the substance, of his commission. As the career of Wolsey was to show, a cardinal legate need pose no challenge to royal authority and might indeed connive at the perpetuation of that *de facto* headship of the church which Henry V had exercised during the vacancy of the Holy See.

It seems clear that Beaufort failed to anticipate the king's adverse reaction. Whether or not he wrote to Henry is unknown; certainly he made no move to return north to see him, but began preparations for his pilgrimage to the Holy Land. Martin V had given him the custody of the deposed John XXIII on 9 January 1418, but a month later he had secured a papal safe conduct and by 20 March had arrived at Venice with an escort of sixty horses. He was received with great honour by the doge and council and resided at the monastery of San Giorgio. There he negotiated the hiring of a heavily armed galley named the *Querina* for his party of eight pilgrims. He was reputed to have with him a treasure of 45,000 ducats, equivalent to £7,500, and to avoid attracting the attention of pirates he slipped away without other accompanying ships.[10]

It was probably in February 1418 that Martin V's letters to Henry V announcing his own election reached Caen, followed by the news of Beaufort's elevation. Chichele, writing from England on 6 March, had not been notified of the former, but had received reliable news of the latter, and quickly protested to the king that the installation of a permanent legate would be dangerous and unprecedented, derogating from his own primacy, and opening England to papal taxation and other demands.[11] This was not without substance, for one of Martin's very first appointments had been that of Walter Medford, dean of Wells and Beaufort's chancellor and vicar-general in spirituals, to be papal nuncio and collector in England. Then at the end of January Martin proposed sending Fleming and Spofford to England 'for the affairs of the pope and the Roman church', though Spofford was at present accompanying Beaufort to the Holy Land. Martin further made it clear that he regarded Chichele's confirmations of elections during the papal interregnum as technically insufficient, thereby causing the recently elected Chaundler and Ware to secure papal provision; at the same time the pope reserved to himself all churches vacated by translation and provision. By the middle of March he had signalled his neutrality in the Anglo-French conflict by appointing Cardinals Orsini and Fillastre—the former a close friend of Catrik and Beaufort, the latter Francophile—to mediate for peace.[12] The hope of influencing papal policy thus appeared chimerical; instead it must have appeared that Beaufort and the English delegation had become the tools of papal policy.

It was small wonder, therefore, that Henry V gave ready ear to Chichele's complaint, and saw Beaufort's legateship as a challenge to the rights of the crown. During the following months the king's views must have been communicated to the pope, for when, having returned to Venice on 10 September, Beaufort rejoined the papal court at Mantua in late October, no move was made to publish his appointment nor did he take his seat in consistory. Perhaps only at this point did Beaufort become fully

[10] McFarlane, *England in XV Century*, 86; Antonia Morosini, *Extraits de sa Chronique*, ed. H. Lefevre-Pontalis, ii. 158–61. He had probably visited the duke of Milan en route: *CPR 1446–52*, 308. For shipment of scarlet cloth for himself and his retinue, see *CCR 1413–19*, 4000; *Foedera*, ix. 491.

[11] A. Duck, *Life of Henry Chichele*, 125–37; McFarlane, op. cit., 82. Martin's letters announcing his election were dated 22–3 December and were copied in the chancery at Caen (*Foedera*, ix. 534–6). Henry had returned to Caen by 24 Feb. from the siege of Falaise: *CSL* no. 821; Wylie and Waugh, *Henry V*, iii. 72.

[12] *CPL* vii, 1, 5; *Foedera*, ix. 567; Crowder, thesis, 404–13; *Register of Robert Hallum*, ed. J. M. Horn, 631; *Reg. Chichele*, i. xlii, xc–xci; *BRUO* ii. 1253. Catrik died in 1419; on his tomb in Santa Croce, Florence, he is described as 'ambassiator serenissimi domini regis angliae'. His heraldic shield figures three cats.

aware of the king's opposition, for he at once made preparations to seek Henry's presence, even if this meant a winter crossing of the Alps. On 2 December he wrote to the corporation of London that he and his servants were in good health and had lately set out from Mantua. By which route he reached Calais in late February is not known; it was on 3 March that he finally met the king at Rouen.[13] Henry now made it plain that if Beaufort published his bulls and attempted to exercise his powers he would incur the penalties of provisors and praemunire and face lasting ruin. This was sufficient to induce him to give promises of good behaviour.[14] For the next three months, while he remained in the royal camp under the watchful eye of the king, Beaufort took his place alongside Chichele and his brother Exeter in the negotiations leading to the meeting with John the Fearless and Charles VI at Meulan. It was during this period that he and Henry explored the possibility of his resigning the see of Winchester and surrendering his wealth.[15] They even got as far as a consideration of possible successors: Kemp and Fleming were mentioned, and Beaufort later had in mind a third, a layman. Nothing was decided about this, and Beaufort had returned to England by mid-August to consider it further, giving a binding promise not to publish his bull.[16] Thomas Chaucer, who had returned to England in March 1419, was now charged by Henry V to keep Beaufort under surveillance and report regularly to the king. To Chaucer's alarm Beaufort showed some signs during the following winter of reneging on his promise to Henry. He had kept his own copy of the offending bull and, probably during the October parliament, which he attended, he took into his confidence a person 'of good estate' who, to Beaufort's satisfaction, professed surprise that the king had forbidden him to use his powers and offered to tell Henry, if asked, that it seemed to him no derogation of royal authority nor any detriment to the realm. This was quite possibly Bedford himself, whom Henry had just summoned to France, for to no one of lesser degree could Beaufort have broached the

[13] *Cal. L. Bk. I* 208. The letter is dated from Rympton, the episcopal manor in Somerset, presumably having been brought by Beaufort's messenger and copied on arrival in England early in Jan. The city's reply is dated 15 Jan. Martin V was at Mantua between 14 Oct. and 6 Feb. 1418/19. His itinerary has been traced by F. Miltenberger, *Mitteilungen des Instituts für Osterreichische Geschichtsforschung*, 15 (1894), 661–4. One of Beaufort's attendants on pilgrimage, John Coventre, was back in London on 6 Mar., broken in health (*Cal. L. Bk. I* 209). McFarlane, *England in XV Century*, 86–7.

[14] This is implied in Beaufort's letter to Henry in 1420 and in that of Chaucer: McFarlane, op. cit. 89, 94.

[15] *Foedera*, ix. 704, 761. He had been named as one of the commissioners to treat with the dauphin in Jan. 1419, but his name does not figure in the negotiations: ibid. 670, 687, 704. About this time he delivered some of his silver vessels to the wardrobe for wages of war, receiving repayment of £1,458 on his return to England: E 403/643 29 Feb. 1420.

[16] McFarlane, *England in XV Century*, 88 n. 5. He imported a sealed chest with cloth purchased abroad: *CCR 1419–22*, 29. He was met at Winchester by the fellows and members of the college wearing new liveries of green cloth: Winchester College muniments, no. 22100.

matter or received an answer in these terms. It was from Bedford's hands that he was ultimately to receive the coveted dignity. But by the time Chaucer wrote to Henry V on 11 March 1420 this alarm had proved groundless, and Beaufort was anxious that Chaucer should reassure the king of his fidelity to his promise.[17]

Having enforced obedience, Henry had left the question of resignation to Beaufort's free choice, and by the spring of 1420 Beaufort had almost resolved to resign and surrender his wealth to the king within the context of another pilgrimage to Jerusalem. Moods of otherworldliness alternating with schemes for retrieving something from the wreckage seem to have filled Beaufort's days. Chaucer voiced his scepticism of the former—'credite operibus', he wrote—and we have the testimony of Poggio Bracciolini that Beaufort's behaviour at this time was characterized by restless wandering rather than by finding solace, as he himself was doing, in study and contemplation. Pilgrimage, one may guess, was to be the cover for a visit to Rome, where he would take up the cardinalate alone, without the legateship. Henry's concordat with Martin V, ratified in April 1419, had envisaged—albeit in general terms—the creation of some English cardinals at the Curia.[18] Yet the more Beaufort thought about it the stronger grew his doubts and fears. Chaucer urged him to seek Henry's personal sanction or his move might be misinterpreted. The king had indeed invited him to the peacemaking and marriage at Troyes, yet Beaufort hesitated to set out in case Henry again misjudged his actions, countermanded his journey, and exposed his disgrace. His letter of excuse, cringing and apprehensive, reveals how dramatically their relationship had changed since Beaufort had confidently exhorted the king on the morrow of Agincourt.

And trwly, my sovereyne lord, but if yowr hynesse hadde commandid me the contrarie, if I myht have be to Goddis wrshyp and yowrys at that blessid gladde mariage, I nolde for no thyng be thennys. But Godde, blessid mote he be, wylle not that I have in thys worlde that that I moste desirid, of the whyche to see that joyfull day of yowr mariage haht ben on. Besechyng yow, my sovereyne lord, to have in yowr noble remembrauncce wyht what conclusion of reste I departid laste owte of yowr graciouse presence and aftir that I have demenid me syht I kam in to thys yowr reaume and wyht Goddis grace shall to my lyvys ende. . . . Also, my sovereyne lord, whanne I was on the grette see I made a wowe that aftir time I were onys in yowr reaume of Engeland I sholde no see passe save on pilgrimage un to I

[17] *Rot. Parl.* iv. 116–17; McFarlane, *England in XV Century* 92–5. Parliament opened on 19 Oct.; Beaufort was in London on 13 Oct. and on 7 Feb. 1420: C 85/156/11, 13. Chaucer's letter shows that the conversation took place 'in the towne' and some time previously when Chaucer himself had been in London, probably during the parliament. By January 1420 Chaucer was negotiating a loan in Oxford: McFarlane, op. cit. 101 n. 82.

[18] His reported intention was 'to abyde halfe a yere [in Jerusalem] and than to come home a preste and noght a bysshope': Chaucer's letter is printed by McFarlane, op. cit. 92–5. For the concordat, *Foedera*, ix. 730; Harriss, 'Henry Beaufort, Cardinal of England', 117.

hadde be at Seint Jamys. . . . And therefore, my sovereyne lord, wyht all humblesse that any subgit kan thenke or devise I beseche yowr hynesse to take not to displesaunsse my nowht comyng. For Godde knowht I ne fene not ne no colour seke.

Nor was there any certainty that he would be welcomed at the papal court or exercise influence there, for his usefulness to Martin V had disappeared when he forfeited the king's trust and favour. Unnerved and uncertain, torn between his fears, his pride, and his ambitions, Beaufort did nothing. His instinct was to retain the basis of his wealth in England rather than bid for uncertain influence at the papal court. Moreover, though his plan to build himself a princely estate from gratifying the aims of his two masters lay in ruins, their aims had not changed, and their need for someone in Beaufort's position remained.

This became steadily apparent over the next two years as Anglo-papal relations settled into a stalemate following Henry V's rebuff to Martin's request for a repeal of the statute of provisors in 1419. Although the murder of John the Fearless by the dauphinists brought Henry within measurable distance of his greatest ambition, Martin maintained a conspicuous refusal to approve the condemnation and disinheritance of the dauphin, pronounced in Paris, or to recognize the treaty of Troyes, concessions which Henry must have ardently desired to strengthen his position in France. Beaufort must often have reflected how Martin's precipitate assertion of papal power and Henry's equally ready defence of the English church had fatally prejudiced their chances of gaining their larger objectives, which might have been secured by the patient services of a trusted mediator. No wonder that he fretted as he went about his routine diocesan duties, took recreation in hunting around Winchester, or visited the dowager Queen Joan under house arrest at Leeds castle.[19] Probably by the autumn of 1420 he had come to a decision to put aside thoughts of the cardinalate and rebuild his position in the king's counsels. Despite the plague which prevailed in London, he and Bubwith attended a meeting of the council at Blackfriars on 17 August 1420, a sufficiently unusual occurrence to suggest that its dispatch to Rome of Richard Clifford, bishop of London, was related to Beaufort's own affairs. Did he carry Beaufort's formal renunciation of the bulls? Certainly Beaufort was no longer under surveillance by Thomas Chaucer, who had returned to France in mid-July, and from the autumn come the first signs that he was resuming his place in

[19] Beaufort's traceable movements during 1420 are: 6 Apr. Chertsey (*Chertsey Cartularies*, i. 53 no. 71); 6 June Bishop's Waltham (McFarlane, op. cit. 90); 2 July, 9–11 Aug. Leeds Castle (A. R. Myers, 'The Captivity of a royal witch: the household accounts of Queen Joan of Navarre, 1419–20', in id., *Crown, Household, and Parliament in the XV Century*, 98, 110); 17 Aug. Blackfriars (E 28/23); 7 Sept., 8 Oct. Bishop's Waltham (*Reg. Fleming*, i. no. 72; *Winchester College Muniments*, no. 16724); 6 Nov. Southwark (*Register of Richard Fleming*, ed. N. H. Bennett, i. no. 459).

government. He probably attended the important council meeting on 27 October where writs of summons for a parliament were authorized, and on the same day received a joint grant of the farm of the lands of the late William Cheyne for £400 p.a.[20] He was present at the parliament which met on 2 December for two weeks, acting as a trier of petitions, and was in London when Henry V returned in mid-February 1421. He and Chichele sat at the queen's right hand at the coronation banquet, and on 23 April he officiated at the election of the knights of the Garter at Windsor.[21] His formal restoration to the king's grace, and Henry's care not to publicize his humiliation, thus opened the road to future service. Only a handful knew what had happened: Beaufort's associates at the papal Curia, those whom Beaufort or the king had taken into their confidence, and probably the king's lieutenants in England during 1419–20, John, duke of Bedford, and Humphrey, duke of Gloucester.

To those outside this circle Beaufort appeared to command increasing influence and favour as the tide of Anglo-Burgundian success swept on. It took little to persuade Poggio Bracciolini to attach his own fortunes to those of Beaufort when he joined the bishop's household at Mantua in November 1418, doubtless on the encouragement and recommendation of the English delegation at Constance. By the end of his first winter in England disillusion had begun to set in, for Beaufort's restlessness and uncertainty whether to cross the Channel meant that he rarely saw his master.[22] The prevalence of plague in London late in the summer of 1420 gave him the opportunity to visit Salisbury—but he found no classical manuscripts, and such men of letters as he encountered were more disputatious than learned. By the beginning of 1421 he had resolved to leave, and sought Beaufort's permission, but his master wanted to retain him for the king's visit, and the ensuing improvement in Beaufort's standing is reflected in a new note of expectancy in Poggio's letters of June and July 1421. In the presence of Simon of Teramo Beaufort had promised him the first living to fall vacant in his gift; but another six months passed until a benefice came his way, and then it proved to be one with cure of souls and of no great value. Throughout 1422 he sought to exchange it and kept hoping for a prebend, but Beaufort remained evasive, and after four years Poggio decided to cut his losses and return to the Curia despite its intrigue and place-hunting.[23]

Poggio caught Beaufort at a time when his fortunes were at a low ebb,

[20] C 81/1543/21; *CPR 1416–22*, 310. He was doubtless present at the rededication of the church of St Cross hospital in Oct. 1420: Kirby, *Annals of Winchester College*, 179.

[21] McFarlane, op. cit., 109; *Gregory's Chron.* 139; *The Brut*, ed. F. W. D. Brie, ii. 445; J. Anstis, *Register of the Order of the Garter*, i. 75. Beaufort was at Southwark on 17, 30 Apr. 1421: C 85/156/14, 15.

[22] *Poggii Bracciolini: Epistolae*, ed. T. Tonelli. i. 30–1, dated 5 Mar. 1420.

[23] Ibid. i. letters vii–x, xiii–xvii, xx–xxii. Poggio had returned to Rome by Feb. 1423.

and his customary affability and urbanity had worn thin. Though impressed by his patron's influence, there was little in the bishop's tastes and character to attract him, nor does it seem that Beaufort's household numbered men with whom Poggio could share his enthusiasms. It was there, certainly, that he met Richard Petworth, Beaufort's secretary since 1415, and it was probably through Simon of Teramo that he came to know Nicholas Bildeston, the king's envoy to Martin V in 1421–2, and William Toly, the clerk of the signet, who was briefly in England with Henry in 1421, both of whom entered Beaufort's service after Henry V's death. All these had interests in common with him and qualities which endeared them to him. But it must have been from the days spent in Beaufort's household that he retained the impression that trade, agriculture, and the management of their estates formed the interminable table talk of the English nobility, and he had little interest in, or understanding of, the bishop's preoccupation with problems of royal government and the political order in Europe.[24]

While Henry Beaufort was facing the first great crisis of his career, Thomas Beaufort in the three years that followed Henry V's departure for France attained the height of his fame and fortune. He had remained with Bedford in England during the late summer of 1417, nominally on pilgrimage in the north, but anticipating the Scottish invasion which he was well placed to check with local levies while Bedford mustered a larger army from the south which forced the Scots to withdraw.[25] The parliament which met in November received the news of this and the king's successes together with that of the capture of Sir John Oldcastle; it was also called on to ratify Bishop Beaufort's patent for repayment of his loan which the Commons commended as a 'comfort, surety and good example to all lieges who will well and loyally acquit themselves to the king in his necessity'. The contributions of the Beauforts, in the field and from their purse, clearly commended them to the Commons, and helped to produce a favourable climate for the grant of two further subsidies to be levied in February 1418 and 1419. While these were under debate in parliament, the duke of Exeter, with the earls of Northumberland and Westmorland and the chancellor, visited convocation on 11 December to report the king's need for a subsidy for the war in France, and three days after that of the Commons the clergy made a similar grant.[26] Exeter probably remained in London throughout the winter, attending Bedford's council until in the early spring, responding to the king's urgent wishes, he indented for a year's service in France to commence on 3 March 1418.[27]

[24] *Poggii Bracciolini, Opera Omnia*, i (Turin, 1964), 'De Nobilitate', 69.

[25] Wylie and Waugh, *Henry V*, iii. 89–92.

[26] *Rot. Parl.* iv. 106, 110–11; *Reg. Chichele*, iii. 39–40, 45.

[27] *CSL* no. 316; C 81/1364/38 ('We would that our uncle of Exeter might come to us . . . as soon as he might'); *Rotuli Normanniae*, ed. T. D. Hardy, 273; Newhall, *Conquest of Normandy*, 197, 204.

His force numbered 500 men-at-arms and 1,500 archers, some of whom were reinforcements for Clarence's retinue. Clearly there were close relations between the two, for Clarence had with him Exeter's nephew, Henry, earl of Somerset. Accompanying Exeter were Lord Fitzhugh, the king's chamberlain and lord treasurer, and Huntingdon's younger brother Edward Holand, styled count of Mortain, and Sir Gilbert Umfraville. Exeter's musters were taken in mid-April and he was probably in France by Trinity.[28] By then Henry V's campaign was on the move after the winter, and Exeter's first assignment was the capture of Evreux. His first rewards followed hard on his arrival, for on 1 July he was granted the barony of Harcourt in tail male. This was the more surprising in being the first grant in such terms, and in following the grant to Clarence in February of the Vicomtés of Auge, Orbec, and Pont-Audemer, which had specifically excluded the barony of Harcourt.[29]

Exeter now joined the advance on Rouen, taking up his siege station at the Porte Beauvoisine on 1 August, and it was here that his retinue was regularly mustered in the months before Christmas. It may have included the following of Sir James Harrington, with the aid of whose Lancashire and Cheshire bowmen he repulsed a French sally on 25 November, and it certainly numbered those who had served him at Harfleur, such as Sir John Blount, Janico D'Artas, and Sir Thomas Rokeby.[30] The presence nearby of Huntingdon and Sir John Nevill, the husband of Elizabeth Holand, suggests that this sector was the Beaufort–Holand–Clarence preserve. Whether through warfare or disease, they suffered the deaths of the young Henry, earl of Somerset, Edward, count of Mortain, and the more elderly Blount during the siege.[31] After the surrender of Rouen on 13 January 1419 (of which he was then appointed captain), Exeter was commissioned to subdue the fortresses to the north up to the line of the Bresle, a task which he had completed by the end of February, probably returning at about the time that his brother arrived.[32] What part he played in discussions in Rouen with Henry V over the bishop's future is unknown, but his own services, favour, and perhaps pleading with the king may have helped to win respite for his brother. At the end of March he was sent to invest Château Gaillard, which eventually surrendered in September, but Exeter was present alongside his brother at the Meulan negotiations in June, and on 4 July he received the grant in tail male of the lordship of Croisy on the Eure, forming the link between Evreux and Mantes.[33]

[28] E 404/33/216–20; *CPR 1416–22*, 201; Devon, *Issues*, 354. *St Albans Chron.* 118.

[29] *Rôles normands et francais*, ed. L. Brequigny, nos. 73, 205; *Rot. Norman.* 259; *Calendar of the Norman Rolls*, 728.

[30] *Strecche Chron.* 170–2, 41; *Brut*, ii. 387–8; *Eng. Chron.*, 46; *Cal. Norm. Rolls*, 717–18.

[31] *London Chronicle*, ed. Nicholas, 95; Kingsford, *English Historical Literature in the XV Century*, 289. Henry's death is given as 25 Nov. 1418: C 139/15.

[32] *Rôles normands*, 726; Newhall, *Conquest of Normandy*, 124–6.

[33] Newhall, *Conquest*, 220; *Cal. Norm. Rolls*, 783, 790.

Throughout the following year he remained with Henry V, participating in the negotiations of the treaty of Troyes and the king's marriage, the siege and capture of Melun, of which he was made captain in November, and Henry's entry into Paris in December. Already captain of Rouen, Conches, and Melun, when Henry departed for England in January 1421 he was appointed military governor of Paris with responsibility for the guard of Charles VI.[34]

Meanwhile his nephews had begun their military careers in Clarence's retinue. Following the death of Earl Henry at Rouen, his younger brothers John, Thomas, and Edmund all came over to Normandy in the course of 1419. Hitherto they had been in the household of their mother Margaret, their living expenses paid partly by an annual sum of 200 marks from Bishop Henry, partly by Clarence himself. Bishop Beaufort helped to equip them for service with horses, carriages, armour, and harness in the autumn of 1419, and they probably crossed in November. At Christmas they are said to have been knighted by Henry V in Rouen, and their first taste of warfare was at the siege of Melun, commenced on 13 July 1420, where their mother joined Clarence.[35] On Henry V's return to England in January 1421, Clarence, who was left as lieutenant-general, at once abandoned the strategy of siege warfare in favour of a *chevauchée* into Maine and Anjou. What the strategic purpose of this was has never been wholly clear; he had mustered a force of some 4,000 men, but this was insufficient either to capture Angers or to fight a major battle. Most probably it was intended to reconnoitre the ground for a major and systematic conquest of Maine in the following summer or next year, but also perhaps to stake out a claim to the territory on behalf of himself and the Beauforts. For he was at the castle of Beaufort, twenty miles east of Angers, when the news of the proximity of the French and Scottish army arrived, and the encounter which cost him his life on 22 March occurred at Baugé a few miles to the north. Both John and Thomas Beaufort were made prisoners, as were John Holand, earl of Huntingdon, and young Lord Fitzwalter, who had been the ward of John, earl of Somerset. The young Lord Roos, whose wardship Thomas, duke of Exeter had surrendered in June 1419, was killed, and so were the veterans Sir Gilbert Umfraville and Sir John Grey and Sir William Bowes, all from Clarence's retinue.[36] Baugé was thus a family as well as a national disaster. Margaret had lost three of her sons to death or captivity, and with Exeter himself

[34] *Cal. Norm. Rolls*, 381, 388, 390–1, 393; *Foedera*, x. 30.

[35] WAM, 12163. This account of the duke of Clarence for 7–9 Henry V does not give a clear date for the young Beauforts' crossing, but the details of their equipment and expenses are on fo. 11–12^{v}, 13^{v}, 18^{v}. 21. *Chronique de Normandie*, ed. B. Williams, 198; Walsingham, *Hist. Angl.* ii. 336; Kingsford, *Eng. Hist. Lit.* 319; *Strecche Chron.* 188.

[36] Wylie and Waugh, *Henry V*, iii. 297–310; Newhall, *Conquest*, 275–6 suggests that Clarence was anticipating a Franco-Scottish incursion. *Chronicles of London*, 74; Kingsford, *Eng. Hist. Lit.* 320; *Henrici Quinti Gesta*, ed. B. Williams, 149, 274.

childless, there remained only Edmund, who had remained behind with his mother, to continue the family into the next generation.

Baugé endangered English authority everywhere, not least in Paris where the news arrived on 4 April. It could only enhance the discontent produced by the near famine conditions prevalent all over northern Europe. Exeter shut himself up in the Bastille, and in June, fearing betrayal to the advancing dauphinist forces, he imprisoned the Burgundian L'Isle-Adam, thereby provoking a riot but keeping control of the city with a show of force. By the beginning of July Henry V was back in Paris with reinforcements, to relieve Chartres and to remove the dauphinist threat from the south-east. Exeter did not accompany him to the siege of Dreux or on the campaign along the Loire, but joined him on 1 September with men from his garrisons at Conches and Rouen to form the vanguard for the siege of Meaux. At the siege, at which he and the earls of Warwick and March were the principal commanders, he covered the ground between the north wall of the town and the river. Despite heavy casualties and the ravages of disease, the siege was maintained throughout a gruelling winter, and it was Exeter who conducted the surrender negotiations on 2 May.[37] At the end of May he was at Paris for the reception of Queen Catherine, brought over by Bedford, and was sent with Bedford to the relief of Cosne early in August, returning in haste to Vincennes on the 20th to the deathbed of the king. It was Bedford, Exeter, and Warwick who received Henry V's last commands and heard his final wishes.

Of all Henry V's aristocratic captains, it was Exeter with whom he had the longest associations, and in whom he showed the most confidence. Henry trusted him, in turn, with his three greatest conquests—Harfleur, Rouen, and Paris—probably because he excelled as a disciplinarian and had made himself a reputation for endurance and steadiness under siege. The same qualities made him formidable on the other side of the lines, for Henry V's sieges of Harfleur, Rouen, and Meaux, in all of which he commanded, were also tests of endurance and discipline. He was perhaps less reliable as a tactician in the field—it was once again tenacity and endurance that saved him from the full consequences of his defeat at Valmont— though these qualities were not called upon in the conquest of Normandy. Although it was Clarence who in virtue of the size of his retinue and his assault on Caen dominated the early stages of the conquest, it was Exeter who emerged more often as Henry's trusted lieutenant. Certainly neither Bedford nor Gloucester could match his record of service.

Bishop Beaufort must have regarded the death of Clarence with some relief. Although the Duchess Margaret was then over 40 and they had

[37] Wylie and Waugh, *Henry V*, iii. 323, 331 n. 2, 337, 339, 349; *Cal. Norm. Rolls*, 431.

ceased to expect children of their own, it meant that at her death the Beaufort lands in which she had dower or jointure and the Holand property which she held in her own right would revert to Earl John's sons, provided that she did not remarry. The danger that the Beauforts might lose all this if she had pre-deceased Clarence was not unreal; for these lands formed the bulk of Clarence's estate and had been enjoyed by him while alive. Thus in the years 1418–19 and 1419–20 the income from Margaret's lands had totalled £1,414 and £1,318 respectively, while from his own properties, Holderness, Hawarden, Somerton (Lincs.) and Guines, Clarence drew less than £300.[38] By his will of 10 July 1417 the duke provided for his executors to discharge his debts from the money the crown owed him and the ransoms of his prisoners of war, as also from his own lands and those he held in ward for the Beaufort heir. They were also to distribute £2,000 among his household servants. When the lands had been freed of these charges, they were to revert to Margaret for life and then to Henry, earl of Somerset, with remainder to the king.[39] The rest of the duke's income derived from his exchequer annuity of 2,000 marks, and he also enjoyed the two annuities formerly held by John, earl of Somerset of £500 at the exchequer and from the petty custom in London. He was also in receipt of 200 marks p.a. from the bishop of Winchester for the sustenance of John's sons. In the two and a half years before his death he had been able to recover no less than £4,838 of arrears from these annuities.[40] Thomas had appointed his widow and a group of his retainers as executors. The will was not proved until November 1423 and the process of discharging his debts was probably prolonged. It is unlikely that in the end Margaret received more than a small residue of the duke's movables. However, on payment of a fine of one year's income she was permitted to retain the lordship of Holderness while she also inherited Clarence's substantial claim to the residue of the ransom of Charles d'Angoulême.[41] She also entered into full possession of the lands of her first husband. Together with her own jointure and the Holand lands this provided her with a landed income of about £1,350 p.a. and a further £1,000 in annuities. Although she was only entitled to retain all these properties until the heir, John, came of age on 25 March 1425, she would even then enjoy her own inheritance, jointure, and dower. In all the duchess would be able

[38] WAM 12163 fos. 4, 6ᵛ. By 1420 a significant part of the estate had been assigned to her by the duke 'secundum ratam inter eosdem factam', for the maintenance of her own household: fos. 7–8ᵛ, 11.

[39] *Reg. Chichele*, i. 293–5.

[40] WAM, 12163, fo. 9.

[41] *PPC* ii. 334. It was probably as a safeguard against the Stafford claim to Holderness that Clarence enfeoffed Henry and Thomas Beaufort and others in the property which they then surrendered to the executors, making a fine in Feb. 1423 for the failure to obtain a licence: *CPR 1422–9*, 59.

to count on an income of comfortably over £1,000 p.a. which her son could only rival if he were able to ensure the full payment of his annuities at the exchequer.[42] In fact, of course, he was a prisoner in French hands.

Henry V returned to England in February 1421 with the double purpose of bringing redress and reassurance to his subjects, and recruiting as many of them as possible for the continuance of the war in France. He found them critical and war-weary, unwilling to support a war fought well beyond the bounds of Normandy, and anxious for the promised benefits of peace. In the parliament of December 1420 the Commons had demanded the king's return, and as soon as he arrived in London Henry issued writs for a parliament to meet on 2 May. He then set out on a visitation of the realm, showing himself to his subjects, redressing wrongs, giving thanks at important shrines, raising loans, and recruiting troops. By the beginning of May he had a force of 900 men-at-arms and 3,300 archers under indenture to muster on the 23rd.[43] The meeting of parliament was thus to be the culmination of his visit, a demonstration of the resolution of the community of the realm and of their gratitude and loyalty to the king. The tangible expression of this would be the grant of a tax for the cost of the royal expedition. No taxation had been granted by either parliament or convocation since November 1419, and for the past year virtually none had been collected. The result had been an unprecedented slump in exchequer revenue. Whereas in each Michaelmas term since the beginning of the reign the exchequer had received between £50,000 and £86,000 in cash, in Michaelmas 1420–1 it had received under £20,000.[44] It says much for the self-discipline of the treasurer that there had been no significant increase in assignments or fictitious loans; the temptation to 'print money' had been resisted. But since wages of war had to be paid in cash, and there was no reserve to draw upon, it had been clear from the first that the expedition could only be launched by loans raised on a scale at least as extensive as in 1415 and 1417.

For this the auguries were not good. The debasement of the French and Flemish coinage had produced an outflow of bullion from England, and the recent parliament had been exercised over the shortage of coin and the general poverty of the realm. Henry's own presence and persuasion now secured many contributions, and in April commissions were issued to leading magnates in each county, instructing them to interview all persons of substance who had not yet contributed, and return the names of those willing to lend and those who refused.[45] In the first of these commissions,

[42] C 139/15 (IPM Earl Henry); C 139/101 (IPM Duchess Margaret). These estimates of income are derived from the account for 1419–20 in WAM 12163.

[43] Wylie and Waugh, *Henry V*, iii. 318–19; Newhall, *Conquest*, 281.

[44] Steel, *Receipt*, 439, 458.

[45] *Rot. Parl.* iv. 123, 125–6; *St Albans Chron.* 126; *CPR 1416–22*, 385; *Foedera*, x. 96–8; *CCR 1419–22*, 337; *Strecche Chron.* 184–6.

issued from York on 7 April, Bishop Beaufort was named as sole commissioner for Hampshire, indicating that he had given at least the promise of a major loan by this date. Those contributing were required to pay their loans into the exchequer on 1 or 8 May, and a total of £35,836 was recorded from the 572 lenders. Beaufort himself contributed £14,000, but only twenty-four others exceeded £100, and only four of these were for more than 1,000 marks. The numerous small contributions from clergy, towns, gentry, and local communities of vill and hundred reveal an extended operation to induce taxpayers to advance what they habitually paid towards a subsidy.[46]

There are a number of other indications of Henry's intention to seek a grant from parliament. Three chronicles affirm this, two even stating incorrectly that a tax was granted.[47] The king had pointedly refrained from asking for a tax in the previous December, and though the chancellor made no direct reference to taxation in his opening address, he extolled Henry as a veritable Julius Caesar, and dwelt on his steadfastness in the face of the news of Baugé.[48] Thomas Chaucer, once again Speaker, is likely to have been the king's choice as he could report at first hand on the making of the treaty of Troyes and the king's marriage. Moreover, on 6 May the council received a statement from the treasurer, clearly designed for the parliament, showing that a deficit was inevitable unless taxation was provided.[49] But at some point during the first week of parliament the government must have received indications that the Commons were unwilling to make a grant. With the loans ready to be paid into the exchequer, there began an urgent search to provide for other security for their repayment. The Lords declared their readiness to stand surety for the repayment of all loans made by authority of parliament, but the provision of actual revenue was left to the clergy. On Friday 9 May Bishop Beaufort appeared in convocation to ask for a subsidy. In what was probably a carefully rehearsed move, William Lyndwood, as proctor for the lower clergy, produced a cedule of clerical *gravamina* incorporated in the grant of a tax. Lyndwood was a Canterbury official, but well known to Beaufort as holding the prebend of Taunton. Beaufort may verbally have indicated the royal acceptance, though the king's answers, together with the grant of two subsidies payable at November 1421 and 1422, were probably not formally ratified until convocation reassembled on 13 May.[50] The loans could now be registered in the exchequer, and repayment made by assignments on the November subsidy.

[46] E 401/696; Steel, *Receipt*, 163. As late as 13 May sheriffs were ordered to ensure that the promised loans were sent to the exchequer: E 28/34.

[47] *Henrici Quinti Gesta*, 152; *Strecche Chron.* 186; Walsingham, *Hist. Angl.* ii. 337.

[48] *St Albans Chron.* 126; *Rot. Parl.* iv. 129.

[49] *PPC* ii. 214–5.

[50] *Reg. Chichele*, iii. 66.

While the clergy's grant could provide security for the mass of smaller loans, it could not suffice for those of any size. The larger lenders held back: London produced only £2,000, Whittington and Bubwith 1,000 marks each, and that was all. It was here that the lack of a lay subsidy had its effect, for in its default larger loans would all have to be charged against the customs and these were already heavily engaged for the repayment of outstanding debts and the Calais appropriation; moreover, their yield had been seriously reduced since 1419 by a slump in trade.[51] Had he been forced to, Henry V could doubtless have placed London, the Staplers, foreign merchants, and the greater ecclesiastics under various degrees of compulsion to lend, but with the wages for the first quarter now due there was no time for prolonged negotiation. Nor did the king wish to mar the impression that he had cultivated during his visit that he had come to redress complaint, reform abuses, and rekindle loyalty and enthusiasm for the war. Providentially one man's wealth was sufficient to furnish the money to launch the expedition, and that man was perforce amenable to royal pressure.

Precisely when the size of Beaufort's loan was determined is impossible to say, but it undoubtedly set the seal on the process of his restoration to royal favour and hence to a full role in government. His influence in parliament and convocation was again manifest, he again took his place at the St George's day celebrations at Windsor, and he now reassumed his regular attendance in council.[52] Nevertheless the price was steep. By the beginning of 1421 he had recovered no more than £5,693 of the £14,000 which he had lent in 1417, so that a total of £22,300 of his wealth was now in the king's hands. Nor was this all, for even as the musters went ahead at Dover in the last week of May, it became apparent that there was still insufficient for wages, and the king borrowed a final 5,500 marks from Beaufort to enable his army to sail.[53] Whatever political benefits he anticipated, Beaufort knew that the prospects for the repayment of this sum of £26,000 were hazardous. Confined of necessity to the customs, and

[51] The £6,000 of fictitious loans this term were all on the customs: Steel, *Receipt*, 163; E. M. Carus Wilson and D. Coleman, *England's Export Trade 1275–1547* (henceforth *Eng. Export Trade)*, 57. The appropriation of 23*s*. 4*d*. of the subsidy made in 1417 was reduced in the following year to 16*s*. 8*d*.: *PPC* ii. 208–13, 217, 317.

[52] The Commons declared that his loan was 'pur l'aise de vostre povre communalte d'Angleterre': *Rot. Parl.* iv. 132. A number of Beaufort's retainers and friends sat in the parliaments of 1419–21: Richard Baynard (1421), William Chamberlain (1419), Thomas Chaucer (1421), Robert Darcy (1419, 1421), William Coggeshall (1420, 1421), John Golafre (1421), Lewis John (1420), John Uvedale (1419, 1421), Thomas and Richard Waller (1419, 1421), William Whaplode (1420), John Wilcotes (1419, 1421), William Yerde (1419). For his attendance at the Garter, see Anstis, *Garter*, 75–6.

[53] *PPC* ii. 298–9. On 24 May letters to lenders in Kent asked for loans to be delivered at Dover by 1 June: E 28/34.

with his loan of 1417 still unrepaid, he insisted that his patent should give him unequivocal preference over all other claimants. That issued on 19 May put into his hand all the customs of Southampton, with the right to appoint a collector, and gave him control of the cocket and preference over all future assignments including grants of annuities. Yet since 1417 the yield of the Southampton customs had averaged £2,200 p.a., so that full repayment could hardly be expected for some ten years. Beaufort was highly conscious of the risks attendant on so long a delay; should the king die, the subsidy granted to him would expire, and should the war in the Channel revive, the Southampton trade might collapse. He even suspected that Italian merchants might be diverted to London on royal orders, to boost the customs there which the king controlled. His patent therefore contained clauses enabling him to extend his rights to other ports if the Southampton trade were to be impeded or the subsidy suspended, while in the event of the king's death he was to have full repayment of the whole sum of £22,306 within a year, failing which he would have the right to dispose of the golden crown which was delivered to him as security.[54] The 5,500 marks lent at Dover was covered by a separate agreement, repayment being made by tallies on the customs of London dated in three instalments, November 1421–2.[55] Considering the size of his loan and the hazards of a prolonged period of repayment, these were not unduly favourable terms. It would have been surprising had they been so, for although Henry found himself dependent on Beaufort's money to secure his return to France, he still held the whip hand. Beaufort's ambition was now centred on regaining political influence in England. He had learnt from the events of 1417–19 that his usefulness to Martin V depended on his good standing with the king, and though he recognized that of the two the royal power was supreme, he still hoped for influence in a wider sphere. The domestic confines of the English council were unlikely to satisfy him for long.

The question inevitably presents itself at this point of how and when Beaufort acquired his great wealth. To this no conclusive answer can be given, for the accounts of his treasurer at Wolvesey, which alone might have provided the key, have long disappeared. Undoubtedly the estates of the bishopric of Winchester and, to a much lesser extent, those of Lincoln, which he held for six years, formed the bedrock of his fortune. Winchester was the wealthiest of the English sees, valued at £4,192 in the *Valor Ecclesiasticus*, and assessed for the common services at 12,000 florins. The clear income received by the bishop in the first decades of the century was

[54] *Rot. Parl.* iv. 132–5; *CPR 1416–22*, 372; *PPC* ii. 288; E 356/17 m. 28^{v}–29^{v}, E 356/18m. 26. His collector in Southampton was John Foxholes.

[55] *PPC*, ii. 298–9, iii. 42; E 404/39/140.

upwards of £3,700 p.a., on which the only substantial charge was the cost of the household, perhaps of the order of £1,500 p.a.[56] The revenues of the bishopric alone thus placed him in the ranks of the higher nobility, and there is little doubt that under Beaufort they were carefully managed.[57] Moreover, unlike the lay nobility, he did not face the cost of equipping himself for war, although he financed his 'pilgrimage' from his own resources. Nor, prior to 1421, had he made any significant purchases of lands or undertaken any major building projects. Yet even if his surplus income from his see had been allowed to accumulate as jewels, plate, and cash, it is unlikely that by 1417 it could have reached from this source alone at least £25,000 and by 1421 over £30,000 in coin. Where else could it have come from ?

Usury on his loans to the crown may be ruled out, simply because these had been neither sufficiently large nor numerous to have yielded such an increase of his fortune. Spread over thirteen years before 1417, they had totalled only £6,876. All had been repaid within a few months from the lay and clerical taxes and the duchy of Lancaster estates, like those of other lenders, and advances of this type carried no interest. Nor are the grounds for crediting him with large-scale trading ventures, licit or illicit, any stronger. Although he had been deeply involved in Anglo-Flemish trade negotiations, and was well known to the leading Staplers, the customs accounts afford no evidence that he was exporting wool, and his first licence to do so comes ten years later. Not before 1417 did he have the nomination of one of the collectors in Southampton for the repayment of his loans, and that in itself is no ground for suspecting him of evasion of the customs. On the other hand it is certain that the six years during which he occupied the office of chancellor must have presented many opportunities for personal enrichment. Although he received few grants of profit from the crown, he would have been the recipient of a constant stream of fees and gifts of all kinds for his goodwill. A careful husbandry of his receipts from land and office could have made Beaufort a rich man in his own right, but there is the further possibility that what he loaned to the crown was not strictly his own.

According to a well-informed chronicler, his eldest brother's will committed to his hands £20,000 in cash. Clarence laid claim to half of this in respect of his marriage to Earl John's widow and the custody of his heir,

[56] *Valor Ecclesiasticus*, ed. J. Caley and J. Hunter, ii. 2; W. E. Lunt, *Financial Relations of the Papacy with England, 1327–1534*, 792, 829. For the income of the bishopric from the pipe rolls, see Appendix III. There is no evidence for the cost of Beaufort's household. It is likely to have been nearer the £2,392 of Archbishop Stratford's and the £1,849 of Humphrey earl of Stafford's than the £300 of Bishop Bourchier of Worcester. See F. R. H. Du Boulay, *The Lordship of Canterbury*, 256–7; C. Rawcliffe, *The Staffords*, 46; C. Dyer, *Lords and Peasants in a Changing Society*, 200.

[57] In 1408 his officers' exactions had produced riots at Taunton: *CPR 1408–13*, 179 (I owe this reference to Mr G. Belfield).

and the matter was put to arbitration.[58] How much Beaufort retained, and how he used the money apart from the payments he undertook to make for the sustenance of John's heirs, cannot be known. It is at least possible that part of the loan which Henry V extracted from him was not strictly his but was the inheritance of the young Henry, earl of Somerset, still a minor in 1417, and that of his surviving brother John who in 1421 was held prisoner in France.

The first indication of Beaufort's restoration to royal favour was the king's visit to Farnham in May 1421. With Henry V's return to France Beaufort took his seat as a regular member of the council, at first under Bedford and from April 1422 under Duke Humphrey. Although its business is well recorded, the names of those attending are given only occasionally. Beaufort appears alongside Chichele, Bubwith, Langley, and Morgan throughout July 1421, when he rendered judgement in the dispute between the countess of Arundel and Lady Bergevenny over the possession of Bromfield and Yale. He spent August and September on the episcopal manors in Hampshire and Somerset and reappeared in council on 13 October. Following the birth of Prince Henry on 6 December, he and Bedford stood godfather to the infant.[59] Five days earlier parliament had met and, uniquely of all medieval parliaments, granted on the first day a whole subsidy, payable in two halves at February and November 1422, even before electing its Speaker. Presumably this was in fulfilment of a promise given by its predecessor, and it was perhaps designed to coincide with the birth of Henry V's heir. The Speaker, Richard Baynard, may have had connections with Beaufort through the family of Fitzwalter, the custody of whose lands had been committed to Beaufort as executor of John, earl of Somerset. Langley, Beaufort, and Bubwith were triers of petitions. Both parliament and council were preoccupied during the winter months with problems of the recoinage, with settling a significant number of property disputes which posed threats to the peace, and with investigating and reforming the finances of Calais. All these were the aftermath of Henry V's visit, from whom came a stream of signet letters rendering justice or awarding patronage to petitioners.[60] The repayment of his great loan had meanwhile begun at an encouraging rate. By the end of 1421 he had recovered £3,099 from the Southampton customs, £612 from his custody of the lands of Henry Beaumont, and £446 from arrears of the

[58] *Chron. Angl.* 62.

[59] HRO Eccles. II, 159422; *PPC* ii. 286–97, 303; E 28/35; C 81/1543/34, 35, 37. He was at Marwell on 10 Aug., Taunton on 1 Sept.: *Reg. CS* 62.

[60] For Fitzwalter see *CPR 1413–16*, 170, *CPR, 1416–22*; 78. In July 1422 Beaufort, with John Leventhorpe, Lewis John, Robert Darcy, and Richard Baynard also had custody of the lands of Thomas Coggeshall and the marriage of the heir: *CPR 1416–22*, 440; *CFR 1413–22*, 437. *Rot Parl.* iv. 151, 154–6, 159–63. For Calais, see *PPC* ii. 310, 317, 363; PRO acquisition 30/26/184–5; E 101/187/3, 4. For disputes, see *PPC* ii. 306, 321, 333; *CPR 1416–22*, 413; for recoinage, *PPC* ii. 317–8, 324, 332; for royal warrants, *CSL* 185–7.

clerical tenth.[61] But though busy once more in the affairs of the council and able to prosecute his own interests, Beaufort had to all appearances been reduced to the status of just one among a group of hard working servants of a determined king.

At the same time he had begun to rebuild Martin V's confidence in him. He ingratiated himself with the papal collector, Simon of Teramo, who had been so bold as to commend to convocation the papal claims to provisions. Martin had been led to expect that Henry V would raise the matter in parliament during his visit, but neither there nor in parliament is there any record of discussion, and when the royal envoy, Nicholas Bildeston, returned to the papal court, to Martin's surprise and chagrin he made no mention of it. Bildeston may not yet have formally joined Beaufort's service, but he was already a close acquaintance of Poggio, whose own friendship with Simon of Teramo surely assisted Beaufort's cultivation of the papal collector. Certainly Simon carried back to Rome warm recommendations of Beaufort as 'keen and vigilant for the honour of the Holy See and the liberty of the church in England' and in return Martin exhorted Beaufort to 'restore the church in England to her former liberty' and promised future rewards for good service.[62] English interests at the Curia were still handled by Catrik and Polton, both strong supporters of Beaufort. Catrik had received backing from the Curia in his bid for the see of Salisbury in 1417 and Polton secured that of Hereford in 1420 when Lacy, a favoured royal chaplain, was translated to Exeter. It was through Polton that Beaufort had procured his exemption from Canterbury's jurisdiction, and Chichele believed that Polton was traducing him at the papal court.[63] Martin V probably thought the archbishop too much the king's creature, and saw his spirited defence of the rights of his see as a potential obstruction to papal authority; there was friction between them over a wide range of issues.[64]

Chichele's close attendance on Henry V in France during 1419–20 had served him well. He was able to promote his protégé John Kemp to the sees of Rochester, Chichester, and London in quick succession, and to secure Rochester in 1421 for John Langdon, a monk of Christchurch, against the papal designation of Spofford, another client of Beaufort at the Curia. The contest between the royal and papal candidates over Rochester was only resolved by Clifford's death in August 1421, which enabled Kemp

[61] E 401/696, 699, 702.

[62] *Reg. Chichele*, i. p. xlii; iii. 66; J. Haller, *England und Rom unter Martin V*, 260, 302 suppl. 3, and letter of 6 Dec. 1421, suppl. 1.

[63] *Foedera*, ix. 487; *Chichele Reg.* i. p. xliv; McFarlane, *England in XV Century*, 84.

[64] Thus, Martin's release of the spiritualities to Fleming and Polton before their oath of obedience to Chichele; his refusal to accept Chichele's candidate for the see of Lisieux, and to sanction the celebration of St Thomas's jubilee: *Reg. Chichele*, i. xliii–iv; Jacob, *Henry Chichele*, 44–8.

to be moved from Chichester to London and Polton from Hereford to Chichester, thus vacating Hereford for Spofford. For a time Henry V withheld consent to the consecration of Spofford, who failed to secure it from the bishops whom he approached. Eventually, on 24 May 1422 Beaufort consecrated him at Blackfriars and secured his acceptance by the Hereford chapter. He also paid for his feast; not surprisingly Spofford looked to Beaufort as his 'protector singularissimus'.[65] Ostensibly, then, Beaufort stood at the head of a 'papal party' in the episcopate, but this had small substance or reality. These were second-rate sees, and those appointed were able opportunists rather than men of stature. It was royal servants like Fleming and Morgan who secured Lincoln and Worcester in 1419, just as on a lesser scale it was the nominees of king and archbishop who secured the archdeaconries and prebends which fell vacant in the dioceses of Salisbury, Wells, and Chichester in which Beaufort looked to exercise patronage.[66] Though he might try to persuade Martin of his zeal and influence through the reports of his friends and clients at the Curia, Beaufort knew full well that the king was, and meant to be, master of his church and would determine the limits of papal power within it.

Suspicion and frustration had marked relations between the king and the pope over the past two years. Faced with Henry's intransigence over provisions, Martin maintained his refusal to condemn the dauphin or recognize the treaty of Troyes, and tried steadily to build up support among the English episcopate. Yet Martin's demonstration of papal authority in the case of Rochester had made his point: as he said, Henry V could not always expect the pope to do what he wanted, for the pope was only asking for what was just and due to him, and Henry, whom God had exalted, should remember that all kings and kingdoms were in God's hands. In the last year of Henry's life there were signs that the respective interests of pope and king would require the resumption of negotiations. Martin was pressing Henry not only to review the statute of provisors but to receive the mission of Cardinal Albergati for the establishment of peace with the dauphin as a prelude to a Hussite crusade. It was later claimed that Henry had been ready to consider both matters, though whether he would have been willing to barter control over his bishops for anything less than full papal recognition of his title to the French throne must remain doubtful.[67] As he consolidated his hold on northern France and awaited

[65] Haller, *England u. Rom*, 260; *Reg. Chichele*, loc. cit., *Register of Thomas Spofford*, ed. A. T. Bannister, 5, 28: 'protector singularissime vestre dominacionis benignitas, que me in singulis meis peragendis negotiis favoribus prevenit gratissimis'. He asks Beaufort for 'vestre sanum et salubre consilium et auxilium'.

[66] *CSL* nos. 813, 823, 830.

[67] *Foedera*, ix. 730, 806–7; Wylie and Waugh, *Henry V*, iii. 171, 374–7; G. du Fresne de Beaucourt, *Histoire de Charles VII*, i. 327–31; Harriss, 'Henry Beaufort, Cardinal of England', 121.

the death of Charles VI he may have felt that his position would strengthen further; yet sooner or later the talking would have to start and Bishop Beaufort might then expect to resume his role as intermediary. As it happened the king's sudden death transformed the domestic and international situation and placed Beaufort's ambitions in a wholly different context.

6

The Establishment of Conciliar Government, 1422–1424

HENRY V's sudden death faced the nobility with two major questions: how was the war to be continued, and how was England to be governed? On neither did the dying king leave detailed instructions. The military problem was probably foremost in the minds of Bedford, Exeter, and Warwick, who attended the deathbed, and the burden of Henry's advice to Bedford as regent of France seems to have been broadly defensive: to maintain the Burgundian alliance, to hold Normandy at all costs and make no peace which would not guarantee it to the English, and to release no important prisoners until his son came of age.[1] Nor did the king attempt to prescribe the forms of government at home. His last recorded thoughts are in the codicils to his will made on 26 August, dealing with the disposal of his residual chattels, wards, and ships. Two sentences, conferring the 'chief guardianship and protection of our dearest son' ('tutelam et defensionem nostri carissimi filii principales') on Humphrey, duke of Gloucester, and 'the rule and governance of his person' ('persone sue regimen et gubernationem') on Thomas, duke of Exeter, are embedded in detailed clauses bequeathing all the king's plate, chapel furniture, and books to his heir.[2] It is clear that in these codicils the king's thoughts were on the custody of his infant heir and his personal effects, and that the *tutela* conferred on Gloucester related solely to these. Gloucester's interpretation of his charge as extending to the government and administration of the kingdom, as the property of the king, though it gave some trouble to the council, was never accepted by them as Henry V's intention. Nor could ambiguity have been intended, for Henry's secretary William Alnwick, who was at his bedside and must have been well aware of the legal implications of the term *tutela* in civil law, evidently did not foresee the contention over it.[3]

[1] Wylie and Waugh, *Henry V*, iii. 417; J. S. Roskell, 'The Office and Dignity of Protector of England, with special reference to its origins', in *Parliament and Politics*, i. 200–1.

[2] P. and F. Strong, 'The last will and codicils of Henry V', *EHR*, 96 (1981), 99–100. It is worth emphasizing that these were very distinct functions. Exeter's task was the rule and education of the young king and he had the keeping of his body (cf. Tito Livio cited by Roskell, *Parliament and Politics*, 201) while Gloucester was given the guardianship of his interests and property and responsibility for his safety. Various chronicles attribute a share in the upbringing of the king to Bishop Beaufort, the earl of Warwick, and Sir Walter Hungerford: Roskell, ibid. 201–2, 205–7.

[3] For an exposition of the legal implications of *tutela*, see Roskell, *Parliament and Politics*, 206. For Alnwick's presence, see *PPC* iii. 248. Alnwick was a DCL and a Notary Public by papal authority: *BRUO* i. 11.

During September, when the obsequies had been performed and while the cortège to convey the king's body to England was being assembled, discussion must have taken place about the future pattern of government. Burgundy's withdrawal and the death of Charles VI put Bedford's position as regent of France beyond dispute. In England Gloucester's authority as *Custos Angliae* was deemed to have ended and the lords of the council who assumed authority to summon parliament and renew official appointments in Henry VI's name recognized that they did so under an authority that was provisional until confirmed by parliament.[4] Gloucester had accepted a summons to parliament on these terms, but at the first full meeting of the council after the return of the cortège, on 5 November, he intimated his claim to a greater authority, protesting that it would be contrary to his 'status et libertas' to receive the power to open and dissolve parliament 'de assensu concilii'.[5] A letter from the duke of Bedford to the city of London which would have arrived at this point suggests that he was already apprised of Gloucester's pretensions. In it Bedford asserted his own right to pre-eminence in England, the governance of which belonged to him as nearest in blood to the late king and according to the 'lawes and ancient usage and custome of the same reaulme'. Warning the citizens to 'geve in noo wyse assent, conseil ne confort' to any proposals against such laws and customs and his own rights, he nevertheless disclaimed any intention of going against 'the ordinaunce or wil of oure saide soveraine lord that was, savyng our right, to the which as we trowe and truste fully that hit was not our saide soverain lordes entente to deroge or doo prejudice'.[6] It is plain that Bedford had been alerted, albeit belatedly, to the construction which Gloucester was intending to place upon the codicil bestowing upon him the *tutela* of Henry VI. Evidently news of the contents of the will and codicil must have spread beyond the circle of those at the deathbed to the council in England long before the cortège itself arrived.

The will and codicils were only openly read following Henry V's burial on 10 November but, perhaps deterred by Bedford's warning, Gloucester did not then lay claim to the regency and the lords of the council gave formal assent to the codicil and requested Gloucester to take up his charge, which they clearly interpreted as strictly applying to Henry VI's person.[7] Chichele's sermon at the opening of parliament on 9 November likewise reflected the assumption that the government would be through a council of all estates along the lines of Richard II's minority, though he carefully

[4] Roskell, *Parliament and Politics*, 196–7.

[5] *Rot. Parl.* iv. 169; Roskell, op. cit. 197–8.

[6] R. H. Sharpe, *London and the Kingdom*, iii. 367; and in *Collection générale des documents francais qui se trouvent en Angleterre*, ed. J. Delpit, i. 232–3.

[7] Gloucester's memorandum was printed by S. B. Chrimes, 'The pretensions of the duke of Gloucester in 1422', *EHR* 45 (1930), 102–3.

left the nature of its headship undefined.[8] Gloucester's claim was first openly advanced in response to the Commons' request early in the parliament to know who should have the governance of the realm under the king, and was made on grounds of his birth and Henry V's will. For some three weeks the lords debated the issue, concluding that 'for divers causes' they dared not agree to the employment of the term *tutela* in any commission giving Gloucester powers of government, and denying that Henry V had power to devise the governance or rule of the land after his death. Nor did they find Gloucester's claim to the regency well grounded in precedent or the law of the land.[9] These objections had all been foreshadowed in Bedford's letter. In endeavouring to meet them, Gloucester again appealed to the terms of the codicil, arguing that the title proposed for him, 'Defender and Chief Councillor', did not adequately meet these terms or the Commons' desire for a 'governour', and proposing William Marshal's title of *Rector Regni.*[10] But the lords were not to be moved, and by 5 December he had bowed to their decision and agreed to accept the title of 'Protector and Defender' during pleasure.

All along Gloucester had been advancing his claim against the settled policy of the principal lords that government should be committed to a named council. Those who had led the opposition to Gloucester were Exeter, March, Warwick, and Bishop Beaufort, the first three of whom had been with Bedford at Henry V's deathbed. Of these Exeter was first in dignity and importance; to him had been committed the rule and upbringing of the young king and he knew and must have represented Bedford's wishes to the council. But it may well have been the bishop who, in late September or early October, having got wind of Gloucester's intentions, conveyed these directly or through his brother to Bedford in Normandy. Hardyng credited the Beauforts with leading the opposition, and it was probably Henry who organized the search into precedents and the law of the land. He too may have persuaded the Commons that Gloucester's claim to the regency was 'against the right and freedom of the estates of the same land' and secured their acceptance of the lesser title.[11] The Speaker, Roger Flore, had previously occupied the office in November 1416 when Beaufort was chancellor, as also in 1417 and 1419 under the duke of Bedford. With Beaufort he had been a feoffee for the will of the late duke of York, and as chief steward of the duchy of Lancaster north of Trent was to be closely involved with the feoffees for Henry V's will. The feoffees' receiver-general, John Leventhorpe, also sat in this parliament, as did Beaufort's retainers John Golafre and Thomas

[8] Roskell, *Parliament and Politics*, 208–9.
[9] Ibid. 210–11.
[10] Gloucester's memorandum, loc. cit. n. 7 above; Roskell, op. cit. 213–14.
[11] *Rot. Parl.* iv. 326.

Chaucer.[12] It would nevertheless be wrong to exaggerate the bishop's influence, which in general was less than that of his younger brother in the eyes of both Bedford and Gloucester.

Bishop Beaufort must have reacted to the news of Henry V's death with distress and bewilderment, followed by expectancy. Henry had restored the English crown to its former greatness, and Beaufort, like others, saw this as evidence of divine approval and protection for one who had consciously striven to fulfil the ideal of Christian kingship. Even in an age which accepted untimely death as God's inscrutable purpose, the removal of His minister when poised to unite the two mortal enemies of Christendom in a perpetual peace must have shaken the confidence of those who had been persuaded by the king's vision. Yet Henry V's political heirs had no choice but to dedicate themselves to the realization of his great purpose. Their devotion to his memory and inspiration was underpinned by the recognition that withdrawal or defeat would call into question the legitimacy of Lancastrian rule abroad and at home. Co-operation and continued service was inescapable for all Henry V's lieutenants, but more especially for those of the royal blood. Here the king's demise had improved the bishop's prospects. He whom Beaufort rightly regarded as in many respects his pupil had also proved his master, depriving him of his anticipated reward and sharply reminding him that his role was that of a royal servant. Though spared public and material punishment, his ambition and self-confidence had been severely shaken and he had returned to a muted and subsidiary role in Henry V's council. He had swallowed his resentment and learned circumspection, but the crisis in his relations with the king must have deepened his jealousy of his other nephews of the full blood. Now, with the king an infant, the bishop was determined that his relationship with Gloucester and Bedford was to be one of partnership, or substantial equality, and not one of obedience. Gloucester's claim to be regent and accountable only to the king was probably felt as a threat by many, but by none more than Bishop Beaufort. In conciliar rule and shared responsibility he saw safety, and the opportunity to recover his own influence and standing.

The council named in parliament on 9 December 1422 was mainly composed of those who had the confidence of the late king. At the time of Henry's death Exeter, March, Warwick, and the Earl Marshal had all been serving in Normandy. So, among the bishops, had Kemp, while Chichele, Beaufort, Langley, Wakering, and Morgan each had long and distinguished careers as royal administrators and diplomats. They were reinforced before the end of the year by the appointment of John Stafford as treasurer and William Alnwick as keeper of the privy seal, both of a

[12] J. S. Roskell, *The Commons and their Speakers in Medieval English Parliaments*, 178–80; id. *Parliament and Politics*, iii. 255–64.

younger generation and marked out for bishoprics. Stafford had ties with Chichele, Beaufort, and the chancellor, Langley; Alnwick had been Henry V's secretary. Below the greater nobility Lord Fitzhugh, Sir Walter Hungerford, Sir Walter Beauchamp, and Sir John Tiptoft had all been household officials; the first three were among Henry V's executors, and the last three had all been Speakers of the Commons. With all these men, whose abilities, wealth, and tried service in war, administration, and parliament marked them out for promotion to the peerage, Beaufort already enjoyed close connections. Hungerford, his co-feoffee in the estates of the duchies of York and Lancaster, was to be joint overseer with him of Bishop Bubwith's will and joint custodian of the temporalities of Bath and Wells. Beauchamp, an old associate of the Beauforts in Henry IV's household, had been Speaker in the parliament of March 1416. He was likewise a co-feoffee for Henry V's will, in which his sister Elizabeth figured as a beneficiary if she married by the advice of the two Beauforts; when she did it was to their nephew Thomas Swynford. Tiptoft had recovered favour with Henry V only in the second half of the reign, but in 1422 his marriage to Joyce, coheir of Edward, Lord Charleton of Powys, whose mother Eleanor Holand was sister to the duchess of Clarence, linked him into the Beaufort circle where his familiarity with Burgundian-imperial diplomacy was also appreciated. All three men were also substantial landowners in the south-west. The fifth member of this group, Ralph, Lord Cromwell, had a different background, having come to France in the retinue of the duke of Clarence, who had made him captain of Pontoise and named him one of his executors. Although Henry V had appointed him one of the negotiators of the treaty of Troyes and later governor of Charles VI, it may have been through Exeter's influence that he had been given the captaincy of Harfleur and now entered the council. He was soon to emerge as a close associate of Bishop Beaufort.[13]

The council was not merely formally balanced between the three estates; it contained equally strong groups of household servants, administrators and diplomats, and soldiers. The interests of Normandy and the northern marches were both well represented, while the clerical element, reinforced by officials, was matched numerically by the lay. Above all it comprised those whom the late king had selected for their fidelity and abilities, who knew his objectives and were committed to their fulfilment. In the first year of its existence it strove consciously to avoid factionalism and maintain continuity in policy and membership. Up to the middle of 1423, while the council was defining the structure of government and making provision for its financial commitments, it met almost daily and attendances were large.

[13] For their careers: A. C. Reeves, *Lancastrian Englishmen*, 65–119; Roskell, *Parliament and Politics*, ii. 95–136, iii. 107–50; R. L. Friedrichs, 'The career and influence of Ralph, Lord Cromwell, 1393–1456', Ph.D. thesis (Columbia, 1974).

Only the Earl Marshal, Lord Fitzhugh, and Sir Walter Beauchamp were infrequently present and the presence of thirteen councillors in addition to the officers was not unusual. Thereafter the withdrawal of Exeter, the Earl Marshal, and Hungerford to France, of Northumberland and Westmorland to the border, and of Kemp to Normandy helped to give greater prominence to the clerical and knightly element and prompted a new nomination of the council in parliament early in 1424. This introduced Lord Scrope, Thomas Chaucer, and William Alington, though only the first attended regularly.[14] The addition of Chaucer and Alington gave further coherence and weight to the Beaufort–Cromwell influence in the council. Chaucer brought diplomatic and parliamentary experience, and the marriage of his daughter Alice to the earl of Salisbury late in 1424 linked him to the greater peerage. Alington had been treasurer of Normandy under Henry V; he was a long-standing servant and executor of Clarence, who had enfeoffed him, together with Cromwell and both the Beauforts, in his estates in the East Riding and Lincolnshire, which they conveyed in 1423 to a syndicate to discharge the duke's debts. At the same time Alington was Cromwell's feoffee in Tattershall, along with Kemp, William Philip, and John Tiptoft. In July 1424 they conveyed it to Cromwell and Bishops Beaufort and Langley, Lord Scrope, Walter Hungerford, and others to the use of Cromwell and his wife, with remainder to Beaufort and Langley.[15] Clearly this section of the council had close working relations with each other based partly upon their local interests and partly as followers of Clarence.

They were also beginning to organize the distribution of patronage. In November 1423 the temporalities of the see of York were committed to Cromwell and Sir William Harrington (Exeter's follower) at farm, and Cromwell also had the farm of Somerton (Lincs.), formerly held by the duke of Clarence, while Cromwell and Scrope acted as the mainpernors of Sir Walter Hungerford for the grant of the wardship and marriage of Philip Courtenay. In February 1424 Tiptoft received custody of two-thirds of the Ingoldsthorpe lands and Cromwell secured the farm of the manor of Bolsover.[16] The Beauforts seem to have strengthened their interests mainly in Wales. In February 1423 Exeter was appointed justice in North Wales while he and the bishop were given joint custody of Carmarthen priory. In November 1423 the bishop's son-in-law, Sir Edward Stradling, was appointed chamberlain and receiver of South Wales, and a year later steward and receiver of Cantreselly and Penkelly.[17] This evidence for a

[14] For membership of the council, see *Rot. Parl.* iv. 175, 201; *PPC* iii. *passim* and C 81/1544; also A. L. Brown, 'Privy Seal' thesis, ii. 259, appendix VIII. Biographies of Chaucer and Alington are in Roskell, *Parliament and Politics*, iii. 151–92, 317–30.

[15] *PPC* iii. 30–5; *CPR 1422–9*, 59–60, 212.

[16] *CFR 1422–30*, 39, 59, 63, 73, 76; E 28/44.

[17] *CPR 1422–9*, 63, 128, 168, 254, 257; *PPC* iii. 24, 129; R. A. Griffiths, 'The rise of the Stradlyngs of St Donats', *Morgannwg*, 7 (1963), 15–47.

surge in the influence of the bishop and his associates after the middle of 1423 followed the withdrawal of his brother from the council for a period and preceded the first of his own loans to the minority government. It prefigured his appointment as chancellor on Langley's resignation in July 1424.

The grip which Beaufort and his associates were establishing on the work of the council was also reflected in the new procedures for the conduct of business, introduced in the parliament of 1423–4. On its appointment in 1422 the council had confined its procedural rules to the requirements that the protector's advice be sought on all matters normally referred to the king, and that the majority of the councillors be present for great matters and a quorum for those of lesser importance, their names being recorded. At the same time the council asserted its right to appoint all the principal local officials and to control all the fiscal prerogatives of the crown. On its reappointment in the 1423–4 parliament more detailed procedures were introduced to take account of the pressures of individual interests and differences over policy during the past year. To prevent individual members answering petitions these were to be read before the whole council each Wednesday; nor was the council to determine petitions for which the common law provided redress. The requirement for a quorum on all except urgent matters, and for the unanimity of the officers of state was reaffirmed, and all matters on which a unanimous decision could not be secured were to be postponed until a majority of the council was present. All communications with foreign powers were to be in the name of the whole council and any disputes which arose between lords were to be submitted to the protector and the council, who undertook to resolve them impartially.[18] These regulations were a response to some of the developments of the past year: the competition for patronage, Gloucester's pursuit of his wife's interests in Hainault, and the renewed feud of the earl of Warwick and Lord Berkeley. How far the council had itself been split in its deliberations the records do not reveal, but these resolutions show that the majority of the councillors recognized the dangers of factionalism and the necessity for corporate responsibility if the objectives of Henry V were to be achieved. If Beaufort was beginning to gather support it was as much for his commitment to the principle of conciliar authority and his financial and diplomatic skills as by his organization of a following within the council.

Having asserted its corporate responsibility against the protector and having grasped the levers of power, the first task of the council was to take stock of its financial resources and obligations. The most pressing of these was the debt to Calais, which stood at £28,718 at the end of 1421 and had been only marginally reduced in the following year. The authorization of an immediate payment of 2,000 marks on 21 December 1422, increased to

[18] *Rot. Parl.* iv. 176, 201; *PPC* iii. 148–52.

£2,000 in January and £5,000 in February when Warwick renewed his indentures, showed the council's growing awareness of the garrison's truculence. Although parliament confirmed the appropriation of one mark from the customs for Calais in all ports except Southampton, where Beaufort's prior claim was reserved, Calais received no payments from the exchequer and late in March or early in April the garrison mutinied and seized the wool. This was redeemed by the Company of the Staple for £4,000, the council giving obligations on the customs in repayment. In the following year Calais received almost £16,000 from the exchequer and the council undertook to increase the Calais part of the subsidy if and when parliament raised the rates of the customs.[19] The other standing charges for defence were less onerous and less pressing. New indentures were entered with the earl of March as lieutenant in Ireland for nine years at 4,000 marks p.a., with Sir John Radclyf as seneschal of Guyenne and captain of Fronsac at an annual charge of £3,406, with the earl of Northumberland for the East March at £2,500 p.a., with Sir Richard Nevill for the West March at £2,150 p.a., and with Lord Greystoke for the keeping of Roxburgh castle at £1,000 p.a. All these were at economical peacetime rates, and the council aimed to secure continuity of service by prompt payment and a steady discharge of their arrears.[20]

It was even more important to demonstrate its commitment to the war in France. The temporary recapture of Meulan by the French in January 1423 augured a spring offensive, while Bedford was concerned to consolidate the Anglo-Burgundian position in the north. For this, and for the defence of Champagne, he asked for reinforcements, and by March the council had indented with Exeter, Norfolk, Willoughby, and Hungerford for one year's service from early May with a force of 380 men at arms and 1,140 archers.[21] Exeter's ill health delayed his sailing. In April 1423 he was reputed to be 'grievously ill' and unable to attend the Garter ceremonies, and though sufficiently recovered by mid-May to attend the council and intending to cross the Channel, it was not until mid-July that he sailed. For the next eighteen months his whereabouts remain unknown. Though summoned to parliament in November 1423, it is not certain that he attended and his omission from the peace commissions suggests either absence or incapacity. He reappeared in council only in 1425. The leadership of the force thus fell to the Earl Marshal who, with Lord Willoughby, helped Salisbury win the battle of Cravant on 30 July.[22] That guaranteed the Anglo-

[19] *PPC* iii. 2, 19, 40–51, 67–95; E 28/40 27 Apr.; E 403/661, 28 Apr.; H. L. Ratcliffe, 'The military expenditure of the English crown, 1422–1435', M.Litt. thesis (Oxford, 1979), 112–15.

[20] *PPC* iii. 44, 49, 68, 162–3; E 28/41; E 404/39/280. For payment to these charges, see Ratcliffe, thesis, 131–2, 148, 173, 177.

[21] *PPC* iii. 37–8, 67; E 28/39 9 Mar.; *CPR 1422–9*, 121.

[22] For Exeter in council, see C 81/1544/32 (13 May); Brown, thesis, ii. 259; *PPC* iii. 86, 101, 113 (10 July). The army mustered at Dover in late May: E 404/39/317; E 403/661 11 June; Archer, 'The Mowbrays', thesis, 204. Exeter sailed from Sandwich in July: E 101/51/7; E 403/661 17 July.

Burgundian ascendancy in eastern France and gave substance to the alliance between Bedford and Duke Philip, personalized in Bedford's marriage to Anne and the triple league with Duke Jean of Brittany.

Before indenting for service both Exeter and the Earl Marshal claimed payment of their arrears from the council. Exeter elected to receive £600 due to him from the Agincourt campaign from Henry V's goods, while the 1,000 marks claimed by the Earl Marshal was paid to him by Bishop Beaufort, who recouped this from the plate and movables of the late king.[23] Under Henry V's will his executors were to sell these for the discharge of his debts, but the council had redeemed them for the sum of 40,000 marks, paid to the executors. The Beauforts' eagerness to acquire some of the late king's effects for themselves was understandable and it served to discharge the council's obligations. Henry V's death precipitated a demand for the discharge of debts which he himself had been able to disregard, and throughout 1423 the council and the treasurer were dealing with numerous claims for wages of war and payment for supplies.[24] For the sake of his soul and his honour, as well as for its own credit, the council was bound to try and honour these obligations. Parliament further authorized the assignment of dower for 10,000 marks to Henry's widow, and honoured Henry V's verbal livery of lands to the earl of Stafford without charge, while the council accepted Exeter's testimony that the late king had expressed remorse over his seizure of Lord Scrope's entailed lands and authorized their restoration.[25] It is within this context of the council's consistent concern to honour the wishes, promises, and obligations of Henry V that we must examine the repayment of Bishop Beaufort's loans.

At Henry V's death Beaufort was owed £8,306. 18*s*. 8*d*. from the loan of 1417 and £11,513. 18*s*. 3*d*. from those of 1421. His patent, which gave him the receipt of all the customs and subsidies in Southampton, provided for the extension of this to London and other ports 'if it should happen that by reason of war or ordinance or any other contingent cause whatsoever the course or exercise of merchandise in the aforesaid ports should have ceased, or that the merchants seeking access to the aforesaid port should have been hindered or disturbed to the detriment of the customs or subsidies in the same port'.[26] In renewing the wool subsidy on 18 December 1422 the Commons reduced the rate for denizens from 50*s*. to 40*s*. and abolished tunnage and poundage. Probably in anticipation of this, Beaufort had a month previously been granted the custom on alien and cloth exports in London and five other ports, in which he was empowered to nominate one of the collectors, and had received his first payment from

[23] *PPC* iii. 60, 101; J. L. Kirby, 'An account of Robert Southwell . . . 1422–3', *BIHR* 27 (1954), 192–8, citing BL Add. Ch. 17209.

[24] *Rot. Parl.* iv. 178. Crown jewels redeemed: *PPC* iii. 115, 124, 145; E 28/44 21 Feb. Other debts: E 404/39/347; E 404/40/176, 202.

[25] *Rot. Parl.* iv. 183, 195; *PPC* iii. 26; E 28/42 13 June.

[26] *Rot. Parl.* iv. 134 (trans.).

Hull by indenture on 8 December. Then on 16 February the council reduced the alien subsidy from 63*s.* 4*d.* to 53*s.* 4*d.* and on 8 February Beaufort's patent was extended to cover these same customs in other ports but also, crucially, the subsidy on wool in London. It was this last which was challenged in council a week later, as being contrary to the Commons' appropriation of the subsidy strictly for the defence of the realm. However, the law officers ruled that Beaufort's loan had been made for this purpose, thereby establishing the important precedent that his loans could in future be secured on this revenue.[27] Since wool exports from London in 1422–4 numbered 11,993 sacks against Southampton's 1,363, this gave him immeasurably quicker repayment of his loan. Without this extension it is unlikely that the debt to Beaufort would ever have been cleared; for after 1422, due to the decrease of customs duties, the grant of an annuity of 500 marks to the queen, and the decline of exports from Michaelmas 1423, the clear yield of the Southampton customs fell from an average of £2,000 p.a. to a mere £563 p.a. in 1422–6. In London however the clear yield of the customs from Michaelmas 1423 to Easter 1426 was £22,615. Between February 1423 and May 1425 the payment of £17,594 to Beaufort cleared the loans of 1417 and 1421. Beaufort's 'long commission' on the ports was thus neither so embracing in its terms nor so opportunistic in its timing as McFarlane suggested.[28] Undoubtedly Henry V's death enabled him to press claims which might otherwise have been disregarded until he would have been induced to compound them for a lesser sum. But this was equally true of many lesser creditors whom the council now sought to satisfy for the sake of political harmony. It may also have been mindful of the other clause in Beaufort's patent which permitted him to retain the gold crown if he had not been repaid within a year of the king's death. Beaufort had a real grievance and a real lever which it would have been unwise to ignore.

The council had also shown itself determined to continue Henry V's pattern of sound finance. At the time of his death there was £6,000 in the exchequer of receipt and for the first eighteen months of the new reign the inflow of cash was maintained at the preceding high level, helped by the collection of the lay and clerical half-subsidies granted in 1421, while assignmements were kept down and fictitious loans were not substantial.[29] The council granted no new annuities and throughout 1423 showed its determination to maximize revenue from the fiscal prerogatives. Heavy fines were imposed on those who alienated lands or married without

[27] *CFR 1422–30*, 18–20; *PPC* iii. 34–5; *Rot. Parl.* iv. 173–4.

[28] *Eng. Export Trade*, 57; E 356/18 m. 10–11, 26–7; E 401/677, 696; E 403/658, 660, 663, 666, 669, 671. Cf. McFarlane, *England in XV Century*, 122–4.

[29] Steel, *Receipt*, 166, 440, 459. The council ordered collection of the taxes granted in 1421: C 81/1544/21; *CFR 1422–30*, 4.

licence; the sale of some wardships and marriages brought notable gains to the exchequer and the lands of Lords Roos and Nevill, in the king's hands, furnished part of the salary of the protector.[30] In March 1423 it was ordained that all farms of 10 marks and above had to be negotiated with the treasurer, as did all wardships and marriages after June 1424.[31] Finally the buoyancy of royal finance was assisted by the continuing boom in wool exports following the treaty of Troyes, which averaged 16,600 sacks p.a. in 1422–4.

The council was thus able, without apparent strain, to find £12,000 in cash for the reinforcements sent to Bedford in 1423 under the Earl Marshal and Lord Willoughby, but by 1424 it was beginning to feel the effects of diminished taxation.[32] No tax had been sought in the first parliament of the reign, and the Commons' mood had been reflected in their reduction of the wool subsidy for denizens. But the council undoubtedly hoped for a grant from the second parliament in October 1423 and when, at the end of eight weeks during which the Commons had been informed of the 'busoignes et grandes necessitees' of the realm, nothing had been granted, the protector dispatched them for the Christmas recess in order that they should notify their communities and make provision on their return. Yet again the session ended on 28 February 1424 with no grant of direct taxation, merely the renewal of the wool subsidy at the existing rates on 8 February.[33] The Commons must have been well aware of the military requirements, for the council had already begun negotiations with captains, and on the very day of this grant it indented for a force of 400 men at arms and 1,200 archers for six months' service commencing on 1 May. It was with these troops, led by the earl of Warwick and Lords Willoughby and Poynings, that Bedford won the battle of Verneuil on 17 August. The total cost of the expedition was, as in 1423, about £12,000, equivalent to one-third of a lay subsidy.[34] The tight-fistedness of the Commons left the council with no option but to raise this by a loan on the security of the customs, £9,333 of the total of £11,944 being loaned by Bishop Beaufort and the remainder by Archbishop Chichele and eight others.

The terms had been settled by the council on 26–8 February and on 1 March Beaufort's loan was paid into the exchequer.[35] At that date his loan of 1421 had been fully repaid but he was still owed £8,000 from that of 1417. An act on the last day of parliament provided for the repayment of

[30] *PPC* iii. 45, 49, 100, 103, 129–30; *CPR 1422–9*, 108, 111, 136, 159, 201, 189; *CFR 1422–30*, 58, 62, 76, and E 28/42 24 Nov. (Courtenay); *CFR 1422–30*, 28 (Clifford), 64 (Westmorland).

[31] *CCR 1422–9*, 67; *PPC* iii. 147.

[32] Ratcliffe, thesis, 8.

[33] *Rot. Parl.* iv. 249.

[34] E 28/44 14 Feb.; *PPC* iii. 135; Ratcliffe, thesis, 12–15.

[35] *Rot. Parl.* iv. 210–11; *PPC* iii. 144, 146; *CPR 1422–9*, 214; E 401/707; Steel, *Receipt*, 167.

the total sum of £17,333. 6*s* 8*d*. and tallies were at once delivered to him for 8,000 marks on the customs and subsidies in London, Hull, and Ipswich, with preference over all other creditors including Calais. The new loan extended Beaufort's grip on the ports and it enhanced still further his influence in council. Nor was he willing that the new advance should protract the repayment of his outstanding loans. His patent was designed to secure the total discharge of all his dues by midsummer 1425, and in fact he had received 20,000 marks from the customs of Southampton, London, Hull, and Ipswich by that date. That was probably as much as these revenues would bear, and for the balance of 6,000 marks Beaufort was promised repayment in cash at the exchequer at Christmas 1424 and midsummer 1425. As security the full council, headed by Gloucester, agreed to deliver crown jewels deemed to be worth 6,000 marks but acknowledged to be of greater value. The most important was the gold collar worth perhaps £5,000, half of which Beaufort was allowed to retain as pledge for £1,000. Some of the other jewels which made up the nominal total of £4,000 were similarly undervalued.[36] What significance should we attach to these conditions? Were they sufficiently unusual or advantageous to suggest that Beaufort was planning to appropriate the jewels by contriving the crown's default, as Gloucester later claimed?

Although the jewels were undoubtedly worth less than the 22,000 marks which Gloucester alleged, Beaufort certainly stood to gain handsomely if the exchequer defaulted on repayment at the prescribed dates. Even so the terms cannot have appeared so markedly abnormal or unreasonable as to have excited the council's suspicions. In the first place, with his loan of 1417 still not repaid, Beaufort had good reason to insist on early and firm repayment dates under severe penalties. Secondly, the use of jewels as security for a loan of lesser value was not uncommon practice, even though in this case the disparity was greater than normal. Finally, although like other creditors Beaufort was promised free disposal of the jewels should the crown default, few creditors chose or dared to exercise this option; indeed on occasion the crown insisted on reclaiming the jewels before the debt was discharged.[37] However much he coveted them, Beaufort could hardly expect to appropriate some of the most important regalia. Nor could either the council or Beaufort have envisaged that the treasurer would default on the repayment of such comparatively small sums at the prescribed times. It seems most likely that the terms were framed to ensure speedy and effective repayment and that the other opportunities which

[36] *CPR 1422–9*, 214; *CCR 1422–9*, 118; E 28/45 20 July; E 101/335/15/1; *Kal. and Inv.*, ii. 117–20; McFarlane, *England in XV Century*, 125–8.

[37] For jewels held in excess of wages owed for the Agincourt war: *Rot. Parl.* iv. 178. Creditors relinquishing jewels before repayment of their dues: *PPC* iii. 145 (bishop of Durham); E 28/44 21 Feb. (prior of St John).

they presented lay only at the back of Beaufort's mind. The circumstances which led the exchequer ultimately to default will be considered later.

The political rewards from his loan were more predictable than the financial. Bedford's resultant victory at Verneuil underlined his obligation to Beaufort, whose commitment to the war in France was now firmly established. The Commons' gratitude was likewise reinforced. On this occasion they were led by John Russell, known to Beaufort for his long service in the duchy of Lancaster, while among the shire representatives William Flete (Hants), Richard Baynard (Essex), William Carent (Somerset), and possibly William Yerde (Surrey) had direct connections with the bishop. Above all his loan confirmed his pre-eminence in the council. With Gloucester preparing for his Hainault venture and Exeter absent, Beaufort was the only remaining member who was of the royal stock. When, at the beginning of the summer recess in 1424, Langley indicated his wish to lay down the chancellorship, Beaufort was his obvious successor.

In addition to this political and military legacy of Henry V, some of the king's most trusted servants found themselves responsible for the execution of his will. In this too Henry Beaufort came to occupy a central and decisive role for the next twenty years. By his will of 1415, which he revised before he sailed to France for the last time in June 1421, Henry V named sixteen executors and three overseers, of whom eleven were members of the council in 1422–4. The executors were divided into an official group holding posts in the royal household and the duchy of Lancaster who were charged with the day-to-day administration of the will, and a group of leading nobility, to the four principal members of which, Gloucester, Exeter, Beaufort, and Langley, the administrators were to report twice a year. To the executors Henry had willed all his movable goods not specifically devised, for the discharge of his debts, but realizing that these would be insufficient he had additionally placed lands of the duchy of Lancaster to the estimated gross value of £6,000 p.a. in the hands of certain feoffees to whom the executors were to apply when their own resources had been spent. Of the feoffees originally named in 1415, nine still survived at Henry V's death: Exeter, Westmorland, Chichele, Beaufort, Langley, Fitzhugh, Hungerford, Wodehouse, and Leventhorpe. No others were thereafter co-opted. All the feoffees were executors or overseers of the will and all save the two duchy officials were also members of the council.[38] It was inevitable, if not entirely foreseeable, that of the two overlapping bodies the feoffees would emerge as the more powerful and permanent. They commanded an independent and substantial income and were answerable to no one but themselves. Their position, too, had political implications, since the feoffment was controlled by the Beaufort–Nevill

[38] J. S. Roskell, *The Commons in the Parliament of 1422*, 113–20; P. and R. Strong, 'Last will', 86–7; Somerville, *Duchy of Lancaster*, 199.

interest and excluded the royal brothers, Bedford and Gloucester, to whom Henry V had accorded a residuary interest in the duchy lands failing his direct issue. This development was ensured by the inability of the executors to fulfil the task assigned to them under Henry's will.

In the 1422 parliament Henry V's goods were redeemed from the executors' hands by the payment of 40,000 marks with which they were optimistically instructed to discharge the debts of both Henry IV and Henry V and render account at the next parliament. In fact they had by then received only £18,404 from the treasurer; moreover, the exchequer now faced an acute shortage of cash and they had to accept the balance in assignments on some relatively inaccessible sources.[39] Starved of money, the executors were bound sooner or later to have recourse to the feoffees. That happened in September 1424 when the executors of Henry IV complained that they had received only 10,000 marks from those of Henry V, and the feoffees agreed to pay them 9,000 marks in three annual instalments from the revenues of the enfeoffed lands. Significantly, they required Henry IV's executors to render account to themselves and no one else, not even their own supervisors. These payments were duly made and by 1429 Henry IV's debts had been discharged. Henry V's executors were in December 1426 still owed £2,050 of their share of the 40,000 marks and faced claims for household debts estimated at more than £10,000.[40] Even so, it was not until 1432 that responsibility for the execution of the will was finally transferred to the feoffees, of whom there then remained only five, Beaufort being the most important. The long delays over the will also meant that the income from the duchy lands accumulated in the feoffees' hands from 1422 to 1429, subject only to the payment of 9,000 marks to the executors of Henry IV and a solitary loan to the crown of £1,000 for the recovery of Crotoy made on 1 March 1424.[41] Thus whereas Henry V had envisaged the feoffees as auxiliary and subordinate to the executors, they eventually emerged as a wealthy, influential, and unaccountable body.

The death of Henry V removed the focus of loyalty for a nobility who had sunk their inherited feuds in common service to the crown. Would the tensions and divisions which could be expected in a ruling council of equals emerge as factions, fuelled by territorial rivalries and dynastic ambitions? The council was alert to these danger and, helped by its own self-discipline and the constraints imposed by the French war, it largely managed to avoid them, at least during the first years of the reign. Its coherence was further strengthened by the dynastic ties between its members, and here the Beaufort–Nevill connection was of peculiar importance.

[39] *Rot. Parl.* iv. 206–8, 213–42; *CPR 1422–9*, 136, 176. These sources were fines, jewels, and sales of the king's ships.

[40] *Rot. Parl.* iv. 280–2; E 28/47 18 Dec. 1426, cf. E 404/43/176, P. and F. Strong, 'Last will', 87 n. 2.

[41] *PPC* iii. 135; E 401/707; Ratcliffe, thesis, 10–12.

The main line of the Lancastrian house had only very tenuous connections with the rest of the nobility. Henry IV's marriage with Mary Bohun had led to a relationship with the Staffords when her niece Anne married successively the third and fifth earls. Despite disputes over the partition of the Bohun inheritance, the Staffords remained staunch allies of Lancaster and when Earl Humphrey's long minority ended in 1423 his marriage to Ann Nevill, one of Joan Beaufort's numerous children, strengthened this connection. It had probably been arranged by Henry V.[42] The other alliance made by the second generation of the house of Lancaster, that of Elisabeth with John Holand, duke of Exeter, had at first less propitious consequences, for he perished as a rebel in 1400. Yet her subsequent marriage to Sir John Cornewaile and tenacious advocacy of her son's rights meant that, when he reached manhood in 1417, John Holand, earl of Huntingdon was viewed with favour by Henry V and encouraged to seek the restoration of his dignities and estates by service in war. Captured at Baugé in 1421, Huntingdon was liberated in exchange for the count of Vendosme early in 1426 and his marriage to Anne Stafford, widow of the earl of March, quickly followed.[43] Clarence's own marriage to Margaret, daughter of Thomas Holand, earl of Kent, and widow of John Beaufort had further linked the two houses of Lancaster and Holand, but since there had been no issue her own interests after 1421 centred on the protection of her sons' inheritance. Without exception the remaining children of Henry IV had married into foreign dynasties, so that apart from a degree of consanguinity with the Staffords and the Holands, Bedford and Gloucester stood related to the remainder of the English nobility only through their grandfather.

By contrast the alliances of the Beaufort half blood were more numerous and widespread. This was due less to the marriages of John and Thomas than to the prolific and political qualities of their formidable sister Joan. Married to Ralph Nevill, earl of Westmorland in 1396, she continued to bear him children until 1415. Her daughters were systematically married to the heirs of Mowbray (1412), Percy (1414), Stafford (before 1424), and York (before 1424), all of whom were ending their minorities and three of whose families had suffered forfeiture. Of Joan's sons, by 1422 the eldest, Richard, was married to Alice, daughter and sole heiress of Thomas, earl of Salisbury, by Eleanor Holand, and although Thomas's subsequent marriage to Alice Chaucer (which Beaufort may have assisted) could have

[42] For Stafford claims to Penkelly and Cantreselly and to Holderness, see Rawcliffe, *The Staffords*, 13–18; *CPR 1422–9*, 254; *CCR 1422–9*, 59; *PPC* iii. 30. Beaufort interests were affected in both cases, but Exeter secured Humphrey livery of his lands without fine: *CPR 1422–9*, 75.

[43] The negotiations for Vendosme's ransom were long and complex. His petition to Henry V in 1420 is in E 28/33 5 Oct. Most of the references are given in Reeves, *Lancastrian Englishmen*, 169 ff. and see further Nicolas, *Agincourt*, Appendix, 24–8. For Huntingdon's marriage, *CCR 1422–9*, 273–4, 277. For Cornewaile's close relations with the Beauforts, see Reeves, loc. cit. and *CPR 1422–9*, 316.

produced issue, it did not and Richard was able to claim his father-in-law's title. His younger brother William had married, for a title, Joan, the mentally retarded but sole heiress of Lord Faucomberg, while in 1424 Westmorland and Warwick agreed on the marriage of the third son, Edward, with Elizabeth Despenser, Warwick's stepdaughter.[44] By that date, therefore, most of the leading families of the peerage stood in a proximate relationship with the Beauforts, namely Holand, Nevill, Percy, Stafford, Mowbray, York, Despenser, and Montagu, and these included all the surviving members of those families which had opposed the Lancastrian usurpation. The Beaufort marriages thus served to link these families to the royal house in a degree of consanguinity sufficient to betoken favour while remaining separated from the royal line of the whole blood. For the Beauforts they marked an important stage in their integration with the English nobility.

The only active members of the higher nobility not directly linked to the Beauforts were the earls of Suffolk, March, and Warwick. Suffolk was still unmarried, making a military career in France with Bedford and Salisbury. Despite the confidence which Henry V had shown towards the end of his reign in the earl of March, and his appointment to the council in 1422, he was regarded with some reserve as being the natural figurehead for any dynastic challenge to the house of Lancaster. His numerous retinue aroused the suspicion and jealousy of Gloucester, and his appointment as lieutenant in Ireland for nine years in May 1423 was a convenient way of removing him from the council. He did not sail until the autumn of 1424 and within six months he had died of plague.[45] His nephew and heir, Richard of York, was the ward of the earl of Westmorland, his father-in-law.[46] The Beauchamps, by contrast, had a long tradition of loyalty to Lancaster, and Richard, earl of Warwick was at the mid-point of a distinguished career in camp and council chamber, even if he was also at the centre of some of the more disruptive disputes of the early twenties. On the death of Thomas, Lord Berkeley in 1417 Warwick had entered Berkeley castle and its Gloucestershire manors in right of his wife Elizabeth, Berkeley's sole child, against the claim of Berkeley's nephew James. Warwick secured the backing of Bedford, Berkeley that of Gloucester. Henry V had attempted mediation on his visit in 1421 and the council in May 1423 persuaded the parties to accept arbitration. However, it was not until November 1424 that, 'by the great and unwearied labours'

[44] In August 1424 Warwick bought the wardship of Elizabeth for 1,100 marks and Westmorland cancelled Warwick's debt to him of twice this sum when the marriage was contracted. Beaufort as chancellor doubtless facilitated the deal: Longleat MS 342. (I owe this reference to Dr A. Sinclair.)

[45] His petition for the remission of the balance of his marriage fine was rejected by the council: *Rot. Parl.* iv. 212.

[46] *CFR 1422–30*, 64.

of the bishop of Winchester, now chancellor, an interim award was accepted, and a final one made a year later. Although James was given Berkeley castle, he lost virtually all the remaining lands to Warwick, in whose favour the award was certainly tilted.[47] Warwick's position on the council and the need for his services in France, to which he returned in 1424 for the Verneuil campaign, undoubtedly influenced the council in his favour, but Lord Berkeley seems to have borne the chancellor no ill will, for his son William later entered the cardinal's household. In his search for allies, however, Lord Berkeley had, in 1423–4, married Isabel, the eldest daughter of Thomas Mowbray, earl of Nottingham (d. 1400), and aunt of the present Earl Marshal. Although the Mowbray–Beauchamp dispute over Gower had been settled, the ancient rivalry between the two families was to find renewed expression in claims to precedence in the 1425 parliament, where Mowbray's victory owed much to Gloucester's support. Warwick was also involved in the feud between John, Lord Talbot and James, earl of Ormond. This had its origins in a struggle for power in Ireland but with Talbot's marriage to Warwick's daughter Margaret, it fused with Warwick's own quarrel with Joan, Lady Bergavenny, Ormond's mother-in-law. Both parties were summoned before Bedford and the council in 1426 and placed under recognizances, their quarrel being put to arbitration.[48] Although in these and other disputes the parties inevitably sought support among the lords of the council, in both cases it had been by the authority of the council and parliament, as a whole, that a settlement had been reached.

Finally the council sought to stabilize relations with Scotland by fashioning a treaty with the captive James I along lines already indicated by Henry V. Henry had cultivated his friendship, making him a knight of the Garter, and, in return for his services at the sieges of Melun and Meaux, had promised him release on parole after his final campaign. The negotiations undertaken between May and September 1423 by leading members of the council, which resulted in a treaty of marriage and a seven-year truce, undoubtedly represented the fulfilment of the king's own plans. The treaty signed at York on 10 September 1423 and ratified, on the Commons' recommendation, in parliament on 28 January 1424, freed James for a ransom of £40,000 payable in six instalments of 10,000 marks.[49]

[47] J. Smyth, *Lives of the Berkeley's*, ed. J. Maclean, ii. 42–8, 100; J. H. Cooke, 'The great Berkeley law suit', *Trans. Bristol and Glouc. Antiq. Soc.* 3 (1878), 305–24. For the recognizance of Apr. 1423, E 28/40 19 Apr.; for the awards, *CCR 1422–9*, 62, 74–5, 122. The most recent account is in A. Sinclair, 'The Beauchamp Earls of Warwick in the later Middle Ages', Ph.D. thesis (London, 1987).

[48] A. J. Otway-Ruthven, *A History of Medieval Ireland*, 348–61; *CPR 1422–9*, 423; *CCR 1422–9*, 317–18; M. C. Carpenter, 'Political society in Warwickshire, 1401–72', Ph.D. thesis, (Cambridge, 1976), 113–14.

[49] *Foedera*, ix. 694, x. 299, 301.

The first of these was then remitted as the dowry of his bride, Joan Beaufort. The treaty had much to commend it, for as well as establishing the northern frontier and reducing the cost to the exchequer, it prohibited the further recruitment of Scots into the dauphin's armies, while the ransom would make a significant contribution to exchequer finances. The choice of his bride undoubtedly reflected James's own will and affections, but it was politically adept. It linked him both with the Nevills and Percies across the border and with the half-blood of the royal house. It was a notable coup for the Beauforts, a vindication of their quasi-royal status and an extension of their diplomatic influence. Neither brother had been personally involved in the negotiations but it fell to Bishop Beaufort to marry the couple at St Mary Overy early in February and to provide the marriage feast at Winchester house. It seems unlikely that Gloucester's later strictures on the remission of the dowry were widely shared or voiced at the time.[50]

The council took no other initiatives in foreign policy, leaving to Bedford the attempt to win acceptance for the treaty of Troyes from continental princes. Even in regard to the duke of Burgundy, it became involved in terms only of Gloucester's personal schemes and quarrel. Relations with the papacy were a more inescapable concern, but it was not until 1425 that these began to mount slowly towards a crisis. Both are more conveniently considered in the context of the quarrel between Beaufort and Gloucester.

Prior to Henry V's death Henry Beaufort's hopes of recovering the king's trust and favour were centred on a renewed role as intermediary in Anglo-papal relations. Overnight this prospect disappeared. Released from the shadow of his masterful nephew, he became a leading and essential member of the junta responsible for maintaining the late king's political and military legacy. The English council, rather than the Roman Curia, became his power base, from which he could hope to influence and direct, rather than merely execute, policy. How clearly he foresaw the long and bitter feud with Gloucester which ensued is difficult to know. There is no indication of antagonism between them prior to 1422 and even by the summer of 1424 there are still few signs of tension in the surviving records. The council had been preoccupied with asserting and defining its corporate authority, maintaining political harmony, discharging its obligations under Henry V's will, and implementing his policies. Gloucester and Beaufort had undertaken their conciliar duties with equal regularity, but by the beginning of 1424 the distinctive role and policy of each had begun to

[50] R. Nicholson, *Scotland: The Later Middle Ages*, 252, 258–60; W. Balfour Melville, 'The later captivity and release of James I', *Scot. Hist. Rev.* 21 (1924), 96–8; id., 'James I at Windsor', ibid. 25 (1928), 226–8; Toy, 'Winchester House, Southwark', 75.

emerge.[51] Where Gloucester's bid for the regency had alarmed and antagonized the council, Beaufort had stood firmly for its corporate responsibility. Gloucester's pre-eminence in status and blood combined with his inability to assert a natural leadership in the council made him a semi-isolated figure, while Beaufort increasingly forged connections among the nobility. As Gloucester's attention became increasingly focused on his Hainault venture, Beaufort demonstrated his readiness to provide financial support for Bedford's defence of Normandy. Beaufort, too, had closer links with Henry V's professional servants—the knights and lesser nobility on the council and in the duchy of Lancaster. These connections and his own ecclesiastical status and semi-royal blood commended him as an arbiter and reconciler and won him acceptance as a *primus inter pares* where Gloucester was suspected of harbouring personal ambitions.

Added to this was Beaufort's long experience of royal government, his historical perspective reaching back to the Lancastrian revolution, his acumen and addiction to business, and the wide range of his contacts in the church, the mercantile community, and parliament. These qualities, backed by his financial resources, exactly met the requirements of the minority council in its first two years. His recovery of influence from the shadow into which he had fallen under Henry V is thus in no way surprising, but it brought in an increasingly acute form the problems of relations with the protector. In the discussion of any business within the council the bishop would command the greater expertise, the greater experience, the greater following, the crucial financial resources. Only the protector's closely defined authority and personal status could counter-balance these. Gloucester's *amour propre* was a prominent element in his character, and he was prone to see divisions on matters of policy as challenges to himself. Unless he was content to become a figurehead he was not likely to concede the *de facto* leadership which Beaufort would be bound increasingly to assume. His withdrawal on the expedition to Hainault seemed to offer an escape from these tensions, and in apparent harmony Gloucester invested Beaufort with the office of chancellor and headship of the council at a ceremony at his residence in Hertford castle on 16 July 1424. Thereafter he ceased to attend the council and by mid-October had set sail for the Low Countries.

[51] In the first two years of the reign Gloucester is recorded at 322 sessions of the council and Beaufort 303, these being only surpassed by the chancellor and treasurer: Brown, thesis, ii. 259, table VIII. All Beaufort's episcopal instruments in these years are dated from Southwark apart from one at Waltham in Aug. 1423.

7

The First Quarrel with Gloucester, 1424–1425

THE council had left to Bedford the task of securing adhesion to the treaty of Troyes from the peers of France and the princes of Europe. The first step, the triple alliance of the dukes of Bedford, Brittany, and Burgundy, in April 1423, was more important as a political declaration than as a pledge of military support. Both Jean V and Philip the Good were primarily concerned with the independence, defence, and—in the case of Burgundy—the expansion of their own territories, rather than with the completion of the English conquest. Indeed a total victory over the dauphin such as Henry V might have achieved would have threatened their own autonomy. Bedford expected some degree of military assistance while also accepting some degree of neutralism from his allies, but he could not afford any renunciation of their allegiance to Henry VI. Henry V had used military force to recall Jean V in 1421, and Bedford was to do likewise in 1427.

Relations with Duke Philip of Burgundy were more complex. The treaty of Troyes had effectively forced him to relinquish the aspirations of his father and grandfather to control French government and he made no attempt to challenge Bedford's assumption of the regency; instead, Philip's ambitions centred on the consolidation and extension of his lands in the Low Countries. This delimitation of their respective interests suited Bedford well, provided that Philip maintained his military commitment to the defence of the Anglo-Burgundian territories to the east of Paris and to the Burgundian presence in Paris itself. In his relations with England, Philip should, under the treaty of Troyes, have become a vassal of Henry VI, but he studiously avoided swearing fealty and from the first assumed the role of an independent ally. Likewise, although the treaty ended the long-standing commercial truce by bringing both territories under a common authority which would regulate trade and protect merchants, in practice little changed. English merchants saw the treaty as an opportunity to ensure their monopoly of wool exports to Flanders, extend their export of cloth at the expense of the Flemish industry, and control the trading of Flemish and other alien merchants in England. Henry V, anxious not to alienate his new ally, had withstood their demands, although to stabilize the currency and prevent an outflow of English silver to the Low Countries, he had established a mint at Calais so that purchases of wool at the Staple should be paid for in English coin. Disputes over these commercial issues—the rights of Flemish merchants in England, the penetration of English cloth into Flanders, and the bullion regulations at Calais—were to inflame feelings on both sides of the sea over the next two decades. But they were not of sufficient importance in the eyes of either government to jeopardize their alliance. Far more serious was the claim of Humphrey, duke of Gloucester to the inheritance of Jacqueline of Hainault, for this struck at the very centre of Philip's ambitions, the integration of the Low Countries under his own rule.

From 1421 to 1423 the English had concentrated their military effort in Picardy and Champagne in a determined and ultimately successful attempt to consolidate the Anglo-Burgundian hold over these territories. By 1424 Bedford was ready to resume the English conquest to the south and south-west of Paris, notably in the vulnerable area of Perche, and to push westwards into Maine and Anjou. For this he neither expected nor needed Burgundian aid, and the English having achieved victory at Verneuil looked to reap the fruits of it for themselves. Yet it was essential that Burgundian pressure should be maintained to the east and that substantial reinforcements should come from England. Both these were put at risk by Duke Humphrey's venture. In all probability Henry V had connived at Jacqueline's flight to England from her husband, John IV of Brabant, early in 1421: she had been assisted by Sir Lewis Robessart, given a pension, and invited to stand godmother to his son. How Henry expected to use her is not clear, but Gloucester married her in January 1423 with the intention of establishing himself as the ruler of Hainault, Holland, and Zeeland in her right—or perhaps, at the very least, of being bought off with a large sum. The success of this project would depend on effective military intervention, a papal verdict in favour of his marriage, and the calculation that Philip would be inhibited from action by his position as a vassal of Henry VI. For the last two he would need his brother Bedford's support, and initially Bedford may have given this out of fraternal solidarity and as a means of putting indirect pressure on Duke Philip. When Bedford's efforts to find a solution through the arbitrament of himself and Burgundy failed, and the matter was referred to the pope in June 1424, Gloucester began to assemble a force with the Earl Marshal as his second in command.

Following Gloucester's landing at Calais on 18 October, Bedford and Burgundy made a final attempt at arbitration, but Gloucester rejected the terms proposed and Philip declared his determination to assist John of Brabant in repelling the invaders.[1] The full extent of the danger to the Anglo-Burgundian alliance now became apparent. The hostility towards the Flemish in London was paralleled by the suspicion and contempt with which the duke of Burgundy was regarded by some of the English

[1] K. Vickers, *Humphrey, Duke of Gloucester*, 131–59; R. Vaughan, *Philip the Good*, 34–9.

commanders in France. Although the evidence of a plot by Salisbury and Suffolk to assassinate Duke Philip was shown to be a clever fabrication, it derived plausibility from its circumstantial detail and reflection of the confident chauvinism of the English captains after Verneuil, some of whom regarded the duke as an enemy second only to Charles VII.[2] An English conquest of Flanders had remained an option even under Henry V, and in placing it on the military agenda Gloucester could count on a measure of support among the soldiery in France. That the English council under Beaufort was at one with Bedford in regarding this as dangerous folly, and was co-ordinating with him its reassurances to Duke Philip, may be inferred from the dispatch of Chaucer and Tiptoft to Bedford in December 1424 to discuss 'certain special matters'. Throughout Gloucester's campaign Bedford bombarded his brother with messages and warnings to desist.[3] Gloucester's early success, as Mons surrendered and the Earl Marshal ravaged to the gates of Brussels, encouraged him to turn a deaf ear to mediation, while Philip, having secured a truce with the French, summoned his vassals and took the field. Bedford now retracted his support and Burgundy's action called Gloucester's bluff. The English troops became demoralized and Gloucester withdrew to Mons and, on 12 April, 1425, to England. The whole episode of Gloucester's intervention in Hainault demonstrated that, even at the height of English success in France, with the dauphin's army disorganized after Verneuil, Bedford could not afford to imperil the alliance with Philip of Burgundy. Gloucester's venture was at best an irrelevance, at worst an impediment to his great task, and the outcome must have convinced Bedford of his brother's volatility, ineffectiveness, and lack of commitment to the war in France. For Bedford had swiftly followed up Verneuil by dispatching Lord Scales and Sir John Fastolf to conquer Maine, while the earls of Salisbury and Suffolk advanced towards the Loire. With scarcely an interruption during the winter months the English besieged fortress after fortress until the capitulation of Le Mans in August 1425 and Mayenne in October signalled their effective mastery of Maine. The capacity of the English to mount a number of simultaneous sieges on different fronts depended on adequate reinforcements from England, and for this Bedford looked to the English council.

Such was the background to the first fifteen months of Beaufort's chancellorship, culminating in his confrontation with Gloucester in October 1425. As head of the council he saw his prime task as being to raise money and troops for Bedford's offensive. This meant a sustained

[2] M. A. Desplanque, 'Project d'assasinat de Philippe le Bon par les Anglais, 1424–6', *Mémoires couronnés et mémoires des savants étrangers*, 33 (Brussels, 1865–7), 1–78.

[3] Roskell, *Parliament and Politics*, iii. 175–6; *Wars of the English*, ed. J. Stevenson, i. pp. lxxxii–v, ii. 399–405; Jehan de Waurin, *Recueil des Croniques* . . ., ed. W. Hardy, iii. 133–4.

effort to secure taxation and minimize the effects of Gloucester's intervention on trade with Flanders. The first convocation of the reign was summoned for 16 October 1424 and three days after it opened all the regular councillors with Beaufort at their head attended while he eloquently expounded the need for a subsidy. Two days later the lower clergy made their reply, to the effect that they were not empowered to make a grant. On 30 October Beaufort and the other councillors returned and exhorted them to consider the great perils threatening the realm, but no decision was reached, nor yet again on 4 November when long deliberation failed to change the lower clergy's answer. To obtain a fresh mandate for a grant Chichele then prorogued convocation to 16 January 1425. On that day Beaufort and other royal councillors again appeared and, *tam opportune quam importune*, repeated the demand for a subsidy. Beaufort deployed all his skills of persuasion: 'first with smooth words and then with harsh and threatening ones, and with no small urgency, he pleaded', but finally on 17 February the proctors of the lower clergy refused on grounds of poverty to make any grant.[4] After subjecting the clergy to so much pressure this was a considerable blow to the council's authority, the more so as it had clearly hoped to use the example of a clerical grant to extract a lay subsidy from parliament. Even so, a week after convocation ended, writs were sent out for a parliament to meet on 30 April, and a further assembly of convocation on 28 April. Already in February the council had begun preparations for sending reinforcements to Bedford in the early summer, and though it was already too late to secure a tax which would directly pay for their wages, a grant would provide security on which loans could be raised.

Parliament had already opened when, on 4 May, Beaufort appeared in convocation with the treasurer and Lords Scrope and Cromwell. This time they coupled their demand for a subsidy with a warning to the clergy to purge their own abuses, but this made little impression and Lyndwood, the spokesman for the lower clergy, again pleaded poverty. As a result convocation was kept in session for two further months, partly to wear down its resistance, partly owing to the continuing crisis in parliament. Finally, on the penultimate day of parliament, 13 July, the three officers of state with Scrope and Cromwell again appeared, Beaufort reminding the clergy of the great burdens that must necessarily be supported and the perils looming in France if Bedford was not succoured, and Cromwell expounding these in ornate language while apologizing for having spoken in 'verbis opprobriosis et inhonestis' on his earlier visit. Eventually, on the insistent pleading of Chichele himself, convocation agreed to a half-tenth to be levied at Michaelmas, with exemption for the poorer benefices.[5] That

[4] *Reg. Chichele*, iii. 91–8.
[5] Ibid. 103–13.

was all that the bullying and pleading had yielded, and it came too late to influence parliament.

When parliament opened on 30 April, Beaufort and other members of the council had already agreed to loan sufficient for the first quarter's wages of an expedition, and in the course of May and June further loans from him, the city of London, and the Italian companies raised the total to 20,000 marks.[6] A force of 1,400 men under Lord Grey of Ruthin, many from the duchy of Lancaster, could thus be dispatched in June and early July at a cost of just over £10,000.[7] The attempt to secure a grant for this was prefigured in the chancellor's opening address. Its formal construction and exposition of the triple requirements for the king's honour and peace of the realm as being wise counsel, obedience from subjects, and ready aid and sustenance was characteristic of Beaufort's sermons. For the councillors and the Commons he had a special message. Councillors should take as their model the elephant, a creature free from malice, rancour, and envy, of inflexible purpose and prodigious memory; only in a body of such councillors was there safety. This was undoubtedly aimed at Gloucester. To the Commons he described how Bedford had enlarged the *pays de conquête* since Henry V's death and how this should stir them to 'voluntariam subventionem et sustentationem'. The phrase is significant. In convocation Beaufort had pleaded the royal necessity; but parliament had once already refused to acknowledge any obligation in time of peace, and it was to the goodwill of subjects that Beaufort now appealed.[8]

Beaufort himself had forfeited the goodwill of at least some of the members, and opinion in the capital had been excited against him. Gloucester's expedition commanded strong popular support and he had returned apparently to raise men and money for a resumption of his campaign. The council had provided no money for his first venture, for which Gloucester had compelled the estates at Mons to grant him 40,000 crowns; nor is there any hint in the formal records of this parliament of public debate as between 'the war of Hainault' and 'the war of France'. Yet this issue lay behind the personal rivalry and overshadowed the long debate over taxation. There was still no conclusion to this when parliament adjourned for the Whitsun recess on 21 May, on which day Beaufort delivered into the exchequer the second instalment of his loan which now amounted in all to £8,933. 6*s* 8*d*. Beaufort's two loans thus guaranteed the departure of reinforcements to Bedford, and the second quarter of their

[6] Beaufort's loan was in two parts: £4,000 on 22 Mar. and £4,933. 6*s*. 8*d*. on 21 May. The first is not entered on the only extant receipt roll (E 401/711), though its repayment is on the issue roll (E 403/673) with reference to the receipt roll under 22 Mar. Steel, *Receipt*, 168 therefore omits this from the total for this term. For loans of other councillors in Mar. and June, see *PPC* iii. 167–8; *CPR 1422–9* 271, 286, 293.

[7] Ratcliffe, thesis, 16–20; *CPR 1422–9*, 299–300.

[8] *Rot. Parl.* iv. 261.

wages was paid on 21 May and 21 June. His concern must now have been lest any provision for Gloucester's venture should impede his repayment. On its reassembly parliament passed an act securing the loans of all subjects to the total of £20,000, and by letters patent on 6 June Beaufort was granted repayment of all his outstanding loans, said to amount to £11,032. 16*s*. 1*d*., from the customs and subsidies in all ports levied since Easter last, reserving only any assignments made before 1 May. He could also claim the revenue from all wardships not granted before that date, from his own debts to the crown, and from any lay and clerical subsidies to be granted in future. Beaufort further fortified himself with the personal obligations of his fellow officers and a number of councillors who must be reckoned his supporters on the council: Kemp, Morgan, Cromwell, Scrope, Tiptoft, and Alington.[9] Although kept in session until 14 July, the Commons ultimately braved the council's displeasure and refused to grant direct taxation, contenting themselves with renewing the wool subsidies until 1429 and granting tunnage and poundage, though only for a year. A powerful mercantile lobby, probably encouraged by Gloucester, attached conditions to the grant, requiring alien merchants to be put to host and compelled to sell their merchandise within forty days.[10] Perhaps in the end Beaufort did not regret this refusal of a tax, for Gloucester's influence was visibly growing and it could well have been diverted to his use. As it was, on the last day of parliament, the lords agreed to a loan to Gloucester of 20,000 marks spread over four years to be repaid at the king's discretion, and a cedule was hurriedly prepared to secure the Commons' assent.[11] On 5 November the council, bowing to Gloucester's pressure, authorized the payment of the first instalment, of 5,000 marks, from the clerical tenth extracted from convocation on the last day of parliament. It was doubtless with this money that Gloucester dispatched the young Lord Fitzwalter with 1,500 soldiers to the relief of his wife early in January 1426. Together with local forces they made an army of 4,000 men which joined battle with the levies from the cities and Burgundian knights from Philip's own retinue. Bedford had in fact given Philip warning of the landing, and the result was the massacre of the English, though Fitzwalter made good his escape. It is all too likely that Bedford's own information had been received from Beaufort.[12]

Beaufort's unpopularity in London seems to have arisen from his attempts to stem the wave of anti-Flemish feeling sparked off by Gloucester's expedition. This may have been purposefully fomented, for

[9] The figure of £11,032 probably included the £1,000 advanced on 1 Dec. 1424 and the balance still outstanding of the other loans of 1417 and 1424. *CPR 1422–9*, 293–4; *Rot. Parl.* iv. 271, 275, 277–80; *PPC* iii. 199–200.

[10] *Rot. Parl.* iv. 275–6.

[11] Ibid. 289. Cf. *Gregory's Chron.* 158: 'that Parlyament hadde an evylle faryng ende.'

[12] *PPC* iii. 179; *CCR 1422–9*, 259; E 404/42/138; Vaughan, *Philip the Good*, 40–4.

the establishment of Hainault, Holland, and Zeeland as an English fief promised substantial gains to English merchants. The most important was as a market for English cloth, exports of which had leaped dramatically after the treaty of Troyes and, though falling back in 1423–4, were now making a good recovery. London merchants trading to Holland and Zeeland had recently secured recognition from John of Bavaria and feared correctly that the establishment of Burgundian control over these areas would bring an extension of the ban on English cloth enforced by Duke Philip in Flanders. English domination of these territories, on the other hand, would place Philip under pressure to lift this, and would further two long-term aims of the Staplers, to exclude Spanish and Scottish wool from Flanders, and to enforce the monopoly of sales at Calais against the practice of shipping wool direct to Middleburg. As to the object of popular hostility, the Flemish merchants in London, they were a fluctuating and unorganized community, more active in the carrying trade than as cloth exporters.[13] Yet attacks on them could stimulate reprisals in the Low Countries and on English shipping, prejudicing relations with Duke Philip and discrediting Henry VI's claim to afford them protection as his subjects. From past experience Beaufort knew how quickly the vicious spiral of piracy and reprisal could take hold, and with what labours it had been successfully contained by Henry V.

As Gloucester's early triumphs in 1424 became known in London, bills against the Flemings appeared in the city and on 13 February 1425 were fixed to the gates of Beaufort's house and those of other bishops. An exodus of Flemings began. Beaufort, fearing a riot and suspecting the connivance of the city authorities, summoned the mayor and aldermen and placed some under arrest, allegedly on charges of treason made by approvers from sanctuary. At the same time Beaufort strengthened his own bodyguard from the royal household, and the council placed an armed force in the Tower under Bedford's chamberlain, Sir Richard Wydeville, with instructions to admit no one except on the authority of the chancellor and council. Despite some treasonous language and disturbances when Gloucester returned with his undisciplined troops in mid-April, London was quiet but tense; one chronicler remarks that the 'chancellor bore a heavy heart against the city'.[14] Wydeville's refusal to admit the protector to the Tower could have precipitated an armed coup by Gloucester, though it may equally have prevented one. Gloucester certainly exploited the citizens' grievances, declaring that Beaufort had fortified the Tower in the manner of a *châtelain* and contrasting this with the treatment they had received from Henry V and could look for from himself. On 5 June,

[13] *Eng. Export Trade*, 138; N. Kerling, *Commercial Relations of Holland and Zeeland with England*, 64–88, 147–52, 173–99; J. L. Bolton, 'Alien Merchants in England in the reign of Henry VI', B.Litt. thesis (Oxford, 1971), 270.

[14] *PPC* iii. 167; *Gregory's Chron.* 158; *Brut*, ii. 432, 567; *Great Chron.* 136–40.

accompanied by the earl of Stafford and other noblemen, the protector paid a formal visit to the court of the mayor and aldermen and addressed them on certain matters; his influence probably induced them to make a loan of £3,000 ten days later.[15]

Parliament met on 30 April in an atmosphere of violence, with public threats to the chancellor's safety and petitions complaining that subjects had been falsely accused and arbitrarily imprisoned on charges of treason and Lollardy without trial. Gloucester and Exeter carried the infant king into Westminster hall: a reaffirmation both of royal authority and of their own responsibilities for his protection. All this enhanced Gloucester's influence, which was exercised strongly to attract and support new allies. The precedence dispute between the Earl Marshal and the earl of Warwick, besides consuming much parliamentary time, contained a potential threat to the unity of the council, for it neatly personified the rival claims of Bedford's campaigns in France, to which Warwick had led the 1424 expedition, and Gloucester's venture in Hainault, from which Mowbray had just returned. Mowbray's successful recovery of his grandfather's dukedom thus had partisan implications, while the evidence cited on both sides recalled disturbingly the vendettas in 1388–97.[16] Moreover, the restoration of the Mowbray dukedom could be guaranteed to raise the expectations of the Holands. The final stages of Huntingdon's release were ratified in this parliament and Gloucester quickly sought to attach Huntingdon to himself. He was probably also backing the attempts of John, Lord Scrope to recover some of his father's forfeited property which Henry V had given to Lord Fitzhugh, now recently deceased. Scrope was to become one of the duke's supporters in the council in the following years.[17] The common thread to all these alliances was in the former opposition of the families of Mowbray, Holand, and Scrope to the Lancastrian crown. Gloucester was not, of course, seeking to revive this tradition, but was wooing support from those who had claims to lost lands and dignities. The risk lay in harnessing these expectations to a feud within the house of Lancaster. For the moment the council consciously proclaimed its solidarity, declaring that the welfare and peace of the realm during the king's minority stood 'principaly in the goode onehed and accord among the lordes the whiche during the tendre age of the Kyng governe and rule under him and by his auctorite,' and calling upon them to settle personal quarrels peacefully.[18] The assertion and exercise of the council's corporate authority was Beaufort's strongest defence against

[15] *Cal. L. Bk. K* 47; Corporation of London Record Office, Journal of the Common Council, fo. 43. C. M. Barron, 'The government of London and its relations with the Crown, 1400–1450' Ph.D. thesis (London, 1970), 157.

[16] *Rot. Parl.* iv. 267–74.

[17] Ibid. 283–5, 287; *CPR 1422–9*, 228; *CCR 1422–9*, 154. Following his release Huntingdon immediately married March's widow.

[18] *PPC* iii. 175–7.

Gloucester, and the document may represent his own initiative as chancellor.

Although an open quarrel had been avoided, the parliament had done nothing to ease the situation in London or to lessen Gloucester's determination to remove the chancellor. Throughout the summer months tension increased in the city, where Gloucester and Beaufort remained, watching each other's movements. Some disturbances took place, though the evidence for them is very fragmentary. During June the steward and marshal of the household held sessions of the court of the verge just outside the city, at Southwark, Highgate, and Stratford to hear a series of indictments of treason and felonious insurrections. Subsequently, shortly after Michaelmas, there were further indictments before an oyer and terminer commission headed by Sir John de Boys, Sir Thomas Chalton, and Robert FitzRobert relating to an affray in Westminster hall and one in Holborn on 1 May. None of these were said to have been expressly directed against Beaufort, but the city was evidently in a disturbed state.[19] Beaufort was widely vilified, particularly for the protection which, as chancellor, he felt it his duty to extend to friendly alien merchants. Complaint against the chancellor's failure to provide redress for acts of piracy by aliens had been made in parliament, and was aggravated by his refusal to enforce the hosting of alien merchants, which had been the condition for the grant of the wool subsidy.[20] In these circumstances Beaufort's issue of proclamations in London and some other ports on 30 July forbidding seizures of goods and ships of Flemings, on the ground that they were subjects of Henry VI, was an act of considerable political courage and indicative of how seriously he viewed this threat to the alliance with Burgundy.[21]

Gloucester was said to be compiling evidence against the bishop from his past, evidently hoping to frame a charge of treason from the events of 1412, and probing into the proceedings against Queen Joan in 1419 to see if Beaufort (then in disgrace) had been implicated. From somewhere he got an implausible story that at an unspecified date Beaufort had been behind an attempt to assassinate Prince Henry.[22] None of this was of much substance, as the two envoys sent over by Bedford to investigate, and if possible compose, the quarrel must have concluded after visiting Gloucester at his inn on Sunday 28 October. But Gloucester was determined to force the issue and on the 29th, the day of the mayoral procession, he

[19] There are only very fragmentary remains of the indictments for Michaelmas 1425: KB 9/221/936; also KB 27/658 Rex rot. 6^{v}, 8^{r}–v, 11; KB 27/659 Rex rot. 9.

[20] *Gregory's Chron.* 157–8; cf. *Calendar of the Plea and Memoranda Rolls 1413–37*, 239; *Rot. Parl.* iv. 191–2; *Chronicles of London*, 85.

[21] *CCR 1422–9*, 263, 323.

[22] *Chronicles of London*, 78. In Aug.–Sept. a number of Beaufort's supporters were in the north negotiating with the Scots: *PPC* iii. 171–3.

warned the mayor to guard the city well and set watches, and the city remained at arms during that night. Much violent language was used against Beaufort in the streets. The confrontation came next day when Gloucester sought to ride to Eltham to remove the king. Beaufort construed this as an attempt to take Henry VI into custody and perhaps usurp the crown; Gloucester declared that he was acting to prevent a similar seizure of the king by Beaufort. At Southwark Beaufort had gathered retainers of the duchy of Lancaster to bar the way, and they took up defensive positions in the gates and houses on London bridge. It was Chichele, Bishop Stafford, and Beaufort's own nephew, Prince Pedro of Portugal, then on a visit to London, who acted as intermediaries, riding between the two camps eight times on 30 October to arrange terms. Inevitably the onus was on Beaufort to retract. By taking up an armed posture he had challenged the authority and duty of the protector to maintain peace and order in the realm. Moreover, under the terms of Henry V's will Gloucester could claim specific responsibility for the safety of the king's person. The settlement permitted Gloucester to bring the king to London in the company of the prince of Portugal and the lords of the council, and in the following days Gloucester presided over meetings of the council at his house and elsewhere in which he was granted the proceeds of the clerical tenth and crown jewels were recovered from the duke of Exeter for a gift to Prince Pedro.[23]

Gloucester's triumph placed Beaufort in jeopardy and he appealed to Bedford in a letter written on 31 October and transmitted by the hand of Bedford's chamberlain, Sir Ralph Butler. His confidence that the bearer's own report of the situation would be sympathetic to him and that Bedford shared his own view of Gloucester is implicit in the terse sentences in which he urged Bedford to return:

> as ye desire the welfare off the kyng oure sovereyne lorde and off his Rewmes off England and off Fraunce, and your owne wele and oure also, hast you hedir; ffor be my trouth and ye tarye, we shall putte this land in aventure with a ffelde. Such a brothir ye have here. God make him a goode man. For your wisedom knoweth wele that the prosperite of Fraunce stant in the welfare of England.[24]

Whether or not Beaufort genuinely believed that Gloucester was intending to divert the resources of England to his own interests, this tellingly played on Bedford's own fears. Equally, his warning of a potential clash of retinues—for that was his plain meaning however he later glossed it—may have been alarmist, but probably reflected his determination to defend his

[23] *Chronicles of London*, 77–8; *Gregory's Chron*. 159; *PPC* iii. 178–80; Jean le Fèvre, *Chronique*, ed. F. Morand, ii. 118 interprets it as a struggle for control over the person of Henry VI. HRO Eccles. II 159427 shows that the steward and constable of Taunton were at Southwark on 2–4 Oct.

[24] *Chronicles of London*, 84.

position. Bedford's decision to return showed that he had taken Beaufort's point. The effect of his declared intention was to suspend the authority of Gloucester and the council until he arrived on 20 December. Even the customary appointment of sheriffs was postponed.

Before considering Bedford's composition of the quarrel there are further aspects of Beaufort's chancellorship which call for comment. Gloucester's decision to take custody of the infant king was prompted by his suspicion that Beaufort was proposing to remove Henry VI from Eltham 'to thentente to putte him in suche governance as he lust'. Did this reflect Gloucester's genuine alarm at the growth of Beaufort influence in the royal household? No formal changes had occurred during Beaufort's chancellorship, although Sir Walter Hungerford, who was appointed steward in April 1424, was his close associate. But it is also possible that Queen Catherine's familiarity with the young Edmund Beaufort was already attracting attention. After the capture of his brothers at Baugé Edmund had returned to England with his mother, and between then and his departure to France in the company of Bishop Beaufort in March 1427 his activities are totally obscure. He is most likely to have lived in his uncle Exeter's household, and thus to have come into frequent contact with the court and the queen mother. By 1425 Edmund was aged 19 and Catherine 24. Her evident desire to marry him threatened to bring the governance of the young king more directly and permanently under the influence of the Beauforts than Gloucester, or perhaps even Bedford, was inclined to contemplate. It was this that prompted the inclusion of the queen in the solemn articles of mutual trust between the two brothers, and the passage of an act in the parliament of 1427 forbidding her to marry during her son's minority, and imposing penalties of forfeiture on any spouse. But any connection between this *affaire* and Gloucester's action late in 1425 must remain conjectural.[25]

Gloucester's withdrawal had inevitably consolidated Beaufort's leadership in the council. From the autumn of 1424 to the spring of 1425 this was probably a remarkably harmonious body. Virtually none of the higher nobility attended other than the earl of Warwick, and he only occasionally. Apart from his fellow officers, Stafford and Alnwick, Beaufort's episcopal colleagues were Chichele, Kemp, Morgan, and Langley, with all of whom except the archbishop his relations were cordial. With the members of the lesser nobility he was even more closely linked as a business associate and through the distribution of patronage. Lords Cromwell and Scrope, Sir

[25] *Chron. Angl.* 17 gives no precise date for the *affaire* and it possibly took place in 1426 rather than 1425. See R. A. Griffiths, *Reign of Henry VI*, 60–1; A. Crawford, 'The King's burden?', in R. A. Griffiths (ed.), *Patronage, the Crown, and the Provinces*, 37. The statute is printed by Griffiths, 'Queen Katherine of Valois and a missing statute of the realm', *LQR* 93 (1977), 248–62.

Walter Hungerford and Sir John Tiptoft, William Alington, and Thomas Chaucer had a multiplicity of connections with him.[26] As a body the council could deploy a wide range of professional experience in the fields of diplomacy and papal relations, administration and finance, parliamentary experience, and war. What it lacked, in the absence of the nobility, was the authority to compose disputes among them if such arose. The parliament of 1424 had heard complaints about disorders and demands for a new itinerary of the King's Bench to enforce the law. Perhaps in anticipation of the protector's impending absence, new commissions of the peace were issued in every shire on 24 July 1424. The addition to these of the local ordinary with whom, in fourteen of the southern shires, the new chancellor was associated, was a striking innovation. Bishops had never previously been named to the peace commissions and this probably reflected Beaufort's own views of their responsibilities.[27] The commissions were further strengthened by the appointment of any members of the higher nobility who had lands in the shire and were not serving abroad, notably the duke of Exeter and the earls of Warwick and Stafford. Lord Cromwell's name was added in four shires, and everywhere more local knights and important gentry were included. In November the appointment of sheriffs in some of the southern shires also reveals the chancellor's influence. Richard Wyot in Buckinghamshire, John Golafre in Oxfordshire, John Clipsham in Surrey, Edward Stradling in Somerset, and John de Boys in Hampshire were all officials or retainers of the bishopric. By these means Beaufort sought to strengthen his authority as head of the council; however, he appears to have made no attempt to secure the election of any of his followers as knights of the shires in the 1425 parliament.

The coherence of the Beaufort group on the council was, not surprisingly, manifested in their enjoyment of patronage during the protector's absence. In June 1424 the council had relinquished to the treasurer the power to grant farms of lands falling into the king's hands, and between October 1424 and July 1425 there occurred a number of highly valuable casualties. Custody of the temporalities of the sees of York, Wells, and Norwich were distributed between Sir Walter Hungerford, Sir John Stourton, Lord Cromwell, Lord Scrope, Sir Walter Beauchamp, and the duke of Exeter. These were all farmed at realistic rents.[28] Among lay escheats the most important was the lands of the earl of March, who died in January 1425. The wardship and marriage of March's

[26] Council attendance is mainly recorded in *PPC* iii. 159–69; both E 28/31 and C 81/1544 are extremely thin for these months.

[27] *Rot. Parl.* iv. 254; *CPR 1422–9*, 559–73; *Proceedings before the Justices of the Peace in the Fourteenth and Fifteenth Centuries*, ed. B. Putnam, pp. lxxxi–ii. Cf. Beaufort's earlier involvement in Feb. 1422: *CPR 1416–22*, 413.

[28] *PPC* iii. 147; *CFR 1422–30*, 96, 101, 108.

heir, Richard of York, was already held by the earl of Westmorland to whose daughter Cecily the young duke had been contracted by 1424. On Westmorland's death in October 1425 York seems to have been transferred to the duke of Exeter. The greater part of the March lands had been placed in feoffment in 1415, but this was now largely overridden by the council, for on 1 May the duke of Exeter was granted the custody of those in East Anglia valued at £357 p.a. and Sir Edward Stradling had those in Pembrokeshire, while the much larger block in the marches and Wales was placed under the stewardship of Sir John Tiptoft.[29] The council's intention was to use the revenues from these, with £1,000 from the marriage fine of the earl of Oxford and £500 from the farm of the Roos lands held by Lord Cromwell, for the repayment of loans advanced by the members of the council for the expedition to Normandy. However, on 23 June Gloucester celebrated his return to the council by securing the custody of the remainder of the estates, including those parts previously enfeoffed by the late earl for the discharge of his debts, to the value of £3,092 p.a.[30] Understandably Gloucester must have resented the monopoly of patronage by the close knit body of councillors, even if in their own eyes it was the natural reward of office and service. The chancellor did not himself receive any further custodies, but in February 1425 he was granted an additional salary of 2,000 marks p.a. during Gloucester's absence in recognition of his responsibilities.

Beaufort's tenure of the chancellorship also enabled him to obtain repayment of the loans of 1417 and 1424 for which he held assignments on the customs. From July 1424 to May 1425 he received no less than 20,000 marks but, coming at a time when wool exports to Flanders had been disrupted by Gloucester's expedition and parliament had refused direct taxation, this deprived the exchequer of its most valuable source of revenue. It once again became totally dependent on his and others' loans for military expeditions and immediate expenses. The treasurer exercised some restraint in making assignments, and many payments must have been simply deferred, but tallies issued to the lords of the northern marches tended to be uncashable. In November 1424 the council felt obliged to offer the earl of Northumberland very favourable terms for the renewal of his keeping of the East March. He was guaranteed assignments on the north-eastern ports for three years and was given repayment of Henry V's debts to him totalling £3,073 from the customs and the Scottish ransom, while his own obligations to the crown in respect of his ransom of 1414,

[29] *CFR 1422–9*, 64, 85, 98, 100, 102, 119; *CPR 1422–9*, 254, 264, 266, 271, 343; *PPC* iii. 194. Exeter held the lands at the time of his death: E 101/514/22.

[30] *PPC* iii. 169; *CPR 1422–9*, 271–2, 518; *CFR 1422–30*, 103–4; E 404/42/152. P. A. Johnson, 'The political career of Richard, duke of York, to 1456', D.Phil thesis (Oxford, 1981), 19–22, citing C 47/9/33.

totalling £4,000, were put in respite. Among these was a bond for £1,000 in his name presently held by Beaufort, which the bishop now agreed to restore to the earl, accepting in its place the promise of a further assignment on the customs which was eventually made in May and July 1425.[31] Beaufort evidently held Northumberland's bond as part of the instalment of £2,000 due at Christmas 1424 in part repayment of the £4,000 he had loaned in March. McFarlane identified this arrangement as that referred to by Gloucester many years later when he accused Beaufort of contriving the exchequer's default on the repayment of this £4,000 in order to secure for himself the rich collar and other jewels which he held in pledge. Yet the renewal of Northumberland's indentures does not wholly match Gloucester's recollection that Beaufort, 'seeing your said money ready to have quit with the said jewels, caused the Treasurer of England that time being to pay the same money for part of another army'.[32] Moreover, since the payment of the £1,000 had been deferred by Beaufort's assent it as yet gave him no claim upon the jewels. That claim would only arise if full repayment of the whole sum was not made by midsummer 1425. By then the treasurer was indeed seeking money for 'part of another army', namely the reinforcements sent to Bedford under Lord Grey of Ruthin. For this Beaufort loaned £8,933. 6*s*. 8*d*., and was given security for repayment from the customs; but he was also permitted to retain the crown pledged to him by Henry V (though the loans from the previous reign had all been repaid) and the rich collar and other jewels pledged in 1424. These terms were agreed on 6 June in full council, at which Gloucester was now present, and formally recorded on the rolls of parliament.[33] The jewels had therefore not been lost sight of; indeed they had been further engaged as security for a loan more nearly corresponding to their true value. What was apparently overlooked in this new agreement was any provision for the repayment of the balance of £3,000 from the 1424 loan due in cash at midsummer.

By April 1426 Beaufort had received repayment of all his loans of 1425 and also for the £1,000 for which he had surrendered the earl of Northumberland's obligations. He returned the obligations of the lords of the council covering his loan on 11 July 1426 and on the same day the treasurer was authorized to treat with divers persons who held jewels as pledges, and to recover these. It was at this point that Beaufort was found to be still owed the balance of the £4,000 loan of March 1424. The chancellor, now Archbishop Kemp, ordered repayment to be made to Beaufort, but at precisely this point the treasurer, Sir Walter Hungerford, was desperately trying to get money together for the dispatch of

[31] Steel, *Receipt*, 167–8; *PPC* iii. 162–3; cf. *CPR 1422–9*, 176, 267.
[32] McFarlane, *England in XV Century*, 126; *Wars of Eng*. ii. 443.
[33] Above, ch. 7 no. 9.

reinforcements under the earl of Warwick and Sir Richard Stafford for service in Champagne and Brittany. Although the muster had been ordered for 1 August, the departure of this force was delayed until 30 August by lack of ready cash for wages. Indeed as late as 23 July commissioners had been sent into the shires to negotiate loans for this, which were to be paid into the exchequer not later than 1 September. With difficulty a total of £3,404 was raised during August, just sufficient to enable the exchequer to pay out £5,475 in wages for the force of 800 men.[34] This time Beaufort did not lend, for he had withdrawn from the council following his resignation of the chancellorship. The failure to redeem the jewels at this point was thus a reflection of Beaufort's own loss of influence and the responsibility for it was shared by Bedford, Gloucester, Kemp, and Hungerford. No further attempt was made to repay him the balance of his 1424 loan, and it was probably assumed that he could be induced to surrender the crown jewels without repayment. Indeed on 26 February 1427, shortly before he left with Bedford, Beaufort did surrender the gold crown, and later on 10 May 1430 when he accompanied Henry VI to France he returned the rich collar and other jewels needed for the king's coronation, receiving a payment in respect of these of £908. 2*s*. 1½*d*. The tablet of St George, with the remainder of the jewels delivered in 1424, he retained until his death, to be redeemed by the king in 1449 for £2,043. 8*s*. 9*d*.[35]

The story of this loan can therefore bear a somewhat different interpretation from that which McFarlane placed upon it. In 1424 jewels of greater value than the sum advanced by Beaufort were pledged to him because there was no revenue which could be assigned for its repayment—only the promise of cash liveries in two instalments by the treasurer over the following fifteen months. Beaufort did not contrive the exchequer's default on the first of these instalments in December 1424; he accepted payment of half from the customs and agreed to recycle the remainder in the context of further advances he was to make in the New Year. The occasion which Gloucester later referred to was probably the default on the payment due at midsummer 1425, since this occurred at precisely the time when the exchequer was paying the second quarter's wages of the reinforcements sent to Bedford. Gloucester was seeking money and troops for his own venture and had cause to remember the dispatch of this army. Beaufort may have connived at this because it presented him with a useful card to play at a time when his political position was under threat. In any case the jewels could not be redeemed since they had again been pledged

[34] McFarlane, *England in XV Century*, 128–9, citing E 403/694 10 May for the writ ordering repayment to Beaufort. *PPC* iii. 199–200, 203; *CPR 1422–9*, 345, 354–5; Ratcliffe, thesis, 21–2.

[35] McFarlane, *England in XV Century*, 129–31, 136–7.

to Beaufort for the repayment of his fresh loans. By 1426 the position was different, for Beaufort had lost power, he was unwilling to make further loans, and could claim repayment of all those outstanding. It was now discovered that he was still entitled to retain the jewels pledged for the residue of the 1424 loan; but again the council was prevented from redeeming them by the need to finance reinforcements. For this Beaufort was in no way responsible; it was the consequence of the acute shortage of cash at the exchequer, and Bedford's determination to send troops to France. Beaufort's claims were set aside and for the time being he was allowed to retain the jewels, though probably in the knowledge that he could be forced to surrender them when Bedford and the council decided.

The repayment of all his outstanding loans by 1426 (except for the £3,000) brought to an end the first period when Beaufort emerged as an outstanding creditor of the crown. Since 1417 he had advanced a total of £51,600, and on occasion almost £26,000 of his money was in the hands of the crown. Virtually all these loans had been charged on the customs, at first in Southampton and subsequently in all ports of the realm, where he had established a 'long commission' on the ports, which gave him preference over other creditors and enabled him to appoint his own collectors. But the customs were not his chosen security; they fluctuated with trade and had a tendency to become overcharged with other assignments. Beaufort would have preferred the lay and clerical subsidies, but Henry V had been determined to keep these for his current military expenses, and after 1422 both the Commons and the clergy refused any grants. Beaufort's concern for secure and speedy repayment expressed itself in the elaborate preferences, the additional obligations from the council, and the crown jewels which he obtained as collateral security. His experience under Henry V had made him distrustful, for had Henry V lived, Beaufort could have waited five or six years for repayment of his loans. All Beaufort's loans had been contributed for the war in France, but whereas under Henry V he had little option but to lend and derived little political reward from them, under the minority council his loans were an important factor in his growing political influence. They contributed directly to his entente with Bedford and his own authority in council. This, rather than financial profit, provided the inducement to lend.

8

Bedford's Intervention, 1426–1427

THE quarrel between Beaufort and Gloucester did not arise from divisions within the council or feuds between the nobility. Nor did Gloucester accuse Beaufort or the council of financial malpractice or misgovernment. He capitalized on the chancellor's bad relations with London, but otherwise his charges centred not on government in his absence but on the challenge to his authority since his return. The refusal to yield him the Tower presented him with a *casus belli*, but his real objective was the destruction of Beaufort's authority as the head of the council. Bedford's intervention brought a setback to Gloucester's plans which was reflected in the latter's refusal to attend council until Beaufort had been dismissed. This Bedford refused to do, citing Henry IV's rejection of the similar demand from Prince Henry against Archbishop Arundel, while inviting Gloucester to lay his charges at a meeting of the whole council at Northampton on 13 February where they would be dealt with 'by the way and meene of justice or by the meene of amyable demenyng and trety'.[1] Bedford had the backing of the council for this plea, and when it failed he formally required Gloucester to attend the parliament already summoned to meet at Leicester on 18 February in the king's presence.

Gloucester plainly distrusted Bedford who, since his return, had taken up residence at Westminster palace, next door to Beaufort at the abbey. Together they had laid the foundation stone of the Brigettine convent at Isleworth, and Beaufort had continued to attend council.[2] They had strengthened their support in parliament, the usual forum for settling disputes of the nobility, by sending personal writs of summons to Tiptoft and Hungerford. Whether or not the chancellor also took steps to influence the shire elections, there was a notable increase in the number of his followers as representatives. Thomas Chaucer sat for Oxfordshire in company with William Lisle, Richard Wyot for Buckinghamshire, and John Golafre for Berkshire; both these had been sheriffs in 1424–5.

[1] *PPC* iii. 185. The invitation was issued at a great council, meeting at St Albans on 29 Jan. 1426. The endorsment on BL Cotton MS, Vespasian C XIV fo. 157, not printed by Nicolas, gives further names of those present, including the bishops of Durham, Worcester, St David's, Exeter, Bath, and Rochester, the keeper of the privy seal, the earls of Stafford and Northumberland, Sir William Philip, Sir John Cornewaile, and others. Unfortunately a hole in the manuscript preceding the name of Durham leaves it uncertain whether Beaufort or one of the archbishops was also present.

[2] *Great Chron.* 137; William Worcestre, *Itineraries*, ed. J. H. Harvey, 335.

Similarly in Hampshire and Surrey the sheriffs of that year, John de Boys and John Clipsham, both Beaufort servants, were returned. In the west country John Stourton for Wiltshire and William Carent for Dorset had connections with Beaufort, as did Lewis John from Essex and John Russell from Herefordshire. The Speaker, Sir Richard Vernon, had inherited a family connection with the Beauforts as heir to Sir Fulk Pembridge, and was the steward of High Peak.[3] The sympathies of the lower house were not so hostile to Beaufort as in the previous year; perhaps the disaster suffered by Lord Fitzwalter and the losses endured by merchantmen from the decline in trade and Flemish piracy had tempered the support for Gloucester's military ambitions.[4] In any case mercantile grievances would carry less weight at Leicester than in London, and its associations with the duchy of Lancaster made it appropriate for the settlement of a family quarrel.

Beaufort's opening sermon deliberately echoed that which he had delivered at Leicester twelve years before, warning against Lollardy and emphasizing the importance of discreet and wise council for the maintenance of peace and justice. He concluded by asking subjects to give aid in both their goods and bodies for the defence of the realm. Although the formalities of the opening had been maintained, no public business was transacted—not even the election of a Speaker—while efforts were concentrated on composing the Beaufort–Gloucester quarrel. The bands of followers were limited and disarmed, and during this interval the Commons sent a delegation under Roger Hunt to urge reconciliation. Hunt was the 'Father of the House', known to Bedford as Speaker in 1420, servant and counsel to the duke of Norfolk, and an associate of Tiptoft. The council searched for a copy of Henry V's will, doubtless for its reference to the custody of the king and definition of Gloucester's authority, and considered Gloucester's articles and Beaufort's replies.[5] By 7 March both contestants had agreed to arbitration by a carefully balanced committee of the council. This framed the terms of a solemn declaration by Beaufort to the effect that he had never intended an affront to Gloucester's dignity and authority. Gloucester formally accepted this, respiting his 'heaviness' against the bishop and accepting reconciliation with him. No damages or recompense were sought from Beaufort, but he immediately resigned the chancellorship, this clearly being one of Gloucester's stipulations. Beaufort for his part was allowed to purge himself of Gloucester's charges of past treasons, and Bedford accepted this in the king's name.[6]

[3] Roskell, *Parliament and Politics*, iii. 178–9, 267–9.

[4] For the effects of Flemish piracy on East Anglian shipping, see E 28/47 23 July.

[5] *Rot. Parl.* iv. 295–6; Roskell, *Commons and their Speakers*, 188, 207–10.

[6] *Chronicles of London*, 89–94; *Rot. Parl.* iv. 297–9. Commenting on the articles in a letter,

Bedford's task had been to woo Gloucester back into the political community while allowing Beaufort to make an honourable retreat. He had saved Beaufort from punishment but at the price of an arbitrament which centred on the readmission of Beaufort to Gloucester's good lordship, thereby underlining the difference of degree between them. Beaufort's disavowal of his intention to dishonour Gloucester was not paralleled by any retraction on Gloucester's part of his charges against Beaufort. Even apart from his loss of the chancellorship and withdrawal from the council, this represented a bitter blow to Beaufort's pride. It could not but recall the humiliation inflicted upon him by Henry V for his presumption in accepting promotion as cardinal legate. There was now, of course, no threat to his wealth or ecclesiastical status; indeed Bedford enhanced the latter by procuring Beaufort's nomination as cardinal priest of St Eusebius by Martin V eight days after he had surrendered the chancellorship. John Stafford's simultaneous resignation of the treasurership has been variously interpreted. He has been seen by some as the tool of Beaufort and by others as the ally of Gloucester, and indeed he had close connections—though of different kinds—with each. More probably his departure was due to Bedford's desire for a clean sweep and to Stafford's own wish, as a newly enthroned bishop, to give himself some time in his diocese after a wearing and frustrating three years of office. He was not disgraced and continued on the council.[7]

Throughout Beaufort's chancellorship Stafford had faced a permanent deficit with very little room to manœuvre between contending claims. Ostensibly this was due to Beaufort's own long commission on the customs, but that itself was only the consequence of attempting to finance the expeditions to France without direct taxation. Now all this was set to change, though not dramatically. Beaufort's loans had been repaid and his departure from the council meant that he would lend no more. The customs, now substantially returned to the treasurer's control, had begun to pick up as the prospect of further intervention by Gloucester receded: a boom in exports could be predicted to follow the lean years. Some yield could be expected from the residue of the clerical tenth of Martinmas 1425 and the reintroduction of tunnage and poundage, but if Bedford hoped to

Dr Alan Rogers pointed out that their form is that of an appeal before the council by written bill, and that though some could be construed as treasonous (setting hands on the king's person, plotting the death of Henry V, conspiring to procure the abdication of Henry IV), the charge of treason was never made. Gloucester's complaint was of 'causes and maters of heavynesses', but Beaufort showed that he was aware of the implications in declaring that he 'never purposed treson nor untruthe' against the king. Beaufort may have been required to rebuild the south gate on London bridge: Worcestre, *Itineraries*, 269.

[7] McFarlane, *England in XV Century*, 129; Roskell, *Commons and their Speakers*, 190; E. F. Jacob, *Essays in Later Medieval History*, 44.

maintain the momentum in France, direct taxation offered the only hope of avoiding further deficits.

The new chancellor, Archbishop Kemp, and the treasurer, Lord Hungerford, adopted the same tactics as Beaufort and Stafford. During the long parliamentary recess which followed the arbitration, convocation met and the lower clergy were exhorted by them first to amend their style of living, secondly to pray for the good estate of the realm, and thirdly to grant a subsidy without which, and a similar grant from the Commons, Bedford would refuse to return to France to hold and recover the king's rights. They obtained the grant of a half-tenth payable at Candlemas 1427 but even so failed to move the Commons to do more than renew the wool subsidies and tunnage and poundage.[8] In consequence the council, with the authority of parliament, launched a general loan on the security of the customs and the crown jewels, while the clergy were asked for an advance on the half-tenth payable at Candlemas. For the first time since 1421 commissioners were sent out to argue and plead with substantial gentry and communities. They encountered a wide variety of excuses, and their surviving reports make it surprising that as much as £3,404 was raised.[9] By comparison with the £9,000 extracted from the localities in 1421, it revealed the weakened grip of Henry V's heirs. The whole exercise, in parliament and the shires, must have impressed on Bedford the limited basis of support in England for the great task he had inherited in France, confirming his reliance upon Beaufort's political and financial support, and his apprehension of the consequences of Gloucester's sole rule.

Bedford had returned to resolve not only the crisis between Gloucester and Beaufort but an impasse between the council and Martin V. Essentially this arose from the position at Henry V's death. In the king's last years it had become clear that papal recognition of Henry's title to the crown of France would depend on the king's recognition of papal rights of provision in England, which Henry refused to contemplate. During the first year of the minority both issues were in suspense, but in October 1423 the death of Henry Bowet, archbishop of York, gave Martin V the opportunity for a decisive assertion of his claims. While the chapter elected the council's nominee, Philip Morgan, bishop of Worcester, Martin in February 1424 translated Fleming from Lincoln. Morgan was an experienced royal diplomat and councillor, Fleming a flexible careerist who had served Martin's interests at the council of Pavia-Siena. Martin saw him as a sympathizer and may also have believed that he would receive support from Beaufort. In fact the council remained united behind Morgan, and

[8] *Reg. Chichele*, iii. 177, 180.

[9] *Rot. Parl.* iv. 300; *CPR 1422–9*, 318, 353; Steel, *Receipt*, 170. There were widespread refusals in East Anglia, Hampshire (where Beaufort was a commissioner), and Leicestershire: E 28/47 23 July, E 28/48 4, 6 Sept., 2 Oct.

proceeded to nominate John Stafford, the treasurer, to Morgan's see of Worcester. It threatened Fleming with the penalties of praemunire forcing him to renounce his bull of provision, and sent Nicholas Bildeston once again to Rome to declare the royal rights.[10]

In the first half of 1424 the council's firm stand was probably strengthened by Gloucester, the validity of whose marriage to Jacqueline of Hainault was even now under arbitration. If—as had happened by midsummer—that failed, a submission to the pope could be expected, from whom Gloucester hoped for a favourable response. Fleming was told to use his influence at Rome on Gloucester's behalf, and Gloucester dispatched a series of letters to the papal court urging a quick verdict.[11] Had Gloucester been content with diplomatic pressures, Bedford would probably have lent his support; but his resort to arms brought a shift in Bedford's attitude and seemingly in that of the English council under Beaufort. On 27 October 1424 rumour reached Gloucester at Calais that Simon of Teramo had reported to the pope that if Martin pronounced against Gloucester the council would cede him full liberty in filling English benefices.[12] The rumour was certainly exaggerated, and on receiving Gloucester's protest, Martin hastily recalled Simon. The papal collector was known to be in Beaufort's confidence, and Gloucester was probably convinced that Beaufort was now working against him. This may even have been the origin of their vendetta. In any case the confusion into which English policy was thrown by Gloucester's invasion undoubtedly encouraged Martin to postpone his judgement on Gloucester's suit and to stand firm over provisions.

The dispute with the council was helped towards a resolution by the death of Bishop Bubwith of Wells on 24 October 1424, for Martin now accepted the council's recommendation of Stafford, already dean of Wells, and provided him. Martin was anxious not to alienate Beaufort, whom he regarded as his staunchest supporter in the episcopate, and Beaufort was Stafford's patron and colleague; he himself consecrated the new bishop at Blackfriars at Whitsun. With the Beaufort–Gloucester quarrel paralysing the council during 1425–6, it was through Bedford's own negotiations with Martin V that the tangle over provisions was finally resolved. On 20 July 1425 Kemp, who was with Bedford, Warwick, and Hungerford in Paris to adjudicate the Burgundy–Gloucester duel, was translated to York, while Fleming was retranslated to Lincoln, and William Gray, dean of York and

[10] R. G. Davies, 'Martin V and the English Episcopate', *EHR* 92 (1977), 318, 323–6; Jacob, *Essays*, 41–2.

[11] *PPC* iii. 210–11. This document must be dated some time in 1424; it is plainly separate from the document printed immediately above: see Davies, 'Martin V', 326 n. 2. *Wars of Eng.* ii. 388–93, 400–14.

[12] Thomas Bekynton, *Correspondence*, ed. G. Williams, i. 279; J. Ferguson, *English Diplomacy 1422–1461*, 126. Cf. *CPL* vii. 29 n. for a different interpretation.

a friend of Kemp and Bedford, was promoted to London. In April Norwich had been vacated by the death of Wakering, and in November Ely similarly by the death of Fordham, but no moves to fill either were made by the council; all awaited the arrival of Bedford. It was only at a meeting on 14 January 1426, presided over by Bedford, that the council finally endorsed Kemp's translation to York, giving Ely to Morgan, Norwich to Alnwick (whom it had earlier recommended to Martin V), and Worcester to Thomas Polton. In all cases the temporalities were restored by 23 April.[13] This was part of an attempt by Bedford to settle all outstanding differences with Martin V and place relations with the papacy on a new footing. Alarmed by Martin's cordial relations with Bourges, he had conceded papal rights of provision in Lancastrian France, to secure the pope's co-operation in controlling the church there and pave the way for his recognition of Henry VI's title. He had permitted the provision of Martin's nephew Prospero Colonna to the archdeaconry of Canterbury, which Chichele had steadfastly opposed, hoping to deflect Martin's campaign for the abolition of the anti-papal legislation in England. Finally, in expectation of greater co-operation and harmony between the papacy and the Lancastrian crown, Martin on 26 March 1426 elevated both Jean de Rochetaillée and Henry Beaufort to the cardinalate. This too was with Bedford's approval. Evidently he took a different view from Henry V of the function and advantages of an English cardinal.

The archbishop of Rouen, who sat on Bedford's *Grand Conseil*, was to preside over the church in Lancastrian France, but whether Bedford and Martin shared a common view of Beaufort's role is less easy to judge. Martin's confidence in Beaufort's goodwill towards papal policy was apparently unshaken, fortified undoubtedly by the reports of Simon of Teramo and his successor John de Obizzi whom Beaufort had cultivated, and possibly also by those of Bildeston. How accurately the English political situation was understood in Rome is questionable; Martin may have assumed that with Bedford's return Beaufort's position would be protected and his influence restored. In the spring of 1426 he wrote thanking Beaufort for favouring the cause of Prospero Colonna and promising further benefits. When Cardinal Cesarini arrived in May 1426 to press for the repeal of the statutes, he in turn was persuaded of Beaufort's goodwill and identified Chichele as the centre of opposition.[14] By December 1426 Martin V had resolved to press hard for the repeal of the statutes. He warned Bedford that the question should be resolved at the next parliament and exhorted Chichele and Kemp to give a lead. In March 1427 he even suspended Chichele from the exercise of his legatine powers.

[13] Davies, 'Martin V', 328; *Reg. Chichele*, pp. xci–ii.

[14] Haller, *England u. Rom*, 269; *Reg. Chichele*, i. pp. xliii–v, 86; Jacob, *Archbishop Chichele*, 50–1.

By contrast his letters to Beaufort were full of his joy at hearing from Cesarini that Beaufort held the pope in singular affection and was a veritable fighter for the rights of the Roman church. Martin was moved to promise to be an Alexander III to Beaufort's Becket.[15] Cesarini had grossly misled Martin about Beaufort's political influence and intentions and had traduced Chichele as an enemy and traitor to the Holy See. Indeed Bedford and Beaufort had adeptly exploited Martin's gullibility for their own purposes, leaving the council and Chichele to handle the rejection of the pope's demands and his consequent displeasure. It was small wonder that Beaufort was to be coolly received by the council when in due course he returned as cardinal.

The changes in the episcopate from 1423 to 1425 had also a personal significance for Beaufort. Death had removed three of his long standing friends, Bowet, Bubwith, and Wakering;[16] but these losses were more than compensated by the promotion of others who were to be more active as political allies. With the chief of these, Kemp, he was to forge a long and trusting partnership, and scarcely less so with Stafford, who owed his advancement more directly to Beaufort. Stafford was a notable pluralist: by 1423 his preferments were worth 664 marks p.a. including prebends in the dioceses of Salisbury and Chichester perhaps obtained through Beaufort's influence. He also held the deanery of Wells, which he occupied for the brief interval between Beaufort's chancellor Richard Medford and his vicar-general John Forest. Alnwick, already an associate of Beaufort as keeper of the privy seal, had succeeded Stafford as archdeacon of Salisbury in 1420, while Polton, whom Chichele had long regarded as his enemy at the Curia, had devotedly served Beaufort's interests there. Bedford's disposal of these sees in 1425–6 bears many signs of Beaufort's proposing. This parallels other evidence of Beaufort's increasing influence following Henry V's death at slightly lower levels of ecclesiastical patronage. This was mainly exercised in the prebends of the dioceses of Salisbury and Wells. In Salisbury the prebend of Bedwyn was held by Simon of Teramo from 1423 to 1425, when it went to Nicholas Bildeston; in 1423 that of Durnford was held by Edward Prewys, probably the brother of John Prewys, clerk of Beaufort's household, and that of Grimston by Richard Leyot, Medford's successor as Beaufort's chancellor. Leyot was Bedford's chancellor by 1424 and in that year William Lyndwood, also on Bedford's council, received the prebend of Bishopstone and John Hody that of Warminster. By 1426 Hody had become chancellor of the diocese of Bath and Wells where John Forest, Beaufort's vicar general, succeeded Stafford as dean in 1424. Forest received the prebend of Combe in March 1425,

[15] Haller, *England u. Rom*, 270 ff, suppl. nos. 8, 9; *CPL* vii. 26.

[16] Bowett commemorated Beaufort in his chantry : *The Certificates of . . . Chantries, Guild, and Hospitals, in the County of York*, i. ed. W. Page (Surtees Soc., vol. 91, 1894), 12.

previously held by William Toly, Henry V's clerk of the signet, who may already have transferred his services to Beaufort.[17]

In the absence of Beaufort's register it is difficult to trace his movements following his resignation as chancellor on 16 March 1426. He was not at the Garter ceremonies on the eve of St George's day although his brother was well enough to attend, and it is unlikely that he was present for the second session of parliament. Nor is there any evidence of his personal activity in his diocese, where his new vicar general, Robert Keton, was acting for him throughout 1426.[18] It is likely that for much of the summer he resided at Bishop's Waltham and was occupied in putting his affairs in order pending his withdrawal, for on 14 May 1426 he had received licence to go on his long-postponed pilgrimage. Perhaps he was at his brother's deathbed at Greenwich in December, and after the obsequies at St Paul's in the new year he made a pilgrimage to St Albans[19] late in February.

The only record of his attendance at council prior to the eve of his departure was at a meeting of the great council at Reading on 24 November which reaffirmed some of the regulations for the transaction of business laid down in 1422 and 1424.[20] These regulations foreshadowed Bedford's decision to return to France in the spring, but they evidently did not allay the fears of the councillors. So disturbed were they by reports that Gloucester had declared that he was answerable to no one except the king, and that on Bedford's departure he would govern as seemed good to him, that on 28 and 29 January eleven of the twenty-two councillors named in November met in the Star Chamber and presented to Bedford a definition of their powers, to which they invited him to subscribe.[21] The essence of this was the declaration that the execution of the royal authority 'stondeth as now in his lordes assembled, either by authority of his parliament or in his consail and in especiale in the lordes of his consail' and 'resteth not in oon singular persone but in all my said lordes togidres', reserving only the authority given to Bedford and Gloucester as protector by act of parliament. Unless they were free to govern by this authority and answer collectively to the king when he attained his majority, the councillors declined to assume their charge. Bedford swore solemnly to be ruled by the council in all matters belonging to the rule of law and, armed with this declaration, the council sought a similar promise from Gloucester, then ill at his lodgings. This he had little choice but to give, promising to be ruled and governed by the lords of the council in all things that might touch the king, his realms, lordships, and laws.

[17] Le Neve, *Fasti*, dioceses of Salisbury, Bath and Wells, Chichester.

[18] Anstis, *Garter*, 96; *Reg. Chichele*, i. 236, 243, 348.

[19] *Foedera*, x. 358; *Johannis Amundesham . . . Annales*, ed. H. T. Riley, i (Rolls Ser., 1870), 10–11; HRO Eccles. II 159427 records the expenditure of £161 on his household at Bishop's Waltham.

[20] *PPC* iii. 213 ff.

[21] Ibid. 231–42.

Those who had extracted this declaration from Gloucester under threat of resignation were those who were to remain in England as the protector's council. The non-noble element, like Chaucer and Alington, had disappeared from the November list. Headed by the two archbishops, with Stafford, Morgan, and Alnwick among the bishops, and Cromwell, Scrope, Hungerford, and Tiptoft now all members of the baronage, they formed a body with strong traditions of conciliar authority and with closer associations with Bedford and Beaufort than with Gloucester. To this core the five earls of Huntingdon, Stafford, Warwick, Salisbury, and Northumberland varyingly added their presence; only the first two of these had been present on 28 January. Gloucester's own attendance at council had been intermittent during the year when Bedford was protector, and he had exercised little influence over policy or patronage. Bedford had prevented the dispatch of further aid to Jacqueline throughout 1426 while her forces held their own against the ducal armies, and had maintained contact with Duke Philip through an embassy of his three principal counsellors, Wydeville, Oldhall, and Estcourt.[22] Bedford likewise secured for himself some of the major offices and perquisites. Even before Exeter's death in December 1426 he had the reversion of his office of admiral, and in February 1427 he exchanged his annuity of 1,000 marks at the exchequer for the keeping of the lands of the earl of Oxford which Exeter had previously enjoyed. He received lands of the honour of Richmond after the death of the earl of Westmorland in October 1425 and the farms of the gold and silver mines in Devon and of the estates and wardship of the heir of Lord Grey of Codnor. On Exeter's death Gloucester succeeded to his office of justice of North Wales, and later that of Chester, but had no direct financial rewards.[23] In fact the new treasurer, Lord Hungerford, doubtless with Bedford's support, began a rigorous exploitation of the fiscal prerogatives through commissions to inquire into concealed rights and by individual compositions for licences to marry and fines for marriages, enfeoffments, and alienations without licence—thereby provoking complaint in the second session of parliament.[24]

Having failed to obtain direct taxation from parliament, Bedford had to follow a financial policy of strict economy, rigid preferences, and conservation of royal rights if he was to find money to take an army back to France. By restraining payments to Calais and appropriating the wool subsidies to his immediate needs, assiduously exacting casual revenues,

[22] E 28/47 11 June; E 28/49 6 Feb. In Feb. 1426 the Roman court gave a preliminary sentence against Jacqueline, sequestering her lands: *CPL* vii. 29.

[23] *PPC* iii. 207, 210, 227, 267; *CPR 1422–9*, 395; *CCR 1422–9*, 231–2; *CFR 1422–30*, 119.

[24] *Rot. Parl.* iv. 306; *CPR 1422–9*, 282, 334, 350, 352, 388, 393–4, and, for commissions, 356, 359–61; *PPC* iii. 253.

and using the clerical tenth levied at Candlemas, Bedford gathered over £18,000 in cash at the exchequer during the Michaelmas term 1426–7.[25] This sum was sufficient and to spare for the 1,200 men who sailed with Bedford and Lords Talbot, Clinton, Roos, and Camoys on 19 March.[26]

All these leaders shared a close attachment to Bedford, Beaufort, and Warwick. Talbot had married Margaret Beauchamp, probably in September 1424, and on his return from Ireland had taken up the Beauchamp quarrel with Lady Bergevenny leading to the clash at Snitterfield and the death of his brother William in January 1426. Both parties submitted to Bedford's award under bonds of £1,000 in November 1426 when Bedford made Talbot his retainer. Bedford also acted as godfather to his first son. Talbot was then turning 40 and an experienced soldier.[27] His brother-in-law, Thomas, Lord Roos, had just attained his majority, having inherited the title from his brother John, who had died at Baugé. Thomas, like John, had been the ward of Exeter; he had been knighted at the Leicester parliament and had married Margaret Beauchamp's sister Eleanor, who bore his first son in September 1427.[28] Even younger was Sir Roger Lewknor, claimant to the title of Lord Camoys by virtue of his marriage to Eleanor, coheir of the late Hugh, Lord Camoys, an old retainer of the house of Lancaster and a west country neighbour of the Beauforts.[29] In the same company were Sir Thomas Beaumont, Sir Edmund Beaufort, and Henry Bourchier. Sir Thomas had just taken over the wardship of his nephew John from Bishop Beaufort, while Henry Bourchier, the son of Exeter's captain Sir William, had recently come of age and made his first appearance in the council.[30] Service with Bedford was undoubtedly seen as an opportunity to secure recognition of family claims as well as lands and rewards in France. Edmund Beaufort's presence had its own significance. The death of his uncle, Exeter, and the departure of his other uncle, the bishop, left him no household other than his mother's. Having attained his majority, it was fitting that, as a younger son, he should seek his fortunes in war. Moreover if his *affaire* with Queen Catherine had indeed been an undercurrent in the crisis of 1425–6, his removal became part of Bedford's

[25] E 28/47 25 July 1426; *Calendar of Documents relating to Scotland*, ed. J. Bain, iv. 199, 204; Payments to Calais were suspended from May 1426 to May 1427 but a delegation from Calais came to the council in Feb. 1427 and secured additional finance: Ratcliffe, thesis, 114; *PPC* iii. 243, 260; E 28/49, 25 Feb., 8 Mar.

[26] Steel, *Receipt*, 170; Ratcliffe, thesis, 22–4; *CPR 1422–9*, 404; E 404/43/158–75. The total cost was £9,000–£10,000.

[27] A. J. Pollard, *John Talbot and the war in France, 1427–1453*, 11; *CCR 1422–9*, 317. Talbot was in dispute with Lord Grey of Ruthin over precedence in the 1426 parliament: *Rot. Parl.* iv. 312.

[28] *PPC* iii. 225–6.

[29] *CP* ii. 508.

[30] *CFR 1422–30*, 164; *CPR 1422–9*, 270; E 28/49 6 Feb.; *CP* ii. 147–8.

design to pacify and heal these quarrels. Bedford and Gloucester, having bound themselves by a treaty of mutual friendship and trust, now significantly extended this to include the queen mother.[31]

Yet Edmund's departure to France must have been viewed with apprehension not merely by his mother, the dowager duchess, whose two remaining sons were both still held prisoner, but by his uncle. For, with Exeter's death without heirs, uncle and nephew represented the whole of the male line of the Beauforts at liberty, and the continuation of that line rested with Edmund, yet unmarried. Failure in the male line was not uncommon among the nobility at this period, and though it had saved the Beaufort lands from Clarence's designs, it dissipated the estates gained by Exeter. Like his uncle Exeter, Edmund Beaufort had to make his way by arms, and he was now equipped to do so. His retinue was as numerous as that of Lord Roos and second only to Talbot's; very probably it was furnished by the generosity of his uncle and may well have included some of Exeter's followers. If he could avoid death or capture the prospects for Edmund's military career with Bedford were encouraging, for the tide of war was still with the English and Bedford's return could be expected to herald a new advance. Yet the disaster at Baugé had done the Beauforts irreparable harm, for it had excluded them from the profits of war and the grants of land which others had reaped by the victory at Verneuil and the conquest of Maine in 1424–6. These were all in the hands of Bedford, Salisbury, Warwick, and Suffolk, who rejoiced in their acquired titles of duke of Anjou and count of Maine and Alençon, count of Perche, count of Aumale, and count of Dreux. Exeter's retinue in France had disintegrated, and his barony of Harcourt now went to Bedford.[32] Edmund Beaufort arrived in France with little but the expectations of a younger son, and these must have been focused on the conquest of Anjou.

The plight of his brothers was not forgotten. The battle of Baugé had left the duchess Margaret not merely a widow with two captive sons but the custodian of the count of Angoulême, Clarence's hostage since 1412 for the fulfilment of the treaty of Buzançais. Of the sum of 210,000 *écus* then due, less than half had been paid by the time of Clarence's death, following which Margaret raised her demands by 70,000 *écus* in order to purchase the return of her sons. But partly owing to a failure to raise the money and partly through Henry V's reluctance to sanction Angoulême's release, this scheme had come to nothing and for the next ten years Angoulême languished under the guard of the Beaufort servant Richard Waller

[31] Bekynton *Correspondence*, i. 138–45.

[32] *Appendices to Rymer's Foedera*, ed. C. P. Cooper, 373–7; *Wars of Eng.* ii. 434, 532; A. Longnon, 'Les Limites de la France et l'entendue de la domination anglaise', *Rev. des quest. hist.*, 18 (1875), 444–510.

at Groomsbridge or at the duchess's Northamptonshire manor of Maxey.[33]

A different difficulty was presented in 1423, when John, earl of Somerset was purchased by Charles VII from his captor the Scot, Lawrence Vernon, and transferred to the duchess of Bourbon, whose husband and son, the count of Eu, had both been made prisoner at Agincourt. More than once—the last time in January 1421—Henry V had come close to agreeing to Bourbon's ransom on condition that he accepted the king's title, though in his will he had effectively prohibited the release of Eu during his son's minority. Hopes for the release of Somerset and his brother now centred on an exchange with the duke of Bourbon. Although the duke himself was now past fighting, the political implications of his release were considerable. His duchess had pursued a policy of friendship towards Burgundy, maintaining a truce covering the Bourbonnais, while his son the count of Clermont had attached himself to the dauphin. John the Fearless had sought to win Bourbon as an ally through a marriage of his daughter Agnes to the count of Clermont, first proposed in 1412, revived in 1418, and finally consummated in February 1425 with the consent of the captive duke. The duchess and her son thereupon agreed to observe all the treaties concluded between the duke of Bourbon and the king of England. In this context the release of the duke of Bourbon offered the hope of securing the adhesion of one of the leading principalities to the Anglo-Burgundian cause, at a time when the fortunes of Charles VII were at an ebb and Bedford was preparing to renew his offensive.[34] At a meeting of the council at Canterbury on 10 March 1427, immediately prior to Bedford's departure, the councillors individually gave cautious approval to the terms for Bourbon's release. He was to fulfil his promises to Henry V and to bring the count of Clermont into Henry VI's obedience. He should pay the balance of the ransom for the two Beauforts, who were in turn to give security to answer to Henry VI for their ransoms when he came of age.[35] Thus one way and another the prospects for the new generation of the Beaufort family in France seemed hopeful.

The death of his brother at Greenwich on 31 December 1426, much as it must have saddened Bishop Henry, had little consequence for either his own political position or the fortunes of the family. The position which Exeter had filled since the death of Earl John in 1410, as a lay ally to his brother in the council and the royal camp, had by 1426 devolved on

[33] G. Dupont-Ferrier, 'La Captivité de Jean d'Orléans, comte d'Angoulême', *Rev. Hist.*, 62 (1896), 45–60; M. Jones, 'Henry VII, Lady Margaret Beaufort, and the Orleans ransom', in R. A. Griffiths and J. Sherborne (edd.), *Kings and Nobles in the Later Middle Ages*, 254.

[34] *Foedera*, x. 85, 100; A. Leguai, *Les Ducs de Bourbon pendant la crise monarchique du XV siècle*, 86; P. and F. Strong, 'Last will', 92; Charles VII purchased Somerset for 40,000 *écus*: *Appendices to Foedera*, 167.

[35] *PPC* iii. 255–6.

Bedford. The partnership of the two brothers had been closest in the years 1410–11 and 1422–3. Undoubtedly each assisted the rise of the other, their complementary and equally strenuous service to the crown winning their family recognition from the full blood and establishing it securely in the upper peerage. In moments of crisis Thomas had supported Henry, and their political attitudes and loyalties rarely diverged. Yet they had never formed a Beaufort faction, for Thomas's loyalty had been reserved exclusively for the crown. To his contemporaries he appeared the model of knighthood, displaying valour, discipline, good lordship, largess, fidelity, and compassion, and earning the sobriquet of 'the good duke of Exeter'.[36] He kept a firm rule in his household where he would have no swearers, liars, or tale bearers, and would accept no bribes. He sustained those who served him faithfully, supplying the daily needs of his soldiers, and caring for his retainers in their old age. His reputation helps to explain why Henry V not merely vested him with his most important commands but entrusted him with the upbringing of his son. Exeter's devotion to royal service, coupled with his childlessness and position as a younger son, meant that his advancement and enrichment brought little permanent benefit to his family.

With Exeter's death the interests of the family in England were now in the hands of Joan, countess of Westmorland, and Margaret, duchess of Clarence. Margaret held all the prospective Beaufort inheritance, comprising her own Holand lands, her dower and jointure, and the lands of her son John. When, on 25 March 1425, John had come of age, inquisitions had been taken to establish his rights as heir to his brother Henry, and livery of the lands had been ordered in September.[37] Since John was in captivity his mother presumably assumed responsibility for their administration. John gained very little from his uncle's death. Exeter's landed estate had come principally from two sources: the grants of forfeited lands made to him by Henry IV and the lands held in right of his wife. Some of the former, notably grants of Mowbray and Holand lands, had been transient, and the largest and most permanent were those of Lord Bardolph, comprising Stowbardolph and the honour of Wyrmegey held in fee-tail.[38] As he died without direct heirs this reverted to the crown, but it was first committed to his executors for the payment of his debts. Some individual manors in Kent, Sussex, and Hampshire which he had received after their forfeiture

[36] Worcestre, *Itineraries*, 161, 223, 249, 355–9.

[37] PRO C 139/15: *CCR 1422–9*, 230–1. John received two-thirds of Enderby (Lincs.), Orwell (Cambs.), Oveston, Maxey, Eydon (Northants); half of Brampton and Torpell (Northants); Corfe and the Somerset properties of Curry Rivel, Martock, Langport, Abdyke hundred, and Bulston; with two-thirds of annuities to a sum of 1,000 marks. For Bishop Beaufort's protection of his lands, as chancellor, see C 1/6 no. 177.

[38] Mowbray and Holand lands: *CPR 1397–9*, 414; *CPR 1399–1401*, 247; Bardolph lands: *CPR 1405–8*, 105, 443; *CFR 1405–13*, 316.

by Robert Bealknap in 1399 had apparently been alienated without licence before his death and were ultimately seized into the king's hand.[39] Since his wife's death he had held by courtesy of England a group of Yorkshire manors which, before his own death, he had granted to Sir William Harrington, again without licence. This was disputed by his wife's cousin, John Langton, and the lands were taken into the king's hand in 1431 until a settlement was reached between the two claimants in 1433.[40] The terms on which he held his grants from the crown largely precluded their descent to his nephews. The only lands which John, earl of Somerset could claim as his heir were a few individual manors in Hertfordshire, Herefordshire, and Bedfordshire and the manor of Stockton in Yorkshire, the reversion of which had been granted by Gaunt to Thomas with remainder to the sons of Earl John, and to Bishop Beaufort and the Countess Joan. John was granted seisin of these lands in June 1427 but their value was small. For the rest Thomas's income had come from his annuities at the exchequer and in Devon which ceased with his death, from his offices including the profits of the admiralty which Bedford now took over, and from the custody of lands of royal wards, the most notable at his death being those of the earl of March in East Anglia, which his executors retained until 1429, and those of the earl of Oxford, which went to Bedford.[41]

Like his brother John, Thomas held much of his wealth in cash and plate. The accounts of his executors record a sum of £504 in coin and the sale of jewels and silver to a total of £2,675. They were also able to recover large sums from his creditors: £1,127 from loans he had made and a further £665 in tallies and obligations. The issues of his own lands yielded them £638 and from the estates of the earl of March they drew £339, while the sale of the important manors of Greenwich and Mutford together brought £800. Altogether his estate amounted to £6,787. Exeter's will gave instructions for conventional if restrained obsequies, and his executors spent just over £500 on equipping the funeral cortège, from Greenwich to London and thence to Bury St Edmunds, with black cloth worn by his executors and household, and on the distribution of alms at each of the resting places. The tomb itself, made in London, cost £106. His special bequests to the Carthusian houses at Mountgrace and Hinckley, and to recluses, hospitals, and paupers, indicate that Exeter conformed to the devotional attitudes of the Lancastrian royal house.[42] His will is notable,

39 *CCR 1396–9*, 435, 449; *CPR 1399–1401*, 176, 549–50; *CFR 1422–30*, 257.

40 *CFR 1422–30*, 264–5; *CPR 1422–9*, 97; *PPC* iii. 52–3; *CPR 1429–36*, 257; *CFR 1430–7*, 31, 75, 87, 137–9. In general, C 139/30 and A. J. Elder, thesis. A list of the Beaufort estates is in Appendix II.

41 For the grants to Bedford: *CPR 1422–9*, 349, 395; his executors' account is E 101/514/22.

42 His will is printed in *Royal Wills*, 250–65 and *Reg. Chichele*, ii. 355–64. In Feb. 1416 he had been admitted to the confraternity of Winchester (*Reg. CS* 58) and in Nov. 1426 to that of Durham: *Historiae Dunelmensis Scriptores Tres*, ed. J. Raine (Surtees Soc., 1839), p. ccxv.

too, for the large number (forty-three) of individual bequests to retainers and servants, and its emphasis on his responsibilities to his *familia*. These bequests, totalling £1,138, were to be made after his debts had been discharged and, if sufficient money remained, money was allotted to poor scholars at Queen's college, Oxford, and Trinity hall, Cambridge, to masses for his soul in five monasteries, to paupers, beggars, marriage portions, and the remaining members of his household. His will eloquently reflects his own code of belief and behaviour, but gives no indication of a sense of dynasty. None of his moveable wealth was left to his brother or nephews, and even allowing for the circumstances of their impending departure from England, their absence as legatees or executors is surprising. His choice of Bishops Alnwick and Morgan, Sir Lewis Robessart, and Sir Walter Hungerford as supervisors suggests that he pinned his hopes on the councillors remaining in England, and his executors headed by Sir William Phelip were all leading retainers and officials of his household.[43] The executors did their best to fulfil his instructions. They discharged debts and obligations to the sum of £3,625; they paid the fees and wages of his officials and those of his domestic servants for five weeks following his death; they paid many of the legacies to those whom he had specified and to others whom he had not; they paid up annuities which he had granted, including £160 to Hinckley priory; and they distributed small sums to hospitals, for marriage portions, and to prisoners: in all to a total of £1,657. The residue of the estate went on administrative and funeral costs.[44]

Exeter's influence was mainly exercised in East Anglia and to a lesser degree in the north, from where the majority of his followers in war and peace were drawn. These now attached themselves to the earl of Suffolk, the duke of York, the earl of Stafford, and the Nevills. Two of his officers, Reginald Curteys and Robert Barbot, moved into the service of Cardinal Beaufort, Barbot becoming treasurer of Wolvesey;[45] but essentially nothing of the estates, wealth, or clientage of Thomas, duke of Exeter passed to the family of Beaufort. Indeed by the summer of 1427, thirty years after their legitimation, the Beauforts had to all intents and purposes ceased to have any presence in English politics. No male representatives of the family remained in England and their lands rested in the hands of a dowager duchess who, though she now promised not to remarry, was bound to be vulnerable to other pressures. Gloucester could be pardoned

He gave £100 for a loan chest to Oxford University: *The Register of Congregation, 1448–1463*, ed. W. Pantin and R. Mitchell, 419.

[43] A list of his household is in Worcestre *Itineraries*, 354–9. He bequeathed a 'book called Tristram' to Joan, countess of Westmorland and a cup to his 'brother' Sir Thomas Swynford.

[44] The executors received discharge on 28 Feb. 1428 (*Reg. Chichele*, ii. 376), though money was still being recovered for the estate in 1441: *CCR 1335–41*, 459, 464.

[45] HRO Eccles. II 159427. Beaufort also retained William Wolf.

for thinking that he had seen the back of his rival and could now enter into the fullness of his own authority.

The quarrel between Beaufort and Gloucester in 1425 was the first test of the cohesion of the minority council. It was ostensibly over the respective authority of the protector and the council for the maintenance of order and the security of the king, but it was inflamed by personal antipathy and conflicting ambitions. Gloucester saw his honour as Henry V's brother affronted and the authority which he exercised as protector set aside, while beneath the public injury lurked resentment at his own failure to command the respect and leadership which were his birthright. Beaufort was made to relive the humiliations he had endured in 1419–20 and further back in 1412, impressing upon him his inferior status and vulnerability in any disputes with the princes of the full blood. The quarrel also called in question the structure of government. Under Beaufort's active leadership the council since 1423 had become a tightly knit, professional, and hard-working body, jealous of its responsibilities and its enjoyment of the fruits of power. It feared the usurpation of its authority by the protector, just as he feared his displacement by a body with which he had few ties and in which he could be no more than a figurehead.

Over and beyond these conflicts of personality, ambition, and political power, the dispute raised the question of the whole direction and purpose of Lancastrian policy. Although the completion of Henry V's work commanded an unthinking consensus, there were in practice different degrees of commitment to this and different views about how it should be achieved. Bedford was for the continuation of Henry V's military strategy: the slow conquest of territory by sieges and the distribution of fiefs to English captains as rewards. Diplomatically he sought to win and retain the allegiance of the great French princes and the papacy by concessions to their own interests. He looked to the council in England for continuing supplies of men and money and restraint in traditional areas of dispute, such as commercial rivalries and papal rights. For this Bedford had the full support of Beaufort and the council, which attempted to secure taxation, raise loans, and encourage the nobility to serve in France or on the northern frontier. Moreover, the council continued, as far as possible, Henry V's policy of maintaining exchequer credit by careful financial planning and the exploitation of the crown's fiscal prerogatives. Gloucester's venture in Hainault directly challenged this, by alienating England's prime ally and by threatening to divert English resources from the conquest of France. In the event it was Beaufort's 'long commission' on the ports which proved a barrier to such a change of policy, for his stranglehold on the customs made it impossible to finance any major expedition other than from his loans. Unless Gloucester could secure taxation specifically for his own expedition, he could only change the direction of English policy by breaking Beaufort's political and financial monopoly. Yet the 'long commission' had not been contrived by Beaufort either for his own enrichment or to bolster his political influence; it was the direct consequence of the refusal of parliament and convocation to grant supplies. Moreover, because Beaufort could only afford to lend if his repayment was assured by stringent preferences and his own continuance in power, Bedford had to underwrite Beaufort's political safety. In 1425–6 Bedford could not afford to allow Duke Humphrey to overthrow the council, and even the removal of Beaufort from office was only possible because the regent took his place in the year following. Beaufort's chancellorship and the crisis which terminated it, therefore, effectively cemented his political alliance with Bedford, based on their mutual dedication to the furtherance of the conquest of France. It was with this purpose that they sailed together from Dover in March 1427.

9

Crisis and Crusade, 1427–1429

WITH the return of Bedford and Beaufort to France in March 1427 each of the remaining princes of the Lancastrian blood undertook separate responsibilities. Bedford resumed the task of extending Lancastrian France; Gloucester, once again protector, was left to govern England in conjunction with the council; Beaufort was named as legate in Bohemia, Germany, and Hungary for the crusade against the Hussites. In practice none of these tasks could be pursued in isolation, and they became interlocking elements in Bedford's ambitious design to achieve Lancastrian hegemony in France. That crashed with the retreat from Orléans, which in turn entailed the abandonment of the crusade and Beaufort's re-entry into English politics.

Bedford's first task was to bring Jean V, duke of Brittany, back to the English alliance. In 1426 military pressure from Suffolk had compelled him to seek a truce, and in 1427 the confiscation of his lands in Normandy and the capture of Pontorson by the earl of Warwick induced Jean to seek peace and once again to swear adhesion to the treaty of Troyes.[1] Bedford had resumed the English offensive in Maine, and the capture of Laval in March 1428 left him poised to attack Anjou. Before the winter Bedford had also captured Rambouillet, strengthening the southern frontier towards the Loire, and with the spring he began to assemble troops at Dreux for a further advance. In the east, as well, military support had been obtained for the first time for four years from Burgundian captains under Jean de Luxembourg, whose operations on the borders of Lorraine forced the duke of Bar into an alliance, while to the south the duke of Orange was threatening the Dauphiné. English diplomacy was also encouraging Aragon to attack Castile, prompting the latter to seek a truce, while at Charles VII's court feuds between La Trémoille and the count of Richemont aroused hopes of attracting the constable and his brother-in-law the count of Clermont into the reinvigorated Breton–Burgundian–English alliance. Only in Scotland was Charles VII finding new allies, while the papacy remained diplomatically neutral between the two contendents. On all its borders the kingdom of Bourges was isolated and threatened. Bedford only awaited Salisbury's substantial reinforcements from England in the summer of 1428 to attempt a decisive offensive which would breach the Loire.[2]

[1] G. A. Knowlson, *Jean V, duc de Bretagne et l'Angleterre*, 134–41.

[2] Beaucourt, *Charles VII*, ii. 24–31, 175; Ferguson, *English Diplomacy*, 20, 45–7; M. G. A. Vale, *Charles VII*, 54; Longnon, 'Limites de la France', 473–86.

For Edmund Beaufort the operations of 1427–8, directed to the recovery and defence of earlier gains, had been unproductive; he still awaited the promised advance into Anjou. However, on his arrival in Paris in April 1427, he had received from Bedford the county of Mortain, previously held until his death in 1418 by Edward Holand. At the beginning of the century it had been worth some 3,000 *li.tournois* a year, but as a border county it had suffered depredations and it was only with the conquest of Maine in 1424 that it can again have become profitable. By September 1427 Edmund had joined the large army assembled by Bedford at Chartres, but there is no indication that he took part in the operations which captured Laval and extended the English conquests into western Maine early in 1428. He returned to England some time later in the winter of 1427–8 and did not join Salisbury's army in the summer.[3]

In England Gloucester had given notice that, when his brother left, he would govern as he pleased, and in the course of 1427–8 he actively exercised his authority as protector, both in settling disputes and in finally procuring for himself the custody of the lands of the earl of March.[4] He was also able to strengthen his personal following on the council, particularly among the higher nobility. Throughout 1427–8 there were some fifteen councillors in regular attendance, of whom two or three were usually earls. Huntingdon and Salisbury (during the year he spent in England) were the most assiduous and both gave the protector personal support. Northumberland and Stafford withdrew at the end of 1427, and the duke of Norfolk, on whom Gloucester could also count, rarely attended. Among the bishops and lesser lords Gloucester succeeded in attracting only Lord Scrope to his following; the remainder, led by the officers, Kemp and Hungerford, adopted a stance of wary independence, fortified by the distant authority of Bedford. They were able to withstand the protector on two major issues, namely the prosecution of his wife's claims in Hainault and of his own claim to the regency, while on a third issue, the response to Martin V's campaign against the statute of provisors, the council displayed a resolution for which Gloucester and possibly Bedford must have been privately grateful.

The first of these to arise was the epilogue to the saga of Jacqueline. When the long winter siege of her stronghold of Zevenbergen ended with its surrender on 11 April 1427, duke Philip stood poised to take Holland,

[3] *Actes de la chancellerie d'Henri VI*, ed. P. Le Cacheux ii. 349; R. A. Newhall, *Conquest of Normandy*, 97, 137, 160, 219, 309; H. Sauvage, 'Documents relatifs à la donation du Comté Pairie de Mortain à Pierre de Navarre par Charles VI', *Soc. de l'hist. de Normandie, Mélanges*, 52 (1898), 238; R. Planchenault, 'La Conquête du Maine par les Anglais: la lutte des partisans, 1427–9', *Rev. hist. et arch. du Maine,* 93 (1937), 24–34, 160–72; 94 (1938), 47–60.

[4] *CPR 1422–9*, 404, 422–3; *CFR 1422–30*, 103, 249; *Amundesham*, *Annales*, i. 16; *PPC* iii. 313.

but six days later the death of John of Brabant made her the rightful heir and with her fleet still in being she could, with English assistance, have prolonged the military struggle and forced Philip to make territorial concessions.[5] In April 1427 she once more appealed to the English council and the prospect of renewed English intervention acquired substance with the earl of Salisbury's return. He had been outraged by Duke Philip's attentions to his wife, Alice Chaucer, and was engaged in direct litigation with the duke over the lands and wardship of the duke's stepchildren by his first wife. At the same time Salisbury was contesting the jurisdiction of the duke of Bedford over his own lands as count of Perche.[6] He thus became a ready recruit to Gloucester's camp. Salisbury was back in council on 15 July; already on 23 June the council had agreed to furnish Gloucester with the second instalment of 5,000 marks from the customs, sanctioned by the parliament of 1425, and a further 4,000 marks from his salary, for the purpose of rescuing Jacqueline and sustaining the towns still in her hands, though not for further conquests.[7] The careful limitation revealed the council's dilemma. While under immediate pressure from Gloucester, it was well aware of Bedford's insistence on maintaining the Burgundian alliance. Indeed, after spending a month in Paris Bedford and Beaufort had visited Philip in Lille at the end of May to try and effect a settlement of the problem of Jacqueline.[8] The council now dispatched its own embassy, of Tiptoft and Alnwick, to Arras and received Burgundian envoys in return; then wrote to Bedford to inform him of its actions and urge him to restrain Philip. Bedford responded at once, warning the council of the dangers of alienating Burgundy, reminding them that a papal verdict on Gloucester's marriage was expected, and calling on them to restrain the protector; he also wrote to Gloucester himself, and to Duke Philip. Bedford's stern warnings had their effect; Gloucester's intervention never materialized, a truce was arranged, and on 9 January 1428 the papal verdict affirming the validity of Jacqueline's marriage to John of Brabant faced Gloucester with the humiliating prospect of doing penance for his illicit union and contracting a fresh marriage if he sought to pursue his claims. He did not, preferring to marry his mistress, Eleanor Cobham.[9]

By the time parliament met on 13 October 1427 the prospect of English intervention in the Low Countries had been deferred if not wholly averted,

[5] Vaughan, *Philip the Good*, 44–9.

[6] *English Suits before the Parlement of Paris, 1420–36*, ed. C. T. Allmand and C. A. J. Armstrong (Camden Ser., 1982), 127–31, 141–7.

[7] *PPC* iii. 271–4, 276, 290–2; *Foedera*, x. 375. Monstrelet, *Chronique*, iv. 258–9 mentions Salisbury's involvement in Gloucester's plans.

[8] Waurin, *Croniques*, iii. 211 notes Bedford's departure for Lille on 26 May. Beaufort was in Paris 30 Apr.–20 May and at Malines on 15 June; he therefore probably accompanied Bedford: *A Parisian Journal, 1405–1449*, ed. and trans. J. Shirley, 212; *Actes de la chancellerie*, ii. 34; *CPL* vii. 32.

[9] *PPC* iii. 276; Vickers, *Gloucester*, 201–2.

but Gloucester's influence was strong and there was still much support for Jacqueline's cause, hatred of Flemings in London, and pressure from mercantile interests.[10] The chancellor, however, wanted to send a fresh army to France and reminded members of their duty to contribute to the defence of the realm. The Commons remained wary of acknowledging any obligation to support the war in France and a prolonged struggle took place. 'The arduousness and difficulty' in reaching a decision meant that no tax had been granted by the end of the session on 8 December, by which time the former grant of tunnage and poundage had expired; and when on 25 March 1428 a graduated parish tax and a tax on knights' fees was granted and tunnage and poundage renewed, it carried a proviso to ensure the safety of Jacqueline and the alliance with Hainault by treaty.[11]

Already in the new year Gloucester and Salisbury had begun to see advantages in an expedition to France where Salisbury's true interests lay, and on the same day as the tax was granted Salisbury indented for six months' service with a force of 600 men-at-arms and 1,800 archers, to commence on 30 June.[12] He had spent the winter seeking recruits from Lancashire, Cheshire, and Yorkshire, though he experienced delay in filling his quotas and was not ready to muster until 19 July. There is no evidence that his objectives or strategy were discussed in council. Only the stipulation that no one already holding lands in France should serve, and his heavy investment in artillery, indicated that it was intended to inaugurate a new phase of the conquest. Even more significant was the fact that Salisbury was retained directly by the king and not, as previously, by the regent, for thereby Gloucester and Salisbury had found a way of usurping Bedford's direction of the war and introducing a rival source of authority into Lancastrian France. If Gloucester saw it as an opportunity to revenge himself on Bedford for displacing him in 1426–7, for Salisbury it offered the means to demonstrate his independence of Bedford and to enlarge his own fiefs. Salisbury was thus enabled to ignore the decision taken at a meeting of Bedford's *Grand Conseil* in Paris in May 1428 to commence the conquest of Anjou, and march instead to besiege Orléans.[13] The political motives aside, there were good personal and strategic reasons for his decision. He had bitter memories of Clarence's ill fated foray into Anjou, and though he had participated in the conquest of Maine, his own military operations had been mainly in Champagne and to the south of

[10] Roskell, *Commons and Speakers*, 192; *Amundesham, Annales*, i. 20; *Rot. Parl.* iv. 328. The bonds for Gloucester's advance of 9,000 marks were cancelled on 17 Mar. 1427: *PPC* iii. 291–2.

[11] *Rot. Parl.* iv. 317–18.

[12] *Wars of Eng.* i. 403–14; *Foedera*, x. 392–4; E 101/71/2/28. Ratcliffe, thesis, 25–8 gives full details.

[13] *Wars of Eng.* ii. 77–84; Beaurepaire, *Les États de Normandie sous la domination anglaise*, 34, 168–70; id., *De l'administration de la Normandie sous la domination anglaise*, 55.

Paris. There, in contrast to the grants to Bedford's captains in Maine, his own rewards had been few.[14] If he was now to participate in the conquest of Anjou any lands he gained there would be held as fiefs from Bedford as duke of Anjou, whereas in the Orléannais he would hold what he secured in virtual independence. Psychologically the capture of Orléans would breach the 'frontier' of the Loire, while strategically it might strike a mortal blow at the kingdom of Bourges. The risk—as at all major sieges conducted in an exposed position—was that the besieging force would not be able to maintain itself in strength over a sufficiently long period to wear down resistance and deter relief. A piecemeal reduction of Anjou was more within the limits of English resources and experience.

The outrage which Bedford felt at this decision was the greater since Salisbury's expedition was the largest since 1421 and the result of considerable financial effort.[15] The ability of the exchequer to finance it without any loan from Beaufort was largely due to Lord Hungerford's stringent collection of royal revenue and systematic preference for military needs. This policy had commenced under Bedford's direction, with the addition of increments to farms of lands, increased fines, and the revision of rents in Calais.[16] In July 1427 the treasurer launched a widespread investigation into concealed rights of the crown and fraud among its revenue collectors, and further commissions were issued for particular shires in the following year.[17] Large fines for marriages and alienations of lands without licence continued to be imposed and provoked complaints in the October parliament.[18] The treasurer was also materially helped by the high level of wool exports which, in the two years from Michaelmas 1426 to Michaelmas 1428, reached a thirty-year peak. Disposable revenue for the two years between Easter 1427 and Easter 1429 totalled some £115,000, the highest of the reign hitherto, and much of this was received in cash at the exchequer. From this it was able to pay some £18,000 for Salisbury's army between March and July 1428 without substantial recourse to borrowing.[19] It was a significant demonstration of how, by advance planning and stringent control, the exchequer could finance military expenditure from its own resources without resort to Beaufort's wealth.

This was the more striking in that almost £42,000 was also spent on the standing charges of defence. At Calais, where the duke of Bedford

[14] The many grants to Warwick, Suffolk, Scales, Willoughby, Fastolf, Grey of Ruthin, etc., in *Actes de la chancellerie*, ii. 363–74 contrast with the few to Salisbury: ibid. 325, 338.

[15] Ratcliffe, thesis, 32; *Wars of Eng.* i. 417–21. As many as 400 men-at-arms had joined Salisbury in France, led by Bedford's captains: Beaurepaire, *Administration*, 55.

[16] *CFR 1422–30*, 144, 165, 167, 172; *CPR 1422–9*, 404.

[17] *CPR 1422–9*, 406, 467, 494, 499, 546, 548. For a reform of customs administration in France, see *CCR 1422–9*, 429; *PPC* iii. 315–6.

[18] *CPR 1422–9*, 444, 464; *PPC* iii. 281; *Rot. Parl.* iv. 329.

[19] *Eng. Export Trade*, 58; Steel, *Receipt*, 171–2. A general loan raised £7,033: *CPR 1422–9*, 479–82; E 28/50; E 404/44/185.

displaced Warwick, to the latter's considerable annoyance, assignments of £19,260 were delivered over these two years, though even this was insufficient both to pay the current wages of the garrison and to discharge Warwick's arrears.[20] The arrears owing to Sir John Radclyf as lieutenant in Gascony were also considerable when he returned to England in 1425, and though from 1427 to 1429 he was paid a total of £5,100, he was still owed a further £6,620. The payment of the wardens of the marches and the garrisons there was a more urgent priority and these received £11,156 in the two years 1427–9. In the same period two expeditions were sent to Ireland at a cost of £5,750.[21] Over and above these continuing charges were the two expeditions of Bedford and Salisbury, costing some £27,000, so that in all some £70,000, or 60 per cent of disposable revenue, was spent directly on war. There is little doubt that this reflected the control exercised over finance by Lord Hungerford with the backing of the council, who in this saw themselves as more answerable to Bedford than to the protector.

In regard to both relations with Burgundy and financial provision for the war, therefore, Bedford had circumscribed Gloucester's freedom of action before he left, and continued to influence policy from France. Similarly, his backing for the council before his departure enabled them to withstand the protector's demand for a redefinition of his powers. Gloucester broached the matter at the beginning of parliament, but it was not until the end of the second session, on 3 March, that he withdrew to await a satisfactory answer. Despite the psychological and financial pressure of this tactic—for the tax had not been granted and Salisbury's plans were placed in jeopardy—the lords answered with a forthright and unanimous rebuke, reminding Gloucester of the settlement of 1422, exhorting him to be content with this until the king's approaching adolescence, and requiring his presence in parliament.[22] Gloucester had grossly underestimated the council's own apprehension of his rule and the strength it had acquired from Bedford's support in January.

By contrast the council was in broad harmony with the protector in its attitude to Martin V, and perhaps harboured resentment against Bedford and Beaufort who, having cultivated Martin's favour for their own ends, left England at the point where papal pressure for the repeal of the statutes was intensified. The papal envoy, John de Obizzi, who brought the bull suspending Chichele from his legatine functions, was imprisoned, and when on 16 May 1427 the council debated on what securities he should be released, Hungerford, Cromwell, Tiptoft, and Bourchier took an even

[20] Ratcliffe, thesis, 112, 114, 116, 123; *PPC* iii. 242–3; *Letters of Margaret of Anjou*, 37–45; C 76/111 m. 1.

[21] For all these charges, see Ratcliffe, thesis, 131–6, 148–51, 163–79; *PPC* iii. 339.

[22] *Rot. Parl.* iv. 326.

more rigorous line than Gloucester and Huntingdon. Martin might rage at the 'Saracen like' treatment of his official, and aver that such could not have occurred had Beaufort and Bedford been in England, but he had left himself with few cards to play.[23] His closest allies were on the continent; in England were only his enemies like Gloucester and reluctant servants like Chichele.

The trust and favour which Martin showed to Beaufort threatened, indeed, to alienate his former associates in the council. This was clearly shown in the dispute over the provision of Robert Nevill to the see of Salisbury. In July 1426, hard on the decease of John Chaundler, the council had nominated Robert Nevill, Joan Beaufort's fifth son, despite the fact that he was only 22 two and still at Oxford. This was one of Bedford's *douceurs* to the dethroned chancellor. Then, on 16 September, the chapter elected their dean, Simon Sydenham, though they did not dare to press his claim, while Martin forebore to make any provision as a mark of displeasure at the council's procrastination in the matter of the statutes. Then, following Bedford's return to France, the members of the council, on 19 May 1427, individually gave assent for Sydenham to pursue his election at the Curia—a calculated rebuff to Beaufort and even to Bedford. Immediately he heard of it Beaufort wrote to Martin V on 15 June from Malines, accepting the legateship and urging the claims of his nephew. On 14 July the pope 'moved solely by the cardinal's prayer and, in virtue of his commitment to the crusade, desiring to please him alone rather than many others', provided Nevill to the see despite his youth. From boyhood his career in the church had been planned and fostered by his uncle, who, with the complaisance of Archbishops Bowet and Kemp, had procured for him from the age of 10 a sequence of Yorkshire prebends. He had accompanied his uncle to the council of Constance. His provision to Salisbury placed that see more firmly under the cardinal's clientage than it had been when held by either Hallum or Chaundler, and Nevill was to work closely with Beaufort's officials over the next eleven years.[24]

While Martin could exercise his right of provision in this case, his instruction to Chichele to present his demand for the repeal of the statutes to parliament in person produced no more than a half-hearted ritual at the opening of the second session. Though Gloucester formally backed the papal request, its rejection was predetermined. When, on 29 July 1428, Martin restored Chichele's legatine status, it was a recognition that his long-drawn-out campaign had failed. In the end the final effort had been sadly mistimed. Martin could wield neither threats nor favours to influence the English parliament; the one inducement he could offer was that which

[23] *Reg. Chichele*, i. pp. xlv–vi; *PPC* iii. 269; *Amundesham, Annales*, i. 13; Haller, *England u. Rom*, 301–2, suppl. 12.

[24] Davies, 'Martin V', 331–41; *CPL* vii. 32–3; *BRUO* ii. 1350.

Henry V had sought in vain—recognition of the English king's title to the crown of France. For that Bedford, Beaufort, and probably the council as a whole might have been prepared to compromise. But the papacy was unlikely to make so momentous a judgement while the struggle between the two soi-disant kings of France was so evenly balanced. Had the planned offensive of Bedford and Salisbury succeeded, the question of provisors could again have become negotiable. In that sense Martin's attempt to force the issue in January 1428 was premature; it had no willing advocates, and on both sides of the Channel was seen as an impediment to Anglo-papal co-operation. Much as he deplored English intransigeance, Martin himself may have begun to take a similar view. For with the verdicts rendered on the statute of provisors and Jacqueline's marriage, the way was clear for seeking the support of England and Burgundy in a crusade against the Hussites.

When, on 25 March 1427, Bedford invested Beaufort with his cardinal's hat and scarlet cope furred with grey, at St Mary's church in Calais, two bulls were read to him. One appointed him legate for the kingdoms of Bohemia, Germany, and Hungary with the management of the crusade, the other permitted him to keep all his English dignities and benefices *in commendam*.[25] However, Beaufort's immediate attention was directed to strengthening the ties with Burgundy, and it was not until early July that he left the Low Countries with a significant contingent of troops, reaching Nuremberg by 13 July and joining the already advancing crusading army on the 28th. Part of the army under the archbishop of Trier had laid siege to the town of Stříbro between Tachov and Pilsen, but Frederick of Brandenburg, who disapproved of this move, had remained at Tachov pleading illness, and was there joined by Beaufort. Reports of the mustering of a Hussite army led to the abandonment of the siege and a retreat to Tachov on 4 August. In the face of a demoralized and rapidly disintegrating army, Beaufort and the elector's son tried to rally the German forces and make a stand. Beaufort unveiled the papal banner, but to no avail. Reputedly exclaiming that if he had had ten thousand English archers there the outcome would have been different, the new cardinal was stung by the defeat to organize a further crusade which would be under his command and in the military effectiveness of which he could have confidence.[26]

[25] *CPL* vii. 30–1; *Brut*, ii. 434; Davies, 'Martin V', 336; *Chronicles of London*, 95, 131. These chronicles describe the 'Cardinal's habyte' as 'in maner of a ffrer's coope of ffyne scarlett furryd with puryd'. Pured was the belly fur of the grey squirrel in winter: *OED*. G. A. Holmes, 'Cardinal Beaufort and the crusade against the Hussites', *EHR* 88 (1973), 721.

[26] Holmes, 'Cardinal Beaufort', 723–4; F. C. Heymann, 'The crusade against the Hussites', in K. M. Setton and H. W. Hazard (edd.), *A History of the Crusades*, iii. 612. Waurin, *Croniques*, ii. 324–6 places Beaufort's remark in 1421, but he did not leave England in that year. He had evidently brought some men from England in his service: one George Weaver of Chester was excused appearance in the shire court on account of his accompanying the cardinal: E 28/54; PRO CHES 29/130 m. 20, 28 (reference from K. B. McFarlane's notes).

Beaufort at once set about this with determination. Encouraged by Martin V's reaffirmation of his faith in him and the wide discretionary powers to organize the German bishops which he now received, he seized the initiative from the hands of the discredited German princes and on his own authority summoned a meeting of the Reichstag at Frankfurt on 16 November. At first progress was frustrated by the mutual distrust and self-interest of the princes and towns, but by 1 December agreement had been reached for a tax to furnish an army under Cardinal Beaufort and the Margrave Frederick of Brandenburg, which would be spent by authority of a committee of princes, towns, and the two commanders. On 6 December Beaufort published his indulgences for this crusading tax and an encyclical letter threatening excommunication for non-payment. In the imperial context a tax embracing both clergy and laity for the defence of the Reich was unprecedented; it introduced a new concept of obligation and formed the precedent for the later 'common penny'.[27] Beaufort's achievement in knocking together the heads of princes, churchmen, and burgesses to secure this measure of co-operation was long remembered. He was present for further meetings with the princes at Heidelberg in the new year, and was settling disputes between the archbishops of Cologne and Trier and the duke of Cleves in the first half of February 1428. For all this he received warm praise from Martin V who, in October 1427, had imposed a tax of a tenth of clerical incomes on the whole church for the project.[28] Yet by the spring of 1428 Beaufort had come to recognize that the political fragmentation of Germany was an almost insuperable impediment to the formation of a unified army under strong leadership, even when exercised from outside, while the amount of money being raised by taxation was falling below expectations. He therefore decided to broaden the basis of the crusade and seek military support from north-western Europe.

At this point Beaufort's plans for a crusading army directly impinged on Bedford's proposed offensive in France, and the wider implications of the crusade, as a manifestation of the Lancastrian ascendancy, began to emerge. In appointing Beaufort, Martin had commended his wisdom and prudence, his royal lineage, his experience of great affairs, and the renown of his nation in arms. The crusade would bring lasting glory to himself and to England. The pope had accompanied his invitation to Beaufort with letters to Henry VI, the duke of Bedford, and the council.[29] Clearly he wished it to be seen as a commission not just to Beaufort himself but to the

[27] Holmes, 'Cardinal Beaufort', 724; *CPL* vii. 35–6; S. Rowan, 'Imperial taxes and German politics in the fifteenth century', *Central European History*, 13 (1980), 206–11.

[28] E. Schnith, 'Kardinal Heinrich Beaufort und der Hussitenkrieg' in R. Baumer, (ed.), *Von Konstanz nach Trient*, 124–38; A report on his visit to Trier, where he assisted Archbishop Otto in the reform of the diocesan chapter, is in J. Leideker, *Historia Cartusiae S. Albani* (1765), Trier Stadt Bibl. MS 1666/353, pp. 101–2. (I owe this reference to Dr A. I. Doyle.)

[29] *CPL* vii. 30–2.

English nation as a whole. As such it had profound political and religious undertones. As the pope pointed out, England, the incubator of heresy, had a particular duty to expunge it. The Lancastrian kings had indeed shown themselves hammers of the Lollards and had identified themselves with the crusade through Henry IV's service in Prussia and Lithuania and his son's dying avowal of his intention 'to rebuild the walls of Jerusalem'. For Henry V's far-reaching vision of his mission embraced, in his own claim to the French crown, the traditional role of Capetians and Valois as leaders of European chivalry in a holy war. Beaufort's appointment was a recognition that he was the custodian of, if not heir to, this Lancastrian tradition. The crusade thus inaugurated a new phase in Anglo-papal relations. For a whole decade co-operation had been inhibited by papal insistence on the repeal of the statute of provisors, but Martin was now a more chastened and wearied figure, ready to recognize the inevitability of defeat on this issue and intent above all on the extirpation of heresy before he died. He was even prepared to accept tacitly that a successful crusade under Lancastrian leadership would have to await the resolution of the conflict in France. Earlier missions under Cardinal Albergati to persuade Henry V to make peace with the dauphin to this end had met with rebuff. But a successful English offensive in 1428–9 might induce Charles VII to sue for peace on terms which, under papal pressure, would prove more favourable to Lancastrian claims. If that were to be followed by the eradication of Hussitism by an Anglo-Burgundian–Imperial army Martin would find it difficult to withold recognition of the Lancastrian title to the throne of the most Christian king. Henry V's dream of a *Pax Anglicana* under which Christendom would unite for a crusade in the east seemed for a moment within the bounds of possibility.

This was a heady prospect and one cannot know how far it beguiled any of the principals, all of whom were hardened realists whose eyes were fixed on immediate contingencies. It is clear, for instance, that Bedford had made the launch of the crusade dependent on the success of the English offensive, and that from this point Beaufort saw his task as being to co-ordinate and fulfil the distinct aims of the regent and the pope. Bedford had readily levied a double tenth from the French clergy—though not without opposition—using half for the crusade and half for the war against Charles VII, but he was adamant that no troops should be withdrawn from Lancastrian France. Beaufort therefore turned to Burgundy, and at the end of the first week in March 1428 had arrived in Bruges to enlist Duke Philip's participation. In his reply, sent to Beaufort at Calais on 19 March, Philip affirmed his willingness but professed his inability to assist until the succession of his dynasty was secure and his quarrel with Gloucester settled. For, despite the truce with Gloucester and the definitive verdict on Jacqueline's marriage, she still held out obstinately in Gouda and it was not until 3 July, through Beaufort's own negotiation, that Jacqueline and Philip signed the treaty of Delft. Indeed Beaufort had almost certainly spent the whole of the early summer in helping to re-establish Anglo-Burgundian co-operation, notably at the meeting of the Paris *Grand Conseil* in May and June, at which Duke Philip was present and where the strategy for the forthcoming campaign in France was discussed.[30]

As part of this attempt to settle all outstanding differences between them, Bedford and Beaufort took up Philip's complaints about the treatment of Flemish merchants in England, and wrote to the council requiring it to give them, as Henry VI's own subjects, immunity to buy and sell freely at once, and not prospectively from 1429 as the English merchants had argued. By the end of the summer Beaufort had won Philip's confidence to such a degree that the duke was seeking the hand of Beaufort's niece, Isabel of Portugal, the daughter of João I and Philippa of Lancaster.[31] Hopes of fulfilling Philip's need for an heir were matched by the presence of a substantial Burgundian contingent at the siege of Orléans. In the autumn of 1428 Anglo-Burgundian co-operation had rarely been more cordial and more fruitful, and this was in the main the achievement of Beaufort himself. It was both a comparatively recent achievement—for he had had little previous contact with Duke Philip—and one which had abiding importance in the troubled time ahead.

Assured in principle of the commitment of both dukes to the crusade, Beaufort now sought the support of the council in England. In the scheme which he had laid before Philip and his counsellors in March, Beaufort had proposed that he himself should lead a contingent of no less than 4,000 to 6,000 English archers. At the same time he wrote to Henry VI expressing his desire to return to England and, in guarded terms, requested support for the crusade and promised to use his influence in Rome on the king's behalf. He now received papal authorization to preach the crusade in England and to grant indulgences.[32] In fact it was not until 1 September 1428 that Beaufort arrived in London, where attention had already been drawn to the crusade by a procession led by the young king and the queen mother, as well as by the arrival in May of the papal envoy Kunes of

[30] Holmes, 'Cardinal Beaufort', 725 n. 4, 727; Y. Lacaze, 'Philippe le Bon et le problème hussite: un projet de Croisade Bourguignon en 1428–9', *Rev. hist.* 241 (1969), 76–7, 85; Beaurepaire, *États de Normandie*, 33, 171–2.

[31] *Wars of Eng.* i. 77. On 1 July 1428 the English chancery issued detailed letters of protection to all Low Countries merchants: C 76/110 m. 3; *PPC* iii. 304–8; *Foedera*, x. 403; Lacaze, 'Philippe le Bon', 92, and 86 for the statement that Beaufort journeyed to Nuremberg in June 1428 to discuss plans for a new Diet.

[32] *Œuvres de Ghilibert de Lannoy,* ed. C. Potvin, 227–49. Holmes, 'Cardinal Beaufort', 727–9 prints Beaufort's letter from BL Add. MS 14848 fo. 121. Beaufort significantly addresses Henry VI as 'most christian king' and signs himself 'Cardinall called of your realm of England'. The council replied to Beaufort on 30 Apr.: *PPC* iii. 294. For the papal letter, see *Reg. Thomas Langley*, ed. R. L. Storey, iii. 130–4.

Zwolen seeking permission from the council to levy the papal tenth. But convocation, which met from 5 to 20 July, deferred a decision on both Kunes's request for a papal subsidy and that presented by Hungerford, Tiptoft, Cromwell, and Scrope for a tenth for the war in France, parallel to the tax granted in the March parliament. Indeed it was soon clear that these former associates of Beaufort, whether through distrust of his papal connections, or resentment over the treatment of Chichele, or mere prudence in the face of Gloucester's animosity, were conspicuously distancing themselves from him and his project. When Beaufort rode into the city with his legate's cross and cardinal's hat carried before him, wearing a cape of crimson velvet with draped sleeves and a broad 'scholastic' velvet hat, and attended by knights holding his jewelled and enamelled bridle, he received a tumultuous welcome from the crowd and a reception of honour from the mayor. The city had apparently obliterated from its mind its recent hostility, but otherwise he was met only by his two nephews, Edmund Beaufort, count of Mortain, and Robert Nevill, bishop of Salisbury, both of whom owed their new dignities to his favour.[33]

The cardinal at once sought an interview with the young king at Windsor. He then travelled to Hertfordshire, arriving at St Albans on 22 September. He was received in solemn procession to the strains of a new organ, his scarlet cape furred with miniver denoting his new dignity. Beaufort gave his blessing to the people and offered at the shrine. Next morning he visited the nuns at Sopwell and after dinner journeyed to the Queen Mother at Langley. If Edmund Beaufort was still accompanying him he now had the opportunity to resume his liaison with Catherine, for the cardinal proceeded alone to Walsingham and thence to King's Lynn which he had reached by 1 October.[34] By the first week in November he was back

[33] *Gregory's Chron.* 162; *Amundesham, Annales,* i. 26; *Brut*, ii. 436; *PPC* iii. 295; *Reg. Chichele*, iii. 183–8; Holmes, 'Cardinal Beaufort', 732–3. *Reg. Fleming*, i. 624 shows Beaufort at Southwark on 2 Sept. 1428.

[34] *Amundesham, Annales*, i. 28; NRO, KL/C 7/2 (King's Lynn Hall Book), fo. 222. Considerable uncertainty surrounds the date of Queen Catherine's secret morganatic marriage to Owen Tudor and the birth of her eldest son, Edmund. The DNB gives the latter as 1430, at Hadham; Crawford 'The King's burden', 37, says the marriage took place 'about 1428–9' and Griffiths, *Henry VI*, 60–1, 'round about 1431–2', following in this Chrimes, *Henry VII*, 5–9. But Catherine had four children before she retired to the convent at Bermondsey after a protracted illness in 1436, so that the earlier date woud seen preferable (cf. Griffiths, 'Queen Katherine'). It is clear that in the course of 1428–31 she had a number of meetings with Cardinal Beaufort, a period in which Edmund was apparently in his household: *Amundesham, Annales*, i. 28, 33–4, 56. Her choice of his name for her first-born may have been mere sentiment, but it must raise the suspicion that the father was Edmund Beaufort and that she contracted her disparaging marriage to Owen Tudor to save her lover the penalties of the statute of 1427. Indeed the chronicler explains her choice of Owen on the grounds that these would fall less harshly on a penniless esquire: *Chron. Angl.* 17. The secret of the boy Edmund's parenthood would be safe while the queen lived and the official tolerance of her marriage to Owen and subsequent birth of their children, and the protection afforded to Owen, suggests that this was a solution which, for different reasons, was agreeable to both

in Southwark where John, duke of Norfolk came to dine with him, almost losing his life when his barge sank on the return journey. It was not until 11 November, on the eve of the reassembly of convocation, that Beaufort met Gloucester and the lords of the council at Gloucester's house by St Paul's wharf. There Beaufort was formally reminded that no papal legate could enter England without royal permission, and that he was now received solely as cardinal. He in turn disclaimed any intention of contravening the jurisdiction of the crown and affirmed that he came not as legate but solely as cardinal and for the matter of the crusade. Next day Chichele suspended convocation while he and other prelates accompanied Beaufort to the council.[35]

The hard negotiation over the grant of a tax and the raising of an army now began. It has been pointed out that the sympathetic hearing given to Beaufort's mission was assisted by current alarm about Lollard activity. There was a spate of heresy hunts, and convocation was currently examining three London Lollards. In Beaufort's eyes Lollardy was principally dangerous as a threat to civil society: by challenging the law of God it subverted civil law. That had been the theme of his sermon at Leicester in 1426, and it recurs in his letters to Henry VI in March and to the Hanse towns to whom he wrote seeking support for the crusade in May. In the last he had depicted the Lollards as subverting 'not only the faith but alle polytyke rewle and governance, steryng the peple to rebellione and disobeisaunce of her lordes and governours', and in a letter read to the assembled clergy Martin V warned that the growth of the sect would endanger the whole kingdom and England suffer the fate of Bohemia. In the event convocation was not readily moved by this alarmist

Gloucester and Cardinal Beaufort. Following the death of Catherine in Jan. 1437, however, Gloucester may have seen an opportunity to discredit and ruin the Beauforts if the secret of Edmund 'Tudor's' parentage could be wrung from Owen. It seems clear from the elliptical minute of the council in July 1437 (*PPC* v. 48–50) that Gloucester had been behind the summoning of Owen before the council, the promise of safe conduct, the winkling of him from sanctuary, and his examination before the king and council, a sequence of events which must have commenced in the early spring. It may be of significance that early in April. Cardinal Beaufort suddenly mooted his intention of going to the papal court and surrendering his see into the pope's hands (below ch. 13 n. 76). Uncertainty seems also to have affected Edmund Beaufort's movements at this point, for in April there was discussion in council about him serving with Warwick in France; but in the event nothing came of this (below ch. 14 n. 14). If Owen did harbour a secret, it was too risky to allow him to remain at liberty, and by July he had been arrested and lodged in Newgate, probably on a plea of debt. Later, possibly before the end of the year, he broke prison, only to be recaptured by Lord Beaumont in Feb.–Mar. 1438. On 24 Mar. 1438, in the cardinal's secret chamber at St Mary Overy, at a council meeting from which Gloucester was absent, Owen was committed to the custody of Suffolk in Wallingford, thus ensuring his safety and silence: *Foedera*, x. 686; E 28/59. By its nature the evidence for Edmund 'Tudor's' parentage is less than conclusive, but such facts as can be assembled permit the agreeable possibility that Edmund 'Tudor' and Margaret Beaufort were first cousins and that the royal house of 'Tudor' sprang in fact from Beauforts on both sides.

[35] *Wars of Eng*. ii. 760; Holmes, 'Cardinal Beaufort', 735; *Reg. Chichle*, i. p. xlviii, iii. 190; Bodleian MS Tanner 165 fos. 81–3 (new foliation).

talk; faced with concurrent demands from the cardinal and the council, it granted a half-tenth to the king payable at Martinmas 1429, while the pope had to be content with the promise of a tax of eight pence in the mark on clerical incomes. Though Chichele, writing to the pope, looked forward to 'a notable subsidy' when convocation reassembled in ten months' time, Martin had every reason to be angry that his letters to the clergy had been fruitless and his levy of a crusading tenth effectively ignored. In fact, as Chichele reported, this reflected a compromise between Beaufort and the council, which had stipulated that he could have either money or troops from England, but not both. Beaufort needed men rather than money, and the council had accepted in principle his proposal to raise a fighting force, though it cut down the numbers from 500 men-at-arms and 5,000 archers to 250 and 2,000 respectively, and prohibited the recruitment of any of these from France. It also permitted him to preach the crusade, proclaim rates of pay, take out protections, enforce discipline, and provide shipping. He could elicit voluntary contributions to the crusade in lieu of service, though such money would have to be spent in England, and the wages of the force were to come from Rome itself. In fact 14,000 florins had already been dispatched to him in October. On these conditions Beaufort and Chichele, on 9 December, jointly issued instructions to all diocesans for the preaching of the crusade.[36]

One further stipulation by the council was that Beaufort should ensure the neutrality of the Scots before he withdrew men for service on crusade. This had been placed in jeopardy by a marriage contract, initialled on 19 July and confirmed on 30 October 1428, between James I's 3-year-old daughter Margaret and the son and heir of Charles VII, the fruit of negotiations pursued at the French court by Sir John Stewart since April. Even more worrying was the proposal that Margaret should be conveyed to the French court in a fleet carrying 6,000 Scots, thus renewing the danger to Lancastrian France which Bedford had averted at Verneuil.[37] The credibility of Beaufort's policy of binding James I to neutrality by the marriage of 1424 was thus at stake. It had, indeed, already been undermined by the failure of James to maintain payments of the ransom. Despite repeated complaint—the last by Henry VI in December 1427—only 9,500 marks had been delivered since 1424, and though the English council prospectively allocated the 10,000 marks due on 15 August 1428 to various creditors, this likewise never materialized.[38] As both sides well knew, James had neither the means nor the need to pay, since any threat

[36] Holmes, 'Cardinal Beaufort', 725, 728, 735–40; *Reg. Chichele*, iii. 210; *Reg. Langley*, iii. 128–45; *PPC* iii. 330–8. Writing to Martin V, Chichele professed to have been guided wholly by Beaufort in the matter of the tax: Bekynton, *Correspondence*, i. 255.

[37] Beaucourt, *Charles VII*, ii. 397–9; Nicholson, *Scotland*, 289.

[38] *Foedera*, x. 384, 406, 409; *PPC* iii. 303; Balfour-Melville, *James I*, 126, 143–8, 160–8.

by the English to enforce payment would only drive James more deeply into the French camp. Beaufort's principal task—for which the council commissioned him on 10 February 1429—was to negotiate Scottish neutrality, and this he hoped to accomplish through a personal meeting with James at Coldingham in early March. He did in fact prevent an alliance between James and Charles and was able to return with assurances which were given substance in the eventual renewal of the truce for five years in December 1430. Although this covered only England and the sea, and did not inhibit Scots presently serving in France, the death of Sir John Stewart in February 1429 removed the principal agent and instigator of the French alliance. Although James had given no satisfaction over payment of the ransom, Beaufort secured the minimum needed to vindicate his own honour and remove the last obstacles to the crusade.[39]

On his return to London at the end of March the cardinal could start recruiting his army, assisted by a further 16,000 florins from the receipts of the papal tenth, paid into Ubertino de Bardi's company in London on 21 February.[40] At this point the general expectation must have been that the crusade would go ahead, furthered by Beaufort's energetic organization and the unenthusiastic acquiescence of the council. Yet the overall Lancastrian strategy into which it had been woven was already unravelling. Following Salisbury's death on 2 November the siege of Orléans had lengthened into winter and, despite Fastolf's victory at the battle of the herrings on 12 February, its capture was becoming progressively less likely and the English position daily more precarious. Even before Salisbury's death a steady stream of desertions significantly reduced the 4,000 strong force with which he had commenced the siege, and when Bedford refused to permit the surrender of the town into Burgundian hands in April, Duke Philip's withdrawal of the 1,500 Burgundian troops fatally undermined the English posiition. Bedford had already significantly depleted the garrisons in Normandy to reinforce the siege and now appealed to the council in England for a further 200 men-at-arms and 1,200 archers for the next half-year, without which the siege could not be maintained. In addition he spelt out the need for Henry VI to be crowned king of France.[41] Bedford, it is clear, had already apprehended that a failure before Orléans would place the whole of Lancastrian France in jeopardy. His request, discussed at an urgently convoked meeting of the council at Westminster, had momentous implications. First, it would imply Henry's prior coronation in England and

[39] Beaufort spent Christmas at Chertsey where he composed a dispute between the abbey and the vill: *Amundesham, Annales*, i. 32; *Chertsey Cartulary*, i. 58 no. 72. He left for the north on 13 Feb. For the negotiations, see *PPC* iii. 318–20; *Cal. Docts. Scot.* iv. 212 no. 1031; *Rotuli Scotiae*, ii. 264; *Exchequer Rolls of Scotland*, iv. 466–7, 477; Balfour-Melville, *James I*, 168–88; C. Macrae, 'The English council and Scotland in 1430', *EHR* 54 (1939), 415–21.

[40] *Amundesham, Annales*, i. 34; Holmes, 'Cardinal Beaufort', 743–5.

[41] Beaurepaire, *Administration*, 20–1; *PPC* iii. 322.

therewith the ending of the protectorate. Second, since the cost of a royal expedition could not be met from normal revenues—which the treasurer had recently reported as falling short of existing expenses by 20,000 marks p.a.—a further appeal to parliament would be necessary. Finally, any proposal to send reinforcements to France at this juncture must raise doubts about the expediency of Beaufort's recruitment for the crusade.

At precisely the same time Beaufort's own position had been called in question. Although he had made no attempt to claim a seat in council, he now sought to exercise his accustomed right to officiate at the St George's day ceremony at Windsor. This raised two issues: first, that his retention of an English see as cardinal was unprecedented; second, that in procuring the bull to hold Winchester *in commendam* Beaufort had laid himself open to the penalties of praemunire. The matter was basically political, for the retention of Winchester effectively entitled him to a seat in the council. In the event the council ducked the problem. Neither Beaufort himself nor Gloucester's principal allies were present at the great council on 17 April where, in the king's presence, all individually gave their views. Their verdict—that he should abstain from attending the Garter ceremony as they could not pronounce on a matter so '*ambigua et indecisa*'—was conveyed to him by his friends on the council, Northumberland, Stafford, Tiptoft, and Cromwell. Evidently the council was seeking to avoid a major political crisis and hoped that the whole question of praemunire would not be raised. Privately Beaufort was probably urged to avoid a confrontation which could endanger himself and his crusade. Yet their answer was not to Beaufort's liking, and next day he insisted on seeking the king's presence and demanding the reasons for his suspension from a right which he had exercised for twenty-four years. He was told explicitly that the retention of his see, as cardinal, was unprecedented and that the council could not prejudice the young king's rights in the matter.[42] Hitherto, as Kemp reported to the bishop of London, William Gray, then at the Curia, Beaufort had borne himself in every matter most prudently, notably, and honourably, showing a keen appreciation of the anti papal-feeling, waiving his legatine status, bowing to the council's conditions for conducting his mission, and making a long winter's journey to Scotland at its specific request.[43] His insistence on facing up to the issue of the Garter ceremony—which he could easily have avoided, as he had in 1427—shows both that, as the council acknowledged, this was a matter touching his own dignity and the rights of his see, and that Beaufort was reasonably

[42] *PPC* iii. 323–4.

[43] Holmes, 'Cardinal Beaufort', 738 n. 4 from BL Cotton Cleopatra C IV fo. 162^{v}. His title as legate 'per universam Germaniam, Hungariae et Bohemiae Regna cum plena potestate a latere ac in materia fidei per orbem universam' is recited in C 81/156/21, and cf. Holmes, 'Cardinal Beaufort', 728.

confident that he could outface his enemies. He had some grounds for this. He had at once grasped that Bedford's appeal for help, signalling as it did the collapse of the Orléans offensive (which Gloucester had supported) and the probable end of the protectorate, had revived the influence of Bedford's supporters in the council. He may also have foreseen—and so may the council—that the turn of events in France would again render his financial resources indispensable.

From the time of Beaufort's mission to Scotland there are a number of indications of his increasing influence in the council. While visiting Burgundy in the previous year, he had sought to advance negotiations over the duke of Bourbon's release in exchange for his nephew John, earl of Somerset, and in March 1429 the council took the first positive step of moving the duke to Calais. Bourbon had agreed to recognize Henry VI and render liege homage, and arrangements were being made for receiving the first instalment of his ransom.[44] The cardinal's influence was also directly responsible for the permission granted to Obizzi on 20 April to acquire benefices in England to the value of 200 marks p.a.,[45] and it was probably exercised indirectly to secure the title of earl of Salisbury for Sir Richard Nevill, Joan Beaufort's eldest son, who was married to the deceased earl's only daughter, Alice. Nevill had already secured writs giving him seisin under this title in February, but faced claims from the late earl's uncle Sir Richard Montagu. The council's decision in favour of Nevill was given on 3 May and by July Montague had died without male heirs. Beaufort was also called upon to arbitrate a partition of the Montague lands between the new earl and the dowager countess, both his relatives.[46] As his rival's power revived, Gloucester found his own control of patronage slipping. In March 1428 Gloucester had removed the young duke of York from the custody of Joan Beaufort, to whose daughter Cecily he was already married, for attendance in the royal household, and on 4 November his 1425 grant of the earl of March's lands at farm was renewed, as well as the keeping of the New Forest, vacated by Salisbury's death. This was again confirmed on 15 February 1429, yet on the following day Gloucester was required to surrender the March lands, which were then placed in the keeping of the young duke of York jointly with Bishop Alnwick and the earl of Northumberland until the end of his minority. Their mainpernors for this were Lords Tiptoft, Cromwell, and Sir John Radclyf. The Beaufort–Nevill

[44] *Foedera*, x. 426; *CPR 1422–9*, 550. On 4 July the council assigned 5,000 marks of the expected ransom to Calais; in fact no more than £400 was received: *PPC* iii. 344; E 364/65/4; E 403/689.

[45] *CPR 1422–9*, 532.

[46] *CFR 1422–30*, 262, 273; *PPC* iii. 324; M. Hicks, 'The Nevill earldom of Salisbury, 1429–71', *Wilts. Arch. Mag.* 72/3 (1980), 41–2. In Beaufort's award of 7 Dec. 1428 he is already entitled earl: Northants RO, Fitzwilliam MS 2046. Salisbury had made Beaufort his principal feoffee for his wife's jointure in Aug. 1428: *CPR 1422–9*, 474, 477, 504.

interest had thereby contrived to wrest the young duke's inheritance from Gloucester's hands.[47] Cromwell's own fortunes were also on the upturn, for in June and October he received the profitable grant of the keeping of Bolsover castle and Horncastle, while Radclyf was awarded the customs in Melcombe from which to discharge his arrears as lieutenant in Gascony at the rate of £1,000 p.a.[48]

On the very day on which discussions took place over Beaufort's attendance at the Garter ceremonies, the council agreed to dispatch a force of 100 men-at-arms and 700 archers to Bedford, and by 8 May it had persuaded Radclyf to indent for six months' service as their captain.[49] To finance this the council borrowed 4,000 marks from the feoffees of the duchy of Lancaster. Already the retreat from Orléans, which was to culminate in the disaster at Patay on 18 June, had begun, and even as Patay was being fought Beaufort was sealing his own indenture with the crown to take 250 men-at-arms and 2,500 archers to the Bohemian crusade. In fact the diversion of this force to France was already all but decided, for three days earlier royal writs ordering the arrest of shipping and the provision of victuals and lodging for the cardinal's force in Kent had spoken incautiously of his proceeding overseas '*in obsequium nostrum*', and on 26 June orders were given for his and Radclyf's forces to muster together on Barham Down on 1 July. By then the news of Patay had reached England and on 1 July at Rochester Beaufort signed a secret agreement with the council to lead his crusaders to Bedford's aid. The diversion was to be made public only when the army had crossed the Channel, and was then to be effected by a prohibition in Bedford's name that no one should pass the borders of France before the end of the year. It was also agreed that the king and council should write to the pope and German princes explaining the circumstances and exculpating Beaufort, who was to be represented as having agreed only with the greatest reluctance.[50]

For Beaufort the decision was indeed momentous. He can have had no illusions about Martin's reaction, for he was betraying the pope's trust in him which he had carefully fostered over the past ten years. Undoubtedly he would forfeit further employment or rewards in papal service. Even so, the blow to his own fortunes was incidental to the wider reversal suffered by the double monarchy. The crusade was intended to crown its triumph over the Valois king, but at a stroke Bedford and Philip had been thrown

[47] *PPC* iii. 194, 292–3, 311, 313–5; *CFR 1422–30*, 249, 259–62, 286; *CPR 1422–29*, 401, 518, 525.

[48] *CFR 1422–30*, 269, 278; *PPC* iii. 339 cf. 303.

[49] *PPC* iii. 326.

[50] *PPC* iii. 337–44; 347; *Foedera*, x. 417–18, 423–4; *CPR 1422–9*, 553–4. How early the diversion was contemplated is uncertain; from May money was set aside in the treasury at Caen for 50 lances and 950 archers promised by Beaufort: Beaurepaire, *États de Normandie*, 35. Licences for the cardinal and Edmund to go abroad are dated 18 June: C 76/111 m. 4.

on to the defensive and neither could now contemplate the diversion of resources to the east. There was a large measure of truth in Beaufort's excuse to Martin that the danger to Lancastrian France, and the king's orders, left him no option, and that his troops would not have followed him to Bohemia.[51] Yet his agreement with the council also shows that he sought to make capital from the gratitude of Bedford and the council. It was put on record that he had condescended to the agreement 'for the moost singuler love, zeele and tendrenesse that he bereth to the seuretee, welfare and prosperitee of the King and of alle his landes and subgittes and in especial of my lord of Bedford and of the reaume of France and the King's subgittes there'. Beaufort's choice at this juncture lay between service to Martin V or to Bedford, between a career at the Curia or in the Lancastrian kingdoms. One or other had to be sacrificed and the choice, when it came, was not in doubt. Even apart from the immediate pressures on him, the whole orientation of Beaufort's policy and personal fortunes had been towards the regent of France and the accomplishment of his appointed task. The cultivation of papal favour, and even the leadership of the crusade which it had brought him, had been ancillary to this end. Indeed Beaufort's concern for his own safety left him little choice. The dispute over his attendance at the St George's day ceremony had indicated how vulnerable was his position in England. To have chosen papal service at this juncture would have left him exposed to praemunire charges and the forfeiture of his see, whereas his claim on the gratitude of Bedford and the council would forearm him against further attack and prepare the ground for a return to English politics. On the whole he accomplished skilfully the manœuvre of changing horses in midstream. But the Hussite crusade, like so many in the late Middle Ages, fell victim to the exigencies of national interests and perished in the débâcle which overwhelmed the grandiose Lancastrian bid for the hegemony of Europe.

When the council assumed the responsibility for the diversion of Beaufort's army to France it also assumed financial responsibility for its wages. The exchequer had no money for this; indeed it had already borrowed from the city of London and the duchy feoffees for the wages of Radclyf's force.[52] All the council could promise was that it would reimburse Beaufort and the papacy for the total cost in two instalments, on 28 February and 1 May 1430; and on 6 July the lords of the council entered obligations to this effect. Since no money had been raised by papal taxation in England, and very little from preaching the crusade, Beaufort had been dependent on payments from the special account administered by the four cardinals for receipts from the crusading tenth. From this he had received

[51] *CPL* vii. 38; Holmes, 'Cardinal Beaufort', 746.

[52] 4,000 marks from the feoffees, 8,000 marks from London: E 403/689 12 May; *CPR 1422–9*, 518, 534, repayable from the clerical tenth and customs.

14,980 florins before they suspended payments in August 1429 on hearing of the diversion of the crusading army. This was equivalent to about £2,750, sufficient for the payment of the first quarter's wages and the cost of shipping. To cover the cost of the second quarter's wages the council, on 5 July, warranted payment of £2,431 together with a reward to Beaufort of 1,000 marks. But this warrant was merely promissory and no payment was made upon it, for Beaufort undertook to try to extract this from Bedford, keeping the council's promise secret.[53] When and by whom these wages for the second quarter were eventually paid is not certain, but it was probably the treasurer of Normandy.[54] At all events the secret obligations into which the lords entered on 6 July—which were to be replaced by others bearing a later date once Bedford had openly commandeered the crusading army—were for a total of £7,233. 6*s*. 8*d*., and this was duly paid to Beaufort in two instalments, on 8 March and 1 May 1430.

This directly reflected the influence he by then commanded in the council. He had returned to England on 23 February 1430 to procure the first payment due on the 28th, and the second payment was made on the day he advanced a loan of £9,950 for the royal expedition.[55] Beaufort can therefore have suffered no loss himself; but did he faithfully repay what he had received from the papacy? It seems likely that he did. Repayment was certainly expected both by Martin V and the Medici bank, and there is no evidence for subsequent demands from either. It was also in the interests of both Beaufort and the council to minimize the damage to relations with the papacy at this stage. Suspicions that Beaufort enriched himself from the crusade are equally unwarranted. It is true that the council had to accept Beaufort's figure for the total debt to himself and the pope, but without evidence of how the figure of £7,233. 6*s*. 8*d*. was arrived at it cannot be assumed that Beaufort was overcharging the council. Gloucester made no reference to it in his subsequent accusation against the cardinal. In any case the scale of the whole operation was quite small, affording opportunity neither for 'the gathering of much treasure' by the cardinal (as Hall later alleged) nor for substantial loss by the pope.[56] Its importance was

[53] Holmes, 'Cardinal Beaufort', 744–5; *PPC* iii. 345; *Foedera*, x. 427.

[54] The treasurer of Normandy paid 11,000 *li. tournois* (almost £2,000) for Radclyf's force in August, but as they had been already paid six months' wages this may have been for Beaufort's contingent: Beaurepaire, *Administration*, 63. He also borrowed 9,388 *li.t.* from Beaufort early in Sept. for reinforcments to be sent to Paris: *Wars of Eng.* ii. 141–2.

[55] *PPC* iv. 16; warrant, 25 Feb., E 404/46/288 (printed, Holmes, 'Cardinal Beaufort', 747); Payments, E 403/693 8 Mar., E 403/695 1 May (*Issues of the Exchequer*, 409). What the total of £7,233. 6*s*. 8*d*. comprised is unclear; certainly the 14,980 florins, £2,431 for the second quarter's wages, and 1,000 marks reward; perhaps, too, 3,000 florins from the Apostolic chamber in 1428, and money raised from preaching the crusade.

[56] Discussed by Lunt, *Financial Relations*, 569–70; Holmes, 'Cardinal Beaufort', 746–9. E. Hall, *Chronicle*, ed. H. Ellis, 139: 'For by a bull legatyne, which he purchased at Rome, he gathered so much treasure that no man in maner had money but he'. As Holmes pointed out,

measured in political and personal rather than financial or, indeed, military terms.

The size of the force that Beaufort led to France is uncertain, but the council's agreement to pay wages of £2,431 for the second quarter suggests that it cannot have equalled Radclyf's force of 800 strong for which £5,579 was paid for six months' service. Radclyf shipped with 2,000 horse, Beaufort with 1,500. Probably, then, it numbered hardly more than 600 men; certainly it fell far short of the numbers for which he had indented in June. In fact the crusade had attracted very few recruits, some of whom were probably of doubtful calibre. This must already have been apparent when Beaufort agreed to change its destination, and the kernel of his force was formed by the retinues of Edmund Beaufort and Robert, Lord Willoughby.[57] There were probably few actual crusaders in it. Militarily the combined contingents of Beaufort and Radclyf were an opportune, if not very substantial, addition to English strength. Of equal importance was the assistance rendered by the duke of Burgundy, to whom Bedford had sent immediately on hearing the news of Patay. Duke Philip arrived in Paris on 10 July with 800 troops from Artois to the accompaniment of a dramatic re-enactment of the murder at Montereau. He stayed in Paris a week, thereby avoiding the coronation of Charles VII at Rheims, and on his departure Bedford returned to Rouen to raise troops for the expected battle with the French royal army.[58] Meanwhile Beaufort and Radclyf, having reached Calais, proceeded to Amiens where Beaufort took the opportunity to ride forward with his household attendants to Corbie to meet Duke Philip returning from Paris, and hold discussions with him on future strategy. He then pressed on to Rouen where Bedford received him 'with much joy and consolation', and the combined force, now numbering some 4,000 men, moved straightway to Paris, which it entered on 25 July. Further Burgundian reinforcements were on the way under the Bastard of Saint-Pol and L'Isle-Adam.[59] Beaufort now committed himself formally to the defence of Lancastrian France. On 29 July he undertook to remain in Bedford's service for five months, receiving 3,000 *li. tournois* per month from 1 August from French revenues, with an advance payment of two

Poggio later spoke of Beaufort financing the crusade at his own cost. Something like 50,000 florins had been collected in taxes on church estates in Germany in 1428–9 (Rowan, 'Imperial taxes', 210) and according to Schnith, 'Heinrich Beaufort', 137 n. 7, Sigismund and the German princes were reclaiming 130,000 gulden from Beaufort in 1431. Lannoy's memorandum mentions large sums collected from churches and towns in Germany, but it would seem doubtful if any of this reached Beaufort after 1428.

[57] Ratcliffe, thesis, 38–9; *Amundesham, Annales*, i. 39; *Foedera*, x. 423, 433.

[58] Waurin, *Croniques*, iii. 307–8; *Parisian Journal*, 238; Beaurepaire, *Administration*, 21, 62 for Burgundy's indenture; Lacaze, 'Philippe le Bon', 92.

[59] Waurin, *Croniques*, iii. 309–10; *Parisian Journal*, 240; Clément de Fauquembergue, *Journal de 1417 à 1435*, ed. A. Tuetey, ii. 316.

months' salary 'for the great and notable services and expenses in bringing troops to the aid and recovery of the conquest'.[60]

Beaufort stayed only briefly in Paris; by 3 August he had left for Rouen with only his household attendants, where he probably remained until 25 August when Bedford summoned him to a council of war at Vernon. The French had failed to attack Paris in mid-August, and when they did so at Jeanne d'Arc's instigation on 8 September, the English had been reinforced and the assault failed. But with the English hold on Normandy increasingly threatened by rebels and 'brigands', Bedford decided to hand Paris over to Duke Philip and withdraw to Rouen to consolidate his position. He now recalled Beaufort from Honfleur where he had been persuading the estates of Caen and the Cotentin to grant a subsidy before embarking for England. Beaufort had returned to Rouen by 12 September and, with Bedford, appealed to Duke Philip to come to Paris.[61] He arrived on 30 September with a numerous and magnificent train and was welcomed by Bedford; six days later Beaufort joined them with an equally impressive retinue. At a meeting of the *Grand Conseil* in mid-October the duke of Burgundy, at the request of Bedford and Beaufort, accepted the governorship of Paris and the post of lieutenant governor of the *pays de conquête,* leaving Bedford free to depart to Rouen on 17 October, while Beaufort once more headed for England. Although Beaufort's direct military contribution in the crisis had been small, it had symbolized the determination of the house of Lancaster to defend the conquest and lent weight to his strenuous efforts to ensure the fidelity of Duke Philip to the alliance at a time when, through the duke of Savoy, he was being offered large concessions to desert.[62]

The diversion of a crusading army to a national war understandably scandalized Martin V, and although his attitude later softened as the size and nature of Beaufort's force became known, the whole incident swung papal sympathies perceptibly towards Charles VII. It also marked the end of Martin's trust in Beaufort and ended his career in papal service. Beaufort himself showed no further concern for the crusade nor interest in the Hussite problem. How serious had been his commitment to it? There had been nothing previously in his career to indicate that he had been either influenced by Philippe de Mezière's vision of a *Pax Christiana* as the prelude to the recovery of the holy places or was concerned with the doctrinal challenge of heresy. It is true that in July 1427, before the battle of Tachov, he had written in conciliatory tones to the Hussites in Prague,

[60] BN MS Fr. 4488 (account of Pierre Surreau for 1428–9), 20327 (warrant for payment, 14 July), 26549 (receipt).

[61] Beaurepaire, *Administration*, 10, 55, 63; id., *États*, 39; BN MS Fr. 4488; Allmand, *Lancastrian Normandy*, 172.

[62] *Wars of Eng.* ii. 126–7; *Parisian Journal*, 242; Fauquembergue, *Journal*, ii. 326; Beaucourt, *Charles VII*, ii. 413; Vaughan, *Philip the Good*, 21–1.

but this was less to engage in doctrinal debate than to exercise his own skills as a diplomat before he put the military prowess of his German allies to the test.[63] His own view of heretics was strongly conventional: they were subverters of divine law in both religious and secular society, and he had little reluctance in using the secular sword against them. It was for the military reputation of his family that Martin had chosen him, and Beaufort was determined to live up to this in his own person. Thus far we may say that his commitment to the crusade was full hearted, and the time and energy which he spent on its organization and preparation from the winter of 1427 to the spring of 1429 leave no doubt that he saw it as a practical venture. Yet it is questionable whether he would have accepted the leadership of the crusade, even with the bait of a cardinal's hat, had he not been forced out of the chancellorship by his quarrel with Gloucester. Certainly Bedford supported his elevation as a means of removing him from England. Beaufort's greatest dignity came to him in 1427, just as it had been withheld from him in 1418, through the machinations of his superiors in church and state, then at cross purposes, now in harmony. In this sense the crusade was wished upon him, principally by the pope, but with the willing acquiescence of the regent.

Then, in the course of 1428–9, Bedford came to see that the alliances forged by Beaufort as leader of a German crusade could interlock with Lancastrian pretensions to the crown of France, strengthening co-operation with Burgundy, bringing prestige to the English cause, and placing the papacy under a debt of gratitude. As Beaufort's plans advanced they became ever more enmeshed in these political and national interests. Thus the need to reinvigorate the Burgundian alliance and to ensure the continued neutrality of Scotland were as important for the defence of Lancastrian France as for the recruitment of a crusading force. Beaufort's diplomacy was already underpinning Bedford's plans before the diversion of his crusading force. Similarly, although the crusade was an opportune recompense for his exile from English politics, his organization of it drew him back there. This was probably not his original intention, but from the beginning of 1429 he was using his mission to England to rebuild his influence in council, and as the crisis in France deepened, his concern to render assistance to Bedford overruled his obligations to Martin V. The pope could hardly expect otherwise; he had already given Beaufort the dignity he desired and had little more to offer. Certainly to take up his cardinalate in Rome would be small material recompense for the loss of his wealthy see and the influence he sought to exercise over the fortunes of his great-nephew's realm. Yet to assure his position in the Lancastrian

[63] F. M. Bartos, 'An English cardinal and the Hussite revolution', *Communio Viatorum* (1963), 47–54 builds too much on what was probably a tactical offer.

dominions against the enmity of Gloucester Beaufort needed Bedford's support. That had been the lesson of 1424–6, and in 1429 Beaufort showed that he had taken it to heart. Even so, his decision to go to Bedford's aid was not only because that was where his own wealth and political interests lay; it was because his heart was in the future of Lancastrian France rather than in Bohemia or Rome.

That future had suddenly become uncertain. The forward movement which had continued since Henry V's death had been checked; no longer would it be possible to plan for the realization of his grand design. His successors' task was henceforth the defence of the conquest. This was the burden which Beaufort and Bedford now jointly shouldered, conscious that they were the trustees of the Lancastrian dynasty in the person of the young king, now leaving childhood and approaching puberty. As this ominous prospect unfolded the crusade and papal service came to seem no more than an interlude, its failure of little consequence.

10

The Coronation Expedition, 1429–1432

THE crisis of 1429 destroyed English expectations of final victory over the kingdom of Bourges and showed their unreality. Bedford, recognizing that he would never realize Henry V's ambitions, now sought to maintain the inheritance intact for the heir who might himself fulfil his father's dreams. The allies and supporters of Henry VI had likewise to make a serious reassessment of their position, for the prospect of a prolonged struggle to defend the conquest could only undermine confidence in its durability and in the credibility of the treaty of Troyes as a basis for peace under the aegis of the heir of Lancaster and Valois. Whether the treaty could even survive as a military alliance was in doubt. Charles VII was already tempting Duke Philip with generous terms for a reconciliation not substantially different from those later agreed at Arras. For the moment Burgundy was restrained by the memory of his father, uncertainty about political and military developments, and the personal influence exerted by Anne, Bedford's wife, and Cardinal Beaufort; but as the Anglo-French stalemate continued the ducal council was increasingly divided between rival factions arguing for and against the repudiation of the treaty. As loyalties became fluid and fragile, the legitimacy of Henry VI's title assumed a special legal and psychological significance. It constituted an absolute barrier to the peace between England and France which papal diplomacy sought to promote, and an obstacle to Philip's reconciliation with the royal house. Only the papacy could cut this knot by a pronouncement on the validity of the treaty, a matter of increasing concern to the Lancastrian government. To hold Burgundy firm, retain papal sympathies, and prevent any hostile verdict on the treaty of Troyes, became the aims of English diplomacy in the following years. To all these Cardinal Beaufort could make a unique and indispensable contribution.

The crisis also set the seal on the political alliance of Bedford and Beaufort. Beaufort's response, in diverting his crusading army and sacrificing papal favour and his curial career, though it had greater symbolic than military importance, won him the pledge of Bedford's support. Nor was this given solely out of gratitude, for the resurgence of the French monarchy underlined the dangers of any dispersal of English resources and of opposing counsels in England and France. To restore the territorial limits of Lancastrian rule and the credibility of its claims would demand a major military effort from a united nobility and council. This was to be manifested in an expedition by the young king to secure his coronation as king of France, for the finance and organization of which Bedford looked to the cardinal. Plainly he distrusted Gloucester's ability and disinterestedness, whereas Beaufort had always shared Bedford's aims and had been willing to follow his policies. However, Beaufort would only put his wealth and abilities at Bedford's service if his position in England was secure. His visit had brought home to him his vulnerability to the charge of praemunire and the erosion of his support in the council. Temporarily he had countered these, but his status and ultimate security depended on Bedford, and it was as the regent's representative that he returned to England in October, charged with organizing English resources for the expedition to France. Harmony between Beaufort and Gloucester could not be expected, but peace and a degree of co-operation were essential if the political authority of the council was to be maintained and Bedford's policy fulfilled. For the next two and a half years, therefore, Beaufort's energies were directed towards organizing the diplomatic and military counter-offensive, and this restored him to a recognized, if not central, place in the English council. Nevertheless his visits to England were intermittent, and his main achievement was to oversee the coronation expedition. He can be credited with whatever success it achieved.

Beaufort's first task was to secure taxation from the English parliament. Early in September 1429 he had been at Honfleur, pressing the estates of Caen and the Cotentin to grant aid, and waiting ship for England where parliament was due to open on 22 September. But Bedford had recalled him to Paris to help persuade Duke Philip to assume responsibility for its defence, while sending two personal envoys to the parliament to urge the need of taxation for the defence of the conquest.[1] Beaufort probably left Paris on 17 October in the company of the dukes of Bedford and Burgundy, though he did not arrive in London until 5 November. On the following day he assisted at the coronation of Henry VI and sat in state at the king's right hand at the ensuing banquet. Yet it was not until 18 December, two days before the prorogation of parliament, that he was admitted to the council.[2] There are indications that Gloucester had stubbornly opposed this. Following the coronation Gloucester had necessarily surrendered the protectorship, without prejudice to Bedford's rights, and in the following weeks he was at variance with the council over a number of small issues of patronage and over the more important

[1] P. Le Cacheux, *Rouen au temps de Jeanne d'Arc et pendant l'occupation anglaise*, 157–8; Beaurepaire, *États*, 139; id., *Administration*, 10; Beaucourt, *Charles VII*, ii. 413; *Wars of Eng.* ii. 126–7.

[2] *Amundesham, Annales*, i. 44; *Gregory's Chron.* 165–8; *Rot. Parl.* iv. 338. At the coronation he appeared attired as a cardinal, 'yn hys abyte lyke a chanon yn a garment of rede chamelett, furryd whythe whyte menyver'.

election of Marmaduke Lumley, a Nevill protégé and follower of Beaufort, to the see of Carlisle.[3] When it was at length unanimously agreed to invite Beaufort to the council, the unprecedented nature of his position as a cardinal and a royal councillor was stressed, but justified by reference to his consanguinity with the king, his industry, discretion, fidelity, and circumspection, and the merits of his recent and future services in France. At the same time the council ominously reaffirmed the decision of 17 April that his retention of Winchester was res *inusa* and should not prejudice the crown's rights. He was also debarred from attending when matters relating to the Holy See were under discussion.[4]

Support for his recall was also voiced by the Commons whose choice of Speaker, William Alington, had already indicated the strong influence exerted by Bedford's and Beaufort's allies on the council. The Commons, on 12 December, granted a whole subsidy to be collected at Hilary 1430, and on 20 December, the last day of the session, they followed this with a further whole subsidy for collection at Christmas 1430 and with the grant of tunnage and poundage until the following parliament. This grant of a double subsidy, unparalleled since 1416, was prefaced by the Commons' special recommendation of the cardinal. It is probable that he had urged upon them the insufficiency of a single subsidy for the size of the expedition needed to ensure the king's safety and recover the lands of the conquest; for even as parliament debated, Louviers was lost. The Commons' generosity was also testimony to their confidence in Beaufort's own commitment to the venture. For the second subsidy provided security on which the council was now authorized to borrow up to £50,000, and Beaufort had already indicated his readiness to resume lending on a large scale. With the financial provision secured, military planning could now go ahead, and letters were immediately sent to Paris and towns in Normandy announcing the royal expedition. Parliament was then adjourned with the promise that measures for the defence of the realm and the establishment of good governance in all areas would be taken in the next session.

That lasted only five weeks, at the end of which the Commons further marked their appreciation of the scale of the task ahead by renewing the wool subsidy until Martinmas 1433 and advancing the second lay subsidy to Martinmas 1430. At the same time they put their generosity to good account by presenting one of the longest common petitions of the reign, mainly requesting reforms in law-keeping and local administration, but also including a series of demands by the Company of the Staple. The chroniclers expressed satisfaction over the statutes enacted on these; indeed for both crown and Commons the parliament had proved the most

[3] E 28/51 8, 14 Dec. *PPC* iv. 8.
[4] *Rot. Parl.* iv. 338; *PPC* iv. 11.

co-operative and constructive since 1422.[5] This reflected not only the sense of crisis but the presence of so many experienced and influential leaders of the shires among the representatives. Besides Alington himself, four former Speakers (Chaucer, Hunt, Russell, and Tyrell), the chancellor of the exchequer, Henry Somer, and some esquires and officers of the royal household provided effective leadership in the house. With some Beaufort had personal links, and his ability to command their confidence must have done much to win support for the expedition. Bedford had good reason to be grateful for Beaufort's attested ability to establish a rapport with the Commons.

It is equally possible—though the evidence is less direct—that it was Beaufort who procured a comparable grant from convocation. This had been in session since 19 October, and since 25 October had been debating unavailingly a request for a subsidy conveyed by a delegation largely consisting of the cardinal's friends on the council: Archbishop Kemp, the duke of Norfolk, the earls of Warwick, Stafford, and Salisbury, and Lords Cromwell, Hungerford, and Tiptoft. Only on 20 December, in line with the Commons and under the influence of their example, was it finally agreed to grant a whole and a half subsidy and a graduated tax on stipendiary priests. The whole subsidy, which subsumed the half granted in 1428, was to be payable on 1 May 1430.[6]

With a full lay and clerical subsidy due in the spring, preparations for the expedition went ahead throughout the second session, and by 19 February indentures could be signed with seven earls, twelve lords, and twenty-five captains of knightly rank, together with officials and members of the royal household. In all a force of some 5,000 men was to be shipped to France, and this was in addition to the 2,259 men who had already been sent as reinforcements under the Bastard of Clarence at the beginning of the year at a cost of £11,600. The wages alone for the royal expedition amounted to some £35,000 for six months, and despite the availability of the first lay subsidy at Hilary 1430 the council now found it necessary to anticipate up to half of the second subsidy by loans.[7] In addition to the many small loans raised in the shires under writs of privy seal in March and April 1430, three exceeded £1,000 and between them produced the highest figure for loans since 1421. These were 10,000 marks received from the city of London, 2,000 marks from the feoffees of the duchy of Lancaster, and 12,500 marks from Cardinal Beaufort. The first two were paid into the receipt on 20–4 April along with many smaller loans, and repayment was made by tallies on 1 May, confirmed under letters patent on 19 May. The feoffees of the

[5] *Rot. Parl.* iv. 336–9, 341–58.

[6] *Reg. Chichele*, iii. 211–13.

[7] Ratcliffe, thesis, 40–1, 46–60; *PPC* iv. 8; *CPR 1429–36*, 41. On 21 Apr. some minor clergy were called to the council to contribute loans: E 404/46/336.

duchy were still owed £1,695. 6*s*. 11*d*. from their loan of May 1429, giving a total of £3,028. 13*s*. 7*d*., for which they now received tallies on the tax. In fact these were never cashed, and in December 1430 were changed to an assignment on the customs in Southampton, where they controlled the coket seal and appointed as their collector the archbishop's brother, John Chichele. This was the third loan made by the feoffees, doubtless at the instigation of Cardinal Beaufort, and it heralded their increasingly frequent contributions in the years ahead.[8]

Beaufort himself received tallies for £2,000 on the customs and for £9,950 on the lay subsidy in sixteen shires and boroughs in southern England. This sum included the repayment to him of £3,616. 13*s*. 4*d*., forming the second instalment of the sum for which the council was indebted to the pope for its use of the crusading force in the previous year. Beaufort now used it to pay the wages of his own retinue in the impending expedition. His loan of 12,500 marks had been delivered personally to the duke of Burgundy at Lille for the wages of 1,500 men at English expense.[9] Beaufort seems to have had no difficulty in securing repayment from these assignments, since he could exert influence upon all the collectors; the lay subsidies offered him greater security than the customs, which were destined to shrink rapidly in the following years.

Duke Philip's agreement to a military alliance in March 1430 was a triumph for Beaufort's diplomacy and the *sine qua non* for Henry VI's expedition. From the outset of the crisis Bedford had looked to Burgundy for military aid, but Duke Philip had been willing to give this only on receipt of cash payments. Bedford had secured his assistance in July 1429 with 40,000 *li. tournois* from the Norman treasury, half in cash and half in jewels, and in the autumn relinquished the military custody of Paris into his hands. Bedford's resources were strained to the limit, and he had even borrowed 9,388 *li. tournois* from Beaufort for the wages of the Paris garrison in September.[10] Military operations died down with the winter, leaving the question on which side Duke Philip would fight when they resumed in the spring. In August 1429 Franco-Burgundian negotiations at Arras had already offered Philip most of what he was to secure in 1435, and in October Charles VII's envoys to Paris proposed a peace conference at Auxerre in April 1430. This was the more disturbing in that Martin V was urging Charles to make peace and would endorse any settlement with his authority.

[8] *Foedera*, x. 452; *Cal. L. Bk. K* 110; *CPR 1429–36*, 61–2; E 401/724; E 403/695; E 28/52 19 May.

[9] E 401/724; E 403/695; Devon, *Issues*, 409; *CPR 1429–36*, 60. Since only the repayment, and not the loan itself, was entered on the receipt roll, Steel's figures for Easter term 1430 need to be increased by £8,333. 13*s*. 4*d*.: Steel, *Receipt*, 174; 459. *Foedera*, x. 454–5; *PPC* iv. 31–2; Vaughan, *Philip the Good*, 17.

[10] *Wars of Eng*. ii. 102 ff, 141; Vaughan, loc. cit.

Duke Philip's interests pulled him in both directions. The memory of his father's murder, his sister's marriage to the duke of Bedford, the vital commercial links with England, his oath to the treaty of Troyes, and the gains he held in France by virtue of it, all kept him faithful to Henry VI. But the French resurgence had brought loss and destruction to his territories and imposed great financial strain, and it had exacerbated tensions within his own territories and among his own councillors, divided into pro-French and pro-English elements. For the moment the latter, in the persons of Jean de Lannoy and Jean de Luxembourg, were ascendant, and throughout the winter Beaufort maintained close contacts with the Burgundian court. Lannoy came to England early in December to discuss the strategy of the royal expedition and on 15th the council authorized Beaufort to return to the Burgundian court, possibly envisaging that he would remain in Normandy for the next three months to prepare for the king's arrival. Duke Philip's bride, Isabel of Portugal, Beaufort's niece, was at the same time in London, on the last stage of her journey to Flanders where she was married to Philip on 6 January. In December the council had also taken up the papal proffer of peace negotiations with the suggestion that Beaufort should be appointed mediator, or at least Henry VI's representative, commending him as one who had for thirty years been involved in the affairs of the kingdom and was already engaged in the arduous task of bringing peace to France. Bildeston, Beaufort's personal agent, was to deliver this message, but in the event the suggestion proved unnecessary. The conference at Auxerre never materialized, for by April Philip was at war with the French.[11] In fact Beaufort remained in England throughout January, attending the council and parliament, and only left for Flanders in the first week in February. The ground for his mission had been well prepared by Lannoy and the presence of Bedford's own personal representative, the French secretary Gervase le Vulre, underlined the importance of the meeting. As a result, on 12 February, Duke Philip formally indented to serve Henry VI with 1,500 men on the payment of 12,500 marks. Beaufort returned to England for the ratification of this by the council and later in March delivered this sum in person to Philip at Lille, while in May Jean de Luxembourg was separately retained with a payment of £500.[12] These advances came, as we have seen, from Beaufort's own treasure. Thus when Henry VI and his nobility crossed to Calais on St George's day, Duke Philip was already in the field and

[11] Vaughan, *Philip the Good*, 21–3; Beaucourt, *Charles VII*, ii. 400–20; J. G. Dickinson, *The Congress of Arras, 1435*, 82, 210; *PPC* iv. 9, 12–13; E 404/46/167 21 Dec.

[12] *PPC* iv. 9, 18, 44, 72, 76; E 404/46/178–9, 360; E 28/51. BL Add. Ch. 7959 is Bedford's authorization for le Vulre, dated 15 Jan. and speaks of Beaufort's visit to Burgundy. *Foedera*, x. 454–5 shows that Beaufort had returned to England by 5 Mar. E 28/32 contains a draft letter, undated, by Henry VI to Duke Philip expressing joy at the letter from the duke and the cardinal; almost certainly it refers to this mission: cf. *Amundesham, Annales*, i. 48.

advancing to besiege Compiègne, and there existed a broadly concerted plan for Anglo-Burgundian forces to clear Picardy and, hopefully, Champagne while the English, having recovered Château Gaillard and lower Normandy, would retake Louviers. The recapture of Rheims remained the objective, though the difficulties of this were fully appreciated, as was the imperative need to succour the threatened capital.[13]

The provision of taxation and the reactivating of the Burgundian alliance were prerequisites for the royal expedition; but before Henry VI could set foot in France the safety of Calais, his residence for the next three months, had to be assured. The French resurgence in Champagne had rekindled Armagnac loyalties in Picardy where Charles VII's forces had seized Compiègne and attacked isolated places in the neighbourhood of Dieppe. The need to strengthen the defences of Calais followed several years of declining expenditure on the town. The mutiny of 1423, met initially by a Staple loan of £4,000, had been followed by increased payments to discharge some of the garrison's arrears and the allocation of one mark from the wool subsidy and the profits of the Calais mint for a period of five years from July 1426. The garrison also received the greater part of 10,000 marks from the first instalment of the ransom of James I, but no further payments of this materialized, as neither did the 5,000 marks promised from the Bourbon ransom. The demands of Bedford's and Salisbury's expeditions further reduced payments to Calais from the customs, while its internal revenues also declined. Where the receipts of the treasurer of Calais from 1421 to 1424 had been almost £14,500 p.a., by 1428–9 they had fallen to £10,500. Already by 1429 the garrison's arrears since 1421 had built up to £20,000, while £16,636 from those of the preceding treasurer, Salvayn, was still unpaid in 1433. There was as yet no threat of mutiny, but the need to take positive measures to ensure the safety of Calais in the immediate future was pressing. At the end of the first session of parliament in 1429 the allocation from the wool subsidy was raised from one mark to one pound per sack, the increase being designed to provide a sum of 10,000 marks, partly for the discharge of arrears and partly for repairs to the fortifications.[14] At the same time the greater merchants of the Staple successfully petitioned for the enforcement of the Partition Ordinance.

The ordinance was the response to a situation which had obtained for almost a decade and had three main facets.[15] First was the general

[13] Beaucourt, *Charles VII*, ii. 37, 416; Vaughan, *Philip the Good*, 22–4, both citing Lannoy's memorandum, BN MS Fr. 1278; Lannoy, *Œuvres*, 486–7.

[14] By 1428–9 the receipts of the treasurer of Calais had fallen to £10,500 p.a.: Ratcliffe, thesis, 107–25. *PPC* iii. 242–3, 344–5; *Rot. Parl.* iv. 340–1; E 404/46/166.

[15] The Partition Ordinance has been discussed by E. E. Power, 'The wool trade in the fifteenth century', in *Studies in Eng. Trade*, 83–90; J. H. A. Munro, *Wool, Cloth, and Gold*, ch. 3, 4; T. H. Lloyd, *The English Wool Trade in the Middle Ages*, 256–61; id., *The Movement of Wool Prices in Medieval England*, 20–8, tables 2, 3.

debasement of coinage in north-west Europe produced by the war, economic disruption, and the attempts by the French and Burgundian rulers to meet increased expenditure. Fears of a drain on the stronger English currency, particularly through wool sales at the Calais Staple, were already expressed in the last years of Henry V's reign, and legislation was passed to require resident foreign merchants to purchase English merchandise with their gains. Regulations for payment in English coin for purchases of wool at Calais were probably introduced when the mint was set up at Calais in July 1422, for in the following two years its profits quadrupled as foreign money was drawn in and minted into English coin. These and other measures suggested that a strict bullionist policy was prudent and profitable. It was also popular, for foreign merchants were widely suspected of profiting from credit dealings. Indeed the second feature of the period was the surge of chauvinism among English merchants for whom the duke of Burgundy's status as a vassal of the Lancastrian crown held considerable commercial allure. Proposals to levy a toll on shipping passing the straits, to compel the duke to admit English cloth to Flanders, and to bar the import of rival Spanish and Scottish wool were all side-stepped by Henry V. Later, hostility to the duke fuelled support for Duke Humphrey's invasion, while Beaufort's protection of Flemish merchants in London and refusal to enforce the hosting legislation brought upon him popular hatred and were used to engineer his resignation. In 1428 Duke Philip's attempt to extend the embargo on English cloth to Holland and Zeeland, unsuccessful though this proved, confirmed the predictions of those who had opposed the Bedford–Beaufort policy of appeasing Burgundian expansion in the Low Countries. Thirdly, the period had been one of fairly consistently depressed prices for wool, mainly due to over-production. The greater merchants believed that the price could be increased, particularly for the finer quality wools which they handled

The Staplers' demands were in two parts. First they asked for a concerted effort to enforce the monopoly of the Staple on the ground that this would increase the customs and subsidies. Secondly they asked for the strict enforcement of the recent ordinance requiring all purchases of wool at Calais to be in cash, with a proportion in English coin; the price to be fixed for each grade of wool; and the profits from all sales to be divided proportionately to the stock held by each Stapler, but only after all the wool from each shipment had been sold.[16] Here again the ostensible reason was to increase the revenue at the Calais mint and raise the price of wool, perhaps with an implicit promise of an increased rate of subsidy. Yet the prime purpose of the ordinance was to organize the English merchants

[16] *Rot. Parl.* iv. 350 (43), 352 (47), 358 (59–68); *SR* ii. 253–7.

trading at Calais as a joint stock company and penalize foreign buyers. It strengthened the twenty or thirty greater merchants whose resources enabled them to endure the delays inherent in the partition system at the expense of the smaller merchants who had to operate on a quick turnover basis, while the Flemish merchants could no longer buy on extended credit and had to pay a higher price.

It has usually been assumed that in all this the greater merchants had the support of Cardinal Beaufort, and that his interests and views coincided with theirs. Yet particularly in the previous decade, but also over a much longer period, Beaufort had sought to protect the interests of Flemish merchants in England, and his concern to maintain a high level of trade with Flanders and good relations with the duke of Burgundy had been guiding principles in his and Henry V's policy. At this very moment, when he was attempting to rebuild the political and military alliance with Duke Philip, he can only have viewed the predictable Flemish reaction to the Partition Ordinance with apprehension. Indeed it is more likely that the greater merchants would have sought support from Gloucester than from Beaufort, and the chronology of the legislation, as far as it can be detected, lends support to this suggestion. The enactment of the ordinance for a period of three years from 2 February 1430 suggests that it must have been negotiated during the first session alonside the increased allocation to Calais from the subsidy granted on 20 December. If the council's agreement with the Company of the Staple had been thrashed out in the course of the first session before the admission of Beaufort to the council on 1 December he would have faced a *fait accompli* which his own still precarious position would prevent him from challenging. It is possible that, as with other members of the council, he was persuaded by the self-interested arguments of the Staplers; and indeed the passage of the statute was, as predicted, followed by a short-lived increase both in the price of wool and the revenue of the Calais mint. Moreover, it was probably judged that the grievances of the Flemish merchants would be contained by the close alliance forged with the duke of Burgundy, while those of the lesser merchants of the Staple would be outweighed by the backing which the government could expect from its oligarchy. Fairly immediately that was expressed in a loan of 3,500 marks delivered at Calais on 12 July by the Company of the Staple for troops sent to strengthen Paris for the king's arrival.[17] At this critical juncture the council had no option but to pay the price which the Staplers demanded, and probably neither Beaufort nor others foresaw that the ordinance would precipitate a slump in wool exports which far outweighed any of its benefits.

In the first seven years of the reign wool exports had averaged just under

[17] Munro, op. cit., 93, 110 sees Beaufort as 'the probable author of the ordinance'. *PPC* iv. 52; *CPR 1429–36*, 111; E 404/47/149.

15,000 sacks a year, with peak periods in 1422–4 and 1426–8. In the six years between Michaelmas 1429 and the rupture of the Burgundian alliance this average fell to just over 9,000 sacks, and the fall to this level in 1429–30 was both immediate and permanent. Revenue from the customs was consequently between £9,000 and £10,000 p.a. less than under Henry V. Nor was the level of the subsidy raised when, at the end of the parliament in 1430, it was extended to run concurrently with the ordinance until 1433. Although this collapse of trade can be attributed with reasonable certainty to the impediments imposed by the ordinance, how precisely this operated is difficult to identify. Probably Flemish purchasers turned to the cheaper Spanish and Scottish wools which the Staplers had sought to exclude in 1421; doubtless smuggling increased, as did by various means shipments through Holland and Zeeland. Only shipments to Italy from Southampton, which were not affected by the ordinance, tended to increase.[18] All these effects were, very largely, those which the Staplers had sought to avoid, even if their own command of the trade and their profits from it were increased.

At last, by the end of March 1430, Beaufort could feel that the royal expedition had been underwritten financially by parliament, the city of London, and the Company of the Staple, and that the military resources of the English nobility and the duke of Burgundy had been mobilized. His final concern, before departure, was to allay the personal quarrels which could sap its purpose, and to safeguard his own position in England during his absence. Over the last four years rifts had developed among the nobility: between the duke of Norfolk and the earl of Warwick, between the earl of Stafford and the earl of Huntingdon, and perhaps between Norfolk and Huntingdon, while Gloucester's quarrel with Beaufort now embraced their followers and associates in the council. Accordingly, at Canterbury on 16 April, as musters were being prepared, he set down his conditions for accompanying the expedition. First, all disputes between members of the council—and Norfolk, Warwick, and Huntingdon swore individually to this effect—were to be submitted to the judgement of the council. There followed certain provisions for the conduct of business by the two councils in France and England. Each was empowered to take decisions except on matters requiring joint consultation. Of paramount importance was the requirement of joint agreement for the dismissal or appointment of any of the officers of state or members of the continual council, and for all appointments to bishoprics. Thirdly, Bedford's regency was to terminate with the king's arrival in France. Although the council minute records that Beaufort only agreed to go to France 'at the busy prayer and instance of my lord of Gloucester and other lords of the

[18] *Eng. Export Trade*, 59; these are the reasons adduced by the Company of the Staple in 1432: *Rot. Parl.* iv. 410.

council', these conditions express not his reluctance to attend the king (where the centre of power would be located) but his suspicions that Gloucester would take advantage of his absence.[19] They were designed to perpetuate the existing distribution of power which effectively reduced Gloucester to a figurehead. The three officers of state were still those appointed or confirmed by Bedford in 1426, while Cromwell and Tiptoft (who was to act as a link betwen the councils in England and France) were both firm adherents of the cardinal. Apart from these the only regular members were three bishops, Chichele, Gray, and Langdon, and Lord Scrope who now supported Gloucester. Gloucester enjoyed the dignity and patronage of the office of king's lieutenant, but in government he was sworn to do all things with the assent of the council, and not otherwise. On the other hand Beaufort's role as organizer and orchestrator of the expedition, and the effective head of the council in France, was implicit in these conditions and recognized by the award of a salary of £4,000 p.a.

The French captains were well prepared for the Anglo-Burgundian counter-offensive and hard fighting took place over a wide area during the spring and summer of 1430. The French pursued their aim of detaching the duke of Burgundy from the alliance by concentrating their attacks upon his territories and supporters. Barbasan cleared the Burgundians from Champagne and the basin of the Oise, while Roderigo de Villandrado, defending the Dauphiné, won victories against the counts of Orange and Savoy. Attacks were launched on the ducal lands in Burgundy and Namur and alliances made with his enemies, Frederick of Austria and Sigismund, while his subjects in Liège were incited to revolt. But the crucial trial of strength centred on Compiègne, to which an Anglo-Burgundian army lay continual siege from May to October. Despite the capture of Jeanne d'Arc and the pressure from the forces of Jean de Luxembourg and the earl of Huntingdon, the successful resistance of the garrison did more than anything else to break the duke's will to fight. Even during the siege he had withdrawn part of his forces to suppress the revolt of the Liégeois and had himself returned to the Low Countries to secure Brabant on the sudden death of his cousin Philip of Saint-Pol. On 4 November he wrote a long letter of complaint to Henry VI detailing his losses and reproaching the English for failure to honour the fiscal undertakings given by Cardinal Beaufort in March.[20]

Due in part to the concentration of the French effort against their ally, the English had made steady if piecemeal progress in recovering lands and fortresses in Normandy, the Île de France, and Brie. Bedford retook

[19] *PPC* iv. 35–41; *CPR 1429–36*, 53.

[20] *Wars of Eng.* ii. 156–81; Beaucourt, *Charles VII*, ii. 37–9. Over £2,700 had been paid to Duke Philip and the Bastard of St Pol during the summer: Ratcliffe, thesis, 71–2 citing E 101/52/35.

Château Gaillard, Etrépagny, and Aumale in June and July, enabling Henry VI to move to Rouen, and in August the earl of Stafford resumed the governorship of Paris, to which Bedford himself returned in January 1431. On this reckoning the expedition had proved a limited success, but it had not matched the ambitious strategy envisaged by Lannoy, and the duke of Burgundy had been effectively immobilized as an ally by the heavy losses which he had sustained. It looked as if the French had fought the Anglo-Burgundian offensive to a standstill; at the very least they had ensured that Henry VI would never be crowned at Rheims and that even to make Paris secure the English would have to maintain their advance for a further summer. Could the English find a second wind for this final offensive, which they would have to fight largely on their own? It was on that question that 1430 closed.

Cardinal Beaufort apparently remained with the king throughout the first eight months of his stay in France. When Henry moved to Rouen on 17 July the English councillors who had accompanied him merged with the *Grand Conseil*. In accordance with the decision of the Canterbury council, Bedford's office and powers as regent were suspended and both military appointments and gifts were taken out of his hands. The *Grand Conseil*, using the great seal of France, assumed responsibility for all payments from the Norman treasury and formally reappointed officials. The very imperfect evidence about who attended the *Grand Conseil* at this period imposes caution, but it appears that the English members comprised Beaufort, who was normally present, one other bishop, the earl of Warwick as Henry's governor, and often another official. As president of the council Beaufort assumed control of the government, although the chancellor, Louis de Luxembourg, and the other members of Bedford's *Grand Conseil* must have remained an influential element.[21]

Beaufort also made a financial contribution. At the end of August the treasurer of Normandy was ordered to repay loans from him totalling £2,866. 13*s*. 4*d*. sterling and 3,000 *li. tournois*, some of it advanced for the payment of Duke Philip's forces at Compiègne, some towards the purchase of Jeanne d'Arc, and some for the wages of the Bastard of Saint-Pol and Thomas Beaufort, count of Perche.[22] By November 1430 the first six months for which the expedition had indented was expiring and the responsibility for the continued payment of its wages devolved on the treasurer of the household, also constituted treasurer of war. Over the next six months, to the end of May 1431, he received further sums from the

[21] *Amundesham, Annales*, i. 52; B. Rowe, 'The *Grand Conseil* under the Duke of Bedford, 1422–35', *Oxford Essays in Medieval History presented to H. E. Salter*, 224–5, 232–4. A further list of 24 June 1430 is in E 28/52.

[22] BN MS Fr. 20327 no. 150; MS Fr. 26549 no. 15. The muster of Beaufort's retinue at Caen in Sept. 1430 is in MS Fr. 25769 (ref. from Allmand, *Lancastrian Normandy*, 198).

English exchequer while also drawing on the revenues of Normandy. But this was insufficient to meet the full cost of the royal household and retinue, and in November Beaufort lent the treasurer £2,815.[23]

By 7 November 1430 Beaufort was preparing to leave Rouen and by 16 December he had arrived at Calais, where he received messages from Duke Philip. Five days later he crossed to England with Bishop Stafford and Lords Ormond and Tiptoft. Having spent Christmas at Canterbury, and paid a visit to Queen Catherine at Waltham, he retired to Chertsey to await the parliament summoned for 12 January.[24] He was to spend the first four months of 1431 organizing the substantial wave of reinforcements needed to take Henry VI to Paris. The duke of Gloucester presided at the opening of parliament, and his follower, Sir John Tyrell, was chosen Speaker, while William Lyndwood delivered the charge in place of the chancellor, Kemp, who was reported sick. His themes—the need for unity, peace, and justice in the realm—reflected the domestic preoccupations of Gloucester, rather than those of Beaufort. Nevertheless at its dissolution on 20 March, parliament granted a tax of one pound on each knight's fee or twenty pounds of annual income to be levied at midsummer, and a whole tenth and fifteenth to be levied at Martinmas, with another third at Easter 1432. It also increased the rate of tunnage and poundage for alien merchants. Little is known of the course of this parliament, but Beaufort must have argued the king's needs to good effect to secure this further grant of taxation at the wartime level. Once again he was not without supporters in the Commons, where Thomas Chaucer and Thomas Stonor continued to represent Oxfordshire, John Russell Herefordshire, Roger Hunt Huntingdonshire, and John Newburgh Dorset. His other known associates were Lewis John, Hamo Sutton, and Renfrew Arundell.[25] Yet, as in 1430, Beaufort's own readiness to lend was of crucial importance in guaranteeing the dispatch of the expedition and thus in persuading the Commons to make their grant. Before the close of the session parliament authorized the raising of loans to the sum of £50,000 and Beaufort had delivered his own contribution to the exchequer.

Convocation had assembled a little later than parliament, and two days after its opening, on 21 February, a delegation from the council led by the chancellor and numbering Bishop Lumley, the earl of Suffolk, Lords Tiptoft, Hungerford, Cromwell, and Scrope sought prayers and aid for the king in France. All save the last were firm supporters of the cardinal, but despite their powerful advocacy and the urgency of the need, no conclusion

[23] Hotoft received £18,238 from the exchequer in Michaelmas and Easter terms 9 Henry VI and £13,771 from Norman revenues for his whole period in France: E 404/408/9; *PPC* iv. 79; Ratcliffe, thesis, 66.

[24] L. Gilliodts van Severen, (ed.) *Inventaire des archives de la ville de Bruges*, v. 9; *CPR 1429–36*, 99; *Amundesham, Annales*, i. 56.

[25] *Rot. Parl.* iv. 367–9; *Members of Parliament* 318–20.

was reached when their request was debated five days later. Not until 21 March was a subsidy granted, to be collected in two halves at Martinmas 1431 and 1432. Perhaps because they were already due to pay a half-tenth in May, the clergy had been less generous than the Commons.[26] On 8 February, even before these grants had been secured, indentures had been made for reinforcements for six months' service. Payment for the two quarters was made on 20 February and 16 March, the latter being most unusually a full five weeks before the muster, fixed for 22 April. The speed with which this force was assembled owed much to the fact that its leaders were the cardinal's nephews, Edmund, count of Mortain, and Thomas, count of Perche, whose release he had recently negotiated. Both of them had attended the parliament. Each led a contingent of 128 men-at-arms and 460 archers, with Lords Audley, Fitzwalter, and Clinton bringing somewhat smaller retinues. The total size of the expedition was 519 men-at-arms and 2,133 archers, and its cost in wages £17,082. In the event part of the force under Lord Clinton failed to sail before August, but in late June or early July another sizeable contingent of 800 men was dispatched under another nephew of Beaufort, Richard Nevill, earl of Salisbury, at a further cost in wages of £5,584. The total cost of the expeditions in 1431 in wages and shipping was almost £24,000.[27]

The cardinal's renewed involvement in the defence of Lancastrian France had revived moves for the release of his nephews. The proposal in 1429 for the exchange of Bourbon and Somerset had never borne fruit, although more than once in the following years, Philip had urged delivery of Bourbon to himself in payment of the English debts to him[28]. However, in April 1430, on the eve of his departure with the royal expedition, Cardinal Beaufort and the Duchess Margaret had given obligations of 2,000 marks, to be paid if required when Henry VI came of age, for a proportion of Bourbon's ransom to be remitted in respect of Somerset's brother Thomas. Thomas had indeed been released by the summer, but this was more probably as part of an agreement under which he and the earl of Suffolk were ransomed by Charles d'Orléans (Suffolk's captor at Jargeau) to raise money for the liberation of Jean d'Orléans, count of Angoulême.[29] That, in fact did not take place, for the Duchess Margaret retained custody of Angoulême as providing the best hope of her securing the release of her son John. Although John remained hopeful from 1430 to 1434, during which time formal protections were issued to him as being in

[26] *Reg. Chichele*, iii. 216–28.

[27] Ratcliffe, thesis, 46 ff; *Foedera*, x. 493; E 404/47/166–8. A force of 500 men under Radclyf was also sent to Gascony: *PPC* iv. 53; Ratcliffe, thesis 137; E 404/47/197.

[28] *Wars of Eng*. ii. 173.

[29] *Foedera*, x. 457; *CCR 1429–35*, 31; Dupont-Ferrier, 'Captivité de Jean d'Orléans', 60. In Mar. 1431 the council granted Thomas Beaufort the custody of Charles, count of Eu: E 404/47/232, E 404/48/298.

the king's retinue, in the end neither he nor Angoulême obtained their liberty by the time Bourbon died in 1434.[30] The cardinal's role in these negotiations is largely obscure. Very probably he provided some money for Thomas's ransom, set at 7,000 marks, £3,000 of which Thomas took back with him when he sailed with his uncle to France in March 1431.[31] Whether he could have done more to assist Somerset's release is impossible to say.

It was to be expected that both Suffolk and Thomas Beaufort should now join the royal expedition. Suffolk was with Huntingdon at the siege of Compiègne and in August 1430 Thomas had 120 men-at-arms and 360 archers with him at La Charité-sur-Loire. By November he was back in Paris, bound for England in his uncle's company, and in February 1431 he joined his brother Edmund in indenting for service on the cardinal's return to France. This was performed mainly at the siege of Louviers where he died on 3 October, three weeks before its fall.[32] His brother Edmund had been in continuous service in Normandy from his return there with the cardinal in 1429. Bedford had at once appointed him constable of the army at a salary of 250 *li. tournois* per month and sent him and Willoughby to the siege of Etrépagny. From the autumn of 1429 to December 1430 he held the captaincies of Neufchâtel, Gisors, and Gournay while also fielding a force of 27 men-at-arms and 117 archers in February and a larger force at the siege of Château Gaillard in May. Returning with his uncle in December to recruit for the spring campaign of 1431, he then proceeded to the siege of Louviers, though in September he was detached to assist the duke of Burgundy with a small force at Liège.[33] The cardinal likewise acquired his own captaincy at Honfleur, which he held from September 1430 until 1438.[34] The Beaufort brothers and their cousin Richard, earl of Salisbury, thus made a marked contribution to the coronation expedition. But their effective careers in France had only commenced when the English had been thrown on to the defensive and fresh conquests had ceased. The grants of the county of Mortain to Edmund in 1427, of Ivry to Huntingdon, of Perche to Thomas in December, and of Laval to Warwick in March 1428 were all of escheated fiefs.[35] When Thomas died in 1431

[30] C 76/113 m. 20, / 115 m. 13 /116 m. 15, /117 m. 11; Dupont-Ferrier, op. cit. 59–62.

[31] The Duchess Margaret had assigned Thomas 2,000 marks from her annuity on the customs and this was paid in Feb., July, and Oct. 1431 by the hand of Edmund: E 404/47/163; *CPR 1429–36*, 112; A. E. Marshall, 'The role of English war captains in England and Normandy, 1436–61', MA thesis (Swansea, 1975), 109.

[32] Marshall, loc. cit., citing BL Add. Ch. 11671; E 404/48/298; BN MS Fr. 20327 no. 150; 26549 nos. 4, 5; 4488 no. 617.

[33] Marshall, thesis, 113–4, citing BL Add. Ch. 11731 and BN MS Fr. 25768–9; R. A. Newhall, *Muster and Review*, 128; Le Cacheux, *Actes . . . d'Henry VI*, ii. 154–6; *Appendices to Foedera*, 387. BN MS Fr. 26549 nos. 6–8, 10–13.

[34] Le Cacheux, *Actes . . . d'Henry VI*, ii. 371; Marshall, thesis, Appendix II; *Wars of Eng.* ii. 540. The cardinal's retinue was mustered at Caen in Sept. 1430: Allmand, *Lancastrian Normandy*, 198.

[35] Le Cacheux, op. cit. ii. 353; Longnon, 'Limites de la France', 510.

Perche was granted to Humphrey, earl of Stafford, the husband of Beaufort's niece. The cardinal's relatives formed only a small fraction of those—the great majority of the English nobility—who accompanied Henry VI to France and served there from 1430 to 1431 without substantial reward. But the military presence of the Beauforts served to reaffirm the tradition of the family as strenuous supporters in arms of the royal house and title and to underline the cardinal's own commitment to the royal expedition and his claims on royal and public gratitude.

Not only were the reinforcements of 1431 led by Beaufort's family and associates, they were paid for by loans from himself and those whom he could personally persuade to lend. Between 8 February and 16 March 1431 a total of £28,000 was received in loans at the exchequer which, over the same period, paid out £18,628 in wages of war. This included both quarters' wages for the Beaufort brothers and the first quarter for Richard Nevill. The cardinal himself provided no less than £12,758 of this which, with £2,816 loaned by him in Normandy and £4,326 for his fee as councillor while attending Henry VI, all totalling a precisely calculated £20,000, was repaid from the lay subsidy in nineteen shires by tallies fortified by letters patent dated 24 April. At the same time he received licence to export 800 sacks of wool at any port. The same type of security was afforded to the city of London, which lent £3,323, the feoffees of the duchy of Lancaster, who lent 5,000 marks, and the Staplers Nicholas Wooton, William Estfeld, and Nicholas James, who now lent £3,018.[36]

The key figures in the loans from London and the Staple were evidently Wooton, mayor of London, and Estfeld. A royal letter from Rouen in November 1430, doubtless framed by Cardinal Beaufort and perhaps conveyed by him, had requested a loan of 10,000 marks from the city as a matter of dire need: 'it would do more ese and service in our present necessite than peraventure shuld the double and much more at other tyme'.[37] The two loans now organized by Wooton fell just short of that sum. In all, these major lenders had produced £22,500 between them. None the less the treasurer, Lord Hungerford, now reported that over and above all these loans he would need to find a further £16,380 for the second quarter of the earl of Salisbury's contingent and the payments due on the indentures for the lieutenant in Ireland and the seneschal of Aquitaine.[38] The council ordered him to give priority to the king's needs in France and initiated a further phase of borrowing with general commissions in all shires under the authority of the act of parliament. By midsummer these had yielded a total of £9,875, of which the feoffees of the duchy contributed a further 2,000 marks, the Staplers headed by Estfeld

[36] E 401/725; *PPC* iv. 79; *CPR 1429–35*, 115, 118; E 404/47/191. A previous loan from the Staple of 3,500 marks was still not repaid and this was deferred until Martinmas: *PPC* iv. 88; *CPR* ibid. 120.

[37] Sharpe, *London and the Kingdom*, iii. 372–4.

[38] *PPC* iv. 79.

produced £2,333, and a major effort by the earl of Suffolk in East Anglia and Lord Greystoke in Yorkshire just on £2,000.[39] This was used for the wages of Salisbury and Lord Clinton. The massive scale of this borrowing must be stressed. Since Beaufort's return in December, loans of almost £46,000 had been recorded at the exchequer, the highest total of the century and surpassing even those for Henry V's expeditions. Moreover, this was the culmination of a sustained effort which, from the sailing of the expedition until June 1431, had raised almost £65,000. For the most part the government's indebtedness was short-lived: it represented a massive anticipation of the lay and clerical subsidies for as far ahead as Easter 1432. But it had needed a concerted effort to tap all the major holders of liquid wealth, and Beaufort's readiness to advance no less than £21,000 of the total had probably been effective in persuading others to lend.

In addition to paying for the reinforcements leaving England the exchequer had been sending money across the channel for the royal army and household, to a total of at least £26,000 between November 1430 and December 1431.[40] Yet it was clear that the enormous effort into which Beaufort had galvanized the council on his visit could not be sustained. Parliament empowered Bedford, Beaufort, and Gloucester to negotiate peace, 'considering the burden of the war and how grievous it is to this land', and at a meeting of the council shortly before the expedition sailed some central questions were raised about how and by whom this burden should be met. Gloucester seems to have undertaken to meet from English resources the cost of the present reinforcements after the end of their six months' service, but to have resisted any suggestion that the charges of the Paris administration should fall on England. The council also warned that if the cost of the royal army could not be met from French resources, it would have to return at the end of six months, and those who remained in France must be given conquered land to hold and defend at their own charge.[41] The councillors returning to France were left in no doubt about the impossibility of financing active war indefinitely. This reinforced the strategy of a six-month summer campaign which should clear the way to Paris for the king's coronation there, if not at Rheims.

This time Beaufort returned with some of his principal supporters on the council: Tiptoft, Cromwell, and Alnwick.[42] All were to lose their posts in Gloucester's purge a year later. It was therefore significant that on 1 May,

[39] *CPR 1429–36*, 124; Steel, *Receipt*, 176; E 401/728; E 404/47/336, E 404/48/108.

[40] *PPC* iv. 71–2, 78, 89, 103–4, 108; E 404/47/123, 145, 154, 182, 336; E 404/48/141, 249; E 403/700.

[41] *PPC* iv. 91–7. In Apr. 1431 the *Grand Conseil* at Rouen was looking to Cardinal Beaufort to pay wages at the court: Fauquembergue, *Journal*, iii. 11.

[42] *PPC* iv. 80, 83; *Gregory's Chron.*, 172. On 24 Apr. the ship *Little Jesus* was commissioned for his return and he was excused accounting for his various embassies: E 404/47/296–7.

the day before sailing, they had the articles of April 1430 read and subscribed to afresh in the presence of Beaufort, Kemp, the bishops of Ely, Bath, and Rochester, and Lord Hungerford. Gloucester was ominously absent, though he had attended three days before.[43] The preceding months must have brought home to him the enormous influence which Beaufort had come to wield through his organization and direction of the royal expedition; he was glad to see his rival go and determined that he should not return. Indeed the articles relating to decisions of importance to be taken in France, which the departing councillors put to those remaining in England, contained two proposals which could well assist Gloucester's purpose. The first related to Bedford's status after Henry VI's return to England. He had, on the council's requisition, vacated the regency while the king was in France, but he had always claimed a prescriptive right to this and now refused to hold it under a commission from the king, since such would be revocable. Gloucester and the council evaded a decision about this, remitting it to the cardinal's discretion and thereby placing upon him the onus of affronting the duke. For Beaufort this was an important and sensitive issue. He saw Henry's double coronation as terminating the claims of Bedford and Gloucester to exercise autonomous authority in virtue of their birth, and believed that they should now receive their authority from the king and the council. His own future position following Henry VI's return to England would be directly involved, for the royal expedition had enabled him both to impress his authority on the young king and to control the council that acted in his name. He now saw the opportunity to build upon this and to free himself from the old anxieties and resentments over his dependence on the goodwill of the full blood, with whom his relationship had always been ambivalent.

Beaufort's immediate object may have been to remain president of the *Grand Conseil* with an independent commission from the king, controlling administrative and diplomatic policy, parallel to Bedford's military command. But Bedford refused to surrender the exercise of his full power as regent, and Beaufort's attempt to force him to do so resulted in a profound and bitter quarrel. The accounts of this in both Hardyng and Hall are confused: they relate it to Bedford's vacation of the regency during Henry's visit, and the former links it to the coronation itself. In fact it must have centred on Bedford's acceptance of the commission to govern France in the king's absence, which was delivered to him at Rouen on 12 October 1431.[44] For Bedford received this only under protest that it should in no way derogate from his natural right to the regency, if such a right existed, and he significantly added to his old title of regent that of '*gouvernant*', underlining that his was not merely a military and protective function as

[43] *PPC* iv. 38–9.

[44] Rowe, '*Grand Conseil*', 226–7 discussed the evidence.

Gloucester's had been in England. Beaufort had technically gained his point, though he was to pay heavily for the resentment which Bedford now nursed against him and which may, indeed, have erupted at the coronation, provoked by Beaufort's assertive role in the ceremony. For in picking a quarrel with Bedford over a principle on which the political and personal interests of the royal brothers were for once aligned, Beaufort had exposed himself to Gloucester's enmity.

Gloucester's hopes of keeping his rival at a distance were also strengthened by the papal initiative for a negotiated peace. In November 1430 Martin V had finally decided to entrust the delicate role of intermediary between England, France, and Burgundy to Cardinal Albergati, who, by the late summer of 1431, had embarked on a series of visits to the three courts. The parliament of 1431 had empowered Bedford, Gloucester, and Beaufort to treat for peace and, if the terms were acceptable, to conclude the same. The council, at least, had no illusions about the prospects for this or the purpose of the negotiations. No meaningful concessions could be made to the French while Henry VI was under age and, as the French would not accept Henry's title, the English could only win a respite from fighting by means of a truce, which the French consistently refused.[45] Charles VII's real purpose in encouraging tripartite negotiations was to detach Burgundy from the English alliance. As a cardinal, as the principal representative of Henry VI, and as a friend and relation of Duke Philip, Beaufort was well equipped to conduct the long and tortuous struggle to retain Burgundy's loyalty. Gloucester must thus have seen Beaufort depart in May 1431 with every expectation that his rival's career would, for good or ill, shape itself in France, leaving him free to consolidate his own position in England.

Immediately on his return to Rouen in mid-May, Beaufort participated in the trial and burning of Jeanne d'Arc. The preparation of charges against her and the breaking of her spirit during her long and rigorous imprisonment had taken place in his absence, although it is doubtless right to say that, like Warwick and the other English leaders, he was resolved on her death. The ultimate act of the drama was probably delayed until he was present to witness it. As the leading dignitary among those who assembled to hear her abjuration in the cemetery of the abbey of Saint-Ouen on 24 May, it was to him that Bishop Cauchon appealed when Jeanne's apparent dissent from the recital of her abjuration provoked a cry from the English for her immediate death. Beaufort quieted this and ordered Cauchon to continue and to receive her abjuration and penance. Following her relapse six days later, Beaufort was also present at her execution, moved as others were by her demeanour at the point of death. On his order her ashes were

[45] Dickinson, *Congress of Arras*, 82–3; *Rot. Parl.* iv. 371; *PPC* iv. 95–6, 279–81.

carefully collected and thrown into the river, to avoid the risk of popular veneration. Beaufort seems to have assumed responsibility for ensuring that the procedures of the trial and execution were legally and politically conclusive, even to the point of issuing letters of protection in Henry VI's name against citation to Rome or to the council of Basel for all who had participated. Those named were all his English associates: the earls of Warwick and Stafford, Bishop Alnwick, and Lords Cromwell and Tiptoft.[46]

During the next six months Beaufort must have mainly remained at Rouen, although the only references to his presence are in June and July. The Beauchamp household accounts show how the residence of Henry VI and the court made Rouen the capital of Lancastrian France. Although Bedford himself was only occasionally present, and Duke Philip studiously avoided meeting the king, the duke of Brittany came in the summer and autumn and there was a steady passage of members of the English nobility. Among these the young duke of York and the earls of Warwick, Stafford, and Arundel were on cordial terms with the cardinal; he also enjoyed the presence of his conciliar colleagues, Lords Cromwell and Tiptoft, and of his young nephews along with their companions in arms, Lords Clinton, Audley, Willoughby, and Fitzwalter. It was in their company, sharing fully their efforts and anxieties in wresting the key town of Louviers from the French and opening the way to Paris, that Beaufort both demonstrated his commitment to Lancastrian rule in France and hoped to lay the basis for his renewed influence when he returned to England.[47]

The army of 2,600 men which Beaufort brought with him to France had one overriding purpose: to secure the route to Paris. It could afford little aid to Duke Philip against whom, from the beginning of 1431, the French resumed their pressure in Burgundy, Picardy, Artois, and Namur. Emissaries from the duke had come to England in the spring to seek further subventions, and the council had agreed to pay for 1,800 soldiers under Jean de Luxembourg to operate with the Burgundians on the marches of Picardy. On Beaufort's return to Rouen in May, the council again sent a conciliatory answer to the duke's complaints, promising to send aid into Burgundy once Louviers had fallen and to investigate and settle the duke's outstanding claims under the indentures signed with Beaufort in the preceding year. Clearly Beaufort was making every effort to placate Philip, accompanying the council's reply with personal assurances of his own wish to serve Philip's interests, though whether he found

[46] *Procès de condamnation et de rehabilitation de Jeanne d'Arc*, ed. J. Quicherat, ii. 6, iii. 185, 240–3; *Procès de Condamnation de Jeanne d'Arc*, ed. P. Tisset, i. 443, ii. 335, 348, iii. 51, 136.

[47] Warwickshire RO, Beauchamp Household Book, CR 1618/W 19/5 entries for 7 and 29 June. For his presence in July, *CPL* viii. 342. For the other lords, and for the Beaufort brothers at Louviers, see SC 8/7180; *Appendices to Foedera*, 392, 396.

time to visit Flanders in the summer is unknown.[48] For now English efforts were concentrated on the recapture of Louviers, and at the end of five months, on 28 October, this fell. During the siege La Hire had been captured, and near Beauvais the earl of Warwick had defeated and made prisoner Xantrailles. Duke Philip likewise had his triumphs in Champagne, where on 2 July the count de Vaudemont captured René d'Anjou and the redoubtable Barbasan was slain. But Philip was now ready to retire from the war, and on 8 September signed a truce for two years, to be transformed in December at Lille into a treaty of general suspension of war for six years. With this Philip in effect declared his military neutrality in the Anglo-French struggle. The question of his political allegiance remained undecided, and the ominous agreement which Cardinal Albergati now secured from both French and Burgundians to a peace conference at Auxerre in March 1432 received reluctant endorsement by the English on 3 December. Beaufort must have met Albergati during the latter's visit to Rouen in October, and he himself could anticipate a prominent role in the negotiations as the principal Lancastrian representative. At this point Beaufort's expectations of re-entering English politics seemed remote, for Henry VI's sojourn in France, now approaching its climax, had invested him with the prime responsibility for the government of Lancastrian France, while Bedford conducted its defence.

This had been underlined by a series of loans which he had made to the treasurer of the household, both for domestic and military costs, in the six months preceding the coronation. Between June and September he advanced almost £6,000 in gold from his own coffers on seven different occasions. These were for the fees of members of the council and officials of the *parlement* and *chambre des comptes*, for the purchase of the captured La Hire, for the wages of reinforcements to be sent to his nephew Thomas at Louviers, and for the garrison of the earl of Warwick at Meaux. Except for one advance of £1,083. 6*s*. 8*d*., later paid in England, all of this was entered in the treasurer's account, and most of it was repaid by Tyrell before Henry VI's return to England.[49] Further, on 28 September the council in England, on Gloucester's advice, wrote to Beaufort asking him to defer the repayments due to him at Michaelmas until Easter, with the purpose of using the subsidy for current expenses in France. But Beaufort, conscious of 'the great necessitee that the king stood inne the whiche necessitee myght not abide the sendyng of good oute of England', decided to lend a further 10,000 marks from his own coffers. The only security he received for this was letters obligatory from the lords of the council in

[48] Vaughan, *Philip the Good*, 26; *Wars of Eng*. ii. 188–95.

[49] E 404/48/156–8; E 401/731; E 101/408/13; *PPC* iv. 109. Beaufort's receipts for five of his loans, totalling £3,366 remain in Bodleian Lib. Misc. Ch. Eng. C 1 nos. 19–22. (I am indebted to Dr A. Wathey for this reference.)

France for its repayment by 22 May 1432. His earlier loans seem to have been delivered solely on the bond of the treasurer of war, indicative of his close control over the royal expedition. It is significant that the only loans made in this period which were secured by jewels were two last, small advances, totalling £733. 6*s*. 8*d*., made during the king's stay in Paris, for which the sword of Spain and other jewels were pledged. Both these were made after the news had reached him that Gloucester had begun proceedings against him under praemunire in November. Thus, during the six months following his return to France Beaufort had lent almost precisely 20,000 marks from his own treasure 'withoute the whiche lones', it was later acknowledged, 'neither the siege of Lovers might have ben cundited to good conclusion neother the king have abiden to receive his corone and sacre, the which was withal instance required of my lord Bedford . . . ne have returned agen to his Reaume of England'.[50] Beaufort might justifiably feel that he had rendered equivalent service to those lay lords who were fighting for Henry VI and accompanying him to his coronation, and had earned the gratitude of the crown and the council in England. Indeed the indispensability of his service in France must have induced a sense of security which made the news of Gloucester's attack all the more traumatic.

It was just this indispensability which all too probably laid the seeds for his fall, for the council's request for the loan of 10,000 marks must have arrived at precisely the moment when the question of Bedford's future commission and status was under discussion at the *Grand Conseil*, and may well have given Beaufort the leverage with which to force Bedford to accept the commission from the king. His quarrel with Bedford undoubtedly gave Gloucester the signal to move against him. The clouded relationship with Bedford which overhung the young king's entry into Paris on 2 December was worsened by Beaufort's insistence on personally crowning Henry, superseding the right of the archbishop of Paris. His assumption of the leading role was a salve to his pride, hurt by the ancillary position he had occupied at the coronation in England two years before; but it must also have served to imprint on the young king's mind the sacred character and authority of the uncle from whom he now received his French crown. Aware of the political significance of the event, Beaufort saw to it that Henry's entry into his capital bespoke the legitimacy and authority of the double monarchy, and that the coronation 'was wortheley done with all the solempnite that might be doon and ordeyned'. Yet Burgundy's absence was manifest, there was little largess for the citizens, and the banquet that followed became disorganized and was perhaps marred by an open quarrel with Bedford. Beaufort remained in Paris,

[50] SC 8/7180.

presiding at the council, until 26 December when Henry VI began his homeward journey.[51] He had arrived at Rouen by 4 January and at Abbeville on 18th, but he took leave of the king when the royal party crossed the Channel on 9 February, making his way directly to Ghent.

His visit came at a critical point in Anglo-Burgundian relations. Duke Philip had not merely signalled his military neutrality by the truce of Lille, he had absented himself from Henry VI's coronation (as he had earlier from that of Charles VII at Rheims), much to the anger of the English and their alarm at the prospect of his defection in the impending peace talks. For although the royal expedition had accomplished Bedford's specific requirement of a coronation, it had by no means brought security to Paris nor added credibility to Henry VI's title. Indeed the fact that Henry had publicly and indelibly received the crown of France became a further impediment to meaningful negotiations; for thereby the hands of any future English emissaries were effectively tied. It similarly sharpened the dilemma of those who increasingly sought to attune their loyalties to the shifting political and military situation, among whom was now the duke of Burgundy. Beaufort could not by himself expect to reconcile the diverging positions of the allies, but he could hope to limit the damage to the English cause, ensure the duke's genuine neutrality, and forestall his desertion while Bedford secured the safety of Paris. For any further military effort in 1432, to strengthen and enlarge the English position or even to meet the full weight of French arms now relieved of the Burgundian war, taxation would have to be sought from a spring parliament. On the security of a lay subsidy loans for wages of war could be raised from Beaufort and others. Such had been the pattern of 1430 and 1431, and such was probably the sequence envisaged by Bedford and Beaufort at the outset of the consultations at Rouen in October prior to Henry VI's move to Paris. But all these prospects were thrown into disarray by the quarrel between Bedford and Beaufort and Gloucester's consequent attack on the cardinal.

[51] *Cal. L. Bk. K* 135–7; *Parisian Journal*, 269–71; *Brut*, ii. 461; B. P. Wolffe. *Henry VI*, 60–2; A. Longnon, *Paris pendant la domination anglaise*, 320–40. Beaufort gave Henry VI a gold ring garnished with a fair ruby on the day of the coronation: *Foedera*, x. 71, 76.

11

Gloucester's Second Attack, 1432

Few meetings of the English council are recorded during the summer and early autumn of 1431. Gloucester himself was occupied with the supression of Jack Sharpe's rising and a judicial visitation of the west midlands.[1] The first indication of a move against Beaufort came at an enlarged meeting of the council on 6 November when the king's sergeants and attorneys, clearly acting on Gloucester's behest, raised two questions: whether in accordance with precedent Beaufort should not have relinquished his see on his elevation to the cardinalate and could now be required to repay the revenues he had received since 1427; and whether he had obtained from Martin V exemption from the jurisdiction of Canterbury, in breach of the statute of praemunire. On the latter, Bishop Polton of Worcester, cross-questioned by Gloucester, admitted that his fellow proctor at Rome in 1418, John Catrik, had told him that Beaufort had indeed procured and paid for such a bull. Asked for their individual views on what should be done, most of those present advised that the records should be searched and the justices consulted before the cardinal was summoned to answer. While they were bound to maintain the king's rights, it was important to act legally, and they were mindful of Beaufort's blood affinity with the king and the notable services he had rendered. Kemp and Hungerford concurred in this and only Lumley dissented, desiring no action to be taken until Beaufort could be present.[2] Gloucester could probably count on active support from Norfolk, Huntingdon, and Scrope, and may have hoped to play upon the resentment harboured against Beaufort by Chichele and possibly other bishops; but the clergy would be wary of endorsing any attack on one of their order or of arousing a conflict with the papacy. Bedford's attitude was another factor, particularly if it had been reports of his quarrel with Beaufort on 12 October over the commission that had prompted Gloucester's action.

The strength of Gloucester's following was further tested on 28 November when Lord Scrope proposed that, on the king's return, Gloucester's salary as principal councillor should be raised to 5,000 marks. This was eventually agreed by all except Kemp and Lumley. Pressing his advantage, Gloucester now persuaded the council to authorize the sealing of writs of *praemunire facias* against the cardinal, although he bowed to

[1] *PPC* iv. 86–91; C 81/1545/24.
[2] *PPC* iv. 100.

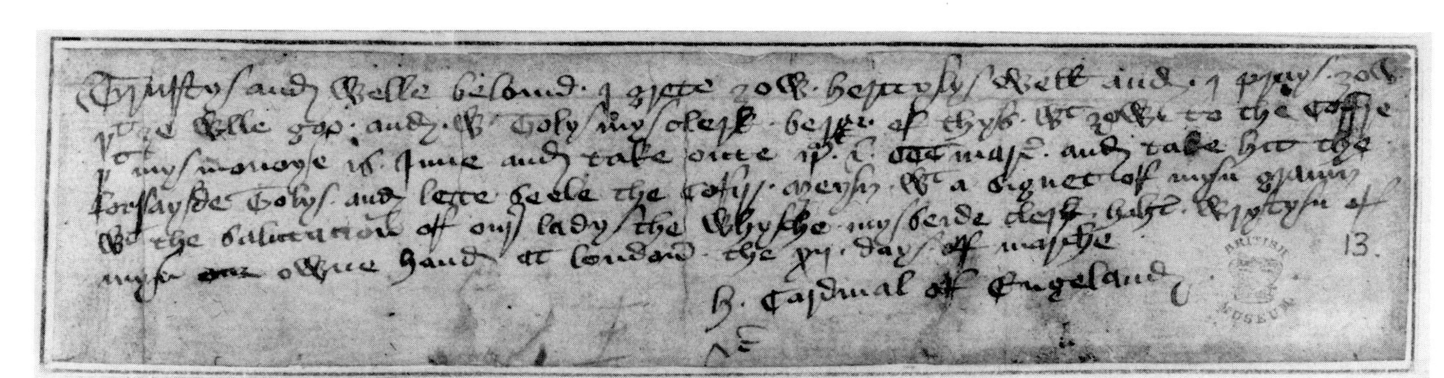

Holograph Letter of Cardinal Beaufort written in his later years.

Trusty and welle belovid I grete ȝow herttyly well and I pray ȝow þt ȝe wlle goo and W Toly my clerk berer of thys with ȝowe to the coffre þt my monoye is inne and take oute iiM^{l} and CCC marc and take hit the forsayde Toly and lette seele the cofir ageyn with a signet of myn gravin with the salutacion of our lady the whyche my seide clerk haht. Wrytyn of myn owne hand at London the xii day of Marche.

H. Cardinal of Engeland.

Stone Effigy of Cardinal Beaufort from Bishop's Waltham Palace.

Portrait of a Cardinal, probably Henry Beaufort, by Jan Van Eyck

The Hospital of St Cross, Winchester: Gate Tower, Hall, and Brethrens' Chambers.

their request that these would not be issued until the king's return.[3] On this occasion Beaufort was represented by his vicar-general, John Hermandsworth, abbot of Chertsey, and indeed the news of the meeting of 6 November must have reached him at Rouen shortly before the king set out for Paris. Technically the praemunire had to be answered on pain of forfeiture by personal appearance in the royal court within two months, and Beaufort's decision not to return in the king's company is at first sight surprising. His influence over the young king, the support of the lords who were returning with him and of his committed followers on the council, and the gratitude for his services during the expedition, may have seemed sufficient guarantees of his safety. In the event, recognizing the strength of the legal case against him, Beaufort chose a different tactic. At Calais, shortly before the royal host was due to embark, he claimed that he had been repeatedly summoned to the Curia by the new pope, Eugenius IV, and he now sought permission from the king's councillors to obey. This was granted, and Beaufort was thereby temporarily absolved from answering the praemunire writ. Eugenius's efforts were concentrated on the forthcoming peace conference at Cambrai in March under the presidency of Cardinal Albergati. Beaufort could be expected to play a major role in this, and possibly Eugenius wished for prior consultation with him over the Lancastrian attitude. The pope was also anxious to assure himself of the fidelity of the English episcopate following his bull dissolving the council of Basel.[4] However, Beaufort did not go to Rome in the following weeks, but stayed in Flanders. He had remained at Calais after the king's departure, waiting to receive his treasure, which he had ordered secretly to be shipped from England.

This was contained in four great coffers, or 'standards'. Besides quantities of plate—twenty ewers of gold, ninety-nine cups of gold, divers gold chalices, candlesticks, cruets, salvers, and so on, and a great coffin full of small parcels of gold—it must have included in coin at least the £20,000 which he had recently been repaid from the lay subsidy. On 6 February Gloucester had come to Dover to meet the king and got wind of the operation. Riding over to Sandwich, he was in time to 'espy' the standards being secretly loaded on board the *Mary of Winchelsea* under cover of night. The cardinal had secured no licence to export the precious metals, and Gloucester, profiting from this illegality, ordered the standards to be arrested as the ship prepared to sail. On the following day they were taken

[3] Ibid. iv. 104–6. Gloucester's salary had been raised from 2,000 to 4,000 during the king's absence in France: ibid. 12.

[4] A. N. E. D. Schofield, 'England and the Council of Basel', *Ann. Hist. Conc.* 5 (i) (1973), 10–12; C. T. Allmand, 'Normandy and the Council of Basel', *Speculum*, 40 (1965), 3 notes that the Paris doctors had sought Beaufort's support for the council. A letter from Eugenius IV summoning Beaufort to the Curia without delay is undated but ascribed by Haller to June 1432: J. Haller, *Piero da Monte*, 43 suppl. 16.

into the king's hands and when Henry VI landed at Dover two days later the writs against Beaufort were promptly issued.[5] His ruin seemed assured.

There are two possible explanations of Beaufort's intentions. He may indeed have resolved to enter papal service and was in the process of transferring his wealth to Rome prior to resigning his see and quitting English politics. The seizure of his treasure brought these plans to a halt and caused him to return to England. This was the impression he wished to give. Perhaps more probably, he was intending to seek asylum in the friendly Burgundian court, where he would be well placed to keep in touch with England, and was prudently withdrawing his treasure before it should be seized. There was much to draw him there. He could reinforce the influence of the Anglophile element in the duke's council prior to the peace conference, though because of Albergati's illness this had now been postponed to July at Auxerre; he might also endeavour to placate the complaints of the Flemish merchants against the Partition Ordinance which they had put to him in December 1430 and again in June 1431 on his journeys through Calais, and try to avert a ban on English cloth throughout Burgundian territories which was under discussion. But more especially the warm welcome which he seems always to have received from Duke Philip would on this occasion be reinforced by their common enmity towards Gloucester and by the impending birth of Isabel's second child. Early in May Beaufort stood godfather to the infant, who, however, died shortly after.[6] If, as seems possible, the superb portrait by Jan Van Eyck purporting to be of Cardinal Albergati (see Plate III) is in truth a portrait of Cardinal Beaufort, his prolonged stay in Ghent from mid-February to mid-May 1432 would be a likely occasion for a work possibly intended as a gift to his hosts or even for his godson.[7]

Two of Beaufort's letters from this period survive. The first, written on 16 February to his 'entirely well beloved and friend' Archbishop Kemp asks him to appoint as Beaufort's attorneys in the matter of the *praemunire* the persons Beaufort had named in an earlier letter. He concludes by assuring Kemp of his future favour and adds a postscript in his own hand: 'your trewe brothir that suffyseth not to thanke yow'.[8] On 18 February, four days after the king arrived in London, Kemp complied and appointed

[5] PRO Mem. Roll, KR (10 Henry VI), E 159/208 Com. Rec. Pasche mm. 2–2e; The original schedules of jewels and plate, and the depositions are in Exch. Bille E 207/14/4 19a–22a. This material was discovered by K. B. McFarlane from whose unpublished paper on 'The Political Crisis of 1432' I have drawn for this account.

[6] Munro, *Wool, Cloth, and Gold*, 93; Gilliodts van Severen *Inv. Archives Bruges*, 9 shows Beaufort there on 16 Feb. and in May; Monstrelet, *Chronique*, v. 50; A. B. Taylor, 'The diplomatic career of Isabel of Portugal, 1435 to 1457', Ph.D. thesis (Colorado, 1978), 7.

[7] The grounds for identifying the portrait as that of Cardinal Beaufort are fully discussed by M. G. Vale in a forthcoming article in the *English Historical Review*. I am indebted to Dr Vale for informing me in advance about his researches.

[8] SC 1/44 no. 4.

William Tresham, Thomas Rolf, Nicholas Radford, and John Asshe.[9] In fact Kemp's own days as chancellor were numbered, for a week later Gloucester had dismissed from office all the cardinal's supporters. Besides Kemp, Hungerford lost the treasurership, Alnwick the privy seal, Cromwell and Tiptoft were removed as chamberlain and steward of the household, the king's secretary, William Hayton, was dismissed, as were his almoner and dean of the chapel, and the signet was deposited in a bag under Gloucester's seal in the exchequer. Although four months later Cromwell entered a protest against his dismissal as being contrary to the council ordinance of 1430, Gloucester had been careful to await the king's return to give his action full legality. Indeed it underlined the importance attaching to the person of the young king since his double coronation. Bedford and Gloucester had surrendered their offices as regent and protector, which they claimed to hold of right in virtue of their birth, and had accepted their headship of government by the king's commission and hence at his pleasure. Both were probably apprehensive of the influence which might be exerted over the king by his immediate attendants. In this context Gloucester's purge was not a purely vindictive extension of his hatred of Beaufort but a bid to place in the offices of state and household those upon whom he could rely, and to forestall any moves among Beaufort's supporters in the household to plot his own dismissal. Both Gloucester and Bedford may have viewed with misgivings the cardinal's increasing presumption and his hold over the young monarch during the last half of 1431.

Gloucester's simultaneous seizure of Beaufort's treasure and the dismissal of his supporters appeared to give him the whip hand; in fact both proved prime errors of strategy. It is just possible that, had Beaufort succeeded in withdrawing his treasure from England, the praemunire charge might have persuaded him to resign his see, take his seat in consistory, and commit his last years and energies (for he was now about 57) to the diplomatic and military defence of Lancastrian France. The past five years had left him with stronger ties and interests on the continent than in England, with more inducement to build upon the authority he had acquired in France than to attempt to rebuild that which he had lost on his resignation in 1426. In France, too, he might hope to advance the prospects of his nephews by grants of conquered or vacated fiefs. It was the seizure of his treasure which forbade this course, for his authority and influence had always rested upon his wealth, deployed at crucial moments to enhance his reputation, secure political allies, and sway decisions in his favour. Trusted as were his judgement, persuasiveness, and organizing ability, the respect and authority which he commanded would disappear were he no longer

[9] *Foedera*, x. 500.

'the rich cardinal'. Having seized his enemy by the jugular vein, Gloucester had left him with no option but to fight back. Secondly, by his wholesale removal of the Bedford–Beaufort group from office, Gloucester had transformed his personal vendetta against Beaufort into a wider political crisis. Had he confined himself to pressing the firmly established praemunire charge, Gloucester might have effectively removed his rival from English politics and intimidated his leaderless supporters. Instead he made them into a desperate and coherent opposition and ensured that Beaufort would return to lead them. It was a classic instance of the folly of overkill; plainly Gloucester lacked the arts of Macchiavelli.

The scene for this trial of strength was the parliament which assembled on 12 May. The council had already in November envisaged summoning a parliament on the king's return, but when the writs were issued on 25 February (the same day as the dismissals), Gloucester must have seen it as the setting for the trial and condemnation of the cardinal. The charge was to be no less than treason. Here again Gloucester was in danger of overreaching himself. The penalties of praemunire—forfeiture and outlawry—were technically sufficient to ruin Beaufort; perhaps Gloucester feared that their disproportionate severity would make a pardon likely.[10] A charge of treason was certainly prepared, and was anticipated by Beaufort, though the grounds for it are obscure. The reference in the *Brut* to 'offences and blames that were put upon him for things done in France by the complaint of certain lords' is too specific to be helpful.[11] Beaufort had awaited the parliament as offering the best occasion for meeting Gloucester's challenge. Not only would his own supporters be present in both houses, but the value of his services in France and England could be publicized before a wider audience and set in the context of the present needs of Lancastrian France. He had begun to lay the grounds for this in a letter written from Ghent on 13 April, the second to survive, addressed to John Welles, the mayor, and the sheriffs and aldermen of London. Complaining that he was ill repaid for the services that he had rendered in France, and that the 'adversitees that I soffre ageinst reson and gentilness' had compelled him to abandon his journey to Rome, he announced his intention of returning to England 'aboute the bigynnyng of this parlement to know the causes why I am thus straungely demeened and declare myself as a man that have nought deserved soo to be treted'.[12]

Warned that the parliament would see a trial of strength between the two factions, Gloucester sought to present himself as the guarantor and upholder of public order. Writs were sent to the higher nobility and Lord

[10] *PPC* iv. 104; E. B. Graves, 'The legal significance of the Statute of Praemunire of 1353', in C. H. Taylor (ed.), *Haskins Anniversary Essays*, 74–5.

[11] *Brut*, ii. 465.

[12] *Cal. L. Bk. K* 139; Sharpe, *London and the Kingdom*, iii. 374–5.

Cromwell forbidding them to come to parliament with more than their accustomed number of household servants, and at the opening of parliament Gloucester called on the Lords to affirm individually their unanimity as a demonstration and encouragement to the Commons. The stinging rebuke delivered to him by the council in 1428 had wrought a change in the duke's tactics. Instead of harping continually on his rights and challenging conciliar authority, he had behaved with propriety and restraint, submitting to conciliar control and building up a body of his own supporters. Now, while asserting that 'by virtue of consanguinity and birth' he was, in Bedford's absence, principal councillor to the king—a declaration calculated to win Bedford's support—he yet promised that he would do nothing by his own mind and will but only by common deliberation and advice of the Lords. He fortified his claim to political leadership by appearing as the defender of the law. The new chancellor, Bishop John Stafford, having first denounced the violation of God's law by heretics (whom Gloucester had suppressed), had further emphasized the need for due observance of the king's law for the good health, security, and prosperity of the realm. This theme Gloucester now took up when, on 14 May, he visited the court of the exchequer in person and made a long speech to the barons about Beaufort's attempt to smuggle his treasure from the country. Referring to the damage to the realm from the drain of precious metal, and describing in detail his seizure of the treasure at Sandwich, he cited five statutes of Edward III, Richard II, and Henry IV, demanding its confiscation and claiming one-third of it as his reward under 5 Henry IV c. 9. No one appeared for the cardinal. John Vampage, on behalf of the crown, asked for a sentence of forfeiture, and in the presence of the treasurer, Lord Scrope, this was pronounced, though when Gloucester sought his share the court postponed the case to 9 June. On that day Gloucester again appeared in person and Beaufort took the precaution of making a legal gift of all his goods and chattels to his nephew Edmund, Lord Cromwell and Archbishop Kemp; but the decision was again postponed. Even so, it meant that Gloucester could go to parliament with a legal verdict.[13]

Unfortunately the chronology of proceedings in the parliament remains obscure. Beaufort was not present at its opening as he had anticipated in his letter, and with the council dominated by Gloucester's followers it was some time before the cardinal could muster support. Perhaps the first sign of this was the disquiet expressed by the earls and lords who had stood surety for Beaufort's loan of 10,000 marks made for the coronation in Paris, that it had not been repaid by Easter as promised, despite the great

[13] Above, n. 5. As McFarlane observed, Gloucester conveniently forgot the more recent statute, 2 Hen. VI c. 6, which prescribed a quarter, rather than a third of the goods, to the informer: *SR* ii. 219. Beaufort's gift is in *CCR 1429–35*, 234.

services he had rendered to the king.[14] Gloucester's failure to secure his share of Beaufort's treasure on 9 June and Lord Cromwell's protest in parliament on 16 June against his dismissal were other signs that Gloucester's control was weakening. By the time a delegation from the council of Basel arrived on 23 June it was to the cardinal that it first addressed itself, and when it was received in audience by the king early in July Beaufort was at Henry's right hand.[15] It was probably in the latter part of June that Beaufort appeared before the king, Gloucester, and the Lords to demand that those who would accuse him of treason should now do so to his face, and that he should have the opportunity to answer. Gloucester and the Lords, having consulted together, announced that no one accused him of treason and that the king held him a true liegeman. At Beaufort's request this was exemplified under the great seal. It paved the way for the settlement of other issues on 3 July.

His offence under the statute of Praemunire was dealt with by a Commons' petition which asked the king, in virtue of his services and consanguinity, to absolve him from the penalties he had incurred, and to quash proceedings already started against him. After mature deliberation the council agreed to recall and cancel the writs of praemunire to which most had agreed only with great reluctance in the first instance. Secondly, despite the declaration of the exchequer court, his treasure was restored to him in return for a deposit of £6,000—a fraction of its true value—which would be recoverable if, within the next six years, he was able to demonstrate his innocence to the king.[16] Thus he had avoided disputing the matter in parliament and could choose his moment to secure his vindication. The price for these decisions in his favour was the loan of a further £6,000. This total of £12,000 was not the sum of his wealth held by the crown, for he had as yet received no repayment of the £8,476 loaned to the king in France in the course of 1431. Had the verdict on the charge of praemunire been sustained, the crown need have repaid none of these loans nor released his treasure. That was the degree of Beaufort's vulnerability in 1432 and of the magnitude of the decision which faced parliament. If it followed Gloucester, the cardinal's position would be destroyed, his services would be lost, but his wealth would be available to the crown. Instead it chose to restore formal harmony within the Lancastrian family, acknowledging Beaufort's services as banker and elder

[14] C 81/1545/30, 31 records the presence of Gloucester, Norfolk, Huntingdon, Stafford, Suffolk, the archbishops of Canterbury and York, the bishops of Ely, Bath, and Lincoln, and Lord Scrope. SC 8/7180 for the protest of Warwick, Stafford, Salisbury, Arundel, Beaumont, and Tiptoft, all of whom had attended the coronation in Paris: cf. Fauquembergue, *Journal*, iii. 26.

[15] Schofield, 'Council of Basel', 19–20.

[16] *Rot. Parl.* iv. 390–1; *Foedera*, x. 516; E 404/48/349; C 81/1545/32. Gloucester, amongst others, subscribed to the withdrawal of the praemunire.

statesman, and his concern for the defence of the dual monarchy and the common weal of the realm. The pressures for the latter course were considerable. Bedford, despite his recent coolness to Beaufort, was unlikely to support his ruin at Gloucester's hands. The Commons had expressed their dismay and concern over the disunity among the Lords, and their petition for Beaufort's exculpation probably reflected the general temper of the lower house, though this contained few of his followers. Both Bedford and the Commons had come to rely on the cardinal's willingness to lend.[17]

On balance the parliament had been a victory for Beaufort, seemingly won against the odds. The treason charges had been dropped; so were the proceedings of praemunire; and his right to hold Winchester *in commendam* was never again called in question. He thus became the first English bishop to retain his see together with the dignity of cardinal. His treasure, too, had been restored, and his loans of 1431 together with the current advance of £6,000 were now securely assigned on the lay subsidy payable at Martinmas 1432 and Martinmas 1433. For with the royal expedition past, and evidence of hardship in the shires, the Commons had been reluctant to grant more than a half-tenth and fifteenth spread over the two years.[18] Yet Bedford's need for reinforcements to maintain the English recovery in France remained as pressing. Chartres had already been lost when the parliament opened, and Bedford had laid siege to Lagny, which it was vital for the English to recover since it nullified the possession of Meaux higher up the Marne. Bedford pressed the siege for three months, but was forced to retreat on 4 August on the approach of a relieving army under Raoul de Gaucourt and Roderigo de Villandrado. At that date Lords Camoys and Hungerford with 1,200 men were just embarking for France. Their indentures had not been sealed until 8 July and their wages and costs, totalling just over £8,000, were paid on 19 and 21 July from the money loaned and deposited by Beaufort on the 15th.[19] That this force only sailed when the campaigning season was already half spent was largely due to the parliamentary crisis; whether its wages were to come from the cardinal's forfeited treasure or from a fresh loan awaited the resolution of the cardinal's case. Bedford's crucial failure to recover Lagny, which in turn sealed the fate of Meaux, may be directly attributed to this delay.

That was the price which the nation had to pay for the quarrel; but should its outcome be judged a personal victory for either Beaufort or Gloucester? If Gloucester intended to ruin Beaufort and drive him from England, he had failed. Very probably this was his aim, for he had pursued

[17] *PPC* iv. 109; *Rot. Parl.* iv. 391; E 401/731; *Foedera*, x. 502; E 404/48/156–8.

[18] *Rot. Parl.* iv. 389; E 401/731 19 July.

[19] Beaucourt, *Charles VII*, ii. 45; Ratcliffe, thesis, 81–3; Roskell, *Parliament and Politics*, ii. 121; *CPR 1429–36*, 218.

his campaign relentlessly on a number of issues from November to June, and the settlement was only forced upon him by the support for Beaufort in council and parliament. Yet in the more limited aim of excluding Beaufort and his supporters following the king's return, Gloucester was succesful. Beaufort secured his wealth, but he lost influence over the king and in the council which he had been rebuilding since 1429. As in 1426, Gloucester had re-established his own control, with this difference, that Beaufort was now left with no wider role to play as leader either of a papal crusade or a royal expedition. He was forced, uncharacteristically, to attend to the affairs of his diocese. McFarlane reckoned that the abandonment of his curial ambitions was Beaufort's greatest penalty: 'he had been about to depart to Rome, not on a visit but to take up the employment he had forfeited in 1429. Now he had to stay at home; he had again to abandon his Roman ambitions.'[20] It is clear that Beaufort, notwithstanding the parliamentary guarantees, did not dare to leave England for another year. Yet there seems to be no certain evidence that he was either offered or was himself anticipating employment by Eugenius IV, or indeed that an office at the Curia was ever anything but a bolt hole from Gloucester's enmity. If we are to judge from where he directed his energies, Beaufort's ambitions lay in establishing and securing recognition for the Lancastrian dual monarchy. His world was encompassed by the courts and councils of northern Europe. For the moment Gloucester had forced him out of this world too, but by saving his wealth intact and by legalizing his tenure of his see, Beaufort had guaranteed his future. In that sense the real victory in 1432 rested with him.

Although the settlement of July 1432 had ensured Beaufort's safety, for the following years he remained excluded from the council on which the remnants of his following enjoyed no influence. Until July 1433 those who attended regularly were mainly Gloucester's friends.[21] Only Kemp and Cromwell, both dismissed from office in 1432, could be reckoned staunch allies of Beaufort. Gloucester also kept tight control over patronage and policy. The council endorsed grants to him of the farm of the duke of Norfolk's lands in November 1432, and the lands of Bernard Lesparre and the castle of Mauléon in Gascony in February 1433, while petty sinecures went to members of his household. His principal ally, the earl of Huntingdon, relieved the earl of Salisbury in France and was granted 1,300 marks for his services and the crown's debts to him.[22]

Unfortunately for Gloucester this was also a period of deepening

[20] From 'The Political Crisis of 1432'.

[21] *PPC* iv. 120–61; C 81/1545/34–45; E 28/53, 54. The regular attenders were: Gloucester, Suffolk, Huntingdon, Cromwell, both archbishops, the bishops of Ely and Lincoln, the treasurer, and chancellor.

[22] *PPC* iv. 132, 142, 145–6, 152; E 28/53, 54.

financial embarrassment. Little revenue was available. Despite efforts to tighten up collection, the customs showed no signs of recovering to their pre-1429 level. Most of the half clerical tenth and quarter lay subsidy due for collection at Martinmas 1432 had already been assigned in repayment of earlier loans from Beaufort and the feoffees of the duchy of Lancaster. The council therefore took advantage of a meeting of convocation in September 1432, at which delegates were to be appointed to the council of Basel, to send the three officers of state to demand a further grant. They secured a half-subsidy, one-quarter of which was to be collected at Martinmas, and this helped to raise cash receipts in the Michaelmas term to almost £11,000.[23] Meanwhile there were still debts to dicharge from the royal expedition, for the household, and for wages of war, and in November the arrears of the Calais garrison, which had been accumulating at the level of £3,000 p.a., brought a deputation to the council under a member of the garrison, John Madley, demanding payment under threat of mutiny. Obligations on the customs for 4,000 marks were given to the soldiers, but when issued as assignments on 23 February they proved uncashable, and before Easter the soldiers had seized the Staplers' wool. This was redeemed by a loan from the Staple of £2,918, and the ringleaders of the revolt, including Madley, were in due course mercilessly executed by the duke of Bedford.[24] Finally, in March the accumulated debt of £7,029 to John Radclyf, as seneschal of Gascony, was met by assigning him the profits of Merioneth and Caernarfon and the issues of Chirk and Chirkland.[25] This financial crisis had already undermined the authority of the council when it faced Bedford's annual demand for reinforcements in the spring of 1433.

On 18 February the council had indented with the earl of Huntingdon for a force of 200 men-at-arms and 900 archers, the total cost of which came eventually to £9,647, and at the same time gave him 1,300 marks reward.[26] The need to find over £10,000 in cash led to a series of extraordinary measures. The council could not, of course, look to Cardinal Beaufort for a loan, but through Archbishop Chichele it could put pressure on the other feoffees of the duchy of Lancaster. During the royal expedition they had lent £7,133. 6*s*. 8*d*. at Beaufort's instigation, and Gloucester had continued to exploit them, borrowing £3,800 in March and July 1432.[27] By midsummer 1432 the crown owed the feoffees £9,232, and they asked to be left free to meet the remaining claims of Henry's creditors. But by the

[23] E 28/53 21 July for letters to collectors; *Reg. Chichele*, iii. 233–6; Steel, *Receipt*, 203.

[24] *PPC* iv. 121, 132, 139, 189; E 401/732; E 403/706; *Rot. Parl.* iv. 473–4; *Chronicles of London*, 135. By the end of 1433 the garrison's arrears totalled £45,100, of which £25,464 was incurred under Richard Buckland, the present treasurer: Ratcliffe, thesis, 125–6.

[25] *PPC* iv. 155; *CPR 1429–36*, 269–70.

[26] *PPC* iv. 145–6; Ratcliffe, thesis, 84–6; E 28/54.

[27] *Rot. Parl.* iv. 280–2; E 401/725, 728, 729, 731.

beginning of 1433 their loans made from May 1431 to July 1432, amounting to £8,266, had been repaid and they were thus ripe for a further demand from the council.[28] On 15 February 1433 they agreed to make a loan of £3,000 for Huntingdon's expedition for which they received repayment by a strictly worded preference on the customs in Southampton, guaranteed by the retention of the coket seal and the appointment of one of the collectors. As one of the feoffees, Beaufort's assent must have been obtained for these terms, which conformed closely to those which secured his own loans of the 1420s on this source. Yet he was not present at the council at which they were ratified, and Gloucester's negotiations seemingly took place wholly through Archbishop Chichele, who himself lent £2,000.[29]

Other bodies were brought under similar pressure, and loans of almost £8,000 were raised in February from which £2,500 was despatched to Bedford, and the first quarter's wages were paid to Huntingdon on 2 March. By Easter, however, the exchequer had exhausted its credit and on 15 April the treasurer, Scrope, admitted to the council that he could not find the money for the second quarter for Huntingdon, nor for the costs of the embassy to the council of Basel. He appealed to Gloucester to negotiate further loans before he and other councillors left for the meeting with Bedford at Calais.[30] The admission of bankruptcy, the drying up of credit, and the revolt of the Calais garrison showed that the days of Gloucester's control of government were numbered. Yet it was not within Beaufort's power to displace him, and he had few opportunities even to undermine his rival's position. The record of the cardinal's movements and activity in the latter part of 1432 is almost wholly lacking. In October he may have been with Bedford at Rouen, but he sealed documents at Farnham in December, at Chertsey in January 1433, and at Havant and Southwark in February.[31] Apart from whatever time he gave to the affairs of his diocese, his attention was focused on developments across the Channel.

By the summer of 1432 it was becoming necessary to decide whether the

[28] *Rot. Parl.* iv. 399–400; DL 28/5/1. Somerville, *Duchy of Lanc.* 212, citing DL 29/12034 gives the feoffees' clear receipt for 1431–2 as £3,297.

[29] *Rot. Parl.* iv. 393–4; *PPC* iv. 141–4, 152; E 28/54 15 Feb. 1432, attested by Gloucester, Suffolk, York, Chichele, Kemp, chancellor. *CPR 1429–36*, 260–1, 349–50. The loan was not entered on the receipt roll until 21 Apr.: E 401/733. Since the feoffees had still not been repaid their loan of £3,028 from April 1430 assigned on the Southampton customs, they were now owed £6,028: *CPR 1429–36*, 294; *Rot. Parl.* iv. 437.

[30] Steel, *Receipt*, 203; Ratcliffe, thesis, 89; *PPC* iv. 157. For the council's exploitation of feudal rights to raise money, see E 28/54 15, 16, 18 Feb. A mere £2,643 reached the exchequer in cash this term, mainly from sheriffs' proffers: E 401/733. Scrope left in the treasury only £175 in cash and a bond for £200: E 401/735.

[31] *Reg. CS* 70–2. On 28 Jan. he appeared at the exchequer in person to answer for the customs due on his shipments of wool: E 159/209 Com. Rec. Hilary 9^{v}.

crown should support and recognize the council of Basel, which had formally opened a year before under the presidency of Cardinal Cesarini. Ever since 1417 English policy, under the guidance of Bedford and Beaufort, had been strongly papalist, led by the hope of papal recognition for the Lancastrian title to the crown of France and fear of a contrary verdict. That was still of prime importance, but after Beaufort's forfeiture of Martin V's confidence in 1429 relations with the papacy had been distant and both Sigismund and Duke Philip had pressed for support to be given to the new council which, as always, enjoyed the backing of the university of Paris and the clergy of northern France. Within the English council Chichele, despite his treatment by Martin V, remained papalist at heart and no friend of Cesarini, while Gloucester's personal history made him conciliarist in sympathy. All this meant that the English attitude towards the council of Basel had been at first non-committal, but early in 1432 the Basel fathers followed their defiance of Eugenius's bull of dissolution by appeals to the princes of Europe for recognition, and a delegation under Gerardo Landriani, bishop of Todi, arrived in England in June. It at once got in touch with Beaufort and by July had procured an audience with the king. Further, it returned to Basel bearing Henry VI's recognition of the status of the council and the promise of an English delegation. The dispatch of a letter to the pope urging him to a more conciliatory line towards the council underlined the discomfiture of the papal envoy Peter de Mera, and possibly of the two archbishops who may have favoured a more neutralist stance. Yet it was not merely Gloucester's personal prejudice that carried the day, for in seeking English support the delegation from Basel had stressed the council's concern with the suppression of subversive heresy and its offer of mediation between England and France. This was well tuned to Beaufort's ears, and his presence at Henry VI's right hand during the reception of the embassy was indicative of the influence he might exert in this matter. In fact the English crown could not ignore the Basel council, which had already secured recognition from Charles VII and seemed likely to become a forum for international agreements, whether with the Hussites or in the Anglo-French quarrel.[32]

England needed the goodwill of the council the more because delays and suspicion were currently breeding disillusionment with the papal peace mission led by Cardinal Albergati. The conference scheduled for 2 July 1432 at Auxerre was frustrated by Albergati's illness and Bedford's opposition to its location. Adjourned until November, it was rendered fruitless by the French insistence on the presence of the princes captured at Agincourt and on the surrender of English claims to the French throne as

[32] Schofield, 'Council of Basel', 17–26; Allmand, 'Council of Basel', 4–10.

the basis for negotiation of peace terms; nor would the French negotiate a truce, which the English mainly had in mind. A further conference at Seine-Port in March 1433, at which the prisoners were to be available, was all that could be agreed.[33] These negotiations seem to have been supervised by Bedford, for whom the year 1432 had brought singularly little comfort. An attempt to betray Rouen in March had proved abortive, but conspiracies at Pontoise and Paris later in the year showed spreading discontent with English rule. Normandy became vulnerable to a raid to the walls of Caen by the French captain de Lore, and in Maine Lord Willoughby and Matthew Gough lost ground. More serious was the loss of Chartres in April, and Bedford's failure to take Lagny after a lengthy siege from May to August was followed in October by the loss of Provins. The capture of Montargis and Maurepas were the only English successes.[34] The death of Bedford's wife Anne of Burgundy in November not only inflicted a cruel personal loss but severed a crucial link in the Anglo-Burgundian alliance.

All these circumstances conspired to bring Beaufort back into Bedford's service as the diplomatic representative of the Lancastrian monarchy. As the former leaders at Constance passed away, as pope and council fell again at odds, and as yet another crusade against the Hussites came to nought, Beaufort's long experience and past efforts gave him an increasing standing and authority in the travails of Christendom. Nor would Bedford overlook his past contribution to the increasingly strained Anglo-Burgundian alliance. Even Gloucester may have urged that he was the obvious choice to represent English interests at Basel, where he would be safely removed from English politics. The English delegation to Basel thus emerged as a predominantly Beaufort enterprise. At the end of November 1432 Beaufort and Kemp had licence to export money for their costs in journeying to Basel, and this was renewed in February 1433 when further licences were issued to Bishops Nevill of Salisbury and Fitzhugh of London and Sir John Colville, and finally in May to Bishop Lumley of Carlisle.[35] The assurance given to Beaufort that he would not be impleaded by the crown for two years for any previous acts, and his licence to take 20,000 marks in cash and jewels (raised to £20,000 in February) indicates his nervousness about a renewal of proceedings on the 1432 charge, and possibly an expectation that he would remain abroad for a considerable time. On 1 March 1433 he again appointed John Asshe and Nicholas Radford as his attorneys and by 7 March he had crossed the Channel.[36]

[33] Beaucourt, *Charles VII*, ii. 441; *Foedera*, x. 524, 530; *Wars of Eng*. ii. 252–3.

[34] Beaucourt, *Charles VII*, 42–5.

[35] *Foedera*, x. 525, 537–9, 549. Lord Hungerford was also added: Schofield, 'Council of Basel', 38–40, 112.

[36] *Foedera*, x. 541; *CPR 1429–36*, 254, 257, 262.

From then until his arrival at Calais from France on 12 April he is lost to view. Although armed with a safe conduct to Sigismund, to whom the news of Beaufort's arrival in Basel was sent on 23 May, it seems unlikely that Beaufort ever attended the council.[37] Probably he sought out Bedford and attended the conferences at Seine-Port on 21 March. For the English now offered to bring the Agincourt prisoners from Dover to Calais where the regent proposed to hold an extraordinary meeting of the combined council from England and Normandy in April. In part this was to prepare the ground for what was regarded as an important and positive phase in the Anglo-French negotiations. Cardinal Albergati had designated the next meeting for July at Corbeil, but attention was also focused on the council of Basel. The threat of a schism between the council and the pope raised the possibility that the council might itself become an independent venue for mediation. If this happened the English would have to review their strategy, for developments at the council had not been favourable to Lancastrian claims. The English delegates had clashed with the envoys of Charles VII over the right to represent the French 'nation', and partly to circumvent such disputes the council had adopted voting by deputations rather than by 'nations', thereby reducing English influence. But though the consideration of peace negotiations was an important reason for the extaordinary session of the two councils at Calais, that was not its main purpose.[38]

Bedford had read the signs of retreat and demoralization in France, and of war weariness and bankruptcy in England, with increasing alarm. The military position of the English had become precarious, the alliance with Burgundy was under threat, and both had to be strengthened if the credibility of Lancastrian claims in the peace negotiations was to be sustained. Yet to renew the offensive it was first necessary to revive the will to fight and pay for the war in England. Beaufort had doubtless conveyed to Bedford a full and critical account of Gloucester's administration, and Bedford later indicated that it was the inability of the council to assure him of adequate supply from England that had brought his decision to return.[39] The implications of this were momentous, entailing as it would the displacement of Gloucester and the reinstatement of Cardinal Beaufort to the council. Gloucester's opposition, though probably strenuous, must have been overriden in the session of the combined councils during the first

[37] A. Zellfelder, *England und das Basler Konzil*, 84. Beaufort was certainly at Saint-Omer at the end of May (below, ch. 12 n. 1). Kemp likewise got no further than Calais, and his prest of 1,000 marks for the cost of his embassy to Basel was diverted to pay for the siege of Saint-Valery: E 404/52/397.

[38] Beaucourt, *Charles VII*, ii. 453; *Wars of Eng.* ii. 234–5; Schofield, 'Council of Basel', 36–44 was the first to draw attention to the significance of this meeting, documented in Emmanuel Coll. Camb. MS 142 and Bodleian Digby MS 66.

[39] *PPC* iv. 224: 'and for lakke of comfort there amonges other causes'.

part of May. Beaufort's reinstatement was signified by his loan 'at the request of my lords of Bedford and of Gloucester' of a further 10,000 marks—part of the treasure which he had exported under licence—for the siege of Saint-Valéry.[40]

Beaufort's loan thus purchased his readmission to the council, but it was indicative of the bankruptcy of the exchequer that no specific revenue could be found from which repayment could be assigned. The cardinal had to be content with letters of obligation from some of the lords of the council who, as in 1431, were his particular supporters. They bound themselves to make repayment from any future grant of a subsidy or from revenue accumulated at the exchequer. In effect this put the office of treasurer in commission, and on 11 July, immediately following Beaufort's return, a warrant was sent to the exchequer listing the standing charges for which the treasurer could alone make payment on his own authority. As additional security these lords were to hold jewels in pledge, with ultimate authority to sell them for the repayment of the loan.[41] Beaufort may have hesitated to hold crown jewels himself, feeling that his position was still too precarious for the political risks this would entail. These terms had strong political undertones. They heralded the close alliance of Bedford and Beaufort and the consequent displacement of Gloucester from leadership of the council, the reinstatement of Beaufort's supporters, and the removal of Lord Scrope as treasurer.

The Calais council thus opened a new phase in Beaufort's career, ensuring his return to English politics in a manner which he could hardly have foreseen when he crossed the Channel hoping to resume his direction of Lancastrian diplomacy, with missions planned to Basel, Sigismund, and Duke Philip. In the event it had been his financial resources which proved indispensable. His future was now shaped by Bedford's determined attempt to revive support for the war in England and resume the offensive in France, objects to which the duke was to devote the remaining two years of his life.

[40] Half was paid directly to Louis of Luxembourg and half was delivered into the exchequer on 16 July and later sent to Louis: *PPC* iv. 162, 167; E 404/50/326; Devon, *Issues*, 425. Saint-Valéry was captured on 20 Aug. 1433.

[41] These lords were: Archbishop Kemp, Bishops Morgan, Stafford, and Gray, Suffolk, and Hungerford. In 1434 they were given assignments on the lay subsidy for repayment to Beaufort: E 404/50/356; Devon, *Issues*, 425. For the warrant of 11 July: E 404/49/169.

12

Bedford, Beaufort, and Burgundy: The Last Phase, 1433–1435

BEDFORD remained at Calais for at least another month after the departure of Gloucester. His marriage to Jacquetta, the niece of Louis of Luxembourg, at the end of April, though designed to reinforce the loyalty and service of the house of Luxembourg to Henry VI, had estranged Duke Philip by the insult to the memory of his sister, the slight to his status as Jacquetta's feudal lord, and the threat of the subtraction of Luxembourg from his own allegiance. Beaufort's assiduous efforts at reconciliation brought both dukes to Saint-Omer at the end of May, but neither could be persuaded to visit the other.[1] The rift proved temporary, occasioned by personal pique rather than divergent interests, and Beaufort's own friendship with Philip and Isabel was not jeopardized. Indeed the summer months of 1433 witnessed an unusual degree of Anglo-Burgundian co-operation in the field. From May to August the count of Saint-Pol and Lord Willoughby laid siege to Saint-Valéry until its surrender, while from June to September Duke Philip himself led an army to challenge the French in Champagne and expel them from Burgundy. In the latter he was assisted by 1,600 English troops under the recently ransomed Lord Talbot.[2] Although Burgundy could claim to have borne the brunt of the fighting in 1433—for the French hoped thereby to erode his commitment to the treaty of Troyes—Burgundian arms had more than usual success. It was in this more aggressive mood that Philip dispatched the Anglophile Lannoy to England to demand further military assistance and to report on whether Bedford's promise of a renewed English offensive was likely to take effect. Lannoy crossed the Channel along with Bedford and Jacquetta on 24 June. Beaufort had returned in the previous fortnight.

In England policy was firmly under the control of Bedford, Beaufort, and Warwick. It was to them that Lannoy brought a confidential message from Duke Philip about his hopes for alliances with the count of Richemont and the count of Savoy, and through them that the royal reply

[1] Waurin, *Croniques*, iv. 39–40; Monstrelet, *Chronique*, v. 58; Schofield, 'Council of Basel', 41 n. 109 from Emman. Coll. MS 142 adds that Beaufort also endeavoured to reconcile Gloucester and Burgundy. M. R. Thielemans, *Bourgogne et Angleterre*, 60 shows that Beaufort was at Bruges on 21, 24, 26 May.

[2] Beaucourt, *Charles VII*, ii. 46–8; Vaughan, *Philip the Good*, 66; *Wars of Eng.* ii. 249–62; A. J. Pollard, *John Talbot and the War in France, 1427–53*, 19.

was sent. Beaufort and Warwick treated Lannoy with studied coolness, which he reported to his master, as was doubtless intended; but Bedford deplored the recent quarrel and proffered an olive branch.[3] Clearly they were anxious to impress on Duke Philip the new resolve and policy which Bedford had come home to initiate. This was to be effected through a parliament which, on Bedford's orders, had been summoned to meet on 8 July. Its purpose was not only to accomplish a change of ministry but, as Lannoy reported, to take a formal and public decision on fundamental policy: whether to approve peace on the best terms that could be obtained or to provide money for a large and powerful army to seize the initiative in the following year. In fact the decision to reactivate the war was implicit in Bedford's return. Lannoy soon reported that there was no question of England making a separate peace, and Henry VI, replying to Duke Philip's letter, affirmed that he would not meet the basic French demand for the surrender of his claim to the French crown.[4] For the moment negotiations were suspended both at Corbeil, where the proposals brought by Albergati from Charles VII proved unacceptable, and at Basel. The original English delegation had made no headway at the council and had returned, while Kemp and others who were *en route* for Basel had, like Beaufort, turned back.[5] Although the earl of Suffolk and the captive duke of Orléans were formulating new proposals for an ambitious conference with the French nobility at Calais in October, the attention of Bedford and Beaufort was directed towards a renewed offensive for which they now sought a substantial grant from parliament.

Chancellor Stafford's speech commended the need for unity among the lords, but made no mention of provision for war, and Bedford used its first session to re-establish his authority. He could claim no formal title as in 1426, and Gloucester may have seen the parliament as offering a last chance to halt his displacement. Roger Hunt, who had been Speaker under Bedford in 1420, was again elected, and on 13 July Bedford took the initiative with a declaration that he had returned to confront malicious rumours over his conduct of the war in France. This he did by the formal issue of a challenge to any who would accuse him, whether such were of equal status to him or not. He thereby elicited an expression of confidence in himself and for the moment disarmed opposition to the war policy. What happened during the next four weeks is obscure, but there may have been a prolonged struggle before Scrope yielded the crucial office of treasurer to Ralph, Lord Cromwell on 11 August. Both Stafford and Lyndwood remained in their ofices. Two days later parliament was adjourned.[6]

[3] *Wars of Eng.* ii. 227–9.

[4] Ibid. 218–62 (esp. 239); *Brut*, ii. 466.

[5] Beaucourt, *Charles VII*, ii. 454, 462; Schofield, 'Council of Basel', 46–9; *Foedera*, x. 556.

[6] *Rot. Parl.* iv. 419–20.

The autumn session saw Bedford's powers defined. On 24 November the Commons had declared that his presence had been 'full fructuous for the restful rule and governaile of this land' and had petitioned for him to remain. On 18 December he presented for approval articles which specified his power 'unto the tyme that hit shal lyke my Lorde to take the exercise of the governaunce of this reaume in his owne persone'. The effect of these was to bring under his direct surveillance and sanction the appointment and dismissal of the king's councillors, other principal officers, and bishops, and the summoning of parliament. On all these matters Bedford was to be notified wherever he was at the time.[7] The council's authority was thereby more drastically curtailed than at any previous time during the minority. The ability to influence the young king provided a further element in these manœuvres for power. In March 1432 Gloucester had replaced the principal officers of the household and in November the earl of Warwick, as Henry's governor, had protested against the attempts to influence the king on matters beyond his judgement, and sought to restrict access to him. Henry was showing himself a responsive and intelligent boy, and now that he had been crowned and was in his twelfth year could appropriately be introduced to some matters of state. In February 1433 the council was listing matters on which he should be informed, and when he received the second delegation from the council of Basel in October 1433, his demeanour was said to be modest and grave. But for the moment Bedford was merely concerned to remove him from contrary influences, and to economize on household expenses; hence throughout the winter of 1433–4 the king enjoyed a prolonged sojourn at the monastery of Bury Saint-Edmund.[8]

Bedford thus established himself as effective vice-gerent for both kingdoms, seeking to mobilize their resources in the crisis that faced Lancastrian France. The existence of an autonomous council in England, following its own policy and serving its own interests and led by a brother whose judgement and jealousy Bedford distrusted, was now brought to an end. When the council was reappointed in parliament its clerical members were dispensed from attendance out of term; Bedford probably envisaged governing with a council composed of the principal officers, Beaufort, and himself.

Bedford's personal ascendancy was further employed to benefit his supporters. John Mautravers established his claim to the earldom of Arundel and the possession of Arundel castle, despite the protest of the new duke of Norfolk, still a minor in the king's ward. Arundel's father had been excluded by Mowbray influence from 1416 to 1429; now he was commended for his outstanding service in France 'tam armorum

[7] Ibid. 423.
[8] *PPC* iv. 132–7, 159; Schofield, 'Council of Basel', 51 n. 5; Wolffe, *Henry VI*, 74–5.

strenuitate quam maturitate consilio', and rewarded for further services in 1434 with the title of count of Touraine. A favourable reponse was given to a petition in the name of the earl of Somerset, probably presented by his brother Edmund, defending the Beaufort title to the Sycharth and Glyndwrdwy lands against Sir John Skidmore, the husband of Glyndwr's daughter. For good measure Edmund Beaufort procured Skidmore's dismissal from the office of constable of Carmarthen castle in virtue of the statute of 1402, and himself received the office in August 1433.[9]

The first task of the new administration was to replenish the exchequer and restore a measure of financial discipline. Cromwell faced a daunting situation. Not only was the exchequer empty but its revenues had been assigned two years ahead, including the taxes immediately due. Under the influence of Beaufort the feoffees of the duchy of Lancaster had lent a further £3,000 and held letters patent, confirmed by act of parliament, for the repayment of £9,028 from the Southampton customs. So likewise did the merchants of the Staple for the repayment of their loan of £2,918 from the customs of Boston and Hull.[10] No clerical subsidy was due for payment in 1433 and the Martinmas quarter of the lay subsidy granted in 1432 had already been pledged to Cardinal Beaufort in repayment of his loan of July 1432. Little cash could be expected at the exchequer, and the treasurer's difficulties were accentuated in 1433–4 by a spectacular drop in wool exports, whether occasioned by murrain or by a restraint of trade.[11] Cromwell endeavoured to meet this situation by a three-pronged strategy. First he sought to apply the measures of surveillance and economy which had been the basis of Henry V's policy. Already within two days of assuming office he had secured parliamentary authority for a stop on the exchequer until £2,000 could be provided for the expenses of the household. Collectors of customs were then ordered to bring all receipts in cash to the exchequer, with their rolls and tallies for the Michaelmas audit.[12] During the rest of the summer vacation the officers of the receipt worked hard to produce a detailed 'state', or valor, of royal revenue, expenditure, and debts. This, as presented to parliament, showed an annual deficit of £21,447 leaving aside revenue from direct taxation and expenditure on the war in France. It served to justify both a demand for taxation and a rigorous hierarchy of preferences between creditors. Cromwell insisted on all warrants for expenditure from the council passing his scrutiny, on security of tenure for himself in the treasurership, and the support of the council for the policy of preference and restraint.[13] This

[9] *Rot. Parl.* iv. 377, 443, 440; *CPR 1429–36*, 286.

[10] *Rot. Parl.* iv. 463, 474. The loan was probably made in the summer but only entered on the receipt roll in Dec.: E 401/734.

[11] A mere 1706 sacks were exported: *Eng. Export Trade*, 59, 123.

[12] *PPC* iv. 175–6; *Rot. Parl.* iv. 420; E 28/54 13 Aug. 1433 (formerly E 404/50/354).

[13] *Rot. Parl.* iv. 432–9; J. L. Kirby, 'The Issues of the Lancastrian Exchequer and Lord Cromwell's estimates of 1433', *BIHR* 24 (1951), 133.

policy was rigorously pursued throughout the winter. First Bedford then Gloucester voluntarily reduced their salaries to £1,000 p.a. A tight control was exercised over all payments, only particular annuities and debts to important commanders such as the earls of Huntingdon and Northumberland, or those ready to do further service, like Lord Talbot and Sir John Stanley, being authorized. Not until July 1434 was the restraint of annuities even partially relaxed. In February Cromwell ordered an inventory of crown jewels to be made, and investigations into malpractices at the exchequer led to the appearance of the under-treasurer and tellers before the council in July. These are all indications of a drive for greater financial discipline which was paralleled by a similar exercise in budgeting and economies in Normandy.[14]

Cromwell saw these economies and reforms as complementary to renewed support for the war from parliament. Early in the second session, on 18 October, he presented his financial survey and asked for provision for the royal household, the government, and the defence of the realm. Despite the pressure which this was designed to bring upon the Commons, in a session which lasted almost to Christmas only a single tenth and fifteenth was granted, to be collected in quarters at Easter and Martinmas 1434 and 1435. Moreover, the Commons reduced the subsidy by £4,000 as a relief to impoverished areas. That meant that scarcely more than £8,500 would be available at each quarter payment. An increase in the subsidies paid by alien merchants did little to compensate for this.[15] Anti-alien feeling, noted by Lannoy during his visit, was also manifested by petitions to impose trading restrictions on alien merchants, and the Commons made a further attempt to get the statute of truces annulled. Both these Bedford rejected, but the Partition Ordinance, which had technically expired at Lady Day 1433, was renewed on a Commons petition, to run for three years from 1434.[16] Although the effects of the ordinance must by now have been plain, complaints in the preceding parliament about the decline of the customs, the increase of smuggling, and the export of wools direct to Holland and Zeeland never associated these with it. A mission from the Four Members in December, which sought to prevent the renewal of the ordinance, made no impact. Yet so serious was the effect on the cloth industry of Flanders and the ducal mint that Philip was induced to make the ban on English cloth imports effective throughout his territories.[17] Bedford and Beaufort were well aware of the consequences of these

[14] *Rot. Parl.* iv. 425; *PPC* iv. 178, 181, 185–6, 190, 198, 201, 261; E 404/50/117–30, 170 (dispensations from retraint of payments, Oct., Nov., 1433). For Normandy: *Wars of Eng.* ii. 532, 540, 559.

[15] *Rot. Parl.* iv. 425–6.

[16] Ibid. 450, 453–4. On 18 Feb. 1433 Gloucester had issued commissions against sea rovers and letters of marque to many merchants: E 28/54.

[17] *Rot. Parl.* iv. 410, 453–4; *CPR 1429–36*, 131, 200; Thielemans, *Bourgogne et Angleterre*, 60–1; Munro, *Wool, Cloth and Gold*, 93–100.

growing commercial tensions, but they faced a well-organized mercantile lobby in the Commons which probably had Gloucester's support. Moreover the mutiny at Calais and the growing debt to its garrison reinforced their dependence on the Company of the Staple. In the event Bedford secured neither an adequate grant of taxation from parliament nor a further loan from the Staple; yet a revocation of the Partition Ordinance, had it revived the flow of trade, would have reshaped Cromwell's budget.

Even less success attended the council's efforts to secure a grant from convocation. Two separate delegations of lords, the first including both the chancellor and the treasurer, addressed convocation on 19 November and 7 December, expounding the king's necessities and the dangers from the French and Scots, and asking for a liberal grant. However, the lower clergy, pleading the extreme scarcity, would grant only three-quarters of a subsidy in addition to and following on from the quarter due for collection in Martinmas 1434; not even Chichele's pleas and the prorogation of convocation until 21 December could induce them to concede earlier terms for its collection.[18] Despite Bedford's insistent urgings, his own example of frugality, and Cromwell's stringent reforms, the exchequer could expect only a half lay and a quarter clerical subsidy in 1434 and a half lay and half clerical subsidy in 1435, with a further final quarter clerical subsidy in 1436. By the end of 1433 Bedford had been forced to accept that, whether from indifference or exhaustion, support for an ambitious counter-offensive in France could not be revived. In this Gloucester had grasped the mood of the country better.

Nevertheless Bedford and Beaufort were committed to the active prosecution of the war, which would now have to be supported by loans. For the years 1433–4 and 1434–5 the exchequer's cash receipt amounted to a mere £9,400 and £7,900, these being the lowest of the century hitherto, apart from 1424–5. In the same two years it borrowed £25,255 and £30,032, the highest figures of the reign apart from the years 1430–2.[19] In other words it had become locked in a situation where virtually all its current revenue had been assigned, and current expenses could only be met by borrowing. In so far as these were for the war in France they were inescapable, and had to be paid in cash. In December 1433 the exchequer borrowed a further £3,000 from the feoffees of the duchy and 2,000 marks from the captive earl of Somerset, both doubtless negotiated by the cardinal.[20] It then dispatched 8,000 marks to Louis of Luxembourg for the garrisons of northern France, partly in cash but mainly by bill of exchange on Bedford's own treasury in Normandy. On 4 February 1434 Lord Talbot indented for six months' service with 920 men. Wages for his force,

[18] *Reg. Chichele*, iii. 247–52.
[19] Steel, *Receipt*, 441, 460.
[20] E 401/735; i.e. the feoffees' loan negotiated in July, above n. 10.

totalling £5,500, were issued within three weeks from two major loans, one of £4,000 from Cromwell and the other of 2,000 marks from the city of London.[21]

At the same time commissions were issued for a general loan in all shires, naming the leading supporters and associates of the cardinal: Edmund Beaufort and the abbot of Chertsey in Surrey, Bishop Nevill and Lord Hungerford in Wiltshire, the earls of Salisbury, Devon, Warwick, and Suffolk in their respective shires, Lord Cromwell in Lincolnshire, Thomas Chaucer in Oxfordshire, and Lord Tiptoft in Huntingdon. Lenders were offered repayment from the 'customs, subsidies, revenues, jewels, and moveables of the crown' as well as the recent parliamentary grants. Since the first instalments of those had already been assigned in repayment of the cardinal's loan of 1433 and the loans made in February, it was not surprising that few men were found to accept security 'of so long and so far days' and that the total paid in during the early summer was under £5,000.[22] Beaufort himself had not been a commissioner; he was to make his own contribution in June for the force despatched under the earl of Arundel.

On 10 May Beaufort agreed to lend 10,000 marks and four days later Arundel and a number of Bedford's captains sealed indentures for an army of 234 men-at-arms and 934 archers. A total of £7,560 was paid to them in June and July after the conditions for Beaufort's loan had been agreed and he had delivered the money to the exchequer.[23] Beaufort's stipulations had been debated by the council during May but not essentially modified. Since the whole of the Martinmas subsidy was already pledged for the repayment of his loan of 1433, this new advance had to be assigned on lay and clerical subsidies due for payment in 1435. The risk to his capital, from the insolvency of the exchequer and the likely revival of Gloucester's influence on Bedford's return to France, explains Beaufort's requirements that his assignments should not be altered, that he should be repaid in gold, and that in the meantime he was to hold jewels valued at 7,000 marks and bonds from the council for 3,000 marks. Jewels to the value of £4,924 were delivered to him on 7 June, including the 'rich collar' and the 'sword of Spain'.[24] With this loan Beaufort also secured a final settlement of the crown's claim to his goods and jewels seized by Gloucester's authority in 1432. With his own mouth Henry VI now ordered that the £6,000 for which they had been redeemed should be repaid by assignments on the lay and

[21] *PPC* iv. 187–8; Ratcliffe, thesis, 90–3; Pollard, *Talbot*, 19. A debt of £1,000 to Talbot was discharged at the same time: E 404/50/159, 164. The loans raised some £7,500: Steel, *Receipt*, 205.

[22] *CPR 1429–36*, 353–4; *PPC* iv. 202–3; E 401/735.

[23] *PPC* iv. 238–9; E 401/737 2 June; Ratcliffe, thesis, 93–6.

[24] *PPC* iv. 214, 233–9, 247–54; E 404/50/317, 320; *Foedera*, x. 590. *Kal. and Inv*. ii. 142–6.

clerical subsidies due in 1435. This brought the total assigned to Beaufort from the direct taxes due in 1434–5 to £19,333. 6*s*. 8*d*., while on 20 June 'at the special contemplacion of my seid lord of Bedford' he lent a further £2,000 for the duke's own return to France, to be repaid from the same scource.[25] At this point more of his wealth was in the crown's hands than at any time since the death of Henry V. Although Bedford's needs had enabled Beaufort finally to lay to rest the threat of expropriation raised by Gloucester, his loans also demonstated his gratitude to his protector and his own commitment to the war in Normandy.

Arundel's expedition had provided the occasion for an attack on Bedford and Beaufort by Duke Humphrey, the gravity of which has been masked by its ineffectuality. The great council which met from 24 April to about 8 May 1434 was attended by a large number of knights and esquires whom Bedford had summoned to rekindle support for the war and to discuss future strategy. On 26 April Gloucester submitted to it a memorandum highly criticial of the recent conduct of the war, which Bedford conceived to be derogatory to his honour. Bedford answered this in writing on 8 May in terms which Gloucester likewise took to impugn his honour, and Henry VI formally took the matter into his own hands, abrogating both sets of articles. On 5 May, while these proceedings were in progress, the lords, knights, and esquires petitioned the king. They stated that Gloucester had himself offered to lead a mighty army to France with the purpose of winning a decisive victory. He had courted popular support for this by raising expectations among the commons of 'being discharged of any taille or tallage for many yeres', and they feared that the council's rejection of Gloucester's offer might thus 'cast us into murmur and grucchyng of your people and in peril and danger towards your highness in time to come'. They therefore wished to put on record the council's reasons. Primarily these were financial. Gloucester's proposal was reckoned to cost £48,000–50,000, indicating a force of about 7,000 strong, comparable to that which Henry V had led to Normandy in 1417. Recent experience showed that there was no means of raising a sum of this size by taxation, general loans, or from the exchequer's revenues, and they challenged Gloucester to say how he proposed to finance it.[26]

No answer from Gloucester is recorded, and the impression left is that the duke's cheap demagoguery had been exposed by the hard facts. Yet Gloucester did have an answer, of which the council was certainly aware, although how openly he stated it is difficult to judge. For six years later Gloucester recalled the argument he had put in 1432 and 1434:

'whanne the said cardinal had forfaited al his gode bicause of provision, as the

[25] *PPC* iv. 244–8; *CPR 1429–36*, 414; E 404/50/331; Devon, *Issues*, 425; *Foedera*, x. 593.

[26] *PPC* iv. 210–16. Gloucester said that 'he trowed that the poople of this your land wold take hemself right nyghe for so greet a gode to theim as shuld be the discharge that thei shuld have by the seid offre'.

statute thereupon made can more pleynly declare, he, havyng the rieule of you, my lord so doubted, pourechaced hymself, in grete defraudacion of youre highnesse, a chartre of pardon; the whiche gode, and it had ben wel gouverned, might many a yeere susteyned your werres without eny talages of youre poure people'.[27]

Gloucester, in effect, proposed to finance his expedition by foreclosing on Beaufort's wealth. Although Beaufort had received a pardon on the praemunire charge in 1432, no decision had yet been taken on the crown's claims to the treasure which he had attempted to export illegally. This could still provide the excuse for his ruin. Yet what expectation could Gloucester have had of this in 1434? He appears to have been calculating on support from two quarters: first, the popular desire for relief from taxation coupled with envy of the rich cardinal; secondly, Bedford's dedication to a final effort to reverse the tide of French advance. Gloucester was suggesting that the rejection by parliament and convocation of Bedford's appeal for taxation on a wartime scale need not be fatal to his plans: the cardinal's wealth would of itself be sufficient and the excuse for seizing it was still at hand. That was the temptation which Gloucester offered the regent, and it was no chimera. For by the end of June not only did the crown hold £21,333 of the cardinal's money on loan, but he had renewed his licence to export the sum of £20,000 if he should go overseas on pilgrimage or to the council of Basel.[28] On this evidence alone his resources were indeed sufficient to mount a major expedition or to relieve parliament of taxation for several years.

Bedford, of course, refused the bait. He was clearly nettled by Gloucester's inept criticism of his own strategy, but quite apart from this he stood to lose the cardinal's diplomatic services and influence, and the action would shatter the fragile harmony of the Lancastrian house. Moreover, Gloucester's proposal had disturbing implications for his own position. For if Gloucester led such an army he would displace Bedford in France, while if Bedford led it he would once more have to leave Gloucester in control in England, his power unchecked by the council and his popularity enhanced. On all these grounds Bedford preferred political and financial co-operation with Beaufort on the prevailing pattern; indeed he may even have used the threat from Gloucester to enforce his new demands on the cardinal's wealth. Beaufort's loans of May–June 1434 were in this sense the price for Bedford's defence of his status and treasure. Gloucester's challenge helped to cement the trust and common purpose between them, just as it deepened the suspicion and hostility of the two rivals. Even so the council had done nothing to resolve the question to which Gloucester had at least ostensibly provided an answer. What new source of revenue could be found for continuing the war with France?

[27] *Wars of Eng.* ii. 450.
[28] *PPC* iv. 235.

One answer was proposed by Bedford on the eve of his return to France in June. In a long memorandum to the council, designed both to vindicate himself and to appeal for more support, Bedford reviewed the decline of English fortunes in France since the siege of Orléans.[29] Disclaiming responsibility for that débâcle, he described the poverty of Lancastrian France, its inability to defend itself, and its need for 'more chargeable and abyding socours than ever before'. This was the message he had brought to Calais and which he had laid before parliament and convocation, though to no avail. Even now, on the eve of his departure, nothing had been provided towards this. In heartfelt and eloquent language he recalled the great sacrifices made to realize his late brother's claims; nor did he doubt that today Englishmen would keep faith to their utmost to defend these. But they too were poorer and could not sustain heavy taxation. There remained one source of revenue, already tapped, which now needed to be fully exploited: the duchy of Lancaster. He proposed that the feoffees should surrender their estates, receiving sufficient assignment to discharge the remaining debts of Henry V, and that the revenues be wholly applied to maintaining a permanent force of 200 men-at-arms and 600 archers in France. He further proposed to use the garrisons in Calais and the march for service in France, and to support a similar force from the revenues of Normandy granted to him by Henry VI. Bedford was plainly taking advantage of Beaufort's dependence on his protection; the cardinal had certainly no mind to surrender the duchy lands, but the timing and generosity of Bedford's offer seemed to leave the feoffees no option. Hence, with the simple condition that the tallies which they held for the repayment of their loans should first 'be suffisantly paied and content', they agreed to surrender their trust at Michaelmas and receive acquittance at the next parliament.[30] Whether Bedford sailed to France believing that his scheme would be realized is a moot point. In fact, as the cardinal must certainly have known, there was no chance that more than a fraction of the huge debt of £9,028 which the previous parliament had assigned on the port of Southampton from Easter 1434 would be paid by Michaelmas.[31] Long before this debt was discharged the feoffees were bound to be asked to make a further loan. Here too there was no escape from the vicious circle of the crown's anticipation of its revenues.

The campaigning season of 1434 proved remarkably successful. In north-eastern France it was marked by a large measure of Anglo-Burgundian co-operation. In Picardy Talbot recovered Beaumont-sur-Oise, Creil, and

[29] *PPC* iv. 222–9.

[30] Ibid. 229–32.

[31] A mere 523 sacks were exported in 1433–4 from Southampton: *Eng. Export Trade*, 59. The feoffees' collector, John Chirche, received £2,648 in Mich.–Easter 1433; £3,905 in Mich.–Mich. 1433–4; £5,190 Mich.–Mich. 1434–5: E 356/29, 30, 31.

Clermont, removing the threat to the Vexin, while Willoughby acting jointly with Burgundy's lieutenant the count of Étampes and Jean de Luxembourg recovered Saint-Vincent, Mortemer, and Saint-Valéry, which had been lost again to the French in January. Duke Philip continued the war against the duke of Bourbon, forcing him to sue for a truce at the end of September. Meanwhile Arundel and Lord Scales effectively cleared the French from Maine and part of Anjou in what has been described as 'the last systematic effort of the English in this area'.[32] By the time Bedford returned to France the inroads made upon the English position in 1433 had been fully restored.

Nevertheless this demonstration of the military effectiveness of the Anglo-Burgundian alliance took place against the background of negotiations for peace and shifts in court factions which were before long to lead to its rupture. Direct peace negotiations between the English and the French came to a halt following the failure of the conference at Calais proposed by Suffolk and the duke of Orléans. Beaufort, Suffolk, and Warwick had waited in vain at Calais in late October 1433 for an embassy from Charles VII. With Albergati's peace mission likewise stalled, attention now shifted to the council of Basel. In June 1433 the English delegation had withdrawn in protest against procedures which discriminated against its status and influence, and when Landriani arrived in London once again in October 1433 to plead for support against Pope Eugenius, the official response was lukewarm, although he received a cordial welcome from Gloucester. The English council could not neglect the potential importance of Basel for negotiations, and agreed to send another embassy; but convocation, influenced by Peter Beverley, Bedford's confessor, gave unequivocal support to Eugenius. The delegation now sent certainly reflected the influence of Bedford, Beaufort, and Chichele. It was led on the clerical side by the bishops of London and Rochester and Thomas Brouns, dean of Salisbury, on the lay side by Edmund Beaufort, Sir Henry Brounflete, and Sir John Colville.[33]

Even as this embassy was being assembled the English council found itself embarrassingly in conflict with the pope over the provision of one of its members, Thomas Brouns, to the see of Worcester, vacated by Polton's death at the Curia in September 1433. Eugenius had at once provided Brouns, confident that he would be acceptable since he had been the royal candidate for Chichester in 1431; he was an experienced and trusted

[32] Beaucourt, *Charles VII*, ii. 49–51, 508; 511–12: Vaughan, *Philip the Good*, 66–7; U. Plancher, *Histoire générale et particulière de Bourgogne*, iv, *preuves*, cxli–iii for letter of Bedford, Gloucester, and Beaufort to Philip 11 June 1434. R. Planchenault, 'La lutte contre les Anglais en Anjou pendant la première moitié du xv siècle', *École des Chartes; position des theses*, 75 (1923), 80.

[33] Schofield, 'Council of Basel', 47–54; *CPR 1429–36*, 340, 342; *CCR 1429–35*, 273.

diplomat who was watching over royal interests at Basel. But an action which should have been a happy symbol of Anglo-papal accord instead started an eighteen-month wrangle; for on 22 November the royal council authorized the election of Thomas Bourchier, the 23-year-old half-brother of Humphrey, earl of Stafford, who was brother-in-law to Cardinal Beaufort. Almost certainly this was a bid by Bedford and Beaufort for the Staffords' support in the current parliament; it was said to be on the request of the Commons, although no petition for it survives. In the new year the council urged Bourchier on the pope, the cardinal writing separately to remind Eugenius of the value of Lancastrian support in his present vicissitudes, and restating the firmness of the council's resolve. Eugenius remained obdurate, professing that his honour was at stake. He told Beaufort to accept Brouns for Worcester while promising that his young kinsman would be provided for in due course. The council reaffirmed its stand in May 1434, and it was only the death of Langdon of Rochester in September, at Basel, that untied the knot.[34] Letters were immediately sent to Brouns requiring him to resign Worcester and inhibiting him from recommending a candidate for Rochester, to which Eugenius was invited to provide him. By March 1435 Eugenius had accepted this compromise, though in notifying Beaufort through Adam Moleyns of Bourchier's provision he took the opportunity of urging him to show his gratitude by working for the abolition of the statutes of provisors and the restoration of the pristine liberty of the Roman see in England. It is unlikely that he seriously expected a response.[35] Beaufort was the chief consecrator of Bourchier at Blackfriars in May 1435.[36] The affair had been an acute embarrassment to all parties, producing an unforeseen clash between Bedford's twin policies of consolidating political support at home and cultivating papal goodwill in the approach to decisive peace negotiations.

The English attitude towards the council of Basel was bound to be essentially negative. The instructions to the embassy, issued on 31 May 1434, reaffirmed support for papal authority and defined its objectives as the upholding of Henry VI's title and rights and the furtherance of negotiations for peace or truce. Its members were advised to co-operate closely with Sigismund and the envoys of the dukes of Burgundy and Britanny, and were given ninety collars of esses for distribution among

[34] *CPL* viii. 213–15; *PPC* iv. 213–14; Haller, *Piero da Monte*, 204, suppl. 19. See also E. F. Jacob, 'Thomas Brouns, bishop of Norwich, 1436–45' in H. R. Trevor-Roper (ed.), *Essays in British History presented to Sir Keith Feiling*, 61–83.

[35] *CPL* viii. 216–18; *PPC* iv. 285–6; *Reg. Chichele*, i. 118, 121; E 28/55 10 May, 8 Nov.; Haller, *Piero da Monte*, 209, suppl. 23.

[36] Bourchier presented his bull and took the oath to the king at Gloucester on 14 Apr.: E 28/55; A. Hamilton Thompson, *The English Clergy and their Organisation in the Later Middle Ages*, 21.

Sigismund's retinue.[37] They made an impressive entry into Basel on 5 August, accompanied by a large body of archers. Although their credence entitling Henry VI King of France evoked protest from the French delegation, and a violent dispute broke out with the Castilians over precedence, they secured incorporation under a specially modified oath on 22 October and separate representation on the deputations during the session. But by the end of the year their number had been significantly reduced. The earl of Mortain and Thomas Brouns left in November and Colville possibly earlier, while the bishop of Rochester had died. The insignificance of the English delegation, particularly in contrast to the impressiveness of the French, made a mockery of their claim to be a 'nation', and reduced their role to that of a watching brief for Lancastrian interests. The initiative which the English had held at Constance, and through which they had imposed their view of the justice and authenticity of the Lancastrian claim on Sigismund and others, had now quite disappeared. They found themselves isolated and unheeded, forced to reiterate claims which, once a mark of English confidence and arrogance, were now merely a matter of embarrassment and ridicule.[38] This foreshadowed the position at Arras.

Already each of Henry VI's allies was moving towards making peace separately with Charles VII. Sigismund did so early in May 1434, thereby securing French support for the council and freeing himself for action against his inveterate enemy Duke Philip. This posed little immediate threat to Burgundy, but he could not remain indifferent to the continual financial drain of the war and the gradual isolation into which his alliance with England was forcing him. By the end of the year he had concluded truces with Charles VII covering Burgundy and Picardy. The other principal English ally, Jean V, duke of Brittany, had urged Henry VI to make peace with Charles in an embassy in June 1434 at the same time as he signed a formal truce with the French king, an act in itself suggestive of the duke's disengagement from the status of vassal under the Treaty of Troyes.[39] As both Burgundy and Brittany reassessed the value of the English alliance, the displacement of Duke Philip's enemy at the French court, La Trémoille, by the count of Richemont opened the way to the duke's reconciliation. Through Richemont's mediation, and that of the indefatigable Amadeus of Savoy, a conference was arranged at Nevers where, on 6 February 1435, Burgundy and Bourbon made peace. This

[37] Schofield, 'Council of Basel', 55–7; Bekynton *Correspondence*, ii. 260–9; Knowlson, *Jean V*, 152; Devon, *Issues*, 424.

[38] Schofield, 'Council of Basel', 59–84.

[39] Beaucourt, *Charles VII*, ii. 482; Vaughan, *Philip the Good*, 67–71; Knowlson, *Jean V*, 154–9; *PPC* iv. 255–9.

opened the way for the reconciliation of Duke Philip and Charles VII, since the agreement at Nevers provided not merely for a peace conference on 1 July at Arras but for the terms on which Burgundy should transfer his allegiance should the English not accept the 'reasonable offers' of the French. Burgundy was to be rewarded with the cession of the Somme towns, the county of Ponthieu, and other places. Invitiations to the conference were to be sent to the English and to both the pope and the council of Basel.[40] With the trump card of Burgundy's allegiance in their sleeve, the French had thus seized the initiative in the peace stakes from the council of Basel and now looked primarily to the papacy to sanction Duke Philip's release from the treaty of Troyes.

Cardinal Beaufort's own movements for the four months following the departure of Bedford and the embassy to Basel are unrecorded. He had not accompanied Bedford to Gravesend at the end of June 1434 with the rest of the council, perhaps because on 15 June he had received licence to proceed overseas, taking £20,000 to fulfil certain vows which he had made. It is likely that he now took the opportunity to make his long deferred pilgrimage to Compostella, for during the early summer a large fleet of vessels had been assembled to transport no less than 3,050 pilgrims for the celebration of the Jubilee of St James on 25 July.[41] His name does not appear in the records of the only two council meetings held between June and October, and neither does that of Gloucester. The duke may have been at Kenilworth, where the young king was spending the summer hunting, and have taken advantage of his position to urge Henry to throw off the constraints of the minority and rule in person. Reports of this had reached the council early in November, causing it to take the highly unusual course of riding as a body to Cirencester where a solemn remonstrance was read to Henry VI warning him against 'such mocions and sturings apart as have been made [to him] but late agoo'. The council reminded him that he was not yet of an age to choose between good and harmful courses of action; they urged him to be patient and to continue to learn to discriminate, and to heed the advice of the continual council. This was delivered in the names of Beaufort and all other members of the continual council apart from Gloucester and Huntingdon.[42]

Little evidence survives for either the composition or the business of the

[40] Beaucourt, *Charles VII*, ii. 516–17.

[41] *PPC* iv. 236, 239, 259; *Foedera*, x. 567–70, 572, 574–5, 580, 590; *CPR 1429–36*, 414. For Beaufort's absence from his diocese at the end of July: *Reg. Chichele*, i. 284. For these mass sailings in years when the feast of St James fell on a Sunday and special indulgences were accorded, see C. M. Storrs, 'Jacobean pilgrims from England' MA thesis (London, 1964). Other years had been in 1423, 1428, and 1445. The passage took up to two weeks each way. The licences are enrolled on C 76/116.

[42] *PPC* iv. 287–9; C 81/1545/50. Henry VI had moved from London on account of the plague in July: Devon, *Issues*, 426. Gloucester was probably in London in Nov.: *Wars of Eng.* ii. 274.

continual council during the winter months of 1434–5. The few surviving lists show the attendance of more of the higher nobility and fewer bishops than previously, a pattern set at Bedford's departure.[43] Neither Gloucester's nor Beaufort's name occurs until May. Its foremost concern was a threefold commitment to the war in France. First there was the charge of 5,000 marks which Bedford had undertaken to pay each half-year to the chancellor of France for the garrisons of northern France when he left in June 1433. Sums of 5,000 marks and 8,000 marks had been dispatched between July and December of that year and the instalment for Easter 1434 was authorized and paid during June-July 1434.[44] But the exchequer had been unable to find the instalment due in December 1434 and in February 1435 the treasurer, Lord Cromwell, put to the council a proposal by which extra revenue might be raised. This was to purchase and export on the king's behalf 222 sarplers of wool (equivalent to 555 sacks) on which only half the duty would be paid. The purchase was to be made with 5,000 marks assigned on the king's part of the duchy of Lancaster, the revenues of Chirkland and North Wales released by Sir John Radclyf, and the customs in ports other than Southampton.[45] The wool was to be purchased at an average price per sack of £6, to which would have to be added some £1. 10*s*. for the payment of duty, freight, and petty costs. There is no contemporary evidence of the price at which wool was selling at Calais, but at either end of the century this was between £9. 10*s*. and £14 per sack according to quality. At an average price of £12 the treasurer stood to make a profit of some £2,500.[46] It is difficult to know how far this took effect. On 21 February the treasurer of Calais and a royal clerk, John Langton, were credited with lending £3,219 which was then 'paid' to the chancellor of France as his December retainer, and repayment of their 'loan' was charged on the sources specified for the purchase of the wool. If this marked the purchase of the wool, on 30 March Hugh Dyke, Thomas Brown, and Thomas Pounde, all associates of the cardinal, had licence to export and sell the 222 sarplers at the king's venture.[47] How the expected profit was divided remains unclear.

[43] *PPC* iv. 282–95; E 28/55. Beaufort was at Farnham 21 Feb. 1435 (HRO Eccles. II 159433) and Windsor on 23 Apr. (Anstis, *Garter*, 114). Councillors attending in the winter were: earls of Huntingdon, Stafford, Suffolk, Warwick; both archbishops; bishops of Ely and Lincoln; Lords Hungerford and Tiptoft; the treasurer and chancellor.

[44] *PPC* iv. 165–7, 187–8, 233; *Foedera*, x. 565, 568, 590.

[45] *PPC* iv. 291–3, 298.,

[46] This figure is entirely hypothetical. There is no indication of the proportions of higher and lower grade wool nor of whether the Partition Ordinance had in fact raised the sale price at Calais. For price evidence, see H. L. Gray, 'English Foreign Trade from 1446 to 1482' in *Studies in Eng. Trade*, 12–13; A. Hanham, 'The profits of English wool exports, 1472–1544', *BIHR* 55 (1982), 139–47; Lloyd, *Movement of Wool Prices*, 71 figs. 8, 9.

[47] E 404/51/173; *CPR 1429–36*, 454; E 401/741; E 403/718. The enrolled accounts give no names of exporters and the only surviving particulars, of Dyke and Charlton, contain merely lists of annuitants.

The second charge on the council was its undertaking to find the wages of the permanent force of 200 men-at-arms and 600 archers; the money was to come from the lands which the feoffees of the duchy were due to surrender at Michaelmas. Predictably, however, the revenues from the Southampton customs had proved insufficient to repay the feoffees' loans and on 4 February 1435 they were permitted to retain their lands until the following Michaelmas on providing a further loan of £6,000.[48] In fact they could find no more than £5,000 for delivery on 18 February, which the council at once used for instalments on these two continuing charges.[49] By 13 May the council was again pressing them 'for the great necessitee that the king hath at this time to send succour to his reaume of France' to lend a further £3,191 to be repaid from the Southampton customs, to enable it to meet the charges for the first half of the year. In June and July the exchequer duly dispatched a further £5,050 to France for the wages of Bedford's force.[50] Of this total of £8,200 loaned by the feoffees in 1435 they seem to have recovered no more than £1,500 from the lands of the duchy, leaving almost £6,700 to be charged on the customs at Southampton. Here the level of wool exports had recovered since the slump of 1433–4, but a debt of this size was going to take two years to discharge, during which time it was all too likely that they would face further demands from the crown.[51] Since December 1433 the feoffees' loans had been made in the name of Cardinal Beaufort, whose own loans during this period had been consistently repaid from the lay subsidies. It was perhaps no accident that the long delays which he was willing to accept for the repayment of the feoffees' loans had the consequence of prolonging the feoffment. In any case the emergence of the feoffees as major lenders, second only to Beaufort himself, had extended and consolidated his grip on crown finance and confirmed his indispensability to Bedford. Only the Company of the Staple and the Corporation of London had comparable funds at their disposal and both were reluctant to lend for the French war.

The exchequer was now anticipating its revenue to such an extent that it had difficulty in meeting immediate needs from current income. Cash receipts during 1434–5 sank to a new low of £7,900 while borrowing reached over £30,000.[52] Even the boom in wool exports which followed the preceding year's slump produced no marked effect on its total income for the year, since so much of this revenue was pledged in repayment of old debts. The treasurer thus remained locked in the situation which he had

[48] *PPC* iv. 290–1; E 404/51/144; E 28/55 13 May.

[49] E 401/741 (wrongly described by Steel, *Receipt*, 207 as from Beaufort); *PPC* iv. 294–5; E 403/718.

[50] E 28/55 13 May; E 404/51/323–5; E 403/720; E 401/743.

[51] Customs receipts at Southampton Mich.–Mich. 1434–5 totalled £5,191 of which £4,320 was paid 'in thesauro': E 356/18 m. 30.

[52] Steel, *Receipt*, 441, 460.

inherited and forced into further anticipation of revenue by the pressing needs of the new campaigning season.

The exchequer had, between July 1434 and July 1435, dispatched a total of £11,714 to France in wages and supplies for the permanent forces and garrisons under the duke of Bedford.[53] That did not include the garrison at Calais which, along with the other frontier charges, found its receipts severely pruned in this period for the benefit of France. Its receipt from the exchequer, which over the past decade consistently averaged £7,000 p.a., fell in the two years February 1434–6 to £4,500, while the receipt from the Staple showed a tenfold decline from £3,000 to £300 p.a. By February 1436 Buckland's arrears for wages stood at £31,794.[54] The arrears owed to Sir John Radclyf for the keeping of Guyenne and Fronsac castle were proportionately as great. Since 1433 he had held the customs at Melcombe and the revenues of North Wales and Chirkland for the discharge of his debt of £7,029; now in February 1435 he was constrained to surrender half these revenues for the urgent needs of France and the support of Cromwell's wool venture. By Michaelmas 1435 his total arrears had grown to £12,180.[55] Payments to the lieutenants in Ireland and on the northern marches had in general been regularly discharged until 1431, but Sir Thomas Stanley, who had become lieutenant in Ireland in that year, accumulated arrears on his salary of 4,000 marks p.a., so that by July 1435 these stood at almost £1,800.[56] In the north the situation was better. Northumberland had been fully paid by assignment when he surrendered the command of the East March in July 1434, although some of his tallies remained to be cashed. Salisbury took over both marches from July 1434 to the autumn of 1435 by which time his arrears for the West March were still under £2,000. Both earls were protected from the effects of the mounting crisis at the exchequer by the firm preference they had secured over local sources of revenue.[57] These arrears to Calais, Guyenne, and Ireland bear witness to the strain imposed on the exchequer by the commitment to increase English support for the war in France which Bedford and Beaufort had taken in May 1433. Particularly since Bedford's return to France, Beaufort and Cromwell had striven to meet these obligations by pruning and defaulting upon other charges. Such expedients could only be temporary and could only be justified by the urgency of the military position.

Anglo-Burgundian successes in 1434 seemed indeed to justify these

[53] Ratcliffe, thesis, 100–1.

[54] Ibid. 112, 118, 126. The allocation of one mark per sack for Calais had been renewed for two years on 12 July 1434: E 404/51/157.

[55] Ibid. 138–43; *PPC* iv. 298; E 404/51/164.

[56] Ibid. 153–4. Of this £1,294 represented uncashed tallies.

[57] Ibid. 157–83. For Salisbury's conditions for taking the office in 1434, see *PPC* iv. 269, and his licence to export cloth, E 404/50/344. For Northumberland, *PPC* iv. 218.

sacrifices. The Lancastrian monarchy held and recovered ground, and to that extent held its allies, showing that it was not yet a spent force. By the spring of 1435, however, the situation had changed. Burgundy had already made peace and attention was concentrated on the forthcoming conference at Arras, at which the duke's defection seemed increasingly probable. A major military success for English arms might even now save the alliance, and was in any case essential to establish a strong bargaining position. For the English desperately needed a long truce to stabilize the position militarily, financially, and politically, and a major victory, or even the avoidance of a major defeat, might compel the French to yield them this. Yet at this moment the war turned markedly against the English. The French under La Hire captured Rue, Étaples, and Le Crotoy at the mouth of the Somme, and Arundel, who was sent to check them, was killed at Gerberoi on 31 May. At the beginning of June Saint-Denis was taken by surprise, threatening Paris, which Bedford had left in February, while from early in the year risings in Caen and the Cotentin had shown the diminishing English hold on Norman loyalties. The need for fresh troops following Arundel's death was urgent, and on 8 June Lords Talbot and Willoughby indented to take to France in mid-July an army of 282 men-at-arms and 1,705 archers.[58]

For its wages—the third of the council's commitments to France—£11,356 would have to be found in cash, and since the exchequer itself had none, and the quarter lay subsidy due for collection at Easter had already been assigned to the cardinal, this would have to be raised through further loans. Although no general commission seems to have been issued, a carefully selected list of individuals was approached and contributions were recorded at the exchequer from 3 June until the middle of July. Not a few of them had connections with the cardinal, and all were constrained to lend significant sums, rarely less than 100 marks. Among the first recorded was one of 2,000 marks from John, earl of Somerset, presumably from the accumulated revenues from his estates.[59] Once again the cardinal himself was the principal lender, paying in 10,000 marks on 7 July and £500 on the 14th. In all, including the £3,191 from the duchy feoffees, a sum of £21,813 was raised, second only to the great loan organized by the cardinal in the winter of 1430–1. On this occasion his own contribution represented money currently being repaid from his loans of 1434, but since no further grant of taxes had yet been made, Beaufort had to accept obligations under the seals of lords of the council without, this time, the additional security of jewels. In common with other lenders he waited until 1437 to receive assignments on lay subsidies in repayment.[60] The lack of effective security

[58] Ratcliffe, thesis, 101–3; Pollard, *Talbot*, 20.
[59] E 401/743; cf. the identity of many names with the list in *PPC* iv. 303–4.
[60] His loan had been negotiated by mid-June. *CPR 1429–36*, 461; *Foedera*, x. 609; E 28/56 20 Feb.; E 401/743; E 403/720; Steel, *Receipt*, 207.

for repayment underlines the pressures which Beaufort and Cromwell must have brought upon lenders and the scope of their achievement in raising so much. It was the last service they were to perform for Bedford. After a vigorous campaign in the Île de France Talbot successfuly recovered Saint-Denis three weeks after the duke had died.

Talbot's army sailed to France on 20 July, at approximately the same time as the English embassy to the Congress of Arras. Duke Philip's invitation to the congress had not been received in England until the middle of May, when the French had already signified their acceptance and both the pope and the council of Basel had appointed legates as mediators, in the persons of Cardinals Albergati and Hugh of Lusignan.[61] Doubtless plans for an embassy were already well advanced; certainly in April Eugenius IV had expressed his hope that Beaufort would attend, and by mid-June procurations had been issued and expenses paid for a large and dignified embassy drawn equally from Henry VI's realms of England and France. On the English side the principal members were Archbishop Kemp and Bishops Alnwick and Rudborne, the earls of Huntingdon and Suffolk, Lord Hungerford and Sir John Radclyf, and the keeper of the privy seal. From France Louis de Luxembourg was named, though ultimately he did not attend, and the delegation from Bedford's council was led by Bishop Cauchon of Lisieux.

Cardinal Beaufort's role was, for the moment, ambiguous. The English were still hoping to represent all signatories to the treaty of Troyes by a single embassy and three procurations were prepared, one listing Duke Philip at its head, one substituting Beaufort's name for his, and the third omitting both. When the duke emphatically declined to lead the Lancastrian embassy, making clear that his interests were distinct, Beaufort likewise decided not to take part in the direct negotiations with the French. In Kemp, Cauchon, Alnwick, and Hungerford he had tried and trusted associates, and the superior legatine authority of his brother cardinal created problems of precedence and status. Moreover, by keeping himself apart from, though in contact with, the Anglo-French negotiations, he preserved a freedom to conduct his own bilateral talks either with the mediators or with Duke Philip. He was said to hold reserve powers should the negotiations founder, but it is unlikely that he had authority to make further concessions than those which were sent to the embassy on 31 July and later, and certain that he never produced such. Both he and the embassy were authorized to negotiate peace and a marriage alliance with Charles VII.[62] In fact English hopes were focused on, and limited to, the establishment of a prolonged truce which should stabilize the present position, not only in military and territorial terms, but in respect of Henry VI's claim to the French crown and Duke Philip's allegiance to the treaty of

[61] Dickinson, *Congress of Arras*, 20–1, 82–3, 89–90, 218–19.
[62] Ibid. 27–32, 34–49, 216–18.

Troyes. In mid-June Beaufort received an advance of £1,000 for his expenses and licence to take with him 10,000 marks in money. He had arrived at Calais by 28 July with a retinue as large as that of the main embassy, and was to remain there until the breakdown of negotiations between the English and French in the third week of August.[63]

Beaufort was also empowered to negotiate with the duke of Burgundy and the Four Members about the Partition Ordinance. The ducal ban on the import of English cloth throughout his territories and, even more, his truce at Nevers with Charles VII, had made the English willing to listen to Flemish complaints for the first time since 1429. In February 1435 an English delegation was given notably conciliatory instructions for negotiations with the Four Members in April. Nothing came of these and at his last appearance in council before his departure Beaufort received fresh authority to resume talks. Whether he did so during early August while he was at Calais is uncertain; in any case the English offers were mainly designed to persuade the duke to stay loyal to the alliance through concessions to the Four Members.[64] Despite its baneful commercial effects, the Partition Ordinance had never emerged as a political issue between England and Burgundy and it now played little part in determining the duke's position.

In one sense that had already been decided at Nevers, where the terms on which France and Burgundy made peace in September 1435 had already been agreed. Indeed in essentials they had been on the table since 1429; the question was whether the duke would take them up. The question was debated intensively in the ducal council, the Francophile party being led by his chancellor Nicholas Rolin and the Sieur de Croy, and the Anglophile by Hugh de Lannoy and Jean de Luxembourg. The debate was mainly conducted in terms of Burgundian interests: was the English alliance an incubus which subjected Burgundy to the destruction and financial burdens of war and kept the duke from the circle of his natural peers in order that the English could cling to Normandy and Paris, as Rolin argued; or was it the guarantee of the commercial prosperity, political stability, and independence of the Low Countries from a predatory French monarch bent on revenge, as the Anglophile councillors urged? At the root of any answer lay an assessment of the military capacities of the English and French. Was the English conquest permanent; if not how long would it last? On an answer to that would be framed the ducal response to the moral and legal doubts raised by his contemplated renunciation of the treaty of Troyes.

There is little doubt that from the beginning of 1435 the Francophile element was winning this debate, with the powerful assistance of the count

[63] Dickinson, *Congress of Arras,* 35, 103, 219; *PPC* iv. 302; *Foedera*, x. 610; C 76/117 m. 8.
[64] *Foedera*, x. 605, 619; C 76/117 m. 3, 7; Thielemans, *Bourgogne et Angleterre*, 61.

of Richemont at Charles VII's court and the consistent advocacy of peace by his ally the count of Savoy. The papacy likewise favoured and was ready to sanction a Franco-Burgundian reconciliation as a means to a general peace. For the English the best hope of deflecting this lay in a demonstration of the continued viability of Lancastrian pretensions. Duke Philip's letter to Henry VI in May had mirrored his divided counsels; it had dwelt on the might of the French and their military success, the uncertain loyalty of Lancastrian France, and the Burgundian losses, all of which dictated the need for peace; yet at the same time he encouraged Henry to send out a mighty army, so that he might negotiate from strength and be ready for instant war should negotiation fail. Henry's much briefer reply sent through Lannoy concentrated on recalling Philip to his obligations under the treaty of Troyes and promised the dispatch of an army—Talbot's force, which sailed in July. Peace negotiations were not mentioned. The principal English objective at Arras was thus to hold Philip to the treaty. A long truce with France, linked to a marriage, could best assist this and the embassy had detailed instructions for this; but any renunciation of the French crown or the treaty of Troyes was outside its brief.[65]

It was, of course, precisely on these that the French insisted as necessary for a true and permanent peace. For it was this false English claim that had provided the legal *casus belli* and the pretext for rebellion by the French princes over the past hundred years. Unless a peace could be negotiated on the basis of French sovereignty, they were prepared to continue the war; they would not countenance a truce and marriage, which would merely postpone the issue and provide occasion for further disputes. If the English were ready to renounce the title they might still hold great areas of France as fiefs. In this sense the French could envisage a *de facto* division of France, just as the English were prepared to recognize a partition which left them holding lands in sovereignty. That was the nearest both sides came to recognizing that the fortunes of war were still evenly balanced and that, while English pride and the will to fight remained, a military solution would prove long and costly.[66] But to the English the French demands could only spell final surrender. For to relinquish the claim to the crown and acknowledge the invalidity of the treaty of Troyes (the two amounted to the same) would leave the English with no independent right to be in France or any claim to Burgundian allegiance. To hold as vassals of Charles VII was a recipe for interminable disputes and eventual deprivation, quite apart from providing an opening for extruded Frenchmen to

[65] Dickinson, *Congress of Arras*, 21–2, 32–3, chap. 3, 109–16; Vaughan, *Philip the Good*, 98–101; *Wars of Eng.* ii. 431–3.

[66] Dickinson, *Congress of Arras*, 141–52. The final French offer proposed the deferment of homage for seven years until Henry VI came of age: detailed in Beaucourt, *Charles VII*, ii. 539–40.

claim lands and benefices in Lancastrian France. Despite the logical force of their arguments, the French could thus have little expectation that the English would accept them; rather were they designed to convict the English as enemies of a true and general peace and justify the abrogation of the treaty of Troyes and the release of Duke Philip from his oath. Already it could be said—as Philip himself had in writing to Henry VI—that the treaty which he had signed in the hope of peace had become a recipe for continued war. English insistence on it now played into French hands. For in truth the French had so framed the argument that the English could not win: if they renounced the claim to the crown of France they deprived themselves of any title to the land they held, while if they maintained the claim they branded themselves as enemies of peace.

The fact that the Anglo-French peace negotiations were an ill-tempered charade, doomed to failure, perhaps explains why Cardinal Beaufort took no formal part in them. His particular mission was to save the Anglo-Burgundian alliance. It was at the point where it had become clear that a general peace was impossible that Beaufort left Calais and arrived at Arras on Tuesday, 25 August. He was met by Duke Philip, Cardinal Hugh of Lusignan, and the English delegates and went direct to the *cité* where the English embassy was housed, while the French and Burgundians fraternized in the abbey of Saint-Vaast where the congress was held. Beaufort occupied the episcopal palace. There followed two days of courtesy visits between the cardinal, the duke, and the duchess, and on the 27th and 28th there were intensive discussions with certain of the French embassy and among the English themselves, with a further meeting between Beaufort and the duke. On the 29th Beaufort accompanied the English delegates to a plenary session at Saint-Vaast, but after exchanging words with Cardinal Albergati he left for another meeting with Duke Philip. By then Beaufort had ruled out any concession of Henry VI's rights and, as hopes for a general peace faded, the departure of the English was widely predicted. All Beaufort's efforts were now concentrated on retaining the loyalty of Burgundy. On 31 August, the anniversary of Henry V's death, he celebrated solemn mass for the late king's soul in the episcopal chapel, but only the English attended. It was followed by a general meeting of the English and French embassies, at which Beaufort and Philip were present, which finally dispelled all hopes of peace. For the duke the moment of decision had at last arrived. On 1 September he gave a great banquet for the English before their departure, showing every honour to the cardinal and his companions. Even now Beaufort did not despair of a final appeal to the duke's loyalty. Casting protocol aside, the two men, joined by Kemp, held earnest talk in the middle of the room, having sent their attendants out of earshot. For an hour and more Beaufort pressed on Philip arguments with which he must have become wearisomely familiar from the deliberations with his own councillors and in his own mind. All that we know of Beaufort would allows us to infer that these were now expounded with a cogency and persuasiveness that did justice to the great issues involved. The cardinal pleaded with a passion that brought sweat in great beads to his forehead, until the attendants discreetly brought wines and spices to terminate the discussion.[67] For Beaufort the duke's impending desertion spelt not merely the explicit failure of Henry V's great design, which he and Bedford had striven to sustain; it marked the end of an alliance which had become the corner-stone of his policy and his peculiar responsibility, terminating a relationship of friendship and trust which he had cultivated for more than a decade and had fortified by the duke's marriage to his niece. So much was at stake for Beaufort, and so great must have been his forebodings of the consequences for the English position, that Burgundy's desertion must be reckoned among the bitterest moments of his life.

His fortitude was tested even further by the death of Bedford two weeks later. It is unlikely that Beaufort journeyed to the deathbed of him on whose friendship and protection he had counted for the past ten years. But when, on 10 September, Bedford drew up his last will, he named Beaufort as one of his three principal executors, along with Louis of Luxembourg and Archbishop Kemp, the others being Lord Cromwell, Sir John Fastolf, Andrew Ogard, and Robert Whittingham. In this small circle of confidants Bedford's trust remained unshaken to the last.[68] The double blow, of Burgundy's desertion and Bedford's death must have brought many to despair of the future of Lancastrian France, but for Beaufort they additionally raised the spectre of his personal vulnerability. Of his inner misgivings at this juncture we can only guess, but his public demeanour bespoke a commitment to uphold the cause to which Bedford had devoted his life. As the embassy left Arras on 6 September in a rainstorm on its way to Lille, each member of the cardinal's retinue, dressed in his vermilion livery, had the word 'honour' embroidered on his sleeve, and the cardinal himself, claiming that he still had 'deux milions de nobles' in his treasure, vowed to use it to sustain the war for his nephew's rights.[69]

The three years after his return to England in 1432 were among the most critical in Beaufort's career, and set the scene for his dominance of English politics in the rest of the decade. Between 1427 and 1432 he had visited

[67] Beaucourt, *Charles VII*, 37–9; A. de la Taverne, *Journal de la Paix d'Arras*, ed. A. Bossuat, 54–62; le Fèvre *Chronique*, ii. 325; Plancher, *Hist. Bourgogne*, iv. 203–6.

[68] *Royal Wills*, 270–6; *Reg. Chichele*, ii. 595–88. Bedford had not named Beaufort as an executor in his earlier will of 1429: B.-A. Pocquet du Haut Jussé, 'Anne de Bourgogne et le testament de Bedford, 1429', *Bibl. École des Chartes*, 95 (1934), 319–26. The journey from Arras to Rouen was very hazardous at this time: *Appendices to Foedera*, 413–4.

[69] Taverne, *Journal*, loc. cit.; *Livre des trahisons de France entre la Maison de Bourgogne: Chroniques relatives à'histoire de la Belgique*, ed. Kervyn de Lettenhove, ii. 210.

England on only three occasions, none longer than seven months, and his energies had been given to the papal crusade and the defence of Lancastrian France. Overspanning that period, from 1426 to 1433, Gloucester had headed the council in England and on three occasions, in 1426, 1429, and 1432 had made clear his implacable opposition to the cardinal's return to English politics. It was only under the protection of Bedford, and as the instrument of his policy, that Beaufort was restored to the council and could start to rebuild his following. Their partnership was built upon a final, heroic attempt to preserve the credibility of the double monarchy by military and diplomatic efforts which made severe demands on the resources of England and Normandy. These years were ones of intense strain for Bedford, Beaufort, Kemp, and Cromwell, binding them into a formal political alliance. Similarly the increasing and unremitting financial demands of the war drove the exchequer ever more heavily into debt and dependence on the loans supplied by and through the cardinal. Bedford thus found himself increasingly committed to, and dependent on, the support of the cardinal and his allies, provoking outright criticism from Gloucester who saw himself displaced from influence in council and now espoused policies diametrically opposed to those of the dominant group. When English policy collapsed in the autumn of 1435 with the desertion of Burgundy, the death of Bedford and the imminent loss of Paris, the political future of Beaufort and his followers was inevitably thrown into jeopardy. Even so Beaufort had no choice but to remain in England and face the predictable enmity of his rival. Though his policy was discredited and his protector removed, there was no longer any place for him at the papal Curia or in Lancastrian France, and no refuge at the Burgundian court.

13

The Anti-Burgundian Reaction and the Ending of the Minority, 1435–1436

On his return from Arras it must have seemed to Cardinal Beaufort that he stood in considerable danger of being made the scapegoat for a policy that had disastrously failed. For the past ten years the cultivation of Burgundian friendship had been the guiding principle of his and Bedford's policy, expressed in support for Duke Philip's territorial aims and, since 1429, in the repeated dispatch of money and troops. Both could be viewed as detrimental to England's own interests and neither had ultimately prevented Burgundian defection. Beaufort in particular was personally identified with this through his visits to the Burgundian court, the marriage of his niece to Philip, and his final mission to Arras. By the same token, the outcome of the congress could be seen as a long-delayed justification for Gloucester's persistent and deep-rooted hostility to Duke Philip, sustained ever since his own ambitions in Hainault had been frustrated by Bedford and Beaufort. Burgundy's defection would certainly release pent up anti-Flemish feeling which would look to Gloucester for leadership.

Similarly, Beaufort's standing at the Roman Curia had appeared to provide an assurance of papal respect for Lancastrian claims, even if hope of a positively favourable verdict had long been abandoned. But following the breakdown of the Anglo-French negotiations at Arras, Cardinal Albergati had come down firmly against Henry VI's title to the French crown and had proceeded to make a separate peace between Burgundy and France, releasing the duke from the treaty of Troyes.[1] Kemp's incredulous protest that neither the pope nor the council could authorize the rupture of Burgundy's solemn oath, and Beaufort's long and harrowing pleading with the duke, suggest that even at the last the English were unprepared for the eventual outcome. For this was the nemesis of that grand strategy of harnessing papal policy in support of Lancastrian interests, on which Beaufort had built his position and reputation and for which Gloucester's marital intentions had been sacrificed.

Thirdly, in the past two years Beaufort, Cromwell, and Kemp had strained the resources of the realm to support Bedford's conduct of the war in France. Bedford's strategy had been to conduct a piecemeal but persistent defence of Lancastrian strongholds wherever they were threatened

[1] Dickinson, *Congress of Arras*, 129.

and to recover or extend English lordship by sieges. Gloucester, by contrast, had advocated a major thrust to seek and destroy the French army, but had seen his proposal (to be paid for from the cardinal's wealth) rejected by the council in 1434. With Bedford's death he was now heir apparent and, as the last of Henry V's brothers, the natural successor to his military and political leadership. Already in the summer of 1435 Gloucester had been asserting his political status by assiduous attendance at council meetings, and Bedford's death terminated the constraints on major decisions and changes of officers and councillors without his sanction.

Over the past decade, therefore, Gloucester had stood for a different orientation of English policy and strategy from that which had been pursued and which now stood discredited. Although nominally head of the council in England for most of that period, he had repeatedly seen the exercise of his natural leadership limited by his elder brother in league with his uncle of the half-blood. His resentment against Bedford had been openly expressed in 1426, 1427, and 1434 and he had sought the ruin and exile of Beaufort in 1426, 1429, and 1432, while the cardinal's supporters, Kemp and Cromwell, had suffered dismissal at his hands. Now that his hour had at last arrived Gloucester might be expected to replace the officers of state, exclude his enemies from council, and give to English policy an anti-Burgundian and anti-papal bias, coupled with a major military effort under his direction or command. Beaufort in particular had reason to fear for his wealth and status, so recently under threat.

In the event little of this happened. Gloucester indeed secured some of the spoils from Bedford's decease. On 1 November 1435 he was appointed captain of Calais and lieutenant in Picardy, Flanders, and Artois for nine years, and on 23 November he had a grant of the Channel Islands in rebatement of 500 marks of his exchequer annuity. The council now, on occasion, met under his own roof; but none of the officers of state were removed nor did the membership of the council change.[2] Gloucester made no direct threat to Cardinal Beaufort, needing to rely upon on his wealth in the crisis that now faced the realm. Within two years, by the time the minority had formally ended, Beaufort had not only safeguarded his position but had once again established a commanding influence over policy and broad support within the council. Gloucester's hour passed as swiftly as it had come, bringing no permanent increase in his authority or change of policy or personnel. For this there were broadly three reasons. First, the magnitude of the military and political crisis which faced Lancastrian France enforced political unity at home, while the financial demands on the English exchequer made Beaufort and Cromwell

[2] *Foedera*, x. 624; *Rot. Parl.* iv. 483–4; *PPC* v. 5; E 28/57 10 May 1436.

indispensable. Secondly, Beaufort, Kemp, Cromwell, and Louis of Luxembourg saw themselves as not only Bedford's executors but his political heirs, presenting a united front against Gloucester in England and commanding the confidence of Bedford's council in France. Gloucester lacked the personality and supporters of their calibre to override them. Thirdly, as Henry VI's own intervention in politics gradually increased Beaufort began to acquire influence over the young king and to exploit royal patronage. We shall consider each of these in turn.

English reaction to the failure at Arras was divided and confused. There was probably a widely held, if uninformed, belief that an opportunity to secure reasonable terms on which Normandy could be retained had been lost. A letter from the Norman estates to Henry VI recalled the French offer to guarantee Normandy as an English fief and underlined its people's need for peace and relief from the burden of war; the royal answer spelt out the English offers that had been refused, and the French demands for the restitution of lands, offices, and benefices.[3] Lannoy reported in 1436 (for the benefit of Duke Philip) that in England the majority of the people, overburdened with taxes, blamed the council for not accepting the last French offer which the duke had transmitted.[4] Gascoigne, with hindsight, censured 'an English duke and a bishop' for refusing peace at Arras, and indeed, when the Burgundian letters containing the final French offers were read out in council, both Gloucester and Beaufort pointedly walked out. Yet in returning from Arras with honour rather than peace, Beaufort matched the mood of the council. Even the young king, who, in July, had eloquently urged the cause of peace on his aunt the Duchess Isabel, had burst into tears when Philip's letters omitted his French title, and now burned with anger and revenge for the affront.[5] But anger was no substitute for policy, and the lords were divided about whether to proceed against Burgundy by diplomacy or war. Beaufort would certainly have advocated diplomacy, and throughout the winter seems to have got his way, for efforts were made to renew the alliances with Sigismund, the duke of Bavaria, the duke of Gueldres, and the Count Palatine, and letters of support were sent to the towns of Holland and Zeeland, while through Louis of Luxembourg contacts were maintained with the Anglophiles on the ducal council.[6] Nevertheless, both there and in the English parliament which met on 5 October, warnings were sounded of the likelihood of an Anglo-Burgundian war, and royal letters had strictly summoned all lords to

[3] *Lettres des rois, reines et autres personages*, ed. M. Champollion-Figeac, ii. 426–8, 433–5.

[4] Vaughan, *Philip the Good*, 104–5.

[5] Gascoigne, *Loci e Libro Veritatum*, 219; Waurin, *Croniques*, iv. 98–101; Monstrelet, *Chronique*, v. 191–4; Le Fèvre, *Chronique*, ii. 363–4, 377.

[6] *Foedera*, x. 626, 634; Thielemans, *Bourgogne et Angleterre*, 72–3, 77–9, 437–8.

attend in person.[7] The gravity of the challenge to Henry VI's title was underlined when, for the first time, he attended the continual council which met at Kingston on the eve of parliament to consider its response to Burgundy.[8]

This provided the theme for the chancellor's speech expounding the infamy of the duke of Burgundy and the need to take measures for the defence of Calais. Anti-alien excitement in London was reflected in a spate of bills in the Commons. Although a petition for the repeal of Hanseatic privileges was refused, other petitions secured the forfeiture of goods of friendly aliens in enemy vessels, the repeal of the statute of truces, and the strict enforcement of the Partition Ordinance and the Calais monopoly, with the revocation of all licences of exemption.[9] But in the end the Commons were more ready to protest than to pay, merely granting a whole subsidy to be levied in quarterly instalments at Whitsun and Martinmas 1436 and 1437, with a graded income tax on offices and land which would yield approximately £9,000 payable at the quinzaine of Easter. At the same time convocation, which had met on 12 November, granted a whole and a half-tenth, payable at Annunciation 1436 and midsummer 1437 respectively, and a tax on chantry priests. The fact that both assemblies lasted until two days before Christmas, when the grants were finally made, suggests considerable pressure from the council, perhaps for a more immediate or higher contribution.[10] For, in the course of the session, the military situation had worsened dramatically and the exchequer was totally without financial resources to meet it. Throughout the concluding weeks of the Congress of Arras the French had kept up pressure on Normandy, taking Pont de Meulan on 14 September, but it was the surprise seizure of Dieppe on 28 October which triggered the rising in the Pays de Caux and the loss in rapid succession of Fécamp, Tancarville, Montivilliers, and Harfleur. In desperation the estates of Normandy wrote to Henry VI appealing for the swift dispatch of a large force, to be led by a great lord, related in blood to the king, and with a formidable reputation. This was to be at English expense, for Normandy was now too impoverished to support itself.[11]

Henry's reply, justifying the rejection of the French terms at Arras, promised an army by 1 January, and on the day of the parliamentary grant he wrote more specifically that provision had now been made for a large

[7] Vaughan, *Philip the Good*, 101–2; E 28/56 28 Sept.; *Rot. Parl.* iv. 481.

[8] C 81/1545/55 1 Oct. Not at Eltham, as Wolffe, *Henry VI*, 81.

[9] *Rot. Parl.* iv. 491–3.

[10] Ibid. 486–8; *CFR 1430–7*, 269–71; H. L. Gray, 'Incomes from land in England in 1436', *EHR* 49 (1934), 612; R. Virgoe, 'The parliamentary subsidy of 1450', *BIHR* 55 (1982), 134 n. 60.

[11] *Lettres*, ed. Champollion-Figeac, ii. 420–8. For a similar letter to Gloucester from Bishop Cauchon, see Bekynton, *Correspondence*, i. 289.

and powerful army, greater than any in living memory, to wit, 2,000 men at arms and 9,000 archers to be sent under York, Salisbury, and Suffolk to abide in Normandy. The advance party would sail before the New Year and the main body, if weather permitted, by the end of January.[12] Thus in the course of the parliament the council's military priority had shifted from the threat to Calais to the defence of Normandy, where the military and political exigencies had suddenly rendered Gloucester's cherished proposal opportune.

An army of such a size, even for half a year, would cost in the region of £65,000 and virtually all of this had to be raised before it could sail. At the beginning of Michaelmas term there can have been virtually no cash in the exchequer, for not more than £20,000 had been received over the past two and a half years. No lay subsidies were collected in 1435, the council having evidently ruled out a spring parliament in order to await the result of the Congress of Arras. A quarter clerical subsidy was due at Martinmas, but an appreciable portion of this was already assigned in repayment of Beaufort's loan of 1434. The one productive source of revenue came from the backlog of wool exports which over 1434–5 must have yielded some £29,000 in customs, though much of this had already been anticipated by loans during the summer. Not until the end of March 1436 did the receipts from the clerical tenth and chaplains' tax bring in most of the £24,297 recorded for this term, to be followed by £16,249 in the summer term from the proceeds of the clerical tenth and income tax.[13] Cromwell was clearly aiming to mobilize cash for the expedition and to break out of the recurrent anticipation of lay and clerical subsidies into which he had been forced by Bedford's demands since 1433. Yet the size and urgency of the reinforcements needed left him no option but to borrow extensively, both for the proposed Normandy army and to meet the developing threat to Calais. Since the fleets of the Cinque Ports, with Gloucester's backing, had already declared 'bloody and open war' in the Channel, trade at Calais had virtually collapsed and the customs could provide no security for a fresh round of borrowing. The treasurer was thus forced to pledge all four instalments of the lay subsidy up to Martinmas 1437. The loans raised in Michaelmas and Easter terms 1435–6 amounted, in fact, to over £48,000, so that in all the exchequer could dispose of practically £89,000 in cash during this year.[14] This figure exceeded that mobilized in either 1429–30 or 1430–1, and more was borrowed in this than in either of these years. Such in outline was the scale of the financial effort in response to the threat to Normandy and Calais in 1436.

[12] Ibid. ii. 428–31, 433–5. Letters were sent out to the leading men in the shires to array themselves for service in Normandy: *Wars of Eng.* i. 510–12 (misdated to 1450).

[13] Steel, *Receipt*, 441; E 401/744, 748.

[14] Thielemans, *Bourgogne et Angleterre*, 77 (cf. *Rot. Parl.* iv. 489); Steel, loc. cit.

In the weeks following the end of the parliament, agreement was reached with York, Salisbury, and Suffolk to make their indentures on 20 February, and to these was now added a force under the separate command of Edmund Beaufort, count of Mortain. The main army had been reduced to 4,500 men, of which almost four-fifths were archers, but it was to remain in Normandy for a year as promised. Edmund Beaufort received an independent command in Maine and Anjou for two years, and his force of 2,000 men was only slightly smaller than that of York himself. The Beauforts were making a bid for the fiefs there held by the duke of Bedford which were now in the king's hands. Indeed on 19 March the English council granted Mortain lands formerly confiscated from Jean d'Alencourt in lower Normandy.[15] It seems clear enough that the addition of Mortain's force and the terms of his separate command were the price exacted by the cardinal for financing the army to Normandy.

This was slow to assemble. After the dispatch of a small body of troops in December, storms delayed the passage of the advance force under Sir Thomas Beaumont until 10 March.[16] On 20 February the main commanders, York, Salisbury, and Mortain, received £19,160 for their first quarter's wages from a sum of £22,676 loaned five days earlier.[17] Of this £12,666. 13*s*. 4*d*. had come from the cardinal himself and a further £4,000 from the feoffees of the duchy through him. Of the cardinal's loan £7,353. 13*s*. 1*d*. was to be repaid from the lay subsidy due at Whitsun 1436 and the remainder in equal parts from the two later instalments of the subsidy under the security of jewels. At the same time the council's outstanding obligations to him were confirmed: 1,000 marks from the loan of 1434 for which he held tallies on the clerical tenth payable at Martinmas 1436, and 10,000 marks from 1435 for which no payment had as yet been arranged.[18] In all the crown was thus in debt to the cardinal in the sum of £20,000, for little more than one-third of which he could expect repayment in the current year. The feoffees, half of whose loans of 1435 had still not been repaid from the Southampton customs, stipulated that this should be their last loan to the crown until their obligations to Henry V's creditors had been fulfilled.[19] Langley had retired as a feoffee in November 1435 and Chichele seems to have become a sleeping partner, leaving the duchy

[15] E 404/52/196, 208, 211, 226. BN MS Fr. 26549 no. 19. Witnessed by Gloucester, Beaufort, Kemp, Stafford, Warwick.

[16] A force of 970 men under Richard Wasteneys and Henry Norbury sailed in Dec., costing £4,800; Beaumont had 800 men: E 404/52/156. 161, 165; E 403/722 16 Dec., 10 Mar. Henry VI sent repeated assurances to the chancellor of France of the dispatch of the army: *Lettres*, ed. Champollion-Figeac, ii. 435–40; E 28/56 16 Jan.; *Wars of Eng*. i. 427–8.

[17] E 403/721. Ships were to be ready for 1 Apr.: *CPR 1429–36*, 533–5.

[18] E 401/744; *CPR 1429–36*, 602; E 404/52/204, 393; E 28/56 20 Feb.; *Foedera*, x. 632. Full payment had been made by July 1437 when Beaufort restored the jewels: *Kal. and Inv*. ii. 163–7; E 101/335/158.

[19] E 404/52/199.

resources in the hands of Beaufort and Hungerford. The influence which Beaufort wielded through his wealth was never more strikingly displayed than at this point in his career. Not merely had the council's obligations to him and the financial exigencies of the war protected him and Cromwell from their inveterate enemy, but his new subventions had determined that the defence of Normandy would receive priority over punitive action against Burgundy, and that his two nephews, Salisbury and Mortain, would be given leading roles among a new generation of captains in France.

The wages for the second quarter of the great army were due to be paid early in April when shipping was to be provided and it was expected to muster for departure. They were to be met by a general loan for which, on 14 February, letters of privy seal were individually addresed to nobility, clergy, towns, and gentry.[20] But little had been received by the end of March when news of the duke of Burgundy's impending attack on Calais transformed the situation.

Throughout the winter Beaufort had striven to avoid occasions of conflict with Burgundy in order to concentrate English resources on the defence of the conquest.[21] But in the spring Philip decided to take advantage of the impending French attack on Paris and Normandy to attempt the capture of Calais. Exploiting the Anglophobia in Flanders inflamed by English piracy and the Partition Ordinance, the duke formally sought military aid from the Four Members at a meeting at Ghent early in March, holding out the promise of banning English cloth and of looting Calais of its wool.[22] On hearing of this the council's first reaction was to reinforce the garrison with 200 men-at-arms and 20 archers. The cost of this force was about £900, but pending the receipts from the Lady Day taxes, even this sum could not be found and on 15 March Beaufort advanced a further 1,000 marks 'for its dispatch in all haste in this present great necessity'. The money was delivered to the treasurer of Calais on 19 March and on the same day he received repayment by five tallies on the customs due from Italian galleys in London.[23] Beyond this stopgap the council faced the prospect of dispatching a substantial army to Calais. Undertakings had already been obtained from the lords in parliament to provide six weeks' service at their own costs in the event of a threat to Calais, and on 26 March further letters were sent to towns (and probably gentry) describing the Burgundian preparations, asking them to array troops, and to be present at a council on 25 April to certify their

[20] *PPC* iv. 316 ff; *CPR 1429–36*, 528–30, 533.

[21] For the letter of Gloucester and Beaufort to Philip on 17 Mar. see *PPC* iv. 329–34 appealing to his honour. Protection was given to Flemings in England who took an oath of allegiance to Henry VI: *CPR 1429–36*, 541–88.

[22] Thielemans, *Bourgogne et Angleterre*, 81; Vaughan, *Philip the Good*, 75; G. A. Holmes, 'The Libel of English Policy', *EHR* 76 (1961), 195.

[23] E 401/744; E 403/721; E 404/52/187, 222, 394.

contribution and receive instructions. Those who could not do service were to compound with a grant of money. The letters, desiring the help of all true subjects 'at this tyme of verrey necessite', reminded them 'what a preciouse jeuell the saide towne of Calais is to this reame, . . . what a bolewark and defense it is to this lande,' and what its loss would entail for the burden of coastal defence.[24] The urgency of the danger and its emotive force unlocked purses more readily than the earlier appeal for the relief of Normandy. From mid-April to mid-May the exchequer recorded a series of substantial loans from many of those to whom letters had been sent in February; in all sixty-three individual loans brought in £4,277. Despite their earlier reservation, the feoffees lent £2,380 and on 14 May agreed to defer their claims on the Southampton customs in order to make 4,000 marks immediately available to the treasurer of Calais.[25] With all the Low Country ports closed and the Calais mint likewise, the treasurer was receiving nothing from the customs, and only the Italian galleys yielded revenue. On 15 March, at the time of his own loan, Beaufort had arranged for a further sum of £4,000 to be lent in the name of John, earl of Somerset, probably for the second quarter's wages of his brother the earl of Mortain, who had sailed from Winchelsea possibly by the 7th and certainly by 23 April.[26] He alone of the leaders of the great army seems to have been ready to muster at the appointed date. In any case the exchequer had no means of paying the second quarter's wages for the rest of the army until the cash receipts from the lay and clerical taxes arrived at the end of April. The cardinal had at least ensured that his nephew's contingent was ready, paid, and dispatched on time.

However, Edmund Beaufort was not free to employ his force to extend his holdings in Maine, for his destination had been countermanded to Calais. According to the *Brut*, this was done by Gloucester 'to strengthen the town till rescous might be had', but probably also to check the Beaufort ambitions. It was a step he lived to regret. Mortain commanded a substantial force of 2,000 men, with two other barons in his retinue, of whom Lord Camoys was one. The high proportion of archers, numbering 1,600 made it more effective for field than garrison duty, and from the first he conducted raids into Flanders, the most effective being to Loon and Gravelines a fortnight after his arrival. These services were recognized by

[24] *HMC Various Coll.*, iv. 197–200; *PPC* iv. 352b–e; cf. *Brut*, ii. 574.

[25] E 401/748 17 Apr.–23 May; cf. *PPC* iv. 317 ff.; E 404/52/316.

[26] Somerset's loan (E 401/744) was not repaid until 29 May 1441. Mortain's departure is given as early April (*Brut*, ii. 468), 23 Apr. (ibid. 574), after 8 Apr. (*Gregory Chron.* 178). His wages for the second quarter are recorded on the issue roll under 10 May. He had been recruiting his army during Jan.–Mar. along with Wasteneys and Beaumont: C 76/118. 11–18. It was doubtless the loans of the cardinal and earl at this point that procured for Edmund Beaufort and Margaret duchess of Clarence the grants of the wardships of Robert Lord Morley, John Hill, and John Arundell to the value of £1,600 in discharge of the arrears of their annuities: E 403/721, 26 Mar.

his election to the chapter of the Garter, the insignia being sent out to him on 5 May.[27] The garrison under Sir John Radclyf was not equipped for such operations and Mortain's independent command enabled him to establish himself as the *de facto* defender of Calais during the early summer, a development which Gloucester could hardly have welcomed. It was probably hoped that Mortain's presence would deter Duke Philip's venture, for no plans for further reinforcements were made until early June.[28] The situation in France still took priority, even though the dispatch of York's army was agonizingly delayed.

This was no longer from lack of money. In March and April the exchequer was receiving the lay and clerical grants and was using the proceeds of the general loan as they came in. On 22 April the council fixed York's muster for 3 May at Winchelsea.[29] This was already a month behind schedule, during which time the whole of the English position in France had crumbled. Sir Thomas Beaumont's force had been wiped out near Saint-Denis and the loss in swift succession of Pontoise, Charentan, and Saint-Germain-en-Laye finally made Paris untenable. The English withdrew on 17 April. From this point of view the diversion of Edmund Beaufort to Calais had proved a costly mistake; it had certainly wrung expressions of incredulity and dismay from the chancellor of France at the unaccountable English inactivity during the first four months of 1436. Further urgent appeals warned that Rouen itself was now endangered. Yet York not merely failed to muster by the appointed date; he had still not finalized the terms of his commission as the king's lieutenant governor which had been under discussion since late April. These were finally approved in council on 8 May, but a further two weeks elapsed before he was ready to sail, during which a series of exasperated letters were sent to him by the council. He was accused of causing 'gret hurte and losse' to the crown, since' for your long tarrying of passage our charge waxeth dayly gretter and gretter'; his captains' complaints about the insufficiency of shipping were dismissed and he was told 'to be serviceable' to the royal officers and take ship forthwith. Almost daily the king wrote to the chancellor of France that York was coming. Eventually York, Salisbury, and Suffolk drew their pay on 24 May and sailed a week later.[30] Although

[27] Thielemans, *Bourgogne et Angleterre*, 88 n. 37 dates the raid 14 May; this is too late, for Gregory says it was fourteen days after his arrival, the Garter being sent to him following the news of it. Anstis, *Garter*, 116; *Foedera*, x. 60.

[28] Mortain had fortified Merk (*Brut*, ii. 577) and victuals and arms were sent to him (E 28/58 15 Nov.). On 12 May £2,240 destined for Normandy was diverted to pay for ships to safeguard Calais and on 14 May the duchy feoffees made 4,000 marks due to them available for Calais: E 404/52/352, 356, 370.

[29] E 401/748; E 28/56 28 Apr.; *Cal. L. Bk. H*, 204.

[30] Documents from these weeks, some wrongly attributed to 1438, are in *Wars of Eng*. ii. lviii–lx, lxxii–iii, 438; E 28/56 10, 25 Apr.; E 28/57, 12, 14, 19, 20 May. E 403/724; Devon, *Issues*, 428–9; *Foedera*, x. 642; *John Benet's Chronicle*, ed. G. L. and M. A. Harriss, 185.

his army fell short of what had been promised in December, it proved sufficient to check the French advance, to re-establish control over the Pays de Caux, and prepare for the siege of Harfleur. Creil was retaken and raids conducted to the environs of Paris. Early in 1437 Talbot was to recapture Tancarville, rout La Hire at Ry, and surprise Pontoise. In the chroniclers' eyes it was he, rather than York, who made Normandy secure.

That was not surprising, for York lacked the authority and military experience to step into Bedford's shoes, and his appointment as lieutenant governor may have been an afterthought. There is no hint in the records of how soon after Bedford's death the question of a successor began to be discussed, but in the autumn of 1435 it was the military situation that was uppermost in the minds of the English and Norman councils and the need was for a commander to save the duchy rather than a governor to rule it. Louis of Luxembourg had gathered the threads of power into his own hands and had no wish to see his authority displaced. The estates of Normandy had asked for an army under a duke of the royal blood, probably with Gloucester in mind, but his appointment was unlikely on many grounds. He had not visited Normandy since 1421 and was now poised for a war against the duke of Burgundy; moreover it was doubtful whether the cardinal would advance money for an army under his command. Both Cardinal Beaufort and Louis of Luxembourg are likely to have preferred York, Salisbury's brother-in-law, whose youth and gratitude for the cardinal's goodwill would guarantee his pliability.[31] Although York had been named to the post by early March, or even before, the terms of his commission were only being negotiated in late April when the original date of his muster had already passed. This may suggest that his insistence on succeeding to Bedford's position had led to dispute over the extent of his powers. For the eventual terms of his commission specifically debarred him from making appointments to the principal civil and military posts in the duchy or from making grants of escheated fiefs above the value of 1,000 *salus*. His salary was fixed at 30,000 *li. tournois* and the term of his appointment was set at one year.[32]

Having dispatched York, the council returned to the threat to Calais, summoning the lords and all who held fees from the crown to assemble at Canterbury on 22 July. Gloucester was the clear choice as leader; he was

[31] Beaufort had helped York recover the earldom of March lands in 1429 (above, ch. 9 n. 47), secured livery of his estates in May 1432 (*Rot. Parl.* iv. 397–8) for service with Henry VI in France, and invested him with the York estates in July 1433 (*CCR 1429–35*, 260). York was in the Nevill–Beauchamp circle and enfeoffed Warwick, Alnwick, and others with lands before crossing to France in 1436: E 28/57 4 May; Johnson, thesis, 26–7.

[32] The duke's commission is BN MS Fr. 5330 fo. 137 (I have to thank Dr P. A. Johnson for a photocopy of this). A warrant for payment of York on 23 Feb. 1436 speaks only of his indenting for service of war; another to Salisbury on 5 Mar. refers to York as lieutenant of the realm of France: E 404/52/208, 211. For payment of his salary, see Johnson, thesis, 62.

already captain of Calais and was now invested with the county of Flanders.[33] During the early summer Duke Philip had captured the outposts of Oye, Balinghem, and Sandgate and now invested Calais itself. The scene was thus set for the great confrontation between the two princes from which Gloucester had been deflected in the past. Now he was the nation's leader at a time of direst emergency, against an enemy whose deceit he had often denounced. This was to be the hour of his vindication. In the next few days only a small advance party under Lord Welles sailed and Gloucester, with the main body, did not cross until 3 August. In that space the whole situation was transformed. A Flemish attempt to blockade Calais by sea was mishandled and on 28 July Edmund Beaufort and Lord Camoys seized a bastille manned by the men of Ghent with a bold sally, inducing such confusion among the Flemish levies that the whole besieging army retired in disorder on the following day. Gloucester arrived to find the threat to Calais removed. Cheated of the glory of saviour by the cardinal's nephew, he led the army in a systematic devastation of Flanders in which all the pent up national hatred and personal rancour was ferociously vented. By 27 August Gloucester and the army had returned with the spoils.[34] Though he had not met Philip in battle, he now vaunted his role as the successor to Henry V, the defender of England against both Burgundy and France.[35]

The lords had offered to muster at their own expense, but wages for the period overseas were paid immediately on their return. These totalled about £6,000 and a further £1,100 was paid for shipping. This was drawn from two major loans, one of 1,000 marks from Archbishop Chichele, the other of £6,000 from Cardinal Beaufort, both made on 28 August though arranged while the army was assembling at Canterbury on 24 July.[36] It can only have been with considerable reluctance that Beaufort made this further advance. It is true that he had by then been repaid £7,219 of his

[33] Gloucester was acting *in loco regis*; he was commissioned king's lieutenant on 27 July (*Foedera*, x. 651–2) and in the *Brut*, ii. 574 is termed 'Protectoure and Deffendoure of England'. Summons to all fee holders: E 28/57 30 June; general proclamation 3 July *Foedera*, 647–8.

[34] The army numbered 745 men-at-arms and 6,910 archers: *Wars of Eng.* ii. p. xlix. There is considerable confusion among the English chroniclers on Mortain's role: *Chronicles of London*, 142; *Gregory's Chron.* 178–9, both date the raid 12 July and treat it as crucial. Davies, *Eng. Chron.* 55 gives credit to Radclyf; *Brut*, ii. credits Mortain and Camoys with breaking the siege, but the version on pp. 504–5 does not mention them, while that on p. 581 attributes it to the arrival of Lord Welles. Mortain's role is generally emphasized in 'The Ballad of the Siege of Calais', 'Mockery of the Flemings', and 'Scorn of the Duke of Burgundy': *Historical Poems of the Fourteenth and Fifteenth Centuries*, ed. R. H. Robbins, 78–90. For modern accounts, see Vickers, *Duke of Gloucester*, 251–3; Vaughan, *Philip the Good*, 75–83; Thielemans, *Bourgogne et Angleterre*, 90–107.

[35] R. Weiss, 'Humphrey, duke of Gloucester and Tito Livio Frulovisi' in D. J. Gordon (ed.), *Fritz Saxl, Memorial Essays*, 42–4 (discussing the 'Humphroidos').

[36] E 401/748; Steel, *Receipt*, 209; E 28/57 24 July; *CPR 1429–36*, 604.

loan of the previous February from the Whitsun lay subsidy and he probably asked for the new loan to be assigned on the next instalment due at Whitsun 1437. But the treasurer hoped to keep this available for a spring expedition, and Beaufort had to accept assignments on the Southampton customs, even though these were still charged with the loans made by the duchy feoffees. Beaufort stipulated that repayment of his own loan should take priority; even so he waited until May 1438 to regain his money. In a period of seven months he had advanced just on £20,000, and the tally of his loans awaiting repayment was as follows:

(i) £666. 13*s*. 4*d*. lent in May 1434, assigned on the clerical tenth due at Martinmas 1436;
(ii) £6,666. 13*s*. 4*d*. loaned in July 1435 for which he held bonds by the lords of the council but no other security for repayment;
(iii) £2,646. 6*s*. 11*d*. of the loan of 20 February 1436, assigned on the lay subsidy due at Martinmas 1436;
(iv) £2,666. 13*s*. 4*d*. of the loan of 20 February 1436, at first assigned on the lay subsidy due at Whitsun 1437 but changed on 15 May 1437 to the Martinmas 1437 lay subsidy, for which he held jewels as security;
(v) £6,000 loaned in August 1436, to be repaid from the Southampton customs.

Thus at the beginning of 1437 the crown still had some £14,000 of his wealth in its hands.

Nevertheless, it was mainly through his wealth that Beaufort had managed to retain and strengthen his political position after Bedford's death. The year following the Congress of Arras had been one of prolonged crisis, as threats to Normandy and Calais varied with unpredictable intensity. At times the whole fate of the Lancastrian conquest had seemed to hang in the balance. The council had been in virtually continuous session with both Gloucester and Beaufort habitually present and rarely less than six lords in attendance.[37] The need for a common front had dampened political rivalries and precluded action by Gloucester against Beaufort and his supporters. In particular the council depended on the cardinal's wealth to meet military emergencies. Beaufort was undoubtedly under pressure to provide these loans, and insisted on strict safeguards for his payment. All were discussed extensively in the council, their terms were minuted and the names of the lords asenting to them were carefully noted. Moreover, for the large loan of 1435 the lords of the council were still under bond to him. While the danger to Calais enhanced Gloucester's influence in foreign policy and his claim to act as defender of the king and realm, Beaufort's ready purse and close liaison with the council preserved

[37] The files covering Sept. 1435–Aug. 1436 are extremely full: E 28/56, 57; C 81/1545/56–9.

his own standing and that of his supporters. Beaufort, Kemp, and Cromwell were not only assiduous in attendance but were mainly responsible for planning and implementing the council's response to the crisis. Their vigour and command of the administrative and financial machinery made them indispensable.

Further, the crisis enabled Cardinal Beaufort to involve his nephews in the defence of France and revive the long-standing Beaufort interest in Maine and Anjou which Bedford's death had opened up. Indeed the cardinal's ambition probably stretched further ahead to grasp for the Beauforts the position which Bedford had held. In 1436 the family had no candidate to match the claims by birth or dignity of Gloucester or indeed York. The cardinal was ready to support York's military command and was constrained to accept his investiture with Bedford's title, though with Maine and Anjou withdrawn from his command and the major fiefs and offices reserved to the council. When, in fact, York attempted to override the grant of the d'Alencourt fiefs to Edmund by bestowing them on the Duchess Jacquetta, the council on 2 April 1437 upheld Edmund's grant.[38] Such a clash of interests in no way predicated a rivalry between them. Indeed while York's service in France was both fitting and obligatory for a young and able nobleman, it could hardly be anticipated that he would seek a long-term career there. His extensive English and Irish estates dictated a role in English politics; whereas for the landless Beauforts France afforded major opportunities. Both York and the council must have envisaged York's commission as temporary, the response to a military emergency. Even so its significance for the interests of his nephews is unlkely to have escaped the cardinal. A successor to York would have to be found if the ambitious young duke were not to become the heir to Bedford by default.

Despite Gloucester's captaincy of Calais and feud with Burgundy, and Beaufort's friendship with Louis of Luxembourg and dynastic interests in France, there is little to suggest that in these months there was a struggle between rival groups favouring the commitment of resources to Calais or Normandy. The council recognized that their fate was interdependent and that neither could be abandoned in 1436 without endangering the other. It was ready to switch resources as the threat shifted to either, and though Beaufort's loan was originally made for Normandy, most of it was in the event spent in the defence of Calais. Nevertheless tension between Beaufort and Gloucester persisted beneath the surface and was manifested in minor ways. Gloucester's indentures for Calais were debated at length in parliament and reduced from twelve to nine years. At a council meeting in May 1436, from which Beaufort and Cromwell were absent, it was decided

[38] BN MS Fr. 26549 no. 19.

as a matter of policy to prefer the payment of life annuities (such as Gloucester held) to the repayment of loans.[39]

Tension is more discernible between the cardinal and the Company of the Staple. In December 1435 the treasurer, with the support of Beaufort, Kemp, and Alnwick, again sanctioned an evasion of the Partition Ordinance to raise money for the standing subvention to the chancellor of France. This time he raised a loan of 8,000 marks from three Staplers, Hamo Sutton, Hugh Dyke, and William Estfeld, by licencing them to sell their wool at Calais freely and 'without any restriction and partition'.[40] Repayment was guaranteed to them by act of parliament from the lands of Bedford and others in the king's hand, and collateral security was provided by Beaufort himself who, on 8 November, granted to Kemp, Cromwell, Alnwick, Edmund Beaufort, Hugh Dyke, Richard Buckland, John Asshe, and Thomas Walsingham 1,000 marks p.a. for the term of his life to be levied from certain episcopal manors.[41] The merchants thus purchased the opportunity to dispose of their wools unhampered by the ordinance at a time when trade at Calais was at a standstill, while the treasurer was enabled to dispatch £5,248 to Louis of Luxembourg by their hands.[42] Beaufort's readiness to abet a breach of the ordinance would clearly not have endeared him to the company which, indeed, conspicuously refused any contribution to the sustained effort to raise loans throughout the spring and summer of 1436. This was despite the council's specific request to the mayor of the Staple, Nicholas Wooton, for a loan of 10,000 marks for the wages of York's army, followed up by a letter conveyed through the cardinal's servant William Flete. This too met with refusal, Flete complaining that he had received 'little tendernesse or noon but rather malice and wrong' from the merchants.[43] Though Beaufort had close

[39] *Rot. Parl.* iv. 483–4; *PPC* iv. 339; E 404/52/399.

[40] *Studies in Eng. Trad*, 86–7; *English Economic History: Select Documents* ed. A. E. Bland *et al.*, 185–6; Holmes, 'Libel', 203; C 76/118 m. 19. E 401/744 18 Jan. for the loan.

[41] *Rot. Parl.* iv. 485–6; *CPR 1429–36*, 498; E 404/52/371. Beaufort's grant is in *Reg. CS* 78–9; *CCR 1435–41*, 38–9; E 28/57. It is capable of more than one explanation. The fact that Beaufort, Kemp, Alnwick, and Cromwell were trustees for the repayment of the merchants' loan and that Beaufort, Cromwell, and Buckland were Bedford's executors links it to this transaction. Yet one would expect all three merchants to be among the grantees, not just Dyke, and it was unusual to grant life annuities to discharge a specific debt. McFarlane (thesis, pp. K 12–15) interpreted it as an investment of 1,000 marks p.a. by Beaufort in the wool trade; but it was an inauspicious moment for such a venture, only two of the grantees were merchants, and the bishopric pipe rolls show no payments from these manors to any of them (HRO, Eccles. II. 159429). This similarly militates against the suggestion by Greatrex (*Reg. CS* loc. cit.) that these were pensions to those named. Whichever explanation is favoured, it is clear that Beaufort was closely linked with these leading merchants. Repayment was warranted 22 June and assigned 11 July mainly from Bedford's lands: E 404/52/371; E 401/744.

[42] E 403/722, 16 Dec., 26 Mar.

[43] E 28/56 1 Mar.; C 1/16/448 cited by Holmes, 'Libel', 211. Payments for Flete's journey in E 403/721.

connections with individual Staplers, the company itself viewed his Flemish sympathies with distrust.

Among the nobility Cardinal Beaufort enjoyed a direct family relationship with the Nevills and through them a more distant one with families some of whom had been former opponents of the house of Lancaster. Joan Beaufort's determination to endow her own children at the expense of her husband's heir by his first marriage brought a potentially dangerous split in the Nevill family. The settlement made after her marriage had remained unchallenged during the first earl's lifetime, but when in 1429 Ralph, second earl of Westmorland inherited his grandfather's title, he quickly showed himself determined to challenge his disinheritance from the bulk of the patrimonial estates in favour of Joan's son Richard, earl of Salisbury. In August 1430 both Westmorland on the one side and the Countess Joan on the other were bound in recognizances of £2,000 apiece not to pursue their quarrel by force, and were assigned a day to plead before the council. Westmorland complained that his inheritance had been reduced from 4,000 marks a year to a mere 600 marks p.a., while Salisbury's landed resources were fortified by his tenure of the wardenship of the West March.[44] The successful renegotiation of the Scottish truce for five years in December 1430 released Salisbury to join his uncle, the cardinal, on his return to France in May 1431. He safeguarded his position by securing reappointment as warden until 1434 and by requiring the council to place Westmorland under obligations not to pursue his claims either by force or legal judgement during that period. Westmorland complained bitterly at being deprived of his rights, but merely succeeded in getting the bond reduced from 10,000 marks to £4,000.[45] Three years later the cardinal's influence once again deterred Westmorland from pressing his claim. Some time in 1434 there came to light in the monastery at Durham a will of Ralph, first earl of Westmorland dated 1400, and thus prior to the enfeoffments of 1404 which had deprived the elder branch of the inheritance. Pressed by the second earl to open it and read it in public, Prior Wessington in October sent his attorney to report to the cardinal and the Countess Joan in London and thence to the council, which forbade him to surrender the document without the consent of both parties. Nevertheless soon afterwards Wessington delivered the box of documents to the countess and her son and the will disappeared without trace.[46] In July 1434 Salisbury had added the East March to his commission, and when

[44] *CCR 1429–35*, 67. For the original enfeoffment disinheriting the elder line, *CPR 1401–5*, 470. Accounts of the dispute are in Storey, *End of the House of Lancaster*, 109–14 and J. Petre, 'The Nevills of Brancepeth and Raby, 1425–99', *The Ricardian*, 5 (1981), 418–35. See also E 28/53 nos. 72–5 dated 9 Henry VI.

[45] *CCR 1429–35*, 125; E 404/47/321; *PPC* iv. 79. He had returned to council by May 1432: ibid 113.

[46] R. B. Dobson, *Durham Priory, 1400–1450*, 189–90.

Westmorland's recognizance expired at Michaelmas he was forced to renew it on the same terms until Easter 1436. By then, in response to the military crisis in France, Salisbury was preparing to serve abroad with Suffolk and York, and the recognizance was again extended until a year following his return.[47] When he did so he at once became a prominent member of the council and the years from 1438 to 1443 saw a series of attempts by the council to settle the Nevill dispute, in which the cardinal's associates and family used their influence.

In May 1438 Westmorland was persuaded to abide the arbitrament of Kemp, Alnwick, Hungerford, and Lyndwood, but such a group so evidently lacked the requisite impartiality that, not surprisingly, within a few months the quarrel flared up, with 'grete rowtes and compaignies upon the field', and both parties were summoned before the council in February and May 1439 and placed under new bonds until Easter 1440.[48] The death of the Countess Joan in 1440, leaving Beaufort and Kemp to act as supervisors of her will, helped to hasten a settlement. Shortly beforehand she had demised Sheriff Hutton and her Yorkshire lands to Salisbury, who now also secured Middleham, while Westmorland inherited her dower lands. In 1441 both sides fortified their positions by enfeoffments of these acquisitions: Salisbury to Cardinal Beaufort and his own retainers, Westmorland to his son and daughter-in-law whose father, the earl of Huntingdon, together with Northumberland and Stafford, acted as witnesses.[49] Finally, by an award made in August and September 1443, facilitated by Prior Wessington's tireless mediation, Westmorland acknowledged the estate of Cardinal Beaufort, Salisbury, Latimer, and Faucomberg in all the lands received from the first earl, with small exceptions, under a penalty of £400 p.a. if he attempted to reverse it.[50] Thus, through almost a decade and a half, Beaufort's influence in council had been used at critical points to protect Salisbury's acquisition of the Nevill lands and to confirm the disinheritance of the second earl, a position he was finally forced to concede. Territorially this meant the entrenchment of Nevill–Beaufort influence in north Yorkshire and Durham, where it was further strengthened by the translation of the cardinal's nephew Robert to the see in succession to Langley in January 1438.

In the preceding years the defence of the north had been very largely organized under the Nevill–Beaufort aegis. Despite the five-year truce procured by Beaufort in 1430, by 1433 border raiding had begun to assume

[47] *CCR 1429–35*, 346–7; *CCR 1435–41*, 56; *Select Cases before the King's Council*, ed. I. S. Leadam and J. F. Baldwin (Selden Soc., 1918), 101–2.

[48] *PPC* iv. 289–90, v. 90–2; *CCR 1435–41*, 178–9, 199, 276–9; *Excerpta Historica*, 1–3.

[49] *CCR 1435–41*, 407–9, 478–81; *CCR 1441–7*, 12–13; *PPC* v. 179–80; *Formulare Anglicanum*, ed. F. Madox, 141–6.

[50] Dobson, *Durham Priory*, 191; *PPC* v. 282–3; *CCR 1441–7*, 150–1, 195–9; 43rd *DKR*, 243.

serious proportions and in August Beaufort's negotiators, his nephew Edmund and his clerk Stephen Wilton, were sent to register a protest.[51] As full-scale raiding engulfed the border, further embassies were dispatched in 1434 and 1435. Salisbury was made warden of both marches and negotiations were entrusted to a group of northern barons and churchmen of the Nevill–Beaufort interest: Salisbury, Lumley, Richard Leyot, and Stephen Wilton.[52] Finally in 1436 Burgundy's siege of Calais encouraged James I to attempt the capture of Roxburgh. When the siege commenced in August, Northumberland, Kemp, Langley, and Lumley improvised a council for the defence of the north; but it was the dissensions in the Scottish camp, provoked by the years of James's harsh rule, rather than military considerations, which caused the siege to be abandoned and set in train the conspiracies which were to lead to James's murder.[53] Thus at Roxburgh, as at Calais, the English had been saved more by their enemies' weakness than by their own military efforts, and Beaufort had narrowly escaped the devastating verdict on his policy that the fall of either place would have represented. His influence in the north was, if anything, confirmed when Lumley took over the wardenship of the West March for seven years in November 1436.

The marriages of Joan Beaufort's daughters had served to bring former opponents of Lancaster into a relationship with the new royal house, but the Nevill family quarrel and the rise of Salisbury's power in the north threatened to reactivate some of these divisions. The earl of Northumberland was married to Joan's daughter Eleanor Nevill, but Gloucester had made some efforts to win over him and the earl of Huntingdon by appointing them joint wardens of the marches in succession to Salisbury in July 1435. In November 1435 they were joint guarantors for the duke's licence to create a jointure for his duchess, Eleanor, for which he undertook to recompense the crown with 2,500 marks. Both were, moreover, drawn into links with the senior branch of the Nevills through the marriage of Northumberland's sister to the second earl of Westmorland in 1426 and that of Huntingdon's daughter to Westmorland's son John in 1440.[54] Another of Joan's daughters, Catherine, had been the wife of Gloucester's ally John, duke of Norfolk, but on his death in 1432 the cardinal himself undertook the administration of the Mowbray estates during the minority of his heir.[55] Beaufort's two remaining nieces were the wives of the duke of York and the earl of Stafford. York was indebted to

[51] *PPC* iv. 178, 347, 351; *Rot. Scot.* ii. 282–3.

[52] *Rot. Scot.* ii. 288; *Foedera*, x. 620; *PPC*, iv. 308–15.

[53] Storey, *Langley*, 159–62; Nicholson, *Scotland*, 323.

[54] *CPR 1429–36*, 503–5. In May 1429 Northumberland had been one of those invested with rents from the episcopal estates (*Reg. CS* 66–7) but never otherwise appears among Beaufort's feoffees.

[55] *CPR 1429–35*, 197. Below, ch. 18 n. 51.

him for procuring delivery of his inheritance, and Stafford by his hopes of recovering the Holderness lands on the death of the aged duchess of Clarence. Stafford's affinity to the Beauforts was to be further strengthened by the marriage of his eldest son to Margaret, the daughter of Edmund Beaufort, in 1444. Meanwhile the careers of his half-brothers, the Bourchiers, were advanced by the promotion of Thomas to the see of Worcester in 1435 and the summons to parliament of Henry in 1433. Thus Joan Beaufort's sons-in-law were for the most part favourably disposed towards the cardinal.

Beaufort influence was further extended through the connections of Salisbury's own family. In 1436 strong links were forged between the Nevills and Beauchamps by the double marriage of Salisbury's children Cecily and Richard to Henry Beauchamp and his sister Anne. These were the children of Richard, earl of Warwick's second wife, Isabella, whose daughter by her former marriage, Elizabeth, was married to Edward Nevill, Lord Bergavenny, another of the cardinal's nephews. Edward Nevill's elder brother George, Lord Latimer, had married one of the three daughters of the earl of Warwick's first marriage, his brothers-in-law being John, Lord Talbot and Edmund Beaufort, count of Mortain. Many ties of kinship thus linked the Beauchamp–Nevill–Beaufort houses, strengthening in the 1430s a tradition of support for the house of Lancaster which dated back to the beginning of the century. Warwick himself, not merely a veteran of Henry V's wars, but governor of the young king, was a close and long-standing colleague of the cardinal, even if after 1434 he attended council infrequently. In the younger generation these ties were manifested in the companionship in war of Lords Talbot, Latimer, Faucomberg, and Mortain.

Two other members of the upper nobility, the earls of Devon and Suffolk, both had links with Beaufort of another kind. The young earl of Devon, Thomas Courtenay, was married to the cardinal's niece Margaret, daughter of John, earl of Somerset, but he played no prominent part in either English politics or the French war in the 1430s.[56] Suffolk was distantly linked to the house of Beaufort by his marriage to Alice Chaucer; though in general favouring the cardinal's diplomatic policy, there is little direct evidence of a close association between the two at this date.[57] Suffolk's independent influence only began to be demonstrated after 1437. Thus, as head of his family, the cardinal enjoyed extensive connections, forged principally through Joan Beaufort, with a broad swathe of the

[56] For his weak position, see M. Cherry, 'The struggle for power in mid-fifteenth century Devonshire', in R. A. Griffiths (ed.), *Patronage, Crown and Provinces*, 125–6. His first clash with Lord Bonville came in 1440.

[57] Beaufort, Gloucester, Warwick, and Stafford had been Suffolk's feoffees, releasing the lands to him on 6 July 1435 (BL Add. Ch. 2016) and Suffolk appears with Beaufort as joint feoffee for Lewis John in 1433: *CCR 1435–41*, 67.

higher nobility, which undoubtedly fortified his political position. Gloucester, by contrast, was not directly related to any of the nobility, even those whom he claimed as political allies.

As bishop of Winchester and the principal feoffee of the duchy estates, Beaufort exercised a clientage in many localities, while from his years abroad he had acquired a following from those who had been in his military and diplomatic service. A number of individuals can be mentioned though the extent of the cardinal's 'affinity' and the nature of its service defies analysis. His cousin and lifelong associate Thomas Chaucer died in November 1434 and to his post as constable of Taunton Beaufort appointed his son-in-law Sir Edward Stradling. In the bishopric William Whaplode became steward in that year and William Mareys keeper of Wolvesey. Whaplode, along with Renfrew Arundell, accompanied Beaufort to Arras. The cardinal's main legal and financial advisers were John Asshe and William Flete, and other business associates included Hamo Sutton, Lewis John, William Tresham, Nicholas Radford, and Richard Buckland. A number of these sat in the parliaments of the 1430s, though there is no evidence that they owed this to the cardinal's influence. Doubtless they formed a sympathetic element in the Commons, but none of them succeeded to the role filled by Thomas Chaucer in the previous decades. Among the bishop's retainers quite a few served as sheriffs, notably Sir John Seymour and John and Thomas Uvedale in Hampshire, John St Loo and William Caraunt in Somerset and Dorset, Thomas Uvedale and Richard Waller in Surrey and Kent. All these were men of standing in their shires and known to the central administration as reliable servants. Beyond and below the support of his colleagues in the council and the nobility, the cardinal was able to draw on the abilities and experience of his retainers and associates for both his personal and public concerns.

The cardinal's influence was likewise extensive within the church. The years 1433–5 were not prolific in episcopal vacancies. However, Morgan's death left a vacancy at Ely in October 1435 and the council again found itself at loggerheads with the pope. Royal letters recommended Thomas Rudbourne to the chapter and a bull of provision was sought for him. Rudbourne, a chaplain of Henry V, canon of Salisbury, and bishop of St David's since 1433, accompanied Beaufort to Arras and was probably his candidate for the see. But in August 1436 the Ely chapter elected Thomas Bourchier, whom the pope then agreed to translate, proposing at the same time to translate Rudbourne to Worcester.[58] Whose influence lay behind this is not easy to say; it may have been Gloucester's, for in April 1437 Eugenius wrote to him and Henry VI urging the acceptance of this

[58] *CPL* viii. 230–1; *BRUO* 1582; *Reg. Chichele*, i. p. xciv; Hamilton Thompson, *English Clergy*, 21–2.

arrangement and further promising to translate Rudbourne to Ely when Bourchier could be moved to a suitable vacancy. Yet in June 1437 Henry wrote to the pope, from Kennington, and after apologizing for a change of mind, now proposed that Louis of Luxembourg be appointed as administrator of the see of Ely, to be held *in commendam* with that of Rouen, the revenues of which were said to be insufficient, accompanying his letter with similar ones to Cardinals Orsini, Castiglione, and others. This proposal, and the orchestrated pressure on the Curia, clearly emanated from Cardinal Beaufort. It was successful, but Chichele deplored it as 'an evil precedent, to the great detriment and loss of the English church', and felt so strongly that he refused to deliver the spiritualities to Louis, compelling Eugenius to authorize Beaufort and Kemp to do so in his place if their exhortations, made 'with due modesty and good arguments', failed to move the archbishop.[59] The affair further distanced Beaufort from Chichele and attested the latter's ineffectuality and withdrawal.

By contrast, a series of translations in 1436 were accomplished smoothly, perhaps through the medium of the papal collector, Piero da Monte, who arrived after the Congress of Arras and with whom Beaufort quickly established close relations.[60] The death of William Gray of Lincoln in February allowed the translation of Beaufort's colleague Alnwick to that see and the translation of Thomas Brouns to Norwich, all effected by papal bulls of 19 September 1436. A bull of the same date provided William Wells to Rochester. Wells was abbot of St Mary's York, and an experienced diplomat: he had attended the council of Constance in 1414–17 and was the king's envoy to the council of Basel in company with Edmund Beaufort in 1434. He was subsequently to conduct negotiations with the French at Calais in 1440.[61] Rochester was traditionally within the patronage of the archbishop, but Wells was more the cardinal's follower than Chichele's. The fourth vacancy, that of London, occurred with the death of Fitzhugh in January 1436 and was filled by the provision of Robert Gilbert on 20 June. Gilbert was an exact contemporary of Rudbourne as fellow and warden of Merton and had been ordained by Beaufort in St Mary's, Oxford, in 1402. Like Rudbourne, he became a chaplain of Henry V and dean of the chapel royal and had been at Constance. In the 1420s he had become dean of York and of Tickhill, of which Beaufort was warden, but in 1432 Gloucester had removed him from the chapel royal and his career came to a halt.[62] His promotion to London must have been unexpected, and bears the mark of an overdue recognition of past services

[59] Bekynton *Correspondence*, i. 4–11; *CPL* viii. 252, 254.

[60] Haller, *Piero da Monte*, 15–17, 192–3, 215 (suppl. nos. 6, 8, 28); Schofield, 'Council of Basel', 92.

[61] *CPL* viii. 613; *Reg. Chichele*, i. 121–2; *Foedera*, x. 589; *BRUO* iii. 2012.

[62] *CPL* viii. 613; *BRUO* ii. 766; LAO, Reg. Beaufort, fo. 102^{v}.

and perhaps of Beaufort's long standing friendship with him. Finally, the death of Langley in November 1437 allowed the translation of Robert Nevill, Beaufort's nephew, from Salisbury to Durham. The bull was issued on 27 January 1438 on the recommendation of Henry VI, who wrote of the desirability of having a native of the area and one from a leading family in the see.[63] Nevill was indeed to prove a powerful bishop, not least in promoting the interests of his family. From 1433 to 1437 Beaufort's influence had finally determined every promotion to the episcopate, and the character of those appointed indicates where his own preferences lay. The two aristocrats bespoke his political alliances; the remainder were professionals in the mould of Henry V's churchmen, Beaufort's associates in diplomatic and ecclesiastical business. They were men of an older generation overdue for reward, and they reflected the narrowing circle among whom the cardinal now tended to move. These appointments in the last years of the minority represented neither new blood nor fresh channels of advancement, such as were to be manifested in the first promotions of 1438, of Ayscough to Salisbury and Praty to Chichester.

The dioceses of Salisbury, Wells, and Chichester had for long provided Beaufort with prebends for his clerks, and during 1432–7 he could count on the willing co-operation of Bishops Nevill, Stafford, and Sydenham. In the Winchester diocese his vicar-general John Forest and his chancellor Nicholas Bildeston continued to hold the two archdeaconries of Surrey and Winchester. Forest was to die in 1443, bequeathing Beaufort, 'my most special prince and lord', £40 to buy a jewel, though enjoining a limit of £20 for his own funeral expenses.[64] Bildeston remained active, succeeding Thomas Brouns as dean of Salisbury in 1435 and securing canonries in Lincoln, Wells, and York in 1434–5, while Louis of Luxembourg appointed him his vicar-general in the see of Ely.[65] Bildeston was the most important and trusted of Beaufort's officials, and directly involved in the efforts to repair relations with Flanders in 1437–8. In these years Stephen Wilton was being groomed as his successor, serving alongside Bildeston in the Anglo-Flemish negotiations of 1438–40, by which time he had succeeded him as the cardinal's chancellor and a year later as archdeacon of Winchester. He acquired numerous canonries in the dioceses of Lincoln, London, Salisbury, and York.[66] Nicholas Caraunt also started his career in these years under Beaufort and Nevill patronage, with canonries in Salisbury and Wells, where he later became dean and then secretary to Queen Margaret of Anjou.[67] Adam Moleyns, who had been the king's proctor at the Curia

[63] Bekynton, *Correspondence*, i. 92.
[64] *BRUO* ii. 706; *Somerset Medieval Wills, 1383–1500*, ed. F. W. Weaver, 152–4.
[65] *BRUO* i. 188.
[66] *BRUO* iii. 2053.
[67] *BRUO* i. 653.

in 1435, where his addiction to Beaufort's interests had brought a protest from Chichele, received his first canonry at Wedmore in 1436 on returning to England to become clerk to the council.[68] Between them Beaufort and Kemp largely controlled promotion in the English church in these years, just as they also controlled its relations with the papacy.

During the year following the Congress of Arras the English retained a lively hostility to Cardinal Albergati, as Aeneas Sylvius testifies, but the crown's support for Eugenius against the council of Basel was never in doubt. This was determined partly by Beaufort's own influence, partly by that of Piero da Monte, and considerably by Eugenius's readiness to acquiesce in royal demands. It also reflected the young king's own deep religiosity and respect for priestly authority.[69] It may be assumed, though it cannot be attested, that this was encouraged by Beaufort, whom Henry undoubtedly regarded and treated with reverence. It is certain that the events of 1435, when Henry was nearly 14, made a powerful impact on him and brought home his impending responsibilities. The cardinal's central role in them helped to mould Henry's response, and some of his first letters were on matters which Beaufort had most at heart. In July 1435 he wrote to his aunt Isabel, duchess of Burgundy, expatiating on the blessings of peace, and subsequently his mortification on receiving Duke Philip's letters explaining his desertion was bitter and personal. In the following months he used his signet to summon the lords to council and parliament, and to write to the garrisons and commanders in Normandy, and to the duke of York, chiding him for his delay in sailing. Henry was deeply moved by the crisis of his heritage in France, and Lannoy was not alone in appreciating that with his fifteenth birthday his views and wishes would become of prime importance. It was in anticipation of this that Warwick surrendered his formal governorship in May 1436 and the council began to refer undecided or contentious issues to the king.[70]

More immediately, however, Henry's personal authority was manifested in a series of grants of revenues and privileges to the lords assembled for the invasion of Flanders in the summer of 1436. It was a fitting occasion to reward loyal service, and York, Salisbury, and Gloucester all benefited from the payment of their arrears or the pardon of their dues to the crown. The earls of Devon, Oxford, and Suffolk had licences to alienate lands and the duke of Norfolk to enter his inheritance.[71] Cardinal Beaufort procured a number of benefits for himself and his family: grants of wardships to the

[68] *CPL* viii. 233; Haller, *Piero da Monte*, 211 (suppl. 25).

[69] See da Monte's description of Henry VI in 1437: Haller, *Piero da Monte*, 43–5, quoted by Schofield, 'Council of Basel', 93–4. For Eugenius's letter to Beaufort in 1435 seeking support against the council, see Haller, op. cit. 210 (suppl. 24).

[70] For Henry's intervention in these months see in general E 28/56, 57 (e.g. 19 May, 30 June for his decision on the amount granted to Sir Thomas Rempston for his ransom). Lannoy's memorandum is translated by Vaughan, *Philip the Good*, 105.

[71] Grants to York, and his lieutenant John Popham: E 404/52/344, 395–6, *PPC* iv. 337; to

duchess of Clarence and Edmund Beaufort, and the repayment of £1,000 for his attendance on the king in France in 1430–1 from sources of his own choosing.[72] All these grants were authorized by the council during the well-attended sessions of the early summer of 1436. The last recorded day on which Gloucester was present was 27 July, and on the day following Henry warranted one final grant, signing the warrant 'Henry' with his own hand, this being the first occasion on which his signature appears on an official document. This recited that, in consideration of the multiple and gratuitous services rendered by the cardinal, the king had granted him '*de nostro ac mero motu*' the manor of Canford and town of Poole, formerly held by Bedford, for life and without any render.[73] The date suggests that this was the reward for his final loan for Gloucester's expedition, and the form of the grant indicates that it was secured after the dispersal of the council, by Beaufort's private suggestion to the king. It had symbolic importance, as being the first life grant of a crown property in the reign, the first alienation from Bedford's lands, and the first grant authorized solely by the king's sign manual. In each respect it was merely the first of a flood of such grants, and Beaufort must bear the odium and responsibility for encouraging the young king's prodigality. Nevertheless, the enormity of the precedent can easily be exaggerated. Canford and Poole were worth about £50 p.a. and the life expectancy of the cardinal was not great. A significant proportion of his wealth was at present in the crown's hands and its repayment was likely to be prolonged; nor was he receiving any interest on his loans. The precedent had none the less been set and Henry had been alerted to his powers of patronage and favour. The effective *terminus a quo* from which Henry appears to have exercised free disposal of patronage by his own warrants appears to have been a crown wearing at Merton on 1 November 1436.[74] This was the culmination of a great council held in the second half of October in the parliament chamber at Westminster, which probably made a conscious decision on this. The first beneficiaries were the members of Henry's chapel and household who were at Kennington in the following weeks. Between 7 and 30 November Henry signed twenty-seven petitions from members of his entourage. While these grants were being made at Kennington, the council met regularly in the Star Chamber, and when the king joined them on 21 November they thought fit to advise him that offices should be granted strictly according to the degree of the petitioner. They had perhaps been taken aback by his indiscriminate largess.[75]

Salisbury: E 403/721; E 28/56 9 Mar., E 28/57 26 June; to Gloucester: E 28/55 11 July, E 28/57 24 July, *CPR 1429–36*, 503–5; to Norfolk, Devon, Suffolk, and Oxford: E 28/57 20 May, 26 July.

[72] *CPR 1429–36*, 510; E 28/57 26 July, 17 Aug., E 404/52/338–9.
[73] E 28/57 28 July; *CPR 1429–36*, 601.
[74] *PPC* v. 63.
[75] These are all in E 28/58 (cf. Wolffe, *Henry VI*, 88). On 16 Nov. an additional sum was

By the end of 1436, then, Cardinal Beaufort could feel confident that his own position was secure and that, despite the death of Bedford, the network of his political allies remained intact, while his influence in the church was probably more unchallenged than at any previous point in his career. Even so he can have been under no illusions about the damage wrought to the English position in France and to his own credibility as its diplomatic defender by the events of the past eighteen months. That commitment became daily more onerous, its ultimate viability less predictable. The cardinal's advancing years, Bedford's death, and Gloucester's enmity must at times have oppressed him. Moreover, whether he sensed it or not, he was now moving into a new era, when the assumptions of Henry V's great vision would no longer command unthinking acceptance and the men who had devoted their lives to fulfilling it were passing from the scene. A young king of a very different temper, a new generation of nobility, and churchmen of a different mould and training were quickly coming to the fore, with their own demands and priorities. It is entirely credible that at this point Beaufort began to have thoughts about withdrawing from the council and even of resigning his see. By April 1437 he had reached the point of indicating his desire to journey to Rome, possibly to resign his see into the pope's hands and in effect to nominate his successor.[76] From that the council dissuaded him, for the problems of France and Burgundy still posed their inexorable demands and the cardinal's wealth, experience, and prestige were some of the greatest assets left to the English. The cardinal himself realized that the last service he could render to the memory of Henry V and to his heir was to safeguard the duchy of Normandy for the foreseeable future. The interests of his own family could likewise be defended and advanced, and the malevolence of Gloucester forestalled, if the young and impressionable king remained accessible to those whom Beaufort trusted. Retirement was impossible if all that he had striven to safeguard was not to be jeopardized; he would have to tread the mill for six years more.

provided for chamber expenses and on 23 Nov. Gloucester procured the grant of the Channel Islands. The council's reprimand is *PPC* v. 3.

[76] *PPC* v. 9; *CPL* viii. 260. For the possibility that this was connected with investigations into Queen Catherine's marriage to Owen Tudor, see above, ch. 9 n. 34.

14

Finance and the French War, 1436–1439

As the passions aroused by the Anglo-Burgundian rupture began to cool, both sides quickly appreciated the need for a new *modus vivendi*. The wool trade was the life blood of both states, yet from 1436 to 1439 this barely reached 1,600 sacks in any year.[1] Only thereafter did trade revive. This crippled Burgundian finances and excited disaffection in the Flemish cloth towns, already bitterly divided by recriminations over the Calais fiasco. Rebellion, famine, and unemployment in Flanders undermined ducal authority and increased Philip's dependence on Charles VII to an unwelcome degree. To restore Burgundy to a position of true independence and neutrality, such as had been the duke's aim at Arras, commercial intercourse and political relations with England had to be renewed. All these considerations were urged upon the duke by Lannoy in September 1436 and in the next two years his influence and that of other Anglophile councillors was given a powerful lead by the Duchess Isabel.[2]

For the English the arguments for a *rapprochement* were no less powerful. The subsidy on wool exports was the largest single item of revenue and a prime security for loans; its virtual disappearance jeopardized the whole of royal finance. At the same time the unresolved hostilities with Burgundy required the maintenance of a strengthened garrison at Calais and the protection of the continuing cloth trade with Holland by a fleet. Moreover, there was every reason to expect that the French would follow up their diplomatic victory at Arras and their recovery of Paris with a sustained attack on Normandy, which would likewise call for increased military expenditure. To restore trade with Flanders and some informal understanding with the duke would neutralize his ties with the French court and enable the English to concentrate on the defence of Normandy. This, essentially, was to be Beaufort's policy over the next three years, and it was pursued with a fair measure of success. Such a policy was bound to arouse opposition from particular interests. Gloucester sought to keep alive the anti-Burgundian sentiments which had made him the man of the hour in 1436 and, as captain of Calais, he

[1] *Eng. Export Trade*, 60: sacks exported by
(*a*) denizens: 66 (1436–7), 156 (1437–8), 505 (1438–9);
(*b*) aliens: 1571 (1436–7), 1392 (1437–8), 1071 (1438–9).

[2] For Lannoy's memorandum: Vaughan, *Philip the Good*, 102–7; Thielemans, *Bourgogne et Angleterre*, 111; Taylor, thesis, ch. 5 1, 2.

demanded priority for strengthening its defences. The Company of the Staple supported that, and remained suspicious of any sell-out to Flemish demands for a mitigation of the Partition Ordinance and bullion requirements, though it greatly desired a resumption of trade.

These counter-pressures on both the English and Burgundian sides, and the intensity of hatred generated by the events of 1435–6, explain the long delays in initiating negotiations and the caution with which Beaufort and Isabel approached their task of reconciliation. Yet fundamentally no alternative policy was practicable, and the wilder measures advocated in the *Libelle*, such as imposing a blockade on foreign shipping bound for Flanders, received no more support from the council than they had from Henry V when first made in 1420. Indeed it was essentially to Henry V's pre–1420 policy of securing Burgundian neutrality through commercial ties that Beaufort and the central core of the council reverted in these years. It viewed the defence of Calais and the seas as essential, but subsidiary to the threat to Normandy, and sought to safeguard Calais by negotiations with Burgundy rather than through intimidation.

The parliament which met from 21 January to 27 March 1437 saw the high point of Gloucester's influence. A sympathetic Commons, led by his servant Sir John Tyrell, raised the Calais allocation from the wool subsidy from one mark to one pound and sought guarantees from the treasurer that any deficiency arising from the slump in wool exports would be made good from crown revenues.[3] More immediate and tangible relief was provided by a loan of 2,000 marks from the feoffees of the duchy of Lancaster, now effectively Beaufort and Hungerford, while not long after the end of the parliament a much larger loan of 20,000 marks was negotiated from the Company of the Staple, a measure of its concern with the situation at Calais. Gloucester was probably instrumental in obtaining it, though by the time that it was paid over, in July and late October, his influence was already waning.[4] The Commons had prefaced their grant with a commendation of Gloucester for his defence of Calais and also of Beaufort for his boundless generosity.

While under the aegis of Gloucester the attention of parliament had been mainly directed towards the security of Calais, that of the council was concentrated on the reinforçing of Normandy. Early in April it negotiated loans from its members including one from Beaufort for 10,000 marks, intended for an army to accompany the new lieutenant.[5] York's commission of 1 May 1436 had been for one year, and on 7 April 1437 the

[3] *Rot. Parl.* iv. 499, 502. The subsidy bill reveals doubt about whether the increase was necessary and in July the council was still undecided between one mark and one pound: *PPC* v. 43.

[4] *Rot. Parl.* iv, 496; *PPC* v. 26; *CPR 1436–41*, 175. The loan is recorded on the receipt roll for 19 July and 29 Oct. It was repaid from the lay and clerical subsidies: E 401/752, 754; E 404/54/136.

[5] *PPC* v. 13, 16.

council ordered him to remain at his post until his successor was named. The choice must have been under considersation towards the end of the parliament and Gloucester himself had obvious claims to an office which he had sporadically coveted. Yet quite apart from the question of his military suitability, neither Cardinal Beaufort nor Louis of Luxembourg were prepared to countenance the bestowal of the rich patronage of lands and offices enjoyed by Bedford on Duke Humphrey, and Louis travelled to London to make his representations to the council.[6] In the event Louis was well content with the choice of the aged earl of Warwick for a further limited period of eighteen months, with powers similar to those of York. The choice of Warwick, the size of his retinue, and the terms of service had been decided by 18 April when Beaufort made his loan, and in the following three weeks agreement was reached on Warwick's financial claims against the crown. Beaufort, who had been intimately concerned in framing the terms, sent his ring via Suffolk to indicate his approval when the earl's indentures were finally sealed with the council on 11 May.[7]

The appointment of Warwick was clearly stage-managed by Beaufort, Kemp, and Cromwell, with the active support of Louis of Luxembourg. Warwick himself clearly took some persuading, complaining that it was 'fulle farre from the ease of my years, and from the continuall labour of my person at sieges and daily occupacion in the war'; but there was no pretence that he was to engage in war himself or to be more than a figurehead. His eighteen-month commission gave a further breathing space in which the claimants to Bedford's position could be promoted. Given the general presumption that the office should be held by a peer of the royal blood, the candidates (excluding Gloucester) would be the dukes of York and Norfolk and the earls of Huntingdon and Somerset. There is no doubt that the cardinal already had his nephew in mind, but in 1437 he was still in captivity in France.

Negotiations for his release had, in fact, been resumed two years before. With the end of the minority approaching, the cardinal and the count of Mortain put pressure on the young king to authorize an exchange with the count of Eu whose release Henry V had forbidden until his son came of age.[8] In February 1435 Eu was transferred from the custody of the earl of Huntingdon to that of Edmund Beaufort, and at a meeting of the council

[6] Ibid. 7. Louis also asked for Kemp and Alnwick to be added to the council in Normandy. He visited Henry VI at Merton and was given an annuity of a thousand marks: E 101/408/24; *Foedera*, x. 666.

[7] Ibid. v. 16–17, 26. Warwick's articles for the post are in *Wars of Eng*. ii. p. lxvi; the warrants for settling his financial claims on the crown are E 404/53/296–7. He was owed in war wages £1,504; for his captaincy of Calais, £5,175; and for the wages of the garrison, £7,480. These were to be discharged from the issues of South Wales and the marriage of the earl of Arundel, while he was also given protection in his dispute with Lady Bergavenny: *PPC* v. 27–30, 32, 40–1; *CPR 1436–41*, 80, 82.

[8] P. and F. Strong, 'Last Will and Codicils', 92; *Foedera*, x. 602; *CCR 1435–41*, 331; *PPC* iv. 293.

on 9 February 1436 it was agreed that Somerset should purchase Eu from the crown for 12,000 marks, to be paid half in hand and half as a charge on his inheritance. Another year elapsed before Mortain received permission in April 1437 to take Eu to France to negotiate the exchange.[9] By December this had been arranged through the medium of Gilbert de la Fayette, marshal of France, who on 3 April 1438 received a safe conduct to bring Somerset to liberty, though it was probably not until the late autumn that he arrived in England.[10] Somerset had also to recompense his captor Charles, duke of Bourbon, and in all he later claimed to have paid £24,000 to procure his release. Somerset hoped to discharge the remainder of his debt from the sum to be paid for the release of the count of Angoulême, still remaining in his mother's custody. It had been proposed to free Angoulême at the beginning of 1436 on payment of 23,000 *li. tournois*, but this having been put into suspense, it was only when the Duchess Margaret's death in 1439 brought him into Somerset's custody that negotiations were resumed and a new agreement reached with Orléans to settle Somerset's debts.[11]

Somerset was later to claim that, following his release, he was employed practically continuously in the defence of Normandy. Immediately, however, he seems to have remained in England, for he visited Henry VI at Kenilworth on 6 January 1439 and on 26 February he and the cardinal dined at Eltham. Shortly afterwards he joined Warwick's council at Rouen.[12] By then his brother Edmund had emerged as one of the ablest commanders of the new generation in Normandy. At the end of 1435 his marriage to Warwick's daughter Eleanor had produced a son, christened Henry in honour of the king his godfather, and while other children were to follow, this released him for the service at Calais which had first brought him renown. As Warwick's son-in-law it would have been natural for him to have accompanied the earl to France in 1437, and this seems indeed to have been his intention. Warwick's own retinue was relatively small, and on 10 April the names of other captains were canvassed in the council, but of these only Lord Willoughby agreed to go and shortly after Edmund Beaufort's name was suggested.[13] A minute of 17 April shows that the

[9] M. Jones, 'John Beaufort, duke of Somerset and the French expedition of 1443', in Griffiths (ed.), *Patronage, the Crown and the Provinces*, 81 n. 17; *Foedera*, x. 664; C 76/119 m. 4; *PPC* v. 19; E 404/56/329.

[10] C 76/120 m. 8, 11; E 28/58 21 Oct. is a petition from Somerset for protection for la Fayette.

[11] *CPR 1436–41*, 515; *PPC* v. 113; Jones, 'John Beaufort', 81 n. 19. Somerset compounded his claim on the annuity due to him during his imprisonment for £4,000. For Angoulême's ransom, see Dupont-Ferrier, 'Captivité de Jean d'Orléans', 65, and below, ch. 17 nn. 50–3 and text thereat.

[12] C 81/1367/10 6 Jan. 1439, safe conducts for his servants 'at the instance and prayer of the earl of Somerset'; E 101/408/25.

[13] Henry VI's role as godparent is noted in E 28/56 18 Feb. 1436; *PPC* v. 8; *Wars of Eng.* ii. p. lxvi.

separate commission in Maine and Anjou issued to him in 1436 was under discussion, but in the event he did not accompany Warwick's army, which sailed for Normandy in the autumn.[14] Possibly he was engaged on the matter of his brother's ransom.

The delay in the arrival of Warwick's reinforcements blunted the vigorous counter-attacks which Talbot and Kyriell had mounted throughout the summer. At Pontoise, in the Vexin, and in the Pays de Caux the English registered successes, and repulsed the attack of La Hire and Xantrailles near Rouen. Warwick arrived as Montereau fell to the French, but Tancarville was recovered. The first crisis after Warwick's arrival was a threat to Crotoy from Burgundian captains in December, relieved when Talbot and Kyriell made a thrust into Ponthieu.[15] More serious was the danger to Guines from Burgundian forces early in 1438. Perhaps on Gloucester's suggestion, the names of Norfolk and Huntingdon were mentioned as possible leaders of a relieving force, but on 22 March it was with Edmund Beaufort that the council indented for a half-year's service with 500 men-at-arms and the equivalent ratio of archers. His force must have already been assembled, for he mustered four days later with 346 men-at-arms and 1,350 archers and received his first quarter's pay.[16] That came mainly from a loan from the cardinal, made on the same date, for the sum of £7,333. 6*s*. 8*d*., 'for the relief of Guines and for the army which shall hastily be sent to the realm of France and duchy of Normandy in the company of the earl of Dorset'.[17] It is clear that Edmund's expedition had been planned for some time, although its intended destiny was neither Calais nor Normandy but, as in 1436 and 1437, Maine. For his commission on 22 March was made out to him as captain general and governor for the king in Maine and Anjou for a period of seven years, and earlier in that month he had been created earl of Dorset.[18] With his brother's impending liberation, both Beauforts were now being established in the English peerage and as leading Norman landowners. Edmund was the recipient of further royal favour when he was pardoned for his marriage without royal licence, and then in July succeeded Lord Hungerford as constable of Windsor castle for life, converting his other constableships at Carmarthen and Aberystwyth to life grants at the same time.[19]

[14] *PPC* v. 15. Warrants for the payment of the captains accompanying Warwick are E 404/53/308–12; among them was Mortain's captain, James Standish. Warwick drew his own pay on 16 and 25 July; he mustered on 17 Sept., but was still awaiting shipping in Portsmouth and Winchelsea a month later *CPR 1436–41*, 144; E 403/727; E 404/54/96.

[15] Beaucourt, *Charles VII*, iii. 10–11; E. M. Burney, 'The English rule of Normandy, 1435–50' B.Litt. thesis (Oxford, 1958), 96–7.

[16] *PPC* v. 73–5, 90–2; *CPR 1436–41*, 149; C 76/120 m. 7; E 404/54/175; Newhall, *Muster and Review*, 150 n. 3.

[17] E 404/54/179, 180, 182; Steel, *Receipt*, 211.

[18] M. Jones, 'John Beaufort', 90; BL Add. MS 11542 fo. 90 is a fragmentary privy seal of his commission, dated 22 Mar. 1438 at Maidstone.

[19] *CPR 1436–41*, 160, 188.

It was two months before sufficient shipping could be mustered for Dorset's force and by then Warwick's council at Rouen had negotiated a truce with Burgundy which relieved the threat to Guines. That left Dorset free to pursue his original objective of establishing himself in Maine.[20] Landing at Cherbourg with a sizeable force which included Lord Camoys and eight bannerets, he advanced from the Cotentin along the borders of Brittany, capturing first Saint-Aignan-sur-Roe held by 300 Scots and then La Guerche. La Guerche was lost again 'through misgovernance', with the capture of Lord Camoys, and Dorset seems to have conducted no further offensive operations, using his force to secure his position in Maine. At the end of December he concluded a four year-truce and agreement with Jean duke of Alençon, and Charles of Anjou count of Maine, to regulate the *appatis* levied by each side.[21] The city of Alençon was probably his headquarters: it was held by his lieutenant Thomas Everingham and his forces were mustered there between 1437 and 1441. Mortain, which he had nominally held since 1427, had suffered in the border warfare and its castle had been destroyed as recently as 1433 as untenable.[22] His preferred investment was in less exposed parts of Normandy. Following Bedford's death Edmund had made good his claim to his uncle's holding of the county of Harcourt and lordship of Elbeuf, probably by grant from Henry VI, for he was using the title by February 1438 when he began to construct a substantial fortified dwelling at Elbeuf on the border of the Seine, at a total cost of 6,700 francs.[23]

If the cardinal's loan had served to establish Dorset in Maine, in the context of the overall defence of Normandy it was a costly diversion of the only sizeable force dispatched from England in that year. The London chronicler's verdict that Dorset had done 'but lytell gode' was more bluntly expressed by Gloucester when he cited this expedition to demonstrate the perversion of resources under the cardinal's influence.[24] For the greatest military pressure in 1438 was in the Pays de Caux where the liberated count of Eu quickly made himself felt, to the south of Paris where Dreux and Montargis were lost, and in Guyenne where Charles VII's forces had swept

[20] *PPC* v. 94, 100, 102; C 76/120 for protections for his retinue. Wages amounting to £10,612 paid 28 May: E 403/731; payments for his shipping at the end of E 403/734.

[21] *Chronicles of London*, 145 reports the campaign in detail. A. Joubert, 'Documents inedits pour servir à l'histoire de la Guerre de Cent Ans dans la Maine de 1424 à 1452', *Rev. hist. et archaeolog. du Maine* 26 (1889), no. xvii and cf. no. xvi. This was an attempt to stabilize and repopulate the area.

[22] Marshall, thesis, 114 and Appendix 2; BN MS Fr. 26549 no. 21 is his receipt for wages of the garrison of Alençon, Mar.–Sept. 1438; Allmand, *Lancastrian Normandy*, 177.

[23] M. C. Regnier, 'Devis pour la construction d'une maison forte à Elbeuf', *Soc. de l'histoire de Normandie; Mélanges*, 6 (1906), 333–4. Dr M. Jones tells me that in 1437–8 the receipts from the county of Harcourt were 6,000 *li. tournois*.

[24] *Chronicles of London*, 145; *Wars of Eng.* ii. 449: 'the gode . . . . loste by that armee that was last sent thider by the erle of Dorset'.

all before them, even though they retired in the winter without permanent gains. Had Dorset's force been deployed in any of these areas, its impact must inevitably have been greater. Nevertheless, the English garrisons at Meaux, Pontoise, Creil, and Gisors had been kept supplied and the spring of 1439 found the council once again organizing reinforcements to strengthen the English position as the peace talks drew closer.

A large number of lords assembled at Eltham for a meeting of the council from 22 to 24 February 1439, including Gloucester, Beaufort, York, and Huntingdon. They must surely have had in mind the need for a successor to Warwick, but the more immediate decision was to dispatch Huntingdon to Guyenne as lieutenant for six years commencing in June, to counter the French inroads of 1438. His force was of a size comparable to that of Dorset, 300 men-at-arms and 2,000 archers, but at Guyenne rates would be more expensive; in fact it was the largest force sent there since the beginning of the reign. Huntingdon indented on 27 March when discussion on how to finance him must already have begun.[25] On the same day the cardinal lent 7,000 marks, though this was not for the Guyenne expedition. It was almost certainly used for the payment of Warwick's salary under the terms of his indenture on 21 March. It is possible that Somerset took the money with him when he returned to France that month; he was at Rouen ready to take over 'la charge et administration des besongnes de la Duchie de Normandie' at Warwick's death on 30 April.[26] There he was joined by Edmund, and a further force was dispatched from England in the early summer at a cost of £4,359.[27] The cardinal himself was preparing for the peace conference at Calais for which he was to be paid 500 marks per month, with an initial advance of three months' salary. He drew this on 20 May, having made a loan of £3,000 a week earlier to cover this and the cost of these reinforcements.[28] Beaufort's loans of March and May 1439 were thus directed towards the military security of Normandy, where his nephews were in command, and to his own diplomatic initiative at Calais.

Somerset had wasted no time in enlarging Beaufort interests in Normandy. During the first half of the thirties these had been virtually defunct, represented only by the cardinal's captaincy of Honfleur from 1430 to 1437, and that of Edmund at Gisors in 1430. But from March 1437 to June 1438 the cardinal was captain of Cherbourg, which he then

[25] *PPC* v. 108; E 404/55/160; C 61/129 m. 21.

[26] *PPC* v. 115; *CPR 1436–41*, 277–9; E 403/729 21 Mar.; Waurin, *Croniques*, iv. 257.

[27] In late Apr./May Dorset was reviewing the garrison at Rouen: Cooper, *Appendices to Foedera*, 439. Warrants for reinforcements under Wydeville, Chamberlain, and Peyto: E 404/55/186, 291, 293, 296; E 403/734. They were ordered to conform to the orders of the chancellor of Normandy: E 28/61 17 June. Chamberlain was sent to Meaux.

[28] E 28/60 22 May; E 404/55/287; E 401/764; E 403/734 20 May. He drew a further instalment on 10 Oct.: E 404/56/37.

transferred to Somerset, who also secured the captaincy of Renneville, and then those of Avranches and Tombelaine, both in succession to the earl of Suffolk, while from Talbot he took over the captaincy of Falaise in 1439. From 1 June 1439 he was drawing a retainer of 5,000 *li. tournois* per annum for service in the field.[29] The Beauforts attracted to their service some of those professional captains engaged in the defence of the duchy under Bedford: men like Thomas Kyriell, John Cheyne, Christopher Barton, Richard Greenacres, Lewis John, and John Yerde. Edmund had built up his own particular following, notably Richard Frogenhall, Thomas Everingham, Richard Ditchfield, Thomas Delahaye, James Standish, and Thomas Gower. He had also established close ties with his fellow commanders, his brothers-in-law Lords Talbot and Latimer, and Lords Willoughby and Camoys. By the summer of 1439, largely due to the cardinal, the Beaufort brothers had acquired a recognized and growing stake in Normandy and Maine, while the council at Rouen was wholly composed of the cardinal's allies: Louis of Luxembourg, Pierre Cauchon, the abbots of Fécamp and Mont Saint-Michel, John and Edmund Beaufort, Lords Talbot, Faucomberg, and Scales.[30]

Between April 1437 and May 1439 the cardinal had loaned the crown £25,866. The bulk of this comprised three large loans: 10,000 marks in April 1437 to furnish the army for Warwick's appointment as lieutenant in Normandy; 11,000 marks in March 1438 to furnish the army for Dorset's appointment as captain and governor of Maine and Anjou; and 11,500 marks in two loans in March and May 1439, part for Warwick's salary and part for his own embassy to Calais. Some smaller incidental loans in November–February 1439 made up the total, but as a whole this represented an investment in a policy and in its executants of his own choosing, enabling him to shape the crown's commitments in these crucial years. What was the context of crown finance which made Beaufort's loans so necessary, and at how great a risk were they made?

The collapse of wool exports from 1436 to 1439 meant that royal finances had to be supported from the lay and clerical subsidies. The parliament of January 1437 granted a whole subsidy to be collected in halves at Michaelmas 1437 and 1438 and shortly afterwards convocation granted a clerical subsidy for collection at March 1438 and 1439.[31] Over the two years from March 1437 these provided a total of about £75,000, though from some of it the loans raised in 1435 had still to be repaid. Fresh loans could now be raised on its security. When Beaufort lent 10,000 marks on 18 April

[29] Marshall, thesis, Appendix 2; Jones, 'John Beaufort', 83 n. 35. For Cardinal Beaufort at Honfleur, BN MS Nouv. Acq., 1482 no. 97; for Henry Norbury as his lieutenant in Cherbourg, BL Add. Ch. 5832; For Somerset's captaincies, BN MS Fr. 26549 no. 22, 25, 27.

[30] Marshall, thesis, 18, 114–24. A petition of Standish describes his service to Bedford and Mortain: E 28/58 21 Nov.

[31] *Rot. Parl.* iv. 502; *Reg. Chichele*, iii. 526; *CFR 1430–7, 269, 309; CFR 1437–45*, 8, 12–14.

1437 some 20,000 marks of his wealth was already in the king's hands, from loans made over the previous two years. That may have given him pause, and his loan is a measure of the importance he attached to Warwick's appointment. However, his influence secured him assignments totalling 20,000 marks on the first halves of the lay and clerical taxes, together with a pardon for retaining crown jewels which he held at security for any undischarged loans.[32] The total of loans recorded on the receipt roll for the Easter term 1437, almost £21,000, was the third highest of the reign to date. In the event virtually all this money was sent either to Warwick or Louis of Luxembourg in Normandy.[33]

The consequence of this massive anticipation of revenue was a decline of available income in 1437–8 to one of the lowest levels of the reign hitherto.[34] The great council which assembled at Sheen on 21 October 1437 was charged to consider three matters: the threat of schism between pope and council; the proposal to permit the duke of Orléans to return to France to negotiate peace; and a statement of the king's finances showing the predictable charges for the year ahead and how these were to be met. In insisting that a budgetary exercise of this kind had been one of the 'lawdable customs and usages of the king's progenitoures and predecessores', Cromwell and his fellow councillors were endeavouring to set guidelines for the young king and demonstrate the need for fiscal planning and restraint. The council was made directly aware of the financial constraints on royal policy by the treasurer's declaration that he lacked the money to provide troops to safeguard the proposed transfer of Orléans to Cherbourg, unless he cancelled the assignments already made to those who had lent to the crown. Beaufort, Kemp, and Gloucester thereupon insisted that Orléans should pay his own costs for the mission.[35] The wholesale pledging of the lay and clerical subsidies now began to limit the council's power to raise further loans. Beaufort's loan of 11,000 marks in March 1438 was mainly charged on the Southampton customs, though it was not until 8 August that his loan of £6,000 made in the summer of 1436 was finally repaid from this source. For his new loan his conditions were as

[32] *PPC* v. 16, 41–2; E 404/53/302; E 401/752 15 May; *Foedera*, x. 670 and *PPC* v. 33–4 for the pardon which, as McFarlane pointed out, embraced the jewels retained for the 1424 loan. Beaufort now secured repayment of the loan of 10,000 marks made on 17 July 1435 for which the lords of the council had entered obligations.

[33] Steel, *Receipt*, 460; *PPC* v. 13–14, 42. Part of this total represented the the loan of July 1435, now entered on the receipt roll for repayment. A loan of 20,000 marks from the Company of the Staple was made on 19 July and 29 Oct: E 401/752, 754. On 8 July £4,119 was paid to Warwick for his first quarter and on 8 and 17 July £11,906 to Louis of Luxembourg for his standing force of 800 men-at-arms and 2,400 archers at the rate of £8,500 per quarter: E 403/728. He had been in England in May to press his claims: E 404/53/324, E 404/53/104; *PPC* v. 24.

[34] Steel, *Receipt*, 450, table C6.

[35] *PPC* v. 64–5, 68.

stringent as ever: he was permitted to name one of the collectors, and he had preference over the competing claims of Genoese merchants. He received a single tally for £5,000 levied upon John Chirche, the collector appointed by the duchy feoffees, who by the time he resigned in November had delivered to Beaufort £2,775, leaving the residue to be reassigned on the new collectors William Estcourt and William Soper, both the cardinal's close associates.[36]

Thus by the end of 1438 all Beaufort's loans made between July 1435 and March 1438 for the defence of Calais and Normandy, to a total of £40,500, had been repaid, apart from some £2,000 still charged on the Southampton customs. Whereas in 1435–6 he had to lend under pressure and at some risk to his capital, in 1437–8 he was able to lend on good security, to advance his own interests and those of his nephews. But by 1439 this position was already changing, for it was becoming impossible to provide security for further loans. To the prolonged dearth of customs was now added the ending of the lay and clerical subsidies voted in 1437. The replenishing of both these sources of revenue would only come from a resumption of trade and the restoration of Burgundian neutrality or goodwill. That could serve as a basis for either a more aggressive policy in France or the negotiation of a truce or peace with the French, to either of which parliament might respond more generously than to the current defensive stalemate. Before the end of 1438, therefore, Beaufort had shifted his attention from the defence of Normandy to the pursuit of peace. He and Kemp journeyed to Gravelines in December for wide-ranging discussions with the Duchess Isabel on the resumption of trade and the renewal of the Anglo-French peace talks. For his embassy Beaufort lent a further 4,000 marks and made other small advances to the treasurer of Calais, receiving repayment from the customs in Southampton and London and in cash at the exchequer.[37]

When he returned to London about mid-February 1439 the principal charges facing the council in the summer were already taking shape. Money and troops had to be sent to the earl of Warwick (£4,353 was issued for this on 21 March), the cost of an impressive embassy to Calais had to be met, and the council had just agreed to dispatch the earl of Huntingdon to Guyenne in June for six years with a sizeable army. These commitments would have to be financed by borrowing, but since the only security that could be offered was long-term and uncertain assignments on the customs, this narrowed the choice of lenders to those with direct interests in the success of these ventures or personal obligations to the council. As we have seen, Beaufort himself now advanced 7,000 marks in March for the

[36] *CPR 1436–41*, 173, 227; *CFR 1430–7*, 185, *CFR 1437–45*, 58; E 404/54/175, 179, 188; E 401/754, 756; E 403/730. All the remaining £2,224 was paid to the cardinal by Estcourt and Soper within the year of their account: E 122/140/55.

[37] *CPR 1436–41*, 194, 230; E 401/761; E 403/734; E 364/77 H.

reinforcements sent to France and a further £3,000 on 13 May, almost certainly to provide the wages for himself and the other negotiators at Calais. The latter loan was secured on the two collectors of his choice at Southampton; for the larger sum the exchequer could provide no secure assignment and Beaufort had to accept jewels in pledge of repayment by Easter 1440; other lenders had to be content with even less favourable terms.[38]

The most important of these were the feoffees of the duchy of Lancaster. A series of their loans is recorded on the receipt roll on 19 November and 4 December 1438 and 21 March 1439 amounting to £3,517, and on 21 May and 26 June they produced another £4,482. Together these must have represented almost the whole available revenue in the hands of the feoffees. They were all assigned for repayment on the Southampton customs after the cardinal's own loan of £2,000.[39] Between November 1438 and June 1439 the cardinal himself had lent £11,866 and the feoffees £8,000, in all almost £20,000 out of a total of all loans raised of £30,258. None of the other loans were individually of any size, and by midsummer it was becoming clear that the government had exhausted its credit. Its cash reserves, following two years in which no more than £10,300 had been received in coin, must have been negligible, and in the year up to Easter 1439 'fictitious loans' had reached the dangerous figure of 28 per cent of all assignments. It was now entirely dependent on the one creditor who had the resources and readiness to lend, but even Beaufort could no longer find revenue for his repayment.[40]

Massive as these loans were, by midsummer of 1439 it was apparent that they would be insufficient to meet the crown's military commitments. By far the most expensive of these was the earl of Huntingdon's army to be sent to Guyenne. This bore the marks of Gloucester's advocacy, and the decision to send it may well have been taken at a meeting at Eltham from 22 to 24 February after Beaufort's return from Gravelines, attended by Gloucester, Huntingdon, York, and the cardinal.[41] To the military and strategic reasons for strengthening this area would be added the importance of having an imposing force in France during the peace negotiations. The cardinal very probably lent his support to the proposal, both as a concession to Gloucester which might deflect his opposition to the peace

[38] E 401/764, 768; *CPR 1436–41*, 277–9; *PPC* v. 115; E 404/55/158, E 404/56/163. The jewels, valued at £4,589, are listed in *Kal, and Inv*. ii. 182–6 and in J. Caley, 'Extract from the Liber Memorandum Camerariorum, Receptae Scacarii' *Archaeologia*, 21 (1827), 34–8. They were returned by William Port on 30 Jan. 1441.

[39] E 401/761, 764; *CPR 1436–41*, 227.

[40] Steel, *Receipt*, 441 table B6, 460 table D6. The remaining lenders included the Staplers, the city of London, the Genoese community, Chichele, Dyke, and the executors of John Frank: E 401/761, 764.

[41] *PPC* v. 108; E 101/408/25.

negotiations and as a means of distancing Huntingdon from Normandy where he might challenge the role of Somerset as Warwick's destined successor. Warwick's death on 22 April 1439 gave this even greater force. The payment of £8,955 as the first quarter's wages for Huntingdon's force was made on 20 May, and about half of this large cash disbursement is likely to have come from the loans raised from the duchy feoffees.[42] If Huntingdon's army was thus enabled to come into being, paying its second quarter's wages and shipping it to Gascony was another matter. By midsummer the exchequer was empty, its credit had been exhausted, and all sources of taxation had dried up. The cardinal still had money, but he was not prepared to lend it when there was no security for repayment. The one alternative he was prepared to consider was a sale of crown lands.

Gloucester later alleged that, on 25 May 1439, he was 'al sodeinly called' to the council at Kennington where a discussion was held about the sale to the cardinal of Chirk and Chirkland and a group of manors in Dorset, Somerset, and Wiltshire for the sum of 13,000 marks. When the terms of the proposed sale were read aloud by the clerk of the council Gloucester, as he explained, 'eschewing the breking and the losse of youre armee into Guyenne thanne, seeing noon other remedye, gaf thereto myn assent, thenkyng that who that ever laboured, moeved, or stured this matre first unto youre lordship [i.e. the king] counsailled you neither for youre worship nor proufite'. The decision was indeed recorded as taken by the king 'de motu suo proprio', although on the same day the additional sale to the cardinal of the manor of Salden for 350 marks was made 'de avisamento concilii'. Gloucester further asserted that Beaufort insisted on being made

> 'as sure of alle the landes toforesaid by Estre nowe next comyng [i.e. 1440], as can be devised by eny lerned counsaille; and elles, that suretee not made, the saide cardinal to have and to rejoyce to hym and his heires in fee for evermore the landes of the duchie of Lancastre lyeinge in Norfolke, to the value of vii or viii c markes by yeere; whiche things semen right straunge, and unseen and unherd weyes that eny liege man shulde so seche upon his souverain lord, both in his enheritaunce and jewailles and gode'.[43]

[42] E 403/734; E 401/764. These loans totalled £4,482.

[43] *Wars of Eng*. ii. 448. Although both the council warrant (E 28/60 25 May) and the letters patent (*CPR 1436–41*, 311) state that Beaufort paid 13,350 marks for Chirkland and the west country manors, it is clear from the receipt roll that the statement made in 1492 (*Rot. Parl.* vi. 446) that the purchase price was 13,000 marks is correct. That sum was paid into the exchequer on 24 July 'pro certis maneriis, terris, et tenementis per ipsum de domino rege emptis in comitibus Wilts' Dors' et alibi', while on the same day a further £233. 6*s*. 8*d*. was paid for Salden, Bucks: E 401/762. This was separately warranted by the council (E 28/60) and formed a separate letter patent in which the price is stated (ibid. 260). Those present at the council were Gloucester, Beaufort, Kemp, Northumberland, Salisbury, Suffolk, and the three officers.

The truth of this is confirmed by a patent of 7 June dated at Windsor, releasing some duchy manors to Beaufort for certain reasons, the release to be held by Kemp under certain conditions appointed by the king. These were, in fact, parcels of the enfeoffed lands, and even Hungerford made difficulties about their delivery to his co-feoffee while Henry V's will remained unfulfilled.[44] But in the event this safeguard proved unnecessary; on 10 June the cardinal with the three officers of state and Moleyns, meeting in council at St Mary Overy, ordered the evidences relating to Chirkland to be delivered to Beaufort, though it was only after all who held offices and annuities therein had surrendered their own patents and received compensation that, on 3 December, the patent of 25 May was finally handed over.[45] On 30 May the council had authorized Huntingdon to muster and on 24 July, when the purchase price was paid into the exchequer, Huntingdon set sail.[46] By then Beaufort had reached Calais, leaving his servant William Port to conclude the Chirk transactions.

Historians have uniformly endorsed Gloucester's judgement on the sale, impressed by the unequivocal condemnation by Fortescue:

> Nor ther shall no livelode be kept so holl as the kynges consideryng that he mey not onestly sell is lande, as other men mey doo; and also his sellyng wolde be the hurte of all his reaume. Soche was the sellynge off Chirke and Chirkes landes, weroff never manne see a president, and God defende that any man see mo soche hereaftir. Ffor sellynge off a kynges livelod is propirly callid delapidacion off his crowne, and therfore is off gret infame.[47]

Yet such a verdict can only be sustained if the sale was either unnecessary or was to the crown's financial disadvantage. Even Gloucester had acknowledged that there was no alternative source from which to finance Huntingdon's expedition, and exchequer records would appear to confirm this. Gloucester further admitted that to spend the crown's assets might be justified by 'right urgent and extreme necessite'—from which he prayed the king would be preserved. Indeed convention even accounted it to a ruler's credit if he was ready to sacrifice his own lands and wealth and spare his people when the necessity of the realm and their safety demanded. Edward I had proclaimed his willingness to do this, and in the next century both Henry VIII and Elizabeth sold land more extensively than Henry VI to meet military needs.

The lands were not, in fact, part of the ancient inheritance of the crown. Chirk had been part of the Fitz Alan estates which Henry V had purchased from the executors of the earl of Arundel at a price of 4,000 marks. The

[44] *CPR 1436–41*, 276–7; Somerville, *Duchy of Lanc.* 205.
[45] E 28/61 10 June, E 28/63 3 Dec; E 404/55/299.
[46] C 81/1367/13; E 401/762 24 July; Vale, *Eng. Gascony*, 110-12.
[47] Sir J. Fortescue, *The Governance of England*, ed. C. Plummer, 134.

other manors had been held by the duke of Bedford, those in the west country having escheated to the crown in 1429 as part of the Montagu lands, and being charged with pensions to Salisbury's and Bedford's widows. Moreover, Beaufort appears to have paid a fair price, and his intention at this stage was that they should form part of the re-endowment of St Cross hospital, rather than swell his family's estates.[48] That may have persuaded Henry VI, whose mind was already turning to the endowment of a collegiate religious establishment. Even so it is not surprising that it aroused Gloucester's particular resentment and condemnation, for it symbolized the ascendancy which his rival had achieved over the last two years. The sale was decided in council a mere four days after Beaufort and Kemp had been commissioned to negotiate a peace which Gloucester vehemently opposed. Moeover, Gloucester himself had his eye on Bedford's lands. In November 1437 the Richmond lands had been committed to Lord Bardolph at farm, but a month later Lord Tiptoft secured a life grant of two of the manors valued at 100 marks, and in May 1439 had his letter patent predated to that of Bardolph.[49] In June 1438 Duke Humphrey had tried to convert an annuity of 2,000 marks into lands from Bedford's estates, only to find that they were so encumbered with charges that he had to surrender them in exchange for rents from alien priories at precisely the time that Beaufort was negotiating his own grant.[50] Gloucester was thus finding himself outmanœuvred in the competition for rewards. He appears to have been kept in the dark about the impending sale to Beaufort and on arrival at the council found that it had been approved by the cardinal's supporters. Probably he was not conversant

[48] Assuming that Beaufort paid the crown's original purchase price for Chirkland, of 4,000 marks, and hence 9,000 marks for the west country properties, the latter should have been worth about £300 p.a. if a twenty-year purchase price is regarded as normal. At the time of purchase all except Henstridge were charged with dower annuities to both Alice, countess of Suffolk and Jacquetta, dowager duchess of Bedford. Both had agreed by Oct. 1440 to accept other grants from the crown in lieu of these. Alice, who held one-third of Canford, Amesbury, and Winterborne Earls, was granted £63. 4*s*. 5½*d*. elsewhere, so that the value of these three properties may be assumed to be £189. 13*s*. 4*d*. A valuation of Jacquetta's lands gives Wilton and Charlton as together worth £26. 16*s*. 0*d*. Two parts of Henstridge were being farmed at £40 p.a., so that the total value of the properties purchased by Beaufort was around £276. 9*s*. 4*d*. p.a. and they were extended at considerably less in 1452. He was thus paying rather heavily for them. For Salden Beaufort paid 400 marks, though one-third was held in dower by Jacquetta and the remainder charged with an annuity of 40 marks for Robert Whittingham, so that its annual value was £40. Unencumbered, its market price would be £800; whether it was 'cheap at the price' (McFarlane, *England in XV Century*, 133) would depend on how long it remained burdened with these annuities. In fact Beaufort was purchasing on behalf of Whittingham himself, to whom it had been passed by Apr. 1440. *CPR 1436–41*, 479–80 and E 28/64 22, 29 Oct; ibid. 394, 520 for Salden. SC 6/1116/13 for Henstridge. *CPR 1441–6*, 46–7, 129; *CPR 1452–61*. 233.

[49] E 28/59 13 Nov.; cf. R. Virgoe, 'The Cambridgeshire election of 1439', *BIHR* 46 (1973), 97–8. Tiptoft had confirmation of his grants in May and June: E 28/60 5 May, E 28/61 10 June.

[50] *CPR 1436–41*, 188–9, 303.

with the full details of the crown's financial position and had assumed when Huntingdon's army had been commissioned that money for it would be available. Committed as he was to the dispatch of the army, he was now forced to agree to the means of raising the money. The cardinal had so arranged it that he was left no option; there was no other source of money, no other lender available, and Beaufort was about to leave. If Gloucester had refused to rubber stamp the arrangement he could be branded as betraying the defence of Gascony and his own associate Huntingdon, who was ready to depart. His resentment at being placed in this false position is readily understandable.

Undoubtedly the sale of Chirkland inflamed Gloucester's jealousy of the cardinal and provoked him to attack the peace terms negotiated by the English embassy in August and to bring charges against Beaufort at the end of the year. These ensured that the sale became enshrined in political mythology as a prime example of the dissipation of royal lands to a self-interested councillor. The Chirkland affair was indeed symbolic of the stranglehold that Beaufort had established over royal finance and the indebtedness to which the crown had been reduced. Yet this sprang not from royal prodigality but from the determination of the council over the past decade to defend Henry V's conquests, albeit at an increasing cost. More particularly, since 1436 Beaufort's loans had served to implement a policy of restoring links with Burgundy, stabilizing the position in Normandy, and keeping its military government out of the hands of Gloucester and under the control of his own associates and family. They had also enabled Beaufort and the duchy feoffees to appropriate the major sources of revenue, thus rendering any alternative policy impossible. These were the military and financial circumstances which brought Beaufort to the height of his political influence under Henry VI. But these policies and the ascendancy which he had built upon them were shortly to be exposed as vulnerable to changing circumstances and the jealousy of his enemies.

15

Politics and the Pursuit of Peace, 1436–1439

THE formal reappointment of the council on 12 November 1437 was an attempt to impress on the young Henry VI his responsibility for good government.[1] Next day the council adopted guidelines for its relations with the king based on the ordinances of 1406. This was probably at the suggestion of Beaufort and Tiptoft, the two members who had experienced the earlier crisis at first hand. Then, a council composed of the king's friends and relatives had taken government out of the king's hands for a year to impose economy and restraint. The situation in 1437 was analogous but different. The king was too young to bear the full burden of government, too inexperienced to take decisions on great and complex problems of state. A council was needed to make good his natural deficiencies, with a more formalized role and wider responsibilities than under an active and adult monarch. By comparison with the appointment of 1406, the demarcation of powers between the king and council was much less defined. The king's independent authority was slightly extended: as well as pardons, collations, and offices it now comprised 'other things that stand in grace'. More crucially, no provision was made for the council to scrutinize or endorse warrants, and thus control the king's disposal of financial patronage. It was to have authority to determine matters brought before it, apart from those of great weight or charge, which were to be referred to the king, as also were any matters on which it was seriously divided. But no clear definition was given of what matters fell within its autonomous competence. In short, the declaration of 1437 imposed no controls on the king; it merely affirmed that there was a council with which the king should share his responsibilities for government.

This was faithfully reflected in practice. During the three years following October 1436 the council was for long periods in almost daily session.[2] At Westminster it met in the Star Chamber or Parliament Chamber, but not

[1] *PPC* v. 71; vi. 312–15. For recent discussions, see Wolffe, *Henry VI*, 91–2; Griffiths, *Reign of Henry VI*, 276–7.

[2] These were: 1436; 11–30 Oct. (E 28/57), 6–28 Nov. (E 28/58; *PPC* v. 3–5). 1437: 7 Apr.–14 May, 5 June–28 July (*PPC* v. 6–51), 21 Oct.–29 Nov. (*PPC* v. 64–83; C 81/1544). 1438: 29 Jan.–mid.-Feb. (*PPC* v. 86–92; E 28/58), 10–28 Mar. (C 81/1544; E 28/59), 5–17 May (*PPC* v. 93–102). 1439: 7 May–13 July (E 28/60–62), 19 Aug. (E 28/62). The council is also likely to have been sitting in four other periods when Henry VI was residing close to London, namely: 4 Dec. 1437–10 Jan. 1438; 8–12 July 1438; 1–14 Nov. 1438; 22–8 Feb. 1439: Wolffe, *Henry VI*, 361–2; PSO 1/5–7; E 101/408/24, 25.

infrequently meetings were held at Kennington, Sheen, or Eltham when Henry VI was in residence. For virtually all the periods when meetings are recorded Henry was at one of these residences, and on many occasions either his presence is recorded or business was referred to him for advice or decision.[3] Clearly meetings of the continual council were formal occasions, for which notice was given, and to which it was expected that all those appointed in 1437 would come. Some councillors were more assiduous than others, and in the main these were the cardinal's supporters: Kemp and Alnwick among the bishops, Salisbury, Stafford, and Suffolk among the earls, and Lords Tiptoft and Hungerford, together with the chancellor and treasurer, both of them Beaufort's friends. Some meetings were attended exclusively by members of this group, including at least four held in February–March 1438 and in June 1439 in the cardinal's residences at Farnham and St Mary Overy.[4] Yet at most meetings either Gloucster or one or other of his allies was present, and only in the summer of 1439 is there perhaps some suggestion of two factions meeting separately to advance their own interests.[5]

While the council thus retained its corporate identity, the king began to answer petitions on his own authority. In the last weeks of 1436 he signed a spate of grants, mainly to household servants and of a fairly minor kind.[6] The council ordinance a year later therefore only sanctioned an existing practice; yet it was not long before the treasurer was drawing attention to the effects of Henry's prodigality on the straitened royal finances, and the council was moved to deliver a respectful reprimand to the young monarch. In February 1438 it warned him against allowing receiverships to be held for life or by deputy, of too ready pardons to financial officers of their debts, and of the particular grant of the stewardship of Chirk to Robert Ingelfield with the loss of 1,000 marks to the crown. There are indications that Henry took some heed, though his liberality was not easily curtailed.[7] Although the council was powerless to stop the flow of royal

[3] E.G. *PPC* v. 28, 30, 40, 88–9.

[4] R. Virgoe, 'The composition of the King's Council, 1437–61', *BIHR* 43 (1970), 134–60, esp. 142 for meetings in Feb. and Mar. 1438 when the king was not in London, held at St Mary Overy and Farnham; also in June 1439 at St Mary Overy, on the matter of Chirkland: E 28/59, 61, 63; C 81/1544/69.

[5] Thus at the meeting of 6 May 1439 Gloucester's supporters predominated and Gloucester received a grant (E 28/60; C 81/1424/27); on 21–5 May Beaufort's supporters were there in strength for the Chirkland grant and a petition of Edmund Beaufort concerning the Berkeley lands (E 28/60). In July at Sheen, there were important grants to Gloucester (*CPR 1436–41*, 296, 300, 303), Cromwell, Northumberland (E 28/62 9–10 July), and Suffolk (PSO 1/7/36; *CPR 1436–41*, 309–10).

[6] E 28/58; C 81/1424.

[7] PPC v. 88–9; E 28/59 14 Apr. carries a proviso 'so that it be not granted afore' and E 28/60 29 May refers a petition to the council. But most petitions were presented to the king when the court was out of London and were endorsed by the chamberlain or senior members of the household; files E 28/59–61 and C 81/1424 contain numerous examples.

grants, it did maintain a real control over policy. All matters concerned with the defence of Normandy and Calais, all embassies dealing with trade and peace negotiations, and relations with the pope and council, were decided by it; in financial matters the allocation of expenditure, the negotiation of loans, and the levying of taxes were regularly discussed; finally it exercised disciplinary authority in cases of riot and endeavoured to compose the disputes of the nobility.[8] On some of these it might refer to the king, and it might equally seek the advice of the cardinal.[9] On important financial items it was prepared to take a firm line.[10]

Although the king was associated with the council's decisions in these matters, there is no indication that he initiated or directed policy or did more than give his official approval. Henry VI's independent role remained largely confined to answering petitions of grace, and this continued during the long periods when he was away from the capital and the continual council was not in session. During such times individual members of the council might visit the court,[11] and the earl of Suffolk as steward of the household was frequently in attendance, but such government as took place was probably at the initiative of the chancellor and treasurer, acting in communication with the cardinal. Well placed to secure royal favours for himself and his clients,[12] Beaufort had few links with the knights and esquires of the household, and it was into the affinity of Suffolk as steward that they gravitated, rapidly becoming a political force in their own right. Beaufort rarely visited the household when it was outside London and for long periods probably had little contact with the king. His thoughts were centred on Normandy and Flanders rather than on Windsor; it was in France, too, that he sought opportunities to endow his nephews. He failed to see that these years were laying the foundations for a totally different systemn of politics from that which he had known since the death of Henry V.

Nevertheless, Beaufort did exercise a powerful influence on the young

[8] The council's diplomatic and financial business is discussed below; for its concern with discord, see E 28/59 3 Apr.; E 28/61 10 June; E 28/62 24 Aug.

[9] C 81/1424/31; C 81/1367/9; *PPC* v. 26, 81.

[10] e.g. over the king's gift to Sir Thomas Rempston in 1437 (*PPC* v. 79, Devon, *Issues*, 434) and over the claim of York for reimbursment in 1437 (E 28/59 10 Feb.).

[11] The royal household accounts record visits of councillors in May 1437 at Sheen; in Sept. 1437 at Berkhamstead; in Oct. 1437 at Sheen; in Jan. and Feb. 1438 at Windsor; in May 1438 at Windsor; in June 1438 at Westminster; in July 1438 at Windsor; in Feb. 1439 at Eltham: E 101/408/24, 25.

[12] For Henry VI's New Year gift to the Cardinal in 1437 of 'a tabulet of gold with an image of our Lady' see *Excerpta Historica*, 148. Benefits for his servants were: 10 Mar. 1437 William Port appoined customer of Calais 'by contemplacion of our uncle, cardinal' (PSO 1/5/242); 12 May 1437 Thomas Tourges pardoned 'by the instance and prayer of Cardinal Beaufort' (PSO 1/5/253; *CPR 1436–41*, 58); 3 Nov. 1438 Roger Hunt appointed baron of the exchequer 'at the instance of Cardinal Beaufort' (*CPR 1436–41*, 219); 30 May 1439 Richard Roos of Southwark pardoned 'at the instance of Cardinal Beaufort' (C 81/1367/13).

king. His age, status, and relationship to Henry counted for much, and of even greater importance was his success in engaging the boy's religious idealism in two matters of policy: relations with the papacy and peace with France. The widening rift between Eugenius IV and the council of Basel came to a head in September 1437 when the pope formally transferred the council to Ferrara where his followers assembled on 8 January 1438 to receive the Greek delegation. The Basel fathers responded by decreeing the pope's suspension and finally, in June 1439, his deposition. Piero da Monte now intensified his efforts to secure a declaration from the English crown in favour of the pope and the assembly at Ferrara.[13] Following the meeting of the royal council at Sheen in October, a barrage of letters was issued in Henry VI's name expressing support for the pope, urging moderation on Sigismund and the council, and leaving no doubt about the king's horror of schism. Piero da Monte came away from an interview with Henry VI in November 1437 impressed with his seriousness and piety.[14] In February 1438 the royal council was considering sending delegates to Ferrara, though it advised the king that Beaufort should not be one of them. When in May 1438 a delegation from Basel arrived in London, Beaufort arranged a royal audience for them, which was marked by Chichele's frequent outbursts against the council. Yet there were sound arguments for supporting the imperial electors' declaration of neutrality, as a step towards renewing the traditional alliance with the German crown terminated by Sigismund's death in December 1437, which could provide a counterweight to Burgundian hostility. For a brief moment the question of Henry VI's marriage was even considered in this context. It is impossible to discern any distinctive attitude of Beaufort in these matters, although his voice must have had greater weight than any. For that reason it is probably best to assume that what happened fairly closely reflected his wishes. That, in fact, amounted to very little. While Henry VI was probably encouraged to believe that he was exerting influence on behalf of the pope, in fact little came out of all the discussion in England: no English delegation went to Ferrara, but neither were facilities given to the delegation from Basel to propagate their cause. In September 1438 Eugenius actually summoned Beaufort to undertake his long postponed visit to the Curia before old age overtook him, reminding him that this was his true *domicilium* where his wisdom and counsel should properly be rendered.[15] But the cardinal's attention was already engaged on matters nearer to home.

In the aftermath of the Calais fiasco Lannoy had pointed out to Duke Philip that Anglo-Flemish trade would have to be resumed and that

[13] Schofield, 'Council of Basel', 119.

[14] Ibid. 92–105; Ferguson, *English Diplomacy*, 114–15, 136–7; Haller, *Piero da Monte*, 63 no. 69, 275, 277; *PPC* v. 64.

[15] Haller, *Piero da Monte*, 217–22, suppl. nos. 30–3.

negotiations for this could form part of a wider pacification. The duke, he argued, could become the fulcrum for peace between England and France, bringing the French to the negotiating table by himself offering to relinquish his claims on René of Anjou and the Somme towns and persuading the English to release the duke of Orléans. Lannoy believed that peace could alone guarantee Burgundian prosperity, and if negotiated through the agency of the duke would re-establish his influence at the French court. The first moves were indeed made within the context of the continuing trade between England and Holland. Uttenhove and Lannoy were received by the English council for talks in March 1438 while concurrent negotiations for an Anglo-Burgundian truce were conducted at Rouen. In July the Four Members added their weight to the Rouen negotiations, then transferred to Ardres, and in August Uttenhove led a further, more substantial delegation from Holland and Flanders which placed an Anglo-Burgundian *intercursus* firmly on the agenda for a meeting between the Duchess Isabel and Cardinal Beaufort.[16] On 21 November her special envoy to Beaufort, Lalaing, arrived in London and two days later Beaufort, Kemp, Bildeston, Wilton, and others were commissioned to treat at Calais.[17] Their preparations must have been already made, for by 29 November the party had arrived at Canterbury and in the week preceding Christmas they crossed to Calais under the protection of a veritable flottilla of armed ships, the wages and provisioning of which cost 500 marks. At Calais, delegations from Holland, Zeeland, and Flanders met those from London and the Staplers, and lists of grievances and demands for compensation were tabled on both sides. The meeting of Beaufort and Isabel at Gravelines in January gave the first signal for a resumption of wool shipments to Calais and by 8 February agreement had been reached for formal negotiations at Calais in three months' time.[18] The presence of the duke of Orléans at these underlined their wider purpose, and the French king was invited to send a delegation.

Charles VII's delay in replying postponed the starting date and the English delegation was not named until 21 May. It consisted of Archbishop Kemp and Bishops Brouns, Cauchon, and Rudbourne, the earls of Stafford and Oxford, Lords Bourchier and Hungerford, Sir John Stourton, Sir John Sutton, Sir John Popham, and Robert Whittingham, with Thomas Beckington, Stephen Wilton, Nicholas Bildeston, William Sprever, and

[16] Vaughan, *Philip the Good*, 102–7; Thielemans, *Bourgogne et Angleterre*, 117–18; Taylor, thesis, 74–81; *PPC* v. 95.

[17] *Foedera*, x. 713–16. On 21 Dec. Lalaing received a safe conduct under the signet at Kenilworth 'at the instance and prayer' of the cardinal C 81/1367/7.

[18] Chronicle of John Stone, ed. W. G. Searle (Camb. Antiq. Soc., 1902), 22; Thielemans, *Bourgogne et Angletere*, 122–3; Taylor, thesis, 97; *Foedera*, x. 718. Licences to the mayor of the Staple and to Beaufort to export wools: C 76/121 m. 18; *CPR 1436–41*, 227. The costs of shipping are detailed in E 404/55/153–4. The embassy re-crossed the Channel on 22 Feb.

John Rinel as the professional clerks.[19] This was an impressive embassy, carefully balanced in terms of rank, and numbering those with lands in Normandy and knowledge of its problems, as well as diplomats well versed in Anglo-French-Burgundian issues; it included associates of Gloucester and members of the household, though weighted overall with those identified with the cardinal's policy. Beaufort himself was not included, for he was to be 'Mediatour and Sterer to Peace', a position corresponding to that of Isabel on the French side. For although Duke Philip formally headed the French delegation, in practice separate French and Burgundian embassies operated in liaison with each other while the duke himself remained at Saint-Omer, available for consultation but not directly participating. Beaufort and Isabel were to act not as impartial mediators, as had the cardinals at Arras, but rather as intermediaries and conciliators, keeping in close touch with their own delegations but ready to take initiatives to break any deadlocks.

This was reflected in the instructions to the English embassy issued at Kennington on 21 May and to Beaufort himself four days later.[20] As was usual, the former consisted of a series of negotiating positions, beginning with the Lancastrian claim to the crown of France recognized by Charles VI at Troyes and descending to the territorial rights of English kings independent of the title to the crown which, as in the treaty of Brétigny, were claimed in full sovereignty. The English were thus prepared to set aside the question of the title and seek a territorial partition; a reversion to what had been proposed at Meulan in 1419. In the current situation in France even this was being over-optimistic. Moreover, any mitigation of their full claim would set the English on a slippery slope that must lead to demands that Henry VI should hold the lands as his Angevin ancestors had, in homage. This in fact proved to be the most that the French would concede. On the issue of Henry's title the instructions affirmed the validity of his coronation but, if it finally became the only matter in dispute, the negotiators were to refer to Beaufort himself 'to whom the king had opened and declared al his intent in this mater'.

The content of Beaufort's full power to treat and conclude on the title is not known, but there is nothing to suggest that this went beyond a recognition of the *de facto* position by which Henry and Charles each used the title within the lands under their control. Henry VI was ready to

[19] *Foedera*, x. 724; Taylor, thesis, 102; C. T. Allmand, 'The Anglo-French negotiations, 1439', *BIHR* 40 (1967), 14. The embassy was named in council on 8 May: E 28/60.

[20] The following discussion is based on Beckington's journal, printed in *PPC* v. 334–407, the documents in *Foedera*, x. 724–32, and those edited by C. T. Allmand, 'Documents relating to the Anglo-French negotiations of 1439' in *Camden Miscellany*, 24 (1972), 79–149. Besides Allmand in *BIHR* 40, there are detailed accounts in Taylor, thesis, 97–152 and A. D. Dicks, 'The question of peace: Anglo-French diplomacy, 1439–49', Ph.D. thesis (University of Oklahoma, 1966), 20–73.

abandon his exclusive right to the title but not to the use of it within his own territories. This indeed was the compromise which Beaufort was to urge upon the French: that the great and populous realm of France had not at all times in the past been under the rule of one sole king, and that there was no reason in natural law or the needs of good government why it should so be. This declaration was to be made by the cardinal himself, fortified by historical precedents from the time of Charlemagne, and urged within the context of a forceful appeal for peace as the overriding goal to which rulers should devote their efforts. For kings ruled as ministers for the welfare of their subjects, and should set aside the pride and lust of dominion and 'this rigorous and extreme continuans and abiding upon the claymes and querele on both side' that had caused the war to endure 'this hondred yere and more'; which, if it were not to end in the destruction of either, must now be settled 'by good appointment and accord'. Such an appeal, made in virtue of his spiritual office, was the more opportune in that neither papal nor conciliar representatives played any official role in the negotiations; indeed the attempted intervention by delegates from Basel was explicitly spurned by Beaufort and the English embassy. There must be a strong presumption that this declaration represented Beaufort's own sentiments and was from his hand, and that it embodied the arguments which he had used to win the young king's acceptance for his mission. While there can be no doubt that Henry VI himself desired peace with all the ardour and idealism of his years and religious temperament, it is unlikely that he had the polished fluency of composition or the command of allusion to have composed the instructions himself.

On two other matters the instructions showed a realistic appreciation of the points likely to be raised by the French. The French claim for the restitution of lands to those who held before Henry V's conquest was to be allowed in so far as it did not affect any who held existing title to lands; while any proposal for a marriage of the young Henry VI was to be deferred until the completion of a treaty. Finally any further French offers were to be reported to the council and the French meantime urged to conclude a truce, during which places held by the English in France might be exchanged for Harfleur, Dieppe, and Mont Saint-Michel, and the duke of Orléans liberated on payment. The instructions testify to the seriousness of the English desire for a settlement and an appreciation of the areas where concessions would have to be made. They indicate that Beaufort was hoping to circumvent the unbridgeable gap over Henry VI's title and the status of the English lands in France by offering a long truce on the basis of mutual respect for each monarch's title and territory, which would stabilize the existing situation. Yet the difficulty with his proposed solution was that the French had little reason to prefer it to a continuation of the war. Moral and religious exhortation and the bonds of blood and amity between the kings counted little with professional diplomats. An offer to release the duke of Orléans would have carried more weight, but Gloucester's opposition and the calculation that he could be used as a bargaining counter kept all mention of this out of the English procurations until, following Burgundian representations, Beaufort emended these on his own authority after the conference had begun.[21] Charles VII probably viewed Orléans's release as a mixed blessing and was anyway ambivalent in his desire for negotiations. His long-term aims were the reduction of Burgundian power, the expulsion of the English, and the limitation of the French crown's dependence on the princes and nobility. Yet it was clearer than in 1435 that the expulsion of the English was likely to be costly and prolonged, and that it would entail his military dependence on the aristocracy and the duke of Burgundy. A truce would indeed relieve these pressures but would bring immobility to a situation whose fluidity could turn to the crown's profit. Nor would an Anglo-Burgundian *rapprochement* be to the advantage of France. The French council was divided, and readier to talk than to reach a decision. Its dogged insistence that the conference should consider only a peace treaty revealed its suspicion of the English proposal for a long truce.

The embassy crossed from Dover at the end of June to the accompaniment of prayers ordered by Chichele for its success and that of Huntingdon's expedition to Guyenne.[22] Out of deference to Beaufort's age and comfort, the conference was held a mile inland from Oye, seven miles from Calais, and four from Gravelines.[23] Beaufort's pavilion, erected on the site on 1 July, was one hundred feet long, constructed of timber and canvas, and lined with his favourite scarlet cloth. He had brought furniture and plate in abundance and at once set a standard of lavish hospitality by a feast in Calais on Saint-Swithun's day. On 6 July he moved to the conference site in preparation for its opening on 10 July. Beaufort's pavilion could accommodate 300 persons and stood at two bowshots from Isabel's.[24] Between them was the conference pavilion in which Beaufort's seat was placed between Isabel and his goddaughter Anne. When the altercation between the two embassies over their procurations had been settled by Beaufort, Kemp made a formal oration on the cause of peace, taking the *Revelations of St Bridget* as the text for an affirmation of Henry

[21] On this see Allmand, op. cit. BIHR 16; *Camden Misc.* 113; *PPC* v. 344–6.

[22] *Register of Edmund Lacy*, ed. G. A. Dunstan, ii. 156.

[23] The conference forms the setting for the story of two esquires in Beaufort's retinue, John Stourton and Thomas Brampton, brothers in arms, who competed for the favours of the wife of their host in Calais: *Les Cent Nouvelles Nouvelles*, ed. P. Champion, 180–5.

[24] *PPC* v. 341–2; Waurin, *Croniques*, iv. 265 was impressed with the cardinal's 'moult riches tentes et pavillons . . . tant de vaiselles d'or et d'argent', and notes that his reception of Isabel was 'moult honourablement a la maniere d'Angleterre, car bien le sceut faire comme prelat sachant qu'il estoit'.

VI's rights as heir to the treaty of Troyes, an ineptitude which he later compounded by angrily denouncing the archbishop of Rheims's counter-citation of the prophecies of John the Hermit to support the view that the English conquest was doomed as being the work of the devil. Again Beaufort intervened with the jocular observation that perhaps all could be resolved by a marriage between the hermit and St Bridget.[25] These inauspicious beginnings were quickly confirmed as the two sides unfolded their negotiating positions and reached an impasse over the status of the lands to be held by the English in France. Despite Beaufort's plea to Isabel to persuade the French to waive the demand for homage, she reported that they were adamant. Nor would they countenance a long truce, which would only prolong the war, and would in any case have to be accompanied by measures of restitution which the English were not empowered to concede. Thus within two days the conference, so long planned and so elaborately staged, was in danger of collapse. Beaufort's plan for a *de facto* division of France had failed to command French interest or consideration.[26]

It was at this stage, on 13 July, that with Beaufort's support the Duchess Isabel had a meeting at Calais with the duke of Orléans, from which emerged a totally new proposal. On the following day Isabel journeyed to Saint-Omer to discuss it with her husband before presenting it to Beaufort on Thursday, 18 July. In the interval Beaufort had stopped all communication with England, ostensibly because of rumours of a French attack, but possibly also to prevent adverse news of the negotiations reaching the king. The new proposal was for a temporary peace of between fifteen and thirty years, during which Henry VI would cease to style himself king of France and Charles VII would waive the demand for homage, at the end of which if Henry chose to renew his title the war would begin anew or a formal peace be made on the basis of a render of homage.[27] This appeared to offer sufficient advantages to the English for Beaufort to ask for the proposals to be put into writing; it would preserve the territorial status quo, it appeared to contain no demand for restitution, and it left in suspense the question of the royal title and the tenure of the lands. Yet when the written text was delivered to the cardinal later that day, it became plain that this was not a new proposal by Isabel and Orléans, or an attempt to make Beaufort's own scheme palatable to the French, but a means to accommodate English objections to the French plan for a final peace. The consistent French terms for that peace—the formal surrender by Henry VI of his title and of all English conquests, the holding of all lands as fiefs of the French crown, the restitution of Frenchmen expelled, and the release of Orléans without ransom—were plainly set forth as the context (which the English would

[25] Allmand, op. cit. *Camden Misc.* 116.

[26] Allmand, op. cit. *BIHR* 18–20; *Camden Misc.* 117–18; *PPC* v. 353–4, 363–4.

[27] *PPC* v. 66–7; *Camden Misc.* 120–1.

have formally to accept) of the proposed moratorium, and during the temporary peace the French remained insistent on restitution and the release of Orléans.[28]

The English complained bitterly at what they regarded as a deception. Beaufort himself, with his eyes still fixed on the chance of a truce, sought to define the lands in the French proposal. The English produced a list of these and the French a counter-list, though they were already rumoured to be preparing to leave. It was on the urging of Beaufort, who promised to submit the terms to Henry VI, that Isabel and Orléans on 29 July secured the French proposal in a final form. The French had, in fact, made significant concessions. All demands that Henry VI should formally renounce his title and acknowledge French suzerainty were now dropped; instead the prologue merely recognized the contrary standpoints of the protagonists and presented the agreement as a suspension or moratorium of their claims. Territorially the French agreed to the English retention of the whole of Normandy except Mont Saint-Michel, though reserving the homage of Brittany. They still, however, required the restitution of dispossessed Frenchmen and the release without ransom of the duke of Orléans.[29]

These were the terms which Beaufort was prepared to submit to the English council through the major part of the embassy, led by Kemp, which returned to England on 5 August. Beaufort himself chose to remain at Calais. There were good reasons for this. The continued presence of both mediators, Beaufort and Isabel, served to emphasize that the conference merely stood adjourned until the delegations reported back, and was designed (though unsuccessfully) to prevent a French withdrawal. Secondly, Beaufort's age and infirmity (he was twice ill in the following weeks) made further travelling burdensome; indeed this proved to be his final visit to the continent. It would therefore be unwise to infer that his decision reflected a distancing of himself from the proposals, which indeed he commended to the king 'in his own writing'. It would be equally hazardous to maintain that by leaving the presentation of them to Kemp he prejudiced their acceptance; for we know that Kemp argued long and eloquently in the council for Henry VI to relinquish the use of the title. Even so Beaufort must have recognized that a strong case could be made against the proposed terms and that Gloucester was bound to make it. Whether from the realization that his presence would make the issue into a personal vendetta, or from a lack of enthusiasm for the terms, he now stepped back from the final decision. Indeed with the rejection of his own plan he seems to have lost the initiative, relinquishing this to Isabel, who displayed shrewdness of judgement and independence. By the end of the

[28] *PPC* v. 376–9; Allmand, op. cit. *BIHR* 22.
[29] *PPC* v. 378–82; *Camden Misc.* 135–9.

conference Beaufort gives the impression of being a spent force, resigned to the rejection of Isabel's terms and apprehensive of the future both in England and France.

No record survives of the actual debates in the English council during the second and third weeks of August, when the king was at Windsor with all his councillors, but three different memoranda, in French, English, and Latin, show that the terms were closely examined and intensively debated.[30] That in French may well have emanated from the Normandy council, emphasizing as it does the need for peace in the light of the predicament of Normandy. It rehearses the impoverishment and depopulation of the duchy, the impossibility of further taxation, and the disaffection of the natives towards English rule. It is openly scathing about the behaviour of English captains and the state of English defences, and sceptical of both the will and ability of Henry VI himself to take up arms, as of the commitment of the English nobility and parliament to maintaining the war. Normandy is pictured as all but indefensible; its people crying out for peace and stability. These were the practical reasons for accepting terms which promised a long suspension of hostilities, and they must have been forcibly presented to Beaufort by the Norman delegation during the negotiations. They probably carried less weight in England than the legal and political problems which would arise from the suspension of the use of Henry's title and the restitution of lands to supporters of Charles VII; and it was on these that objections in all three memoranda concentrated.

Since the suspension of the use of the title tried to circumvent a logical impasse, it was easy enough to demonstrate its inconsistencies and the legal anomalies it would produce. It would mean a loss of face and be tantamount to abandonment of the king's rights, for not to use a rightful title was itself unjust and dishonourable, and the more so in that the king had been crowned and anointed. Such action would throw doubt on the legitimacy of the war, brand Henry's rule as tyranny, and deprive his grants of validity and their recipients of their titles. Within France Charles VII would alone be openly acknowledged as king, so that appeal would be made to him, while abroad it would undermine Henry VI's status with his allies as well as at the council of Basel and the Curia. In short it was absurd to suppose that Henry VI could in any real sense sustain traditional English pretensions while putting them in suspense. Even more severe were the practical problems of attempting to restore lands to those whom Henry V had dispossessed. The French nobility would never agree to any long-term peace without reinstatement, and the English recognized that in respect of some fiefs—Alençon, Harcourt, Eu, Tancarville, Maine—this had to be contemplated. But the memoranda insisted that compensation would have

[30] E 28/61 19 Aug. The memoranda are in *Camden Misc.* 140–6, 147–9 and *PPC* v. 391–5.

to be paid to existing holders, largely by the French, and that the restoration of the lower ranks of the nobility, involving a general compensation, would be a gigantic expense. Moreover, restitution raised acute difficulties for the security and authority of Lancastrian rule in Normandy, since the sympathies of the restored native landlords would rest with Charles VII, making the defence of the duchy by military enfeoffment inoperable, taxation impossible to collect, and reducing English control to isolated garrisons maintained at English expense. In a word the government of Normandy would be undermined. Even the restored clergy would preach disaffection. Beyond this the memoranda voiced objections to the release of Orléans without ransom, and to some of the territorial changes proposed to consolidate English landholding to Normandy and Guyenne. But the main argument against the proposals was that they amounted to a *de facto* surrender of sovereignty within the English territories. At the end of fifteen or thirty years it would be impossible psychologically, politically, and militarily to revive the claims and programme of Henry V. The English were being offered an ordered, legalized, and peaceful winding up of their colonial rule, rather than forceful expulsion in the foreseeable future.

It was not surprising that the English council rejected these terms, and it would certainly be unwise to attribute this solely to Gloucester's opposition and influence. The memoranda, clearly prepared for the council by professional advisers, were all weighted against acceptance, while the young king's love of peace was only exceeded by his high regard for his kingly title, which he was unwilling to jeopardize or renounce. When the English embassy returned to Calais on 9 September it therefore reiterated the basic English demand for Normandy, Guyenne, and Calais in full sovereignty, which the French had already rejected. They then discovered that in fact the French had decamped since 30 July. Although the fiction was maintained that Charles VII had still to deliver his reply to Isabel's proposal, it could now be seen that the failure of the conference had effectively been determined in the first days when neither the terms for a peace nor for a long truce proved acceptable.

How serious a blow was this to Beaufort's political standing? The Calais negotiations had been the goal of his diplomatic policy, the work of his own servants and associates, and the expression of his renewed authority and influence in the council over the past two and a half years. Beaufort had played on the young king's desire for peace to rebuild the alliance with Burgundy destroyed in 1435–6. But the prospects for peace through Burgundian mediation had now been shown to be a delusion, and in this fundamental sense Beaufort's policy was bankrupt. Yet it yielded some positive fruits, important for the future. The council had acknowledged that the duke of Orléans could make a contribution and were prepared to grant temporary release under sureties, though not to relinquish the ransom. It had also accepted that any permanent recognition of English dominion in France would have to be confined to Normandy, Guyenne, and Calais, implying a withdrawal from the residual lands held in the *pays de conquête*, including Maine. Here the outlines of the next serious negotiations, at Tours, were foreshadowed. But of greater and more immediate consequence was the re-establishment of commercial relations with Flanders.

Proposals for an *intercursus* had already been extensively discussed in the missions of Uttenhove and Lalaing in 1438 and powers for this had been given to a special panel of the English delegation on 23 May.[31] But though Uttenhove and Lannoy met Beaufort at Oye on 23 July and delegates of the Four Members a week later, it was only after the return from England of the main embassy in September that negotiations on the commercial issues began. Isabel had arrived at Calais on 15 September with a Burgundian delegation to receive the formal English rejection of her proposals; she then enquired 'with great coolness and indifference' whether the English were interested in maintaining the truces and negotiating intercourse between England and Flanders.[32] By 18 September Uttenhove and Philippe de Nanterre had joined her and next day negotiations began in the Great Hall of the Staplers. The agreement was signed ten days later. It merely reopened the trade routes and guaranteed the safety of merchants and merchandise for three years. Despite the complaints of the Holland merchants voiced in 1438, it did not raise the question of the Partition Ordinance or bullion regulations, nor that of English exports of cloth. Indeed a bullion war continued and Philip formally renewed the ban on English cloth in Flanders in December.[33] But the agreement meant that Beaufort did not return empty handed. The English council approved the agreement on 10 October and in January 1440 it was extended for a further five years, while the Flemish towns marked their gratitude to the cardinal with a reward of 12,000 *saluts d'or,* equivalent to some 2,000 English marks.[34] This ended the period of interruption of trade initiated at Arras. The northern seas were again fully open to English merchants. Moroever in 1437, through Beaufort's urging, agreement had been reached with Heinrich Vorrath, the burgomaster of Danzig, for the confirmation of the rights of English merchants trading in Hanseatic towns and the payment of the arears of indemnity agreed in 1409. Although the agreement was never ratified by the Grand Master of the Teutonic Order, and gave rise to subsequent disputes and reprisals by

[31] *Foedera*, x. 730–1.
[32] *PPC* v. 377–9, 375.
[33] Thielemans, *Bourgogne et Angleterre*, 443–53; Taylor, thesis, 125–6.
[34] Thielemans, op. cit., 138 n. 161.

either side, it had served to maintain an export market for English cloth during the critical years of Anglo-Burgundian hostility. Between 1436–7 and 1440 cloth exports soared to new heights, topping 50,000 pieces for the first time, a peak from which they were not to descend until the disastrous attack on the Bay Fleet in 1449.[35] The restoration of trade with Flanders brought a similar surge in wool exports to over 18,000 sacks, a level not achieved since the Partition Ordinance of 1429. That the commercial consequences of the breach with Burgundy had been repaired, and something like an entente re-established, must be set as credits to Beaufort's diplomacy, even if his wider plans for the political and military stabilization of the English territories in France had been frustrated.

[35] M. M. Postan 'Anglo-Hanseatic Commercial Relations' in M. M. Postan and E. Power (edd.), *Studies in Eng. Trade*, 117–19; Ferguson, *English Diplomacy*, 93–7; *Eng. Export Trade*, 94–5, 122. These accounts have now been modified by T. H. Lloyd, 'A re- consideration of two Anglo-Hanseatic treaties of the fifteenth century', *EHR* 102 (1987), 919–23.

16

Waning Influence, 1439–1442

THE failure of the Calais negotiations proved to be a·turning point in Cardinal Beaufort's career. Although English diplomacy continued the quest for peace through the mediation first of Burgundy and then of the great French feudatories, this eventually became a blind alley, discrediting the cardinal and passing the political initiative to others. It was also a divisive policy, prompting a bitter denunciation of Beaufort's policies, ambitions, and covetousness from the duke of Gloucester. The attack was buried by official silence but it undermined the cardinal's reputation and assisted his displacement from power. His attendance at council became much less frequent and his old associates there—Kemp, Cromwell, Alnwick, Hungerford, and Tiptoft—were now matched by lords with strong ties to the royal household: Beauchamp, Beaumont, Dudley, Sudeley, and Suffolk. The council itself continued to meet in formal sessions and take major policy decisions, but at other times royal warrants were attested by members of the household or the chancellor and keeper of the privy seal. This gradual shift of power, spreading from patronage to policies, and affecting both agencies of government and personnel, makes these years particularly difficult to interpret. Moreover, some among the household group who came to replace Beaufort had personal ties with him and might be regarded as his political heirs, while the cardinal's gradual withdrawal was also conditioned by his advancing years. Even so it was accompanied by discernible political tensions and was to culminate in a dramatic discrediting of the cardinal's policies and a fundamental shift in English diplomacy. The three years following the Calais negotiations form a transition from the heyday of Beaufort's influence to the events of 1443–4 which precipitated his retirement from politics.

The cardinal returned from the Calais conference to Winchester house at Southwark on 7 October 1439 and at once sent his esquire Otwell Worsley to the king at Kennington, who granted him an audience four days later. Kemp and Beaufort then reported to the council, at which preparations were made for the forthcoming parliament, summoned for 12 November.[1] Under Gloucester's influence this had originally been called to meet at

[1] *PPC* v. 406–7. *Chron. John Stone*, 26 records his arrival at Canterbury on 5 Oct. Those present at council were: Gloucester, Kemp, Northumberland, Suffolk, Stafford, Beauchamp, Sudeley, and Fiennes, besides the chancellor and privy seal: *PPC* v. 109; E 28/64; C 81/1545/75.

Oxford, but on 22 October the council changed the venue to Westminster.[2] Although the Commons elected as their Speaker William Tresham, the steward for the feoffees in the midland estates of the duchy, the two sessions of parliament proved singularly uncomfortable for the cardinal. The elections had already produced a clash between Lord Tiptoft and his rivals, Lords Bardolph and Ormond, outraged by his grant of the Richmond lands in Cambridgeshire, and though Beaufort championed Tiptoft in the council, when a new election was ordered it was Ormond's supporters who were returned.[3] The theme of the chancellor's speech was the need for domestic concord, and no report on the Calais negotiations is recorded. Indeed the rolls give no indication of what business occupied the long and inconclusive first session up to 21 December, when it was prorogued to 14 January for further deliberation on the measures to be taken for the defence of the realm and good and substantial governance.[4] This suggests that both the grants of taxation and the linked measures for the finance of the household, enacted in the new year, had already been extensively discussed. The need for taxation was indeed urgent, for the last lay subsidy had been levied a year ago, in November 1438. In the adjourned session at Reading the Commons' grant, agreed by 9 February, was not ungenerous: one and a half subsidies were to be collected between midsummer 1440 and Martinmas 1441; the wool subsidies and tunnage and poundage were extended for three years from Martinmas and April respectively, and a poll tax on aliens was likewise granted for three years. Combined with the upsurge in wool exports produced by the *intercursus*, this brought a marked improvement in exchequer revenue over the next three years.[5]

These grants were facilitated by the crown's readiness to heed complaints about household finance and impose hosting requirements on aliens for seven years. Four bills referred to the 'great murmur and clamour' against purveyances for the household, to allay which the king promised to apply the revenues from the unenfeoffed parts of the duchy of Lancaster, and from the duchy of Cornwall, to the expenses of the household for the next five years.[6] This was a bait for a proposal by the crown to wind up the enfeoffment of the duchy of Lancaster and apply its

[2] *RDP* iv. 898–902; Gloucester had just presented 129 volumes to Oxford, which sent a petition of commendation to parliament: *Epistolae Academicae Oxoniensis*, ed. H. Anstey, i. 184.

[3] Roskell, *Parliament and Politics*, ii. 137–53 (on Tresham); Virgoe, 'Cambridgeshire Election', 95–101.

[4] *Rot. Parl.* v. 3–4; cf. *Brut*, ii. 475: the parliament 'endured unto Christmasse next and myght not acorde'.

[5] Steel, *Receipt*, 441.

[6] *CPR 1436–41*, 303; *Rot. Parl.*v. 7. This use of the duchy revenues had in fact been in operation since 1437: DL 42/18 fo. 123, 124^{v}.

revenues likewise to household expenses, in order that these might be 'contened and assethed and his people noght so greved'. This proposal elicited a forceful reply from Beaufort and Hungerford, asserting the legality of their title, adducing the large loans made to the crown which had impeded the discharge of Henry V's debts, and claiming that they were still owed many thousands of pounds. Nevertheless, they declared that once they had been paid, and reserving £2,000 p.a. for the final discharge of Henry V's creditors, they were willing to deliver the residue of their receipts to the household. They asked for four safeguards: they were to render no account at the exchequer, to be able to withhold payment if the money was not spent on the household, to have letters patent authorizing the prolongation of their trust, and to have it placed on record that the money hitherto received by them had not been spent for their own profit so that they would not thereafter be 'empeched, vexed, ne endamaged' by the crown.[7]

Beaufort and Hungerford had evidently been placed under severe pressure and had negotiated toughly in defence of their position. That pressure can only have come from the household group under Suffolk, adducing the 'clamour' of the Commons and perhaps abetted by Gloucester. The position of the feoffees, though legally sound, was politically indefensible: the king had the right to enjoy his patrimonial estates, and in applying these to the household expenses was following the canons of good kingship and earning the gratitude of the Commons.[8] Thus the generous grants of taxation and the king's readiness to use his patrimony for domestic expenses bear all the marks of a carefully constructed bargain between crown and Commons at the expense of the feoffees, the elements of which must have been under discussion in the first session and finalized early in the second. It was probably in the period when these matters were in debate—from early in December 1439 to late January 1440—that Gloucester mounted his frontal attack on Beaufort.

Gloucester's charges seem to have been preferred first orally—probably in general terms—and then made more specific when he was required to put them in writing. They were then presented in parliament, probably in the first ten days of the resumed session at Reading.[9] Some of Gloucester's

[7] *Rot. Parl.* v. 8.

[8] The Commons further agreed to allocate a quarter of the subsidy for household expenses: ibid. 32.

[9] *Wars of the Eng.* ii. 440–51; *Arnold's Chronicle*, (ed. H. Ellis), 279–86; *Chronicles of London*, 153. The issue of letters patent on 8 Jan. ratifying Elizabeth Beauchamp's estate in the manors demised to her by the feoffees, and exonerating them, suggests that by then the contents were already known (*CPR 1436–41*). They would seem to have been put in writing before the news of Kemp's promotion as cardinal was known at the end of Jan. (Bekynton, *Correspondence*, i. 38–9, 50–2). However, the reference to Orléans being brought to London and to the imminent arrival of a French embassy would indicate early Feb., for Orléans was transferred to the custody of Lord Fanhope between 29 Jan. and 10 Feb. (Ramsay, *Lancaster and York*, ii. 24).

language links his accusations with the parliamentary pressure on Beaufort to surrender the feoffment: thus, in inviting the king to avail himself of the great lucre of the cardinal, he noted that 'ther is grete gode byhoveful at thys time for the wele and sauvacion of your royaumes, the poverte, necessitee, bareness and indigence of your liege people in your highnesse understanden'. Moreover, the thrust of his demand was for the removal of Beaufort and Kemp from the council with the express purpose of enabling 'men to be at their fredam to sey what hem thenketh of trouth; for thogh I dare speke of my trouthe, the poure ne dar not so'. This suggests that Gloucester may have hoped for the imprisonment of his enemy to enable the Commons to prepare an impeachment; for he could not proceed against the cardinal by way of appeal, and any other legal proceedings would have to be initiated by the crown. Such was far from Suffolk's purpose, which at this stage was to loosen the cardinal's grip, not to remove him or replace his authority with that of Gloucester. No formal proceedings appear to have been taken on Gloucester's charges. No reply from Beaufort or Kemp is on record, and it is probable that the king and the council declined to take further action and, having let the charges do their damage, buried them. If Beaufort was denied the right of reply, that itself underlined the weakness of his position: he was being made to realize his dependence on royal grace. It may be significant that on 4 February, when the charges were probably still under consideration, Beaufort agreed in council to defer repayment of the loan of 7,000 marks made in March 1439. At Easter he would have been entitled to foreclose on the jewels which he held as security, but instead he accepted assignments on the lay subsidy to be paid at Martinmas, for which tallies were issued to him on 9 February.[10]

Gloucester's dossier of his enemies' crimes is a long and impressive document, reaching back to the reign of Henry V. Some of the accusations were well researched and cleverly presented, and the intention was to destroy the cardinal's reputation as a diplomat and a statesman as well as to convict him of corruption and defrauding the crown. Gloucester now had the chance to show the young king that, far from being devoted to the preservation of his inheritance, Beaufort's actions had been consistently 'into derogation of your noble estate, and hurte of both your royaumes, and yet doen and used daily'. Pride, greed, and nepotism were shown to be his consistent motives. His presumption in securing the cardinalate with exemption from the jurisdiction of Canterbury in 1417, his claim to attend parliament and council as cardinal in 1429, his avoidance of the penalties of praemunire in retaining the see of Winchester, and his purchase of a pardon after the forfeiture of his goods in 1432–4 were all now recalled.

[10] *PPC* v. 115; E 404/56/163.

Yet these were no longer live issues, and Beaufort had been exonerated on all these counts in 1434.

Passing to the cardinal's financial dealings, Gloucester charged him with arranging for the exchequer to default on the repayment of his loan of 1424 in order to retain jewels which he held as security; he suggested that Beaufort's tenure of the Southampton customs had enabled him to defraud the crown, and he derided his loans as coming too late to be of help. In two ways the cardinal had defrauded the crown of lands: by procuring manors worth £200 for his nephew's wife Elizabeth Beauchamp through a fraudulent manipulation of the terms of Henry V's will, and by the advantageous purchase of Chirk. The first of these charges, relating to the loan of 1424, was susceptible of different interpretations, though Beaufort undeniably retained some of the jewels. Nevertheless, he was probably covered in this respect by his general pardon of 20 June 1437.[11] Gloucester's language indicates that he knew he would be unable to prove that Beaufort had defrauded the king of customs in Southampton ('by likeliness it is to suppose that . . . ye be thereby greatly defrauded'), and the extant customs accounts carry no indication that Beaufort shipped significant quantities of wool in his own name. Although he had repeatedly been empowered to nominate one of the collectors for the repayment of his loans, the other collector throughout the entire period was William Soper, Henry V's chief naval contractor and clerk of the ships, and mayor of Southampton, a man whose integrity was presumably beyond question.[12] Whether or not he believed it to be true, Gloucester could have no evidence for this charge. With the remaining duchy feoffees, Beaufort was technically at fault for having demised duchy lands to Elizabeth Beauchamp and her husband Thomas Swynford, the cardinal's nephew. Under the terms of Henry V's will Elizabeth was to receive land worth £100 p.a. while she remained single but £200 p.a. if she married within a year of the king's death. Although she did not marry Thomas until 1424–5, she and her husband were granted lands by the feoffees in November 1425 and July 1426. Beaufort's influence as chancellor in procuring her marriage to his nephew and these subsequent grants may reasonably be inferred, and during Gloucester's ensuing period as protector the feoffees prudently purchased a pardon, in November 1427, for alienating the lands without licence. With the feoffees under attack in 1440, the crown looked likely to reclaim these lands, and Elizabeth hastened to obtain letters patent ratifying her estate, the grants being ascribed to the negligence of the feoffees in misreading the will.[13] Here again Beaufort had ensured that he was reasonably covered.

[11] Discussed above, ch. 7 nn. 33–5 and text thereat.

[12] Beaufort's collectors in Southampton were John Foxholes (1417–28), John Chirche (1433–8), and William Mareys (1442–7): *CFR passim*; for Soper, see *The Navy of the Lancastrian Kings*, ed. S. Rose (Navy Rec. Soc., 1982), 6–27.

[13] *CPR 1422–9*, 455; *CPR 1436–41*, 364–5.

On political matters Gloucester accused Beaufort and Kemp of estranging him, York, and Huntingdon from the king and of holding council meetings in his own house. As we have seen, the records of the council give some colour to both statements, though Gloucester had ready access to the court, while meetings under Beaufort's roof were very exceptional. The attack on the cardinal's diplomacy stretched back to the release of King James in 1424, the failure to prevent the desertion of Burgundy at Arras, and to the recent proposals brought back from Calais, for the rejection of which Gloucester claimed the credit. He went on to warn against the proposed meeting with the French in the spring and the release of the duke of Orléans. Finally came a group of charges directed against the Beaufort involvement in Normandy. The cardinal himself was accused of appointing to offices in the duchy for profit rather than by merit, of frustrating Gloucester's own offers to do service there and promoting 'other of his singular affection' in his place (a reference, perhaps, to 1436, 1437, and 1439), and of indirectly causing losses in France through Dorset's inconclusive operations in 1438–9. Clearly these were all matters for debate, and the charges on which formal judicial proceedings could be brought were few. On these the cardinal had already secured himself in respect of praemunire, his loans to the crown, and his purchases of land. Gloucester could hardly have expected to reopen these, except in the context of a general impeachment. More immediately he hoped to frustrate Beaufort's plans by undermining his reputation. In particular Gloucester wanted to halt the prospective negotiations for peace and the release of Orléans, and prevent the appointment of John, earl of Somerset as lieutenant-general in France. Only in the last of these was he successful.

Somerset must have returned to England at about the same time as the cardinal, in October 1439, and over the next three months their concerted efforts were directed to securing for him the post of lieutenant-general. Somerset quickly showed himself agreeable to further service and by 13 December had indented 'at the king's commandment' for six months with 100 men-at-arms and 2,000 archers. Not surprisingly this was financed by his uncle, who, on 22 December, loaned 10,000 marks, enabling Somerset to draw wages of war for £5,271 on the same day.[14] He had also been granted warrants for the payment of all sums due to him at the exchequer and for the arrears of his annuity on the petty custom in London, which Beaufort personally instructed Moleyns to expedite.[15] His mother, the duchess of Clarence, lay dying even while these issues were under negotiation, and his indentures safeguarded his rights in his inheritance. Her death occurred on 31 December, and on 19 February 1440 Somerset

[14] E 404/56/155; E 401/766; E 403/736. Somerset had issued ordinances in Normandy on 4 Sept.: *Appendices to Foedera*, 441.

[15] E 28/63 12 Dec.; *PPC* v. 112–13; E 404/56/154.

was granted the keeping of her lands provided he sued livery of them before Easter 1441.[16] The day fixed for his departure was now at hand: he was to have mustered at Poole on 28 December, but shipping was not available until 16 January, and after a further postponement to 8 February his second quarter's payment of £5,152 was made on 24 February.[17] The exchequer was still acutely short of cash and it was the cardinal who once again raised the money for his nephew's departure, sending Adam Moleyns to borrow £3,200 from Margaret, countess of Devon as executor of her mother's estate.[18] Beaufort's own loan was secured partly on the clerical tenth granted on 22 December and payable at midsummer, and partly on the second instalment of the lay subsidy payable at Martinmas. Thus between mid-December and mid-February the cardinal had procured his nephew's return to France at the head of a sizeable force and as the most senior commander in France; he had also ensured that the exchequer could not, in the immediate future, mount another expedition of comparable or larger size.

The significance of this is apparent in the context of Gloucester's own ambitions and his attack on the cardinal made during these weeks. Indirect evidence shows that Gloucester now revived his plan to lead a large army to Normandy himself, with the powers of lieutenant-general. Letters from the council in France, from June 1441, reveal that the king had originally told them to expect Gloucester, and the duke of York's conditions for taking the office in July 1440 asked for the same powers that Gloucester 'had or shulde have had now late'. Gloucester himself, in his protest against the release of Orléans on 2 June, stressed the need for substantial help to be sent to Normandy in men and money if no 'Riall Army' (i.e. such as he would lead) could be dispatched at present.[19] Finally, a fragmentary document probably dating from slightly before this, entitled 'Le Pouer de Monsieur le Conte de Somerset' states that Gloucester was to go to Normandy, but since he was not yet ready to do so 'in such powerful apparaille' as his and the king's honour required, Somerset had been named by the king and council as 'lieutenant gouverner general pour le fait de la guerre' for the whole realm of France and duchy of Normandy. This empowered him 'mener l'estat de notre guerre', to receive castles and towns into obedience, make truces, appoint captains and civil officials (reserving the higher military commands until Gloucester should come), and grant lands up to the value of 500 *li. tournois* p.a. These powers were certainly given subsequent to his indentures, probably at about the time of

[16] *CPR 1436–41*, 382, 515; E 28/63 19 Feb. Dorset's inheritance of the duchess's annuity of 500 marks was confirmed on 19 Jan.: ibid. 375.

[17] Ibid. 370, 408; E 403/736.

[18] *Rot. Parl.* v. 22; E 401/766, for other loans from London and the Italian community.

[19] *Wars of Eng.* ii. 586, 604; Vickers, *Gloucester*, 268 n. 7; *Foedera*, x. 765.

his sailing in February, from which time he used this title and drew a salary of 600 *li. tournois* per month.[20] No record remains of debates on this issue in parliament or council, but it would seem that, even as he faced Gloucester's attack, the cardinal had ensured the rejection of his rival's ambitious project on financial grounds, and had secured extended, if temporary, powers for his nephew. It must have seemed a short step to the confirmation of these on a permanent basis. In the event it was one which Gloucester frustrated. For although his own appointment never materialized, it placed the effective nomination in his hands, and before the end of June that had fallen to the duke of York who formally indented on 2 July 1440. In this sense the battle between the rivals ended in a draw, with York the *tertium gaudens*, but in reality it marked a severe defeat for the cardinal, who had been unable to impose his choice on the council, and a setback to the ambitions of his nephews.

The Beaufort brothers were, for the moment, heavily engaged in the defence of Normandy and Maine against the French attack directed by Richemont in the autumn of 1439. Dorset, Scales, and Talbot had relieved Avranches by 23 December, and on his arrival Somerset concluded a treaty with the duke of Brittany who agreed to place Saint-Malo in the hands of the Anglophile Gilles and promised to give no aid to the French in Harfleur and Dieppe.[21] After a profitable marauding raid into Picardy, the decision was also taken to besiege Harfleur, which was blockaded on sea and land by Dorset and Talbot. In October 1440 their combined forces withstood a powerful relieving army, Dorset having sent for reinforcements from England and his Norman estates. Somerset declined to settle the fate of the town by single combat with the count of Eu, and by late October Harfleur and Montivilliers had surrendered and were placed under Talbot's custody.[22] Somerset and Dorset could thus return, probably in November, with credit and some profit. Somerset had secured for himself a rent of 3,000 *salus* from Saint-Sauveur-l'Endelin, and Dorset an inn at Calais held by Bedford.[23] Though rewarded and in good repute, the Beaufort brothers

[20] BL Add. MS 11542 fo. 81; BN MS Fr. 26549 nos. 26, 29 are his receipts for the Feb. instalment; cf. *Wars of Eng*. ii. 304. Somerset is not designated by the title in the issue roll of 25 Feb. The exact date of his sailing seems uncertain, for mariners were paid from 22 Jan. to 3 Mar., but he seems to have mustered in Normandy by 17 Feb.: E 101/53/25; Cooper, *Appendices to Foedera*, 447–8.

[21] Beaucourt, *Charles VII*, iii. 20; Pollard, *Talbot*, 52; Knowlson, *Jean V*, 170. Dorset's retaining fees for 1439–40 are noted in BN MS Fr. 26549 nos. 23, 24, 28.

[22] Pollard, *Talbot*, 53; *Wars of Eng*. ii. 308–9; Waurin, *Cronicques* iv. 283; *Appendices to Foedera*, 452–60. Somerset held the field with 400 men-at-arms while Dorset, Talbot, and Faucomberg pressed the siege. A naval blockade was commissioned in May (E 28/66 2 Feb.) and the siege commenced in July.

[23] M. Jones, 'John Beaufort', 85; *CPR 1436–41*, 443, 499. Somerset surrendered the captaincy of Rouen in Nov. (Marshall, thesis, Appendix 2) and the lieutenancy at the end of Oct.: BN, MS Fr. 26549 nos. 30–1, 33. By Jan. 1441 he was named as a commissioner in Dorset: *CPR 1436–41*, 535.

knew well enough that York's appointment and the retirement of the cardinal's close ally, Louis of Luxembourg, as chancellor of Normandy, had ended their prospects of enlarging their lands and offices in France for the foreseeable future. York received very extensive powers over the civil and military administration, equal to those enjoyed by Bedford. In particular he stipulated for freedom to remove non-resident captains and replace them with members of his own retinue, while no restrictions were placed on the value of the lands he was entitled to grant. He was determined to create a personal following from the captains who had served Bedford and those he brought with him. Although the Beauforts were not displaced from any of their lands or captaincies except Falaise, they did not form part of York's following and his exploitation of his position from 1441 to 1445 showed the extent of the prize which Somerset had lost.[24]

For the first time the charge of France was placed on the same footing as that of Ireland and the northern marches, as a fixed annual salary under indenture. York was to be paid £20,000 p.a. for his second to fifth years of office, commencing on 1 September 1441. The payment for his large expeditionary force of 900 men-at-arms and 2,800 archers, with an ample proportion of noble and knightly captains, was authorized by the council on 19 November 1440, and £9,898 was delivered to the duke in January.[25] He was expected to muster at Poole on 1 April 1441, but depite repeated urgings by the king and council and the deterioration of the military situation in France, it was not until 16 May that York left London and only in the latter part of June that he eventually sailed.[26] Though the exchequer had been able to draw on the Orléans ransom and the lay subsidy to meet his wages, it also had to raise some £10,000 in loans. Of this Cardinal Beaufort contributed a mere £1,000, the sum extent of his lending in 1441 and the lowest of any year since 1426–29.[27] York's military achievement on his arrival proved unimpressive, for though he hastened to the relief of Pontoise and, with Talbot, conducted a dazzling series of manœuvres to draw the French to battle, it eventually surrendered on 19 September. This seems to have decided York to adopt an essentially defensive and

[24] *Foedera*, x. 786–7; *Wars of Eng*. ii. 585–91; Marshall, thesis, Appendix 2 and chapters 3, 4. Payments to Somerset as captain of Avranches, 1441–3, are in BL Add. MS 4101 fo. 46, and he continued to hold Bailly and Tombelaine as well as Cherbourg: *Appendices to Foedera*, 492, 506.

[25] *PPC* v. 314; E 404/57/130; E 403/740.

[26] An advance party sailed in Apr./May and shipping and wages for the main force were ready: *PPC* v. 142, 146; E 28/68, 4, 11, 13, 22 May. The French council was told to expect him imminently: *Wars of Eng*. ii. 604, 640.

[27] Steel, *Receipt*, 216–17. A commission for a general loan was issued on 28 Nov. 1440: C 81/1545; *CPR 1436–41*, 504. £9,898 was paid to York for his first quarter's wages on 16 Jan. 1441, a further £2,457 in Feb., and the rest of the second quarter, £7,115, in June: Johnson, thesis, 94.

stationary strategy which was to arouse increasing criticism and discontent in the English council.

Although Beaufort lost the struggle for Somerset's appointment, on the questions of the release of the duke of Orléans and further peace negotiations Gloucester's opposition had no effect. Orléans' release was under active discussion in May 1440, and Gloucester's objections to it were formally presented to the king at Kennington on 2 June. The arguments in its favour drew support not only from French and Burgundian insistence that it was an essential preliminary to peace negotiations but from the hope that Orléans might strengthen the princes, led by Bourbon and Alençon, who were even then in arms against Charles VII with the explicit aim of forcing him to the negotiating table. In this English diplomacy was not aggressive and adventurist, as it had been under Edward III and Henry V; rather it sought to stabilize the political and military situation through a long truce, an aim shared by princes such as Bourbon. It was genuinely expected that Orléans would contribute to the pressure for and success of negotiations. Gloucester attacked the assumptions on which this rested.[28] He argued that Orléans would not be bound by his oath taken as a prisoner, that his natural allegiance was to Charles VII, and that he might well heal the divisions in France and help to drive the English out. Further, the ransom demanded was inadequate to meet the pressing needs of the English armies in Normandy and Aquitaine. These were shrewd criticisms, though Gloucester's attitude was essentially negative. For him the failure of the Calais negotiations had been welcome, but the council knew that Lancastrian Normandy was crumbling and that some initiative—any initiative—was essential to procure a truce.

This was publicly admitted in a document issued late in October 1440 to justify Orléans's liberation.[29] Its theme was the necessity for a respite from war, but it marked an important advance from the ritual declarations on the desirability of peace made by Kemp and Beaufort at Arras and Oye. It frankly spelt out the weakness of Normandy in terms similar to those of the memoranda evaluating the French offer at Calais; indeed the bishop of Bayeux had recently rehearsed these in a letter to Gloucester himself.[30] Yet this was the first public admission of the situation, and was now used to

[28] *Foedera*, x. 764–7.

[29] *Wars of Eng*. ii. 451–60. Henry VI affirmed his decision to release Orléans on 2 July; Charles VII ratified this on 16 Aug.; on 18 Sept. Orléans appeared before Beaufort and other councillors for discussions on his ransom, finally settled by 25 Oct., and three days later publicly swore to accept the conditions. On 2 Nov. the first instalment of the ransom was paid; on 3 Nov. Henry VI signed the order of release, and on 5 Nov. he sailed to Calais. The first paragraph of the document suggests that it was drawn up after his acceptance of the conditions but before his actual liberation.

[30] Bekynton, *Correspondence*, i. 289; cf. Jean Chartier *Chronique latine inédite*, C. Samaran, (ed.), 90–3.

justify peace. Secondly, it argued for a peace based on a territorial division of France, adducing not only the treaty of Brétigny but the story that Henry V had intended to make peace with the dauphin following the treaty of Troyes. The claim that before his death Henry 'was so sadded of werre and disposed in all weies to have entended a paix', marked the first time that Henry V's achievements had been cited to exhort subjects not to the continuance but to the cessation of war.[31] Thirdly, the statement repeatedly stresed the heavy expense of war, with its futile drain of resources and ensuing impoverishment of both England and Normandy: 'of this maner of continuance of the werre the Kyng feleth noon other fruyt, but losse of his people and drawyng alonge of the losse and destruction of his cuntre there [i.e.Normandy], and empoverisshing of hymself and of his land here'. Finally, it justified the diplomatic value of Orléans' release, and denied that he was in a position to betray the secrets of the realm to the French.

What was the purpose of the document, and who were its authors? It was avowedly issued to counter 'a noyse and a grutchyng' among subjects over Orléans' release, and its direct language, almost polemical tone, and emphasis on the respite from financial demands that peace would bring suggest its use in some form of public recital. It was clearly designed to meet the kind of arguments put forward in Gloucester's memorandum to the council, which had been given wider dissemination. As to its author, the document proper was in the name of the king, who explicitly accepted responsibility for Orléans's release, as being done 'of hymself and of his owen advis and courrage', so that no charge should be laid against any other person, while protesting also that it was not done 'of symplesse ne of self wille' but for good reasons, some stated, others secret. Henry's personal responsibility was indeed inescapable under the terms of his father's will, and the declared opposition of Gloucester, the heir apparent, made Henry's advisers understandably nervous. Can the document be ascribed to Gloucester's personal enemy, Cardinal Beaufort? The description of the position in Normandy, the lament that the war had continued for a hundred years and more, and the implicit reversion to a proposal for a division of France along the lines of Brétigny all have direct antecedents in 1439 and may indicate the cardinal's authorship. Yet it surely also reflects the king's own feelings about the war he had inherited and the peace he so earnestly desired.

In the year and a half since May 1439 Henry VI had begun to display not merely involvement but initiative in affairs of state. His sanction must have been secured for the demands on the duchy feoffees and the provision for

[31] This was allegedly on the testimony of 'many that yet lyven and were aboute hym, to which it liked him to open his entente in the saide mater'. The assertion had been made by the Burgundians at Arras in very similar language: Dickinson, *Congress of Arras*, 21, 209–10.

the household, and in the autumn of 1440 he took the first steps in the foundation of Eton. Gloucester's charges against the cardinal must have been referred to the king's decision, while the heated debate over the French proposals of 1439 and over the release of Orléans in May 1440 would have served to develop Henry's views on the question of peace, making him aware that he could determine the issue when his councillors were divided. There is no reason to doubt Henry's 'souveraine and singuler desire [for] . . . that oon thing above alle othr erthly thinges, that is to seye, that the good paix might be had, by the which the werre that longe hath contynued and endured that is to saye an hundreth yeeres and more . . . might cease and take ende', and that he saw this as fulfilling his duty as a Christian monarch to heal the schisms of Christendom. Moreover, the document is infused by a generous idealism and a Christian pacifism, the conviction that war itself was wrong and futile, that were surely as characteristic of Henry as they were uncharacteristic of Beaufort. Nowhere was it acknowledged that Edward III and Henry V had a duty to assert royal rights in France by the sword, or defend them if negotiation failed. One may guess that it was prepared as an outline draft from the council, on which Henry and perhaps Suffolk impressed their own feelings. For Orléans's release owed more to Suffolk, his keeper and intimate friend, than it did to Beaufort, who had never shown any appreciation of the role which Orléans claimed to play. The king's decision to liberate him and public justification for doing so thus marked a significant increase of royal pressure for a cessation of war.

Nevertheless, English policy still looked to Burgundian mediation to achieve this, and while this remained so Cardinal Beaufort's unique standing with the duke and duchess would guarantee him an important role in Henry's counsels. Between October 1439 and July 1440 rapid progress was made in rebuilding commercial and political ties between England and Burgundy. The *intercursus* was extended to seven years to cover Lancastrian France and the whole of the Low Countries, the commissioners appointed to negotiate this in April 1440 being all associates of the cardinal, who was in frequent correspondence with Isabel over the renewal of talks with the French.[32] But throughout 1440 Charles VII procrastinated over these, and from April to December English envoys waited in vain at Calais for the French to arrive. Even the liberation of Orléans early in November brought no response from Charles; indeed both the king and the duke of Burgundy reacted with the utmost caution to this new element in their relationship. Duke Philip sought to bind Orléans to himself by marriage to Isabel's niece Mary of Cleves and by inducting him into the

[32] Beaucourt, *Charles VII*, iii. 144; Thielemans, *Bourgogne et Angleterre*, 134–5; Taylor, thesis, 129. Stephen Wilton and Thomas Kyriell, both servants of Beaufort, were probably the key negotiators: *Foedera*, x. 750, 761, 791.

order of the Golden Fleece, but he avoided occasions of conflict with the French crown and held aloof from the *Praguerie*. This Burgundian caution inhibited any temptation the English may have had to exploit princely discontent. The mood of English policy was wholly defensive, obsessed with the need for stabilization and distrustful of all adventures. In the event it derived no profit and suffered no disaster from the release of Orléans.

Over the next two years English hopes for a mediated peace persisted, but shifted gradually from reliance upon Burgundy to expectations that an alliance of the French princes would compel Charles VII to recognize the independence of English territories. Such a concession could itself serve as a model for the autonomy of princely territories, but for that reason Charles refused to contemplate any treaty with the English that would dismember the crown. However, his room for manœuvre between the dissident princes and the hostile English remained small, and the next two years saw a series of aborted negotiations from which the princes emerged discredited, English hopes of peace frustrated, and the authority of the French crown reaffirmed. One of Orléans's first acts after his liberation was to join the dukes of Burgundy, Brittany, Alençon, and later Bourbon to promote new negotiations with England, a fresh conference at Gravelines being proposed to which an embassy of Dudley, Kyriell, Wilton, and Whittingham were named on 10 April 1441. But Charles VII was deeply distrustful and negotiations were deferred amidst recriminations, first to November and then to May 1442.[33] Beaufort and Isabel were in correspondence over the projected talks in the summer months, but by November 1441 the princes' peace initiative had collapsed and the general impasse over relations with Charles VII prompted more adventurous attempts to bring pressure on the French crown in 1442. These were foreshadowed by a meeting of Burgundy and Orléans at Hesdin in November from which they issued an appeal to the princes to meet at Hesdin on 28 January. Here their manifesto criticized Charles's government, complaining of their exclusion from it and other particular wrongs, and demanding the resumption of negotiations with the English in May at Saint-Omer. This Charles effectively refused, leaving the princes to threaten to hold them without him. Burgundian envoys were sent to Beaufort and Suffolk to confirm the proposed meeting at Saint-Omer.[34]

This proved an empty promise. The English delegation, comprising many of Beaufort's own servants, had arrived at Calais in February 1442, but by June it had tired of waiting and returned.[35] Charles VII's successful

[33] Beaucourt, *Charles VII*, iii. 200–1; Thielemans, *Bourgogne et Angleterre*, 144; Taylor, thesis, 154–7; *PPC* v. 139; *Foedera*, x. 844, 847.

[34] Beaucourt, *Charles VII*, iii. 211–31; Vale, *Charles VII*, 82–3.

[35] The embassy included Kyriell, Wilton, Edward Grimston, and William Port: *PPC* v. 176–7; E 404/58/169.

campaign in Gascony brought the count of Armagnac to heel, destroying the credibility of English backing for the dissident princes and the unity of their opposition. Angevin influence at court remained unshaken and by August Burgundy himself was making approaches for the marriage of his son, the count of Nevers, to Margaret of Anjou, while Orléans was reconciled to the court by the offer of help with his ransom. This failure marked the final abandonment of the pretensions of Burgundy and the princes to act as brokers between England and France, and signalled the need for a fundamental reappraisal in England of how to secure agreement with the French. This was not seen as the fault of Burgundy; indeed Anglo-Burgundian relations drew closer as negotiations, carried on through Beaufort and Suffolk in London and subsequently with York in Normandy, brought Normandy and Guyenne into the military truce with Burgundy which was eventually converted into a definitive treaty including England in April 1443. Cardinal Beaufort probably kept a watching brief on these negotiations, for it was he who formally acknowledged their conclusion in a letter to Isabel on 16 June 1443.[36] It was to be one of his last acts of state, and the culmination of a lifetime adherence to the Anglo-Burgundian alliance

Apart from strengthening and stabilizing relations with Burgundy, there seems to have been little positive support for the French princes. On the death of Jean V of Brittany in August 1442 both England and Burgundy hastened to renew their alliances with the new duke, Francis, but his inclinations were more Francophile than his father's for at this juncture the French court looked more attractive than the disintegrating alliance of the princes. The one exception was the proposal for a marriage between Henry VI and one of the daughters of the count of Armagnac. This arose in 1441, probably on the count's own initiative, and was designed to strengthen his prestige and increase the pressure upon Charles VII to respond to the princes' call for negotiations at Nevers. It was accompanied by a show of force in Gascony where the English laid siege to Tartas and pressed the local nobility into alliances and treaties of neutrality. By April 1442, however, Charles had summoned the southern nobility with their military levies to meet at Toulouse from where he launched a political and military offensive with overwhelming success. The English position crumbled, the count of Armagnac was isolated and compelled to submit, and the marriage negotiations petered out. Although Charles ultimately failed to take Bordeaux itself, he had prepared the ground for a campaign in 1443 that could finally end English rule in Guyenne. The episode was significant, indicative of English failure to co-ordinate diplomatic and military policy, to back the former with the latter, and even to foresee possible

[36] Beaucourt, *Charles VII*, iii. 264; Thielemans, *Bourgogne et Angleterre*, 147, Taylor, thesis, 164; *PPC*, v. 212; *Foedera*, xi. 24.

consequences and measure attendant risks. All this was to become characteristic of Suffolk's policies in the years ahead, as the fundamental weakness of the English position tempted him to take opportunistic initiatives.[37]

The main military effort of the English in 1442 was in Normandy, but this again bore witness to the insufficiency of resources, though redeemed by the vigour of Lord Talbot. His Oise campaign of 1441, though it had failed to capture Charles VII or save Pontoise, had deflected further French penetration of Normandy, and with Charles occupied in Gascony Talbot saw a chance to secure the borders of the duchy by attacking the dangerous French salient at Louviers-Conches, and to reduce the last French enclave in the Pays de Caux, Dieppe. Since Michaelmas York had formally invested him with the defence of Normandy as lieutenant-general for the conduct of the war and captain of Rouen, and in February 1442 Talbot returned to England to seek reinforcements. While in England he was created earl of Shrewsbury, and in mid-June returned to Normandy with an army of 2,500 men, mostly archers, with which he besieged and eventually took Conches in September. His further progress in the salient was held in check by Dunois, and abandoning the difficult task of besieging Louviers, Talbot made for Dieppe. With his force now nearing the end of its six months' service, he lacked the men to invest the port and could only establish a bastille outside. As winter approached he withdrew to Rouen, leaving the bastille under Sir William Peyto and 500 veterans, with the expectation of reinvesting Dieppe in the spring. For all Talbot's vigour and skill, the English military effort was slowly grinding to a halt.[38]

Outwardly the rhythm of political life in England remained unchanged. The frequency of council meetings and the political role of the council continued in the pattern established after the ending of the minority. The council usually met on about five occasions during the year for periods of between one week and one month, although in October–November 1441 it was in session for six weeks and in May–July 1442 for two and a half months.[39] In November–December 1439, January–February 1440, and

[37] The episode is covered in Beaucourt, *Charles VII*, iii. 234–45; Vale, *English Gascony*, 160–1; and Bekynton, *Correspondence*, ii. 177–248, in the journal of Robert Roos and Thomas Beckington. This makes it clear that the whole project had the backing of the household clique. The fact that Gloucester and Huntingdon ventured no criticism is indicative of Suffolk's power, particularly since he now replaced Huntingdon's officers—Clifton, Rempston, and Chetwynd—in the duchy: Vale, op. cit. 112–7.

[38] Pollard, *Talbot*, 58–60; *PPC* v. 1866; *CPR 1441–6*, 106; E 403/743 28 Mar.

[39] Its sessions for which evidence survives were: 1439: 14–16 Oct., 17 Nov., 12–19 Dec. (E 28/63; C 81/1544; *PPC* v. 100–13, vi. 112–13). 1440: 20–8 Apr., 8–12 May, 9–20 June (E 28/63; *PPC* v. 118–20); 14–28 Oct., 6–28 Nov. (E 28/64, 65; C 81/1544). 1441: 22–9 Jan., 4–13 Feb., 7–17 Mar., 4–30 May (E 28/66–8); C 81/1544; *PPC* v. 132–9, 142–50); 14 Oct.–28 Nov. (*PPC* v. 153–81; E 28/69). 1442: 4 May–16 July (E 28/70; *PPC* v. 186–92; C 81/1544); 21–8 Aug., 8–18 Oct. (*PPC* v. 196–209, 210–22; C 81/1544).

January–March 1442 there were also sessions of parliament. On all these occasions, apart from a short session in April 1440, Henry VI attended at least some of the meetings and all his visits to the environs of London coincided with known sessions of the council except in mid-April 1442. The king spent less than three months of 1440 in the palaces near London, almost eight months in 1441, and rather over four months in 1442; otherwise he stayed mainly at Windsor, with occasional short journeys to Kent and Essex.[40] Thus meetings of the council remained formal occasions, with the king at hand, attended by most of those nominated in and since 1437, and at them important matters of policy and government continued to be discussed. Cardinal Beaufort attended the council infrequently in these years and normally only for matters in which he had a personal interest. That, at least, is the impression given by the surviving records, which, from his return to England in October 1439 to the early summer of 1442, record only thirteen days on which he was present in council.[41] The council was still, as has been said, the forum for the discussion of important business which was of concern to the cardinal: York's strategy in Normandy and the danger to Guyenne; the threat of mutiny in Calais; the complaints of English merchants against the Hanse; the appointment of an embassy to Burgundy; the quarrel between the earl of Devon and Lord Bonville. Only for the last of these was Beaufort present.[42] Now past 65 and perhaps at times unwell, he is likely to have been fatigued by meetings and his visits were irregular and widely spaced. Possibly he resided at Southwark and maintained contact through Kemp and Cromwell. Yet taken with the decline of his lending in these years and the enforced surrender of the duchy lands, it seems clear that he had ceased to exercise the overall direction of policy and government that had been his before 1439. Ultimately it was the need to meet the mounting threat to Guyenne that brought the cardinal to resume his daily attendance at council meetings held in the last two weeks of August 1442.

For a time Gloucester had figured more prominently on the council, often in conjunction with his allies Huntingdon and Scrope, and though he failed to alter significantly the direction of policy, over patronage he exerted some influence.[43] But on 28 June 1441 some chaplains of his

[40] Wolffe, *Henry VI*, 362–3.

[41] These were: 12, 15 Dec. 1439; 25 Apr., 12 May, 20 June, 22 Oct. 1440; 25 Jan., 14 Feb., 6, 26 May, (20) June, 15 Nov. 1441; 4, 8 May 1442. Some were related to petitions of the earl of Somerset (*PPC* v. 112–13, E 28/63); annuities on the manors he had purchased from the crown (E 28/64); a petition for tax relief from the city of Winchester (C 81/1426/52); petitions concerning the Beauchamp lands and from François de Suriennes (*PPC* v. 147; C 81/1427/26; E 28/68).

[42] *PPC* v. 157–8.

[43] In Jan. 1440, Gloucester secured a grant of all the lands of Isobel, countess of Warwick during the minority of the Beauchamp heir, Henry, despite her own licence to enfeoff these to her executors in Dec. 1439. By July he had extended this to embrace the Warwick lands during

household, chief of whom was Roger Bultingbroke, were arrested for necromancy and treason in predicting the death of the king. The Duchess Eleanor was named as an accessory and promptly fled to sanctuary at Westminster. The records give no hint of what precipitated this or who instigated it. The council seems to have ended its session late in May and from 6 to 11 June the king was at Dogmersfield, a Hampshire manor of the chancellor, Bishop Stafford, probably on the first stage of his summer itinerary. By 13 June Henry had returned to Sheen, apparently for a special enlarged meeting of the council, his return to the capital probably determined by the 'discovery' of the conspiracy.[44] Who was directing the investigation remains unclear. Ayscough was with the court, but no warrants reveal which councillors had remained in London during June, and only after Henry's return to Sheen in mid-July is Suffolk's presence at court noted. The full council had reassembled for Bultingbroke's recantation on 23 July and for the examination of the duchess next day by the leading prelates, Cardinal Beaufort being present on both occasions. This was followed by her examination on the matter of treason by the lay members of the council, following which she was remanded in custody to appear before Chichele on 19–23 October. At that session neither Chichele, who was ill, nor Beaufort (who was probably at Southwark) were present to give sentence and hear her abjuration; though on 6 November they sat jointly to pronounce her divorce from Duke Humphrey. Following her public penance in London on 13–17 November, she was committed to imprisonment in Chester and subsequently Kenilworth and the Isle of Man. Although there is no contemporary suggestion that the prosecution had a political motive, there can be little doubt that the duke was the real target. Even though he had failed to gain the king's ear and had little influence in council, as heir to the throne he posed a standing threat to those in power. If Henry VI was already displaying signs of melancholia, fears and hopes for his early death may have extended beyond the duchess's necromancers. Eleanor's conviction rendered Humphrey's accession to the throne impossible; for whatever the truth of the allegations, their inherent credibility and the strong revulsion they aroused made the duke a political outcast and permanently suspect. Undeniably Beaufort more than any had cause to fear the succession of Duke Humphrey, yet his part in this affair is as opaque as that of others. He appears to have

Henry's minority, overriding a commital of them to York, Salisbury, and others in May 1439: *CPR 1436–41*, 279, 359–60, 367; *CFR 1437–45*, 122. He backed a petition of Lord Scrope, and secured a pardon for Lord Grey of Codnor, Cromwell's enemy: E 28/64/37; E 28/67 7 Mar. For other petitions presented or sued for by Gloucester for his followers, see E 28/68 4 May and C 81/1426/47–8, 53–4.

[44] C 81 1428/4, 6. The abbot of Bury was at the council in June, when Beaufort intimated his intention of staying with him after 29 June: *Docts. illus. Chapters of the English Black Monks*, ed. W. A. Pantin, iii. 220. The known facts of the affair are set out by R. A. Griffiths, 'The trial of Eleanor Cobham', *BJRL* 51 (1968), 381–99.

deliberately eschewed a prominent role, taking second place to Chichele and absenting himself when Chichele was ill. Within the context of the 'low profile' which the cardinal in general adopted after 1439, that may suggest that he was not the prime mover. But of that there can be no certainty.

Although in all periods when the council was in session most of the appointed lords are known to have attended, none equalled the earl of Suffolk in assiduity, and frequently council decisions were attested by Suffolk, the officers, and Adam Moleyns. Suffolk, moreover, was with the king at Windsor more often than other members of the higher nobility. It is unlikely that Beaufort went much to court, where the stream of petitions which Henry answered were witnessed by the chamberlains and household knights and esquires. The household accounts only record him at Sheen on 2 May 1442.[45] The displacement of the cardinal in the interests of the household was carried a stage further in the parliament which met for a two-month session on 25 January 1442. The Speaker was again William Tresham, now firmly attached to the court as an esquire of the household, and there was a strong representation of major household officials and esquires in the Commons. A final attempt was now made to wrest the duchy lands from the three remaining feoffees. As in 1440, it was argued that their revenues could support the household, and the renewed attack on the feoffees was firmly rooted in statistics compiled since the last parliament by the king's surveyor, John Lathbury. It was claimed that the feoffees' annual revenue of £6,000 had yielded them a total of £114,000 since Henry V's death. The earlier demands for surrender of the lands made in 1434 and 1440 were recalled and the feoffees were reminded that they 'have no title ner interesse therynne but only upon trust', the spectre being raised that their number might be reduced to one, thereby creating a fee simple which would allow the lands to be alienated from the crown. Their last loan, made in June 1439, had been repaid and there was no reason why Henry V's remaining creditors should not be given assignments and the feoffment be wound up. To this pressure the feoffees perforce capitulated, surrendering the lands and receiving acquittance.[46] A bastion of the cardinal's power thus fell to an alliance between the court and the Commons, even though this was based on a fundamental deception. For while the Commons were persuaded that it would serve the interests of household finance, the king had in mind to apply the duchy revenue to the construction of his college at Eton.

For twenty years the feoffees had controlled the larger part of the royal

[45] E 101/409/9. He had been at Windsor on 10 Apr. 1441 for the appointment of an embassy to Flanders: *PPC* v. 140. A number of petitions at his instance or for the benefit of his minor followers are in C 81/1427/42–3; *CPR 1436–41*, 526, 559; E 28/70 8 Dec., and in Dec. 1440 he had the grant of the alien priory of Tarrant Launceston for St Cross: C 81/1426/26.

[46] *Rot. Parl.* v. 56–9.

patrimony, setting up their own central organization and appointing the officials within the lands under their control.[47] Those lands had yielded a clear revenue of at least £3,500 p.a. over the whole period, so that the feoffees had disposed of upward of £70,000.[48] How they had expended this sum we do not know, for none of their accounts have survived, but even by 1442 Henry V's debts had not been fully discharged and a further £2,766 was paid towards this in 1443–5.[49] After assuming responsibility for the will from the executors in 1429, the feoffees over the next decade lent a total of £52,580 to the crown, thereby prolonging their discharge of the will far beyond what Henry V could have contemplated. Their loans formed an extension of the cardinal's own, being negotiated in his name, on securities of his choice, and for purposes of which he approved, providing Beaufort with a virtual monopoly of the credit available to the crown in these years.[50]

Cardinal Beaufort's readiness to use the royal patrimony to sustain Henry V's political and military legacy had fortified his claim to be one of Henry's political heirs alongside Bedford and Gloucester. In addition he was invested with the awesome responsibility for the quiet of the king's soul, and in fulfilling the king's intentions for his chantry tomb, Beaufort explicitly recalled the scale of the king's vision and achievement. Some time after 1437, when the control of the enfeoffed lands had effectively devolved on Beaufort alone, the erection of Henry V's grandiose chantry in Westminster abbey was commenced at the charge of the feoffees. Although its location, and the concept of an elevated chapel in which the celebrant would be visible from below, had been specified in Henry's wills, the wealth of sculpture composing an iconographical scheme which has never been adequately elucidated must have been designed at the time of construction. The twin narrative scenes on the north and south faces, representing stages in the coronation ceremony and in the conquest of Normandy, and the placing of St Denis among the traditional English

[47] The organization is revealed in the only surviving declaration of the feoffees' receiver-general, John Leventhorpe junior, for 10 Henry VI.: DL 28/5/1.

[48] A series of annual valors survive for the period 1427/8 to 1438/9 covering the feoffees' lands (DL 29/732/12033–141). These show their gross value as around £6,500 with a value beyond reprises of £5,200 to £5,500. Annuities progressively decreased from £1,834 in 1427/8 to £832 in 1438–9, for the feoffees made no new grants. As a result, disposable revenue paid to Leventhorpe, the receiver-general, rose from £2,759 in 1427/8 to £3,922 in 1436–7 and £3,608 in 1438–9. In the first year of the reintegrated duchy (1443–4) the feoffees' estates yielded £3,822: Somerville, *Duchy of Lancaster*, 206.

[49] DL 28/5/2 fos. 102^{v}, 122^{v}.

[50] Beaufort was also able to appoint his nephew Richard Nevill steward and constable of Tickhill in 1432 and steward of Bowland in 1437, while Edmund Beaufort was made receiver of Monmouth and Grosmont. In 1437 Suffolk became steward of the northern parts and by 1440 Lord Beaumont, James and Roger Fenys, James Legh, Thomas Tuddenham, and Thomas Staunton, all members of the household, had posts in the feoffees' part: Somerville, *Duchy of Lancaster*, 428, 576., DL 42/18.

saints and martyrs on the altar, were probably designed as a visual affirmation of the Lancastrian double monarchy at the time when it was in acute crisis and was even being disowned.[51] It is possible that one of the twin figures of cardinals on the north and south turrets represents Beaufort. The building of the chantry was a major achievement of his final years, an affirmation of his own status as custodian of Henry V's legacy and spiritual protector of the house of Lancaster.

Even as this great monument to past glory was being fashioned, attitudes towards the French conquests were changing. To the generation which had served Henry V, the war had represented first an ambition to be fulfilled and latterly a commitment to be shouldered. Now, increasingly, it was becoming an incubus to be shaken off. With few exceptions the eyes of the nobility were fixed on the court and its perquisites, not on France with its tally of losses rather than gains. The king had proclaimed his own conviction of the futility of war, and his quickening interest in his religious foundations encouraged detachment from the martial tradition and a widening alienation from those who still lived and fought in Normandy. The expectation of peace made all military effort appear irrelevant, and a lack of direction and sense of inertia attended English foreign policy in these years. Even so the old problems could not be wished away and solutions to them were becoming more pressing. While Normandy, Calais, and now Guyenne had to be defended, armies and leaders would have to be found, the council would need to take decisions, parliament to grant taxation, and—it was all too likely—the cardinal would be called upon to open his purse and lend.

In the two years since his loan of December 1439 for Somerset's army, the cardinal had advanced a mere £1,000; but between the duke of York's departure at midsummer 1441 and the military crisis in Gascony a year later the council faced heavy charges for the safeguard of Normandy, Calais, and the sea which strained the exchequer and led to renewed calls on Beaufort's wealth. During its extended session from mid-October to early December 1441 the council took stock of its commitments to York and Calais. The first quarter of York's salary of £20,000 was now due, but discussion of how to meet this, coinciding as it did with the report of the fall of Pontoise, produced a critical reaction. York's indentures were brought in for review and his envoys were questioned as to why he had so few troops indented. Sir John Popham was sent back with warnings to strengthen the seaports against surprise attack. No cash was to hand to pay the £5,000 for the first quarter and the council was forced to divert £4,000

[51] P. and F. Strong, 'Last will', 89–91; W. H. St John Hope, 'The Funeral, Monument, and Chantry Chapel of Henry V', *Archaeologia*, 65 (1913–14), 129–86; Colvin, *History of the King's Works*, i. 488–9. Prof. R. A. Griffiths has pointed out to me that the coronation scene shows the use of the enclosed or imperial crown.

set aside for the household and pledge jewels for the remainder.[52] With the New Year the council faced a demand from Lord Talbot for reinforcements with which to mount a summer offensive. This may have received support from those who, for their own purposes, were critical of York. Neither the parliament nor council records contain references to discussions about Talbot's expedition, but by 19 March Cardinal Beaufort was ready to advance £5,666, the major part of the wages for 200 men-at-arms and 2,300 archers for whom Talbot drew the first quarter's pay nine days later.[53] What were Beaufort's motives for this? Possibly it was the price of his acquittal on surrendering the duchy lands; yet it may also have been influenced by the family relationship and common interests which bound Talbot and Edmund Beaufort. Not only had they fought together at Harfleur, but as brothers-in-law they shared claims to the Berkeley inheritance. Warwick's death had rekindled their dispute with Lord Berkeley, and a commission issued to Gloucester, York, and Stafford early in 1440 to hold an assize of novel disseisin at the instance of Lord Berkeley prompted Talbot and Dorset to threaten to break the siege at Harfleur and return to enforce their claim. Back in England in 1441, Dorset agreed to arbitration by three justices.[54] Talbot's close connection with Dorset suggests that in making his loan the cardinal may have envisaged Edmund's return in Talbot's company. Both were aggressive commanders, advocates of a more active strategy than that pursued by York, of whom Beaufort and the council remained critical. If so, nothing came of it and Dorset remained in England.[55] The wages for Talbot's second quarter had to be scraped together from a variety of lenders, among whom Beaufort contributed a further £2,000, repaid, as was the previous loan, from the Southampton customs.[56] The continued shortage of cash at the exchequer meant that Talbot's expedition was financed at the expense of York's current salary: of the £15,000 due for the remainder of the year he could be paid only £4,551 in hand, the remainder being in assignments on the lay subsidy payable at Martinmas 1443.[57]

Meanwhile at Calais urgent expenditure was needed on two counts. During the Gravelines negotiations in 1439 a breach in the sea walls had caused extensive flooding and threatened to undermine the castle.

[52] *PPC* v. 157–8, 162–5, 171–2, 178; E 28/69 13, 14, 28 Nov., Payment was delivered to York at the end of Nov.: E 404/58/92; E 403/743 27 Nov.

[53] E 401/775 19 Mar.; *CPR 1441–6*, 76; E 403/743; Pollard, *Talbot*, 58–9.

[54] For the dispute, see Pollard, 'The family of Talbot, Lords Talbot and earls of Shrewsbury in the fifteenth century' Ph.D. thesis (Bristol, 1968), 39–5; Smyth, *Lives of Berkeleys*, ii. 47–60; *Rot. Parl.* v. 40; *CCR 1435–41*, 325, 464, 488; *CCR 1441–7*, 60; and above, ch. 6 n. 47.

[55] By July 1442 Dorset was a commissioner in Carmarthen: *CPR 1441–6*, 106.

[56] E 401/779; Steel, *Receipt* 219; *CPR 1441–6*, 76. He now secured the repayment of his loan of £1,000 made in Feb. 1441 for which he still held jewels.

[57] E 403/746, E 401/779 both 18 May; *Wars of Eng.* i. 431.

Cardinal Beaufort had ordered emergency repairs and William Morton was appointed to supervise the works. But the money allocated to him had remained in the hands of the treasurer of Calais, Robert Whittingham, and the damage had worsened so that by 1442 an estimated £30,000 was needed to render Calais safe.[58] In the course of 1441 evidence of corruption and mismanagement at Calais, which implicated Whittingham, led to his removal, while the duke of Gloucester relinquished the captaincy to the earl of Stafford. These events unsettled the garrison, fearful of losing the arrears of wages due to them from Gloucester's lieutenancy and that of Warwick.[59] The council, expecting a mutiny, approached the Company of the Staple, who on 22 November 1441 agreed in principle to lend £10,000 to be repaid from the retention of one mark from the subsidy on each sack of wool; however, it was to be another year before this loan was handed over.[60] The council also conducted an enquiry into Whittingham's misdeeds and discussed who should replace him, but this was taken out of its hands by the king's personal appointment, on 19 December, of his chaplain John Langton.[61] Whittingham was Beaufort's close associate as the active executor of Bedford's will, and though the cardinal was not implicated in his disgrace, his removal had brought Calais directly under the control of the household.

By July Langton had still not negotiated a settlement with the garrison, who now lost patience and impounded the Staplers' wool. The council hastily sent envoys to the garrison and on 18 July Langton was credited with £4,000 for their wages and the loan from the Staplers was entered on the receipt roll. In fact this still represented a promise, not cash, and awaited the council's endorsement of the allocation to the Company of one mark from the wool subsidy with another half mark for repair work on the sea walls.[62] In council, on 12 October, Cardinal Beaufort threw his weight against the proposal, opposing both allocations as liable to impede the repayment of those who (like himself) already held assignments on the subsidies for repayment of loans. The only support he received was from his old ally, the treasurer, Lord Cromwell. He also cast a lone vote against the proposal to abolish the bullion requirement for sales at Calais.[63] The

[58] C 76/122 m. 14; *PPC* v. 386, 400–5; Colvin, *King's Works*, i. 437–41; E 28/70 3 Feb. 1442. E 28/66 16 Apr. is a long and interesting report by Morton.

[59] Mandate to account with Whittingham, 22 Nov. 1441: E 28/65. Proceedings against Whittingham, are in E 101/193/5 and E 159/219 Recorda, rot. 24. In June 1442 the council was inspecting his books: E 28/70 12, 29 May. The council had sent £1,000 to the garrison at the time of Stafford's appointment: E 28/66 13, 18 Feb.

[60] *PPC* v. 163–4, 167; E 28/70 4 May 1442.

[61] C 81/1367/32; E 28/70; C 76/124 m. 16, 21. Langton seems to have had authority over the garrison from 25 Dec. 1441 to 28 Aug. 1442.

[62] E 404/58/179; E 403/746; *PPC* v. 207. The earl of Stafford's appointment was from 28 Aug.; he promised to bring the garrison's wages when he took up his command: *PPC* v. 209; C 76/125 m. 19; his indenture is E 101/71/912–13.

[63] *PPC* v. 214, 216.

parliament of 1442 had seen further measures against alien merchants and a concerted attack on the Partition Ordinance, the evil effects of which were now detailed at length. Probably this came from the lesser merchants, who asked for a partial return to the old system by which merchants would sell their wools individually, for a third of the price in cash and the rest on credit, but maintaining an agreed price for different grades of wool.[64] What lay behind this radical shift in attitude is far from clear; there seems to have been a confused struggle within the Company, which probably accounted for the delay in making the loan. The council itself declined responsibility for a decision, answering the petition by placing the onus to effect the change of policy on the Company. Beaufort warned that to abolish the bullion requirement was to renounce the English bargaining position with the Flemish, for it would prove impossible to reimpose it. His objection was recorded and the matter referred to the mayor of the Staple. When the mayor reported back on 18 October he had dispensed with the bullion requirement on his own authority, and on 26 November the Company delivered the loan of £10,000 for settlement of the garrison's arrears.[65] The package accepted by the council was indeed the only way to provide the security at Calais on which trade depended. The new policy worked: wool exports leaped to 13,166 sacks p.a. for each of the following years, the highest since the revival of trade in 1439.[66] It also drew the Company more closely into crown finance, marking the beginning of its commitment to the maintenance of the garrison which was to reach a logical culmination in the act of retainer of 1466. A new major source of cash had thereby become available to the crown, to fulfil the same role in supporting the Calais garrison as Cardinal Beaufort had performed for the armies sent to Normandy.

A further charge to which the parliament of 1442 had committed the council was for a fleet of eighty ships to keep the sea for six months, to be paid for from tunnage and poundage and the first quarter of the lay subsidy. This was assembled by late July, but in August the news of the threat to Bayonne impelled the council to use the fleet to ship a force of 500 men under Sir Philip Chetwynd to Gascony.[67] Indeed it had already begun to consider the dispatch of a larger force to ensure the security of the duchy against renewed French attack. The earl of Somerset's name was mentioned and Cardinal Beaufort reappeared in the council. It marked the beginning of a project which was to engage his energies in 1443, in which his political and financial influence was deployed for the last time, and which was to precipitate its final demise.

[64] *Rot. Parl.* v. 52–65.

[65] *PPC* v. 210–20, 222; E 404/59/81, 113, 115.

[66] *Eng. Export Trade*, 60.

[67] *Rot. Parl.* v. 59–60; *PPC* v. 190, 193, 196, 198–9, 204–5; E 404/58/170–1; E 28/70 23 Aug.; *CPR 1441–6*, 107–8.

The notorious 1443 expedition, which is treated in the next chapter, forms the sequel to, and in a sense grew out of, three years in which the cardinal's power in every sector had noticeably contracted. At the beginning of 1440 he had faced a sharp attack on his policies and personal integrity from Gloucester, and was progressively forced from control of the duchy lands by the court and the Commons. The leadership he had once exercised in parliament and council was a thing of the past, for the Commons were now led by a group from the household and his old associates in the council were an ageing and dwindling band. Alnwick retired in April 1442 and Hungerford in that summer; Tiptoft had already ceased to attend and was to die in the following year. The cardinal's own presence had become spasmodic, and when his voice was raised it was often in a minority, so that if not unheeded he was overruled. The full council still met with the king for extended sessions, and debated important matters of policy, foreign and domestic; but Henry was now capable of initiatives and personally distributed patronage and offices. Beaufort was rarely at court or with the king. Whether or not Henry's awe and respect for him had been diminished by Gloucester's charges, there is little indication in these years that king and cardinal were at all close. Age and temperament stood between them. It was his own confessors and chaplains who moulded Henry's spiritual and moral views, became the recipients of his favours, and the executants of his cherished projects. Even in the field of diplomacy and finance, where his influence had traditionally prevailed, the tide now ran against the cardinal. Although he had reopened trade and restored political relations with Burgundy, his policy of securing a negotiated peace with France through Burgundian mediation had finally been shattered, and an anti-Burgundian reaction had set in. Finally, his role as the crown's major financier was disappearing. Although all his loans made before the end of 1439 had been repaid by Martinmas 1440, in the next three years he lent only 13,000 marks, less than in any comparable period since 1426–9. Exceptionally, too, these loans brought neither him nor his nephews evident personal or political advantage, while he had to accept provision for their repayment which accorded him a preference below that of other creditors. His failure to secure the office of lieutenant-general in France for Somerset in 1440 had brought the expanding careers of both his nephews in France to a halt; nor did they find a welcome among the new political establishment around the earl of Suffolk. They had no place in the royal household, but neither were they members of the council. Apart from occasional local commissions and grants, their activities in 1441–2 remain obscure.

It is not even easy to trace the movements and occupations of the cardinal himself. The sparse evidence suggests that his time was mainly spent on episcopal manors in Hampshire and Surrey.[68] His influence in church matters was itself receding. It had reached a peak with the promotion of his two leading colleagues, John Kemp and Louis of Luxembourg, to the cardinalate on 18 December 1439. On the receipt of the news, at the opening of the Reading session of parliament, Henry VI had written effusively to the pope thanking him for the honour and asking that they be allowed to retain their sees. But Chichele was bitterly affronted by the precedence now accorded to York and, as a sequel to Gloucester's attack on Beaufort and Kemp, he protested to Eugenius and carried his case to Rome. He received little comfort, and Eugenius reminded him that for fourteen years he had accepted Beaufort's precedence without protest.[69] That may have been rubbing old salt into the new wound, but this was the last time their paths crossed, and Chichele was soon seeking permission to resign on grounds of ill health. Kemp, abetted by Piero da Monte, had now become the main channel for relations with Eugenius IV and he, with Ayscough of Salisbury and the chancellor, Stafford, constituted the normal clerical representation on the king's council. Ayscough was also habitually in the king's presence and the channel for much ecclesiastical patronage. In Salisbury and Chichester Ayscough and Praty now gave prebends mainly to household chaplains, though the cardinal's servants Richard Petworth, William Toly, and Stephen Wilton were not neglected.[70] These, with his chancellor Richard Leyot, were Beaufort's closest clerical servants, but only Wilton had the youth and ability to compete with the new generation of clerks securing promotion through the court.

The cardinal's dwindling power and influence reflected the passage of time and his own increasingly fragile health. For one who had lived for so long at the centre of affairs, who had fashioned royal policy, discomforted his enemies, and publicly displayed his pride in high office, even an honourable and voluntary withdrawal from public life would have been hard to adjust to. But all the signs are that, following Gloucester's attack on him in 1439–40, Beaufort was systematically extruded from power, and that it was Suffolk rather than Gloucester who engineered his displace-

[68] There are records of his presence at Farnham on 3 Sept. 1440, at Wolvesey 28 Sept. 1440 (*Winchester Coll. Muniments,* nos. 3562, 3559), at Wolvesey 8 Jan. 1441, at Chertsey 16 Apr. 1441, and Bishops Waltham 16 Aug. 1441 (*Reg. CS* 80–3; *Reg. Lacy*, ii. 229); at Bury July 1441 (above, n. 44); at Esher Nov. 1441 and Farnham Apr. 1442 (HRO, Eccles. II 159437).

[69] *CPL* ix. 46–7; Bekynton, *Correspondence*, i. 38–9, 41, 50–2; W. Ullmann, 'Cardinal Kemp, Eugenius IV, and Archbishop Chichele' in J. A. Watt, J. B. Morrall, F. X. Martin (edd.), *Studies in Medieval History presented to Aubrey Gwynn*, 359–83, esp. n. 34.

[70] Household chaplains given prebends by Ayscough; by Praty, Fulk Bermingham, Henry Sever, William Walesby; Le Neve, *Fasti*, Salisbury, Chichester; *BRUO sub nominibus.*

ment. He became a casualty of the new political grouping which accompanied Henry VI's personal rule. It was not in Beaufort's character to vent in public the resentment he must have felt, but to bide his time until the opportunity presented itself to retrieve his position. By the end of 1442 he perceived that this was at hand.

17

The Last Throw, 1442–1444

Cardinal Beaufort's reappearance in council in August 1442 showed a shrewd appreciation of the crown's financial difficulties and the opportunity which these presented to reassert his influence. With the archbishop of Bordeaux present on the 22nd, the council launched into a discussion of how the threat to Guyenne was to be countered. So far as the record goes, neither the size of the force nor the identity of the commander was mentioned, only how money could be raised. The exchequer was desperately short of cash: a mere £5,500 had come in during the Easter term and the next instalments of both direct and indirect taxation were already committed to the discharge of debts to the duke of York, the Company of the Staple, and the cardinal. Beaufort evidently had no mind to lend: he grudgingly offered a mere £4,000 in plate provided he was repaid the cost of refashioning. With other lords offering smaller sums, the council decided to send commissioners into the shires to raise loans, but these met with a poor response.[1] Eventually enough was raised to dispatch a small force under Sir William Bonville in January, but the whole exercise underlined the council's inability to raise a major loan without adequate security and without the cardinal's co-operation. Nevertheless a much larger force would be needed to confront Charles VII's projected attempt to conquer the duchy in 1443, and in October the council returned to a discussion of how this could be raised. It was now that Somerset's name emerged as its leader.

Just how this was so is a matter of some obscurity and interest. On 2 June 1442 Somerset was at Windsor when Henry VI granted his petition for the reversion of an annuity, and he may also have been there at the end of June when the council received news of Charles VII's invasion of Guyenne and authorized the provision of ordnance at a cost of £240.[2] On 7 July Henry VI, from Windsor, ordered this to be delivered to the earl of Somerset who 'purposeth hym to goo in to our Reaulme of France in alle goodly haste'.[3] As noted, Somerset's name does not appear in the record of the council's discussions during August which Gloucester attended, though Cardinal Beaufort's presence spelt his own interest in the matter, and his refusal to provide money suggests that Somerset's appointment had run into

[1] *PPC* v. 199–204; E 28/70 undated; *CPR 1441–6*, 92; *Wars of Eng.* ii. 465–6.

[2] C 81/1431/45; E 404/58/172 3 July, when Cardinal Beaufort was present.

[3] E 404/58/173, with the cardinal again present.

opposition. Then on 21 September Henry wrote to Bekynton and Roos in Bordeaux that 'we have apppointed our cousin of Somerset and with hym right a noble puissance of men of werre to passe into our said duchie, which with Godde's mercy shal be ther in al possible haste'.[4] When meetings of the full council were resumed at the end of the first week of October, Gloucester and Beaufort were present on the opening days, 7th–12th but not thereafter. On 16 October Somerset, at the council's request, delivered his bill of conditions for going to Guyenne.[5] It is tempting to infer from this sequence that when the council reassembled it found that the decision on Somerset's appointment had been taken by the king.

When it returned to the discussion of how an expedition could be financed, the council again ran into the problem of what security could be offered to the cardinal for any substantial loan he would make. Beaufort now endeavoured to override the interests of York and the Staple, opposing the reservation of one mark of the subsidy for repayment of the Staplers' loan in the debates on 12 October, and proposing that existing assignments on the lay subsidy (i.e. to York) should be cancelled in his favour. Not surprisingly the council refused to renege on its previous agreements and at this point the question of Somerset's expedition was dropped.[6] Beaufort was probably content to wait, for the situation had not basically altered when discussion of it was resumed at the beginning of February. Charles VII had withdrawn to Montauban in the winter, but was planning to resume the campaign in Guyenne with Castilian aid in the spring, while the council at Rouen had received warnings of a concerted attack on Normandy. At the first meeting on 6 February, attended by both Gloucester and Beaufort, the question of whether to send armies to Normandy or Guyenne was debated. Most of those present would not commit themselves beyond advocating that which stood in greatest need. Beaufort declared that it was for the temporal lords to make the choice, but that the treasurer should first report on what resources were available. Cromwell's loaded comment was that the money last sent to Normandy (whether he meant to Talbot or York is not clear) had been wasted.[7] Between this and the next recorded meeting on 17 February letters had been sent to the duke of York, and the council now formally approached Somerset, reminding him of his offer of last October, enquiring whether his health permitted him to accept the command, and whether he would

[4] Bekynton, *Correspondence*, ii. 216–17. Somerset's name had meantime been deleted from the commission to raise loans in Dorset.

[5] *PPC* v. 210–18; C 81/1545/ 86, 87.

[6] *PPC* v. 220–1. The assignments on the Martinmas subsidy were duly paid and the Staple delivered its loan: E 401/780. Beaufort had got himself into a false position and the council turned against him his old argument of the necessity to honour assignments if the crown wished to borrow from its subjects.

[7] *PPC* v. 223–4.

propose to go to Normandy or Guyenne and with how many men.[8] At no point was any alternative leader considered, perhaps because no other was prepared to go, but more probably because the cardinal would otherwise not lend. Neither Gloucester nor Beaufort was present at the next council meeting on 2 March when the treasurer reported the impossibility of providing two armies and referred the decision to the king, the lords, and Somerset himself. Commissions to raise aid in the shires still only mentioned the needs of Guyenne.[9] The pace of preparations now quickened. The council was in correspondence with Somerset over his terms for service on the basis of the October articles, and had already fixed a provisional date for his muster on 5 May, giving orders for ships from the south and east coast ports to be assembled at Camber on 23 April. It tried to persuade the earl of Devon to go to Normandy, where Avranches was again threatened, and paid the arrears of Dorset for the keeping of Aberystwyth to enable him to prepare for service.[10] All these were clear indications that agreement had been reached with the cardinal for a major loan.

Over the next three weeks Adam Moleyns negotiated with Somerset his conditions for undertaking service in France and the terms of his indenture, and these were laid before the council when it reconvened at Eltham on 30 March. These documents, and the council's discussion of them, furnish a clear picture of the objectives of the expedition and of the inducements which prompted Somerset to lead it.[11] A large army was proposed, of about the same size as that which Henry V had led to France in 1421 and Henry VI in 1430, and double that led by Salisbury in 1428. Its strategy was to be offensive. Crossing to Cherbourg, of which Somerset was captain, it was to pass through western Normandy into Valois France, crossing the Loire and making 'moost cruel and mortel werre that he can and may'. Militarily its objective was to bring the French to battle and to reduce towns and areas to Lancastrian obedience. Somerset's indentures left him the unfettered direction of military operations, detailed his rights in the disposal of the winnings of war and prisoners, and gave him an absolute estate 'to himself and his heires' in all towns, lands, and castles he gained by conquest, other than those of the royal demesne. The strategy was both bold and imaginative: it represented not only a supreme effort but a new direction. Rather than sending modest reinforcements to

[8] *PPC* v, 225–6.

[9] Ibid. 229. The commissions spoke of an aid of men, victuals, and ships, as well as money: E 404/59/153; ibid. 414–18.

[10] Ibid. 233–40. All duchy of Lancaster annuitants were summoned for 5 May, as were some members of the royal household.

[11] Somerset's articles are C 47/26/28; a draft of his indentures is E 101/71/4/916, and the council minutes *PPC* v. 251–6. For a detailed discussion, see M. Jones, 'John Beaufort' loc. cit.

Normandy and Gascony to hold the projected French offensives, it was decided to meet the threat to both duchies by an aggressive attack launched at the critical area betwen them. At best this would draw the French royal army into a major battle—perhaps another Agincourt or Verneuil—and if it did not it would deflect their attack on the duchies and yield Maine and Anjou to devastation. Such an aggressive army needed to be large, particularly since French morale now stood so high, and Somerset indented for 800 men-at-arms and 3,400 archers, even offering to enlarge this to 1,000 men-at-arms of whom seven were to be barons and eight bannerets. It was to serve for a whole year and be well provided with field and siege artillery, and with a bridge of barrels for river crossings. This all-out effort to wrest the military initiative from the French had its diplomatic counterpart, of which Somerset was undoubtedly aware. For if Henry VI 'intended to peace in that country that is by traictie, and yif him like not the offres of his adversaries in the saide traictie', such an army could force the French to terms. Three years of diplomacy and defensive strategy had left Charles VII unreceptive to English offers; it was time to make him talk peace by the pressure of cruel war. If this reflected the 'hawkish' attitude of Cardinal Beaufort, who had once told parliament 'bellum faciamus ut pacem habeamus', it may also have won over Suffolk and Henry VI, who saw no other means to the end they desired. In any case they had little option. Charles VII's offensive demanded some response and Cardinal Beaufort alone could provide the means. They had to dance to the tune he called.

It was not so clear that the duke of York would be willing to do likewise. He had legitimate objections on three scores: that this would divert men and money from Normandy; that it implied lack of confidence in himself as a commander; and that it was a usurpation of his overall authority as lieutenant-general in France. York's position was not dissimilar to that of Bedford in 1428 when Salisbury had been given a commission to conduct independent offensive operations. Then the regent had held aloof from the Orléans campaign and, perhaps with this in mind, the council on 5 April sent Garter king of arms to York to justify Somerset's offensive strategy as providing a shield to Normandy, and to ask for his patience and understanding over the inevitable postponement of his second year's salary. A vague promise of reinforcements accompanied stern exhortations to maintain garrisons and go to Somerset's assistance should the need arise. At the core of this plea lay the problem of the competing authority of the two commanders. Somerset in his articles pointed out 'that no power that he shuld have in his voiage myghte be vailable nor effectual, considered that my said lord of York hath the hool power before of all the said Royaume and Duchie', and he warned that unless he had 'the good will and consentement of the said my lord of York', he could 'in no wise see that he may take upon him your said voiage'. The solution was found in giving Somerset the title of 'lieutenant and captain general of our duchie of Guienne and of our Reaume of France in the parties where . . . the duc of York actualy exercisith not the power that we have given unto him'.[12] In purely military terms the creation of an independent command for offensive operations beyond the frontier of Lancastrian Normandy was entirely justifiable, and had the advantage of not denuding the Norman garrisons. But it raised questions of the relative status of the two commanders and the exercise of authority in areas to be conquered, and these carried disturbing implications for York's future.

First, Somerset held it essential for his repute and authority that he should have the rank of duke, and to this article the king readily agreed, awarding him precedence second only to York.[13] Secondly, although his authority was confined to newly conquered lands, within this area Somerset was to have full civil and military powers, the title to all lands and castles, and—in his final commission of 4 June—the authority to call the estates, raise taxes, and make appointments.[14] It is clear that the region which Somerset had in mind was not Guyenne, but Maine and Anjou. He asked for the reversion of these counties if the recent grant of them to Dorset, which had been challenged by York's council in Normandy, were to be recalled. He also asked for the county of Alençon, the last major part of Bedford's French lands not to have been regranted. Should this or his fief of Saint-Sauveur-l'Endelin be at any time restored to their French lords he was to receive compensation.[15] These clauses make it plain that the expedition was both for the rescue of Lancastrian France and the enlargement of the Beaufort appanage in Maine–Anjou. Breathtakingly ambitious as this was, it foreshadowed a still greater design. In writing to York the council had warned him that it was 'behoveful and necessaire that the maner and conduit of the werre be chaunged' to an offensive strategy. It was no longer possible to count on French divisions to permit an unimpeded reduction of castles and towns as in the days of Henry V, and success could only come from a decisive victory in the field. Should Somerset obtain this, he would not only vastly enrich himself and firmly establish his appanage on the borders of Normandy but would demonstrate

[12] C 47/26/28 art. 4, 9; E 404/59/161; *PPC* v. 259–64. These take up many of the points discussed on 30 Mar. (*PPC* v. 251–6) and raised in Somerset's articles. Among many other concessions to Somerset were the payment of the arrears of his annuity, legal protection and the right to inherit in his absence, deduction of all his expenses from the thirds of war winnings owed to the crown without account, and a general pardon.

[13] C 47/26/28 art. 14. He was invested at Windsor on St George's day.

[14] Ibid. art. 11; E 101/71/4/916; Jones, 'John Beaufort', 87 citing C 76/125 m. 1.

[15] Ibid. art. 15, 22; *PPC* v. 263. As Jones, 'John Beaufort', 90–1 points out, the king's reply about Alençon was ambiguous and probably amounted to a refusal. The petition for Saint-Sauveur-l'Endelin appears to be E 28/73 16 July, wrongly included in the file for 1444. Its value is stated as 3,000 *salus*.

the culpable inertia of York and ensure his own succession when York's indentures expired in 1445. Somerset was being given the means, in men and money, to outshine and displace his rival. If victory were followed by a negotiated peace which secured English territories, the Beauforts would emerge as the principal nobility of Lancastrian France.

It was a last throw and an unseasonable one. The time had long passed when Englishmen expected to win fortunes and territories in France, and Somerset's plans for a following of seven barons and eight bannerets were quickly disappointed. The Beauforts lacked the territorial resources in England which could provide the nucleus of an army, and Somerset failed to persuade either of his relatives, Devon and Salisbury, to join him. This paucity of noble support probably reflected distrust both of Somerset's own abilities as a commander and of the heady expectations of a decisive victory in France. Long years in captivity had left Somerset without the energy, flair, and military experience for such an enterprise, and with an obsessive concern to restore his personal fortunes. He may have drawn his strategic thinking from Sir John Fastolf, who was organizing his army; for Fastolf had long argued that a war of sieges was no longer practicable and that an offensive strategy, bringing 'sharp and cruel war' along the borders of Normandy, could alone secure the duchy.[16] Gloucester, too, had repeatedly called for a major army which would secure a decisive victory. In 1443 these were voices from a bygone age and it is difficult to detect any comparable enthusiasm in the council. Cromwell, almost certainly, was deeply unhappy with the whole project. Beaufort had scarcely needed to argue the case for it; the knowledge that he would only lend for Somerset's venture foreclosed discussion, and virtually allowed Somerset to dictate his terms. Indeed the cardinal's attendance was virtually confined to the period 3–21 May.

Any scruples which Henry VI may have had about waging 'cruel and mortal war' were submerged in the warmth of his trust and affection for his kinsman. Had Henry been of a martial bent, this might have been his first 'riall viage' to recover his lost and threatened rights. In his place he commissioned Somerset in terms which made him the king's surrogate. Henry now delegated his obligation to bring security and right government to France and Guyenne to a lord of the blood, to govern in 'justice, bonne policie et finance', choosing him for his nearness in blood and love for the king, and conferring on him viceregal powers and the obedience of all subjects. It was thus appropriate that the king should use his own wealth for this cause. As Henry informed York, 'by all the weyes and meenes that he hath mow of his own tresore, finances, grants, chevisaunces, hath doo all that hath ben to him possible for settyng forth of his said cousin of

[16] *Wars of Eng.* ii. 575–85; *PPC* v. 233.

Somerset'. Later he reminded Somerset that he had 'sette hym in the state of Duc and of the litill of his demaines remayning in his hands departed with him more than he hath do to any man in cas semblable in his days'.[17] Henry refused little of what Somerset asked for himself, only reducing his request for 1,000 marks of land to 600 marks. The king had made a personal commitment to Somerset's expedition out of confidence and love for his uncle and cousin.

That the last major expedition to France, comparable in its scale and objectives to those with which former English kings had won victories, should have been conceived and fashioned to fulfil the ambitions of the cardinal and his family is a measure both of Henry VI's complaisance and of the financial constraints upon the council. With the subsidies already pledged and cash receipts in the year 1442–3 averaging a mere £7,000 per term, the treasurer could only report the utter insufficiency of the money available. Beaufort's offer to underwrite the expedition had to be accepted and it allowed him to dictate its size and nature. He advanced £10,000 for the first quarter's wages on 6 April and a further £10,000 for the second quarter on 6 June. Only for Dorset's expedition in 1436 had he previously financed both quarters for any expedition, and never had he lent so much in a single year. Loans from other sources totalled a mere £5,250.[18] The wholesale degree of Beaufort's commitment was further underlined by the difficulty of providing security . This was doubly pertinent to the cardinal, whose advance of so substantial a part of his fortune when his life was drawing to a close could not have been made without apprehension. His long career as a lender to the crown had depended on the speedy and effectual repayment of his loans and even when he lent under pressure he had always insisted on, and haggled over, the securities he would accept. In the preceding August, and again in October, he had declined to lend because adequate security was lacking. Basically that situation had not changed. What had changed was the political opportunity, for which he had been waiting, to avenge the reverse of 1440 and to instal his nephews in France. Disappointed in his wider diplomatic policies, and with power inexorably slipping from his hands, his concern at the end of his career concentrated on his family's future. How he assessed the prospects of the expedition as a means of safeguarding Normandy, or as a contribution to the peace negotiations, and to what extent he shared the deluded optimism of his nephew, it is difficult to say. He was now prepared to take a financial and political gamble, swayed by personal and dynastic pride.

His terms for the repayment of the first £10,000 had been agreed by 15 March when letters patent granted him all the customs and subsidies in Southampton and those payable by Italian merchants in London. Payment

[17] *PPC* v. 262, 412.
[18] E 401/781; *PPC* v. 272–3; Steel, *Receipt*, 220, 461.

was to be made in gold and he was to nominate a collector in each port. This monopoly on the customs from aliens was a slender financial base for a loan of this magnitude. In the current year a mere 1,682 sacks of wool were exported by aliens in London and Southampton and 210 sacks by denizens in Southampton, and the total subsidy payable from these two ports would be just under £5,000. It would thus take Beaufort at least two years to recover his loan and probably longer. Not surprisingly, he further stipulated for the right to change these assignments to a lay or clerical subsidy if such were to be granted.[19] The terms of his patent for the repayment of the second loan were read before the council on 25 May and occasioned some dispute. Beaufort insisted that they should be drawn up 'after the minute, or he would not lend'. For this, his lien on the customs from alien merchants was continued and was now extended to the Calais customs, though only after annuities and existing assignments for loans had been discharged. Beyond this he was granted all the revenue arising from the 'casualties' and in particular the profits of Lord Tiptoft's lands in the king's hands. Finally, he could claim £400 p.a. at the exchequer from sheriffs' proffers.[20] The very miscellaneous sources on which Beaufort's loans were secured reveal both the stringencies of exchequer finance and the decline in the cardinal's influence. The security he must have principally desired—the second half of the lay subsidy due at Martinmas—had already been assigned for York's salary, and the council still refused to displace the prior assignments of other creditors.[21] Although Beaufort could engender and fashion the venture by the availability of his loans, he no longer wielded the political influence to tap prime revenues for their repayment. He was being made to venture his personal wealth to an unprecedented degree, so that the expedition was now a high risk venture not only for his nephew but for himself.

The assembly and dispatch of this large force became a tale of mounting difficulties and frustrations. On sealing his indentures Somerset had set the date for the muster at 17 June or earlier, and at the beginning of April considerable quantities of weapons were ordered.[22] Somerset was emphatic about the need for a speedy descent on France and had chosen the Portsmouth–Cherbourg crossing so that the army could cross in two stages if there were a shortage of shipping. From the beginning of May the council met in daily session, with the king frequently present, and received reports of Somerset's preparations. These began on an optimistic note: he

[19] *CPR 1441–6*, 160; *Eng. Export Trade*, 60.

[20] *PPC* v. 276, 279–80; *CPR 1441–6*, 182.

[21] E 401/778 18 May for the assignment to York.

[22] The warrant for payment of the first quarter's wages, dated 8 Apr., gives 17 June, and this date was eventually agreed: E 404/59/163; *PPC* v. 409. In the draft indenture the date 12 June has been erased and 'within two months after this' inserted: E 101/71/4/916. For supplies ordered, see E 404/59/61, *PPC* v. 257.

suggested advancing the muster to 3 June, though by 20 May this was admitted to be unrealistic. On 28 May Somerset himself came up to the council and asked that his quota of men-at-arms be reduced and that of archers increased—the first indication of difficulties in recruitment. On 17 June, when the earl of Salisbury attended to take his muster, there was no sign of the duke or his army, and four days later Somerset appeared in council to ask for a postponement. By 27 June a preliminary muster revealed a particular shortfall of the barons, bannerets, and knights whom he had confidently anticipated. There was a great deal of confusion, with musters being taken in different places and some of his force still in London, and on 9 July the council exploded in anger. Gloucester and Salisbury were scathingly critical, and in its reply to further articles which Somerset had sent from Corfe through John Yerde, the council complained of his inefficiency and the expense and disturbance caused by keeping troops waiting for embarkation in a hot and sultry summer. It strictly ordered him to ship by 18 July, mustering in Normandy if need be.[23] Even Henry VI added his reproaches. Cardinal Beaufort was not present at this tense meeting, but on 6 July (the day Cromwell resigned the treasurership) he had been induced to lend a further £1,000 to meet the costs of shipping, and four days later a final 1,000 marks.[24] Somerset finally mustered at Portsdown on 17 July and in Cherbourg early in August.[25] He was not wholly to blame for the delays, for there were undoubted bottlenecks in the supply of ships, but it was an ill omen that an army comparable in size to those of 1430 and 1436 should depart so ill supported by the nobility, under criticisms of incompetence from the English council, and in the teeth of bitter hostility from the duke of York and his council in Normandy.

A powerful delegation from Normandy, led by the earl of Shrewsbury and Sir Andrew Ogard, had appeared before the council on 21 June. Regrettably there is no record of the representations they made, though these are likely to have focused on the encroachment on York's authority and diversion of financial support in favour of Somerset. Somerset, who was summoned to the council on the same day, made a formal declaration that he understood his commission as being 'no thing to attempte that

[23] *PPC* v. 281, 292–4, 302–4, 409–14; *Historiae Croylandensis Continuatio*, ed. W. Fulman, 519. One contingent crossed on 8 July.

[24] *PPC* v. 307; E 401/781; E 404/59/277; E 404/59/290; *CPR 1441–6*, 194. the final loan was made 'in dicta instanta necessitate nostra'.

[25] E 101/54/5. He had 600 men-at-arms and 3,949 archers. His captains were Sir Thomas Kyriell, Sir John Lisle, Sir Thomas Cusak, Sir Thomas Chetwode, Sir Thomas Kirkeby, Sir John Retford, and Henry Green. John, bastard of Somerset, was among them, but the muster roll contains no mention of Dorset. The exchequer tellers carried £14,000 to Portsdown, disbursing £11,920 in army wages and £1,537 in mariners' wages: E 403/749.

sholde be to the disworship of my Lord the Duc of York . . . but to his welthe worship and proffit desireth to applie him', and invoked the bonds of cousinage and 'rizt especial tendernesse' between them. This verged on being two-faced, for Somerset's final commission, issued as letters patent on 14 June, had directly extended his powers over York's territories. All officials within the realm of France and duchy of Normandy (including those of the *parlement, chambre des comptes*, and the treasurer of Normandy) were now charged to be obedient and diligent in meeting his commands. As late as 21 July Somerset's powers were being further extended to cover coinage in Gascony.[26]

York had good reason to fear for his eventual displacement, but the more pressing concern of the delegation was with the effects of the financial cutback. Garter had told York in April that payment of his salary would have to be deferred, and it was not until the last of Somerset's expenses had been met that Shrewsbury's plea for aid to the bastille at Dieppe was attended to. Then, of the £4,000 which he demanded, only 2,000 marks was delivered in cash on 22 July, the remainder being in dues and credits.[27] This was too little, too late. Within days of Shrewsbury's return to Normandy in early August the bastille had fallen and many of the earl's retinue were captured.This was the only payment made on York's salary for the year 1442–3, so that by September the crown stood in debt to him for £18,333, 6*s*. 8*d*. By December he had been persuaded to relinquish his claim to 10,000 marks of this on the promise of receiving the balance of £11,666. 13*s*. 4*d*. This was credited to him as a loan on 11 December and eventually paid in February 1444.[28] Somerset's expedition thus consumed virtually the whole of the exchequer's war expenditure in France in 1443 and drained royal finance to the limit. Already on 21 May the council had been told that £8,000 beyond what Beaufort had loaned would be needed, and in the following months successive warrants ordered royal jewels to be pledged. For his final loan of 1,000 marks Cardinal Beaufort again received the rich collar as security, though technically he was to hold only one-third of it.[29]

Somerset's campaign proved an anticlimax rather than either a triumph or a disaster.[30] Moving down through western Normandy, from which he levied a transport tax, into the Beaufort fiefs of Avranches and Mortain, he was joined by Dorset and Matthew Gough, and the combined force ravaged the countryside up to the walls of Angers before turning north to

[26] *PPC* v. 289–90; C 76/125 m. 1 *Lettres*, ed. Champollion-Figeac, ii. 467.
[27] *PPC* v. 306–7; E 404/59/273; E 403/749.
[28] Johnson, thesis, 96.
[29] *PPC* v. 276; E 404/59/287, 300.
[30] The best account of what remains a rather obscure affair is given by Jones, 'John Beaufort', and see also Marshall, thesis, 130–40.

besiege Pouancé.[31] Gough inflicted a defeat on a French relieving force, but the army now left Pouancé to seize La Guerche, a town just inside the Breton border but belonging to the duke of Alençon, formally a potential ally of the English. It had been garrisoned on behalf of Charles VII and for some time had been used as a base against Normandy. Dorset had temporarily seized it in 1438 during his operations in Maine, and now Somerset exacted a ransom of 20,000 *salus* from Duke Francis, half of which was paid on 16 October. Probably in November the army again moved into Maine to besiege the fortress of Beaumont-le-Vicomte, which threatened communications between Alencon and Maine, both held by Dorset. No relieving force appeared and the town was captured and garrisoned. The army remained in the field, recruiting unattached troops from Normandy, until late December, without liason with the duke of York and without further successes. Although it had only been campaigning for four months, it was already owed for three months beyond its six months' wages.[32] It was clear that the French were not going to offer battle and that further scope for plunder was limited; Somerset's troops probably demanded to return or go into winter quarters. They were disbanded in Normandy while Somerset himself returned to England at the beginning of January.[33]

For so ambitious and costly a venture its achievements had been distinctly modest. It had enriched the Beauforts and consolidated their possessions in Maine and south-west Normandy; Anjou had been plundered and a sharp shock given to Brittany. Charles VII had remained just out of reach at Saumur, preferring to permit devastation than seek battle, and to await the inevitable exhaustion of Somerset's offensive. Whether he would have fought had Somerset crossed the Loire can only be guessed. In military terms Somerset's campaign was characteristic of the localized operations of the previous decade, the kind of warfare to which English captains had become habiutated. Yet he had come to France with the proclaimed intention of changing the character of the war, with the promise of reducing large areas to English obedience, and the hope of

[31] Dorset had been on an oyer et terminer commission in Yorkshire in June and in council as late as 6 July: E 404/59/223; *PPC* v. 273, 298. On 1 Dec. 1443 he was granted the issues of the sessions in Cardigan: *CPR 1441–6*. There is no evidence for his crossing and some doubt about his participation.

[32] *PPC* vi. 12; Marshall, thesis, 139; *Appendices to Foedera*, 505–6. Somerset's indentures provided for the payment of his wages for the second half-year by the treasurer of England at the beginning of each month and permitted him to return if these were in arrears.

[33] *Benet's Chronicle*, 190. Some of his troops joined the garrison at Falaise (*Appendices to Foedera*, 507) while others were left to live off the countryside. The discontent aroused in Normandy is discussed by M. Jones, 'L'Imposition illégale de taxes en Normandie anglaise: une enquête gouvernementale en 1446', a paper presented to the third Congrès National des Socétés Savantes on the theme 'La France anglaise au Moyen Âge'. I am indebted to Dr Jones for sending me a copy of his typescript.

forcing a decisive battle and a dictated peace. It was the disparity between the huge effort and high hopes and the limited achievement that brought upon Somerset the indignation of the king and the contempt of his peers when he returned. Whether or not a charge of treason was made against him, he (though not Dorset) seems to have been banished from the court and council and to have spent the last months of his life at Wimborne where he died on 27 May.[34]

On a broader view the expedition of 1443 could be claimed to have partly achieved its purpose, for it had both deflected Charles VII from the conquest of Guyenne and had brought his first serious offer of a negotiated peace. At the beginning of 1443 he had given every indication of resuming the campaign in the south, but by 25 May the court had moved to Poitiers, where the duke of Orléans was at last welcomed in his long-advertised role as peace-monger. Having surmounted the princes' opposition, Charles now designed to steal their clothes with a peace offensive in which they would become his agents. The new duke of Brittany, more Francophile than his father, was encouraged to offer his mediation to Henry VI and to send his brother Gilles, already familiar with the English court, to revive the claims to the earldom of Richmond.[35] The mission was shrewdly timed, Gilles arriving in August when disillusionment with Somerset's expedition had already begun. His offers of peace won a fervent response from Henry VI, who poured out his affection for Gilles and half promised him what he sought. Somerset's attack on La Guerche in October further played into Charles VII's hands, drawing Duke Francis into his camp as the aggrieved victim of English aggression and alienating Alençon. The council hastened to offer restitution, granting Gilles a pension of 1,000 marks and sending a stinging rebuke to Somerset which even Cardinal Beaufort was forced to sign.[36] Charles VII's offer of peace talks not only stole the initiative from the princes and threw English policy into disarray, but was designed to strengthen the dominant Angevin faction at court against Burgundy. The duke's pretensions as a mediator for peace had been shown to be hollow and his role was now transferred to the family of Anjou, hitherto the most consistent enemy of the English. Margaret of Anjou's proposed marriage

[34] *Benet's Chronicle*, 190, says 'magnam indignacionem regis incurrit', and *Chron. Angl.* 31, normally favourable to the Beauforts, admits that he returned 'absque sibi aut regno lucro aut honore', while BL Royal MS 13 C 1 (*Chronicles of London*, 341) says 'parvum profuit set stipendium regni inaniter consumpsit'. For the treason charge and story of suicide, see *Hist. Croyland Cont.* 519, a source normally well informed on the Beauforts, and *CP* xii. 48. He died intestate, an inventory of his goods being commissioned on 14 Nov. 1446: Lambeth Palace Lib., Reg. Stafford, fo. 144. Basin, *Histoire de Charles VII*, ed. C. Samaran, i. 280, 284 alleges that his over-confidence and excessive secrecy, cloaked a natural vacillation and timorousness.

[35] Beaucourt, *Charles VII*, iii. 255–6, 265.

[36] *PPC* vi. 3–7, 11–23. Gilles dined with Henry VI at Windsor on 27 Dec., departing just as Somerset returned: E 101/409/11.

with the Count of Nevers had been broken off in February 1443 under pressure from Charles VII and a year later she was being offered to Henry VI. Finally, Charles saw a suspension of war as giving the opportunity to disband the princes' contingents and carry through the reorganization of the royal army, which the princes had frustrated in 1439.

Many factors and considerations thus underlay Charles VII's decision to oppose Somerset's invasion not by arms but by the offer of peace. It was a piece of superb statecraft, for even while the expedition was marching into Anjou Charles had turned it into an irrelevance. As he foresaw, the English council jumped at the prospect of negotiation, and discountenanced Somerset's venture. Factional rivalries contributed to this wholesale shift in the council's attitude and indeed reversed the 'policies' of its members. The Cardinal's opponents, Gloucester and Huntingdon, who had resumed their attendance at council to castigate Somerset, now lent support to Suffolk's peace embassy. With Henry VI's thirst for peace rekindled, and with an open invitation to the court of Charles VII, Suffolk was poised to take control in the area of diplomatic negotiations, where the cardinal had traditionally reigned supreme. He could also count on the support of York, who had been angered and threatened by Somerset's appointment and saw a truce as enabling him to strengthen the duchy's defences and his own authority within it.[37] Thus it was that, in the last months of 1443, as a massive English army was harrying Anjou, the council signified its readiness to send Suffolk to negotiate peace. This represented not any calculated and concerted pressure on the French to come to terms, as it would have in the hands of Henry V, but the tilting of the balance between factions in the council and the wavering response of a vacillating king to the scheming and foresight of his adversary.[38] Moreover, while Charles VII desired a breathing space in which to prepare the next stage of his military and political offensive, for the English it had become a dire necessity, forced on them by military and financial exhaustion. It was therefore inevitable that Charles would dictate the terms.

That Suffolk's mission represented the personal initiative of himself and Henry VI was made clear by his declaration at a meeting of the full council on 1 February 1444. Suffolk sought an indemnity from the king and the lords against any accusation that might subsequently be brought against him. He was particularly vulnerable in going, at Charles's personal invitation, to a meeting in the heart of France, accompanied only by his own followers, 'men of esye degree and few in numbre'. But he went with Henry's personal blessing and invested with the king's vivid sense of his

[37] York had participated in an earlier attempt to establish contact with Charles VII through the duke of Brittany in Sept. 1442, but nothing had come of it: *Foedera*, xi. 13; *PPC* v. 210–13.

[38] *PPC* vi. 32–5; *Foedera*, xi. 53. Expenses for an embassy of Suffolk, Ayscough, and Wenlok 'in the mater of pees' were warranted by Henry VI on 25 Aug.: E 404/59/291–5.

duty, in imitation of Christ, to bring peace. To this end Henry was prepared for a marriage which would be the seal of amity, and Suffolk bore a letter in which Henry addressed Charles as his 'dear uncle' rather than his adversary of France.[39] He landed at Harfleur on 15 March and was at Tours a month later. Suffolk had authority to conclude a perpetual peace or a general truce, but what his instructions were, or whether they were discussed in council, is unclear. The English terms for peace were basically those offered at Gravelines: the retention of Normandy, Guyenne, and Calais in full sovereignty, independent of any claim to the crown of France. The French, as always, refused any cession of land in sovereignty, and offered only the Brétigny territories to be held as fiefs.[40] No attempt was made to overcome this impasse, and both sides moved quickly to negotiate a marriage linked to a truce. Like Cardinal Beaufort in 1439, Suffolk must have set his sights on a long truce, but Charles VII still judged such a perpetuation of the *status quo* to be prejudicial to French interests, and would concede a truce lasting only to April 1446. Two days later this was followed by the marriage agreement between Henry VI and René of Anjou, with the avowed intention that this should lead to negotiations for a final peace. It was clearly Suffolk's assumption that the marriage would guarantee further prolongations of the truce, while for Charles it was a safeguard against any more dangerous English alliance with the princes as had threatened in 1442. But did Suffolk at Tours also make a secret concession of Maine, as his enemies later claimed? The context of the negotiations and the evidence of French sources strongly suggest that he did.

While from Charles VII Suffolk had secured merely a temporary military truce, with King René he had initiated a family relationship, designed to bring twenty years of peace between them. Both houses laid claim to the same territory and could be expected to reach a settlement over this on the occasion of the marriage. Any suggestion that Margaret should bring the county of Maine to Henry VI as her dowry was ruled out by Charles VII; in any case the English held only part of Maine and were the suppliants for the marriage and the peace along the south-western borders of Normandy which it would bring. Already in 1439 they had been ready to relinquish it in the context of a final peace, as Suffolk himself now confirmed, while the earlier negotiations had also raised the question of the claims by the French nobility for restitution of their lands. Thus a verbal promise to Charles,

[39] *Foedera*, xi. 59; Beaucourt, *Charles VII*, iii. 274.

[40] For Suffolk's offers we are dependent on references in the relation of the French embassy in July 1445: *Wars of Eng*. i. 129–33, 151. Suffolk then claimed that, on his last visit to France (Nov.–Mar. 1444–5), he had said that if Henry VI could hold Normandy and Guyenne without homage he would be willing to 'laisser son droit de la couronne de France au roy' (i.e. Charles VII). In 1450 he was alleged to have admitted that his powers gave 'large and sufficient discharge to have departed the king's title': *HMC, 3rd Report*, 280.

count of Maine, who was prominent at Charles VII's court and in the negotiations with Suffolk, that he could expect his prospective father-in-law to restore his fiefs, would have come opportunely. Before the formal sealing of any treaty between the houses such would have been sufficient, particularly as René undertook to send an embassy to England at once to make detailed arrangements for the marriage.[41] According to an *aide memoire* drawn up for French negotiators on the question in 1446, René's envoys, Auvergnas Chaperon and Charles de Castillon, took up the question with Henry VI when they arrived some time later in the year, and in the great French peace embassy which followed the marriage in July 1445 a verbal promise was given to the Sire de Précigny that the surrender would be made before 1 October 1445. When Adam Moleyns returned with these ambassadors to France in September 1445 he was to have effected this, but failed to do so, and it was left to the envoys of Charles VII, Guillaume Cousinot and Jean Havart, to raise it again in October.[42] This was the first occasion on which Charles VII had formally taken cognizance of the question, having previously treated it as a matter for private settlement between Henry and René, and even now Cousinot and Havart negotiated on commission from King René.[43] When the surrender of Maine finally broke surface in official English documents it was in letters to Charles VII from Queen Margaret on 17 December and from Henry VI on 22 December 1445, which confirmed that it had been requested by Cousinot and Havart and by Margaret herself 'many times' out of regard for her father. By that date the Angevins had fallen from favour and had been dismissed from the court, and Charles VII had begun to make the delivery of Maine his own concern.[44]

If Suffolk did give a verbal undertaking at Tours, Henry VI must have been apprised of it before his marriage, and persuaded to assent as a gesture to his new bride and family. From others it had to remain concealed.[45] York might accept it as the price of stabilizing Normandy, but the Beauforts had recently strengthened their position there and would oppose their disinheritance on any but the most generous terms. It would certainly revive and vindicate Gloucester's deep-rooted opposition to negotiation, as requiring concessions. Suffolk had probably judged that it could be made generally acceptable as part of a final peace or a prolonged truce, for which he saw the marriage as an implicit guarantee. The problem he had created for himself was to prevent news of it leaking out before a permanent truce or peace had been secured. The weakness of this was that

41 Beaucourt, *Charles VII*, iii. 277 citing BN MS Lat. 10151.
42 Beaucourt, *Charles VII*, iv. 284 citing BN MS Fr. 18442 fo. 173.
43 Ibid. 164 n. 1, citing A. Lecoy de la Marche, *Le Roi René*, i. 250; ii. 258–9.
44 *Wars of Eng*. i. 164, ii. 639; Beaucourt, *Charles VII*, iv. 103.
45 In 1450 Suffolk persistently denied giving any undertaking at Tours: *Rot. Parl*. iv. 182.

if Charles refused any such long-term settlement Suffolk could only play for time, hoping to maintain secrecy and defer the surrender. Meanwhile he would have to buy friends and stifle his enemies.

Suffolk's dominance over foreign policy and over the king himself was displayed during the negotiations with the French embassy in July 1445. Despite Henry VI's avowed desire for peace and for the friendship of Charles VII, this last attempt to secure a negotiated settlement quickly foundered on the status of the English lands in Normandy. Disappointed in his hope of the French concession which he had expected from the king's marriage and projected surrender of Maine, Suffolk had to be content with the prospect of a future personal meeting of the monarchs to break the deadlock. The negotiations had demonstrated the wide measure of support for his policy. Cardinal Kemp had once again been brought to the negotiating table for a detailed rehearsal of English claims, while Buckingham and Dorset acted as hosts to the ambassadors. Suffolk himself took the opportunity to abuse and deride Gloucester for his opposition, in the king's presence.[46] Cardinal Beaufort took no part in the negotiations, although to the French envoys who called upon him in London on 21 July he spoke words of peace. The only record of his activity was his meeting with the envoys from Isabel, duchess of Burgundy in June–September 1444 and again in March–August 1445. Their purpose was doubtless to gain precise news about the stages of the Anglo-French *rapprochement*, which had ominous implications for Burgundy. For a formal peace and marriage alliance between Henry and Charles might augur an attack on the duke, whom neither had reason to love. There was little that Philip could do to mitigate his isolation. His envoys could only have reported that Cardinal Beaufort now had little influence over policy, and it was doubtless the appreciation of this that in 1444 prompted Isabel to renew approaches to the duke of York initiated in 1442.[47]

Suffolk too was aware of the importance of securing York's support for the peace negotiations. While at Nancy he had floated a scheme for the marriage of York's eldest son Edward to Madeleine, the daughter of Charles VII. This was pursued throughout 1445 but thereafter disappeared.[48] At the same time Suffolk took steps to arrange payment of York's salary suspended during Somerset's expedition. By December 1443 the new treasurer, Lord Sudeley, had reached agreement for the payment of £11,666. 13*s*. 4*d*. in February 1444. The truce made further payments less compelling, and by the time the duke returned to England late in 1445 he was owed a total of £38,666. 13*s*. 4*d*.; even so the very extent of his

[46] *Wars of Eng*. i. 89–167.

[47] Beaucourt, *Charles VII*, iv. ch. 4; Taylor, thesis, 171–89; Vaughan, *Philip the Good*, 116–21; *Wars of Eng*. i. 137.

[48] Thielemans, *Bourgogne et Angleterre*, 147–9; *Wars of Eng*. i. 79–86, 160–70.

claims, coupled with his hope of securing reappointment, encouraged York to support Suffolk. This was confirmed when, late in 1444, York was granted an extensive appanage in eastern Normandy comprising the counties of Évreux and Beaumont-le-Roger, with Bretheuil, Conches, and Orbec, while his son Edmund received the lordship of Saint-Sauveur-l'Endelin lately held by Somerset.[49] As the greatest landowner in Normandy, York had a direct interest in the stabilization of the frontier by a long truce, even if this were secured by the surrender of the English lands in Maine.

There the Beauforts stood to lose heavily, and in other ways Beaufort interests were sacrificed to Suffolk's designs in 1444. The first was in regard to the release of Jean, count of Angoulême. In preparation for his expedition Somerset had, in December 1442, reopened negotiations for the release of Angoulême, whom he had inherited from his mother, the duchess of Clarence, in 1440. During his expedition Angoulême was held at Cherbourg, from where he wrote to his brother, the duke of Orléans, urging support for Suffolk's embassy.[50] It was in fact as the attorney of the dying Somerset that Suffolk negotiated Angoulême's ransom and release during his mission to Tours in May 1444. By 1440 there remained due of Clarence's share of the composition of 1412 the sum of 81,000 *salus d'or* (£13,500). By an agreement at Paris on 7 March 1444 Angoulême was to be released on the immediate payment of 16,000 *salus* and the balance of 65,000 *salus* was promised within a year, under the seals of Orléans, Dunois, Alençon, and Bourbon.[51] But five days later Somerset died in England, and though the agreement was ratified by his widow Margaret, it was not until 31 March 1445 that Angoulême finally obtained his liberty after thirty-three years of imprisonment. At that point he undertook to pay a further 9,844 *salus* and 1,000 *salus* for his maintenance costs.[52] Although 15,000 *salus* was received in 1445 and a further 7,000 in 1447, the remainder was still being sought by the Duchess Margaret, in a suit before the *parlement* of Paris from 1480 until her death.[53] Doubtless the £3,500 or so which she had received had been useful, for Duke John's death had deprived her of considerable wealth, but she must have felt cheated into surrendering a valuable if wasting asset for this sum. It is clear that Suffolk's own concern had been to win the goodwill of Orléans and Dunois in the peace negotiations.

[49] T. B. Pugh, 'Richard Plantagenet, duke of York, as the King's lieutenant in France and Ireland' in J. G. Rowe (ed.), *Aspect of Late Medieval Government and Society*, 122–3.

[50] P. Champion, *Vie de Charles d'Orléans*, 353.

[51] G. Dupont-Ferrier, 'Captivité de Jean d'Orléans',70; id, in *Revue des documents historiques*, 4 (1877), 17–30; M. Jones, 'Orleans Ransom', 256–7. Somerset's commission to Suffolk is in WAM 12321 and the agreement of 7 Mar. WAM 12285.

[52] WAM 12300–1; BL Add. MS 35814. The bastard of Somerset, held prisoner by Dunois, was to be released as part of this agreement: Champion, *Charles d'Orlèans*, 353, 445.

[53] As described by Jones, 'Orleans Ransom'. Documents in WAM 12285–321.

Suffolk also took advantage of Somerset's death to lay hands on the Beaufort lands and heir. Although the duke had stipulated that his widow should have the care of his daughter should he die on campaign (and this may have been respected), the infant's marriage and the custody of all the lands was urgently sought and obtained by Suffolk within four days of the duke's death, while members of the royal household speedily secured grants of annuities and offices from the estates.[54] There was a six-month delay before the first inquisitions post mortem were carried out (perhaps because Margaret was carrying a posthumous child), and Edmund, who claimed as brother and male heir, was denied access to the muniments. But on 24 October 1444 he was granted licence to receive his part of the inheritance and the inquisitions went ahead. The dowager duchess too was granted dower, assigned to her in February 1445, though as late as October 1446 some parts were still detained by Suffolk's steward.[55] Other families moved swiftly to take advantage of Duke John's disgrace. On 6 January 1444 John Holand finally regained the title of duke of Exeter which the family had lost to the Beauforts in 1416, underlining his restoration with formal recognition of his precedence over Somerset; then as Duke John lay dying in May he sued a special assize against him to recover the manor of Cranmere.[56]

In general, Beaufort presence and influence in both court and council was at a minimal level in the year following Duke John's departure. Although the surviving council records are sparse, they reveal fairly consistently that the only regular attenders were Suffolk, Cromwell, Dudley, and Stourton, together with the three officers, Archbishop Stafford, Sudeley, and Moleyns. The enlarged formal sessions of the whole continual council ceased to be held regularly after the winter of 1443–4. After a poorly attended assembly in June–July 1444, Henry VI was away from the capital for virtually all the remainder of the year, and the direction of policy was finally transferred to the inner group of Suffolk's friends.[57] Edmund Beaufort was not among these, and how often he visited the court it is impossible to say. Certainly he was not among those who attested the king's assent to petitions, nor did any of the Beauforts form part of the group involved in the king's other consuming concern, with the new royal foundations. When Henry's intention to found a college of priests at Eton first took shape late in 1440 his feoffees were largely drawn from the ranks of the household. As the project for a further foundation at Cambridge gathered momentum in the following years some

[54] *PPC* v. 252; C 81/1370/11 dated 31 May 1444 is a warrant to the chancellor to grant Suffolk the wardship, endorsed: 'fail not as we specially trust you', and ordering that the bearer should return with the sealed letters patent (*CPR 1441–6*, 283, 268–9). Margaret had been born 31 May 1443.

[55] C 139/114; *CPR 1441–6*, 311; *CCR 1441–7*, 243, 252, 257, 324, 427.

[56] E 28/73 22 May 1444.

[57] E 28/71–3; C 81/1544; *PPC* vi. 17–30.

new names were added, and the final feoffments of duchy of Lancaster lands for the purpose embraced a wide range among the nobility. Yet at neither stage were the Beauforts included.[58]

Thus the signal failure of Duke John's expedition brought an abrupt end to the cardinal's influence and left the family discredited and bereft of support. It also left the crown heavily in debt to the cardinal. What were his chances of securing repayment, with his own life patently drawing to a close? The exchequer entered the year Michaelmas 1443–4 encumbered with debt. In the previous year it had borrowed almost £28,000, of which £21,666 was owed to Cardinal Beaufort, and had accumulated obligations to the commanders in France which it would need £22,000 to discharge.[59] Much of the revenue due was already pledged: the Martinmas lay subsidy to the duke of York as his salary for 1441–2 and the customs to the Staple and Cardinal Beaufort. However, the truce would ease its military obligations and the royal household was still being mainly supported from the revenues of the royal duchies. Until the queen's arrival and the withdrawal of the duchy revenues in 1445 threw royal finance into confusion, the exchequer was afforded a brief opportunity to discharge some, but not all, of its debts. Which of its creditors it paid would depend much on their individual degrees of preference. Beaufort himself recovered £14,848 in Michaelmas and Easter terms 1443–4 and a further £5,326 in February 1445, representing the entire repayment of the two major loans of £10,000 apiece. Virtually all of this is recorded as received in cash at the exchequer and accounts for the above average proportion of its cash dealings in these terms.[60] By contrast, of the £11,666 assigned to the duke fo York on the customs on 7 February 1444, in payment of his salary for 1442–3, £3,593 proved uncashable and the duke was still seeking payment of the remnant of this in 1454.[61] How was Beaufort able to ensure such swift and effective repayment at a period when his political influence was in abeyance?

When Cromwell resigned the treasurership on 6 July 1443 one of the three articles to which he obtained the king's formal assent was that his successor should maintain all the assignments already made 'and specially for moneye borrowed in my tyme may be content as gode shall growe whereof withoute restraint or delay'.[62] It was to be his last service to the cardinal, and upheld the principle which together they had consistently

[58] For these see Wolffe, *Henry VI*, 136 ff.; Somerville, *Duchy of Lancaster*, 210; C 81/1428/28, 33; C 81/1429/33–4; C 81/1340/4–5.

[59] Steel, *Receipt*, 461. York was owed £11,666, Shrewsbury £10,426.

[60] E 403/751, 753, 755. His repayment in full was acknowledged in a warrant dated 12 Feb. 1445: E 404/61/135. He also received repayment in cash in Mich. 1444/5 of £1,000 advanced 6 July 1443: *PPC* v. 307; E 404/59/277.

[61] Johnson, thesis, Appendix D.

[62] *PPC* v. 300.

defended, of the primacy and inviolability of loan repayments. Sudeley was thus bound to honour Beaufort's patents and the cardinal's priority was safeguarded in the warrants for payments to other creditors. William Port received the money from the collectors whom Beaufort had nominated in the ports.[63] As an additional concession to his patent of 23 May 1443—made after Gloucester had left the council chamber—he had procured licence for the Borromei of Florence to export 600 sacks of wool to Middleburg, evading the Calais Staple.[64] It is not certain that this was implemented, but the repayment of Beaufort's loans was heavily charged on Italian exports, which, indeed, reached their highest peak for fifty years in 1443–4, yielding in subsidy over £6,000, two-thirds of it from Southampton. Numerous safe conducts were issued to Italian and Flemish merchants in this year, as the cardinal had also stipulated.[65] Beaufort would appear to have procured privileges for alien exporters in order to stimulate their subsidies, from which his loans were to be repaid. That these arrangements stood the test of his own departure from the council, the appointment of a new treasurer, and the discrediting of his policy, was proof of his own astuteness but also perhaps of his continuing potential importance as a lender.

In fact Beaufort made only one small loan in 1444. This was of 2,000 marks on 27 February, the very day on which Suffolk, Moleyns, and Lord Roos left for Tours. It was not, however, for their expenses but for John Talbot, earl of Shrewsbury who was returning to France with reinforcements for the duke of York. In August 1443 Shrewsbury, like York, had been forced to compound with the treasurer by surrendering part of his claims for wages against payment of the residue. The crown acknowledged a debt to him of £10,426, which was to be charged on the customs and casualties after the satisfaction of the cardinal's loans. Since then he had still received nothing, and now made his return to France conditional on receiving 2,000 marks of this sum in cash.[66] This Beaufort supplied, in effect waiving his preference in favour of an old friend, his nephew's brother-in-law, whose professional military pride and personal fortune had been severely hurt by the priority given to Somerset's expedition. The cardinal was re-building his bridges. This loan was for the moment secured on the remaining two parts of the rich collar, the other third being already held in pledge for the repayment of 1,000 marks loaned in July 1443. The whole sum of £2,000 was repaid from the lay subsidy levied from the

[63] E 404/60/83, 232, 265; *CFR 1437–45*, 234–7, 227.

[64] *PPC* v. 280.

[65] *Eng. Export Trade*, 60; Lloyd, *Wool Trade*, 270. For export licences and safe conducts to Italians and Flemings, see C 76/125 m. 2, 3, 4; C 76/126 m. 12–15.

[66] E 401/784 27 Feb.; *Wars of Eng.* i. 434–6; E 28/71 27 Nov. 1443; E 404/61/135; *PPC* vi. 27; *CPR 1441–6*, 241. £8,000 of the crown's debt to Talbot was for the payment of his ransom: cf. Pollard, *Talbot*, 109–10.

bishopric estates in Martinmas 1445.[67] By then Beaufort had disengaged himself from the court and its policy, and was intent only on gathering in safely the crown's residual debt to him.

[67] E 28/72 3 Mar.; *CPR 1441–6*, 240; *Foedera*, xi. 55. Beaufort returned the jewels on receiving tallies on the lay subsidy on 11 May 1445: E 101/335/15H.

18

Retirement, 1444–1446

THE death of Duke John in 1444 spelt disaster for the Beaufort inheritance. That had never been large, comprising the few manors given by John of Gaunt and forfeited lands in Devon granted by Henry IV, both in fee-tail; the castle and lordship of Corfe granted by Henry IV in tail male: and the annuity of £1,000 also in tail male charged equally on the exchequer and the petty customs in London. The marriage of John, first earl of Somerset to Margaret, a coheiress of Thomas Holand, earl of Kent, brought in some valuable Holand properties which the Beauforts were lucky not to lose when Margaret married Thomas, duke of Clarence as her second husband. These reverted to her son John, the second earl, on her death in 1439 and became securely vested in the Beaufort succession. Both the first earl and his brother Thomas, duke of Exeter had largely supported their dignities from the rewards of service and grants of casual profits. Thus, though he inherited from both his father and uncle, the second earl's landed income from 1427 to 1438, while he was in captivity, barely exceeded 500 marks, to which he added 1,000 marks from annuities.[1] That of his mother, the Duchess Margaret, was higher, for in addition to her Holand lands and the dowers from her two husbands, she held the Devon lands in jointure. In the 1436 tax returns her landed income is given as 2,000 marks, that of Earl John as £1,000, and that of Edmund Beaufort as £205.[2] It was probably Edmund who managed John's estates during his captivity, and a small surplus may even have accumulated during these years, from which in John's absence loans were made to the crown;[3] on the other hand his annuity certainly fell into arrear.

Needing to pay a ransom of £24,000—the value, as he claimed, of his whole inheritance—John initiated an overhaul of his estate administration, selling his Welsh lands to the earl of Suffolk.[4] However his uncle's policy required him to join his brother Edmund in France and by the end of 1439 he was awaiting shipment to Normandy. At this point his mother's death put him in possession of his full inheritance. This comprised Beaufort lands worth some £570 p.a. and Holand lands worth some £618 p.a. To that he

[1] *CCR 1422–9*, 230–1; *CFR 1422–30*, 172; above, ch. 5 n. 24.

[2] PRO, E 359/29; H. L. Gray, 'Incomes from Land in England in 1436', *EHR* 49 (1934), 615–18.

[3] Loans of £2,000 in Dec. 1433 (E 401/734), 2,000 marks in June 1435 (E 401/743), £4,000 in Mar. 1436 (E 401/744).

[4] *CPR 1436–41*, 515, 433; *Hist. Croy. Cont.* i. 499, 518–19, 539–40.

could add the whole of the annuity of £1,000, with another £20 from the issues of Somerset.[5] To this notional sum of about £2,200 he added £50 p.a. from lands inherited from Joan, widow of Thomas, earl of Kent (d. 1400) in 1442.[6] For his rank this was a sufficient but by no means generous income and there was every inducement for him to enlarge it, as his father and uncle had done, by service in war. Unlike them, however, he asked for and received his reward in advance of his service. On being invited to lead the expedition to France in 1443 Somerset asked for his elevation to a dukedom with lands to the value of 1,000 marks p.a. When this was broached in the council, those present 'absteigned hem in alle wise to speke, nor durst avise the Kyng to depart from such livelode ne to open their mouthes in such matiers'. On his own motion Henry VI then granted Somerset lands worth £400 p.a.[7] By 28 May Somerset, having been disappointed in his search for suitable properties, asked to be shown the king's 'books of such lyvelode as that he may gyve', and in particular 'the boke of the lordship of Kendal and of the valeur of hit'. The treasurer, Cromwell, only agreed to do so on the authority of the council. On 20 June, when Somerset had already failed to keep his muster, Henry VI granted him the lordship of Kendal, formerly held by Bedford, in tail male, and the title was confirmed by charter on 28 August. Since one-third of many of the manors was already held in dower by Bedford's widow, Jacquetta, and elsewhere properties had been granted to others for life, Somerset required a further patent to vest him with the rents and alternative lands.[8] His notional income now stood at some 4,000 marks p.a.

Since John's only legitimate issue was his infant daughter Margaret, the prospect of his death on campaign was a matter of acute concern to himself, his wife, and his brother Edmund. Apart from his wife's dower and the few lands and annuity held in tail male, the majority of both the Beaufort and Holand parts of the inheritance were held in fee simple or tail general, and their descent to Margaret might well be contested by Edmund Beaufort. To avoid this John secured licence in October 1442 to entail land worth 1,000 marks p.a. upon himself, his wife, and his heirs, perhaps compensating Edmund by making over to him the manors of Woking and Sutton in Surrey, worth about £48 p.a. Before he left for France in 1443 he also had licence to alienate land worth a further 500 marks p.a. for the performance of his will.[9] By the time of his death on 27 May 1444, therefore, virtually all his lands had been placed in feoffment and only

[5] She died 30 Dec. 1439: C 139/101. Somerset had the keeping of her lands until he sued for livery: *CPR 1436–41*, 370, 372, 382. A figure of £1,200 p.a. in landed income matches his claim that his ransom was the value of all his lands if estimated at twenty years' annual income.

[6] Principally the manor of Bourne (Lincs.): *CFR 1437–46*, 264–5; *CCR 1441–7*, 99, 104, 107. He was also granted £10 p.a. from Bloxham (Oxon.): *CPR 1441–6*, 102.

[7] C 47/26/28 art. 14; *PPC* v. 252–4, 281, 285–8.

[8] *CPR 1441–6*, 233–4; C 139/114.

[9] *CPR 1441–6*, 170; C 139/160; *PPC* v. 255.

some £200 worth of fee farms was held in fee simple. However, the process of creating his wife's jointure was apparently incomplete, for on 19 July 1445 his widow was pardoned for having acquired lands from the duke's feoffees without licence.[10] Since the duke had died without heirs male, the Kendal lordship reverted to the crown and the other properties held in tail male, including Corfe, descended to Edmund.[11] All the remainder of the estate should have come into the hands of the Duchess Margaret, either as dower or jointure.

In fact, four days after the duke's death the earl of Suffolk secured a grant of the marriage of the heiress Margaret and the custody of her lands. This initiated a struggle between the Duchess Margaret and the feoffees on the one hand and Suffolk on the other, the course of which is obscure.[12] Despite the ratification of her jointure in July 1445 the duchess never enjoyed possession of the lands, and by August 1450 Suffolk had obtained a dispensation for the marriage of Margaret Beaufort to his son John. But Suffolk himself was then dead and the custody of the Beaufort lands reverted to the crown, the claims of the Duchess Margaret being set aside. Early in 1453 John and the Lady Margaret were divorced, and the king's half brothers Edmund and Jasper Tudor received the keeping of all the late duke's possessions in the king's hands.[13] By 1455 Edmund Tudor had married Margaret and a valor of 1455–6 shows her in possession of all the manors enfeoffed for the duchess's jointure except Colnwake, Lamarsh, Torpell, and Bourne. The total value of these properties was about £500 p.a. and on Edmund's death in 1456 she carried them to her third husband, Henry, earl of Stafford. She also recovered the Northamptonshire properties from her father's feoffees and was living at Maxey in the 1460s.[14] Duke John's intended entail, together with his attempt to procure the reversion of Edmund's governorship of Maine, suggests that he returned from captivity resentful of his younger brother's achievements and reputation and determined to assert his own interests and those of his immediate family. Edmund's shadowy role in the 1443 expedition may have reflected a coolness between them. In the event John's dispositions ensured that the estates passed from the male line. By 1446 Edmund must

[10] *CPR 1441–6*, 349, 408. these comprised the most valuable parts of the Beaufort inheritance apart from Deeping, the Kendal lordship, and the Northants properties of Gaunt's original endowment, already enfeoffed for the performance of the duke's will. They were worth some £550 p.a. The transaction probably dated from the last months of John's life, when he knew his wife was expecting a child.

[11] C 139/114; *CPR 1441–6*, 311; *CCR 1441–7*, 243, 324.

[12] Above, ch. 17 n. 54. In Apr. 1447 she married Leo, Lord Welles; this would have posed a further threat to the Beaufort inheritance had the duchess been able to retain it.

[13] *CPL* x. 472; *Benet's Chron.* 209; *CPR 1452–61*, 78.

[14] DL 29/651/10533, 10534. The receiver's account for Mich. 1455–6 shows a gross receipt of £600 and payment to the receiver of £523. Cf. *CPR 1452–61*, 368, 504. For her later residence at Maxey, WAM 12181.

have realized that, barring the infant Margaret's death, he would gain nothing more of his brother's estate, and that he must build up his own by other means.

Unfortunately he had no links with Suffolk's coterie or special access to royal patronage. His two principal strengths at this juncture were his connections with the old Beaufort group among the lords, and his military reputation. In October 1445 he appears among the select group of lords summoned to a special meeting of the council on the eve of parliament, and throughout 1446 he was normally present at council along with Suffolk, Buckingham, and Cromwell.[15] It was the Stafford connection which proved of particular service to him at this point. In 1444 his daughter had married Buckingham's eldest son and he was at the duke's side for the reception of the French ambassadors in 1445 and for the arrest of Gloucester in 1447. In that year he was one of Buckingham's feoffees in Burstwick, formerly held by his mother the duchess of Clarence, and when in 1448 the cardinal's executors passed Canford and Poole to Edmund, Buckingham was one of the remainder men along with Lords Cromwell, Moleyns, and Stourton.[16] Robert Hungerford, Lord Moleyns was Edmund's neighbour in Somerset and Stourton was Duke John's principal feoffee and executor. Edmund's other connections among the nobility were with Thomas, earl of Devon, married to his sister, and with his brothers-in-law the earl of Shrewsbury and Lord Latimer.

Edmund Beaufort, therefore, did not lack allies among the upper nobility; yet none of these was numbered among the group which immediately surrounded the king and controlled the patronage which he dispensed so liberally in these years. Edmund received two major grants to sustain the rank of marquess to which he had been elevated on 24 June 1443: an annuity of £224 from the chamberlain of South Wales in December 1443 and the Gournay lands and manors of Babraham and Bassingbourn in October 1444.[17] Thereafter he received nothing until his successful bid for power in 1451. Altogether, from his exchequer and Welsh annuities, his constableships in Wales and Windsor, and his lands held by inheritance, crown grant, and in right of his wife, he enjoyed a notional receipt of rather under 4,000 marks p.a.[18] He could only hope to extend this slender and partially uncertain income in two ways: from his lands in France and by inheritance from his rich uncle. Duke John's death

[15] E 28/77 25 Sept.; C 81/1546; *PPC* vi. 54. In 1445–6 he secured confirmations of his annuities and the Gournay lands, and in May 1446 was granted a wardship and marriage: *CCR 1441–7*, 243, 324–6; *Rot. Parl.* v. 446–7; *CPR 1441–6*, 419, 426.

[16] *CPR 1446–52*, 78; *CCR 1454–61*, 20.

[17] *CPR 1441–6*, 54, 277, 324, 419.

[18] i.e. £1,000 from annuities, £500 as constable of Windsor (also of Carmarthen and Cardigan), £664 from the grants of 144–4; perhaps some £450 from his own lands and those of his wife. Cf. Storey, *House of Lancaster*, 252 n. 7.

appeared to have put an end to the Beaufort ambitions in France. Yet, though his expedition had failed in its larger aims, it had considerably strengthened the Beaufort grip on Maine. Beaumont-le-Vicomte, commanding the road from Alençon to Le Mans, had been recovered and there, as at Le Mans, Alençon, Fresnay, and Essay, Beaufort captains were installed. It was indicative of the disarray of Lancastrian policy that Suffolk was now pledged to surrender to René of Anjou the one area which had recently been militarily reinforced. The implications of this were to lead to Edmund Beaufort's return to Normandy.

As the term of York's appointment as lieutenant-governor of Normandy came to its end, he made clear his desire and expectation for its renewal. He himself arrived in London in October 1445 and remained there until the first session of parliament in April 1446.[19] His commission as lieutenant had been extended for three months, and during the parliament his accounts as lieutenant were scrutinized at the exchequer. Early in June the council endorsed a financial settlement by which he waived payment of £12,666. 13*s*. 4*d*. and received assignment of the balance of £26,000 on 21–2 July.[20] York perhaps saw his gesture as guaranteeing his reappointment, particularly as the council was currently discussing the size of the retinue with which he might accompany Henry VI to a projected meeting with Charles VII.[21] That meeting, agreed by the French embassy in December 1445 and approved by parliament, was expected by Suffolk to result in a declaration of amity and a long truce, if not of formal peace. But when Adam Moleyns and Lord Dudley arrived in France in July 1446 to arrange the meeting, they found that Charles had made the delivery of Maine a pre-condition, and they returned empty-handed early in October. Suffolk now had to ensure that on their next mission in January-February 1447 they would be able to give a firm guarantee for its surrender. This was now promised for 1 November 1447, to coincide with a meeting of the two kings, and on this basis the truce was extended until 1 January 1448.[22] Significantly it was in the interval between these two missions that on 24 December 1446, Somerset was appointed lieutenant-general for three years. A clear indication of the impending decision had been given in the late autumn when Moleyns inspired accusations against York of peculation in Normandy. The duke angrily denounced Moleyns and exacted an apology.[23] The choice of Somerset was dictated not by Suffolk's favour towards Somerset or distrust of York, but by his calculation that Somerset

[19] *Wars of Eng*. i. 161 shows him at Honfleur on 21 Sept. The date of 6 Dec. in *Benet's Chron*. 191 is too late.

[20] E 404/62/88; Johnson, thesis, 97.

[21] *PPC* vi. 52.

[22] Beaucourt, *Charles VII*, iv. 290.

[23] BL Harleian MS 543, printed with some inaccuracies in A. C. Reeves, *Lancastrian Englishmen*, 245–9.

would only willingly relinquish his governorship of Maine and his lands there if he were rewarded with the bigger prize of York's post. None the less, York was enraged at being supplemented and Suffolk thereby alienated a former supporter.[24]

Somerset was to indent with 300 men at arms and 900 archers on 1 March 1447, but in the event the Bury parliament and then his uncle's last illness delayed his departure, while the further extension of the truce until April 1448 removed the immediate need for his presence.[25] The first steps to implement the surrender of Maine were taken on 27 July, when letters were sealed ordering Somerset and his lieutenants to deliver the fortresses into the hands of the royal commissioners appointed to effect the surrender, Fulk Eyton and Matthew Gough. When Eyton and Gough approached Osbern Mundeford, Somerset's *bailli* at Le Mans, he refused to act except on Somerset's own command.[26] The question was now raised of what compensation was to be paid to English captains and settlers. Although Mundeford and other captains had been authorized to negotiate this with Charles VII's commissioners in September 1447, nothing had been agreed by the time the French formally claimed the surrender on 31 October. Resolved to break the deadlock, Charles VII first appointed a high-ranking embassy to negotiate with Gough, and this reached an agreement for a twenty-year truce and compensation by 30 December. But when further prolongations dragged the surrender into mid-February, Charles moved up his army. Only the arrival of Adam Moleyns and Lord Roos with full powers on 15 March 1448 secured the English withdrawal.[27]

Suffolk had correctly assessed the difficulty of enforcing the surrender at the local level, where Somerset's men would not readily yield unless they were bought out. What he had not anticipated was that Somerset was neither prepared to override his followers' interests nor to neglect the chance of furthering his own. Somerset put a high price on his co-operation. On 13 November 1447 the English council awarded him a pension of 10,000 *li. tournois* p.a. as personal compensation to be raised on the bailliages of Caen and the Cotentin.[28] Under the terms agreed on 30 December Charles VII agreed to pay 24,000 *li. tournois* to English landowners in Maine as compensation, calculated at ten years' income; Somerset was later accused of pocketing a substantial part of this too.[29]

[24] *Chron. Angl.* 35; Basin, *Hist. Charles VII*, ii. 65–6; Griffiths, *Henry VI*, 541 n. 132. York was at the council in the first half of Dec. 1446 and Somerset attended on the 14th: Johnson, thesis, 109 n. 5.

[25] E 404/63/11. 19.

[26] Beaucourt, *Charles VII*, iv. 294–5; Griffiths, *Henry VI*, 499–504; *Wars of Eng.* ii. 642–5, 700.

[27] Beaucourt, *Charles VII*, iv. 295–99; *Wars of Eng.* ii. 666, 687, 692, 710–17.

[28] *Wars of Eng.* ii. 685; Allmand, *Lancastrian Normandy*, 78, 281.

[29] *Foedera*, xi. 203; *Wars of Eng.* ii. 722; *The Paston Letters*, ed. J. Gairdner, i. 107.

Finally, on 31 March 1448, with the crisis over, Somerset was raised to the dukedom as he prepared to embark. Like his brother, he had extracted his reward from Henry VI prior to service, but without the wealth or influence of the cardinal behind him. Instead he had cleverly used the pressure on Suffolk to secure first office and then compensation, while avoiding the final responsibility and odium of the surrender.

The cardinal himself had finally ceased to play any role in central politics. His last recorded appearances at the council were in April and May 1444, and in so far as his itinerary in his last three years can be traced, he only occasionally came near London. From November to February 1444–5 he was at Esher; in the following July at Southwark, where the French embassy visited him; at Esher again in September, and in 1446 at Southwark for midsummer and again in the late autumn.[30] In July 1446 he made his last loan for the earl of Shrewsbury, having previously contributed a modest £1,000 on 21 July 1445 towards a general loan for the queen's coronation, for which he accepted jewels as security for repayment.[31]

In the church, as in politics, Beaufort's old associates formed a dwindling band, while new promotions and appointments owed nothing to his influence. Although he undoubtedly favoured John Stafford's elevation to Canterbury in April–May 1443, at a time when he was influential in council, it was rather upon Chichele's previous recommendation and Henry VI's support that Eugenius IV relied in making the translation.[32] Beaufort had always found Stafford a more like-minded colleague than Chichele, and it is significant that it was only after Chichele's death that Beaufort took up residence at Christ Church, Canterbury. His share in ecclesiastical patronage was likewise declining. Bekynton's appointment to Bath and Wells in 1443 diminished his influence in a diocese where so many of his clerks had received prebends. Yet some of the cardinal's servants still held important offices and secured promotion. When Nicholas Bildeston died in 1441 his successor as dean of Salisbury was Adam Moleyns; but on his promotion to the see of Chichester in 1445 the office was filled by Richard Leyot, Bedford's former chancellor. Leyot was able to pass his prebend of Grimston to another Beaufort servant, Nicholas Caraunt. He

[30] In general his itinerary can be traced from the letters in *Reg. CS* though these can reflect the movements of the bishop's chancery as much as of Beaufort. See too *Wars of Eng.* i. 137–8. The statement that he consecrated the cemetery at King's Coll. Cambridge on 2 Nov. 1446 (Colvin, *King's Works*, 271 citing Willis and Clark, *Architectural History of Cambridge University*, i. 466) is incorrect: the text refers to Waynflete and the date must be 1447. He was not among those summoned on 17 Dec. 1446 to the great council to be held on 24 Jan. 1447.

[31] E 401/791; E 403/757; E 404/61/265.

[32] Jacob, *Essays*, 50 citing Bekynton, *Correspondence*, i. 147, ii. 75–7. All the episcopal appointments of 1445–6, namely Bekynton to Bath and Wells, Carpenter to Worcester, Lyndwood to St Davids, Pecock to St Asaphs, Moleyns to Chichester, and Lyhert to Norwich were the work of Henry VI or Suffolk. See L.-R. Betcherman, 'The making of bishops in the Lancastrian period', *Speculum*, 41 (1966), 414–5.

was the brother of William Caraunt, one of Duke John's executors, and by 1446 had become secretary to Margaret of Anjou. A native of Henstridge, he was the choice of the chapter of Wells when the deanery became vacant on the death of John Forest in 1445.[33] In the Winchester archdeaconry the Beaufort succession had also been maintained, with Stephen Wilton his chancellor succeeding Bildeston. Beaufort's former secretary Richard Petworth still held two prebends in Wells and one in Chichester until his death at a ripe age in 1458, while his present secretary William Toly held one of the prebends at Combe, along with Petworth, Forest, Caraunt, Obizzi, and Gilbert Kymer. Kymer was a long-standing servant of Duke Humphrey, but as dean of Wimborne minster he had connections with the Beaufort circle, and became one of Duke John's executors. Although this handful of the cardinal's servants still held and could secure important benefices, the patronage of the court was usually more potent. When Moleyns vacated his archdeaconries at Salisbury and Taunton in 1445 they were filled by Richard Andrew and Andrew Huls, both royal servants.[34]

In the last three years of the cardinal's life his associates were mainly the members of his household, and of the communities of Christ Church, Canterbury and St Swithun's, Winchester. Here too death was removing some of his oldest servants. Nicholas Bildeston died in 1441, William Flete in 1444, John Foxholes and John Forest in 1445–6. Petworth was entering old age, though he still occasionally acted as a scribe for important documents. Those who ran Beaufort's affairs in his last years were Stephen Wilton his chancellor, Richard Waller master of his household, William Mareys treasurer of Wolvesey, and William Whaplode the steward of the bishopric. They were an able and experienced group. Wilton, a DCL by 1429, had served the cardinal on numerous diplomatic missions, notably to Flanders and Calais, becoming his chancellor by 1440 at the latest.[35] Toly was a professional secretary, Henry V's clerk of the signet in 1419–22, succeeding Petworth as the cardinal's secretary after 1435. Port's position in the household is less clear. A Winchester scholar and fellow of New College from 1419 to 1423, he married twice and made a career as a lay administrator. By 1439 he had been in Beaufort's service for at least seven years, as his principal agent for the administration of his loans and purchases of land. Not surprisingly he was to handle the executors' dealings with the crown and others. A more recent recruit from Bedford's service was William Estcourt, who became surveyor of the episcopal estates in 1435, seemingly the first to hold that office. Beaufort presented him to the rectory of Witney in 1436 and he died in the same year as the cardinal, 1447.[36]

[33] *BRUO* 353, 557, 2189; *CPL* viii. 308, 312–14; *Somerset Medieval Wills*, 211–13.

[34] Le Neve, *Fasti*; Salisbury, Chichester, Bath and Wells, Winchester.

[35] *Royal Wills*, 331; *BRUO* 2053; *Reg. CS* 225; C 81/156/28.

[36] For Toly, see *Reg. CS* 77, 80, 121, 215, 222; Otway-Ruthven, *The King's Secretary and*

William Port forms a link between Beaufort's clerical and lay executors. Waller was a veteran of the French war, having fought at Agincourt where he was instrumental in the capture of Charles d'Orléans, and at Verneuil. He held a number of captaincies in France, but after 1431 retired to England and settled on his estate at Groomsbridge and Spedhurst on the Kent–Sussex border. He quickly established himself as a leading member of the two shires. As a former follower of Clarence, he passed into the service of first the duchess and then her son John, acting as custodian of both Orléans and Angoulême, and organizing the ordnance for the 1443 expedition. He probably entered the cardinal's service soon after his return from France; by 1434 he had an annuity of £20 from Farnham and was steward of Downton in 1435. How long he had been master of Beaufort's household is uncertain, but shortly before his death Beaufort made him steward for life of all the episcopal lands and temporalities. He survived until 1462.[37] William Mareys of Faversham was of only a little less importance in Kent than Waller, serving as sheriff in 1442–3. He had been retained by the cardinal since at least 1424 and by 1431 had succeeded John Burton as keeper of Wolvesey, a post he retained until his death. It was he whom Beaufort appointed as collector of customs in Southampton to secure the repayment of the large loans of 1443.[38] Whaplode too had been in the cardinal's service for at least thirty years before 1447. His own seat was at Chalfont in Buckinghamshire. An assiduous and very reliable local official of the crown, he succeeded Richard Wyot as steward of the episcopal manors in 1429. It is somewhat surprising that, when he founded 'Whaplode's chantry' in Chalfont St Peter soon after Beaufort's death, he made no provision for prayers for his deceased lord.[39]

Waller, Mareys, and Whaplode formed the nucleus of a wider circle of gentry connected with the bishopric in these years. The Uvedales had a long tradition of service and Thomas, a JP and sheriff of Hampshire, was praised by Beaufort for his 'diligence and faithulness' when he made him master of the hunt and keeper of all woods and chases.[40] Richard Newport,

Signet Office in the XV Century, 139, 154; *CCR 1441–7*, 355; and Beaufort's letter to him printed in H. Ellis (ed.), *Original Letters*, ser. I, vol. i, 8 (see Plate I). For Port, see *BRUO*, 1501; *CPR 1446–52*, 561, *CPR 1452–61*, 67, 109, 116, 216–17, 233 and for his career under Edward IV, D. A. Morgan, 'The king's affinity in Yorkist England', *TRHS* 23 (1973), 6–7; McFarlane, *England in XV Century*, 137. For Estcourt, *BRUO*, 648; HRO Eccles. II 159433, 159437.

[37] *DNB*, xx. 587; J. C. Wedgwood, *History of Parliament, 1439–1509: Biographies*, 915; Marshall, thesis, 122; *Wars of Eng.* ii. 394; *Reg. CS* 73, 93. He was also steward to Louis of Luxembourg: Magd. Coll. Oxon., Fastolf papers, 19.

[38] *Reg. CS* 1, 195; HRO Eccles. II 159433; *CFR 1437–45*, 234–6, 240; *CPR 1441–6*, 444. For his tomb: S. Robinson, 'Preston church next Faversham', *Arch. Cant.* 21 (1895) 131.

[39] HRO, Eccles. II 159419, 159429, 159433; *Reg. CS* 66–8, 88; *CPR 1446–52*, 232, 568; *CFR 1445–52*, 74. He was dead by Nov. 1447.

[40] *CPR 1441–6*, 266, 417; *Reg. CS* 71–2, 81, 85, 99; G. Leveson-Gower, 'Notices of the family of Uvedale', *Surrey Arch. Coll.* 3 (1865), 86–90; Wedgwood, *Hist. Parl. Biog.* 900. He took the musters of York in 1441 and Somerset in 1443.

a lesser figure in Hampshire, was singled out for his 'faithfulness, diligence and industry', when made bailiff of Bishopstoke and Waltham.[41] Two among the knightly families of Hampshire were retained by Beaufort: Sir Godfrey Hylton of Chawton and Sir John Seymour of Wolfhall, the latter as constable of Farnham castle.[42] John Thornbury, escheator in 1438–9, was made bailiff of the liberty in 1442 and keeper of Bishop's Waltham, and John Woolf keeper of Stoke park, Marwell.[43] In Somerset and Dorset Sir Edward Stradling remained constable of Taunton, but Beaufort's former associate Sir John St Loo attached himself to the court. In Oxfordshire Beaufort's principal retainer was William, Lord Lovell, keeper of Witney, with Thomas Letterford as bailiff of the episcopal manors.[44] In Kent John Yerde had many connections with Beaufort followers, though he was a royal officer and may never have been retained by the cardinal. Sheriff of Kent in 1440–1, he was principal herberger for Somerset's expedition in 1443 and the main channel for communications between the duke and the council.[45] Although the cardinal held little property himself in Kent, Waller, Mareys, and Yerde clearly provided a nucleus for Beaufort influence there from 1437 to 1445. Although we have no check roll of his household, or list of annuitants, it would not appear that Beaufort distributed fees on a wide scale or gave offices as sinecures. His retinue seems to have been administrative rather than political, and did not dominate the shrievalty even in the shires where the episcopal estates predominated.[46]

In the letters patent by which he made appointments to offices towards the end of his life Cardinal Beaufort frequently included phrases commending his servants for their fidelity and diligence in his affairs and expressing confidence in their future loyalty. As his world contracted to one of old allies and long-standing servants, these were the qualities on which he laid emphasis. The same qualities made others choose him as executor or trustee for their last wills. The tally of these is long. Nicholas Bubwith and Walter Medford, bishop and dean of Wells, named him as supervisor in 1423 and 1424, as did also Ralph, earl of Westmorland in 1424, Queen Catherine in 1437, and his sister Joan, countess of Westmorland, in 1440.[47] Others made him the principal feoffee for the

[41] *Reg. CS* 87, 222; Wedgwood, op. cit. 631.

[42] *Reg. CS* 81, 95, 222, 225; Wedgwood, op. cit. 756. Beaufort's patent spoke of his 'diligence, integrity and faithfulness'.

[43] Thornbury: *Reg. CS* 94, 222. He moved to Kent after 1447, becoming Queen Margaret's receiver: Wedgwood, op. cit. 847; *CCR 1441–7*, 450. Woolf: *Reg. CS* 98, 130; Wedgwood, op. cit. 962.

[44] *Reg. CS* 86, 69; *CPR 1436–41*, 44. Letterford, praised for good and faithful service in 1429, was admitted to the confraternity of Christ Church, Canterbury with other Beaufort servants: below, n. 65.

[45] *CPR 1436–41*, 357, 475, 425, 559; *CPR 1441–6*, 416; *PPC* v. 293–4, 409–14.

[46] Most of those named above served as MPs, but only in Kent between 1437/8 and 1442/3 did servants of Beaufort (Waller, Yerde, Mareys) dominate the shrievalty.

discharge of their debts and the erection of their tomb or chantry, notably William, Lord Zouche and Edward, duke of York, in 1415, Lucia Visconti, countess of Kent, in 1424, John, duke of Norfolk, in 1415 and 1429, and Thomas Montague, earl of Salisbury, in 1427.[48] Among the royal family, besides his role as supervisor and feoffee for Henry V's will, he was sole executor of his brother John and principal executor of the duke of Bedford.[49]

Beaufort's work in administering these estates is, for the most part, untraceable. Not infrequently he was associated with Bishops Langley and Kemp and Lord Hungerford, and they probably entrusted much of the task to specialized officials in their employ. For the administration of some of these estates proved long and complex, and was still engaging the cardinal in his last years. The fulfilment of Henry V's will has already been discussed. The lands enfeoffed by Edward, duke of York remained in the hands of Beaufort and the other feoffees for nineteen years. In 1431 they recovered the portion held in dower by the Duchess Philippa, and when Richard of York was granted livery of his lands in May 1432 he negotiated with the cardinal for the restitution of his inheritance. Beaufort placed him under bond in £2,000 for the payment of ten annual instalments of £1,000 for the completion of the church at Fotheringhay, the settlement of outstanding debts, and the continuance of the annuities charged on the estates.[50] The enfeoffment of the Mowbray lands lasted for almost as long. On the duke's death in 1432 the feoffees took over most of his estates, apart from the dower assigned to the Duchess Catherine (Beaufort's niece). In 1438 the cardinal and Sir Simon Felbrigg, the only surviving feoffees, recovered lands reverting to the late duke on the death of Constance Holand. The third duke had meanwhile come of age in 1436, but it was not until June 1445 that the cardinal, now the sole surviving feoffee, made over all the castles, manors, and lordships held in feoffment since 1415 to the new duke's feoffees. Presumably he had by then discharged all the debts of Duke John and his brother Earl Thomas, and furnished their tombs, but the heir had waited till the age of 30 to enjoy his lands.[51] The disposal of the large sums of money bequeathed by Thomas,

[47] *Reg. Chichele*, ii. 255, 299; *Somerset Med. Wills*, 326–9; *Wills and Inventories*, ed. J. Raine (Surtees Soc., 1835), i. 73; *Royal Wills*, 247; *Hist. Dunelm. Scriptores Tres*, p. cclx.

[48] *CCR 1413–19*, 260–3 (Zouche); *CPR 1413–16*, 350, *CCR 1413–19*, 294 (York); *Reg. Chichele*, ii. 278 (Lucia Visconti); *CPR 1413–16*, 319, *Reg. Chichele*, ii. 473, *CCR 1429–35*, 197–8 (Norfolk); *Reg. Chichele*, ii. 395, *CPR 1422–9*, 474 (Salisbury).

[49] *Royal Wills*, 209, 274; *Reg. Chichele*, ii. 587–8.

[50] Licence to enfeoff, 5 Aug. 1415: *CPR 1413–16*, 349; for their release, *CCR 1429–35*, 134, 214, 260, 264. The lands included the most important parts of the duchy: Johnson, thesis, 6–7. A. H. Thompson, 'Statutes of the collegiate church at Fotheringhay', *Arch. Jnl.* 75 (1918), 246–67. L. F. Salzmann, *Building in England*, 505–9 prints York's indenture for the construction of the nave at Fotheringhay dated 24 Sept. 1434.

[51] *CCR 1435–41*, 149; *CPR 1436–41*, 223; *CPR 1429–36*, 603. C 140/5 (IPM returns for John duke of Norfolk, 1461). I owe this reference to Dr R. E. Archer.

earl of Salisbury, in 1428 was more quickly accomplished, but here too Beaufort and the executors were enfeoffed with six manors for the discharge of certain legacies and the building of the earl's tomb and chapel at Bisham at a total cost of £880. Several years must have elapsed until rents to this sum accrued.[52]

The most illuminating picture of Beaufort as an executor is in respect of Bedford's will, for which the evidence is a good deal fuller. Bedford died in 1435 at Rouen, naming as his executors in England Beaufort, Kemp, Cromwell, and Whittingham, his receiver-general. On 29 June 1438 they purchased release from the crown's claims against the duke by a fine of 1,000 marks, but not until 7 October 1441 was probate awarded and Beaufort given sole administration of the estate. He was then required to present an inventory of Bedford's goods by the following Easter.[53] These were stored in three great standards and two coffers which the duke had left in the custody of Whittingham on his departure from England in 1434. Beaufort had them brought from Whittingham's house at Walbrook to Blackfriars. He sent for the London goldsmiths John Pattisleigh and John Wynne to make a valuation, and his own secretary William Toly compiled the inventory. The surviving records provide a glimpse of the great magnificence of the regent's household.[54] The vessels for his dresser, or cupboard, when he dined in state were valued at £848. 12*s.* 8*d.*; his wardrober David Breknok handed over chapel ornaments valued at £751, bed hangings valued at £760. 13*s.* 4*d.*, and the costly 'bed of Alenson' worth £1,000.[55] In all Whittingham accounted for jewels and plate to the value of £3,617 and Breknok a further £1,484.[56] Beyond this was a mass of soft furnishings held in the wardrobe and, most notably, 'the grete librarie that cam owte of France' (i.e. the books of Charles V) 'of which my said lord ye Cardinal had the substaunce'. There was, finally, another coffer removed from Blackfriars by Lord Cromwell containing 1,800 marks of silver. To the duke's estate was also credited his pensions of 800 marks p.a., the revenues of his English lands and offices, the receipt of £648 from

[52] *Reg. Chichele*, ii. 390–9.

[53] *CPR 1436–41*, 189; *Foedera*, x 704; *Reg. Chichele*, ii. 587–8; E 401/756 16 July (cf. Steel, *Receipt*, 212). William Repington was appointed auditor of Bedford's lands in Oct. 1436: E 28/58.

[54] These are: Whittingham's final declaration (E 101/411/7); an earlier shortlist of jewels and stuff which he had delivered to Beaufort (E 154/1/33); a longer statement of Bedford's goods and assets (E 154/1/39). It is not always possible to correlate the items in these statements and no overall valuation of Bedford's movables can be made. A section of K. B. McFarlane's dissertation was based on the first of these. A full examination of the inventories has been prepared by J. Stratford. *Three Inventories of the Goods of John, Duke of Bedford (d. 1435)*, Society of Antiquaries of London (forthcoming). See also her 'The Manuscripts of John, duke of Bedford: library and chapel', in D. Williams (ed.), *England in the Fifteenth Century*, 329–50.

[55] E 154/1/39 fos. 1–5.

[56] E 101/411/7 fo. 4; E 154/1/39 fo. 7^{v}.

the Devon and Cornwall silver mines, and the debts owed to him.[57] No less than £11,235 was outstanding for his keeping of Calais, along with further sums which he had advanced for the siege of Orléans. Edmund Beaufort owed him 1,000 marks for artillery sent to Maine and Gloucester £1,000 for goods he had purchased.[58]

It remains uncertain how much of this Beaufort was able to collect. Our only firm knowledge relates to the gold and silver mines which Bedford held by a patent of 1433 for the term of twelve years. The executors were granted possession of these in July 1437, though Beaufort had already leased them to John Solers for £183. 12*s.* p.a.[59] He eventually acknowledged a receipt of £1,368 from the mines from 1441 to 1445.[60] We are better informed of this discharge of the duke's debts. For these Beaufort delivered to Whittingham money and plate to a total of £2,198, and the latter's payments exceeded this by almost £150.[61] Of Bedford's estate in France there is scant evidence. What appears to be an interim report to Beaufort from Sir Andrew Ogard, the active executor, values Bedfords goods at 115,126 *li. tournois*.[62] Whittingham's statement also records that Beaufort retained at least £1,352 in jewels and plate after the settlement of Bedford's debts, and beyond this were large quantities of books, plate, ornaments, and household effects, not valued, which came to the cardinal's hands. How Beaufort used or disposed of all this is unknown. Bedford's will contained no specific legacies; he merely provided for the residue of his estate to be used for the salvation of his soul. It is doubtful whether Beaufort ever managed to wind up Bedford's affairs satisfactorily. Although he received a comprehensive pardon as executor on 20 June 1446, it was Kemp who gave Whittingham his final acquittance on 8 August 1449.[63]

It is impossible on this evidence to make a fair assessment of Beaufort as an executor and trustee; but it is not hard to see why he was sought after for this purpose. Beaufort brought professionalism, tenacity, and authority to the task, insisting on strict accountability to himself in the recovery of movable assets, the realizing of outstanding dues, and the settlement with creditors. That his administration of these estates was prolonged, that he was not blind or averse to opportunities for personal profit, and that heirs

[57] E 154/1/39 fo. 5r–v. On the library of Charles V, see Stratford, 'Manuscripts', 339–41.

[58] E 101/411/7. These are recorded on a slip of paper between fos. 2 and 3.

[59] *CPR 1422–9*, 393; *CPR 1429–36*, 289; Exch. LTR Mem. Roll, E 368 Com. Rec. Hil. m. 15; E 101/411/7 fo. 7.

[60] Accounts for 1441–2 and 1442–5 in E 364/79/1; E 364/80/C, E 101/265/9. Cf. *CPR 1441–6*, 334; Devon, *Issues*, 457. The foregoing references are taken from McFarlane, dissertation, 'Cardinal Beaufort', pp. A 9–13.

[61] E 101/411/7 fos. 6–7; E 154/1/39 fo. 8. the duke's three largest creditors were the London merchants William Rus, jeweller, Hugh Dyke, draper, and Robert Wursley, mercer.

[62] E 154/1/39 fo. 8^{v}; cf. Stratford, 'Manuscripts', 330.

[63] E 154/1/33. They were still acting in April 1449: *Wars of Eng.* i. 493.

had to prise their inheritance from his grasp, were all beside the point. For what testators sought above all in an executor was the ability to defend their estate at its most vulnerable, and give effect to their last wishes. The very importance which Beaufort attached to worldly goods, in their own right and for the purchase of eternal benefits, together with his status and influence, made him in demand by his contemporaries. Indeed his fellow executors were often content to resign matters into his hands. In Bedford's case old bonds of friendship and gratitude also dictated the choice. Yet the regent must also have felt sure that one who had provoked a quarrel with Clarence rather than share with him the goods he had received as executor of John, earl of Somerset, and who had successfully defended the tenure of Henry V's feoffees against Bedford himself, would see that his own last will was fulfilled. Alongside Henry Beaufort's services as moneylender to the house of Lancaster we must set those as its family solicitor.[64]

In his final years the cardinal spent freely on material comforts. His movements were now circumscribed by the episcopal residences in Hampshire and Surrey: Wolvesey, Bishop's Waltham, Farnham, Esher, Southwark; but he also developed a close relationship with the Benedictines of Christ Church, Canterbury. As early as 1417 he had been admitted to the confraternity with many of his entourage and subsequently the community acknowledged the 'immense benefits' which he had conferred on the house, and a steady stream of his chaplains and servants were also enrolled.[65] He doubtless lodged there on his frequent journeys to France, and on a visit in 1435 he procured exemption for the city from contributing towards a loan. Family piety, too, played its part: Henry IV was buried in the cathedral and prior to her death Margaret, duchess of Clarence was planning the tomb for herself and her two husbands in a chapel of the south transept.[66] At the end of November 1438 Beaufort spent the better part of a month at the priory *en route* for his preliminary negotiations with Isabel at Calais, and he was there to welcome his nephew John from captivity, with a mass in the prior's chapel sung by the cardinal's own choir. On his return from Calais on 22 February 1439, and again on his final embassy to Gravelines later that year, he was ceremonially received by the prior and convent. In 1443 the spiritual benefits conferred in 1433 were extended at his request to his deceased kindred and great protector, John, duke of Bedford.[67] Finally Beaufort's particular attachment to Christ Church

[64] I owe this happy phrase to McFarlane.

[65] Canterbury Cathedral Muniments, Register S. fo. 115; *HMC 9th Report*, 113; C. E. Woodruffe, 'Notes on the inner life and domestic economy of the priors of Christ Church, Canterbury, *Arch. Cant.* 53 (1941), 5–10; BL Arundel MS 68 fos. 59^v, 62^v (I owe this reference to Dr A. Wathey).

[66] *HMC 9th Rep.* 139, 114.

[67] Ibid. *Stone Chron.* 22–6; CCM Reg. S, fo. 132; *CPR 1441–6*, 219 for Beaufort's gift of the manor of Bekesbourne to the priory.

bore fruit in his decision to take up residence there in the last years of his life.

Already in 1435 Beaufort had indicated, in conversation with the chamberlain, John Elham, that he would be willing to pay for the embellishment of a 'place' for himself within the priory, and the building chosen was the thirteenth-century erection immediately to the east of the infirmary chapel known as 'Meister Omers'. This had been under reconstruction since 1376–7, and to it John Buckingham had retired in 1398 after resigning the see of Lincoln to Beaufort. Just when Beaufort fixed upon it for his own occupancy is uncertain, but characteristically he embarked upon a complete rebuilding at his own cost.[68] The earliest of the surviving priory accounts for this period, that of 1444–5, contains payments to tilers, indicating that work on the roof was finishing, and for a painter adorning the cardinal's room, and on 14 October 1445 he at last arrived to take up residence.[69] He would have found a comfortable dwelling comprising a large and lofty kitchen at the west end, separated from a spacious hall by double screens incorporating the pantry and buttery. Above the screens was the cardinal's private chamber, approached from the hall by a broad newel stair with fine stone treads. The chamber was constructed with a ceiling, a fireplace, and a garderobe, and special iron bars were fitted to the window. The dais of the hall was lit by a pair of oriel windows and a fireplace was set at its eastern end behind the cardinal's seat. An existing range of chambers to the north probably housed his servants and may have contained a chapel. The workmanship throughout was of the highest quality, the finest Kentish ragstone being used in abundance and worked by Beaufort's own team of masons. The butt side purlin roof was of a construction unmatched elsewhere in Kent at this time. In design and construction the building could stand comparison with the best examples of contemporary domestic architecture. No expense had been spared to mitigate the rigours of winter for the ailing prelate, who probably spent the whole of the winter of 1445–6 in Canterbury. The priory accounts record payments to his minstrels for Christmas, and a series of gifts for his table: a boar, swans, deer, partridges, trout, and half a porpoise. The cardinal seemed to have settled in for good; he had his vestments and throne brought from Winchester, and during his sojourn the death of prior Thomas Salisbury led to the election of his friend John

[68] *Christ Church Letters*, ed. J. B. Sheppard (Camden Ser., 1877), 8; J. B. Sheppard, 'The Meister Homers, Canterbury', *Arch. Cant.* 13 (1880), 116–21. An indenture of 1453 refers to it as 'mansum nostrum vocatum antiquitus Meister Homers a modernis le Cardynalysplace vulgariter nuncupatum'. I am indebted to Mr T. Tatton Brown for this reference and for guidance on the architectural history of Meister Omers. What follows is based on his investigations, to be published in vol. iv of *The Archaeology of Canterbury*.

[69] CCM, Miscellaneous Accts. iv. fos. 44–5. Payments were made to the minstrels of the cardinal, and the dukes of Gloucester and Exeter on 7 July 1445, and to the prior of Ospringe riding to meet Beaufort. See also *Stone Chron.* 38.

Elham as successor.[70] In the spring he travelled to London, but had returned by 25 July and was still at Canterbury on 17 September when Queen Margaret, on pilgrimage to the shrine, spent the whole day with him. Then some time in the autumn he left Canterbury for the last time, bound for Southwark and finally Wolvesey.[71]

So it was to his own see and episcopal palace that he returned to die. There is no indication that he had been estranged from the convent of St Swithun's. The requirement for the prior to confirm all episcopal *acta* relating to the transfer of property, the appropriation of churches, and the establishment of chantries must have occasioned frequent business between them, and in his last years Beaufort also safeguarded his appointments of officials by securing the prior's confirmation.[72] But the priory register does little to illuminate their relations: the only complaint against Beaufort was of having enticed away the priory's choirmaster, Robert Bygbroke, to his own chapel. Indeed it was only at particular junctures of his life that Beaufort was at Wolvesey for any length of time; even in his last ten years the dating of documents suggests that the winters of 1440–1 and 1446–7 were his only prolonged stays.[73] Nevertheless, Beaufort undertook a major building programme at Wolvesey at this time. This did not commence before 1441–2 when the pipe roll records the sum of £335. 17*s*. 4*d*. spent on a reconstruction of the pantry and great hall, comprising a new roof and a great window in the northern gable. In the following five years it is probable that Beaufort rebuilt the chapel, which still exists, but for this no accounts survive.[74] The work at Wolvesey had been preceded by an even longer and costlier reconstruction at Waltham, Beaufort's favourite Hampshire residence. He had begun the enlargement and embellishment of the palace at the beginning of his episcopate, additions to the lord's chambers in the south-western tower being followed by reconstruction of the chapel. Work on the latter was suspended between 1417 and 1427, but when resumed it was carried forward continuously to 1441. It was still proceeding when a new programme of work began in 1437, with extensive repairs and new building at Marwell at a cost of £170.

[70] CCM Misc. Accts. iv. fos. 93–5ᵛ.

[71] CCM Misc. Accts. iv. fo. 96; *HMC 9th Rep.* 140; *Stone Chron.* 38–9, Woodruffe, op. cit. 5–9. It is possible that he visited Wolvesey in late May and early June (*Reg. CS* 96–7), but was again in Southwark on 4 July (Hutchins, *History . . . of Dorset*, ii. 16). Towards the end of 1446 the prior visited him in London and later Thornbury and Mareys went to Canterbury on his behalf (Misc. Accts. iv. fo. 143–4).

[72] Greatrex, *Reg. CS*, introduction, p. xix. In March 1446 Beaufort procured for the priory a grant from Henry VI of all the fines and amercements from their lands: *CCh.R 1427–1516*, 56.

[73] *Reg. CS* 74; also two mandates from St Cross in April and Sept. 1444: ibid. 86. A *laudatio* of Beaufort is given in a contemporary history of the see of Winchester, in BL Cotton MS Vespasian D IX, fo. 22ᵛ.

[74] HRO Eccles. II 159437: William Mareys's account as keeper of Wolvesey. He received £338 for the work. Cf. M. Biddle, *Wolvesey* (HMSO guidebook, 1986), 19, 30, 36.

In each of the following three years expenditure is likely to have exceeded £300. Two major new buildings were erected at Waltham: a gatehouse and a 'longhouse'. The latter lay on the north side of the palace site, alongside the moat, and consisted of a series of two bays each with its own chimney stack and garderobe probably similar in style to those at St Cross. The building may have served to house the bishop's principal officials and retainers. Detailed accounts which survive show that much other work was undertaken to make the cardinal's lodgings comfortable: passages were tiled, windows glazed, rails fixed for arras hangings, painters employed to decorate the beams and wainscotting; a new chapel chamber was constructed and work done on a garden for the cardinal's recreation. The new buildings had been finished by the end of 1441 at a total cost since 1437 of around £1,200.[75] Beaufort seems not to have undertaken large-scale building at Farnham or Southwark, although embellishments and repairs at the former were made throughout his episcopate.[76]

In Winchester itself he was a beneficent patron to Wykeham's college, granting it tithe from Andover and helping it to acquire the oratory of the Holy Trinity at Barton and the manor of Fernhill for the endowment of Fromond's chantry within the college. His effigy, carved on the central boss above the chantry altar, is still in *situ*. His final gift to the college was of £100 for the purchase of the manor of Buttes in Barkham, Berkshire. Periodically he conducted formal visitations of the college; he regulated its discipline, and arbitrated its lawsuits. The college entertained him on his visits, consulting his cook about what delicacies were to his taste, and even providing his retinue with hunting gear specially purchased in London.[77] Yet in his last years, as his thoughts turned towards a foundation, it was not to the monastic orders, or the education of the priesthood, or even a chantry college where masses might be sung perpetually for his soul that he chose to apply his wealth. Each of these had attracted the patronage of his

[75] HRO Eccles. II 159435–7; 11 M 59/Bp/BW 62–9 (Bishop's Waltham accounts). Both the pipe roll and the manorial account are missing for the years 1439/40 and 1443/4. Expenditure in 1438/9 was £307. 16*s*. 11*d*. and in 1440/1 was £337. 11*s*. 1*d*., so that it is likely to have been over £300 in the intervening year. By 1442/3 it had declined to £48. The late Mrs Martineau made available to me notes on the pipe rolls compiled by H. M. Stowell and Dr J. N. Hare has given me authoritative guidance on Beaufort's work, pending his full account of the buildings. An effigy of the cardinal, probably from the gatehouse or chapel, is now in the museum at Bishop's Waltham palace (see Plate II).

[76] P. D. Brooks and A. C. Graham, 'The Bishop's Tenants at Farnham' (typescript in Hants RO), cite eleven pipe rolls from 1406 to 1447 which contain details of work on the castle. For Southwark, see S. Toy, 'Winchester House, Southwark', 75 ff.

[77] Kirby, *Annals of Winchester*, 179–82; id. 'The oratory of the Holy Trinity at Barton, Isle of Wight', *Archaeologia*, 52 (1890), 309; *HMC Var. Coll.* 1, 370; *Reg. CS* 76–7; H. Chitty, 'Fromond's chantry at Winchester College', *Archaeologia*, 75 (1924/5), 146–7; W. H. Gunner, 'Extracts from the bursars' accounts of Winchester College', *Arch. J.* 8 (1851), 79–87. Relevant documents among the college archives, particularly relating to properties and lawsuits, are catalogued in *Winchester Coll. Muniments*, nos. 2178–9, 2186–203, 2210, 3540–60, 9609–13.

contemporaries: Henry V at Syon and Sheen, Chichele at All Souls, York at Fotheringhay, Warwick at Guy's Cliffe, and Cromwell at Tattershall, while Henry VI's own foundations were coming into being. Beaufort's decision to establish a 'new foundation' at St Cross, 'a house of noble poverty' alongside that of the existing church and almshouse, was unusual and characteristic. It has been plausibly suggested that it may have owed something to the parallels he perceived between his own career and that of its founder, Henry of Blois.[78] Both were of the royal blood and men of great wealth; both were papal legates and enjoyed a long tenure of the see. However Beaufort's purpose was different to that of his namesake; it was to provide impoverished *generosi* with a standard of living more akin to that of a college than a typical 'God's house'.

This is evident from the fine collegiate-style buildings which survive (see Plate IV). The brethrens' rooms on the north, west, and south sides of the quadrangle were arranged in pairs on two floors with a straight staircase between. The plan set new standards in privacy and amenities, for the building was two rooms deep and each set consisted of a large bed-sitting room in front with two small store rooms and garderobe to the rear. The staircase opened into a small lobby in each set, not into a single large chamber as in most other types of lodging.[79] A series of huge chimneys on the inner face provided fireplaces for each set. Between these apartments and the gatehouse lay the hall and kitchen. The hall, with screen doors and open hearth, was lighted by three southern windows in which were depicted the cardinal's arms surmounted by his hat and motto, *A honor et lyesse*.[80] On it's northern face the gatehouse carried a statue of the Virgin, below which were three niches, one of which still contains the weathered figure of the cardinal in prayer. The gateway contained the muniment room and lodgings for the master on the usual collegiate pattern. The absence of any accounts relating to this work makes it impossible to estimate its cost or to give precise dates for its construction. The first indication that Beaufort had such a project in mind was the purchase of lands for its endowment in May 1439, and a period of six to seven years would have been sufficient to erect these buildings. By 1445 the statutes had been drawn up and the first inmates were probably admitted shortly after. In view of the vicissitudes of the hospital after Beaufort's death, it

[78] G. Belfield, 'Cardinal Beaufort's almshouse of noble poverty at St Cross, Winchester', *Proc. Hants. Field Club and Arch. Soc.* 38 (1982), 79–91.

[79] W. A. Pantin, 'Chantry priests houses and other medieval lodgings', *Med. Archaeology*, 3 (1959), 249. For an architectural description, see *VCH Hampshire*, ii. 102–3. the Blois brethren were housed to the south of the church: none of those buildings survive.

[80] Beaufort's arms were: France and England quarterly, a border gabony, argent et azure, surmounted by a cardinal's hat with strings and tassels, the whole set upon a quarry field powdered with scrolls, lettered 'A Honor et Lyesse'. His arms are also in the spandrils of the gatehouse arch and his cardinal's hat in the moulding above.

seems reasonably certain that all the present buildings had been completed, and paid for, before 1447.[81] On his last visit, in the winter of 1446–7, he could well have viewed his effigy on the gate tower and been greeted by the brethren wearing his scarlet livery.

Who was to enjoy the privilege of membership? Thomas Forest, the master since 1426, was to rule over both the old and the new communities. The latter was to consist of thirty-five brethren and three sisters, served by two chaplains. All were to be unmarried, to be of gentle birth or members of Beaufort's *familia*, and to have fallen into need either by accident or natural disability. They were to be in receipt of no money from elsewhere, to take their meat and drink in hall, and have an annual payment of 20*s*. with 6*s*. 8*d*. for a livery of deep red with the cardinal's hat embroidered upon it. Daily they were to pray for the souls of Henry VI, his queen, and the cardinal, and to keep his anniversary. The chaplains were to receive 12 marks yearly, the master £20. Edmund, earl of Dorset and his heirs male were appointed visitors, and the bishops of Winchester were to be its patrons.[82] The first members of the new foundation were probably in occupation before Beaufort's death. They included John Newles his *serviens* and esquire, and John Turke and John Knight, former fellows of Winchester college. One of the chaplains, John Smithford, was likewise a fellow.[83] These names and others help to make clear Beaufort's intentions. His 'almshouse of noble poverty' (or home for distressed gentlefolk) would replace the obsolescent system of corrodies in providing 'sheltered accommodation' for the professional servants of the bishopric in their old age. It marked his appreciation of the 'fidelity and diligence' which he required and commended in his officers. Even so Beaufort left his foundation inadequately safeguarded against the hazards that would follow when his patronage and protection were removed. Already before his death there had been reports of dissensions and cupidity among the brethren, but the two main weaknesses were the failure to incorporate the master and brethren and the inadequacy of the endowment. Although in the course of 1446 Beaufort made over to the master and brethren the properties he had acquired, it was later claimed that, not being incorporate, they could not defend or acquire estates at law, and could not resist the claims of the less well endowed Blois brothers on their revenues. On 8 April 1455 his executors therefore attempted a refoundation,

[81] Presumably payment for the work was made by the treasurer of Wolvesey, but no accounts of his survive. Iron delivered to Winchester for the cardinal in 1439–40 was not specifically destined for St Cross, but nails and tiles supplied from Southampton in Sept. 1444 almost certainly were: Belfield, 'Almshouse', 8 *The Brokage Book of Southampton, 1439–40*, ed. D. M. Bunyard, 65; ibid. *1443–4*, ed. O. Coleman, ii. 298, 307.

[82] Belfield, 'Almshouse', 82; BL Sloane MS 1080 fo. 121, with a copy in the muniments at St Cross Hospital.

[83] Belfield, 'Almshouse', 82–3.

formally receiving the premises and lands from the community and regranting them to the same as a new body corporate. The statutes were reissued and the duke of Somerset, newly released from prison, was made its patron and protector. However a month later the new corporation again surrendered the foundation to Bishop Waynflete who in August also replaced the now dead Somerset as its patron.[84] For as long as the Lancastrian dynasty survived Waynflete gave it effective protection.

The other weakness of St Cross was its inadequate endowment. On 25 May 1439 Beaufort had purchased from the crown the lordship and castle of Chirk, a group of manors in Somerset and Dorset of the Montagu inheritance, and the manor of Salden in Buckinghamshire. The purchase price for all three was 13,350 marks. The political circumstances of this sale have already been discussed; our concern here is with the cardinal's purpose. The Montagu lands, held in tail male by grant of Edward III, had escheated to the crown on Salisbury's death in 1428, with dower being assigned to his widow Alice Chaucer. Though coveted by Salisbury's son-in-law and successor, Richard Nevill, they were granted in 1433 to the duke of Bedford; they again reverted to the crown in 1435, being further charged with dower for his duchess Jacquetta.[85] From that moment Beaufort had had his eye on them, and on 28 July 1436 had procured the grant for life of one manor, Canford and Poole, free of render. When he purchased the remainder in 1439 the crown undertook to grant him lands of equivalent value to the parts held in dower, though in the event he gained entire possession of the properties by procuring alternative grants for the two dowagers. Their value probably approached £350 p.a.[86] Salden, likewise part of Bedford's estate, was worth about £80 but was encumbered with dower and an annuity to Robert Whittingham, on whose behalf Beaufort purchased it for the sum of 350 marks.[87] The third element in the sale, Chirk, had been acquired by Henry V for 4,000 marks and its clear value in the mid-fifteenth century may not have exceeded the 200 marks p.a. which this represented. Here too vested interests had to be bought out, notably Robert Englefield who was granted an annuity of £40 to surrender the life stewardship.[88] By the end of 1442 Beaufort was in possession of the entire properties and on 2 March 1443 he secured two letters patent, one permitting him to pass all these possessions to feoffees, the other licensing

[84] *CPR 1452–61*, 233–4, 252; *CCR 1454–61*, 147–8.

[85] Hicks, 'Nevill earldom of Salisbury', 141–7; Belfield, 'Almshouse', 85–6.

[86] E 28/57 28 July; *CPR 1429–36*, 601; *CPR 1436–41*, 496, 567, 479–80; *CPR 1441–6*, 46–7, 129, 133; *CCR 1441–7*, 9. The value is calculated on the basis of the compensation paid to the dowagers.

[87] *CPR 1436–41*, 260, 394, 520; *CPR 1446–52*, 376; E 28/60 25 May.

[88] The value of Chirk is discussed by O. W. Llinos Smith 'The Lordship of Chirk and Oswestry', Ph.D. thesis (London, 1971). For Englefield, see *CPR 1436–41*, 56, 72, 341; *CPR 1441–6*, 89–90; *PPC* v. 89.

St Cross to acquire lands to the value of £500 p.a. in mortmain. Then his feoffees duly reinvested him with the lands and he passed these to the master and brethren on 1 February 1446, though subtracting Chirk and Canford. Other properties had also been acquired: a fee farm from Southampton and the manor of Tarrant Launceston by grant from the crown, advowsons at Crondal and St Faith's Winchester, and the hospital of St John at Fordingbridge; all these added a further £45 p.a. to the endowment.[89]

Some time before his death the cardinal made over Chirk to Edmund Beaufort. Its character and location made it unsuitable for the endowment of St Cross and it is likely that Beaufort had always intended it for the family inheritance.[90] Between March 1443 and May 1444 he was also minded to retain Canford and Poole for the family, probably in view of their proximity to Corfe and convenience as a point of embarkation for France, though it was also rumoured that he might sell them.[91] Duke John's illness and death stayed these plans and instead the cardinal created a life interest in them for Edmund and Eleanor, with reversion to St Cross.[92] After these deductions the lands vested in St Cross in 1446 were certainly less than £200 in annual value, and an inquisition taken after the cardinal's death gave the extent of the total endowment, including the advowsons and the hospital, at £158. 13*s*. 4*d*. With the costs of the household running at £221. 4*s*. 7*d*. p.a. in 1451, it is clear that the endowment was basically insufficient to fulfil Beaufort's intentions. At the 'refoundation' in 1455 the hospital received licence to acquire a further £300 worth of land in mortmain, but the death of Somerset and the collapse of the dynasty rendered this a forlorn hope. Indeed the Nevills celebrated their triumph in 1461 by procuring licence to enter all the Montagu lands. With the Beauforts attainted and Waynflete discredited, St Cross had no defence against this injustice, and even when in 1485 Lady Margaret Beaufort became mother of the reigning monarch it was for her own estate, and not for the hospital, that she recovered these properties. When Waynflete, as one of his last acts, attempted another refoundation, the revenues from Beaufort's endowment amounted to a mere £44 p.a. and the community was reduced to one chaplain and two brothers.[93] The civil wars took a similar toll of the family's inheritance. Chirk was forfeited in 1461 and granted to Richard of Gloucester and finally in 1475 to Sir William Stanley. Canford and Poole, similarly forfeited in December 1461, were

[89] *CPR 1436–41*, 525; *CPR 1441–6*, 174; *CPR 1452–61*, 233–4.

[90] In June 1445 Beaufort replaced William Burley as constable of Chirk with his esquire Otwell Wursley: E 28/61 13 July 1439; *CPR 1452–61*, 249.

[91] Magd. Coll. MS Fastolf paper, 40. This was written before Duke John's death.

[92] *CCR 1454–61*, 20; C 139/160.

[93] *CPR 1452–61*, 233–4; Belfield, 'Almshouse', 83–9; Hicks, 'Nevill earldom of Salisbury', 145. R. Chandler, *Life of Waynflete*, 224–6.

secured by the Nevills and then in 1485 granted by Henry VII to his mother for life.[94]

Although the vicissitudes suffered by St Cross had parallels in other late medieval foundations, Beaufort's failure to leave it incorporate and adequately endowed was so uncharacteristic that some explanation must be sought in the circumstances of his last years. It was probably Duke John's death, leading to the transference of the major part of the Beaufort lands away from the male line, that led him to divert part of the endowment, and though the cardinal completed the buildings he never found the opportunity to replace the alienated lands. If he relied on his executors to repair the deficiency, he apparently left no explicit instructions, and none of his fortune was ultimately used for this purpose.

Thus only in the last decade of his life did Cardinal Beaufort employ his wealth for building and the purchase of lands to any significant extent.[95] His total expenditure on building cannot be guessed with any degree of probability, but if the work at Wolvesey and Waltham was of the order of £1,500, that at Canterbury and St Cross must have been more costly, and Beaufort may have expended in all around £5,000. By the standards of his predecessor and successor in the see this was modest. For over twenty years from 1379 Wykeham was continuously engaged on three major building schemes, each larger than anything attempted by Beaufort. Waynflete's building at Magdalen College and at Farnham, though similarly undertaken towards the end of his life, was more ambitious in scale. In neither case have we figures for what they spent. As founders the comparison is even more to Beaufort's disadvantage. Wykeham left New College with endowments valued at £627 p.a. and Winchester with an income of somewhat under £200 p.a. At Magdalen Waynflete had ensured the college an income from land approaching £600 p.a. though he had spent less than £6,000 on his acquisitions.[96] Besides these Beaufort's failure to provide for the much more modest needs of St Cross becomes even more striking. Yet neither Wykeham nor Waynflete aspired to the high political role which Beaufort filled, nor did they lend the crown more

[94] *Rot. Parl.* v. 18; *CPR 1461–7*, 8, 16, 37, 228, 292; *CPR 1467–77*, 505; *CCR 1454–61*, 20; Hicks, op. cit. 145–6

[95] Other apparent acquisitions by Beaufort were: Ochecote (Northants), 1423: *CCR 1422–9*, 123; Westbury (Wilts.), 1425 : ibid. 193; Braborne (Kent), 1425: *CPR 1422–9*, 316; Langley (Kent): *CPR 1441–6*, 244; Wells (Norfolk), 1440: *CPR 1436–41*, 385. Other buildings attributed to him are: the southern gate on London Bridge (Worcestre, *Itineraries*, 269); part of London Bridge (Radford, *Henry Beaufort*, 292); part of the nave and screen in Winchester cathedral and the market cross in Winchester. (A. Tindal Hart, *The Rich Cardinal*, 140).

[96] R. L. Storey, 'The Foundation of the Medieval College, 1379–1530' in J. Buxton and P. H. Williams (edd.), *New College, Oxford* (Oxford, 1979), 8; Kirby, *Annals of Winchester*, ch. 3; P. Partner, 'William of Wykeham and the Historians', in R. Custance (ed.), *Winchester College Sixth Centenary Essays*, 22; J. Mills, 'The foundation, endowment, and early administration of Magdalen College, Oxford', B.Litt. thesis (Oxford, 1977), ch. 2 and Appendix 1. Some properties were gifts, others were suppressed priories.

than conventional sums. From early in their pontificates both saw the foundation of a major educational foundation as their primary monument. Beaufort only turned to building as he began to shed the role of statesman and financier, seeking as he approached his sixty-fifth year to mitigate the discomforts of life for himself and his *familia*. That can only have been of choice, for he was far richer than either and building costs represented only a small fraction of his capital. Essentially Beaufort lacked the incentive and interest for such schemes. He did not share Wykeham's sense of the importance of a trained and educated priesthood or Waynflete's vision of the widening horizons of education. Particularly in his last years Beaufort had no view of the future of his society. The future which he had striven for in his early career was crumbling before his eyes. His present concerns were to ensure his physical comfort, advance his family, and reward those who had served him faithfully. He also began to take thought for the destiny of his soul and his wealth.

19

Last Will and Final Judgement

As Cardinal Beaufort prepared for death he received advice from an unexpected quarter. For two decades Poggio Bracciolini had maintained an intermittent correspondence with Richard Petworth and, as old age crept up on them both, he began to urge his friend to turn his thoughts from worldly to eternal things. Writing in July 1445, he reproached Petworth and his master, the cardinal, with being still too immersed in the former: they should remember that on their final journey they could not take their goods with them; that wealth would not profit them but rather condemn, and that true praise and glory lay not in the acquisition but in the bestowal of riches. The message was directed as much to Beaufort, to whom he asked Petworth to read his letter. He was also to say that he longed to see his former employer before he died, 'for I love him cordially; but age and family ties prevent me'.[1] Five months later Poggio wrote to Beaufort himself. The general theme was the same, but now he had the specific purpose of persuading the cardinal to contribute to the papal crusade against the Turks. The papal order to levy a crusading tenth had been sent to England in July 1444, but after consultations with the king Archbishop Stafford offered merely a voluntary contribution from each diocese, to be collected in 1445–6. Eugenius IV regarded this as tantamount to refusal, and in July 1446 sent Lewis de Cordona as papal nuncio to enforce its collection. Stafford declined to collaborate in this illegal action and in December 1446 the crown formally refused the papal demand. Poggio's letter, clearly written at Eugenius IV's behest; was probably an attempt to avoid a confrontation with the English crown, and Beaufort had cause to be apprehensive that he might be put under pressure to use his own wealth to resolve the impasse. More rhetorical and less intimate than the letters to Petworth, it none the less made a telling personal appeal. No act, Poggio wrote, could be more pleasing to God, who had heaped benefits on the cardinal and had indeed prolonged his life to enable him to show that he could give as well as gain treasure. The needs of the church were great and urgent, and Beaufort's pre-eminence in birth, dignity, wealth, and prudence placed the onus on him to give a lead. Poggio reminded Beaufort that he was descended from kings who had striven to liberate the Holy Places and had formerly himself used his wealth

[1] *Poggii Epistolae*, ii. 293–7.

against the Bohemian heretics. Obliquely he referred to the great wealth and labour Beaufort had spent on battles to achieve earthly fame; what then should he spend to win celestial glory?[2] Poggio wrote with the Beaufort he had known in mind: the pilgrim to the Holy Land, contemplating the surrender of his wealth and see, and the later organizer of the Anglo-Burgundian crusade. But twenty years on the cardinal had no thoughts beyond his native soil. Neither humanist eloquence nor papal exhortation would induce him to dispatch his treasure to Rome.

A not dissimilar exhortation came from close at hand. In his latter years Beaufort had as his confessor a monk of the Sheen Charterhouse.[3] Its royal patronage and proximity to the episcopal palaces at Southwark and Esher make this a more explicable choice than the rigour of the order's discipline might suggest. Moreover, the spirituality of the adjacent Brigettine convent of Syon had earlier attracted the patronage of Margaret, duchess of Clarence, for whom one of the monks, Simon Wynter, translated the Life of St Jerome, with a collection of apocryphal miracles and visions of the afterlife.[4] The theme of this collection—'to lyve so that a man be alwey redy to dye'—understandably touched the duchess closely, and its relevance to the cardinal himself was clearly in the mind of his confessor 'W' who, probably late in 1446, addressed three letters to his now distant penitent. These were later transcribed by William Mede, sacrist of the Charterhouse from 1417 to 1473, who was probably also their author.[5] They contained no hint that the relationship had acquired depths of spiritual intimacy, or that the cardinal was attracted to the practices of his sister-in-law. Although relatively outspoken about the cardinal's failings, and solicitous for his salvation, the writer maintained the formal distance of the confessional. Like Jerome, Beaufort had survived a desperate illness, and he urged on him the need for self-examination, repentance, and acts of amendment if the respite offered by God's grace were not to be wasted. Yet his suggestions went no further than the conventional acts of reparation demanded from the rich. He bade the cardinal ask himself whether he had been guilty of simony in securing his dignities, whether he had gathered wealth by unjust means, or, as an executor, had detained goods against the will of the testator. If so he should make speedy amends by distributing his wealth to the church and the poor while he had time,

[2] Ibid. 308–15. For the crusading tenth, Lunt, *Financial Relations*, 131–40. Jacob, *Essays in Later Medieval History*, 52–7.

[3] However, Robert Puriton, sub-prior of Winchester had been his confessor-general since 1430: *CPL* x. 5; *BRUO* iii. 1526.

[4] G. R. Keiser, 'Patronage and piety in fifteenth century England', *Yale Univ. Lib. Gazette* (1985), 32–46.

[5] Bodleian Lib. MS 117 fos. 14^v–18^v. The letters were summarized by E. M. Thompson, *The Carthusian Order in England*, 340–1 but have never been printed in full. For Mede see *Reg. Chichele*, iv. 322. Dr A. I. Doyle has information on Mede's work as a scribe.

and before the greedy and the flatterers, like crows around a corpse, could strip him of it. In particular he urged Beaufort to provide for his new foundation, so that it might practice pure alms and its officials not seek favours as they were reported to do. For (quoting St Jerome) it was easier to divest oneself of riches when approaching death. He therefore enclosed schedules both of consolation and of practical means of helping the poor. However, the cardinal did not find this easy. As his confessor said, he had spent his life in gathering riches with great labour and care, was moved by worldly affection for his relations, servants, and friends, and was slow to dispense in pure alms and without tangible benefits. Indirectly the letters thus give some credence to the reports of Beaufort's 'chaplain', John Baker, on which Hall embroidered, that to the end the cardinal was preoccupied with the loss of his treasure and with how it could serve him in the next world.[6]

Despite his growing physical weakness, Beaufort had ample time—three months and more—to prepare for his death, and he retained his mental faculties, issuing documents relating to the business of the see and adding codicils to his will, almost to the end.[7] These documents betray no sign of spiritual anguish, fear of judgement, or plea for mercy such as was placed on his tomb. Nor is there any expression of his own unworthiness or revulsion against the world and the flesh, such as is found in some other wills of the time. Instead they declare his confidence that worldly goods can be converted into celestial, and that the repose of his soul can be assured by unceasing intercession.[8] Like his royal nephew and great nephew, Beaufort chose the exact location of his tomb with care, ensuring the greatest possible proximity to the cathedral's patron saint at the time of resurrection. Just as Henry V had sited his tomb to adjoin the shrine of St Edmund, displacing the almery and altar of the Trinity and collecting the saint's relics into his own chantry, so Beaufort sited his chantry tomb to adjoin the feretory of St Swithun and built a marble shrine behind the feretory to rehouse the relics. In other respects too his tomb took that of Henry V as its model: his effigy was of wood covered in silver gilt plates, and the tomb chest had marble columns copied from Westminster. Like the altar in the royal chantry, that in Beaufort's was dedicated to the Annunciation, and his will provided for a daily mass of the Annunciation to be said and bequeathed a silver representation for the altar. Prayers

[6] For Baker, see McFarlane, 'Deathbed', 116–17. Poggio had likewise warned Beaufort that 'he closes tight the purse which another will open after him'.

[7] *Reg. CS* 93, 99. His will was dated 20 Jan. 1447 and the codicils 7 and 9 Apr. He died 11 Apr.

[8] *Royal Wills*, 321–44 from Reg. Stafford, fo. 111: 'Bona mea terrestria in celestia commutare.' Like Bedford's will, Beaufort's contained conventional reflections on the uncertainty of life. All that remained of the inscription by 1601 were the words 'tribularer si nescirem misericordias tuas'.

were also to be offered for the souls of his father and mother, his sister Joan, and his protector John, duke of Bedford.[9] Beaufort was intent on being remembered as a member of the royal family; yet no mention was made of the other royal brothers, Clarence and Gloucester, nor of his ill-fated nephew John, duke of Somerset. Even on his deathbed Beaufort was in no mood to forgive his enemies or those who had betrayed his confidence in them.

Immediately on his death ten thousand masses were to be commenced for the safety of his soul, and each religious house to which he made a legacy was to pray for him in perpetuity. Among these the major beneficiaries were, predictably, the priories of Winchester and Christ Church, Canterbury. Winchester received £200, vestments, plate, and gifts to the prior and brethren; Canterbury £1,000 for building and endowment.[10] To St Augustine's Beaufort remitted 500 marks which it had borrowed from him. Small bequests were made to the mendicants in London and Winchester; Hyde abbey received £200 and the Bonhommes of Ashridge £100, in both cases for building. He left £200 to Lincoln cathedral for masses, and in the second codicil Eton and King's college, Cambridge received £1,000 apiece.[11] Although he had thus disbursed liberally to the church, as his confessor had enjoined, it is remarkable that neither Sheen itself nor any other Carthusian house benefited.

Second to masses for his soul were alms for the poor. On the day of his burial £200 was to be distributed to attendant poor mourners; thereafter his executors were to apportion 2,000 marks between the poor tenants on all the episcopal estates, and to use £400 in liberating prisoners from the London gaols. They were instructed ultimately to use the residue of his estate for pious uses: in relieving 'God's houses', providing marriage portions for poor girls, and helping the needy. All these provisions for the poor were contained in the will of 20 January and served to fulfil the charge which his confessor had laid upon him, except that he made no specific mention of St Cross nor charged his executors to complete its foundation.

Thirdly, the cardinal took thought for his servants. In the original will £2,000 was to be distributed to his *domesticos et familiares* according to their rank and length of service, and in the first codicil he further charged his executors to maintain his household for a year after his death. Finally,

[9] For Henry V's instructions, *Foedera*, ix. 289–93 (1415); P. and F. Strong, 'Last will', 89–100 (1421); St John Hope, 'Funeral, Monument, and Chantry Chapel of Henry V', 145–55. On Beaufort's tomb, see R. Quirck, 'The Tomb of Cardinal Beaufort' (Winchester, Friends of the Cathedral, 1954); A. Tindal Hart, *The Rich Cardinal*, 142; *Reg. CS* 102–4.

[10] He had also given to Winchester priory the manor of Hinton Daubeny (*Reg. CS* 114, 231) and to Winchester college money to purchase the manor of Buttes, for which the college was to celebrate his obit (Kirby, *Annals*, 182).

[11] In July 1446 he appropriated the church of Ringswood to King's college but had not otherwise been a benefactor of Henry VI's foundations; *Reg. CS* 120.

he made a number of bequests by name to his relatives and members of his *familia*. In the original will these were confined to his natural daughter, Joan, the wife of Sir Edward Stradling, who received plate, and to one Hans Nulles, an unidentified member of his household. His two principal executors, Kemp and Somerset, were rewarded with £200 apiece and the remainder with £100, while in the first codicil Petworth was also given £100. In the second codicil, made two days before his death, he found it easier to be generous. John, bastard of Somerset, and his nephew William Swynford, received £400 apiece; Thomas Forest was given £40 and John Yerde some plate. Five hundred marks owed by the new Lord Tiptoft and £200 by William Stafford were remitted. Queen Margaret was left a red damask which she had evidently admired at Waltham.

The successive codicils in the main embraced individual beneficiaries as they came to the cardinal's mind, but on one matter, as K. B. McFarlane pointed out, they reveal a nagging worry. This concerned the royal jewels which he held in pledge for the unrepaid loan of 1424. Of the jewels which he had then received, of much greater value than the sum loaned, the most valuable had all been returned in 1430 and in their place he had received others more nearly corresponding to the £3,000 still owed to him.[12] Any potential profit from the original undervaluing had thus evaporated; it was now his right of ownership that concerned him. His confessor had bade him 'see that restitution is made of all things wrongfully acquired under whatsoever title, cause, or form'. In both codicils Beaufort in fact affirmed that his legal title, through the crown's default, was unimpeachable. Although it is possible to see this as an attempt to quell an uneasy conscience, it is perhaps more likely that it reflected genuine fears for the pressure which would be put on his executors to return the jewels without payment. For crown jewels never lost their identity, and were difficult to sell. The executors could only realize their value by persuading the crown to repurchase them. Accordingly Beaufort first bequeathed two items—the Tablet of Bourbon and a ewer of gold—to Henry VI with the request that the king would support his executors in fulfilling the bequests for the salvation of his soul.[13] Then in the first codicil further gifts were made to the king, who was allowed one year in which to have the option of repurchasing the jewels at their original price. Finally, two days later, Beaufort bequeathed £2,000 to the royal colleges for the celebration of his obit from the money which the king would pay for the jewels. Beaufort thus sought to persuade Henry VI to repurchase the jewels by making his

[12] These were: the Tablet of St George (2,000 marks), the Tablet of Bourbon (£528), the Tablet of Lancaster (1,000 marks), The Tablet of the Salutation (£210), the Image of St George and the Image of St Michael (£120); with various pieces of plate: McFarlane, *England in XV Century*, 137; *Kal. and Inv*. ii. 117.

[13] The tablet was 'set with divers relics of inestimable treasure and specially of the precious blood of our Lord and a piece of the cross and of the Virgin and other saints and martyrs' and was intended for Eton: a gift well calculated to please Henry VI: *CPR 1446–52*, 148.

offers progressively more attractive, culminating in an appeal to Henry's devotion to his foundations. Realizing that he was leaving his executors an undisposable asset which they could neither defend nor enjoy as he had done, he used the spiritual sanctions of a testator to force the crown to redeem the jewels at the full price. In the event the new treasurer, Bishop Lumley, faced a mounting crisis of debt and had no money available; it was only in August 1449 that the urgent need to raise money for the defence of Normandy led him to redeem the jewels for £2,043 in order to raise a larger sum on their security in the city of London.[14] William Port and his fellows probably saw them go with considerable relief.

Beaufort's will was wholly in character with his life. His principal concern was for the judicious disposal of his wealth to communities he knew and could trust, for servants who had been diligent and faithful, and for the means whereby he could be perpetually commemorated. He had full confidence in the hierarchies of this world and their ability to influence those of the next; indeed as one of the great himself he could hardly afford to believe other. He had always moved with assurance in courts and councils and when he came to die he displayed a sense for public ritual befitting the 'Cardinal of England'. According to the third continuator of the Croyland Chronicle, who claimed to have been present, as Beaufort felt his death approach he summoned all the priests of the neighbourhood to Wolvesey. On Saturday 25 March, the feast of the Annunciation (to which he gave special devotion), as he lay in bed in the great chamber he had his exequies with the requiem mass chanted, and then in the evening his last testament was read out before all. Later—probably on the Monday after Easter Day—when the prior had celebrated mass before him in full pontificals, he again had the will and its codicils read aloud and audibly confirmed them. The following day he died.[15]

The accounts of his executors do not survive to show how they disposed of his wealth, but some incidental references to their activities appear in the records of the exchequer and elsewhere. They certainly implemented many of his bequests, furnishing his father's chantry in St Paul's, providing for his obits at Canterbury, Winchester, and Wells, discharging his few debts, and giving alms for the virtuous poor.[16] Oxford university was quick

[14] McFarlane, 'Deathbed', 136–7; G. L. Harriss, 'Marmaduke Lumley and the exchequer crisis of 1446–9', in J. G. Rowe (ed.), *Aspects of Late Med. Govt. and Soc.* 169.

[15] *Hist. Croy. Cont.* 582; printed and discussed by McFarlane, *England in XV Century*, 118–19. As the codicils were drawn up on 7 and 9 Apr., the date for the final reading would be the 10th, followed almost immediately by the cardinal's death as described by the chronicler. Beaufort's devotion to the Annunciation (or Salutation, as it is always termed) continued that of his predecessor, Wykeham.

[16] *HMC 9th Rep.* 54–5; *Reg. CS* 102–4, 113–14; *Letters of Margaret of Anjou*, 102; *Canterbury Chantries and Hospitals*, ed. C. Cotton (Kent Rec. Soc., 1934), 27; Kirby, *Annals of Winchester Coll.*, 182, 265; *HMC Rep. Wells*, ii. 50, 90, 97. The prior of Canterbury spent three weeks in London negotiating with the executors for the legacy of £1,000: C. E. Woodruffe. 'Inner Life of Ch. Ch. Cant.', *Arch. Cant.* 53 (1941), 10.

to write to Kemp asking for a contribution towards the building of the Divinity School, and on receiving 500 marks promised that his name should be commemorated in the bidding prayers at university sermons. Exeter college approached the executors through Stephen Wilton and obtained fifty marks, while the city of Exeter petitioned for a contribution to rebuild its bridge.[17] All these, together with the other specified legacies, were probably paid in the two and a half years following the cardinal's death, and by then work would also have commenced on his chantry tomb.

In July 1449 Charles VII reopened the war in Normandy, and to raise loans for a relief force the exchequer redeemed crown jewels from any who held them in pledge. Beaufort's executors delivered the jewels they held for the 1424 loan on 29 July, receiving tallies on the clerical tenth for £2,043 and at the same time lending the crown £1,000.[18] As the military crisis in Normandy deepened desperate appeals were made to all who would lend, and the executors made further loans to a total of £8,333. 6*s*. 8*d*. between 30 September and 13 December. Fittingly theirs was by far the largest contribution to the final expedition for the defence of Normandy led by Somerset's captain Sir Thomas Kyriell and numbering many Beaufort followers in Kent. The money was paid directly to Somerset's receiver Thomas Maunsell and there can be little doubt that it was loaned in response to the duke's own demand. The cardinal would hardly have objected, for he and Henry V's feoffees had bowed to similar pressure. For the repayment of these loans the executors had assignments on the lay subsidy payable at Martinmas 1450 and 1451 and the clerical tenth payable at the Annunciation 1451. All their tallies were, apparently, effective so that by the summer of 1451 they should once more have had at least £9,333. 6*s*. 8*d*. in their hands.[19] They probably also provided the 500 marks borrowed by the royal council from William Port in June 1450 for the suppression of Cade's revolt, while in April 1452 they were again called on to lend £2,000 when the court found itself confronted by the duke of York. By March 1453 this sum had been paid, and in July 1453 they received a general pardon for all offences and penalties.[20] Thereafter death began to

[17] The auditors for the cardinal's bequest certified in 1453 that it had been duly spent on the Divinity School, and the university celebrated his obit on 11 Apr.: *Register of Congregation*, ed. Pantin and Mitchell, 110, 140, 393, 397; *Munimenta Academica*, ed. H. Anstey (Rolls Ser., 1868), 333–6, 567–75, 735, *Register of Exeter Coll.*, ed. C. W. Boase, pp. lxiii, 21, 34; *Letters of John Shillingford* ed. S. Moore (Camd. Ser., 1872), 142. Lincoln College also celebrated his obit and is likely to have received a bequest; its early buildings had been erected by John Forest, and the 'high and low' chambers may have been like those at St Cross: *HMC 2nd Report*, 131.

[18] *PPC* vi. 86; E 101/335/15J; *Kal. and Inv.* ii. 204–10; E 401/810 28 Aug. In fulfilment of his desire, Beaufort's obit was celebrated at Eton and King's: Maxwell-Lyte, *History of Eton Coll.* 29.

[19] E 404/65/221, 229; Devon, *Issues*, 465; E 401/813; Steel, *Receipt*, 233 gives the total of all loans in this term as £24,203. For Somerset's captains, see Marshall, thesis, 151.

[20] *CPR 1446–52*, 561; *CPR 1452–61*, 67, 116, 329; E 404/69/103; E 401/828 4 Aug. The 500 marks was only repaid in 1456; *CCR 1454–61*, 154.

thin their ranks. Kemp died in 1454, Somerset in 1455, and Wilton in 1457. Whaplode had already died in 1447 and Prior Viall had been removed from his office in 1450 for misconduct. It was left to Wilton, Toly, Waller, Mareys, and Port to vest the refounded St. Cross in Waynflete in 1455, and it is possible that this was followed by their discharge. Their last recorded act was in December 1455 when Waller released the dowager countess of Shrewsbury from the bond of 1,000 marks made by her husband to the cardinal in August 1446.[21] How much money they still held by then is uncertain. Thomas Basin alleged that Somerset had forced them to disgorge much for himself, though possibly he misconstrued the loan of 1449.[22] In the absence of the executors' accounts there can be no certainty about the ultimate destiny of the residue of the cardinal's fortune.

Throughout Henry Beaufort's career his destiny and that of his family were linked to the house of Lancaster. The Beauforts came into the world with no rights or expectations and needed to look to each other for support and to the Lancastrian kings for recognition and reward. In the first generation John, Henry, and Thomas defended the new dynasty against French hostility, aristocratic plots, and Welsh rebellion, and sustained its authority in the face of popular and parliamentary discontent. The elevation of two brothers to the higher nobility and the third to the richest see in England signified their reception into the Lancastrian family group, while the fecundity of their sister Joan, and John's marriage with Margaret Holand, linked them in the second generation with the older established families of Percy, Nevill, Beauchamp, Mowbray, Courtenay, Stafford, and York, as well as with the royal house of Scotland. Thomas became Henry V's most reliable commander and won himself a dukedom, while Bishop Henry as chancellor co-ordinated English policy in the ambitious bid for the French crown. His fall from favour, which brought his career to a sudden halt, was followed by the death of John's son Henry and the capture of his second and third sons at Baugé. These were severe setbacks to the advance of the family, though mitigated by Clarence's own death, which ensured that the Beaufort estate assembled by John would remain in the family. However, Thomas's death without issue returned virtually all his acquisitions to the crown. In the new reign it was left to Bishop Henry, as head of the family, to safeguard the interests of his nephews. He took Edmund, the youngest and ablest, into his service, initiating his career in France and procuring him grants of offices and a marriage into the Beauchamp family. But while John remained in captivity, Edmund's career was restricted to the opportunities available to a younger son. Whether the cardinal could have

[21] Thompson, *Carthusian Order*, 305–6; *CCR 1452–61*, 117. In 1453 Kemp had rewarded William Port for his labours by acquiring for him the manor of St Nicholas Court in Thanet: *CPR 1452–61*, 216.
[22] Basin, *Hist*: *Charles VII*, ii. 67.

done more to hasten John's release is difficult to judge, for political as well as financial obstacles stood in the way. It was only when Bedford's death urgently raised the problem of the succession to the command in France that the negotiations were hastened for his eventual liberation in 1438. Undoubtedly the cardinal believed that his nephews should advance their careers by service to the crown, as he and his brothers had done. Through his loans to the crown he secured them commands in Normandy and the opportunity to acquire fiefs there, but he made no effort to endow them from his own wealth. By 1440 he had all but secured the succession in Normandy for his nephew John, only to see the prize snatched away; three years later his wealth procured John a rival command, but his nephew bungled his chance. John's death in 1444 left his daughter and heiress a prey to the earl of Suffolk, so that virtually all of the first earl's estate passed out of the male line of the Beauforts. Edmund, the better soldier and cleverer politician, secured the lieutenantship that had eluded his brother not through his uncle's influence but by his own skill; he was to establish a hold over Henry VI that carried disastrous consequences for the blood royal. The Beauforts were a not unfamiliar phenomenon in late medieval England: a quasi-royal family seeking to advance itself by favour and service. Towards the end of his life the cardinal's influence was exercised powerfully on their behalf, but during his lifetime at least they never displayed the greed and ruthlessness which often accompanied the advance of new dynasties in the shadow of the crown.

The Beauforts' relations with the royal house were necessarily ambivalent. Dependent on the rule of the house of Lancaster, they could yet never aspire to an equality of status with those of the full blood. Within the Lancastrian family they occupied an inferior level and on occasion found their own interests sacrificed, as in their exclusion from the succession in 1407 and the endowment of Clarence from their lands in 1411. Bishop Henry felt this most keenly, and his relations with his royal nephews were marked by a series of quarrels in which his pride and resentment were displayed. His incitment of Prince Henry to displace his father in 1411, his bid for the cardinalate in 1417, his open challenge to Gloucester's authority in 1425, and his refusal to recognize Bedford's birthright to the regency in 1431, all affronted the dignity of the royal house. On each occasion his fundamental misjudgement betrayed an over-confidence in his own indispensability, and was appropriately rewarded by humiliating retraction and retirement. Yet the dynasty needed his services, particularly during the minority of Henry VI, and his birth predicated a role greater than that of ministers like Wykeham or Stratford. Only with Henry VI's adolescence did Beaufort cease to feel overshadowed and, to a degree, menaced by the senior house. Between 1429 and 1437 the young King regarded his great uncle with awe and veneration. From Beaufort's hand he had received the crown of France, and in his precocious dedication to the duties of Christian kingship, the cardinal-statesman was his natural mentor. In particular Beaufort influenced his approach to the papal-conciliar conflict and to the peace negotiations. Only later, as Henry's religiosity and horror of war turned him away from the tradition of military ascendancy, did the cardinal's influence give place to that of Henry's own chaplains and courtiers.

Despite tensions in the dynastic relationship which were at times inflamed by jealousy and political rivalry, the Beauforts' commitment to the Lancastrian crown was never in doubt. They devoted their careers to the survival and strengthening of the dynasty under Henry IV, the enlargement of its authority and claims under Henry V, and the sustenance and defence of these under Henry VI. In each Bishop Henry was prominent. As a member of the council from 1403 to 1411, he directed the diplomacy which kept the trade routes with Flanders open and gained the goodwill of John the Fearless. His other main contribution was to win the confidence of an initially critical house of Commons. Benefiting from his close relationship to Thomas Chaucer, he showed himself sympathetic to the Commons' demand for 'bon governance' which under Prince Henry was adopted by the council as a programme of reform. In frequent and prolonged sessions of the council policy was formulated, revenue and expenditure estimated and balanced, and administration tightened. 'Bon governance' was more than a response to parliamentary criticism; it helped to justify the Lancastrian usurpation and win acceptance for the dynasty. With the accession of Henry V the programme was extended, by a drive against lawlessness and disorder and the eradication of the canker of heresy. Solvency, justice, and orthodoxy, with attention to wise counsels, were the hallmarks of the righteous king, and in this model Henry V was presented by his chancellor in successive parliaments during the first half of the reign. In the same terms parliament was told of the king's duty to prosecute his just rights in France and that of his subjects to support his cause; indeed he and they were called to a solemn and god-given destiny, to bring the ancient quarrel to a just and lasting peace. This was Beaufort's message to Henry V after Agincourt and to the parliaments from which he extracted the life grant of the customs and the copious subsidies which fuelled the expeditions of 1415 and 1417. As English propagandists transmitted the theme of the divine mission of the Lancastrian house to a European audience caught in the travails of the papal schism, Beaufort's own intervention in the election of Martin V aroused expectations that the pope might endorse Henry V's claims and transfer the leadership of Christendom from the Valois monarchy to one who promised to unite and lead it in a new crusade.

That dream was never realized, though before his death Henry V had formally joined the kingdoms of England and France and bequeathed the structure of the double monarchy to his son. To sustain this militarily and diplomatically became the life work of the duke of Bedford and Bishop Beaufort. Their alliance had both a military and a political dimension. Forged in the early years of the minority to counteract Duke Humphrey's venture in Hainault, it served to underpin the council's resistance to his political leadership. Beaufort and the council needed Bedford's backing against the protector, while Bedford needed their support for the war in France. Beaufort made this his supreme task; though failing to get direct taxation from parliament, his readiness to lend his own wealth ensured the reinforcements which won Verneuil and enabled Bedford to push the bounds of Lancastrian France to their widest extent. Although his plans for an Anglo-Burgundian crusade against the Hussites, the success of which would win papal recognition for Lancastrian leadership of Christendom, faded with the harsh awakening to defeat at Orléans and Patay, his quick response to the crisis in France cemented his alliance with Bedford. For the next six years both men were engaged in the ceaseless struggle to hold rather than extend the Lancastrian conquest. Beaufort threw himself into this with energy and determination. His direction of policy was ubiquitous. By personal visits and attentiveness to Burgundy's demands and complaints he held the duke firm to the alliance. For Henry VI's coronation he organized the largest army to cross the Channel since 1417 and presided over the royal council in France during the visit. He lent readily to sustain both the royal household and the military advance to Paris, twice returning to England to induce the Commons to grant the most generous taxation of the reign for the expedition. He endeavoured to repair relations with the new pope and to steer a course between the rival claims of Eugenius and the council at Basle which would serve English interests best.

Those interests were dictated by the need on the one hand to maintain the title of Henry VI in France and on the other to stabilize English rule there by a long truce. Since the French would only concede the latter if the English abandoned the former, a series of negotiations proved ultimately abortive. Here Beaufort, for all his persuasiveness and experience, could not alter the logic of the situation. Diplomacy could not reverse the military decline and political disintegration of the Lancastrian empire under its immature and spineless king, or the steady increase in the resources and confidence of the French monarchy. Nor could Beaufort's wealth, despite his desperate boast, offset Burgundy's desertion at Arras. He had appealed to the duke on grounds of affinity, old friendship, and loyalty to his oath to Henry V, and in trying to mitigate English isolation in Europe in the years ahead, it was again on his personal contacts at the Burgundian court that he sought to build. Yet by the age of 65 his inventiveness and resilience were deserting him, he had no new solutions to the Lancastrian predicament, and under Suffolk English diplomacy was soon to seek other channels. It seems unlikely that Beaufort would have condoned the gamble of short truces dependent on Charles VII's goodwill, nor can he have had much sympathy with Henry VI's religious aversion from war and implicit rejection of his father's enterprise. Indeed the cardinal's last intervention was to underwrite the attempt to wrest victory from defeat by an aggressive expedition on a major scale. Its inglorious conclusion was testimony to the factiousness and exhaustion that had overtaken the English will to war. Even in its aftermath the cardinal would surely have opposed the surrender of the Beaufort lands in Maine which his loans to the crown had enabled his nephews to acquire. But in his final years he found himself diplaced and saw the work and vision of a lifetime discountenanced and abandoned.

As a statesman Beaufort must be judged by his advocacy and defence of the Lancastrian ascendancy from its conception to its collapse, but his career embraced many roles as diplomat, politician, financier, churchman, and patron, and these must form part of our final judgement. As has been said, his early experience of diplomatic negotiations was with Burgundian, Flemish, and French envoys during the period 1403 to 1411. It is interesting to speculate whether, from his mother, he acquired any familiarity with the language of the Low Countries. Certainly the fact that under Henry IV the defence of Calais and the seas and the negotiation of commercial truces became the preserve of the Beauforts and their officials, including Sir Thomas Swynford, suggests that their lineage was considered relevant. As chancellor Henry Beaufort showed a keen appreciation of mercantile interests, whether in suppressing piracy, redressing injuries and awarding compensation, or protecting foreign merchants in England. He successfully negotiated access for English merchants to the Baltic and in his second term as chancellor consolidated relations with the Hanse and sought to convert the commercial truce with Burgundy into a political and military alliance. That had been foreshadowed by the dispatch of Arundel's force in 1411, and though Beaufort's hand in the negotiations which attended it, as in those with the Burgundian envoys at Leicester in 1414 and indeed with Duke John himself at Calais in 1416, is obscure, it may reasonably be supposed to have been important. It is equally difficult to judge what the tortuous diplomacy which preceded Henry V's invasion of 1417 owed to Beaufort. The king was himself adept at it and kept some of his moves secret from his chancellor—as his letter to Tiptoft about the talks with the duke of Bourbon reveals. Nor, with Beaufort's departure to Constance, did English diplomacy decline in deviousness or foresight. If Beaufort envisaged for himself a new role as the diplomatic representative of the house of Lancaster in Europe, his expectations were doomed; though he was present at the Meulan negotiations in 1419, he had forfeited Henry's confidence by his apparent readiness to serve Martin V, and he played no further part in royal diplomacy.

Nor did the early years of the minority make significant calls upon his skill as a diplomat. Bedford himself handled the crisis of Gloucester's intervention in Hainault though Beaufort was clearly kept informed. It was only on his return to France in 1427, and more particularly with his attempt to recruit Duke Philip for the Hussite crusade, that he became a regular visitor to the Burgundian court. With the military crisis of 1429 Beaufort assumed prime responsibility for the retention of the duke as an ally by financial and military assistance, the promise of territory, and the conciliation of his grievances. Among these was the Partition Ordinance of 1429, accepted by Beaufort as the price of the Staplers' backing for the defence of Calais. Beaufort came under repeated Burgundian pressure for its repeal but prevented the issue from endangering the alliance before 1435; doubtless his lifelong insistence on the protection of Flemish merchants in England afforded a guarantee of his good faith. Between 1429 and 1432 Beaufort and Philip met on a number of occasions and developed a relationship of trust and friendship fortified by the duke's marriage to Beaufort's niece Isabel of Portugal. She emerged as a shrewd negotiator in her own right and an important bridge between England and Burgundy in the years after Arras. The death of Anne of Burgundy and the ensuing tiff between the two dukes over Bedford's remarriage underlined the importance of Beaufort's personal standing with Duke Philip, and his ability to act as mediator. It was at the Burgundian court that he sought and received welcome at the time of Gloucester's attack on him in 1432. Thus too, in the crisis of Burgundian loyalties in 1435, it was in terms of their long-standing brotherhood and common loyalty to the memory of Henry V that Beaufort pleaded with Philip, just as his subsequent attempts to heal the breach in negotiations with Isabel were conducted in an atmosphere of personal trust and cordial hospitality. Beaufort's own motto, *honor et lyesse*, aptly reflected his diplomatic style. That this could not withstand the pull of opposing interests was a personal tragedy for Beaufort, particularly as he believed that the fortunes of England and Burgundy dictated a common opposition to France. Indeed the break up of the Anglo-Burgundian alliance marked the failure of his diplomacy and the death blow to the legacy of Henry V.

The alliance with Scotland suffered a similar fate. This too had been cemented by a personal bond, the marriage of his niece Joan to the liberated James I. By 1428 James was faltering in his allegiance and seeking a more independent role. Beaufort's mission to Scotland in that year was a personal success and secured the neutrality of Scotland through the dangerous crisis of the French revival and the king's absence abroad. That it could not survive the events of 1435–6 was perhaps not surprising.

Nevertheless, Beaufort could in substance claim to have forged and maintained the alliances with Burgundy and Scotland on which the Lancastrian ascendancy in France depended.

In English politics Beaufort's role is perhaps less clearly defined and more contentious, though his importance is indisputable. Over a period of forty years, from 1403 to 1443, apart from short periods of political exile, he was an active member of the council and for eight years chancellor. Such a period of sustained influence at 'cabinet level' would be difficult to parallel in the history of modern Britain; in medieval England it stands unique. His political memory and accumulated experience conferred an authority and advantage from a very early point in his career. Even by 1410 he was the senior among the prince's friends, and by 1422 he alone on the minority council had participated in the revolution which provided the infant king with his title. Twenty years later, he could survey the rise and decline of the Lancastrian ascendancy as a historical epic in which his own career provided the continuum. It was small wonder that his passing seemed to mark the end of an age. Yet rarely was his the role of omnicompetent deputy to a prestigious monarch, that of a Wolsey or a Richelieu, dominating and overshadowing his contemporaries. Beaufort's influence was exercised at the head of a group of lay and ecclesiastical lords who shared his aims and qualities. Bishops like Alnwick, Stafford, and Kemp and laymen like Tiptoft, Hungerford, and Cromwell were men of acumen and energy, cautious politicians and effective administrators. For such men service to the crown was both an honourable and satisfying career and a sure means to advancement in wealth and dignity. When the dominating figure of Henry V was removed, their choice lay between serving as acolytes to an all-powerful regent and undertaking the collective control of policy and patronage through a council. Not surprisingly they preferred the latter, a choice undoubtedly made easier because they recognized in Beaufort the qualities of statesmanship that were lacking in Gloucester. That his policies and personality commanded their respect is evident from the few occasions when they mistrusted his motives and withdrew their backing. Beaufort's two-facedness and sycophancy to Martin V over the repeal of the statues in 1426–7 alienated the council, which reacted coolly to his return as papal legate to preach the crusade. Later there was increasing unease over his control of the Lancastrian estates, and by 1440–2 his isolation compelled him to surrender the feoffment. A year later even his oldest and staunchest ally, Lord Cromwell, was moved to resign as confidence in Somerset's expedition drained away.

Over a period of twenty years this group enjoyed almost uninterrupted control of the three great offices of state and principal household posts, imparting a remarkable stability to the political scene. They were well rewarded: Tiptoft and Hungerford obtained peerages and all the ecclesiastics important sees. If they formed a faction, they were well aware of the dangers of factionalism and made efforts to contain it. Their major success was in presenting themselves as guardians of the political consensus and casting Gloucester in the role of its disrupter. This was in no small measure due to the cardinal's own tactics. He was adept at wrong-footing and traducing his enemies: perhaps Clarence to Prince Henry; certainly Chichele to popes Martin and Eugenius, and Gloucester to Bedford. Gloucester's indictment in 1440 gave expression to his cumulative frustration at being repeatedly outmanœvred and isolated over the preceding two decades.

Yet Beaufort also had weaknesses as a politician. He never wholly rid himself of resentment and jealousy in his relations with the royal house, and of the urge to press his own advantage. This led him into major tactical misjudgements, which prejudiced his long-term aims. His advocacy of Henry IV's abdication, acceptance of the legateship in 1417, flouting of Gloucester's authority in 1425, and purchase of Chirkland in 1439 each produced an outraged reaction which brought a crisis in his career. The evidence of pride and ambition, and readiness to make his wealth serve his own political advantage, which Gloucester rehearsed in 1440, had much earlier aroused the distrust of Henry V. When exercised on behalf of his own family, Beaufort's influence could be politically divisive, and he was generally unforgiving to those who thwarted him. He was certainly a formidable opponent, not afraid to fight each of his royal nephews in defence of his own interests, and quick to champion the rights of his office and see. Yet he found himself worsted by Archbishops Arundel and Chichele and the dukes of Gloucester and Suffolk, and for periods in 1412–13, 1419–21, 1426–9, and 1432–3 he was forced out of the council.

Acutely aware of his own vulnerability, at all stages of his career Beaufort was careful to buttress his position with the backing of some member of the higher nobility with an outstanding reputation in the field. Under Henry IV his brother John and then Prince Henry filled this role; under Henry V it was his brother Thomas, and after Thomas's death John, duke of Bedford. The bishop's support for their military ambitions was matched by the protection they extended at crises in his career: as in his quarrel with Clarence, his disgrace under Henry V, and his conflict with Gloucester in 1426. In defeat he showed great political resilience and was adept at escaping its consequences. He judged that humble submission to Henry V, rather than defiance or abdication, was the likeliest route to restoration. In 1426, having pushed his dispute with Gloucester to the point of open war, he forced his opponent on to the defensive by an appeal to Bedford which cheated Gloucester of victory and secured his own safe withdrawal. In 1429 he successfully outfaced Gloucester's attack on his new status, and in 1432 chose to fight the charge of praemunire by an appeal, in parliament and outside, to the politcal consensus and his own loyal service, which highlighted the vindictiveness of Gloucester's dismissal of his supporters. How he answered Gloucester's final indictment we do not know.

Beaufort had many of the qualities for success in politics; intelligence, hardness, self-confidence, foresight, a degree of ruthlessness, and an appearance of honesty and righteousness. He desired power and enjoyed the exercise of it. Yet his abilities and ambitions evidently aroused not merely jealousy but apprehension, as if his masters and rivals perceived that his aim was not to serve but to rule. In fact Beaufort never enjoyed untramelled power or authority, and his major contribution as a politician was the consolidation of conciliar authority during Henry VI's minority. More than any other he deserves the credit or blame for the political structure to which the king succeeded as an adult in 1442. By then the collective authority exercised by the council over the past twenty years was already in dissolution, the cardinal was in semi-retirement, and his old colleagues were a dwindling band. But during the long years of the minority it had been the confidence which they and the duke of Bedford had in Beaufort's judgement which had established his effective leadership of the council and made him the most influential figure in English politics.

Second to Beaufort's influence in council was his relations with the Commons in parliament. Here too his powerful eloquence was used to good effect. During his three periods as chancellor he gave the opening sermon at ten parliaments. These formal addresses were carefully constructed and designed to impress on the Commons their duty of loyal co-operation in the crown's policies. Within the lower house his cousin, Thomas Chaucer, was his unofficial spokesman and thrice the Commons' Speaker. It was probably he who sponsored the Commons' repeated commendation of the Beauforts under Henry IV, and as the bishop emerged as the principal lender to the crown under Henry V and VI, the Commons more than once recorded their appreciation of his generosity. In 1421 it had enabled them to deflect or defer the demand for taxation, and at all times the availability of his loans took pressure off the multitude of small lenders to make advances of their payment of taxes. Beaufort's boast to Henry V that parliament would make no difficulty in granting the taxation he desired was perhaps gratuitous in the circumstances of 1415; but in his first two periods as chancellor he secured the largest grants made in either reign, and though the Commons proved unyielding in 1425, it was mainly through his efforts and example that they furnished Henry VI in 1430–1 with the largest grants of his reign.

How far did parliament provide political support for Beaufort in his policies or at moments of crisis in his career? The evidence is generally oblique. The two parliaments of 1410 and 1411 clearly gave their backing to the prince's friends, though the Commons proved powerless to prevent the king's dismissal of the council in 1411. In the crisis over Gloucester's claim to the regency in 1422 the Commons took an active and watchful interest and numbered many who were shortly to become Beaufort's colleagues on the council: Tiptoft, Hungerford, Beauchamp, and Chaucer. But the issue was decided among the lords of the council and then ratified in parliament. In 1426 parliament was again seen as the proper setting for resolving the dire quarrel in which the bishop's personal future was at stake. He had already angered the Commons and mercantile community by failing to enforce the latest hosting laws and on this occasion may have made efforts to bolster his position by the return of his supporters in certain shires. Although the Commons expressed their concern about the discords between the lords, their own partisanship remains concealed and the settlement was the work of Bedford and the council. In 1432 however the Commons played a more discernible and possibly decisive role. Beaufort had returned explicitly to answer in parliament the charges brought against him, and it was in parliament that Cromwell protested against his dismissal. Once again the Commons expressed disquiet about the discords between lords and on their petition the threat of praemunire was formally removed and Beaufort confirmed in his right, as cardinal, to hold the see of Winchester. Although the choice and powers of the council, the resolution of quarrels, and the conferment of legal indemnity were all undertaken by the king and lords, the sympathies of the Commons were often discernibly with the bishop. Only in the parliaments of 1440 and 1442 was he clearly under pressure from the Commons, for the surrender of the enfeoffed lands of the duchy; here, for once, his own financial interests conflicted with those of the Commons. By then Beaufort was an old parliamentary hand. He had been present at no less than thirty-two parliaments and in many of these his responsibilities and interests had brought him into daily contact with the Commons. Chaucer apart, there is little indication that he sought to lead or sway the lower house through his own servants. All the indications are that from 1404 he established with the Commons a relationship of mutual responsiveness and respect. They endorsed his policies by grants of taxation, expressed gratitude for his loans, and indicated their support for his survival in the crises of his career.

Undoubtedly the most telling political leverage which Beaufort exerted was through his loans. This was exercised in a variety of situations. Those made under Henry IV were small and few; it was on the insistence of Henry V that he first contributed the greater part of his wealth to finance the king's conquests. But the circumstances of 1417 and 1421 were exceptional, and only with Henry VI did he become a regular and voluntary lender to the crown and therewith the moulder of its policy. The circumstances which permitted this were first the replacement of monarchical by conciliar authority, and secondly the refusal of parliament before 1429 to pay for expeditionary forces to sustain the English conquests. Thereafter the sharp fall in the customs and increasing dependence of Normandy on England reduced the exchequer to a state of habitual insolvency in which its cash flow was always in crisis and a choice between military options was frequently necessary. This was the situation which enabled the cardinal to use his ready money with telling effect. His influence at council, where the terms of the loan were authorized, and at the exchequer, where its repayment was administered, enabled him to dictate the conditions on which he would lend, including the purposes to which his money was to be applied. That was true, at least, when his political position was secure. Such were the loans of 1424 and 1425 made as chancellor for Bedford's conquests in France, those of 1430–1 which established his influence with the royal entourage in Normandy, or that of February 1436, used to equip Mortain for the relief of Calais; those of 1437 for Dorset's expedition and the appointment and dispatch of Warwick as lieutenant; those of 1438–9 for his own diplomatic negotiations, and that in the December following which established Somerset as *de facto* lieutenant in Normandy. Above and beyond all these was the massive loan of 1443 which underwrote the last major expedition to Normandy under Somerset's fateful command. Almost as important was his refusal to lend for projects he declined to support: for Gloucester's Hainault venture; for Salisbury's Orléans expedition; for Huntingdon's Guyenne army in 1439 and York's command in Normandy in 1436 and after 1440. In periods when he was out of power, and for persons and purposes which did not concur with his interests, Beaufort was conspicuously absent as a lender.

Yet he could not always or entirely dictate the use of his wealth. In 1421 and 1432 he had to surrender it to buy himself back into favour; his loans of 1433–4 were the price for his reinstatement under Bedford's protection, and in July 1436 his contribution to Gloucester's expedition was probably under pressure from the assembled lords. Moreover, his wealth in one sense placed him permanently at risk. Had Henry V so decided, he could have confiscated Beaufort's treasure; similarly Gloucester's repeated attempts to encompass his ruin could have succeeded had Bedford and the council been more ruthless and less distrustful of Gloucester. Again, at times the bulk of his fortune was on loan to the crown and at the risk of royal default. Three things prevented this and afforded Beaufort some security. These were his affinity to the royal house, the reluctance of Bedford and the council to enhance Gloucester's power, and Beaufort's future utility as a lender. That he did not emerge a loser from his loans was also, of course, due to the exacting conditions which he set for their repayment. When he was in a position to, he drove a hard bargain. Beaufort employed every type of security and preference as the occasion demanded. He principally favoured exchequer tallies on local subsidy collectors or on the customs collected by his own nominees in the ports, and these were usually specified in letters patent, with clauses stipulating that they should not be changed and, if invalidated, should be reassigned. But at times no immediate revenue was available, and he had to accept the bonds of lords of the council or jewels of equal or greater value to the loan. Who occupied the office of treasurer was thus of vital importance to him, and the council undoubtedly appreciated this. Stafford and Hungerford during the first ten years of the minority were both his trusted associates. Scrope, whom Gloucester intruded in 1432, was dismissed by Bedford in 1433 when Beaufort was called on to lend again. With Cromwell Beaufort enjoyed a close rapport until 1443 and even on his departure Cromwell bound his successor to the repayment of the massive debt to the cardinal. It was an article of faith to them both that assignments to lenders must be guaranteed.

However much they served his political interests, Beaufort's loans were made for the military and political needs of the English crown, and mainly within the context of conciliar rule. In character they were more akin to the service rendered by the English nobility than to the activities of the Italian bankers of the fourteenth century. His wealth and lineage imposed an obligation which a king like Henry V was quick to seize upon and exploit. Whatever occasional financial benefits he derived from licences to ship wool, he did not receive a percentage interest on his loans to the English crown. Nevertheless he was, and was known to be, immensely rich, and the source of his wealth aroused speculation in his lifetime, as it still does. The rents and produce of the episcopal estates of themselves placed him among the higher nobility in income, and the profits of sheep farming were also probably considerable, though whether he habitually traded in wool remains uncertain. Careful husbandry of the profits of office and patronage over a long period, and perhaps the employment of money for which he was a trustee, are all more plausible explanations than usury. But ultimately the source and size of his fortune remains a secret, locked for ever in the now destroyed accounts of the treasurer of Wolvesey.

By whatever means it was amassed, Beaufort's wealth was the talk of Christendom. It was remarked on by contemporaries in Italy, France, and the Low Countries, as well as by his Lancastrian compatriots and their Tudor successors. Although it could generate popular envy among the Londoners, who clamoured for his death in 1425 'to play with his riches', as much as that of his political enemies, there is no indication that it was thought unfitting for one of his rank. Indeed he even escaped censure from Gascoigne. Partly his blood and status explain this. Cardinals from princely houses were becoming a feature of the restored papacy, even though an English cardinal of this kind was a novelty. In reaction from the Franciscan ideal, wealth was regarded as fitting for these princes of the church whom the Renaissance came to view as akin to Roman patricians. In his own day Beaufort set a standard which few or none could match. Poggio recounted in awe how, in his household, even the kitchen utensils were of silver, and another Florentine described a public showing of the cardinal's plate followed by a private tour of his treasure chests. But mostly his affluence was exhibited in a public, one might almost say, professional context. His public appearances were consistently impressive. When he entered Venice as a pilgrim in 1418, or Paris in 1427 and 1429, when he arrived for negotiations at Arras in 1435 and at Oye in 1439, witnesses remarked on the size of his retinue and the splendour of its trappings, all rivalling or surpassing a Valois or Lancastrian prince. Beaufort was determined to be their equal. He entertained sumptuously, giving marriage banquets for Joan Beaufort and Lucia Visconti, diplomatic ones for visiting ambassadors in London and on his own journeys abroad. This public display of wealth was fitting, for in a sense he was acting as surrogate for his infant grand nephew, sustaining the dignity of the Lancastrian throne.

Poggio would have approved this use of private wealth for the public good, though Beaufort's Carthusian confessor urged him to employ it in acts of mercy. It was undue attachment to wealth (*avaritia*) and self-indulgence (*luxuria*) that occasioned mortal sin. As his confessor noted, Beaufort had amassed his wealth with much care and labour and the only hint that he ever contemplated voluntarily relinquishing it, in 1420, was treated with scepticism by Thomas Chaucer. It is clear that both Poggio and his confessor thought that a lifetime's attachment to riches would not easily be thrown off even at the point of death: it would be hard for him to pass through the needle's eye. On the other hand there is no indication from these sources or others that he was self-indulgent. Clearly he lived in considerable comfort and ate well; he enjoyed hunting and lay society, and in his early manhood produced a bastard; especially did he covet jewels and precious ornaments. But his life was extremely busy and mentally and physically demanding, his health and physique took him into an active old age, and there are no hints in contemporary sources of excesses.

Beaufort was the first bishop of the royal blood since the twelfth century and the first cardinal to retain his English see. He also held episcopal office for a period (just short of fifty years) unrivalled in medieval England. Yet no well-defined impression of Beaufort as a churchman emerges. The loss of the major part of his Winchester register is a severe limitation, although it would probably have conveyed little of his personal role. Only in periods of political exile did he see at first hand the life of his diocese. Most of his routine spiritual duties were performed by his vicars-general, John Burbache, John Hermandsworth, and Robert Keton. He commissioned Richard Praty, bishop of Chichester, to investigate Lollardy in the diocese of Winchester, though reserving the examination of one suspect for himself. But for the most part his personal intervention in the affairs of his dioceses was in awards and arbitrations, as in the long-running variance between the dean and chapter of Lincoln, or that between the monastery of Chertsey and its neighbouring villagers, or that of Winchester college with the Salisbury chapter. It is clear that he took these seriously, making himself familiar with the documentary evidence, discussing the issues with both parties in person, and using his authority and experience as a mediator to effect a settlement. All these were favoured institutions which could directly invoke his patronage. So was the priory of St Swithun with which his relations were apparently uniformly cordial. Some other houses, like Hyde abbey and the Bonhommes of Ashridge, received benefactions from him, and Beaulieu was taken into his hand and reformed. Despite his personal link with Syon, his patronage was not extended to the Carthusians nor to any of the new forms of personal piety and devotional cults in which the age abounded. He commended the practice of founding chantries and was himself commemorated in not a few. But concern with doctrine, liturgy, and reform, which moved some of the best churchmen of his age, touched him not at all. If he delivered any sermons other than as chancellor, they are not recorded. His view of the bishop's office remained more jurisdictional than pastoral, and he made bishops regular members of the county bench. When possible successors to his see were canvassed in 1419, he was said to favour a man of high estate who was not even a clerk, holding that 'such men had profited most the church of Winchester before his time'. Even Chaucer was taken aback.

Beaufort's hierarchical views and authoritarian temperament set him at the opposite pole to Chichele, who essentially belonged to the age of Hallum, and Henry V had good reason for alarm at the prospect of his exercising legatine authority in England. But in the event, although as cardinal he secured exemption from the archbishop's jurisdiction, Beaufort made no attempt to challenge Chichele's authority over the English church. If there is little sign of their co-operation, except for the crusade, neither is there evidence of open conflict. To judge from the record, Beaufort attended convocation only as the crown's emissary to demand taxation. He had no concern for the defence of the church's liberties and deliberately avoided the confrontation over the statute of provisors, which Martin V forced on Chichele. If Martin at one time deluded himself that Beaufort might be another Becket, he had been disillusioned by the time of his death. Beaufort had learnt the lesson of his vulnerability as a champion of papal claims in 1419 and when he returned ten years later as cardinal and legate he acted with tact and circumspection to avoid giving offence. It was to his credit that the hostility aroused by the novel prospect of a resident cardinal had, by the time of his death, been replaced by national pride in a dignity which would henceforth become normal in the English church.

Beaufort's aim was rather to be the channel of papal communication with the English crown, and in this he would brook no rival. He permitted his agents to discredit Chichele at the Curia, and he assiduously cultivated the papal collectors sent to England. He used his influence to advance his protégés—Polton, Catrik, Spofford, Fleming, Alnwick, Bourchier—to bishoprics, and in the case of Kemp and Louis of Luxembourg to the Curia itself. But in the main he cultivated papal favour not for his own advancement or that of his friends, but in the interests of the Lancastrian ascendancy. It was this which underlay his mission to Constance in 1417 and which became the ultimate goal of his crusade. For this reason he was never tempted to transfer his loyalty to Rome and assume his seat in the Curia. By so doing he would have sacrificed both his political aspirations and his wealth.

Beaufort mainly impressed his contemporaries as a man of great wisdom, probity, and experience. His cast of mind was essentially political and legal, and he found little outlet in religion, learning, or the arts. He shared some of the military aptitudes of his brothers, and showed courage and resource at moments of crisis. Although his own political career was beset with personal feuds, he was in considerable demand as a mediator in both private and political disputes. He brought patience, intelligence, and good humour to this, and to his diplomatic negotiations, and he similarly evoked confidence as an executor of wills and trusts. His acts of kindness are unrecorded and whatever personal warmth informed his relations with his colleagues is now barely traceable. But some of his servants revealed their affection and loyalty to him in letters, bequests, and endowments, and one may guess that he was liked as well as respected and even feared. Against this must be set an obsessive sense of his own dignity, his pride and touchiness over his birth, a readiness to scheme against and malign others for his own defence and advantage, and a concern to amass wealth, all of which aroused the venom of Gloucester and doubtless the distrust of others. As a politician, his career was one of extraordinary vicissitude; few can have been so wracked on the wheel of Fortune. Poggio's insipid historical compilation on this theme held few lessons for him, and he was equally adept at the practice of *virtu*, the stoicism in misfortune and capacity to grasp the ascending wheel as it turned to better things. All these facets of Beaufort's personality are discernible in the 'Albergati' portrait by Van Eyck (see Plate III). The cardinal, wearing Beaufort's habitual dress of a scarlet gown, its slashed sleeves and collar trimmed with white miniver, confronts the spectator with an informal and open expression.[23] The heavy Flemish features are infused with a calm intelligence, and the general air is of one accustomed to exercise moral and political authority, to render judgement and expect obedience. The eyes are shrewd, with a

[23] Above, ch. 11 n. 7, and for descriptions of Beaufort's dress in 1427 and 1429, see above ch. 9 n. 25 and ch. 10 n. 2. It recalls the scarlet gown trimmed with ermine favoured by Edward III.

hint of cunning, but not devoid of humanity. Indeed a latent sense of humour, unique in Van Eyck's portraits, is strongly suggested in both the eyes and the mouth. Yet there is also a hint of stoical detachment, born of many changes of fortune. It is the portrait of one whom a lifetime's experience has not robbed of innate kindliness or confidence in human nature. This is, in truth, *un prelat sachant*; no monk or ascetic.

As a statesman Beaufort lacked neither vision nor consistency. From the first he saw the Lancastrian monarchy as the focus of loyalty, the guarantor of good government, and the instrument to restore England's fame and honour. In Prince Henry he discerned the qualities which could effect this, and as the early triumphs vindicated his judgement, he affirmed and disseminated his belief in his nation's hallowed destiny. Although he played no part in formulating the treaty of Troyes, its concept of a kingship which should transcend and harmonize the patriotism of two traditional monarchies was one to which he readily gave support. It was the first step towards a new political order in Europe, but with Henry V's death the path remained untrodden. Though firmly committed to his memory and legacy, Bedford and Beaufort could never expect to fulfil his ambitions. They remained locked in a war which turned from one of conquest to one for survival. Out of loyalty they shut their eyes to the inevitability of defeat and the advisability of voluntary withdrawal. To accept these would have been to disown the Lancastrian monarchy of which they were part. Inexorably they, and the English people, had to pay the price for the ambitions which had launched the expeditions of 1415 and 1417. For Beaufort it meant the slow unravelling of all that he had striven for and desired. That he remained untiring in his efforts and watched with fortitude his vision turn to dust and ashes must command a certain respect. It is difficult not to feel that the fragment of his epitaph that survived on his tomb, 'I would tremble did I not know Thy mercies', had as much reference to the England he left as to the judgement that he anticipated for himself.

APPENDICES

APPENDIX I

Henry Beaufort's Loans to the Crown

No.	Date	Sum loaned	Method and period of repayment	Sources
1	18 May 1404	£1,333 6s. 8d.	From second part of income tax in southern England and Lincs., and first half clerical tenth in Lincoln diocese by warrants of war treasurers.	E 101/43/38 file 2; E 101/44/20; *CCR 1402–5*, 401, 415.
2	28 July 1406	£600	Tallies 6 Aug. 1406 on first half of clerical tenth in Winchester diocese. Letters patent.	E 401/638; *CPR 1405–8*, 199, 214; *Foedera*, viii. 448.
3	9 June 1410	£1,000	Tallies 17 July 1410 on lay subsidy at Martinmas 1410 in Hants and Wilts. Letters patent with preference.	E 401/652; *PPC* i. 335, 343; E 404/25/388; *CPR 1409–13*, 204–5, 240.
4	17 July 1413	£1,333 6s. 8d.	Tallies 14 Aug. 1413 on clerical tenth (Nov. 1413) in southern dioceses.	E 401/658.
5	8 June 1415	£1,963 6s. 6d.	From receiver-general and local receivers of duchy of Lancaster. Jewels as security for repayment within one year.	E 401/667; *PPC* ii. 167; E 28/31 2 June; DL 42/17/2 fo. 29.
6	5 Nov. 1415	£666 13s. 4d.	Tallies 6 Nov. 1415 on second part lay subsidy (Dec. 1415) in Hants, Wilts., Oxon.	E 401/669.
7	12 June 1417	£14,000	Letter patent 18 July 1417 grants all future customs in Southampton. Tallies by hands of Foxholes, his nominated collector. £5,693 repaid by 1422, remainder in 1424–5. King's gold crown as security.	E 401/677; *CPR 1416–22*, 42–3, 99.
8	13 May 1421	£14,000	Letter patent 19 May 1421, confirmed in	E 401/696; *Rot. Parl.* iv. 130,

No.	Date	Sum loaned	Method and period of repayment	Sources
			parliament prolongs grant of Southampton customs as above with preference and provision for extension to other ports in case of default or delay (extended in Nov. 1422). £1,059 repaid from his clerical tenths. £4,408 repaid by 1422, remainder in 1423–4.	132–5; *PPC* ii. 288; *CFR* xv. 18–19, 22–3; *CPR 1416–22*, 372, 392.
9	13 May 1421	£3,666 13*s*. 4*d*.	Treasurer's agreement to repay in cash by Martinmas 1422. Tallies 17 July 1421 on London customs. £2,000 of this reassigned 22 Feb. 1423.	E 401/696; E 403/39/140; *PPC* ii. 298–9, iii. 42.
10	6 Mar. 1423	£666 13*s*. 4*d*.	Repaid from Henry V's goods by his executors.	*PPC* iii. 60.
11	1 Mar. 1424	£9,333 6*s*. 8*d*.	Letter patent 1 Mar. 1424: (*a*) £5,333 6*s*. 8*d*. to be repaid from customs in London, Hull, Ipswich; (*b*) £4,000 to be repaid at exchequer Christmas 1424 and Easter (later midsummer) 1425. Jewels of greater value as security for default. For (*a*) Tallies on customs 2 Mar. for payment after Easter 1424, with warrants to collectors. For (*b*) The exchequer defaulted on the second instalment of the £4,000 and Beaufort retained the jewels.	E 401/707; E 101/335/15 J; *PPC* iii. 144, 146; *Kal. & Inv.*, ii. 117–20, 136–7, 143–4; *Rot. Parl.* iv. 210; *CPR 1422–9*, 214; *CCR 1422–9*, 118; E 28/45 20 July.
12	13 Dec. 1424	£1,000	Properly a deferred repayment of part of the £4,000 (loan 11) due at Christmas 1424. Tallies for £900 May–July 1425 mainly on the customs, and cash repayment of £100 Jan. 1426.	E 401/710; E 403/673; *PPC* iii. 162–3.
13	22 Mar & 21 May 1425	£8,933 6*s*. 8*d*.	Under act of parliament and obligations of councillors; letters patent 6 June for repayment of loans 12 and 13 from the customs and future taxes.	E 403/671, 673, 676; E 401/711, 712; *Rot. Parl.* iv. 275, 277–80; *PPC* iii. 167–8, 199–200;

No.	Date	Sum loaned	Method and period of repayment	Sources
			Retention of jewels as collateral. Repaid by tallies issued July 1425–Apr. 1426 with a small sum in cash.	*CPR 1422–9*, 271, 293–4, 360.
14	Sept. 1429	9,388 *li.* 10*s.* *tournois*	Lent in Normandy on security of jewels; repayment midsummer 1430 by treasurer of Normandy.	*Wars of Eng.* ii. 141–2.
15	19 May 1430	£8,333 6*s.* 8*d.*	Letters patent for repayment from lay subsidies Martinmas 1430; tallies assigned 19 May.	E 401/724; *CPR 1429–36*, 60.
16	Aug. 1430	£2,866 13*s.* 4*d.* and 3,000 *li. t.*	Lent in Normandy and repaid by treasurer of Normandy in October.	BN MS Fr. 20327 no. 150; 26549 no. 15.
17	Nov. 1430	£2,815 13*s.* 1½*d.*	Lent to treasurer of household in Normandy. Repaid by tallies on lay subsidy 24 Apr. 1431; letters patent.	E 401/725; E 101/408/9; *PPC* iv. 79; *CPR 1429–36*, 115.
18	Feb.–Mar. 1431	£12,758 6*s.* 9*d.*	Repaid by tallies on lay subsidies under letters patent 24 Apr. 1431.	As next above.
19	June–Oct. 1431	£4,851 12*s.* 10*d.*	Lent to treasurer of household in Normandy and repaid by him.	E 101/408/13; Bod. Lib. Misc. Ch. Eng. C 1.
20	June–Oct. 1431	£1,083 6*s.* 8*d.*	Lent in Normandy; repayment ordered Mar. 1432, made 15 July by tallies on lay subsidies payable Martinmas 1432.	E 401/732; E 404/48/158.
21	Nov. 1431	£6,666 13*s.* 4*d.*	Lent in Normandy under obligations of lords of council. Repaid by tallies 15 July 1432 on lay subsidies due Martinmas 1432 and 1433.	E 401/732; SC 8/7180.
22	Dec. 1431	£733 6*s.* 8*d.*	Lent in France; jewels as security. Repayment as under loan 20.	E 401/732; *PPC* iv. 109–10; E 404/48/156–7.
23	3 July 1432	£6,000	Repayment by tallies on lay subsidies payable Martinmas 1432 and 1433.	E 401/732; *CPR 1429–36*, 346.
24	3 July 1432	£6,000	Deposited to redeem his jewels. Repaid by tallies	*CPR 1429–36*, 346; *PPC* iv. 237–9;

No.	Date	Sum loaned	Method and period of repayment	Sources
			10 June 1434 on lay subsidy due Easter 1435.	*Rot. Parl.* iv. 390; E 401/737.
25	May 1433	£6,666 13*s.* 4*d.*	5,000 marks lent at Calais, 5,000 marks lent at exchequer, 18 July. Obligations of lords for repayment midsummer 1434 from lay subsidies; tallies delivered 14 June 1434.	E 401/733; *PPC* iv. 162, 202, 242; E 404/49/139; E 404/50/326.
26	10 May 1434	£6,666 13*s.* 4*d.*	Letter patent and jewels as pledges for repayment; to be made in gold from lay subsidies; tallies issued 10 June also on clerical subs. due 1435–6. Recovers jewels impounded 1432.	E 401/737; E 404/50/331, 317, 320; *PPC* iv. 233–6, 236–9, 244–54; *CPR 1429–36*, 353–4, 414.
27	20 June 1434	£2,000	Repayment terms as in loan 26; tallies issued 22 June on lay subsidy due Easter 1435.	—ditto—
28	7 July 1435	£6,666 13*s.* 4*d.*	Obligations of lords. Apr. 1437 repayment deferred. Tallies on lay subsidy due Whitsun 1437 issued 15 May 1437.	E 401/743, 752; E 403/720; *CPR 1429–36*, 461; E 28/56; *Foedera*, x. 69.
29	14 July 1435	£500	No note of repayment.	E 401/743.
30	15 Feb. 1436	£7,333 6*s.* 8*d.*	Tallies on lay subsidy due Whitsun 1436 issued 6 Mar.	E 401/744, 752.
31	15 Feb. 1436	£5,333 6*s.* 8*d.*	Jewels as security for repayment at Martinmas 1436 and Whitsun 1437. Tallies issued 6 Mar. then reassigned 15 May on lay subsidy due Martinmas 1437.	E 28/56 20 Feb.; E 101/335/158; E 404/52/204, 393; *PPC* iv. 316–29, v. 16; *CPR 1429–36*, 528–30, 602.
32	15 Mar. 1436	£666 13*s.* 4*d.*	Paid to treasurer of Calais. Repayment by tallies on customs in London.	E 401/744; E 404/52/222, 394.
33	24 July – 28 Aug. 1436	£6,000	Letters patent granting all customs in Southampton; tallies issued from 24 Jan. 1437 to 4 Aug. 1438 as receipts.	*CPR 1429–36*, 604; E 401/748; E 28/57 24 July.
34	18 Apr. 1437	£6,666 14*s.* 4*d.*	Council warrant for repayment from lay	*PPC* v. 16, 41–2; E 401/752;

No.	Date	Sum loaned	Method and period of repayment	Sources
			subsidy due Whitsun 1437 and clerical subsidy at midsummer. Tallies issued 15 May along with those for loan 28.	E 403/728; E 404/53/302.
35	26 Mar. 1438	£7,333 6*s.* 8*d.*	Repayment of £5,000 from customs in Southampton, 2,000 marks from London, £1,000 from exchequer. Repayment completed by end 1438.	E 404/54/175, 179, 188; E 401/754, 756; E 122/140/55.
36	10 Nov. 1438	£2,000	Letters patent for repayment from customs of Southampton; tallies issued 21 Nov.	E 401/761; *CPR 1436–41*, 173, 227.
37	19 Nov. 1438	£666 13*s.* 4*d.*	Tally on fine made by earl of Salisbury, levied 21 Nov.	E 401/761; *CPR 1436–41*, 194, 230.
38	29 Nov. 1438	£666 13*s.* 4*d.*	Cash repayment 6 May 1439	E 403/734.
39	Jan./Feb. 1439	£866 13*s.* 4*d.*	Tallies on customs in Southampton and London, 28 Mar.	E 401/761; E 364/77 H.
40	27 Mar. 1439	£4,666 13*s.* 4*d.*	Jewels pledged to him for repayment by Easter 1440; 4 Feb. 1440 tallies on lay subsidy due Martinmas 1440.	E 401/761, 766; E 404/55/158; E 404/56/163; *PPC* v. 115; *CPR 1436–41*, 277–9.
41	13 May 1439	£3,000	Tally on customs Southampton, 15 May reassigned 14 Apr. 1440.	E 401/764, 768.
42	22 Dec. 1439	£6,666 13*s.* 4*d.*	Tallies issued 23 Dec. on lay and clerical subsidies due by Martinmas 1440.	E 401/766; E 404/56/155.
43	24 Feb. 1441	£1,000	Tallies issued 28 Mar. 1442 on lay subsidy due Whitsun.	E 401/770, 775.
44	19 Mar. 1442	£5,666 13*s.* 4*d.*	Tallies for £4,700 issued 28 Mar. on lay subsidy due Whitsun and Martinmas. £1,966 13*s.* 4*d.* assigned on customs of Southampton, confirmed by letter patent 29 May: reassigned 29 Nov.	E 401/775; *CPR 1441–6*, 61–2, 76

No.	Date	Sum loaned	Method and period of repayment	Sources
45	7 May 1442	£2,000	Repayment as part of loan 44, on the Southampton customs.	E 401/779; *PPC* v. 216.
46	6 Apr. 1443	£10,000	Letter patent 15 Mar. granting all customs in Southampton and customs from Italians in London, with appointment of collector. Repayment in gold by indentures with collectors, recorded as exchequer issues.	E 401/781, 784; E 403/751, 753, 755; E 404/59/233, 277; *CPR 1441–6*, 160.
47	6 June 1443	£10,000	Letter patent 25 May granting repayment from other ports, from casualties, and from Tiptoft lands and sheriffs proffers.	As for loan 45. Also *CPR 1441–6*, 182; *PPC* v. 276, 279–80.
48	6 July 1443	£1,000	As in loan 47. Loans 46–8 all repaid by Feb. 1445.	As for loan 46. E 404/61/135.
49	10 July 1443	£1,000	Delivered to Rolleston, clerk of the great wardrobe and recorded on receipt roll as a loan from him. Repayment made via Rolleston in cash Mich. 1444/5.	*PPC* v. 307; E 404/59/277; E 401/781.
50	10 July 1443	£666 13*s.* 4*d.*	The third of the rich collar held as security for repayment by Mich. 1444. Tallies issued 11 May 1445 on lay subsidy due Martinmas.	E 101/335/15 H; E 401/781, 790; E 404/59/290; *PPC* vi. 29; *CPR 1441–6*, 194.
51	22 Feb. 1444	£1,333 6*s.* 8*d.*	3 Mar. letter patent and council warrant to hold remainder of rich collar. Repayment as for loan 50. He had surrendered the collar by May 1445.	*CPR 1441–6*, 240; *PPC* vi. 27–9; E 401/784, 790; E 28/72 3 Mar.; E 404/61/220.
52	21 July 1445	£1,000	Jewels as security for repayment by Christmas. No record of repayment.	E 401/791; E 404/61/265.
53	16 Aug. 1446	£1,333 6*s.* 8*d.*	Tallies issued 19 Aug. on lay subsidy due at Martinmas 1446.	E 401/794; E 404/62/231.

APPENDIX II

Lands in the Possession of the Beauforts

This list has been compiled from the sources listed below; a reference to a property is tabulated in the appropriate column. The list excludes knights' fees, messuages, and all temporary custodies and farms of lands.

(*a*) Inquisitions post mortem for John, earl of Somerset (d. 1410) and Henry, earl of Somerset (d. 1418): C 137/80, C 139/15.
(*b*) *Feudal Aids*, 1412, 1428, 1431.
(*e*) Account of the receiver-general of Thomas, duke of Clarence, 8 Henry V: WAM 12163.
(*d*) Inquisition post mortem for Thomas, duke of Exeter, d. 1426: C 139/30.
(*e*) Inquisition post mortem for Margaret, duchess of Clarence (d. 1440): C 139/101.
(*f*) Inquisition post mortem for John, duke of Somerset (d. 1444) and feoffment 1443/4: C 139/114; *CPR 1441–6*, 170, 349, 408.
(*g*) Valor of the estates of Lady Margaret Beaufort, 1455–6: DL 29/651/10533–4.

Note 1: Inquisition post mortem of Edmund, duke of Somerset (d. 1455): C 139/160.
Note 2: *CPR 1441–6*, 268.

	a	*b*	*c*	*d*	*e*	*f*	*g*
Lands of John, earl of Somerset, d. 1410							
Cambs.							
Orwell	*	*	*				*
Devon							
Aller Peverell	*	*	*		*	*	*
Halberton hundred	*	*	*		*		
Sampford Peverell	*	*	*		*	*	*
Sampford borough	*	*	*		*	*	
Dorset							
Corfe	*	*	*				1
Leics.							
Enderby	*	*	*				
Northants							
Brampton Parva	*	*	*				
Eydon	*	*	*				
Maxey	*	*	*				
Overstone	*	*	*				

	a	*b*	*c*	*d*	*e*	*f*	*g*
Somerset							
Abdyke hundred	*	*			*	*	*
Bulston hundred	*				*	*	*
Curry Rivel	*	*	*		*	*	*
Lamport	*	*			*	*	*
Martock	*	*	*		*	*	*
Staffs.							
Walsall (rent)	*		*				*
Wales							
Glyndwrdwy lands.	*		*				
Lands of Margaret Holand, countess of Somerset and duchess of Clarence, d. 1440							
Essex							
Colnwake			*			*	
Lands in Dunmow		*					
Lamarsh		*	*			*	
Stratford abbey (rent)			*		*	*	
Waltham fee farm			*		*	*	
Glos.							
Cirencester abbey (rent)			*		*	*	*
Hants							
Andover fee farm						*	*
Basingstoke fee farm		*	*			*	*
Bedhampton						*	*
Romsey fee farm							*
Southampton fee farm							*
Kent							
Dartford with land in Cobham Chiselhurst, and Combe					*	*	
Lincs.							
Billingborough						*	
Bourne						2	
Deeping	*	*	*				
Northants							
Buckby	*	*	*				
Torpell	*		*				
Norfolk							
Ormesby (rent)			*			*	*
Somerset							
Bath priory fee farm			*		*	*	*
Burton						*	
Horethorne hundred		*	*		*	*	*
Kingsbury Regis		*	*		*	*	*

	a	*b*	*c*	*d*	*e*	*f*	*g*
Milborne port fee farm		*	*		*	*	*
Queen Camel		*	*		*	*	*
Surrey							
Woking		*	*				1
Sutton			*				1
Sussex							
Iden (rent)			*			*	*
Worcs.							
Droitwich fee farm						*	*
Yorks.							
Cottingham						2	
Lands of Thomas, duke of Exeter, d. 1426							
Beds.							
Wrestlingworth				*			
Hants							
Crokeston		*					
Hereford							
Newland and Welsh Newton				*			
Herts.							
Maydecroft				*			
Theobalds				*			*
Norfolk							
Burdolph lands							
Yorks.							
Scotton				*			

Lands acquired by John, duke of Somerset, d. 1444:
Lordship of Kendal etc. (reverted to crown)

Lands acquired by Bishop Henry Beaufort, d. 1447:

Bucks.	Salden (to Whittingham)
Dorset	Canford and Poole (to Edmund Beaufort)
	Tarrant Launceston (to St Cross)
Hants	Southampton fee farm; advowsons of Crondall, St Faith Winchester, St John's Fordingbridge (all to St Cross)
Kent	Braborne, Langley
Norfolk	Wells
Northants	Ochecote
Somerset	Henstridge, Charlton Camville (both to St Cross)
Wilts.	Amesbury, Wilton, Winterborne Earls (all to St Cross)
Wales	Chirk and Chirklands (to Edmund Beaufort)

Lands acquired by Edmund, duke of Somerset, d. 1455:

Cambs.	Bassingborne and Babraham	all resumed by the crown in 1455
Dorset	Ryme	
Hants	Carisbrooke	
Somerset	Matthew Gournay lands	

APPENDIX III

The Sources of Beaufort's Wealth

Cardinal Beaufort was reputed among his contemporaries to be the richest prelate in Christendom, and his ostentation was remarked upon both at home and abroad. Twice in his career, in 1421 and 1437, more than £25,000 of his wealth was in the hands of the crown, while the £24,000 on loan in 1443 followed six years during which he had spent perhaps around £18,000 on the purchase of land and a series of building projects. This may indicate a treasure in coin, plate, and bullion of around £50,000–60,000 at the height of his career, and not less than £30,000 when he first emerged as a major lender to the crown under Henry V.[1] In the absence of accounts from either the treasurer of Wolvesey or his executors, the size of his fortune must remain speculative, and for the same reason its source remains as much a puzzle to us as it was to his contemporaries. In the charges which he brought against Beaufort in 1440 Gloucester declared that 'it is wele knowen that it nad ben possible unto the saide cardinal to have comen to so grete richesse but by such moyens; of his chirche it might not ryse, enheritance hath he noone'.[2] The 'means' he referred to do nothing, in fact, to explain Beaufort's fortune, for most of Gloucester's accusations related to the abuse of political influence over the previous two decades. Only the 'liklinesse' that he had defrauded the crown of customs on his shipment of wools from Southampton and the allegation that he had sold offices to the highest bidder in Normandy refer to the possible sources of his wealth. Gloucester did not accuse Beaufort of taking a usurious profit on his loans to the crown and the evidence argues against this supposition.[3] That leaves three possible sources for his fortune: the revenues of the bishopric; the profits (licit or illicit) from wool exports; and profits from personal favours. Reliable figures are available only for the first of these.

Revenues from the bishopric

The Winchester pipe rolls contain summaries of the accounts of some eighty bailiffs and farmers of the episcopal manors, though not all of these appear in every year. The rolls give no overall total for the revenue of the estate and to compile this from each roll for the whole period of Beaufort's episcopate would be an immense labour. In order to establish the general dimension of his episcopal income it has been thought sufficient to take one year in each decade. The columns in the appended table represent:

(i) Arrears: these accumulate progressively throughout the period.
(ii) The total charge: i.e. current dues plus arrears.
(iii) Current dues minus arrears: this figure is not in the accounts.

[1] McFarlane, *England in the XV Century,* 132.
[2] *Wars of the Eng.* ii. 450.
[3] Harriss, 'Cardinal Beaufort, patriot or usurer?'

(iv) Current dues less administrative costs and capital investment.
(v) Payments to the treasurer of Wolvesey after local expenditure under warrant (including payment to the household on itinerary).[4]

Year	i	ii	iii	iv	v
	Arrer.	*Rec. c. Arr.*	(Current dues)	*Et debet*	*Lib. den.*
1406–7	390	5,703	5,313	4,327	3,722
1416–17	634	6,452	5,818	5,212	4,068
1425–6	970	5,161	4,191	3,876	2,979
1434–5	1,500	6,029	4,529	4,985	3,580
1441–2	1,734	6,588	4,854	5,075	3,293

The sum reaching the treasurer of Wolvesey was thus of the order of £3,700 p.a. from the episcopal estates.[5] His main expenditure was upon the bishop's household, but the entire absence of household accounts for any bishops of Winchester in the later Middle Ages makes this a matter of guesswork.

Revenue from wool

It is impossible to substantiate Gloucester's description of Beaufort as 'the chief merchant of wolles in youre lande'. A large number of the episcopal manors, particularly in the Hampshire and Wiltshire downs and in Oxfordshire, had sizeable flocks and were mostly kept in demesne. In the 1420s they had between ten and twelve thousand sheep, and after a decline in the early thirties this figure could have been surpassed by the end of the decade.[6] How this crop was disposed of is unfortunately not traceable. The wool from the Oxfordshire estates was usually marketed in London; that from Hampshire was collected at Wolvesey. Whether it was sold locally to clothiers or exported is uncertain. The Southampton customs accounts contain no indication that Beaufort was a regular exporter of wool; indeed in most years the denizen exports from that port were barely more than a couple of dozen sacks. In only three years before 1440 did they exceed fifty sacks: in 1422–3 (382), in 1424–5 (226), and in 1430–1 (261).[7] Possibly all three (but certainly the last) reflect Beaufort's activities. At other times, if the crop was exported it must have been purchased by Italian merchants, though no evidence connects Beaufort with any in particular. The London customs accounts are equally uninformative about the

[4] Payments to the household totalled £396 in 1406–7, £61 in 1416–17, £140 in 1425–6, £515 in 1434–5, £345 in 1441–2.

[5] The lower total in 1425–6 reflected the effects of pestilence and that in 1441–2 the exceptional expenditure on building at Wolvesey and Waltham to the sum of £438.

[6] HRO Eccles. II 159427, 159429, for 1425–6 and 1428–9. See also P. M. Hyde, 'The Winchester manors at Witney and Adderbury in the later Middle Ages', B.Litt. thesis (Oxford, 1955), 181–7.

[7] McFarlane included a consideration of the sources of Beaufort's wealth in his dissertation and the present account draws partly on this. He examined all the particulars of accounts in E 122/140, 141 and the enrolled accounts in E 356/18, 19. I have checked these and also the customs ledgers for 5–6 Henry VI (E 122/184/3), and 17–18 Henry VI (E 122/141/23), 11–12 Henry VI (E 122/141/21), *Eng. Export Trade*, 59–60.

identity of exporters, and Beaufort's name does not appear in the few surviving ledger books and coket files which contain large numbers of names of merchants.[8] He certainly had close connections with the London merchants and could well have used these as his factors.[9]

The only definite evidence of Beaufort as an exporter of wool relates to four occasions when he received special licences. In March 1427, when proceeding to Normandy with Bedford, he had licence to ship 800 sacks to Cherbourg and sell them there; in April 1431 when he rejoined the king in Normandy, he had licence to ship the same quantity from any port in England to wherever he chose; in November 1438, on his embassy to Calais, he had permission to ship 300 sacks from Southampton to wherever he chose; and in November 1446 he had licence to ship 100 sacks of wool to Normandy.[10] On each occasion the licence gave exemption from the Staple but not from the payment of customs and subsidies, though in 1438 his loans were being repaid from the Southampton customs. On the first two, and possibly three, occasions it looks as if he intended to take the wool with him. Only the second and fourth of these figure in the customers' accounts, which record that he shipped 261 sacks of the 800, paying £435 in customs from Southampton in May 1431, and 83 sacks in 1446–7, stated to be from the episcopal estates.[11] These at least establish him as a wool merchant, if not a very considerable one; but the further extent of his dealings remains unknown.

Personal favours

Beaufort held the office of chancellor for six years and for much of his long career enjoyed considerable political influence and patronage. His favour was sought in commercial and diplomatic negotiations and he was repeatedly in demand as an arbitrator. All these were occasions on which gratuities would be offered to him, and a few such gifts are recorded. In addition he acted for long periods as executor of numbers of the nobility, and this too offered opportunities for personal benefit. None of this is quantifiable, but in sum it was probably not inconsiderable, for Beaufort had a reputation for carefully husbanding his income, though not for exaction or avarice.

[8] Ledgers: E 122/73/9 (16–17 H. VI); E 122/184/3 (4–6 H. VI); E 122/73/11 (17–18 H. VI); coket files: E 122/74/12.

[9] Beyond the names mentioned in the main text, it can be noted that Hugh Dyke is mentioned in Beaufort's will as having sold him vestments and that Thomas Walsingham in his will left his son-in-law a great bible given him by my lord cardinal 'wretyn in boleyn hande': PCC 8 Stokton (ex. inf. A. I. Doyle).

[10] *PPC* iii. 253–4; *CPR 1429–36*, 118; *CPR 1436–41*, 227; E 356/19 m. 21; C 76/129 m. 19.

[11] Beaufort was summoned to the exchequer in Hilary Term 1433 to answer for the customs due, making a personal appearance on 28 Jan.: E 159/209 Com. Rec. m. 9v See also E 122/140/43, 44; E 356/19 m. 20v, 21. I have taken these references from McFarlanes dissertation on Beaufort, p. K5.

LIST OF SOURCES

A UNPRINTED SOURCES

London, Public Record Office:

C 1	Early Chancery Proceedings
C 47	Chancery Miscellanea
C 53	Charter Rolls
C 61	Gascon Rolls
C 76	Treaty Rolls
C 81	Chancery Warrants
C 85	Significations of Excommunication
C 137–40	Inquisitions Post Mortem, Series I
CHES 29	Palatinate of Chester, Plea Rolls
DL 28	Duchy of Lancaster, Various Accounts
DL 29	Duchy of Lancaster, Ministers Accounts
DL 42	Duchy of Lancaster, Miscellaneous Books
E 28	Exchequer TR, Council and Privy Seal
E 34	Exchequer TR, Privy Seals for Loans
E 101	Exchequer KR, Various Accounts
E 122	Exchequer KR, Customs Accounts
E 154	Exchequer KR, Inventories of Goods and Chattels
E 159	Exchequer KR, Memoranda Rolls
E 207	Exchequer KR, Bille
E 356	Exchequer LTR, Customs Accounts, enrolled
E 359	Exchequer LTR, Subsidy Accounts, enrolled
E 364	Exchequer LTR, Foreign Accounts
E 368	Exchequer LTR, Memoranda Rolls
E 401	Exchequer of Receipt, Receipt Rolls
E 403	Exchequer of Receipt, Issue Rolls
E 404	Exchequer of Receipt, Warrants for Issues
KB 9	King's Bench, Ancient Indictments
KB 27	King's Bench, Plea Rolls
PSO 1	Privy Seal Office, Warrants for the Privy Seal
SC 1	Special Collections, Ancient Correspondence
SC 6	Special Collections, Ministers Accounts
SC 8	Special Collections, Ancient Petitions

London, British Library:

Additional Charters 2016, 5832, 7959, 11671, 11731
Additional Manuscripts 4101, 11542, 14848, 35814, 46846
Arundel MS 68

Cotton MSS Cleopatra F III, Tiberius B VI, Titus A III, Vespasian C XIV, D IX
Egerton Roll 8794
Harleian MSS 431, 543
Royal MS 13 C I
Sloane MS 1080

Paris, Bibliothèque Nationale:
Manuscrits français 1278, 5330, 4488, 20327, 25768–9, 26549
Nouvelles Acquisitions 1482

Canterbury Cathedral Muniments:
Miscellaneous Accounts
Register S

Hampshire Record Office:
Eccles. II 159407–37 (pipe rolls)
11 M 59/Bp/BW 62–9 (Bishop's Waltham accounts)
Register of Henry Beaufort

Leeds Central Library:
GC DL/3 (duchy of Lancaster account)

Lincoln Archives Office:
Register of Henry Beaufort

London, Corporation of London Record Office:
Journal of the Common Council

London, Lambeth Palace Library:
Register of John Stafford

London, Westminster Abbey Muniments:
Nos. 12163, 12181, 12285–321

Longleat House:
MS 342

Northamptonshire Record Office:
Fitzwilliam MS 2046

Norfolk Record Office:
MS NRS 11061
KL/C 7/2

Nottinghamshire University Library:
Middleton MS. Mi C 5a

Oxford, Bodleian Library:
MS 117
Digby MS 66
Miscellaneous Charters, England C1
Tanner MS 165

Oxford, Magdalen College:
Fastolf Papers 19, 40

East Sussex Record Office:
Glynde MS 3469

Warwickshire Record Office:
CR 1618/W 19/5 (Beauchamp account book)

B PRINTED SOURCES

Chronicles

Johannis Amundesham Monachi Monasterii S. Albani Annales, ed. H. T. Riley, 2 vols. (Rolls Ser., 1870–1)
Annales Ricardi Secundi et Henrici Quarti in Johannis de Trokelowe et Henrici de Blaneforde Chronica et Annales, ed. H. T. Riley (Rolls Ser., 1865)
Arnold's Chronicle, ed. H. Ellis (London, 1811)
THOMAS BASIN, *Histoire de Charles VII*, vol. ii, ed. C. Samaran (Paris, 1944).
John Benet's Chronicle, ed. G. L. and M. A. Harriss in *Camden Miscellany*, 24 (Camden Ser., 1972).
The Brut, ed. F. W. D. Brie, vol. ii (EETS, 1908).
JEAN CHARTIER, *Chronique Latine inedite*, ed. C. Samaran (Paris, 1928).
Chronicle of London, ed. Sir N. H. Nicolas (London, 1827).
Chronicles of London, ed. C. L. Kingsford (Oxford, 1905)
Chronicque de la traison et mort de Richard Deux, Roy Dengleterre, ed. B. Williams (London, 1846).
Chronique de Normandie, ed. B. Williams (London, 1850).
An English Chronicle, 1377–1461, ed. J. S. Davies (Camden Ser., 1856).
Eulogium Historiarum sive Temporis Chronicon, ed. F. S. Haydon, vol. iii (Rolls Ser., 1863).
CLÉMENT DE FAUQUEMBERGUE, *Journal de 1417 a 1435*, ed. A. Tuetey, 3 vols. (Soc. hist. fr., 1903–15).
JEAN LE FÈVRE, *Chronique*, ed. F. Morand (Soc. hist. fr., 1876–81).
Gesta Abbatum Monasterii Sancti Albani, ed. H. T. Riley, vol. iii (Rolls Ser., 1869).
Gesta Henrici Quinti, ed. F. Taylor and J. S. Roskell (Oxford, 1975).
The Great Chronicle of London, ed. A. H. Thomas and I. D. Thornley (London, 1938).

Gregory's Chronicle: Collections of a London Citizen, ed. J. Gairdner (Camden Ser., 1876).
Hall's Chronicle, ed. H. Ellis (London, 1809).
Henrici Quinti Gesta, ed. B. Williams (London, 1850).
Historiae Croylandensis Continuatio: Rerum Anglicarum Scriptorum Veterum, ed. W. Fulman (Oxford, 1684).
Historiae Dunelmensis Scriptores Tres, ed. J. Raine (Surtees Soc., 1839).
Incerti Scriptores Chronicon Angliae, ed. J. A. Giles (London, 1848).
Livre des trahisons de France entre la Maison de Bourgogne: Chroniques relatives à l'histoire de la Belgique, ed. K. de Lettenhove, vol. ii (Brussels, 1873).
ENGUERRAN DE MONSTRELET, *Chronique*, ed. L. Douët-d'Arcq, 6 vols. (Soc. hist. fr., 1857–62).
ANTONIO MOROSINI, *Extraits de sa Chronique relatifs à l'histoire de France*, ed. G. Lèfvre-Pontalis, 4 vols. (Soc. hist. fr., 1898–1902).
The St Albans Chronicle, ed. V. H. Galbraith (Oxford, 1937).
Chronique du réligieux de St Denys, ed. L. Bellaguet, 6 vols. (Collection des doc. inédits, 1839).
Chronicle of John Stone, ed. W. G. Searle (Camb. Antiq. Soc., 1902).
Chronicle of John Strecche, ed. F. Taylor, *BJRL* 16 (1932).
THOMAS WALSINGHAM, *Historia Anglicana*, ed. H. T. Riley, 2 vols. (Rolls Ser., 1863–4).
JEHAN DE WAURIN, *Recueil des croniques et anchiennes istories de la Grant Bretaigne a present nomme Engleterre*, ed. W. Hardy, vols. ii–iv (Rolls Ser., 1868–84).
WILLIAM WORCESTRE, *Itineraries*, ed. J. H. Harvey (Oxford, 1969).

Documents

Acta Concilii Constanciensis, ed. H. Finke, 4 vols. (Munster, 1896–1928).
Actes de la chancellerie d'Henri VI concernant la Normandie sous la domination Anglaise, 1422–35, ed. P. le Cacheux, 2 vols. (Rouen–Paris, 1907–8).
Anglia Sacra, ed. H. Wharton, 2 vols. (London, 1691).
The Antient Kalendars and Inventories of the Treasury of his Majesty's Exchequer, ed. F. Palgrave, 3 vols. (London, 1831).
THOMAS BEKYNTON, *Correspondence*, ed. G. Williams (Rolls Ser., 1872).
The Brokage Book of Southampton, 1439–40, ed. D. M. Bunyard (Southampton Rec. Soc., 1941); ibid. *1443–4*, ed. O. Coleman, 2 vols. (1960–1).
Calendar of Documents relating to Scotland, vol. iv, ed. J. Bain (HMSO, 1888).
Calendar of Inquisitions Miscellaneous, 1399–1422 (HMSO, 1968).
Calendar of the Norman Rolls, Henry V, 41st, 42nd *DKR*.
Calendar of Papal Letters, vols. v–ix (HMSO, 1904–9).
Calendar of the Plea and Memoranda Rolls of the City of London, *1413–37*, ed. P. E. Jones (Cambridge, 1943).
Calendar of the Proceedings in Chancery, vol. i (Rec. Comm., 1827).
Calendar of the Signet Letters of Henry IV and Henry V, ed. J. L. Kirby (HMSO, 1978).

Calendars of Close Rolls, 1396–1454 (HMSO, 1927–47).
Calendars of Fine Rolls, 1399–1452 (HMSO, 1931–9).
Calendars of Letter Books of the City of London, Books I and K, ed. R. R. Sharpe (London, 1909, 1911).
Calendars of Patent Rolls, 1396–1461 (HMSO, 1909–11).
Canterbury Chantries and Hospitals, ed. C. Cotton (Kent Rec. Soc., 1934).
Catalogue des rolles gascons, normans, et français conservés dans les archives de la Tour de Londres, ed. T. Carte, 2 vols. (London, 1743).
Catalogue of Ancient Deeds, 6 vols. (HMSO, 1890–1915).
Certificates of the Commissioners appointed to survey the Chantries, Guilds, and Hospitals in the County of York, vol. i, ed. W. Page (Surtees Soc., 1894).
Chaucer Life Records, ed. M. C. Crow and C. C. Olson (Oxford, 1966).
Chertsey Abbey Cartularies, part i (Surrey Rec. Soc., 1915).
Christ Church Letters, ed. J. B. Sheppard (Camden Ser., 1877).
Collection générale des documents Français qui se trouvent en Angleterre, ed. J. Delpit (Paris, 1847).
A Collection of Royal Wills, ed. J. Nichols (London, 1780).
Concilia Magnae Britanniae et Hiberniae, ed. D. Wilkins, vol. iii (London, 1737).
Le Cotton Ms. Galba B.I., ed. E. Scott and L. Gilliodts-van-Severen (Brussels, 1896).
The Council of Constance, trans. L. R. Loomis, ed. J. H. Moody and K. M. Woody (Columbia, 1967).
Diplomatic and Scottish Documents and Papal Bulls (PRO List and Index 49, HMSO, 1923).
Documents illustrating the activities of the General and Provincial Chapters of the English Black Monks, 1215–1540, ed. W. A. Pantin, vol. iii (Camden Ser., 1937).
Documents relating to the Anglo-French Negotiations of 1439, ed. C. T. Allmand in *Camden Miscellany*, 24 (Camden Ser., 1972).
English Economic History: Select Documents, edd. A. E. Bland, P. A. Brown, R. H. Tawney (London, 1914).
English Suits before the Parlement of Paris, ed. C. T. Allmand and C. A. J. Armstrong (Camden Ser., 1982).
Epistolae Academicae Oxoniensis, ed. H. Anstey (Ox. Hist. Soc., 1898).
Excerpta Historica, ed. S. Bentley (London, 1831).
Exchequer Rolls of Scotland, 1406–36, ed. G. Burnett (Edinburgh, 1880).
Expeditions to Prussia and the Holy Land made by Henry, Earl of Derby, ed. L. Toulmin Smith (Camden Ser., 1894).
Feudal Aids, 6 vols. (London, HMSO, 1899–1921).
Foedera, Conventiones, et Litterae, ed. T. Rymer, 20 vols. (London, 1727–35); *Appendices to a Report on Rymer's Foedera*, ed. C. P. Cooper (London, 1869).
Formulare Anglicanum, ed. F. Madox (London, 1702).
FORTESCUE, J., *The Governance of England*, ed. C. Plummer (Oxford, 1885).
GASCOIGNE, T., *Loci e Libro Veritatum*, ed. J. E. Thorold Rogers (Oxford, 1881).
Hanserecesse, 1256–1430, ed. K. Koppmann, 8 vols. (Leipzig, 1870–97); ibid. *1431–76*, ed. G. von der Ropp, 7 vols. (Leipzig, 1876–92).

Historical Manuscripts Commission, Reports: 1st, 2nd, 3rd, 4th, 5th, 9th, De Lisle and Dudley i, Various iv, Wells ii.

Historical Poems of the Fourteenth and Fifteenth Centuries, ed. R. H. Robbins (New York, 1959).

Issues of the Exchequer, ed. F. Devon (London, 1837).

Joubert, A., 'Documents inédits pour servir à l'histoire de la Guerre de Cent Ans dans la Maine de 1424 à 1452', *Rev. hist. et archaeolog. du Maine*, 26 (1889).

Lannoy, G. de, *Œuvres*, ed. C. Potvin (Louvain, 1878).

Les Cent Nouvelles Nouvelles, ed. P. Champion (Paris, 1928).

Letters of Queen Margaret of Anjou, ed. C. Monro (Camden Ser., 1863).

Letters of John Shillingford, ed. S. Moore (Camden Ser., 1872).

Lettres des rois, reines, et autres personnages, ed. M. Champollion-Figeac, 2 vols. (Paris, 1847).

Members of Parliament: Part I, Parliaments of England, 1217–1705 (London, 1878).

Munimenta Academica, ed. H. Anstey, 2 vols. (Rolls Ser., 1868).

The Navy of the Lancastrian Kings, ed. S. Rose (Navy Rec. Soc., 1982).

Original Letters Illustrative of English History, ed. Sir. H. Ellis, 1st Ser., 3 vols. (London, 1824).

A Parisian Journal, 1405–1449, ed. and trans. J. Shirley (Oxford, 1968).

The Paston Letters, ed. J. Gairdner, 6 vols. (Edinburgh, 1904).

Peterborough Local Administrations, ed. W. T. Mellows (Northants. Rec. Soc., 1939).

The Plumpton Correspondence, ed. T. Stapleton (Camden Ser., 1839).

Poggii Bracciolini Epistolae, ed. T. Tonelli (Florence, 1832).

Poggii Bracciolini Opera Omnia (Turin, 1964).

Proceedings and Ordinances of the Privy Council of England, ed. Sir H. Nicolas, vols. i–vi (London, 1834–7).

Proceedings before the Justices of the Peace in the Fourteenth and Fifteenth Centuries, ed. B. Putnam (London, 1938).

Procès de condamnation et rehabilitation de Jeanne d'Arc, ed. J. Quicherat, 3 vols. (Soc. hist. fr., 1849).

Procès de condamnation de Jeanne d'Arc, ed. P. Tisset, 3 vols. (Soc. hist. fr., 1960–71).

The Register of the Common Seal of the Priory of St Swithun, Winchester, ed. J. Greatrex (Hants Rec. Soc., 1978).

The Register of Congregation, 1448–1463, ed. W. A. Pantin and R. Mitchell (Ox. Hist. Soc., 1972).

Register of Exeter College, Oxford, ed. C. W. Boase (Ox. Hist. Soc., 1894).

Register of Henry Chichele, ed. E. F. Jacob, 4 vols. (Cant. and Y. Soc., 1943–7).

Register of Richard Fleming, ed. N. H. Bennett, vol. i (Cant. and Y. Soc., 1984).

Register of Robert Hallum, ed. J. M. Horn (Cant. and Y. Soc., 1982).

Register of Edmund Lacy, ed. G. R. Dunstan, 4 vols. (Cant. and Y. Soc., 1963–71).

Register of Thomas Langley, ed. R. L. Storey, 3 vols. (Surtees Soc., 1956–70).

Register of Robert Rede, ed. C. Deedes, 2 vols. (Sussex Rec. Soc., 1908–10).

Register of Philip Repingdon, ed. M. Archer, 2 vols. (Cant. and Y. Soc., 1963).

Register of Thomas Spofford, ed. A. T. Bannister (Cant. and Y. Soc., 1919).
Report from the Lords' Committee . . . on all matters touching the Dignity of a Peer, 4 vols. (London, 1820–9).
Rôles normands et français . . . tirées des archives de Londres, ed. L. G. O. F. Brequigny (Soc. des antiquaires de Normandie, Paris 1858).
Rotuli Normanniae, ed. T. D. Hardy (London, 1835).
Rotuli Parliamentorum, 6 vols. (London, 1767–77).
Rotuli Scotiae, 2 vols. (Rec. Comm., 1814–19).
Royal Letters of Henry IV, ed. F. C. Hingeston, vol. i (Rolls Ser., 1860).
Sauvage, H., 'Documents relatifs à la donation du Comté Pairie de Mortain à Pierre de Navarre par Charles VI', *Soc. de l'hist. de Normandie: Mélanges*, 52 (1898), 213–331.
Select Cases before the King's Council, 1243 to 1482, ed. I. S. Leadam and J. F. Baldwin (Selden Soc., 1918).
Select Cases in Chancery, 1364 to 1471, ed. W. P. Baildon (Selden Soc., 1896).
Snappes Formulary, ed. H. E. Salter (Ox. Hist. Soc., 1924).
Somerset Medieval Wills, 1383–1500, ed. F. W. Weaver (Som. Rec. Soc., 1901).
The Statutes of Lincoln Cathedral, ed. A. Bradshaw and C. Wordsworth (Cambridge, 1897).
Statutes of the Realm, vol. ii (Rec. Comm., 1816).
Sussex Feet of Fines, ed. L. F. Salzman (Sussex Rec. Soc., 1916).
Taverne, A. de la, *Journal de la Paix d'Arras*, ed. A. Bossuat (Arras, 1936).
Testamenta Eboracensia, ed. J. Raine (Surtees Soc., 1836).
Valor Ecclesiasticus, ed. J. Caley and J. Hunter, vol. ii (Rec. Comm., 1810).
The Vespesiano Memoirs, trans. W. George and E. Waters (London, 1926).
Wars of the English in France during the reign of Henry VI, ed. J. Stevenson, 2 vols. (Rolls. Ser., 1861–4).
Wills and Inventories illustrative of the history, manners etc. of the northern counties of England, ed. J. Raine (Surtees Soc., 1835).
Winchester College Muniments, ed. S. Himsworth, 3 vols. (Chichester, n.d.).
York Memorandum Book, ed. J. W. Percy (Surtees Soc., 1973).

Secondary Works

Allmand, C. T., 'The Anglo-French negotiations, 1439', *BIHR* 40 (1967), 1–33.
—— 'Normandy and the council of Basel', *Speculum*, 40 (1965), 1–14.
—— *Lancastrian Normandy* (Oxford, 1983).
Anstis, J., *Register of the Order of the Garter*, 2 vols., (London, 1724).
Armitage Smith, S., *John of Gaunt* (London, 1904).
Avery, M. E., 'The history of the equitable jurisdiction of the Chancery before 1460', *BIHR* 42 (1969), 129–44.
—— 'An evaluation of the effectiveness of the Court of Chancery under the Lancastrian Kings', *LQR* 86 (1970), 84–99.
Balfour-Melville, E. W. M., 'The later captivity and release of James I', *Scot. Hist. Rev.* 21 (1924), 45–53.
—— 'James I at Windsor', ibid. 25 (1928), 226–8.

Balfour-Melville, E. W. M., *James I, King of Scots, 1406–37* (London, 1936).
Barton, J. L., 'The medieval use', *LQR* 81 (1965), 562–77.
Bartos, F. M., 'An English Cardinal and the Hussite revolution', *Communio Viatorum*, 4 (1963), 47–54.
Bean, J. M. W., 'Henry IV and the Percies', *History*, 44 (1959), 212–27.
Beaucourt, G. du Fresne de, *Histoire de Charles VII*, 6 vols. (Paris, 1881–91).
Beaurepaire, C. de Robillard de, *De l'administration de la Normandie sous la domination anglaise* (Caen, 1859).
—— *Les États de Normandie sous la domination anglaise* (Évreux, 1859).
Belfield, G., 'Cardinal Beaufort's almshouse of noble poverty at St Cross, Winchester', *Proc. Hants. Field Club and Arch. Soc.* 38 (1982), 79–91.
Bellamy, J. C., *Criminal Law and Society in Late Medieval and Tudor England* (Gloucester, 1984).
Betcherman, L.-R., 'The making of bishops in the Lancastrian period', *Speculum*, 41 (1966), 397–419.
Biddle, M., *Wolvesey* (HMSO, 1986).
Brown, A. L., 'The authorization of letters under the Great Seal', *BIHR*, 37 (1964), 125–56.
—— 'The Commons and the Council in the reign of Henry IV', *EHR* 79 (1964), 1–30.
—— 'The reign of Henry IV', in Chrimes, S. B., Ross, C. D., Grifiths, R. A. (edd.), *Fifteenth Century England* (Manchester, 1972), 1–28.
—— 'The English campaign in Scotland, 1400', in Hearder, H., and Loyn, H. R. (edd.), *British Government and Administration* (Cardiff, 1974), 40–54.
Caley, J., 'Extract from the Liber Memorandum Camerariorum Receptae Scaccarii', *Archaeologia*, 21 (1827), 34–8.
Carus Wilson, E. M., and Coleman, O., *England's Export Trade, 1275–1547* (Oxford, 1963).
Catto, J. I., 'The King's Servants' in Harriss, G. L. (ed.), *Henry V: The Practice of Kingship* (Oxford, 1985), 97–116.
Champion, P., *Vie de Charles d'Orléans* (Paris, 1911).
Chandler, R., *The Life of William Waynflete* (London, 1811).
Cherry, M., 'The struggle for power in mid-fifteenth century Devonshire' in Griffiths, R. A. (ed.), *Patronage, the Crown, and the Provinces* (Gloucester, 1981), 123–44.
Chitty, H., 'Fromond's chantry at Winchester College', *Archaeologia,* 75 (1924–5), 139–58.
Chrimes, S. B., 'The pretensions of the duke of Gloucester in 1422', *EHR* 45 (1930), 101–3.
—— *Henry VII* (London, 1972).
Cloake, J., 'The Charterhouse of Sheen', *Surrey Arch. Coll.* 71 (1977), 145–98.
Colvin, H. M., *History of the King's Works*, 3 vols. (HMSO, 1963).
Cokayne, G. E. and Doubleday, H. A., *The Complete Peerage*, 13 vols. (London, 1910–59).
Cooke, J. H., 'The great Berkeley law suit', *Trans. Bristol and Glouc. Antiq. Soc.* 3 (1878), 304–24.

CRAWFORD, A., 'The King's burden? The consequences of royal marriage in fifteenth century England', in Griffiths, R. A. (ed.), *Patronage, the Crown, and the Provinces* (Gloucester, 1981), 33–56.
Crowder, C. M. D., 'Henry V, Sigismund, and the Council of Constance', *Historical Studies*, 4 (1963), 93–110.
—— 'Correspondence between England and the Council of Constance', *SCH* 1 (1964), 154–206.
DAVIES, R. G., 'Richard II and the Church in the years of the "tyranny" ', *J. Med. Hist.* 1 (1974), 329–62.
—— 'Martin V and the English Episcopate', *EHR* 92 (1977), 309–44.
—— 'After the execution of Archbishop Scrope: Henry IV, the Papacy and the English Episcopate', *BJRL* 59 (1977), 40–74.
DAVIES, R. R., 'Richard II and the principality of Chester', in Barron, C. M. and du Boulay, F. R. H., *The Reign of Richard II* (London, 1971), 256–79.
DESPLANQUE, M. A., 'Projet d'assasinat de Philippe le Bon par les Anglais, 1424–6', *Mémoires couronnés et mémoires des savants étrangers,* 33 (1865–7), 1–78.
DICKINSON, J. G., *The Congress of Arras, 1435* (Oxford, 1955).
DOBSON, R. B., *Durham Priory, 1400–1500* (Cambridge, 1973).
DU BOULAY, F. R. H., *The Lordship of Canterbury* (London, 1966).
DUCK, A., *Life of Henry Chichele* (London, 1699).
DUPONT-FERRIER, G., 'Jean d'Orléans, comte d'Angoulême', *Revue des documents historiques*, 4 (1877), 18–30.
—— 'La Captivité de Jean d'Orléans, comte d'Angoulême', *Rev. Hist.* 62 (1896), 45–60.
DYER, C., *Lords and Peasants in a Changing Society* (Cambridge, 1980).
EMDEN, A. B., *A Biographical Register of the University of Oxford to* A.D. *1500.* 3 vols. (Oxford, 1957–9).
EUBEL, C., *Hierarchia Catholica Medii Aevi*, vol. i (Regensburg, 1898).
FERGUSON, J., *English Diplomacy, 1422–1461* (Oxford, 1972).
FISHER, J. H., RICHARDSON, M., FISHER, J. L., *An Anthology of Chancery English* (Knoxville, 1984).
FORD, C. J., 'Piracy or policy: the crisis in the Channel, 1400–1403', *TRHS* 29 (1979), 63–78.
FRASER, C. M., 'Some Durham documents relating to the Hilary Parliament of 1404', *BIHR* 34 (1961), 192–9.
GILLIODTS VAN SEVEREN, L., *Inventaire des archives de la ville de Bruges* (Bruges, 1876).
GOODMAN, A. W., 'The marriage of Henry IV and Joan of Navarre' (pamphlet; Winchester, 1934).
GRAVES, E. B., 'The legal significance of the Statute of Praemunire', in Taylor, C. H. (ed.), *Haskins Anniversary Essays* (New York, 1929), 57–80.
GRAY, H. L., 'English Foreign Trade from 1446 to 1482', in Postan, M., and Power, E. (edd.), *Studies in English Trade in the Fifteenth Century* (London. 1933). 1–38.
—— 'Incomes from land in England in 1436', *EHR* 49 (1934), 607–39.

GRIFFITHS, R. A., 'The rise of the Stradlyngs of St Donats', *Morgannwg*, 7 (1963), 15–47.
—— 'The trial of Eleanor Cobham, *BJRL* 51 (1968–9), 381–99.
—— 'Queen Katherine of Valois and a missing statute of the realm', *LQR* 93 (1977), 248–62.
—— *The Reign of Henry VI* (London, 1981).
GUNNER, W. H., 'Extracts from the bursars' accounts of Winchester College', *Arch. J.* 8 (1851), 79–87.
GUY, J. A., 'The development of equitable jurisdictions, 1450–1550', in Ives, E. W., and Manchester, A. H. (edd.), *Law, Litigants and the Legal Profession* (London, 1983), 80–7.
HALLER, J., *England und Rom unter Martin V* (Rome, 1905).
—— *Piero da Monte* (Rome, 1941).
HANHAM, A., 'The profits of English wool exports, 1472–1544', *BIHR* 55 (1982), 139–47.
HARGREAVES, A. D., 'Equity and the Latin side of Chancery', *LQR* 68 (1952), 481–99.
HARRISS, G. L., 'Cardinal Beaufort, patriot or usurer?', *TRHS* 20 (1970), 129–48.
—— 'Marmaduke Lumley and the exchequer crisis of 1446–9', in Rowe, J. G. (ed.), *Aspects of Late Medieval Government and Society* (Toronto, 1986), 143–78.
—— 'Henry Beaufort, Cardinal of England' in Williams, D. (ed.), *England in the Fifteenth Century* (Bury St Edmunds, 1987), 111–27.
HARVEY, M., 'Solutions to the Schism: A study of some English attitudes, 1378 to 1409', *Kirchengeschichtliche Quellen und Studien*, 12 (1983).
HEFELE, C. J. (trans. H. Leclerq), *Histoire des conciles*, vol. vii (Paris, 1916).
HEYMANN, F. C., 'The crusade against the Hussites', in Setton, K. M., and Hazard, H. W., *A History of the Crusades*, vol. iii (Wisconsin, 1975).
HICKS, M., 'The Nevill earldom of Salisbury, 1429–71', *Wilts. Arch. Mag.* 72 (1980), 141–7.
HOLMES, G. A., 'The Libel of English Policy', *EHR* 76 (1961), 193–216.
—— 'Cardinal Beaufort and the crusade against the Hussites', *EHR* 88 (1973), 721–50.
HUTCHINS, J., *History and Antiquities of the County of Dorset*, 4 vols. (London, 1796–1815).
JACOB E. F., 'Thomas Brouns, bishop of Norwich, 1436–45', in Trevor Roper, H. R. (ed.), *Essays in British History presented to Sir Keith Feiling* (London, 1965), 61–84.
—— *Archbishop Henry Chichele* (London, 1967).
—— *Essays in Later Medieval History* (Manchester, 1968).
JEFFERIES, P., 'The medieval use as family law and custom', *Southern History*, 1 (1979), 45–69.
JONES, M., 'John Beaufort, duke of Somerset and the French expedition of 1443', in Griffiths, R. A. (ed.), *Patronage, the Crown, and the Provinces* (Gloucester, 1981), 79–102.

—— 'Henry VII, Lady Margaret Beaufort, and the Orleans ransom', in Griffiths, R. A., and Sherborne, J. (edd.), *Kings and Nobles in the Later Middle Ages* (Gloucester, 1986), 254–73.

KEISER, G. R., 'Patronage and piety in fifteenth century England: Margaret Duchess of Clarence, Simon Wynter and Beinecke Ms. 317', *Yale Univ. Lib. Gazette* (1985), 32–46.

KERLING, N. J. M., *Commercial Relations of Holland and Zeeland with England* (Leiden, 1954).

KINGSFORD, C. L., *English Historical Literature in the Fifteenth Century* (Oxford, 1913).

—— 'An historical collection of the fifteenth century', *EHR* 29 (1914), 505–15.

KIRBY, J. L., 'The Issues of the Lancastrian Exchequer and Lord Cromwell's estimates of 1433', *BIHR* 24 (1951), 121–51.

—— 'An account of Robert Southwell, receiver-general of John Mowbray, Earl Marshal, 1422–3', *BIHR* 27 (1954), 192–8.

—— 'The council of 1417 and the problem of Calais', *History Today*, 5 (1955), 44–42.

—— 'Calais sous les Anglais, 1399–1413', *Revue du Nord*, 37 (1955), 19–30.

—— *Henry IV of England* (London, 1970).

KIRBY, T. F., 'The oratory of the Holy Trinity at Barton, Isle of Wight', *Archaeologia*, 52 (1890), 297–314.

—— *Annals of Winchester College* (London, 1892).

KNOWLSON, G. A., *Jean V, duc de Bretagne et l'Angleterre* (Cambridge, 1964).

LACAZE, Y., 'Philippe le Bon et le problème hussite: un projet de Croisade bourguignon en 1428–9', *Rev. hist.* 241 (1969), 69–98.

LE CACHEUX, P., *Rouen au temps de Jeanne d'Arc et pendant l'occupation anglaise* (Rouen–Paris, 1931).

LEGUAI, A., *Les Ducs de Bourbon pendant la crise monarchique du XV siècle* (Paris, 1962).

LE NEVE, J., *Fasti Ecclesiae Anglicanae, 1300–1541*, rev., 12 vols. (London, 1962–7).

LEVESON-GOWER, G., 'Notices of the family of Uvedale', *Surrey Arch. Coll.* 3 (1865), 63–192.

LLOYD, T. H., *The Movement of Wool Prices in Medieval England* (Cambridge, 1973).

—— *The English Wool Trade in the Middle Ages* (Cambridge, 1977).

—— 'A reconsideration of two Anglo-Hanseatic treaties of the fifteenth century', *EHR* 102 (1987), 916–33.

LONGNON, A., 'Les limites de la France et l'entendue de la domination anglaise', *Rev. des quest. hist.* 18 (1875), 444–510.

—— *Paris pendant la domination anglaise* (Paris, 1878).

LUNT, W. E., *Financial Relations of the Papacy with England, 1327–1534* (Cambridge, Mass. 1962).

MCFARLANE, K. B., 'Henry V, Bishop Beaufort, and the Red Hat, 1417–21', *EHR* 60 (1945), 316–48; 'At the Deathbed of Cardinal Beaufort', in

Studies in History Presented to F. M. Powicke (Oxford, 1948), 405–28: both reprinted in McFarlane, *England in the Fifteenth Century* (London, 1981), 79–138.

McGrath, J. R., *A History of the Queen's College*, 2 vols. (Oxford, 1921).

McHardy, A. K., 'Clerical taxation in fifteenth-century England; the clergy as agents of the crown', in Dobson, B. (ed.), *The Church, Politics, and Patronage in the Fifteenth Century* (Gloucester, 1984), 168–92.

McNab, B., 'Obligations of the Church in English society: military arrays and the clergy, 1369–1418', in Jordan, W. C., McNab, B., Ruiz, T. F. (edd.), *Order and Innovation in the Middle Ages* (Princeton, 1976), 293–314.

McNiven, P., 'The betrayal of Archbishop Scrope', *BJRL* 54 (1971–2), 173–213.

—— 'Prince Henry and the English political crisis of 1412', *History*, 65 (1980), 1–16.

—— 'The Scottish policy of the Percies and the strategy of the rebellion of 1403', *BJRL* 62 (1980), 498–530.

—— 'Legitimacy and consent: Henry IV and the Lancastrian title, 1399–1406', *Medieval Studies*, 44 (1982), 470–88.

—— 'The problem of Henry IV's health', *EHR* 100 (1985), 761–72.

Macrae, C., 'The English council and Scotland in 1430', *EHR* 54 (1939), 415–21.

Mallett, C. E., *History of the University of Oxford*, 3 vols. (Oxford, 1923–7).

Maxwell-Lyte, H. C., *A History of Eton College* (London, 1911).

Miltenberger, F., 'Das Itinerarium Martins V von Constanz bis Rom', *Mitteilungen des Instituts für Osterreichische Geschichtsforschung*, 15 (1894), 661–4.

Morgan, D. A. L., 'The king's affinity in Yorkist England', *TRHS* 23 (1973), 1–26.

Munro, J. H. A., *Wool, Cloth and Gold* (Toronto, 1972).

Myers, A. R., *Crown, Household, and Parliament in the Fifteenth Century* (London, 1985).

Newhall, R. A., 'The war finances of Henry V and the duke of Bedford', *EHR* 36 (1921), 172–98.

—— *The English Conquest of Normandy, 1416–24* (Yale, 1924).

—— *Muster and Review* (Harvard, 1940).

Nicholson, R., *Scotland: The Later Middle Ages* (Edinburgh, 1974).

Nicolas, H., *History of the Battle of Agincourt* (London, 1833).

Nordberg, M., *Les Ducs et la royauté* (Uppsala, 1964).

Otway Ruthven, A. J., *The King's Secretary and Signet Office in the Fifteenth Century* (Cambridge, 1939).

—— *A History of Medieval Ireland* (London, 1968).

Palmer, J. J. N., *England, France, and Christendom, 1377–1399* (Oxford, 1970).

Pantin, W. A., 'Chantry priests houses and other medieval lodgings', *Med. Archaeology*, 3 (1959), 216–58.

Partner, P., 'William of Wykeham and the historians', in Custance, R. (ed.), *Winchester College Sixth Centenary Essays* (Oxford, 1982), 1–36.

PETRE, J., 'The Nevills of Brancepeth and Raby, 1425–1499', *The Ricardian*, 5 (1981), 418–35.
PISTONO, S. D., 'Flanders and the Hundred Years' War: the quest for the *trêve marchande*', *BIHR* 49 (1976), 185–97.
—— 'The accession of Henry IV: the effects on Anglo-Flemish relations, 1399–1402', *Tijdschrift vor Geschiedenis*, 89 (1976), 465–74.
PLANCHENAULT, R., 'La lutte contre les Anglais en Anjou pendant la première moitié du XV siècle', *École des Chartes; position des theses*, 75 (1923).
—— 'La Conquête du Maine par les Anglais; la lutte des partisans, 1427–9', *Rev. hist. et archaeolog. du Maine*, 93 (1937), 24–34, 160–72; 94 (1938), 47–60.
PLANCHER, U., *Histoire générale et particulière de Bourgogne*, 4 vols. (Dijon, 1739–41).
POCQUET DU HAUT JUSSÉ, B.-A., 'Anne de Bourgogne et le testament de Bedford, 1429', *Bibl. École des Chartes*, 95 (1934), 284–326.
POCQUET DU HAUT JUSSÉ, J., 'Une renaissance littéraire au cour d'Henri V', *Rev. hist.* 224 (1960), 329–38.
POLLARD, A. J., *John Talbot and the War in France, 1427–53* (London, 1983).
POST, J. B., 'The obsequies of John of Gaunt', *Guildhall Studies in History*, 5 (1981), 1–12.
—— 'Equitable resorts before 1450' in Ives, E. W., and Manchester, A. H. (edd.), *Law, Litigants, and the Legal Profession* (London, 1983), 68–79.
POWER, E., 'The wool trade in the fifteenth century', in Postan, M. M. and Power, E. (edd.), *Studies in English Trade in the Fifteenth Century* (London, 1933), 39–90.
POWELL, E., 'Arbitration and the law in England in the late Middle Ages', *TRHS* 33 (1983), 49–68.
—— 'The King's Bench in Shropshire and Staffordshire in 1414', in Ives, W., and Manchester, A. H. (edd.), *Law, Litigants, and the Legal Profession* (London, 1983), 94–103.
—— 'The restoration of law and order', in Harriss, G. L. (ed.), *Henry V: The Practice of Kingship* (Oxford, 1985), 53–74.
PRONAY, N., 'The Chancellor, the Chancery, and the Council at the end of the fifteenth century', in Hearder, H., and Loyn, H. R. (edd.), *British Government and Administration* (Cardiff, 1974), 87–103.
PUGH, T. B., 'Richard Plantagenet, duke of York as the king's lieutenant in France and Ireland', in Rowe, J. G. (ed.), *Aspects of Late Medieval Government and Society* (Toronto, 1986), 107–42.
QUIRCK, R., *The Tomb of Cardinal Beaufort* (Winchester. Friends of the Cathedral, 1954).
RADFORD, L. B., *Henry Beaufort* (London, 1908).
RAMSAY, J. H., *Lancaster and York*, 2 vols. (Oxford, 1892).
RAWCLIFFE, C., *The Staffords, Earls of Stafford and Dukes of Buckingham, 1394–1521* (Cambridge, 1978).
REEVES, A. C., *Lancastrian Englishmen* (Washington, 1981).
REGNIER, M. C., 'Devis pour la construction d'une maison forte à Elbeuf', *Soc. de l'hist. de Normandie: Mélanges*, 6 (1906), 331–50.
RILEY, H. T., *Memorials of London Life* (London, 1868).

ROGERS, A. R., 'The political crisis of 1401', *Nottingham Med. Studies*, 12 (1968), 85–96.
—— 'Henry IV, the Commons, and taxation', *Med. Studies*, 31 (1969), 444–70.
—— 'Clerical taxation under Henry IV', *BIHR* 46 (1973), 123–44.
ROSKELL, J. S., *The Commons in the Parliament of 1422* (Manchester, 1954).
—— *The Commons and their Speakers in Medieval English Parliaments* (Manchester, 1965).
—— *Parliament and Politics in Late Medieval England, 3 vols. (London, 1981–3).*
ROWAN, S., 'Imperial taxes and German politics in the fifteenth century', *Central European History*, 13 (1980), 203–17.
ROWE, B., 'The *Grand Conseil* under the duke of Bedford, 1422–35', in *Oxford Essays in Medieval History presented to H. E. Salter* (Oxford, 1934), 207–34.
ST JOHN HOPE, W. H., 'The Funeral, Monument, and Chantry Chapel of Henry V', *Archaeologia*, 65 (1913–14), 129–86.
SALZMANN, L. F., *Building in England* (Oxford, 1952).
SCHNITH, K., 'Kardinal Heinrich Beaufort und der Hussitenkrieg', in Baumer, R. (ed.), *Von Konstanz nach Trient* (Munich, 1972), 119–38.
SCHOFIELD, A. N. E. D., 'England and the council of Basel', *Annuarium Historia Conciliorum*, 5(i) (1973), 1–117.
SHARPE, R. H., *London and the Kingdom*, 3 vols. (London, 1895).
SHEPPARD, J. B., 'The Meister Homers, Canterbury', *Arch. Cantiana*, 13 (1880), 116–21.
SMYTH, J., *Lives of the Berkeley's*, ed. J. Maclean, 2 vols. (Gloucester, 1883).
SOMERVILLE, R. *History of the Duchy of Lancaster* (London, 1953).
STEEL, A., *The Receipt of the Exchequer, 1377–1485* (Cambridge, 1954).
STOREY, R. L., *Thomas Langley and the Bishopric of Durham* (London, 1961).
—— 'The Foundation of the Medieval College, 1379–1530', in Buxton, J., and Williams, P. H. (edd.), *New College, Oxford* (Oxford, 1979).
—— *The End of the House of Lancaster*, new. edn. (London, 1987).
STRATFORD, J., 'The Manuscripts of John, duke of Bedford: library and chapel', in Williams, D. (ed.), *England in the Fifteenth Century* (Bury St Edmunds, 1987), 329–50.
—— *Three Inventories of the Goods of John, Duke of Bedford (d. 1435)* (Soc. Antiq. London, forthcoming).
STRONG, P., and STRONG, F., 'The last will and codicils of Henry V', *EHR* 96 (1981), 79–102.
THIELEMANS, M. R., *Bourgogne et Angleterre* (Brussels, 1966).
THOMPSON, A. H., 'The statutes of the collegiate church at Fotheringhay', *Arch. J.* 75 (1918), 246–67.
—— *The English Clergy and their Organisation in the Later Middle Ages* (Oxford, 1947).
THOMPSON, E. M., *The Carthusian Order in England* (London, 1936).
TINDAL HART, A., *The Rich Cardinal* (privately printed, 1985).
TOY, S., 'Winchester House, Southwark', *Surrey Arch. Coll.* 49 (1975), 75–81.
TUCK, A., *Richard II and the English Nobility* (London, 1973).

ULLMANN, W., 'Cardinal Kemp, Eugenius IV, and Archbishop Chichele', in J. A. Watt, J. B. Morrall, F. X. Martin (edd.), *Studies in Medieval History presented to Aubrey Gwynn* (Dublin, 1961), 359–83.
VALE, M., *English Gascony, 1399–1453* (Oxford, 1970).
—— *Charles VII* (London, 1974).
VAUGHAN, R., *John the Fearless* (London, 1966).
—— *Philip the Good* (London, 1970).
VICKERS, K., *Humphrey, Duke of Gloucester* (London, 1907).
VIRGOE, R., 'The composition of the King's Council, 1437–61', *BIHR* 43 (1970), 134–60.
—— 'The Cambridgeshire election of 1439', *BIHR* 46 (1973), 95–101.
—— 'The parliamentary subsidy of 1450', *BIHR* 55 (1982), 125–38.
WEDGWOOD, J. C., *History of Parliament, 1439–1509: Biographies* (HMSO, 1936).
WEISS, R., 'Humphrey, Duke of Gloucester and Tito Livio Frulovisi', in Gordon, D. J. (ed.), *Fritz Saxl Memorial Essays* (Oxford, 1957), 218–27.
WOLFFE, B. P., *Henry VI* (London, 1981).
WOODRUFFE, C. E., 'Notes on the inner life and domestic economy of the priors of Christ Church Canterbury', *Arch. Cantiana*, 53 (1941), 1–10.
WORDSWORTH, C., 'Inventories of plate, vestments etc., belonging to the cathedral church of the Blessed Mary of Lincoln', *Archaeologia*, 53 (1893), 1–82.
WYLIE, J. H., *History of England under Henry the Fourth*, 4 vols. (London, 1884–98).
—— *The Reign of Henry the Fifth*, vols. i–ii (Cambridge, 1914, 1919), vol. iii with Waugh, W. T. (Cambridge, 1929).
ZELLFELDER, A., *England und das Basler Konzil* (Berlin, 1913).

C THESES

ARCHER, R. E., 'The Mowbrays: earls of Nottingham and dukes of Norfolk to 1432', D.Phil. thesis (Oxford, 1984).
BARRON, C. M., 'The government of London and its relations with the Crown, 1400–1450', Ph.D. thesis (London, 1970).
BOLTON, J. L., 'Alien merchants in England in the reign of Henry VI', B.Litt. thesis (Oxford, 1971).
BROOKS, P. D., and GRAHAM, A. C., 'The Bishop's tenants at Farnham' (typescript, HRO).
BROWN, A. L., 'The Privy Seal in the early fifteenth century', D.Phil. thesis (Oxford, 1957).
BURNEY, E. M., 'The English rule of Normandy, 1435–50', B.Litt. thesis (Oxford, 1958).
CARPENTER, M. C., 'Political society in Warwickshire, 1401–72', Ph.D. thesis (Cambridge, 1975).
CROWDER, C. M. D., 'Some aspects of the English Nation at the Council of Constance', D.Phil. thesis (Oxford, 1953).

DICKS, A. C., 'The question of peace: Anglo-French diplomacy, 1439–49', Ph.D. thesis (Oklahoma, 1966).

ELDER, A. J., 'A study of the Beauforts and their estates, 1399–1450', Ph.D. thesis (Bryn Mawr, 1964).

FRIEDRICHS, R. L., 'The career and influence of Ralph, Lord Cromwell, 1396–1456', Ph.D. thesis (Columbia, 1974).

GRIFFITHS, W. R. M., 'The military career and affinity of Henry, prince of Wales, 1399–1413', M.Litt. thesis (Oxford, 1980).

HYDE, P. M., 'The Winchester manors at Witney and Adderbury in the later Middle Ages', B.Litt. thesis (Oxford, 1955).

JOHNSON, P. A., 'The political career of Richard, duke of York, to 1456', D.Phil. thesis (Oxford, 1981).

LLINOS SMITH, O. W., 'The lordship of Chirk and Oswestry', Ph.D. thesis (London, 1977).

MARSHALL, A. E., 'The role of English war captains in England and Normandy, 1436–61', MA thesis (Swansea, 1975).

MILLS, J., 'The foundation, endowment, and early administration of Magdalen College, Oxford', B.Litt. thesis (Oxford, 1973).

NIGOTA, J. A., 'John Kempe, a political prelate of the fifteenth century', Ph.D. thesis (Emory, 1973).

POLLARD, A. J., 'The family of Talbot, Lords Talbot and earls of Shrewsbury in the fifteenth century', Ph.D. thesis (Bristol, 1968).

RATCLIFFE, H. L., 'The military expenditure of the English crown, 1422–1435', M.Litt. thesis (Oxford, 1979).

SINCLAIR, A. F. J., 'The Beauchamp Earls of Warwick in the later Middle Ages', Ph.D. thesis (London, 1987).

STORRS, C. M., 'Jacobean pilgrims from England', MA thesis (London, 1964).

TAYLOR, A. B., 'The diplomatic career of Isabel of Portugal, 1435 to 1457', Ph.D. thesis (Colorado, 1978).

WRIGHT, T. E. F., 'Royal Finance in the latter part of the reign of Henry IV of England, 1406–1413', D.Phil. thesis (Oxford, 1984).

MCFARLANE, K. B., 'Cardinal Beaufort' (incomplete) typescript.

—— 'The Political Crisis of 1432' typescript.

INDEX